NEW PERSPECTIVES ON LAND REGISTRATION

The Land Registration Act 2002 has been in force for almost fifteen years. When enacted, the legislation, which replaced the Land Registration Act 1925, was intended to offer a clear and lasting framework for the registration of title to land in England and Wales. However, perhaps confounding the hopes of its drafters, the legislation's interpretation and application has since generated many unanticipated problems which demand attention.

In this book's twenty chapters, leading land law scholars, Law Commissioners past and present, judges, and Registry lawyers unpick key technical controversies, and expose underlying theoretical and policy concerns. Core issues addressed in these chapters include: the legitimate ambitions of registration regimes; the nature and security of title afforded by registration; the resolution of priority disputes affecting registered titles; the relationship between the general law and the registration regime; and new challenges presented by modern technological developments.

New Perspectives on Land Registration

Contemporary Problems and Solutions

Edited by
Amy Goymour, Stephen Watterson
and Martin Dixon

·HART·
PUBLISHING
OXFORD AND PORTLAND, OREGON
2018

Hart Publishing
An imprint of Bloomsbury Publishing Plc

Hart Publishing Ltd
Kemp House
Chawley Park
Cumnor Hill
Oxford OX2 9PH
UK

Bloomsbury Publishing Plc
50 Bedford Square
London
WC1B 3DP
UK

www.hartpub.co.uk
www.bloomsbury.com

Published in North America (US and Canada) by
Hart Publishing
c/o International Specialized Book Services
920 NE 58th Avenue, Suite 300
Portland, OR 97213-3786
USA

www.isbs.com

First published 2018

British Library Cataloguing-in-Publication Data
A catalogue record for this book is available from the British Library.

ISBN: HB: 978-1-50990-603-1
ePDF: 978-1-50990-605-5
ePub: 978-1-50990-604-8

Library of Congress Cataloging-in-Publication Data

Names: Goymour, Amy, editor. | Watterson, Stephen, 1975- editor. | Dixon, Martin (Martin J.), editor.

Title: New perspectives on land registration : contemporary problems and solutions / edited by Amy Goymour, Stephen Watterson, and Martin Dixon.

Description: Oxford [UK] ; Portland, Oregon : Hart Publishing, 2018. | Includes bibliographical references and index.

Identifiers: LCCN 2017051088 (print) | LCCN 2017051676 (ebook) | ISBN 9781509906048 (Epub) | ISBN 9781509906031 (hardback : alk. paper)

Subjects: LCSH: Land titles—Registration and transfer—Great Britain. | Great Britain. Land Registration Act 2002. | Great Britain. Land Registration (Scotland) Act 1979.

Classification: LCC KD984 (ebook) | LCC KD984 .N49 2018 (print) | DDC 346.4204/38—dc23

LC record available at https://lccn.loc.gov/2017051088

Typeset by Compuscript Ltd, Shannon

PREFACE

The Land Registration Act ('LRA') 2002 has now been in force for fourteen years. When it came into force on 13 October 2003, it opened up new possibilities: a framework for the introduction of e-conveyancing; a stronger title guarantee; and greater certainty for purchasers who rely on the accuracy of the Land Register. But, like many teenagers, the Act faces challenges. Can it cope with new situations and what society has to throw at it? Where will it be in ten years' time? What will its world, its legal landscape, be like when it matures?

It is to be expected that legislation encounters difficulties as it finds it way and is applied to a myriad of different circumstances, some foreseen, some not, but the challenges faced by the LRA 2002 have been particularly acute. Not only have technological advances since 2003 increased the opportunities for conveyancing fraud, but the 2008 recession—and the consequent reduction in Her Majesty's Land Registry's operational resources—undermined the Registry's ability to detect fraud at a time when fraud-reduction tactics were most needed. These challenging socio-economic circumstances form the backdrop to the Act's formative years.

Confounding the hopes of the Act's drafters, the LRA 2002's interpretation and application has generated many unanticipated problems during its first fourteen years. The extent of these problems is demonstrated by burgeoning litigation around the Act, often involving some of the knottiest issues in land law, and with major financial implications turning on the outcome. In 2016, the Law Commission published a major Consultation Paper, *Updating the Land Registration Act 2002* (CP No 227). The paper postulated a pressing need for 'clarification and amendment', and to ensure that any proposed changes 'stand the test of time' such that they 'are fit for purpose not only now, but also for the future', as the Act enters its adult years. One aim of this collection is to offer a set of critical perspectives that might be employed to evaluate both what we currently have, and what might eventually result from the Law Commission's reform proposals.

This book's twenty chapters explore the current land registration regime from a wide range of viewpoints. It is the product of a collaboration that began in November 2014 with a conference at Trinity Hall, Cambridge, co-organised and co-sponsored by the Cambridge Private Law Centre (Faculty of Law, University of Cambridge) and the Cambridge Centre for Property Law (Department of Land Economy, University of Cambridge). This conference gathered together for the first time the leading experts in the field of Land Registration from academia, practice, the judiciary, Her Majesty's Land Registry, and Law Commissions (present and past).

The book's chapters are organised into two Parts. Part I contains four short chapters, which offer different perspectives on modern land registration regimes, and the challenges they face. These chapters span the ambitions of law reform, the Registry's perspectives on the practical challenges of land registration, the emerging (and burgeoning) land registration jurisdiction, and the economic and political drivers of worldwide land registration reform.

Part II then examines contemporary problems and solutions within land registration systems from both technical and theoretical perspectives. It is arranged around five Sections. Section A examines the nature of a title, once it is registered—exploring, in particular, issues of adverse possession and whether the long-standing doctrine of title relativity has any continuing role in relation to land title to which is registered. Section B tackles the vexed questions surrounding alteration of the Register and the availability (or not) of indemnity payouts by the Registry—drawing, in particular, on two important Court of Appeal decisions (*MacLeod v Gold Harp Properties Ltd* (2014), and *Swift 1st Ltd v Chief Land Registrar* (2015)). Whilst most chapters focus on the position in England and Wales under the LRA 2002, one chapter undertakes an evaluation of the new law of land registration in Scotland. Section C explores questions of 'priority' between competing interests in land; one chapter undertakes a critique of the priority rules operative within the LRA 2002 regime; another examines complex issues of subrogation rights and priority contests. Section D then explores at length the under-examined relationship between the 'general law' and the LRA 2002, via an analysis of three promises purportedly made to registered proprietors and/or disponees by the Act: the promise of title by registration (the 'title promise'); the promise of priority (the 'priority promise'); and the conferral of owner's dispositional powers on a registered proprietor (the 'empowerment promise'). Finally, Section E's two chapters grapple with the 'mechanical' challenges of land registration—one explores the *processes* of title registration in Scotland; the other explores the problems associated with *automating* title registration, and draws some important lessons from Australasian 'Torrens'-style title registration systems.

Our hope is that the book will stand the test of time, even after the Law Commission publishes its final report on *Updating the Land Registration Act 2002*, in 2018. Many of the difficult questions facing the registration regime which are examined in this book are likely to persist—the interaction between the general law and the registration rules; the guile of fraudsters, armed with increasingly-advanced technology; the availability of indemnity; and wider issues concerning the rationale of the Act when e-conveyancing, as originally conceived, does not exist.

We are grateful to the Cambridge Private Law Centre (and in particular Sarah Worthington) and the Cambridge Centre for Property Law, for sponsoring the conference in November 2014 which kick-started this project. We are also grateful to everyone at Hart Publishing for their enthusiasm for our project, for their patience, and for being a constant source of help and advice as we have moved forward with the book. We owe particular thanks to Bill Asquith, Claire Banyard, Anne Flegel, and Linda Staniford. Finally, we extend our thanks to the authors of the chapters in this book, many of whom undertook significant revisions to their chapters in the light of judicial developments and the Law Commission's proposals. Without their contributions, this collection would not have been possible.

Amy Goymour
Stephen Watterson
Martin Dixon
1 December 2017

TABLE OF CONTENTS

LIST OF CONTRIBUTORS

Elizabeth Cooke is the Principal Judge, First-tier Tribunal, Property Chamber (Land Registration), and formerly a Law Commissioner for England and Wales (2008–15), during which time she led the Property, Family and Trust Law team.

Simon Cooper is Reader in Property Law at Oxford Brookes University.

Edward Cousins is the former Principal Judge, First-tier Tribunal, Property Chamber (Land Registration), and formerly the Adjudicator to HM Land Registry.

Martin Dixon is Professor of the Law of Real Property at the University of Cambridge, and a Fellow of Queens' College.

Amy Goymour is University Senior Lecturer in Land Law at the University of Cambridge, and a Fellow of Downing College.

Lynden Griggs is Senior Lecturer at the University of Tasmania, Australia.

Charles Harpum is a Barrister at Falcon Chambers, London, Emeritus Fellow, Downing College, Cambridge, and formerly a Law Commissioner for England and Wales (1994–2001), during which time he led the Property and Trusts Law team.

Robin Hickey is Senior Lecturer at Queen's University, Belfast.

Richard Hill is Assistant Land Registrar at HM Land Registry.

Nicholas Hopkins is a Law Commissioner for England and Wales, and leads the Property, Family and Trust Law team, and Professor of Law at the University of Reading.

Emma Lees is University Lecturer in Environmental and Property Law at the University of Cambridge, and a Fellow of Fitzwilliam College.

Rouhshi Low is a legal researcher, and formerly Lecturer, Queensland University of Technology, Australia.

Pamela O'Connor is Professor and Head of Law School at the University of the Sunshine Coast, Australia, and former Victorian Law Reform Commissioner, Australia.

John Pownall is Land Registrar at HM Land Registry.

Kenneth GC Reid is Professor of Scots Law, University of Edinburgh, and formerly a Scottish Law Commissioner (1995–2005), during which time he directed a major programme of land law reform.

Owen Rhys is a Judge, First-tier Tribunal, Property Chamber (Land Registration).

Roger Smith is a Fellow of Magdalen College, Oxford and formerly Associate Professor of Law, University of Oxford.

Rod Thomas is Associate Professor of Law at the Auckland University of Technology, New Zealand.

Emma Waring is Lecturer at the University of York.

Stephen Watterson is University Lecturer in Law at the University of Cambridge, and a Fellow of Trinity Hall.

TABLE OF CASES

ENGLAND & WALES

SCOTLAND

USA

TABLE OF STATUTES AND STATUTORY INSTRUMENTS

ENGLAND & WALES

SCOTLAND

TASMANIA

VICTORIA

CANADA

ONTARIO

NEW ZEALAND

PART I

Four Perspectives on Modern Land Registration Systems

1

A (Former) Law Reformer's Perspective: Reforming the LRA 2002—Catalysts and Questions

ELIZABETH COOKE

Preface

This chapter is an edited version of the introductory talk that I gave at the conference on 'New Perspectives in Land Registration' in Cambridge on 21 November 2014. At that stage, I was the Law Commissioner with responsibility for the Law Commission's new project on land registration in England and Wales. So much has changed since then. I am no longer a Law Commissioner;[1] and the Law Commission has now published its Consultation Paper, 'Updating the Land Registration Act 2002',[2] steered by its new Commissioner, Professor Nicholas Hopkins. Above all, the law has changed. After some reflection, I have left the text of my 2014 talk substantively unamended (although I have noted in the footnotes where the law has since moved on), in order to expose the particular catalysts—as well as the broader background concerns—which led to the Law Commission's taking on this important law reform project in 2014.

I. Problems Arising Within the LRA 2002

The Law Commission commenced a project on land registration earlier in 2014, as part of its Twelfth Programme of Law Reform.[3]

So what is the Law Commission doing? The stated intention is not to reinvent the wheel or to re-run the project steered by Charles Harpum through the 1990s. Rather, it is to take a look at the Land Registration Act ('LRA') 2002, ten years on, and to consider whether any adjustments are needed in the light of our experience of its operation.

[1] I am now the Principal Judge of the Land Registration Division of the First-tier Tribunal (Property Chamber); in this paper I am not writing in a judicial capacity.

[2] Law Commission, *Updating the Land Registration Act 2002—A Consultation Paper* (Law Com CP No 227, 2016).

[3] See Law Commission, *Twelfth Programme of Law Reform* (Law Com No 354, 2014) 9.

Put like that, the project might sound rather prosaic. And indeed, we are looking at some very fine-grained issues. Points that members of the public and of the legal profession have asked us to examine include the following:

— Will the Land Registry register a lease extended under the Leasehold Reform, Housing and Urban Development Act 1993 when the lessee's mortgagee's consent has not been obtained?[4]
— Can the holder of a mortgage (necessarily equitable) of a beneficial interest register a caution against first registration?
— Should discontinuous leases be registrable even where their term amounts to less than three years?[5]
— Can we review the registration of mines and minerals?[6]
— Can a squatter who has applied after ten years to become the new registered owner within schedule 6, paragraph 1 of the LRA 2002, and has been rebuffed by the registered proprietor's statutory counter-notice, make a fresh schedule 6, paragraph 1 application straight away, or must he wait for a further two years (the period in which the registered proprietor must take action if he is ultimately to defeat the squatter's first application) before doing so?[7]

Most technical problems of this kind are problems to which a solution either already exists or can readily be devised. But there are some deeper issues. Some of them are so deep that they raise the question: what sort of title registration system do we want? I refer, of course, to what the Torrens lawyers call indefeasibility and the question: how secure is a registered title? In particular, if I am the registered proprietor, can I be certain that I will not lose it when the registrar registers a forged transfer from me to someone else? And if I buy land from a registered proprietor, can I be sure that I will not lose it because of some flaw in the title that the Register does not reveal? These questions take us to fundamentals. They make us ask what land registration is for, and what sort of registration system we want to have.

II. Fundamental Issues Underlying Land Registration Reform

So what is land registration for? The answer is to some extent subjective: we can see what a system is for by looking at who wants it. The ancient Egyptians wanted something like land registration in order to sort out their fields when the Nile flood subsided each year. William the Conqueror wanted it for information, and as an instrument of power, and so had the Domesday book written. Henry VIII's motivation for the little-known and unsuccessful Statute of Enrolments in 1536 was similar. But the West Riding (Yorkshire) Deeds Registry was inaugurated as a result of the desire of the West Riding cloth merchants to be able to

[4] Yes: see Land Registry, *Land Registry Practice Guide 27: The Leasehold Reform Legislation* (updated June 2015) para 9.7; accordingly it appears that this is not a law reform problem.

[5] It is difficult to see why not, especially given LRA 2002, s 27(2)(b)(iii) which provides generally that leases 'under which the right to possession is discontinuous' are registrable.

[6] This would potentially be a daunting and endless undertaking.

[7] Surely not; but does the statute need to say so?

give security in which lenders could have confidence.[8] And the Land Transfer Act 1858 in South Australia was the product of the need for settlers to be able to buy and sell land quickly and cheaply and without the inconvenience of managing, storing and producing title deeds. Those motivations tell us what particular land registration systems were for, in the eyes of those who demanded them. In that vein, we can perhaps say that the English statute of 1862 was the product of a desire to be able to simplify conveyancing.

Whether each historic registration system has done what it was demanded and intended for is a matter of fact and opinion. Today, what matters most is whether it does what it must do *now*. Above all, it must be reliable, and it must make provision for those occasions when it has been relied upon and yet turns out not to be reliable. A balance has to be struck between defining reality (whereby title is conferred by the Register) and responding to reality (whereby the Register can be altered in certain circumstances in response to off-Register facts and events). There is always a balance to be struck and that is why 'title by registration' is rhetoric rather than a legal principle; no system can claim to take precedence in all circumstances to off-Register events.[9] There are also many different ways of striking that balance, and that is why—even looking at title registration alone and leaving aside deeds registration—we can identify families of title registration systems which embody different choices as to how to make provision for reliability—or indefeasibility, as the Torrens lawyers call it.

Why, though, look at indefeasibility when the LRA 2002 already makes provision for it in schedules 4 and 8, and when the Law Commission in its 2001 report on *Land Registration for the Twenty-First Century* gave thorough and scholarly consideration to the subject?[10] I think there are two different kinds of answer to that question.

The first and obvious answer is that certain things were left uncertain in the LRA 2002.[11] Fundamentally, 'mistake' was not defined, although its meaning was expounded in the Law Commission's 2001 report[12] and the case law has explored it since. It is now reasonably clear that where a transfer from X to Y is a mistake, so too is the registration of a mortgage or transfer effected (innocently and legitimately) by Y to Z. The scope of 'mistake' is crucial, because there can be no indemnity without a mistake which is susceptible to correction. The drafting of the Act did not close down some different ways of analysing situations where alteration is wanted. Bullet-proof certainty in statutory drafting may not always be advisable, because the law needs room to breathe. But there is sufficient uncertainty here to generate real difficulty for landowners and for Land Registry, so it needs to be solved.

The second reason why the Law Commission is looking at indefeasibility is that the answers to the questions at the heart of the issue may well have changed since 2002. The Law Commission rightly highlighted the unique nature of the English version of indefeasibility, where the answer to who keeps the land depends upon who is in possession of it.

[8] See the preamble to The West Riding Register Act 1703 (2 & 3 Anne, c 4). See further E Cooke, *The New Law of Land Registration* (Oxford, Hart Publishing, 2003) 18.

[9] Take the most basic example: a title register that shows A as the proprietor of land becomes inaccurate when A dies.

[10] Law Commission, *Land Registration for the Twenty-First Century: A Conveyancing Revolution* (Law Com No 271, 2001).

[11] This paragraph, in particular, has now been overtaken by changes in the law, as a result of the Court of Appeal's decision in *Swift 1st Ltd v Chief Land Registrar* [2015] EWCA 330, [2015] Ch 602.

[12] See n 10 above.

There is much to be said for the convenience of that principle and for its resonance with human rights concerns.[13] But there is apparently rather more fraud around now than there was in 2001. With frequency comes a heightened concern, and undeniable discomfort with the possibility that a purchaser, however innocent, might keep land that should not have been transferred to him rather than it being restored to the registered proprietor who should not have lost it.

That second answer means that when we interrogate the concept of indefeasibility we shall not be asking: what is the answer that the Law Commission intended in 2001, or that Parliament intended in 2002? Rather, we need to find the right answers for today.

In doing that, we are inevitably going to be looking sideways and considering in detail the answers given in other jurisdictions. What is special about the Torrens systems? Do we need to become Germanic? And how can we resist the Scots, whose new scheme was conceived by the Scottish Law Commission and detailed in its brilliantly-written Discussion Papers and Report.[14] I have already had long conversations with the former Commissioners responsible for that inspirational project. One of the things that the Law Commission for England and Wales has to do is to work out what it means not to be Scottish. Relevant differences include the fact that we are working within a common law system rather than from a civil law basis, and are examining a title registration system that is 150 years old, rather than not-quite-30 years old as was the Scottish system.

The outcome of our enquiry is not yet known. We do not enter it with preconceived ideas. My own views have modified in the last 10 years or so. Whatever solution we arrive at is likely to be essentially English rather than modelled too closely upon any one other system. And it will have to be devised with a view to its systemic impact upon the Land Registry and the conveyancing system. That system itself is going to be under scrutiny too, because inevitably we shall have to look at the current state of play on electronic conveyancing and the extent to which legal change is necessary to facilitate its further development.

Accordingly, although our review of Land Registration might sound prosaic, it is in fact going to touch on fundamentals and resolve some significant problematic issues—but not, we hope, in a way that breaks the current system. When we publish our consultation paper,[15] we expect to have positive proposals for the solution to the uncertainties about indefeasibility as well as for the more peripheral questions. This conference, as a forum for sharing ideas and concerns, is a vital step towards the formulation of those proposals.

[13] See especially the protection afforded to one's 'home' by Art 8 of the European Convention on Human Rights.

[14] Culminating in Scottish Law Commission, *Report on Land Registration* (Scot Law Com No 222, 2010), and ultimately the Land Registration etc (Scotland) Act 2012.

[15] The paper has now been published. See n 2 above.

2

The Land Registry's Perspective: The Practical Challenges of Land Registration

JOHN POWNALL AND RICHARD HILL

I. Introduction

Land registration is about people. Of course, technically speaking, it is about estates and interests, transfers and leases, charges and incumbrances; but at its heart is the society it serves. Property ownership affects all aspects of our lives. It relates to where our children go to school, to our plans for retirement, to our partnerships, our businesses, and our work. Because all of this matters to us, disputes often arise.

In the middle of all this sit the Land Registry lawyers—the 'Land Registrar' and the 'Assistant Land Registrar'—whose job it is to administer the often complex contentious applications which surface when property rights come into conflict.

This chapter will explore the picture of land registration at the sharp end. By considering how Land Registry lawyers interpret and apply a number of key aspects of the Land Registration Act ('LRA') 2002, it is hoped to give an insight into how land registration works in practice when things become difficult.

II. Registration, Alteration and Objection

The LRA 2002 is intended to create an efficient and clear system for the registration and protection of estates and interests. The majority of transactions and dealings relating to land are registered without difficulty, and the Land Registry lawyer will rarely be involved. On occasion, discrete technical points about applications are referred to the lawyer—for example, issues around capacity, execution, overreaching or the like. It is notable that of a total workforce of around 4,000 people, only 116 are qualified lawyers employed as such.

Complexities, contentious applications and disagreements are most commonly met, and lawyers invariably involved, when one delves into issues which lie beneath the surface of the land registration system. In particular, there may be mistakes in the register, often through no fault of the Registrar. Such mistakes may require alteration (and/or rectification) pursuant to schedule 4 to the LRA 2002, and give rise to indemnity rights under schedule 8. Management and supervision of the so-called 'state guarantee' is a core function of the Land Registry lawyer.

Mistakes which might require alteration can be simple clerical errors, or can be more serious. For example, the same piece of land may be erroneously included in two adjacent registered titles—as occurred in the recent Court of Appeal case of *Parshall v Hackney*.[1] Or a title may have been registered based on defective deeds—as where some or all of the land had been sold twice by the same vendor (so-called 'double conveyancing'). A mistake may also arise where an applicant claims that a title based on adverse possession is incorrect because the squatter had not been in adverse possession for the required period of time, such as occurred in another appeal court case, *Baxter v Mannion*.[2] Issues also arise around the presence or absence of entries relating to restrictive covenants or easements, both in terms of whether they should be noted as burdens on the servient title or, in the case of easements, whether they should be guaranteed as appurtenant to the dominant land.

The meaning of mistake is complex and rather unclear. There are differing views, notably explored by Emma Lees.[3] Such complexities are most conspicuous in the context of fraud, a common problem being where rectification of the Register is sought against a bona fide registered proprietor (C), who acquired from a previous registered proprietor (B), whose own title was acquired from the original proprietor (A) via a forged document. A difficult question is whether C's title can be impugned, despite his being an innocent purchaser. This issue is not discussed here at length—it is the subject of other chapters in this book[4]—but it has been the subject of prolonged discussion amongst Land Registry's lawyers.

Interestingly, there is no statutorily prescribed procedure for making an application to the Registrar for alteration, either to correct a mistake or on one of the other statutory bases for alteration. If somebody wants the Registrar to alter the Register they will, though, have to apply to the Registrar, as the Register cannot be altered except by a Registry official. The general procedure adopted by the Registry—and encouraged through the Registry's online guidance—involves using a form, Form AP1, to make an application for alteration.

Generally speaking, whilst the LRA 2002 provides that the Registrar may unilaterally decide to alter the Register on one of the statutory alteration grounds,[5] it is uncommon for significant alterations to be effected without there having been an application from somebody to make that alteration. The reasons for this are explained in our discussion of objections at the end of this section, but all applications will require evidence to prove, on the balance of probabilities, that a ground of alteration actually exists.[6] For example, evidence of a 'mistake' might take the form of a statement of truth, a deed, or a surveyor's report about historic boundaries.

The lawyer at the Land Registry will assess the application and its supporting evidence, and then make a decision about the possibility of alteration in the case. If, for example,

[1] [2013] EWCA Civ 240, [2013] Ch 568.

[2] [2011] EWCA Civ 120, [2011] 1 WLR 1594.

[3] E Lees, 'Title by Registration: Rectification, Indemnity and Mistake and the Land Registration Act 2002' (2013) *MLR* 62.

[4] See chs 7–10, 13 and 16 of this book.

[5] LRA 2002, s 65 and sch 4, esp para 5.

[6] LRA 2002, sch 4, paras 2 (for court-ordered alterations) and 5 (for Registrar-effected alterations).

the alteration would be prejudicial to the registered proprietor, and therefore amount to rectification as defined under the LRA 2002, it is vital to know whether or not the proprietor is in possession. This is because of the special statutory protection afforded to such an owner. Absent consent of the registered proprietor, rectification cannot be carried out against a registered proprietor in possession unless he has either (i) caused or substantially contributed to the mistake by fraud or lack of care, or (ii) it would for any other reason be unjust for the alteration not to be made.[7] An argument will need to be provided to support the conclusion that the applicant falls into one of those categories of exception.

With regard to the second and more commonly pleaded exception—that rectification will be ordered against a registered proprietor in possession where it would be *unjust not to alter* the Register—in one case coming before the Adjudicator (now the Land Registration Division of the First-tier Tribunal (Property Chamber) (the 'Tribunal')),[8] a registered proprietor in possession has had their title rectified because their property was acquired for investment purposes, and because the applicant had emotional and personal links to the property.[9] An estoppel binding on the registered proprietor in favour of the applicant may also satisfy this ground.[10] Whether or not there would be an injustice is an assessment to be made by the fact-finding Tribunal in the light of all of the relevant data.[11]

At the stage of application, however, it is for the lawyer to consider the case and make a judgement as to whether, on balance, the arguments may be viable. The role of the Land Registry lawyer is to act as a kind of gatekeeper. It would be undesirable for flimsy or unmeritorious applications to be permitted into the system, as this would cause an unnecessary blight on the title. It also invariably involves expense, time and trouble for the proprietor. The aim of land registration is, after all, to simplify conveyancing and property ownership as far as possible, not to introduce unnecessary complexity and bureaucracy.

Every application to alter the Register potentially affects the rights of others, so the system has to allow for objections to be made. This provides one of the most challenging aspects of the Land Registry lawyer's job. Section 73 of the LRA 2002 provides that any application can be met with an objection. Significantly, however, the Act goes beyond allowing for persons with interests adverse to the applicant's to be heard. Objection to an application for alteration can be made by *anyone*, whether or not they claim an interest in the land. It is only in the cases of cancellation of cautions against first registration or of unilateral notices that the identity of the objector is limited—to those who are named as beneficiaries of the entries being 'warned off'.[12]

[7] LRA 2002, sch 4, para 3(2) and 6(2).

[8] See ch 3 of this book.

[9] See *Atake v Pavey*, a 2005 decision of the Adjudicator to HM Land Registry. The Adjudicator considered that the intentions of the applicant and respondent in respect of the property were relevant to the exercise of his discretion. The respondent had purchased the property as a speculative investment, whereas the applicant had a lengthy sentimental attachment to the property and long-term plans for his family linked to it. This influenced the Adjudicator's decision to rectify against the respondent registered proprietor who was in possession: see [51].

[10] *Ruoff & Roper: Registered Conveyancing* (London, Sweet and Maxwell, looseleaf) para 36.002.

[11] See, eg, *Walker v Burton* [2013] EWCA 1228, [2013] 1 P & CR 9, initially heard by the Deputy Adjudicator, where registration of a 300-acre fell was left undisturbed in spite of the fact that the first registration was a mistake. The Court of Appeal considered that it would not be unjust not to alter the Register.

[12] This was the language used in relation to the Land Registration Act 1925, s 55, but it remains in currency amongst experienced practitioners.

The Registrar must serve notice of any objection received and the application cannot proceed until the objection has been 'disposed of'[13]—unless, of course, the objection is groundless. Difficulties arise in defining the line between well-grounded and groundless objections. The LRA 2002 does not specify when an objection will be groundless, so it has been up to Land Registry lawyers to decide and, often sitting in the middle of two or more warring parties, ensure that fairness is achieved in the myriad different situations which arise. The consequences can be significant. Where an objection cannot be dismissed as groundless, then unless it is withdrawn, the matter must be referred to the Tribunal for a judicial hearing. Such referrals almost invariably result in the process becoming lengthier, costlier, and more vexatious for the parties concerned, and the title itself usually becomes unmarketable until the matter is resolved.

The general rule of thumb applied by Land Registry lawyers is that an objection will be groundless when it *cannot* succeed, either on the facts, or the law. When making this decision, the Registrar is exercising a quasi-judicial function, potentially subject to judicial review in the High Court. The Registrar's reasoning must therefore be clear, and submissions have to be considered from both sides, impartially, observing the rules of natural justice. As an essentially administrative body, the Land Registry will focus on the *arguments* put forward by the objector; *evaluation of evidence* and *findings of fact* are for judges to make in court. That said, if clear evidence is available which contradicts an objector's case in a material way, the Registrar may be permitted to take note of facts which would result in the dismissal of an objection.[14] However, the Registrar is unlikely to insist on the production of evidence by the objector to support the contentions made in the objection statement. Accordingly, the threshold which an objector has to cross to succeed is low,[15] which is in keeping with the administrative nature of the Registrar's primary function.

Contentious cases vary in difficulty. An easy case of an objection being groundless is where the subject matter of the objection is legally irrelevant to the disputed entry in the Register. For example, an applicant might allege that she contributed towards the purchase price of a registered title, and has thereby obtained a beneficial interest in the property via a resulting trust. Such an interest would justify her applying for a 'Form A' restriction,[16] to ensure that any future registered dispositions of the title satisfy the conditions of overreaching. In such circumstances, if an objector disputes the *amount* of the applicant's contribution, but concedes that *some* contribution was made and therefore that the applicant has *some* beneficial interest in the property, the objection is groundless: it is the *existence* of a trust interest, not its *extent*, that justifies the entry of a Form A restriction.

Another easy case where an objection is readily dismissed as groundless is where the *mechanics of the LRA 2002* render the objection unviable as a matter of law. For example, an objection to the registration of a transfer from A to B on the basis that it was made in breach

[13] LRA 2002, s 73(5).

[14] An example may be where an aerial photograph, dated, manifestly contradicts the claimant squatter's case that he built an extension to his property by a certain date, thus bringing him within the rules for adverse possession. However, even here one would have to be careful. The squatter might argue that his possession prior to the extension was enough to count, or indeed, that the photographic evidence is not entirely reliable for some reason.

[15] See, eg, *Silkstone v Tatnall* [2010] EWHC 1627 (Ch), [2010] 3 EGLR 25, [17], where Floyd J described the 'threshold' which an objector must pass as being 'very low'.

[16] Land Registration Rules 2003, SI 2003/1417, r 91 and sch 4.

of a contract for sale between A and X will be dismissed as groundless if A's registered title is free of any restriction.[17] The objector's (X's) remedy will be via an action against the seller (A) for breach of the sale contract.

In other circumstances, determining whether an objection is groundless may be rather more difficult. Consider a situation where an applicant, having obtained a court-ordered charging order over a joint owner's beneficial share in a registered estate, seeks to enter a 'Form K' restriction[18] in the Register, restricting dealings with the property subject to the charging order. What happens if the person over whose share the charging order was made alleges that he did not own a beneficial interest in the registered estate at the time the order was made—and therefore objects to the Form K restriction? Even if we assume, as the Registrar must at this stage, that the objector's argument is *factually* accurate—and that he had no beneficial interest when the charging order was made—it remains unclear whether the objection is viable as a matter of *law*. On the one hand, it is arguable that the Registrar should simply accept that where a *court* makes a charging order, no objection to the *Registrar* is possible, and that the correct route is for the objector to make a further application to the court to have the order set aside. On the other hand, it is arguable that the objection is viable, on the basis that if the objector had no beneficial interest, there was no interest for the charging order to bite on, and so no basis for a Form K restriction. Cases before the Tribunal have shown variations in approach to this difficult question.[19] As stated earlier, an objection will only be dismissed as a matter of law where the legal case *cannot* be made. Where the law is uncertain, such a confident dismissal cannot be made and the objection must be dealt with—in other words, where we face two conflicting judicial approaches, we cannot rely on one of them to dismiss an objection which would be valid if the conflicting approach were the correct one.

One test which Land Registry lawyers sometimes use to determine issues relating to objections is to ask whether, if the objection is taken to be factually true, the application can nevertheless be said to be viable. However, care must be exercised when applying it. Consider, for example, the well-known situation where a transfer of a registered estate from A to B has been forged, and B, an innocent purchaser who has been registered as proprietor by mistake, sells on to C. Here, what happens if A objects to the registration of C? At first glance, A's objection appears to be groundless: when B was registered as proprietor—albeit mistakenly—he was 'deemed' by section 58 of the LRA 2002 to be the rightful owner; on its face, therefore, the application to register the transfer from B to C seems defect-free. However, it is also possible to argue that A's objection is viable on the basis that, although B and C are innocent and ignorant of the fraud, completion of the registration of C would have the effect of creating a further mistake in the Register, or at least of perpetuating the mistaken registration of B. Historically, deciding whether A has a viable objection in these circumstances has been a difficult issue, and there have been competing decisions and critical academic commentary.[20] However, the decision of the Court of Appeal in

[17] The 'owner's powers' afforded to a registered proprietor are assumed to be uninhibited in such a case: LRA 2002, ss 23–26.

[18] LRR 2003, r 91 and sch 4.

[19] See *Salam v Shah* REF/2008/0944 (unreported, 8 May 2009), and *Commercial First Business Limited v Choudry* [2012] EWLandRA 2011_0713/2011_0716 (27 July 2012).

[20] Discussed in chs 7–10 and 16 of this book.

Gold Harp Properties Ltd v Macleod[21] appears to have settled the point—it appears that schedule 4 is a powerful trump card, which would justify A obtaining rectification of the Register once C is registered. By extension, if A were to *object* to C's registration in advance, A's objection should be treated as viable, and not groundless.

III. Registration, Fraudsters and Indemnity

In the past 10 years, registration fraud has increased considerably. One may speculate as to the reasons for this. However, the incidence and value of fraud on the whole has generally increased—especially identity fraud. To some extent, the unlawful impersonation of property ownership is simply one of many facets of that wider picture.

The Land Registry is often left to pick up the pieces. Typically, a fraudster pretends to be the owner of the property, goes to a bank and purports to create a charge over the property in return for a loan. The money is paid over, the fraudster disappears, the mortgage arrears build up, and the bank starts possession proceedings against an innocent occupying owner. At that stage, the owner contacts the Land Registry, and rectification of the Register is sought, to remove the charge. Often rectification occurs on the assumption that an indemnity will be paid to the bank by the Land Registry, within schedule 8 to the LRA 2002.

These claims can be difficult to handle. Before the Court of Appeal's decision in *Swift 1st Ltd v Chief Land Registrar*,[22] legal uncertainties played their part in affecting the course of such claims, and the availability of an indemnity. The so-called '*Malory*[23] trust' (which controversially treated the defrauded owner as retaining full beneficial ownership when a forged disposition was registered)[24] as well as the rule (also derived from the *Malory* case) that the defrauded owner would retain an overriding interest binding on future disponees,[25] meant that banks in Swift's position were faced with an uncertain battle over their entitlement to indemnity.

Long before *Swift 1st* was heard, there had been much academic criticism of *Malory*. The Land Registry therefore found itself in some difficulties arguing points which seemed wrong in principle—particularly the *Malory* trust argument, which effectively rendered registration a practical nullity in the event of a fraudulent disposition.

Where are we now? *Swift 1st* has decided that banks faced with the situation in the example above are not precluded as a matter of law from receiving an indemnity. The *Malory* trust argument has now been discredited, and the fact that the true owner can be argued to retain some form of equitable right in a forged transaction will not in and of itself deny the bank an indemnity.

Despite the clarity brought by *Swift 1st*, some questions remain unanswered. The problems that remain are as much evidential as technical. Claimants like the bank in the

[21] [2014] EWCA Civ 1084, [2015] 1 WLR 1249.

[22] [2015] EWCA Civ 330, [2015] Ch 602.

[23] *Malory Enterprises Ltd v Cheshire Homes (UK) Ltd* [2002] EWCA Civ 151, [2002] Ch 216.

[24] Applied in *Fitzwilliam v Richall Holdings Services Ltd* [2013] EWHC 86 (Ch), [2013] 1 P & CR 19.

[25] Land Registration Act 1925, s 70(1)(g) and LRA 2002, s 29 and sch 3, para 2 (the owner's 'right to rectify' the Register was treated as a proprietary right which, when coupled with actual occupation, constituted an overriding interest).

example above are denied a schedule 8 indemnity, or may have their indemnity reduced, where they have carelessly contributed to the mistake in the Register.[26] Faced with a claim, how can Land Registry be sure that the bank has exercised proper care when deciding to lend to the ostensible owner? In *Swift 1st* itself, this was not a matter referred on appeal. The High Court found in the bank's favour on the issue of due diligence. If the procedures followed by the bank (or its lawyers) were the industry standard in 2006, then the diligence was 'due'. It did not matter that nobody went around the house and asked the real owner, Mrs Rani, who she was and what she was doing there. Would the same be the case today? Surely, the rule in schedule 8 that permits a reduction in indemnity in the event of lack of care is designed for just this kind of scenario?

Another real issue is the problem of the Land Registry's statutory right of recourse in respect of any indemnity payments it has made. If the Register is rectified and somebody is indemnified by the Land Registry, then the rights of the indemnified person (bank, buyer etc) against any lawyers involved in the fraudulent transaction—rights in tort, contract, or arising from an equitable wrong—are notionally resurrected so that they may be pursued by the Registry, in the hope of recouping some or all of its indemnity payment. The problem here is that it may be difficult to establish any legal liability owed to the indemnified person by the lawyers involved with the fraudulent transaction. In particular, if the right which is being pursued is against a firm of solicitors who did not represent the indemnified person in the transaction, then it may be that one must try to establish a claim in tort (most likely in negligence, for breach of a duty of care) or a claim for breach of warranty or undertaking. These are very difficult areas of law, and establishing liability can be problematic. Readers may well be aware, for example, of the difficulties faced by a non-client, who seeks to establish that a firm of solicitors is liable in the tort of negligence for pure financial losses.[27] Recent cases involving fraudulent property transactions have involved consideration of the law in these areas.[28] Much will depend upon the particular factual circumstances of the case.[29]

IV. Registration and Plans

Lawyers are not surveyors and, by the same token, surveyors are not lawyers. We speak different languages. Lawyers discuss matters in terms of legal principle, the doctrine of precedent, the rules about interpretation. Words are crucial. Surveyors see things through the prism of the theodolite. But both lawyers and surveyors have to work with plans, and sometimes trying to work out who owns what provides the ultimate challenge for both

[26] LRA 2002, s 103 and sch 8, para 5.

[27] *White v Jones* [1995] 2 AC 207 is the leading case in which a duty was found to be owed to a non-client. The facts were, however, unusual; and more generally, the necessity to identify an 'assumption of responsibility' to the non-client claimant can present a significant obstacle.

[28] See *P&P Property Ltd v Owen White & Catlin LLP* [2016] EWHC 2276 (Ch), [2017] PNLR 3, and the cases cited therein.

[29] See, however, recent proposals to reform the LRA 2002 to extend the duties owed by conveyancers and banks in connection with, eg, party verification, discussed by Nicholas Hopkins in ch 12 of this book, and in Law Commission, *Updating the Land Registration Act 2002—A Consultation Paper* (Law Com CP No 227, 2016).

professions. More often than not, it is the Land Registry plan which provides the starting point of reference for anyone engaged in a dispute over a piece of land, whether that be the precise location of a boundary, or the entitlement to a specific curtilage.

Problematically, however, this is often not the right place to start. Many boundaries recorded at Land Registry are 'general boundaries', not 'determined boundaries', and therefore, by statute, do 'not determine the exact line of the boundary'.[30] Land Registry lawyers tire of uttering the words: 'Your title plan is registered with general boundaries only, and cannot be relied upon to [determine who owns the hedge, or confirm the proper location of the fence, or tell you who owns the private road]'. Nevertheless, people understandably expect their title plans to be definitive. Occasionally, parties will instruct surveyors to map the title plan boundary carefully on a much smaller scale plan to assist in a dispute, and this can often be the root of much confusion and contention.

The law governing situations in which boundary lines are disputed is complex and, indeed, sometimes unpredictable. There appear to be two competing approaches.

First, until recently,[31] the Land Registry operated on the basis that disputes about the precise location of a general boundary between two properties were outside the law of rectification and indemnity. The Register does not *guarantee* the precise line of general boundaries (the 'general boundaries rule'). As such, if land at a boundary line is removed from a registered title, this alteration is by definition not 'prejudicial' to the owner: the owner was never conclusively promised by the LRA 2002 that the land on the general boundary that *appeared* to belong to his title was indeed included. The further implications of this are that the change to the Register is treated as a mere alteration and not rectification, because the change will not prejudice the owner's title; and, more importantly, that no indemnity will be available to the aggrieved owner if the general boundary line in his title is altered.

Unfortunately, following the Court of Appeal's decision in *Parshall v Hackney*,[32] the position has become less certain. In *Parshall*, the court adopted a second, and different, approach to boundary disputes. The dispute concerned ownership of a thin strip of land on a boundary, which was 'doubly registered': it appeared on two registered titles.[33] Although the dispute might have been treated as a typical *general boundary* issue, and as such, outside the provisions for indemnity, Mummery LJ in fact dealt with it as a *property dispute*—in other words, he dealt with it as a dispute that went beyond the accuracy of the red lines on the title plans. In a 'property dispute', as opposed to a 'boundary dispute', the general boundary rule is not capable of answering the issue at stake. In a *property dispute*, when the Register is altered to correct the double registration, the owner whose title loses the overlapping land is entitled to be indemnified for his loss—the alteration qualifies as rectification for the purposes of schedules 4 and 8 of the LRA 2002, since such double registrations are by their nature 'mistakes', and removing the overlapping land will be prejudicial. This second approach to the alteration of boundaries shown on title plans is problematic, and contrary to the view which the Land Registry held prior to *Parshall*, that the alteration was not prejudicial and so the owner had no entitlement to an indemnity.

[30] LRA 2002, s 60(2).

[31] More precisely, up until the Court of Appeal's decision in *Parshall v Hackney* [2013] EWCA Civ 240, [2013] Ch 568, and following statements in *Derbyshire County Council v Fallon* [2007] EWHC 1326 (Ch), [2007] 3 EGLR 44. See also *Strachey v Ramage* [2008] EWCA Civ 384, [2008] 2 P & CR 8.

[32] [2013] EWCA Civ 240, [2013] Ch 568.

[33] The disputed land was 'under two metres across at its widest point and four metres long': [2013] EWCA Civ 240, [2013] Ch 568, [1] (Mummery LJ).

Looking to the future, it will clearly be essential to be able to identify which disputes are rightly categorised as 'boundary disputes' (for which no indemnity is available) and which are 'property disputes' (for which indemnity *is* available). And yet drawing a line between the two types of disputes will be tricky. When is the shift in the red line significant enough to constitute a 'property' change?

In *Parshall*, the issue was complicated by the fact that the land concerned formed part of a valuable car parking area adjacent to a west London property. Were those factors material to the dispute's categorisation as a *property dispute*? It is not obvious that the application of established land registration principles such as the general boundaries rule should vary from place to place depending upon the locus of the title. Mummery LJ observed that the land, '[b]eing in Chelsea, London SW3 and part of Smith's Charity Kensington Estate, [was] worth enough for the parties to survive three rounds of civil litigation'. Should this make a difference? There is nothing in the judgment to say it does, but one cannot help feeling that Mummery LJ found it easier to dismiss the general boundaries rule in the case before him, and recast the case as a *property dispute*, because he was dealing with a small sliver of land with real value to the parties. That value was reflected in the very fact of the litigation. Removal of that land from one of the titles did not, therefore, appear to be a mere 'tidying up' administrative process, without cost to the Land Registry (in the shape of an indemnity).

Some might say that that is how it should be. Registration is supposed to be final, and title is supposed to be guaranteed. If something goes wrong, especially where the Land Registry was at fault, then an indemnity to the aggrieved party should follow. Normally, therefore, where it is clear to the Registry lawyer dealing with the matter that there is a mistake, and that indemnity might be payable, it is often sensible to seek to resolve matters prior to the issue reaching the Court of Appeal. Boundary/property disputes can be intractable and expensive, and the real winners are often the litigating parties' lawyers and specialist surveyors, whose time is costly. This is aptly demonstrated in the recent case of *Murdoch v Amesbury*.[34] This involved an application for a 'determined boundary' under section 60 of the LRA 2002, following referral by the Registrar under section 73. The Tribunal decided that the application should be dismissed, but nonetheless proceeded to establish the position of the true boundary, in order to bring the background boundary dispute to a resolution. This was challenged by Mr and Mrs Murdoch, who appealed to the Upper Tribunal on a jurisdictional point—that the First-Tier Tribunal had limited powers, only to decide the specific application itself, and not go beyond this to establish where the true boundary lay. On appeal it was held that the Tribunal's power was indeed so confined. This means that the process for seeking a 'determined boundary' should be seen as having a relatively limited role in the context of boundary disputes. And what it meant in the specific case, of course, was that both parties had spent a great deal of money, and were no further forward in being able establish where their boundaries truly lay, despite a protracted dispute process under section 73. In subsequent First-Tier Tribunal cases, the Tribunal judge has sought to confine the jurisdictional point in *Murdoch* so as to preserve the right of the Tribunal to do more than simply decide whether the application for a determined boundary could properly be made, and thus enable the Tribunal to resolve the underlying boundary dispute between the parties.[35]

[34] [2016] UKUT 3 (TCC).

[35] See, eg, *Bean and Saxton v Katz and Katz* [2016] UKUT 168 (TCC).

V. Registration and Adverse Possession

Until relatively recently, a large proportion of applications or disputes relating to adverse possession were determined under the Limitation Act ('LA') 1980, sections 15 and 17 and schedule 1. The rapid expansion of the coverage of registered land in the 2000s, coupled with the introduction of the adverse possession regime in schedule 6 to the LRA 2002, has altered this pattern considerably. Many new problems have emerged since the advent of the LRA 2002's innovative new regime.

A Land Registry lawyer's first task in a case concerning alleged adverse possession is to ascertain which of four possible procedures may be applicable.

If the land is unregistered, the application will still be governed by the LA 1980, which provides that the 'paper owner's' title is automatically extinguished by the completion of 12 years' adverse possession by the squatter. In such circumstances, a first registration application would be made, supported by evidence; and if the required 12-year period of adverse possession is found, a possessory title would usually be granted by Land Registry.

If the claimed land is registered, however, there are three possible procedures. First, if the squatter had been in adverse possession of the claimed land for 12 years prior to the 'paper owner' registering his title, then the 'paper owner's' title will have been extinguished under the LA 1980, and the 'paper owner' has, accordingly, been mistakenly registered. The squatter can therefore seek alteration of the Register, to correct the mistake. Secondly, if the squatter can show that the 12 year period of adverse possession ended when the land was registered, but before the coming into force of the LRA 2002 on 13 October 2003, then an application for registration as owner can be made under the transitional provisions, based on the rights which that squatter would had acquired under the Land Registration Act 1925.[36] Thirdly, in all other cases of adverse possession of registered land, a squatter can make an application to become the new registered proprietor under the LRA 2002, schedule 6, provided that the squatter can show 10 years' adverse possession up to the date of the application.

It is the last of these possible procedures which most often presents difficulties for the Land Registry and its customers. This is perhaps to be expected, given that the new schedule 6 scheme involves a complex mixture of common law and statutory requirements: the traditional common law requirements for showing 'adverse possession'[37] have been retained—factual possession, an intention to possess, and that the possession was adverse—but additionally, the applicant/Land Registry must now follow the complex statutory procedure within LRA 2002, schedule 6. The procedure involves the squatter applying to become the new registered proprietor within paragraph 1 (using Form ADV1);[38] the serving of a notice on the registered proprietor; a possible counter-notice under paragraph 5, and/or an objection served/made by the true owner (using Form NAP).[39] If a counter-notice *is* served, there are three possible grounds which the squatter must be able to establish in order to succeed at this point.[40] The schedule 6 procedure therefore presents a number of difficulties. Three are highlighted here.

[36] Land Registration Act 2002, s 134 and sch 19, para 1; and Land Registration Act 1925, s 75.
[37] See, eg, *JA Pye (Oxford) Ltd v Graham* [2002] UKHL 30, [2003] 1 AC 419.
[38] LRR 2003, r 188.
[39] LRR 2003, r 190 and sch 1.
[40] LRA 2002, s 97 and sch 6, para 5.

First, the general complexity of the schedule 6 procedure can render the application process lengthy for both the parties and the Land Registry. Faced with a schedule 6 application for adverse possession, a registered proprietor may object on the facts, serve a counter-notice,[41] or do both.

An objection which is not groundless will be referred to the Tribunal for resolution—a lengthy and potentially expensive process. An objection may, for example, go to the issue of the squatter's alleged possession: the registered proprietor may argue that the applicant has not in fact been in exclusive possession for the requisite period of 10 years, or that the squatter was actually in possession with the consent of the owner. The law of adverse possession is very case specific in its application. Leading cases such as *Pye v Graham* have laid down some judicial guidance about the meaning of the essential components of the concept of 'adverse possession'—for example, the need for the squatter to establish that he is sufficiently in control of the land. Nevertheless, facts are often murky. When the Registry is presented with an adverse possession application, the application will be supported by a declaration or statement which seeks to show that the applicant has been relevantly in possession for at least 10 years. Such statements are by their nature self-serving, and so it is necessary for the Registry to commission a survey of the land, to ascertain whether what is 'on the ground' is supportive of the claim. How old are the fences, for example?

In some situations, however, there will be no need for the registered proprietor to object to the facts establishing the squatter's adverse possession: the serving of a counter-notice will suffice to defeat the squatter's schedule 6 application. Such a counter-notice will be effective unless the squatter can bring himself within one of three narrow statutory exceptions/grounds—namely cases relating to a mistaken boundary line; cases where the squatter was otherwise entitled to the land (eg because he had been gifted the land by a will); or cases where the squatter had an independently-acquired estoppel claim to the land.[42] In the event of an unopposed counter-notice being served by the registered proprietor, the squatter's application will be cancelled. But if the squatter seeks to rely on one of the statutory exceptions/grounds, and the evident facts might support his case, then the issue would again be referred to the Tribunal.

Secondly, further uncertainties arise out of the rule that, if a squatter's application is initially defeated by the registered proprietor's serving of a counter-notice, the squatter may re-apply under schedule 6, paragraph 6, to take over the registered title if he remains in adverse possession for a further two years. This time, the squatter's application cannot be opposed by the serving of a counter-notice. The paragraph 6 procedure raises some difficult questions. In particular, is it open to the registered proprietor to object on the basis that there was factually no adverse possession for the required 10 years before the first application was made under paragraph 1, if no objection was made on this ground when that first application was being considered? Ordinarily, the squatter is entitled to be registered if he applies under paragraph 6, subject only to specific exceptions. Does this clear statutory entitlement override any possible 'new' objection, on the basis that adverse possession had not been shown at the outset? In practice, this problem has not arisen, but it remains a potential, unresolved issue that may arise in the future.

[41] LRR 2003, r 190.
[42] See n 40.

Thirdly, Form NAP, which is used by registered proprietors to object and/or serve a counter-notice to a squatter's application, can give rise to some difficulties. The Land Registry must exercise considerable care to ensure that the contents of this statutory form are properly understood and interpreted by both registered proprietors and practitioners. The High Court has recently held that even where the registered proprietor has not ticked the relevant box indicating an intention to serve a counter-notice, the form might still be effective as a counter-notice if the Registrar could be in no reasonable doubt that that was the proprietor's intention.[43] Land Registry lawyers therefore have to consider carefully any written submissions which accompany the form and seek clarification as to intention where necessary. These are always difficult cases. The Land Registry lawyer must act appropriately when conducting such investigations, and never veer into assisting a party in an inappropriately advisory way. This applies in all such situations, especially if matters become contentious.

It goes without saying that Land Registry lawyers need to comply with the most recent judicial decisions on the functioning of the schedule 6 procedure. Two important cases have recently impacted on the interpretation of the schedule, and have caused us to change our practices.

First, in *Zarb v Parry*,[44] the Court of Appeal delivered an important ruling on the functioning of one of the statutory grounds/exceptions which justify a squatter defeating a proprietor's counter-notice—namely where the squatter has adversely possessed land adjacent to his own (on a general boundary) in the 'reasonable belief' that the land was his own. It was originally thought by the Land Registry and commentators that the 10-year period of reasonable belief as to ownership could relate to any time during the squatter's entire period of adverse possession—which of course might exceed 10 years. However, in *Zarb*, the Court of Appeal rejected this view, deciding instead that the period of reasonable belief must, like possession itself, extend up to the point at which an application is made to the Registrar. From the Land Registry's point of view, this creates difficulties. If an applicant has not taken steps to become registered as proprietor as soon as they are aware that they are not owners of the land, or as soon as such a belief is unreasonable, they will not be able to rely on the relevant condition in order to defeat the counter-notice and secure their registration as proprietors under schedule 6. However, how much time can pass between becoming aware of the ownership issue and making the application? There will inevitably be a time gap of some sort: once it is understood that there is a title issue, advice must be sought and an application prepared, all of which takes time. It is a matter of judgement and careful consideration for Land Registry lawyers to ensure such cases are handled appropriately, and to guarantee a level playing-field, impartiality and fairness.

Secondly, and more widely-reported, was the important decision of the Court of Appeal in *Best v Chief Land Registrar*,[45] concerning residential squatting on registered land. In a rare judicial review ruling against the Land Registrar, the Court of Appeal decided that 'criminal acts' relied on as part of a squatter's application for registration did not bar acquisition of title via the law of adverse possession, despite the illegality of the squatter's conduct.

[43] *Hopkins v Beacon* [2011] EWHC 2899 (Ch) applying the 'reasonable recipient' approach (established in *Mannai Investment Co v Eagle Star Life Insurance Co Ltd* [1997] AC 749 (HL)) to the question of the service of counter-notices within LRA 2002, sch 6.

[44] *Zarb v Parry* [2011] EWCA Civ 1306, [2012] 1 WLR 1240.

[45] *Best v Chief Land Registrar* [2015] EWCA Civ 17, [2016] QB 23.

The crucial background to the *Best* litigation is that in 2012, legislation was introduced to combat residential squatting: the Legal Aid, Sentencing and Punishment of Offenders Act ('LASPOA') 2012 made it, in broad terms, a criminal offence to squat in a residential building when living or intending to live in it.[46] Mr Best applied via LRA 2002, schedule 6, to be registered as proprietor of a house which he had squatted in, but which was registered in the name of a deceased proprietor. For part of the period during which he was in possession and on which his application depended, the criminal sanctions for squatting applied, as the relevant legislation had by then come into force. The Land Registry refused to complete the registration, relying on previous authority[47] which had held that a title could not be acquired where such acquisition depended upon the commission of a criminal offence. This decision was challenged by way of judicial review, on the basis that the decision was unlawful. Whilst the challenge was progressing, the Registry took the step of holding up any similar applications which might be affected by the outcome of the proceedings, pending their outcome.

The Court of Appeal, affirming the decision of the High Court, decided that the Registry had been wrong in rejecting the application. The court emphasised the strong public policy reasons for the existence of an adverse possession regime. It was held that Parliament had not intended, by enacting the 2012 squatting offence, to affect the law relating to adverse possession: the criminal offence had been created to address an entirely different mischief, namely short-term squatting in people's homes. This now means, of course, that such applications cannot be rejected because of the criminality of the squatter's conduct. But it also means that a squatter occupying an abandoned house need not be concerned that the absent owner's title was registered, and indeed will only need 10 years' occupation/possession, as opposed to 12 years where the land is unregistered, to turn a squat into a castle—subject of course to the possibility that the squatter may not be able to respond effectively to the service of a counter-notice by the registered proprietor. The *Best* decision may also inform the Land Registry's approach to adverse possession applications in future if, as appears possible, the LASPOA 2012 squatting offence is extended in future to cover commercial as well as residential premises.

In conclusion, the LRA 2002's adverse possession regime has brought many changes to the way in which Land Registry deals with squatters' claims—but not necessarily in the way some might have expected. Although the schedule 6 regime was introduced to limit the circumstances in which squatters could acquire title, it is clear that applications continue to be made in many widely-varying circumstances, and that the Land Registry lawyer will continue to face interesting and varied challenges in the field of adverse possession in the years to come.

VI. Conclusion

What is clear from our whistle-stop tour of the contentious aspects of land registration is that there are many live issues. Since 13 October 2003, when the LRA 2002 came into force, the caseload of the Adjudicator, and now the First-Tier Tribunal, has increased considerably,

[46] Legal Aid, Sentencing and Punishment of Offenders Act 2012, s 144.

[47] *R (Smith) v Land Registry* [2009] EWHC 328 (Admin) (upheld on appeal for different reasons: [2010] EWCA Civ 200, [2011] QB 413).

and the reputation of its decisions has increased. Over roughly the same period indemnity payments for fraud have increased—reflecting in large part, of course, the onward march of property values—although these claims have come down a little in recent years. There have also been many leading cases involving land registration law, among them five key Court of Appeal decisions: *Baxter v Mannion*, *Parshall v Hackney*, *Gold Harp*, *Best* and *Swift 1st*. The law in this area is, accordingly, very much in the public eye, and Land Registry lawyers can be confident that their work is amongst the most interesting and varied on offer for the land law practitioner.

3

The Land Registration Jurisdiction: An Analysis of the First Twelve Years

EDWARD COUSINS

I. Introduction

The Office of the Adjudicator to Her Majesty's Land Registry was established on 13 October 2003 under Part 11 of the Land Registration Act ('LRA') 2002 to deal with contested issues of title arising out of the land registration process. Its demise occurred on 1 July 2013 when the jurisdiction was transferred into the newly established Property Chamber of the First-tier Tribunal, as part of the wide-ranging tribunal reform process conducted pursuant to the Tribunals, Courts and Enforcement Act 2007.

Since its inception the jurisdiction of the Adjudicator was involved with that type of dispute which Civil Judges dislike so much, and often are so unwilling to hear, namely disputes between neighbours over boundaries and rights of way. One does not have to look very far in the law reports to see examples of this judicial loathing. It may be commonplace for the judge, on arriving in court, to make it very clear that he is unwilling to hear the case, and urge the parties to go away and settle.[1]

The nature of the Adjudicator's jurisdiction was summarised by Mummery LJ in *Susan Wilkinson and the Estate of Brian Wilkinson v Frederick Farmer*, in the following terms:

> The Deputy Adjudicator was the fact-finding tribunal. [The] Adjudicator[…] to HM Land Registry and the Deputies have relevant expertise. Although they might sometimes get things wrong, they are usually more experienced and expert at deciding this kind of question than appellate courts are. A measure of weighed deference should be accorded to the findings and conclusions in their reasoned decision. In this case the decision was given after 2 days of evidence and argument, plus a site view ….[2]

This statement has provided considerable encouragement for judges in this jurisdiction, and makes all the hard work and frustrations seem worthwhile.

This chapter sets out to analyse the reasons for the creation and demise of the jurisdiction, and its development over the 10 years of its existence into a tribunal which gained the

[1] See, eg, statements made in *Alan Wibberley Building Ltd v Insley* [1998] 1 WLR 881 (CA) 882 (Ward LJ), [1999] 1 WLR 894 (HL) 895 (Lord Hoffmann), and *Moncrieff v Jamieson* [2007] UKHL 42, [2007] 1 WLR 2620 [45] (Lord Scott).

[2] [2010] EWCA Civ 1148, [2010] NPC 105 [25].

respect and confidence of the senior judiciary, the legal profession and the public. It has established a strong jurisprudential basis for its worthy successor, the Land Registration Division of the Property Chamber.

II. Historial Background to the Jurisdiction

Over the past 13 years, much water has flowed under the adjudication bridge. From very small beginnings much activity has been generated, experience has been gained in the dispute resolution process, and a considerable body of more-or-less adjectival case law has emerged. Some of it has been developed by the Adjudicator and his Deputies. Some of it has emerged from decisions of the High Court and the Court of Appeal.

In retrospect, the Office of the Adjudicator was perhaps a victim of its own success—latterly having been perceived as a 'jewel in the crown'. Whether or not this is a correct interpretation of the historical circumstances, the factual position is that, after much negotiation, the Office of the Adjudicator was finally abolished on 1 July 2013 and the jurisdiction was subsumed into the expanding empire of what has been described as the 'Tribunals Family' following the enactment of the Tribunals, Courts and Enforcement Act 2007. At this point in time, the jurisdiction was transferred to the Land Registration Division of the newly-created Property Chamber of the First-tier Tribunal. The Adjudicator, together with his three full-time Deputy Adjudicators, 29 fee-paid part-time Deputy Adjudicators, and several part-time Costs Judges, were all 'transferred-in' as 'authorised decision-makers' of the new Chamber. The other two constituent parts of the Property Chamber are the Residential Property Division, and the Agricultural Lands and Drainage Division.

At the time of its creation, there was a level of uncertainty as to the precise nature and the extent of the powers of the Adjudicator. Indeed, at an early stage of the jurisdiction it was likened to a type of 'quango', with little expectation of any great work-flow—a perception based on experience under the former regime. It was even suggested to George Bartlett, then President of the former Lands Chamber, that he could assume two roles: his current role as President and the new role of Adjudicator. He wisely turned this offer down.

During its life, the Adjudicator's jurisdiction earned a reputation for sound decision making in cases that frequently involve complex and technical issues of law, as well as convoluted issues of fact. Litigants came to expect the jurisdiction to act as a substitute court for determining substantive issues, and not just as a means of procedural control on the exercise by the Chief Land Registrar of his administrative functions. Apocryphal stories abound where District Judges and Circuit Judges have been heard to say that they wish that they could transfer boundary disputes and the like from the county courts to the Adjudicator's jurisdiction. This is a markedly different perspective from the original process devised under the Land Registration Act 1925.

In order to understand how this has come to pass, it is necessary to understand the historical background leading to the creation of the Adjudicator.

Under the Land Registration Act ('LRA') 1925, if a dispute arose which could not be resolved by agreement, the Chief Land Registrar was obliged to hold a hearing to determine the questions in dispute unless he directed one of the parties to issue proceedings.[3] The Chief Land Registrar's jurisdiction was delegated to the Solicitor to HM Land Registry, and his deputies.[4] There was a right of appeal to the Chancery Division of the High Court.[5] In practice, relatively few disputes were resolved in this way—at the date of the Land Registry Quinquennial Review in June 2001, hearings in front of the Solicitor numbered about 40 a year.

Numerous reports relating to land registration were produced in the two decades prior to the LRA 2002's enactment; indeed, between 1983 and 1998, the Law Commission published eight reports/papers on land registration. None of these—including the Law Commission-HM Land Registry joint consultative paper of 1998, Law Com No 254[6]—mentioned anything about the need for an adjudication process for disputes, or addressed Article 6 of the European Convention of Human Rights.

However, in June 2001, the Lord Chancellor received a document entitled the 'Land Registry Quinquennial Review' from Mr Andrew Edwards CB, which proposed the establishment of an independent adjudicator to deal with the cases then being dealt with by the Solicitor to the Land Registry. This was apparently the first time that the proposal to create the Office of Adjudicator came into the public domain. No public consultation was proposed on this suggestion, notwithstanding the emphasis placed in Law Com No 254 on the importance of wide-ranging consultation.[7]

Thereafter, on 9 July 2001, and following six years' collaboration, the Law Commission and HM Land Registry published their final joint report, Law Com No 271, together with the draft Land Registration Bill.[8] Part XVI of the report recognised that 'in practice remarkably few decisions [of the Solicitor to the Land Registry] have been appealed and virtually none of those successfully'.[9] Nevertheless, 'there could be a perception that [the Solicitor to HM Land Registry] is not sufficiently independent': issues could arise in cases before the Solicitor which involved the decisions of officials of the Land Registry.[10] The report continued:

> As a matter of principle, it is desirable to create a completely independent office for adjudication. The great merits of the present system of determinations by the Solicitor are that they are cheap, swift and a great deal more informal than a hearing before a court. ... It is intended that the practice of the Adjudicator should offer a similar service and thereby obviate the need for, and expense of, court proceedings.[11]

Accordingly, it was decided that, as part of the proposed sweeping review of land registration in England and Wales, the judicial functions of the Solicitor would be separated from his legal and other functions, and an entirely new judicial post established. With the LRA 2002's enactment, the Office of Adjudicator was born.

[3] Land Registration Rules ('LRR') 1925, r 299(3).

[4] LRA 1925, s 126(5).

[5] LRR 1925, r 300.

[6] Law Commission and HM Land Registry, *Land Registration for the Twenty-First Century: A Consultative Document* (Law Com No 254, 1998).

[7] ibid, Foreword, 1 and para 1.15.

[8] Law Commission and HM Land Registry, *Land Registration for the Twenty-First Century—A Conveyancing Revolution* (Law Com No 271, 2001).

[9] ibid, para 16.1.

[10] ibid.

[11] ibid.

It was in this manner that the primary function of the Adjudicator (and now that of his successor, the Land Registration Division of the Property Chamber) was established—ie, to determine disputed applications to the Registrar in accordance with the procedure provided for by section 73(7) of the LRA 2002. This provided a parallel jurisdiction to that exercised by the courts in relation to land registration issues. The Adjudicator was also given a new original jurisdiction dealing with applications for rectification or the setting aside of certain documents in the case of registered land. A third jurisdiction, involving network access agreements needs only passing mention: it has never resulted in any case being referred to the jurisdiction. This last jurisdiction concerns appeals by conveyancing practitioners against decisions of the Chief Land Registrar in relation to, eg, agreements allowing solicitors electronic access to the Land Registry for the purposes of e-conveyancing.

III. The Position Post-13 October 2003

A. The Volume of Work

As it transpired, the title of 'Adjudicator' was a bit of a misnomer. The jurisdiction dealt with fully-fledged adversarial party disputes where, but for the system in place, the 'customers'—as the Ministry of Justice somewhat quaintly refer to the litigants—might well be happy to maim each other over boundary issues, and the like.

It was initially envisaged that the role of Adjudicator would be a part-time one. This soon proved not to be the case—from about Easter 2004, the workload grew exponentially, and it became impossible for the jurisdiction to continue to function without judicial assistance. A number of competitions were undertaken which eventually resulted in the appointment of 32 Deputy Adjudicators (three in full-time salaried posts, the remainder in part-time fee-paid posts), together with four fee-paid Costs Judges. In practice, the Deputies appointed were barristers or solicitors with experience in land law, and specifically, land registration law.

Within about three years, the volume of work referred from the (then) 24 Land Registry Offices—formerly known as District Land Registries—reached a peak of about 1,900 per annum. In 2010, the annual caseload comprised about 1,600 matters, of which about 30% were determined by final hearings. In later years, the figure fell to below 1,000 referrals per annum.

Between its inception on 13 October 2003 and its demise on 30 June 2013 the Adjudicator jurisdiction received a total of 14,135 referrals. Some 2,099 cases were disposed of after a hearing, and 11,260 were disposed of without a hearing.[12] The number of permissions to appeal and successful appeals has been miniscule, compared with the volume of work in the jurisdiction reflected in these figures.

Many of the cases have involved complex and technical issues, not only of land law and land registration law, but also other related areas of law. If not resolved by the jurisdiction, they would need to be resolved in the Chancery Division of the High Court or in the county

[12] A fuller breakdown of the statistics to date can be found in the Appendix to this chapter.

court sitting with specialist judges. The current figures available indicate that the volume of cases being heard in this jurisdiction is by no means insignificant when compared to the volume of similar cases being heard in rest of the civil justice system—ie, the High Court or county court. The number of land-related cases in those jurisdictions—without taking account of possession actions—seems to be in decline.

IV. The Birth of the Property Chamber, and the Adjudicator's Demise

Plans for a Property Chamber had been in gestation for a considerable period of time. Sir Andrew Leggatt's 2001 Report, *Tribunals for Users—One System, One Service*, considered the arrangements for dealing with land, property and housing disputes.[13] It was observed that:

> There are confusing overlaps of jurisdiction between courts and tribunals, as well as between tribunals. The tribunal model is a useful one, because it brings experts within the decision-making process [...] An expert decision-making forum without overlapping jurisdictions, is a precondition of effective procedural reform. The Law Commission should be enlisted [...] to assist the Government in working out a comprehensive solution, with a view to removing the overlaps and scope for forum-shopping to be found in the current arrangements.

In the wake of the Leggatt Review, the Law Commission was asked to consider the position of land, valuation and housing tribunals. The resulting report, *Land Valuation and Housing Tribunals: The Future*,[14] recommended structural reform of the project tribunals, which included those now within the Property Chamber, together with the Valuation Tribunal and the Lands Tribunal.

Probably as a result of developments in the wider Tribunal world, these Law Commission recommendations were not taken forward. In July 2004, the government White Paper, *Transforming Public Services: Complaints, Redress and Tribunals*,[15] heralded the way for the Tribunals, Courts and Enforcement Act 2007. In November 2007, the government issued a consultation paper on implementation of Part I of that Act, *Transforming Tribunals*,[16] and in May 2008, the government published its response to the consultation exercise.[17] Just under six months later, on 3 November 2008,[18] the first two Chambers of the (then) Tribunal Service were statutorily launched.

[13] Sir Andrew Leggatt, *Tribunals for Users—One System, One Service*, Report of the Review of Tribunals (March 2001) para 3.30.

[14] Law Commission, *Land Valuation and Housing Tribunals: The Future* (Law Com No 281, 2003). The writer was a member of the advisory group that assisted the Commission with the project.

[15] Department for Constitutional Affairs, *Transforming Public Services: Complaints, Redress and Tribunals* (White Paper, Cm 6243, 2004).

[16] Ministry of Justice, *Transforming Tribunals—Implementing Part I of the Tribunals Courts and Enforcement Act 2007* (CP 30/07, 2007).

[17] Ministry of Justice, *Transforming Tribunals—Implementing Part I of the Tribunals Courts and Enforcement Act 2007—The Government's Reponse* (2008) ('*Transforming Tribunals*').

[18] 'T1 day'.

During the same period of consultation and preparation for the new Tribunal Service, further work was undertaken by the Law Commission on the reform of housing law and practice. *Renting Homes*[19] made recommendations for the reform of the law relating to security of tenure in both the public and private sectors. *Housing: Encouraging Responsible Letting*[20] explored new approaches to the regulation of the private rented sector in order to improve housing management.

Chapter twelve of *Transforming Tribunals* set out the government's long-term vision for property tribunals. In broad terms, the government's aim was for:

> a two-tier structure for those land, property and housing jurisdictions which are ultimately assigned to the tribunal system. As with other tribunal areas, the First-tier Tribunal should hear first-instance cases and appeals against administrative decisions. [...] The work should be allocated to a chamber dedicated to land, property and housing matters so that a proper level of expertise can be guaranteed through the appointment of a Chamber President. [...] The role of the Upper Tribunal [...] should predominantly be an expert appellate body, dealing authoritatively with issues of law and general practice.[21]

In 2007, the Law Commission was asked to carry out a second review of the way in which residential property disputes are resolved. So far as formal dispute resolution was concerned, the Commission was asked to consider the case for establishing a housing court or housing tribunal with jurisdiction to determine all major disputes, including possession disputes. The Law Commission's report, *Housing: Proportionate Dispute Resolution*,[22] was result of that review. The report made recommendations in three broad areas: for better advice and assistance to parties; for non-formal dispute resolution; and for formal dispute resolution. It endorsed the approach in *Transforming Tribunals* to establishing a Land, Property and Housing Chamber, and recommended that the government should keep under review the possibility that further specific housing matters may be transferred to the Chamber, on the basis that 'a shift to a more specialised tribunal can result in the benefits of greater efficiency, lower cost to the user, and more access to justice'.[23]

V. The Position as at 1 July 2013

A. The Structure of the Property Chamber

On 1 July 2013, the First-tier Tribunal (Property Chamber) was finally established. The Property Chamber is an amalgam of three tribunals: the Residential Property Tribunal Service (within which there were a number of disparate jurisdictions), the Agricultural Lands Tribunal, and the Adjudicator to HM Land Registry. The structural and judicial integrity of the three constituent parts were preserved on transfer into the Chamber.

19 Law Commission, *Renting Homes: The Final Report* (Law Com No 297, 2006).
20 Law Commission, *Housing: Encouraging Responsible Letting* (Law Com No 312, 2007).
21 *Transforming Tribunals* (n 17) paras 308 and 309.
22 Law Commission, *Housing Proportionate Dispute Resolution* (Law Com No 309, 2008).
23 Ibid, para 5.47.

The launch of the Chamber represented the culmination of much preparatory work, particularly between 2011 and 2013. Part of that work included a consultation exercise on establishing the Property Chamber within the First-tier Tribunal. The Ministry of Justice issued its response to that consultation in October 2012.[24] Broadly, it was decided that the structures for Residential Property, for Agricultural Land and Drainage and for Land Registration would remain intact until the transition into the Property Chamber had been achieved. It was proposed that the Chamber President should then carry out a review both of the structure of the Chamber, and of the arrangements for judicial leadership within it. On the appointment of the President of the Property Chamber, Siobhan McGrath, the Senior President of Tribunals, indicated that the review should take place during the first year of the Chamber.

It is important to note that unlike some other Chambers, such as the General Regulatory Chamber and the Health, Education and Social Care Chamber, there is a great deal of commonality between the three Divisions of the Property Chamber. In particular, all three Tribunals deal with property issues and all three are predominantly inter-parties Tribunals—unlike the Tribunals dealing with appeals against administrative decisions. The range and complexity of cases dealt with in the Chamber should not be underestimated. Altogether, the Chamber is concerned with almost 200 separate jurisdictions dealing with property rights and landlord and tenant relationships. High standards of adjudication and case management are required in order to discharge the workload.

When the Chamber was established, it was decided that each of the three Divisions should be led by a Principal Judge. This post served two purposes. First, it reflected the previous arrangement for each of the amalgamated Tribunals and preserved the senior judicial leadership roles that had existed. Secondly, at a time of significant change, it provided continuity and leadership for judiciary and staff. The Ministry of Justice anticipated that the Chamber President would also hold the position of Principal Judge for one of the divisions. Siobhan McGrath took on that role for Residential Property, having previously held the position of Senior President for the Residential Property Tribunal Service. The present author's role as the Adjudicator to HM Land Registry since its creation in 2003 was transmogrified into the role of Principal Judge for the Land Registration Division. Nigel Thomas, who had been the lead judge for Agricultural Lands Tribunals, became Principal Judge for the Agricultural Land and Drainage Division.

The first year 'strategic review' was then carried out. The President sought the appointment of a new judicial post for the Chamber, namely a Deputy President. However, this proposal was not accepted, and the Chamber will continue for the foreseeable future with its present structure remaining in place.

Although not strictly included within the strategic review's terms of reference, it was thought sensible during the review to canvass opinion on the arrangements for the Land Registration Division. The replies indicated very strong support for retaining a centralised structure. The Land Registration Division is run efficiently from London, and the relative size of the jurisdiction makes a regional structure impracticable. Although about 50% of the cases that go to hearing are heard outside of London, it was said that

[24] Ministry of Justice, *Response to the Consultation on establishing the Property Chamber within the First-tier Tribunal* (2012).

this number would not justify splitting up a very specialist jurisdiction. In the Review, the President of the Property Chamber noted that the workload of the Land Registration Division is significant.

VI. Conclusion

There matters stand. Although there has been a decline in referrals received in recent years, the jurisdiction is healthy with a good workload, and is efficiently run within the new Property Chamber. This is a considerable achievement and a tribute to all who have worked so hard over the years to develop it, both staff and judiciary.

Appendix

Decisions published on the web:[25]	294
Applications[26] for PTA to High Court to 30.06.13:[27]	151
Total referrals received and total rectification applications received and accepted for consideration:[28]	17,022
Contested hearings[29] each year: (not including contested interlocutory or costs hearings, cases settled after listing or (for 2013–14) cases adjourned part-heard but not yet decided)	
1 January 2013–31 December 2013	163
1 January 2014–31 December 2014	164
1 January 2015–31 December 2015	105
Total referrals and rectification cases, 1 July 2013 to end of 2015:	2,622

[25] Up to and including close of business on 31 December 2015. It discounts duplicates of decisions appearing under more than one (sub)category, and also discounts the entry containing the Practice Directions.

[26] Notified to the jurisdiction on or before 12 August 2013. There may have been notifications by the High Court after that date, but the figure is unlikely to be affected significantly. Another feature affecting the accuracy of this statistic is that before 1 July 2013, there was some uncertainty about the recording of applications from District Registries (ie, those outside London).

[27] Since 1 July 2013, applications for permission to appeal now are made to the Upper Tribunal, Tax and Chancery Chamber.

[28] Up to and including close of business on 31 August 2015. This does not include purported applications for rectification submitted direct to the jurisdiction which could not be entertained (principally, though not exclusively, applications to rectify the register).

[29] Each hearing is counted as one, even if it dealt with more than one, linked case. If each case were counted individually, this would produce a substantially higher figure—eg, the figure of 149 for 2013–14 would become 181.

4

A Broader Development Perspective: Economic and Political Drivers of Worldwide Land Registration Reform

PAMELA O'CONNOR

I. Interdisciplinary Perspectives

Most countries have adopted a system of land registration, in which either deeds or titles are recorded in a public register. In the UK, the system of title registration is known as 'land registration', although international usage applies the term to include registration of both deeds and titles.[1] Deeds registers record instruments as evidence of claims to interests in land, and instruments are commonly indexed under the names of the parties. A registered title system registers individual land parcels, spatially defined, with a statement as to proprietorship. The title particulars for the parcel are updated upon registration of subsequent dispositions of property rights. Registration is required to constitute a proprietary interest in land, and provides an affirmation of title (as in the Torrens and English systems) or a presumption of validity (as in the German system).[2] The result is a parcel-based record in which registered titles are authoritative; a 'register of conclusions, not merely the information from which conclusions might be drawn'.[3]

Recent decades, particularly since the 1990s, have seen many countries adopt title registration systems, or redouble their efforts to complete the registration of parcels. Multilateral aid and development institutions such as the World Bank have funded many projects in developing countries, and countries in transition from socialism to private property regimes, to introduce title registration systems and register parcels.[4]

[1] United Nations Economic Commission for Europe, *Land Administration Guidelines—With Special Reference to Countries in Transition* (New York and Geneva, United Nations, 1996) 9 (glossary), 25–28.

[2] The title may be subject to rectification on specified grounds. See generally A Garro, 'Recordation of Interests in Land' in R David, H Egawa and R Graveson et al (eds), *International Encyclopedia of Comparative Law, Vol VI* (Martinus Nijhoff Publishers, 2004) paras 8–13.

[3] J Anderson, *Lawyers and the Making of English Land Law 1832–1940* (Oxford, Clarendon Press, 1992) 65; *State ex rel Douglas v Westfall,* 85 Minn 437, 89 NW 175 (Minn, 1902) (Stuart CJ).

[4] In 2010, the World Bank had a portfolio of land projects in multiple countries, totalling $1.5 billion: K Deininger, H Selod and T Burns, 'Making Land Governance Real' in K Deininger, C Augustinius, S Enemark and P Munro-Faure (eds), *Innovations in Land Rights, Recognition, Administration and Governance* (Washington DC, World Bank, 2010) 190, n 2.

Lawyers tend to view registered title systems primarily as a legal institution, a set of rules and procedures for creating and transferring interests in land and determining their priority. From the mid-19th to the mid-20th centuries, lawyers were at the forefront of public debates about whether to introduce land registration and about the merits of different models. The subject was viewed by lawyers as a law reform issue, involving the deficiencies of property law and the potential of land registration to provide solutions.[5]

It is not, however, law reform considerations which have prompted the current global movement to title registration. From the latter half of the 20th century, the system came to be regarded as part of the infrastructure of a market economy and as a tool of land management. Lawyers became marginal players in decisions to introduce, extend or implement the systems, although their expertise was needed to design the legislative framework. Today, the major proponents of title registration are international development agencies, economists, cadastral experts, surveyors, planners, land administrators, title registrars and information technology systems engineers—a group which Peter Dale and John McLaughlan describe collectively as 'the land information management community'.[6]

Two parallel and discrete bodies of scholarship have developed. The land information management community collaborates internationally on the economic, administrative, informational and technological aspects of registered title systems. The community has the ear of national governments and the international aid and development institutions (such as the World Bank) which make the key decisions about the introduction, design and implementation of the systems. In the meantime, lawyers continue to discuss the legal aspects of title registration systems with little reference to the perspectives of the other disciplines.

There is a need to bridge the communication gap. Theoretical perspectives have been underdeveloped in legal studies of title registration. The broader interdisciplinary literature can enrich legal scholarship by suggesting theoretical justifications for the systems' objects and methods. It can provide empirical evidence to evaluate the claimed benefits, and functional criteria for the design of the systems' legal rules. And it can reveal the reasons why national and provincial governments have paid scant regard to the views of lawyers when deciding to implement the systems.

This chapter seeks an answer to the question posed by Stuart Anderson in 1992: why should the state invest in administrative and legal registration facilities for the benefit of private owners?[7] It provides an overview of some of the key theories and practical considerations which have led governments and development institutions to introduce or extend registered title systems. Section II examines the economic theories which seek to demonstrate how registration systems support economic and social development. Section III then discusses another significant benefit claimed for title registration. Title registration systems facilitate the development of computer-enabled land information systems which link multiple data sources by reference to the parcel.

[5] Anderson (n 3) 80.

[6] PF Dale and JD McLaughlin, *Land Information Management: An Introduction with Special Reference to Cadastral Problems in Third World Countries* (Oxford, Clarendon, 1988).

[7] Anderson (n 3) 87–89 (referring to the debates of the mid-19th century).

II. Economic Theories

The interest of national governments and international development institutions in registered title systems results from the interaction of multiple economic concepts, theories and perspectives as outlined in subsections A to C of this section. In subsection D they are drawn together to form a set of 'linkages' from which evaluative criteria for land registration projects have been derived.

A. Transaction Costs and Wealth Maximisation

Land registration projects are premised on the assumption that there is a public interest in supporting the regime of private property. One set of theories holds that private property is justified by its contribution to the material welfare of society as a whole ('aggregate wealth'). The principal theories in this group are utilitarianism and economic theories of efficiency and wealth maximisation. The theories have both positive and normative aspects. Positively, they seek to explain actual phenomena, such as principles upon which markets operate. Normatively, they imply an onus on governments to take certain action to protect the security of property rights.

To evaluate alternative actions or allocations that will produce gains for some and losses for others, scholars of law and economics use the concept of wealth maximisation, or the Kaldor-Hicks criterion.[8] Property rights are said to be allocated efficiently when no reallocation would produce a further gain in aggregate wealth.[9] A modern elaboration of the theory owes much to the writings of economist Ronald Coase. In 1960, Coase published his article 'The Problem of Social Cost'.[10] The article, which demonstrated the use of economic theory in the analysis of law, was a foundation piece for the Law and Economics movement which emerged in the 1960s and 1970s.

Market exchanges occur when there is a 'co-operative surplus', represented by the difference between the vendor's lowest sale price and the purchaser's highest demand price.[11] Coase showed that the efficiency of markets in re-allocating land and resources to those who will use them most productively can be obstructed by transaction costs. These include the cost of investigating and appraising rights or resources ('information costs'), bargaining to acquire them ('bargaining costs') and enforcing the bargain ('enforcement costs').[12] If the transaction costs are high enough to absorb the whole of the potential co-operative surplus, there will be no scope for mutually beneficial exchange to occur.[13] In such a case, the market will not operate efficiently to shift the right or resource to a more highly-valued use. The forgone transaction represents a 'deadweight' loss in aggregate wealth.[14]

[8] The criterion is explained in R Posner, *Economic Analysis of Law*, 5th edn (New York, Aspen Law & Business, 1998) 13–17.

[9] ibid, 5–6.

[10] R Coase, 'The Problem of Social Cost' (1960) 3 *Journal of Law and Economics* 1.

[11] Posner, *Economic Analysis of Law* (n 8) 36–39.

[12] Coase, 'The Problem of Social Cost' (n 10) 15.

[13] R Posner, *The Economics of Justice* (Cambridge Mass, Harvard University Press, 1981) 71.

[14] OEG Johnson, 'Economic Analysis, The Legal Framework and Land Tenure Systems' (1972) 15 *Journal of Law and Economics* 259, 262.

Coase showed that transaction costs limit the ability of the market to achieve a wealth-maximising allocation of rights. From this positive analysis, Coase derived normative implications for the law. The law ought to facilitate private bargaining and the transferability of rights by reducing transaction costs.[15] Robert Cooter and Thomas Ulen call this the 'normative Coase theorem'.[16] Coase said that ill-defined rights will carry higher transaction costs on transfer.[17]

Indirectly, Coase clarified the relationship between security of title and transferability. A property right in land is insecure if its ownership is actually or potentially disputed or difficult to prove, if its scope or incidents are poorly defined, or if its enforcement against third parties is limited by conflict with another person's superior right. These insecurities increase the information burden on purchasers, who must undertake costly investigations in order to appraise the right.

Other scholars have explored the implications of transaction costs for land transfers. Omotunde Johnson, writing in 1972, showed that under the US deeds registration systems, insecure property rights inhibit exchange by reducing the value of the rights in the estimation of the potential purchaser.[18] The lowering of the purchaser's demand price results from two factors: the purchaser's expenditure on title investigations, and the 'risk premium' for the uncertainty that remains after the investigations.[19] Under the US deeds registration systems, title is always an inference from evidence, and investigations must be limited due to diminishing marginal returns from further searches.[20] Johnson showed that the title risks assumed by the purchaser have the effect of a transaction cost in impeding an efficient allocation of resources.

B. Secure Property Rights and Economic Development

For decades after World War II, the importance of secure property rights in promoting economic development was given little emphasis in the writings of economic theorists.[21] Centralised planning, government regulation and industrialisation were key prescriptions for economic development. Developing countries were advised to establish strong central planning agencies, which received significant transfers of capital from aid institutions. The idea that governments should take control of their economies was also supported by the new field of welfare economics, which highlighted the costs of market failure.[22]

Disillusionment with planning set in during the 1980s, when it was discovered that the socialist economies had stalled, and that capital transfers to public agencies in the developing world had done little to promote development.[23] Disappointing results in

[15] Coase, 'The Problem of Social Cost' (n 10) 19.

[16] R Cooter and T Ulen, *Law and Economics* (US, Harper Collins, 1988) 101–02.

[17] Coase, 'The Problem of Social Cost' (n 10) 19.

[18] Johnson (n 14).

[19] Johnson (n 14) 261–63.

[20] Johnson (n 14) 261.

[21] T Bethell, *The Noblest Triumph: Property and Prosperity Through the Ages* (New York, St Martin's Press, 1998) 7.

[22] J Waelbroeck, 'Half a Century of Development Economics: A Review Based on the Handbook of Development Economics' (1998) 12 *The World Bank Economic Review* 323.

[23] ibid, 325–36.

countries that had followed the prescription of development economists contrasted starkly with the success of the trade-oriented development model pioneered by the 'Asian tigers' such as Taiwan and Singapore.[24]

In the early 1980s, a different set of prescriptions for economic development emerged, promoted by politically conservative leaders like Ronald Reagan and Margaret Thatcher. Neo-classical economics called into question the premises of development economics. There was a shift in the focus of development strategies, from planners and policymakers to market actors. Under the new approach, the key to economic growth and the alleviation of poverty was to encourage people, particularly the poor, to participate in markets.[25]

It was necessary to provide a model for bringing this about in the developing countries and in the former socialist countries which, from 1989, were in transition from command economies to market economies. While economists understood how markets worked in the developed world, they had enjoyed little success in their attempts to promote the development of market economies elsewhere.

In the early 1990s, some economists were saying that mainstream economic theory had overlooked the importance of institutions in the process of exchange.[26] 'Institutions' are 'the rules, organisations and social norms that facilitate coordination of human action'.[27] A new post-Coasean School of economics emerged, devoted to studying the interaction between a country's cultural, legal and political institutions and its economic performance. One of its founders, Oliver Williamson, called the school 'the new institutional economics', to express the idea that traditional economics had overlooked the importance of institutions in explaining economic performance.[28]

The new institutional economics movement has strongly influenced development policy by analysing the complex interplay between institutions, transaction costs and economic performance. By the early 2000s, it was recognised that economic development required a broad and complex process of institutional adaptation.[29]

C. De Soto's Influence on the Development Agenda

The interest of development institutions in title registration was strongly influenced by Peruvian economist Hernando De Soto, who synthesised and applied ideas of institutional economics. In his first book, published in 1989, De Soto argued that poor developing countries were trapped in poverty because they were unable to use their assets to create new wealth. Lacking secure title to their land, the poor were unable to use it as security for loans from regulated institutional lenders. Instead, they were relegated to lenders in what Do Soto called the 'informal' economy which operates outside the framework of government regulation.

[24] Waelbroeck (n 22) 323.

[25] Waelbroeck (n 22) 347–48.

[26] D North, 'Economic Performance Through Time' (1994) 84 *American Economic Review* 359; R Coase, 'The Institutional Structure of Production' (1992) 82 *American Economic Review* 713, 718.

[27] Bethell (n 21) 188–92.

[28] As attributed in R Coase, 'The New Institutional Economics' (1988) 88 *American Economic Rev* 72, 72.

[29] *World Bank Development Report 2002: Building Institutions for Markets* (Washington DC, World Bank, 2002) 3–31.

In his second book, published in 2000, De Soto pondered why Western capitalism had proved so difficult to replicate in the Third World.[30] He concluded that economists had overlooked the importance of security of property as the key to economic development. Western economists had taken for granted the institutions that they found in their own environment. They had failed to specify the institutional settings that were required for their economic prescriptions to work in other countries.[31]

De Soto proposed that in order to transform into a market economy, developing countries needed to follow the examples of the West by formalising customary and other informal land rights (such as possessory rights) into a single system of property.[32] Informal property tenures needed to be formalised and represented in ways that were capable of recognition and enforcement by the legal system. He claimed that this action was needed to transform the assets of the Third World from 'dead assets' into economically productive 'live capital'.[33] Formalisation of titles would encourage investment and facilitate landholders to access secured credit on more favourable terms.

De Soto's prescription seemed to offer a concrete programme for action that suited the neoclassical economic worldview. His message was enthusiastically received by the development community, and continues to influence the World Bank's measurement of regulatory reforms through its *Doing Business* report series.[34] By the late 1990s, the World Bank was committed to formalisation of land titles, while accepting that some informal and indigenous rights should be protected, and that formalisation of rights should be sensitive to distributional aspects including gender equity.[35]

D. Empirical Evaluation of Development Projects

Since the 1990s, development institutions have invested substantial sums in land registration projects in many countries. The establishment or extension of title registration is commonly undertaken as part of a broader land administration project. Land administration involves recording and utilising information about the ownership, value and use of land for the purpose of managing a country's land resources.

The multilateral development institutions require that project outcomes be evaluated against their objects. A conceptual framework proposed by World Bank economists Gershon Feder and Akihiko Nishio has been used to guide empirical studies evaluating the impacts of land registration projects in developing countries.[36] Feder and Nishio hold that secure titles contribute to economic growth by raising the productivity of land, and that the effect is mediated through three linkages.[37]

[30] H De Soto, *The Mystery of Capital: Why Capitalism Triumphs in the West and Fails Everywhere Else* (London, Black Swan, 2000).

[31] ibid, 8–9, 36–45, 64–66, 109–13, 173; Bethell (n 21) 200.

[32] De Soto, *The Mystery of Capital* (n 30) 232–36.

[33] De Soto, *The Mystery of Capital* (n 30) 7, 167–68, 184.

[34] A series of annual reports published by the World Bank since 2004, which measures regulations in 189 economies against indicators of regulation which support or constrain business activity and property rights.

[35] See, eg, K Deininger and S Enemark, 'Land Governance and the Millennium Development Goals' in Deininger et al, *Innovations in Land Rights, Recognition, Administration and Governance* (n 4) 3–4.

[36] G Feder and A Nishio, 'The Benefits of Land Registration and Titling: Economic and Social Perspectives' (1999) 15(1) *Land Use Policy* 25, 30–32.

[37] ibid, 26–28.

First, formal proof of title improves security of tenure by reducing the risk that the current holder's property right will be challenged. Improved tenure security gives a landholder greater certainty of being able to reap the benefits of his or her investment. This increases investment, and boosts demand for variable inputs, including labour and secured borrowing. Higher investment increases the productivity of land.[38]

Secondly, by removing a constraint on the ability of landholders to access secured loans, formal titles may enable them to obtain more credit at cheaper rates or for longer terms. This allows landholders to invest in more productive uses of land.[39]

Thirdly, land registration enables clearer definition and allocation of property rights. By providing publicity for the rights, it reduces the information asymmetries that create uncertainty and inflate transaction costs. Property rights become more marketable, able to be traded more securely and at lower cost. This allows markets to perform their function of moving assets from less to more efficient uses. A more efficient allocation of property leads to higher productivity and economic growth.[40]

These three linkages indicate that evaluations of land registration projects should look for positive economic effects through multiple indicators, such as increased investment, access to credit, productivity and land prices. A growing body of research has returned some promising findings on the economic effects of projects in some countries, although evidence of the second linkage (access to formal credit) is scarce.[41]

Development agencies have responded to the mixed results with policy adjustments. Land administration projects remain a high priority for development assistance, but there has been an increased focus on identifying other precondition for achieving the linkages. Deininger and Feder suggest that policy interventions may be needed to develop complementary development institutions, such as formal credit and markets for labour and other inputs to production, for title registration programs to achieve their economic objects.[42] The goals of land administration projects have also been broadened, to include an emphasis on environmental, gender equity and social objectives.[43]

Land administration and land registration projects are now regarded as part of a broader process of institutional change. It is understood that markets need to be supported by legal and economic institutions, which are in turn supported liberal political institutions. Development interventions seek to provide the preconditions for successful markets, by building institutions that lower transaction costs and create incentives to manage resources sustainably and productively.[44] Security of property rights is firmly established as one of the most important of the preconditions, and land registration as a key policy intervention.

[38] Feder and Nishio (n 36) 27.

[39] Feder and Nishio (n 36) 27.

[40] Feder and Nishio (n 36) 27–28.

[41] K Deininger and G Feder, 'Land Registration, Governance and Development: Evidence and Implications for Policy' (2009) 24 *The World Bank Research Observer* 233, 233–35.

[42] ibid, 233, 256–57.

[43] D Ali, K Deininger and M Goldstein, 'Environmental and Gender Impacts of Land Tenure Regularization in Africa: Pilot Evidence from Rwanda' (2014) 110 *Journal of Development Economics* 262.

[44] The World Bank fully embraced a broad institutional reform agenda in its *World Bank Development Report 2002* (n 29) ch 1.

III. The Land Administration Link

Apart from the benefits associated with supporting land markets, title registers also play a valuable role in generating land-related information with multiple applications.[45] A country's title register forms part of its land administration system, which includes the systems for defining land parcels and boundaries, registering property and valuation data, and adjudicating land disputes.[46] The core of a land administration system is the property base or 'cadastre' which includes the land registration, mapping and surveying functions.[47] The spatial data in the cadastre enables each parcel to be geometrically defined and uniquely identified, and the title register provides information about its ownership.

Most land administration projects funded by multilateral development institutions recommend the use of title registration, in some cases replacing an older deeds registration system.[48] Title registers are more readily integrated with other location-based databases because they are parcel-based and provide authoritative title data.[49] It is also possible to establish a cadastral system based on a deeds register, provided that parcels are spatially defined with unique identifiers and deeds are indexed by parcel.[50]

The evolution of cadastres into computer-enabled land information systems has provided an additional incentive to adopt or extend title registration. From the early 1990s, the International Federation of Surveyors (FIG) articulated a vision for a multipurpose cadastre which would provide rich data about land assets, to support integrated governance of land and resources.[51] Under the leadership of FIG and its international partners, cadastres are evolving into comprehensive land information and management systems. Computer technology has enabled the development of a spatial data infrastructure ('SDI'), an architecture of networked databases containing different sets of spatial information, which can be used to support management and planning.[52] The cadastral parcel provides the reference point, enabling a computer-enabled system to integrate and combine data-sets maintained by multiple administering agencies, such as hydrology, forestry, infrastructure, land valuation and topography.[53] The cadastre or 'property base' is the preferred common reference point for linking information in SDI systems, because it represents the point at which people are connected to land.[54]

[45] I Williamson, 'Land Administration "Best Practice": Providing the Infrastructure for Land Policy Implementation' (2001) 18 *Land Use Policy* 297, 297.

[46] United Nations, *Land Administration Guidelines* (n 1) 3.

[47] FIG (International Federation of Surveyors) Commission 7, *Statement on the Cadastre* (FIG No 11, 1995) 2.

[48] Deininger and Feder (n 41) 243–44.

[49] Deininger and Enemark, 'Land Governance and the Millennium Development Goals' (n 35) 6.

[50] G Adlington, 'Case Studies from Newly Renovated Land Administration Systems in the Emerging Economies' in D Steudler (ed), *Cadastre 2014 and Beyond* (Denmark, FIG No 61, 2014) 24, 27.

[51] For the history of the projects, see I Williamson, 'The Cadastre 2014 Journey' in Steudler (ed), *Cadastre 2014 and Beyond* (n 45) 2–4.

[52] ibid.

[53] A Rajabifard, 'Cadastre 2014 in Relation to Spatial Data Infrastructure (SDI)' in Steudler (ed), *Cadastre 2014 and Beyond* (n 50) 49–50.

[54] I Williamson, A Rajabifard, M Kalantari and J Wallace, 'AAA Land Information: Accurate, Assured and Authoritative', (paper presented to 8th FIG Regional Conference 2012, *Surveying Towards Sustainable Development*, Montevideo, Uruguay, 26–29 November 2012) 4.

A. Models for the Design of Land Administration Systems

Over the past decade, the land information community has developed models for the design and evaluation of land administration systems, including functional specifications for the legal rules. One example is the World Bank's *Doing Business* index for rating the quality of a country's land administration system.[55] The indicators include, *inter alia*: whether all privately-owned land is registered; whether interests must be registered before they are enforceable against third parties; whether the legal system requires verification of identities and identity documents; whether title is subject to a state or private guarantee; and whether compensation is available for good faith purchasers who suffer loss through reliance on erroneous information in the register.[56] In its annual *Doing Business Report* series, the World Bank publishes its rankings of certain countries and regional groupings of countries against the indicators. The effect is to exert a normative influence on governments to implement a system which includes a matrix of features associated with a registration of title system.

IV. Conclusion

This chapter set out to answer Stuart Anderson's question: why should the state invest in registration facilities for the benefit of private owners? While many early proponents assumed that registration systems are introduced as reforms to property law,[57] disciplines outside the law propose a fuller explanation. The economic and development literature proposes a number of linkages through which registered title systems are associated with positive economic, social and governance outcomes. The linkages are not purely theoretical, but are supported to some extent by empirical evaluation of outcomes of projects undertaken in many countries by the World Bank and other development institutions. The findings of positive economic effects are patchy, and indicate that formalisation of titles through registration is 'no panacea'.[58] An understanding has developed that land registration is more likely to achieve its objects when integrated into a broader agenda of strengthening economic and governance institutions.

Apart from the economic and social benefits, the development of the information economy has highlighted the potential of computer-enabled land information systems to generate rich location-based data. The cadastral parcel—spatially defined, uniquely identified, and with authoritative title data—offers an excellent reference point for combining and integrating information from layered databases. Governments, particularly in the advanced economies, are interested in harnessing the data for multiple uses in land governance for both administrative and commercial purposes. These benefits provide strong incentives for governments in the developed world, as well as the developing world, to invest in completing the property base by registering spatially defined parcels and titles.

[55] K Deininger, F Meunier and T Hilhorst, 'How *Doing Business* Can Help Improve Quality of Land Administration: Evidence, Challenges and Country Experience' in T Hilhorst and F Meunier (eds), *How Innovations in Land Administration Reform Improve on Doing Business* (Washington DC, World Bank, 2015) 3–9.

[56] ibid, 8, table 1.3.

[57] Anderson (n 3) 55, 87–89.

[58] Deininger and Feder (n 41) 233.

PART II

Contemporary Problems and Solutions

A

The Nature of Registered Title

5

Adverse Possession Under the LRA 2002

OWEN RHYS

I. Introduction

This chapter does not seek to provide a comprehensive guide to the substantive law and procedure relating to adverse possession claims under schedule 6 of the Land Registration Act ('LRA') 2002—a working knowledge of schedule 6 is assumed. Instead, the chapter explores some of the problems and potential anomalies that may arise or have arisen, primarily on squatters' applications under schedule 6. In addition to relevant decisions of the ordinary courts, this chapter will also refer where appropriate to decisions of the Land Registration Division of the Property Chamber of the First-tier Tribunal, and of its predecessor, the Adjudicator to HM Land Registry.

Schedule 6 of the LRA 2002 created an entirely new scheme for the determination of adverse possession claims as they relate to registered titles. More accurately, perhaps, it created a hybrid scheme, in which the underlying law of adverse possession that had developed under the Limitation Acts was married to an entirely new procedural regime. The reason for the change was explained in the joint report of the Law Commission and HM Land Registry to which the Land Registration Bill (later the LRA 2002) was attached, *Land Registration for the Twenty-First Century: A Conveyancing Revolution*:

> The Bill abandons the notion that a squatter acquires title once he or she has been in adverse possession for 12 years. It creates new rules in relation to registered land that will confer greater protection against the acquisition of title by persons in adverse possession. This is consistent with one of the objectives of the Bill—that it is registration alone that should confer title. The essence of the new scheme is that a squatter will be able to apply to be registered as proprietor after 10 years' adverse possession. However, the registered proprietor will be notified of that application and will, in most cases, be able to object to it. If he or she does, the application will be rejected. However, the proprietor will then have to take steps to evict the squatter or otherwise regularise his or her position within two years. If the squatter is still in adverse possession after two years, he or she will be entitled to be registered as proprietor. We consider that this new scheme strikes a fairer balance between landowner and squatter than does the present law. It also reflects the fact that the basis of title to registered land is the fact of registration, not (as is the case with unregistered land) possession.[1]

[1] Law Commission, *Land Registration for the Twenty-First Century—A Conveyancing Revolution* (Law Com No 271, 2001) para 1.13 (footnotes omitted).

The substantive law as to what constitutes 'adverse possession' was largely settled by the House of Lords' decision in *JA Pye (Oxford) Ltd v Graham*,[2] decided prior to the LRA 2002's enactment, where a claim to adverse possession of a registered title succeeded. LRA 2002, schedule 6 is entitled 'Registration of Adverse Possessor' and the phrase 'adverse possession' is used throughout. Authorities on the legal definition of adverse possession, whether decided in relation to registered or unregistered titles, are therefore still applicable. However, whilst the substantive law of adverse possession remains the same under the LRA 2002, the new regime under schedule 6 has introduced a number of entirely novel and previously-untested procedures and concepts.

An application for a registered title based on adverse possession (other than under the LRA 2002's transitional provisions)[3] must now necessarily be made by means of Form ADV1, after 10 years' adverse possession.[4] The Registrar is obliged to give notice of the application to the persons described in paragraph 2 of schedule 6—primarily the registered proprietor or chargee of the title. A person served with such notice then has a limited period within which to object.[5] An objection must be in Form NAP,[6] which requires the objector to state if he wishes to have the application dealt with under paragraph 5 of schedule 6; if he does so, the objection triggers the service of a 'counter-notice' on the applicant squatter. By virtue of paragraph 4 of schedule 6, if the objector does not invoke paragraph 5, 'the applicant is entitled to be entered in the register as the new proprietor of the estate'. However, the prescribed Form NAP also includes an additional tick-box, namely, 'I object to the registration on the grounds stated in panel 6'. In practice, objectors often tick this box, and in panel 6 they set out facts to rebut the claim by the applicant that he has been in exclusive factual possession of the land, with an intention to possess, for the required period. It is not clear that this type of objection is specifically authorised by paragraphs 3 and 4 of schedule 6, although obviously the registered proprietor must be entitled to challenge the underlying factual allegations made by the squatter applicant in support of his application for registration.

If an objector does require the Registrar to deal with the application under paragraph 5, the applicant must satisfy one or more of the three conditions therein stipulated, in addition, of course, to proving the required 10-year period of adverse possession. This is the principal mechanism designed to raise the bar for squatters under the new regime and, in simple terms, to make it more difficult for a squatter to defeat the registered proprietor's title.

The LRA 2002 also introduced a new dispute resolution system, in the form of the Adjudicator to HM Land Registry (the 'Adjudicator'), as the office was described in section 107

[2] *JA Pye (Oxford) Ltd v Graham* [2002] UKHL 30, [2003] 1 AC 419.

[3] Where a squatter had been in adverse possession against a registered title for 12 years prior to the coming into force of the LRA 2002 on 13 October 2003, the registered title would have been held on trust for his benefit under the former Land Registration Act ('LRA') 1925. That person remains entitled to be registered as proprietor under the LRA 2002's transitional provisions without an application being required under schedule 6: LRA 2002, sch 12, para 18.

[4] Land Registration Rules ('LRR') 2003 (SI 2003/1417), r 188.

[5] A period of 65 business days after the issue of the notice: LRR 2003, r 189.

[6] LRR 2003, r 190. The prescribed form is included in LRR 2003, sch 1. The terms of Form NAP are considered immediately below, in section V.

of the Act.[7] The rationale for this new system was explained by the Law Commission in the following terms:

> [T]he Bill creates a new office, that of Adjudicator to HM Land Registry, that is independent of the Registry. The function of the Adjudicator is to determine any contested application to the [R]egistrar that cannot be disposed of by agreement between the parties. At present, this function is performed by the Solicitor to HM Land Registry, who is the senior lawyer in the Registry. Notwithstanding that he adjudicates only in disputes between parties and not those involving the Registry, issues can still arise in such cases which involve the decisions of officials of the Registry. There could therefore be a perception that he is not sufficiently independent. As a matter of principle, it is desirable to create a completely independent office for adjudication.[8]

The functions of the Adjudicator were transferred to the Land Registration division of the Property Chamber of the First-tier Tribunal (the 'Tribunal') with effect from 1 July 2013.[9] The Adjudicator (now the Tribunal) has in some years received more than 1,500 referrals from the Land Registry, and averages well over 1,000 such cases each year.[10] These references, unless disposed of by agreement or dismissed on procedural grounds, will result in a full hearing based on oral evidence. The procedure is governed by the Practice and Procedure Rules,[11] which are based on the Civil Procedure Rules and provide comprehensive case management powers. It has been held by the courts that the Adjudicator (now the Tribunal) may, where it considers it necessary, resolve all underlying issues of fact arising on a reference from the Land Registry.[12] The particular expertise of the Adjudicator/Tribunal has been recognised in the higher courts,[13] and decisions of the Tribunal and of Deputy Adjudicators have been cited favourably in the Court of Appeal.[14] It is, in effect, a specialist property court. The Tribunal has four full-time salaried judges and 30 fee-paid judges, all of whom are specialist property lawyers.[15] Like its predecessor, the Adjudicator, the Tribunal is required to resolve disputes arising under the new schedule 6 regime. In resolving these disputes, it has been necessary to interpret the new provisions of schedule 6 in circumstances where there was no prior body of case law to provide any guidance. Accordingly, it is largely in the decisions of the Adjudicator, and now of the Tribunal, that answers may be found to some of the novel and difficult issues posed by this new adverse possession regime.

The intention in this chapter is to highlight some of these problem areas, where possible by reference to the decided cases. This is not intended as an exhaustive analysis of schedule 6, so much as a discussion of some problems that have arisen in the practical application of the new regime.

[7] For further exploration of this jurisdiction, see the discussion by Edward Cousins in ch 3 of this book.

[8] Law Com No 271 (n 1) para 16.1. See further ch 3 of this book.

[9] Transfer of Tribunal Functions Order 2013, SI 2013/1036.

[10] However, it is understood that this represents only a small fraction of disputed applications. See further ch 3 of this book.

[11] Tribunal Procedure (First-tier Tribunal) (Property Chamber) Rules 2013, SI 2013/1169 (L9).

[12] *Jayasinghe v Liyanage* [2010] EWHC 265 (Ch), [2010] 1 WLR 2106 (Briggs J); *Silkstone v Tatnall* [2011] EWCA Civ 801, [2012] 1 WLR 400.

[13] See, eg, *Wilkinson v Farmer* [2010] EWCA Civ 1148, [2010] NPC 105 [25] (Mummery LJ).

[14] See, eg, *MacLeod v Gold Harp Properties Ltd* [2014] EWCA Civ 1084, [2015] 1 WLR 1249 [70]–[80] (Underhill LJ).

[15] Including Stephen Jourdan QC, co-author of the leading textbook on adverse possession: S Jourdan and O Radley-Gardner, *Adverse Possession*, 2nd edn (London, Bloomsbury Professional, 2011).

II. The Interaction Between the LRA 2002, Schedule 6 and the Limitation Act 1980

Section 96(1) of the LRA 2002 provides as follows:

> No period of limitation under section 15 of the Limitation Act 1980 (c. 58) (time limits in relation to recovery of land) shall run against any person in relation to an estate in land or rentcharge the title to which is registered.

How does the disapplication of this rule in relation to registered land work in practice? Difficult issues arise where the paramount fee simple (the 'paper title') remains unregistered, but a *possessory* title to the land has been registered. In such cases, does section 96(1) of the LRA 2002 bite, on the basis that *a* title to the land has been registered, and oust the Limitation Act 1980's regime? Or does the Limitation Act 1980 have continued relevance because the *paramount* title remains unregistered? The LRA 2002 itself offers no answer to this conundrum.

A. Illustrations of the Problem

The problem has manifested itself in at least two contexts.

i. Example 1

First, take the following fairly common example. A squatter has been registered with a possessory title to previously unregistered land. The paper title owner, who is not in possession, becomes aware of this and applies to close the squatter's title under section 11(7) of the LRA 2002, on the grounds that at the date of registration of the squatter's title, his paramount title had not been barred by section 17 of the Limitation Act 1980—there had not, at that time, been the required 12 years' adverse possession. However, complicating analysis is the fact that the squatter has remained in exclusive adverse possession of the land during the period of his registration with possessory title. Can he take advantage of his adverse possession during the time that his possessory title was registered, in order to argue that the paper owner's paramount title has been extinguished under the Limitation Act 1980 as a result of 12 years' adverse possession? Or is the squatter denied access to the Limitation Act 1980's provisions once a relevant estate in the land has been registered?

ii. Example 2

A second manifestation of the problem arose in a case that recently came before me in the Tribunal: *Sexton v Gill (No 2)*.[16] A person (X) who was not in possession became registered with a possessory title, as a result of a false declaration in the application to the effect

[16] *Sexton v Gill (No 2)* [2015] EWLandRA 2013_0472_0473 (23 November 2015).

that the applicant was in exclusive possession.[17] A successful application was made to close the title by the person *actually* in possession—a squatter. A further question then arose as to whether the squatter was entitled to be registered with a possessory title instead. The squatter had been in undisturbed adverse possession for more than 12 years, and prima facie could apply for registration with possessory title, relying on the Limitation Act 1980. However, the complication was that the 12-year period of adverse possession included the period during which the title was (wrongly) registered in X's name. Given the fact that X was (wrongly) registered as a possessory proprietor for some of the 12-year period, could the squatter rely on the Limitation Act 1980's provisions, when those provisions seem to be ousted by the section 96(1) of the LRA 2002 relation to registered land?

B. Interpreting the Statutory Provisions

Whether or not the period of adverse possession enjoyed whilst a title was registered may be taken into account depends upon the meaning of section 96(1) of the LRA 2002—a somewhat opaque formulation, which has never, as far as I am aware, received judicial consideration outside the Tribunal. Section 15(1) of the Limitation Act 1980 provides that:

> No action shall be brought by any person to recover any land after the expiration of twelve years from the date on which the right of action accrued to him or, if it first accrued to some person through whom he claims, to that person.

Section 96(1) of the LRA 2002 provides that time under the Limitation Act 1980, section 15 shall not run against any person in relation 'to an estate in land … the title to which is registered'.[18]

There are two possible ways of construing these provisions, as the following sub-sections explain. Some Tribunal decisions have adopted the first interpretation,[19] but it is submitted that the second interpretation represents the better view.

i. The First Interpretation

The first possible approach sees the Limitation Act 1980 as inapplicable in both types of case illustrated by Examples 1 and 2. The argument runs as follows. Section 15 of the 1980 Act is expressly disapplied in relation to an estate in land or rentcharge the title to which is registered. It is therefore crucial to ask: what is 'an estate in land'?

On one view, the phrase 'an estate in land' should be construed by reference to the LRA 2002 itself, which only allows the registration of two estates in land, namely a freehold or a leasehold estate. Where a freehold title to the land has been registered, section 11(7) of the LRA 2002 provides that the fact that the class of title is possessory makes no difference to the vesting of the freehold estate in the land in the registered proprietor. The sole difference is that the interest of the prior paper title owner, as at the date of first registration,

[17] Generally speaking, the Land Registry will not inspect the subject land prior to registration, but will rely on the applicant's statement of truth.

[18] The section also refers to rentcharges but these are ignored for the purposes of this discussion.

[19] *Moore v Buxton* [2009] EWLandRA 2007_1216; *The Secretary of State for Transport v Quest Maidstone Ltd* [2011] EWLandRA 2010_0210.

is not overridden by the registration—as would otherwise be the case if the class of title was absolute. In all other respects, registration of the title to the freehold estate, albeit with a limited class of title, operates to vest the legal estate in the registered proprietor. Furthermore, the expression '[n]o period of limitation ... shall run against any person ... in relation to an estate in land' is apt to include persons other than the registered proprietor. If the intention had been simply to disapply the running of time under the Limitation Act 1980 to the registered proprietor, the section could have stated that in express terms. As it is, the phrase 'any person' embraces a wider class, including, for example, the person with the unregistered paramount paper title as at the date of first registration.

This issue has also been the subject of some discussion by Stephen Jourdan QC and Oliver Radley-Gardner in their book, 'Adverse Possession', as follows:

> As explained in Chapter 20 above, there can be more than one freehold estate in land. There is no provision in the 2002 Act directing that an unregistered estate in the registered land held by someone other than the registered proprietor which subsists at the time of registration is extinguished. There is no obvious reason why the registered freehold estate vested in the registered proprietor cannot co-exist with the unregistered freehold estate vested in the paper title owner, in which case [section] 11(7) has the effect that the unregistered paper title owner can recover possession from the registered proprietor with possessory title by virtue of his unregistered estate.[20]

Chapter 20 of the book relates to unregistered title. Clearly, where title to land is unregistered, different legal estates and interests may exist concurrently—indeed, section 1(5) of the Law of Property Act 1925 expressly so provides. For example, in addition to the fee simple in possession, there may be successive leases, a rentcharge with a right of re-entry, a legal easement and a mortgage—all created in relation to the same land. However, that is not to say that different *freehold* estates may exist concurrently. If 'freehold estate' is given its natural meaning—namely, the fee simple absolute in possession in the land, as opposed to some lesser estate or some right in or over the land such as an easement—it is clear that there can only be one such interest. It may be subject to defeasance—by a right of reverter, for example—but it is the sole freehold estate. Section 1(1) of the Law of Property Act 1925 provides that the only estates in land which are capable of being created or conveyed at law are: (a) an estate in fee simple absolute in possession, and (b) a term of years absolute. It might be thought that there are difficulties with the concept of two concurrently existing fee simple absolutes in possession in the same land. Furthermore, there is perhaps some doubt that the authors' analysis can assist once the title to the land has become registered. Take an analogy. A forged conveyance of unregistered land to F, the forger, is lodged at the Land Registry, with an application for first registration. The application is processed and F is registered as proprietor of the freehold title. As a matter of unregistered conveyancing, the forged conveyance cannot be effective to transfer the legal estate to F. It is a nullity: *nemo dat quod non habet*. However, registration converts this nullity into a legal title to the freehold.[21] The true owner has the right to apply to alter or rectify the Register by removing F from the proprietorship register, but until he succeeds arguably he cannot be said to have a legal estate—a freehold—in the land. By the same token, it might be argued that once a possessory title is registered, the paper title owner's immediately pre-existing legal title is

[20] Jourdan and Radley-Gardner, *Adverse Possession* (n 15) para 21.39.
[21] LRA 2002, s 58.

extinguished. His interest might be regarded as continuing to exist in the form of a statutory right to apply to close the possessory title—but is it right to characterise him as retaining an unregistered legal estate in the registered land? Such a concept might be thought alien to the system of land registration. According to this first approach, once *a* title to the land is registered—whether as possessory or absolute title, and whether that title belongs to the squatter (as in Example 1) or another (as in Example 2)—section 96(1) of the LRA 2002 bites in relation to all adverse possession claims over the *land*, and the squatter is unable to rely on the provisions of the Limitation Act 1980.

ii. The Second Interpretation

There are powerful reasons, however, why this first explanation for the (in)applicability of the Limitation Act 1980 should be regarded as over-simplistic and flawed. The Law Commission report which preceded the enactment of the LRA 2002 emphasised that the new adverse possession regime was intended to apply to a registered, as opposed to an unregistered, title. This suggests that section 96 of the LRA 2002 should be approached on the basis that the aim of the provision was the protection of a *registered* title, not an *unregistered* title. On this view, section 96 should be limited in effect to those who adversely possess against *registered* titles. In other words, the new schedule 6 regime of adverse possession applies only to the *registered* possessory title, but not to the unregistered paramount paper title still (on this view) vested in the paper title owner, to which the Limitation Act 1980's provisions remain applicable.

Approached from this perspective, the better analysis is as follows. Let it be assumed that a person becomes first registered with a possessory title, at a time when the paper title owner's title has not yet been barred under section 17 of the Limitation Act 1980, and he himself is not in possession. In many cases, of course, the person registered is also in possession, but there are cases (as in Example 2 above) where the first registered proprietor is not himself in possession, perhaps having falsified the statutory declaration made in support of his application for registration. A squatter is in possession at this time. In these circumstances, three separate titles coexisted at the date of first registration:

1. The first registered proprietor, who was neither the paper title owner, nor in possession, would have a title conferred solely through the fact of registration and the effect of section 58(1) of the LRA 2002. X's registered possessory title, as section 11(7) of the LRA 2002 makes clear, does not take priority over the prior paper title.
2. The squatter would have a distinct legal title based on his physical possession of the land in accordance with the decision in *Asher v Whitlock*.[22] Such a title is good against the whole world—including X, the mistakenly registered proprietor—other than the paper title owner. Upon making a successful schedule 6 application, the squatter acquires the registered title, and his pre-existing possessory title is extinguished. This is the effect of schedule 6, paragraph 9(1).
3. The (unknown) unregistered paper title owner (O) would retain the paramount fee simple absolute, which entitles him to bring an action to recover the land from the

[22] *Asher v Whitlock* (1865) LR 1 QB 1.

squatter and/or from X, the (erroneously) registered proprietor. Notwithstanding the registration of X's possessory title, the squatter remains in adverse possession of the land as against O, with the same quality of title—ie a title based on possession.

Against this background, the effect of registration would appear to be as follows. As far as the registered proprietor (X) is concerned, he has obtained a freehold possessory title, albeit that he is not in possession. From that moment on, section 96(1) of the LRA 2002 provides that time cannot run against him under the Limitation Act 1980. A squatter, alleging adverse possession, would therefore be obliged to advance a claim against X under schedule 6. However, for as long as the squatter remained in possession, he is also adversely possessing the land as against the unregistered paper title owner (O). O's estate was not registered, but it is protected as against X by the fact that X's registered possessory title is by statute subject to any 'estate, right or interest adverse to, or in derogation of, the proprietor's title subsisting at the time of registration or then capable of arising'.[23] If such an 'estate … adverse to, or in derogation of, the proprietor's title' remains enforceable even though its proprietor (O) is not registered, it must follow that the estate exists outside the scheme of registration. On this basis, whilst the Limitation Act 1980 ceased to apply to the squatter's adverse possession as against the registered proprietor (X), it had not ceased to apply to his adverse possession in relation to the unregistered paper title owner (O).

III. Problems Associated with First Registration of Titles

A potential difficulty arises where a person applies to the Land Registry for first registration, and an objection is made by a squatter, in whose favour time has been running under the Limitation Act 1980. It may be that, at the date of the application for first registration, the squatter has not yet enjoyed the full period of 12 years' adverse possession, such as to bar the paper owner's title under section 17 of the Limitation Act 1980. However, if there is a delay in dealing with the first registration—necessitated perhaps by the Land Registry's need to investigate the objection based on adverse possession—does time continue to run against the paper owner? This was precisely the situation that came before the Tribunal in the case of *Port of London Authority v Mendoza*.[24]

In relation to unregistered land, adverse possession is governed by sections 15 and 17 of the Limitation Act 1980. Section 15(1) provides that:

> No action shall be brought by any person to recover any land after the expiration of twelve years from the date on which the right of action accrued to him or, if it first accrued to some person through whom he claims, to that person.

Section 15(6) provides that:

> Part I of Schedule I to this Act contains provisions for determining the date of accrual of rights of action to recover land in the cases there mentioned.

[23] LRA 2002, s 11(7).

[24] *Port of London Authority v Mendoza* [2016] UKFTT 0087 (PC).

The combined effect of paragraphs 1 and 8 of Schedule I is that the right of action only accrues once there is somebody in possession in whose favour the limitation period can run (ie, somebody who is in adverse possession). Section 17 provides that, with certain exceptions, at the expiration of the period for a person to bring an action to recover land, the title of that person to the land is extinguished.

In the *Mendoza* case, the judge decided[25] that the application by the paper owner (the PLA) for first registration could not be regarded as an action to recover land within the meaning of the Limitation Act 1980.[26] Accordingly, time continued to run against the PLA in favour of the squatter. The Land Registry referred the disputed application for first registration to the Tribunal, which also had to resolve the squatter's claim to adverse possession. Notably, by the time of the Tribunal hearing, the squatter had been in adverse possession for more than 12 years, and hence argued that the PLA's title had become barred under section 17 of the Limitation Act 1980. In relation to this point, the judge decided that the position had to be considered as at the date of the original application. Under section 74 of the LRA 2002, registration pursuant to a successful application for first registration is given effect as from the date of the original application, when the application is entered in the Day List.[27] It is, in effect, backdated. The reasoning was as follows:

> There is therefore a question whether an order should be made to give effect to the application if, before a decision has been made but after the date of the application, the applicant has ceased to have title to the land in question. I am satisfied that, in general, such an order should be made. If the applicant had a registrable title which it was entitled to register, or some other right which it was entitled to protect by notice or restriction, when the application was made, it should not be adversely affected by delay in dealing with the application—a delay in this case of over 6 years.[28]

Once the first registration had been effected, the squatter could still rely on his period of adverse possession, but his application for a possessory title would have to be made via Form ADV1 under the provisions of schedule 6. It is suggested that this is clearly the correct outcome, since it would be unjust if the paper owner were to be prejudiced, and the squatter benefited, by the Land Registry's delay in resolving the original application for first registration.

IV. Acknowledgments of Title

Under the Limitation Act 1980, if the squatter acknowledged the title of the paper owner, then the date on which the owner's right of action against the squatter accrued—and when the Limitation Act 'clock' began ticking—was deemed to be postponed to the date of the acknowledgment.[29] The Law Commission considered that the introduction of the new schedule 6 procedure in LRA 2002, and the disapplication of the Limitation Act 1980,

[25] ibid [25].
[26] A contrary view is expressed in Jourdan and Radley-Gardner, *Adverse Possession* (n 15) at paras 1–24.
[27] Kept under LRR 2003, r 12.
[28] *Mendoza* (n 24) [33].
[29] Limitation Act 1980, ss 29 and 30.

necessarily excluded this concept.[30] This has been the subject of a decision of the Adjudicator to HM Land Registry—*Walton v Kerguelen Investments Ltd*[31]—in which it was held that it was no longer possible for the running of time to be postponed by means of an acknowledgment of title. However, under the new regime, a squatter's acknowledgment of the registered owner's title would disentitle the squatter from relying on the third condition under paragraph 5 of schedule 6, and might also have a bearing on the issue of intention to possess.

V. Defects in the Form NAP Counter-Notice

As previously stated, schedule 6 of the Act introduced an entirely new and untested procedure, by which squatters were able to apply for a title based on adverse possession. Title does not automatically vest in the squatter, as it did in relation to both unregistered and registered titles prior to the LRA 2002.[32] Notice of the squatter's application must be given to the registered proprietor and other interested persons, who then have the opportunity to object to the claimant squatter's alleged facts and/or serve a counter-notice using Form NAP. Service of a counter-notice amounts to a request by the owner that the squatter's application be dealt with under paragraph 5—meaning that the squatter's application will fail unless he can bring himself within one or more of the three conditions in paragraph 5, which are discussed in section VI below. If a counter-notice is not served, the squatter's application will succeed.

The terms of Form NAP are prescribed, and issues may arise where the registered proprietor has failed to complete the form correctly. In some early decisions of the Adjudicator,[33] it had been held that unless a registered proprietor ticked the relevant box on Form NAP to invoke the protection of paragraph 5/serve a counter-notice, the squatter's application would automatically succeed. However, in *Hopkins v Beacon*,[34] Vos J held that it was not essential to tick the actual box on Form NAP; applying the *Mannai* test,[35] it was sufficient if a recipient of the form would be aware that paragraph 5 was being invoked. It would be necessary to look at the documents submitted by the objector/registered proprietor in the round, in order to decide whether paragraph 5 was raised. This seems to be an eminently sensible approach. It was followed in a subsequent Tribunal decision,[36] in which the judge took the view that Form NAP contained sufficient information to put the Land Registry and the applicant on notice that paragraph 5 was being invoked.

Problems may also arise where a squatter makes an application under schedule 6 of the Act, using Form ADV1 but in circumstances where he has been in adverse possession for

[30] Law Com No 271 (n 1) para 14.11.
[31] *Walton v Kerguelen Investments Ltd* [2008] EWLandRA 2008_0321.
[32] Limitation Act 1980, s 17 and Land Registration Act 1925, s 75 (as to the beneficial ownership).
[33] See, eg, *Skipwith v Singh* [2010] EWLandRA 2009_0850.
[34] *Hopkins v Beacon* [2011] EWHC 2899 (Ch).
[35] *Mannai Investment Co v Eagle Star Life Insurance Co Ltd* [1997] AC 749 (HL).
[36] *Norton Arms Bowls Club v Spirit Pub Company (Leased) Ltd* [2013] EWLandRA 2013_0318.

more than 12 years prior to 13 October 2003.[37] Indeed, the author is aware of cases where the Land Registry has insisted that the application in relation to a registered title must be made via ADV1. In these circumstances, the squatter may have barred the registered owner's title under section 17 of the Limitation Act 1980, and, as such, would be entitled to make an application for the registered title under the transitional provisions contained in LRA 2002, schedule 12, paragraph 18. A question then arises as to whether the squatter is entitled to use Form ADV1[38] to apply for the registered title—a form seemingly reserved for squatters applying under the new schedule 6 procedure.[39]

Where the Land Registry has insisted that the application in relation to a registered title—whether under schedule 6 or schedule 12—must be made using Form ADV1, despite the form referring specifically only to applications under schedule 6, there is usually a practical solution. In practice, if a Form ADV1 application is referred to the Tribunal, but the evidence provided in the accompanying Statement of Truth supports a claim under the schedule 12 paragraph 8 transitional provision, the Tribunal will generally permit the squatter to amend the Statement of Case,[40] subject of course to questions of prejudice to the other party.

There is, however, an alternative way of dealing with this situation. Where the registered proprietor has served a Form NAP counter-notice, it may well be that the squatter is unable to satisfy either the first or third condition in paragraph 5—'estoppel' or 'reasonable belief' as to ownership of adjacent land. However, if 12 years' adverse possession prior to 13 October 2003 can be proved, then as a matter of law the registered proprietor's title will have been extinguished (if unregistered at that date) or (if registered at that date) will be held on trust for the squatter under section 75 of the Land Registration Act 1925. On this basis, the squatter's application ought to have been made in Form AP1, as a claim to *alter* the register. Nevertheless, where no such application has been made, but a Form NAP application has been made instead, the fact that the squatter has already barred the title of the registered proprietor may enable the squatter to satisfy the second condition in schedule 6, para 5—that there is some 'other reason', outside entitlements generated by schedule 6, why the squatter is entitled to be registered as proprietor. Morgan J took this view in *Balevents v Sartori*.[41] The same view has been taken by the Adjudicator/Tribunal.[42]

VI. Paragraph 5 of Schedule 6

The three conditions in LRA 2002, schedule 6, paragraph 5 have each given rise to some difficult questions. It may be recalled that satisfaction of one of these conditions by the squatter will allow his application to succeed even if the registered proprietor has served a Form NAP counter-notice.

[37] The commencement date of the LRA 2002.

[38] LRR 2003, r 188, sch 1.

[39] Form ADV1 is entitled 'Application for registration of a person in adverse possession under schedule 6 to the Land Registration Act 2002'.

[40] See, eg, *Davies v John Wood Property Ltd* [2010] EWLandRA 2008_0528.

[41] *Balevents v Sartori* [2014] EWHC 1164 (Ch) [86] (Morgan J).

[42] *Cooper v Gick* [2008] EWLandRA 2007_0103.

A. The First Condition: 'Estoppel'

The first condition, set out at paragraph 5(2), will be met if:

(a) it would be unconscionable because of an equity by estoppel for the registered proprietor to seek to dispossess the applicant, and
(b) the circumstances are such that the applicant ought to be registered as the proprietor.

This should also be read in conjunction with LRA 2002, section 110(4), which provides:

> If, in the case of a reference under section 73(7) relating to an application under paragraph 1 of Schedule 6, the [First-tier Tribunal] determines that it would be unconscionable because of an equity by estoppel for the registered proprietor to seek to dispossess the applicant, but that the circumstances are not such that the applicant ought to be registered as proprietor, the [First-tier Tribunal]—
>
> (a) must determine how the equity due to the applicant is to be satisfied, and
> (b) may for that purpose make any order that the High Court could make in the exercise of its equitable jurisdiction.

It might be said that this is a curious condition to be satisfied by a person claiming title by way of adverse possession. The requirements for an adverse possession claim—exclusive factual possession, adverse to the registered proprietor, coupled with an intention to possess—have nothing in common with estoppel. Estoppel is an equitable doctrine; adverse possession is a doctrine historically tied to the law of limitation, as embodied in statute. The first condition thus introduces a hybrid element into this area of law.

In relation to this first condition, it is also worth noting that the squatter is presented with a number of separate hurdles to overcome. First, an estoppel must be established. The general principles should be well-known.[43] They would require, in broad brush terms, that the representor has encouraged the representee to act to his detriment, or has acquiesced in the representee's actions in the knowledge that he has a mistaken belief as to his rights. The representation and the detriment must be proved. Secondly, the recovery of possession by the paper title owner must be 'unconscionable'. It might be thought that proof of an estoppel necessarily imports a degree of unconscionability—certainly, it seems unlikely that an applicant could establish an 'equity by estoppel' without also proving some unconscionable behaviour on the part of the registered proprietor—but paragraph 5 clearly states that unconscionability is a separate matter to be proved. Finally, even if these two elements are proved, the squatter must also establish that 'the circumstances are such that the applicant ought to be registered as the proprietor'. This indicates that there is a discretion as to whether to confer title on the squatter, even where an estoppel and unconscionable conduct are proved. This ties in with the power given to the Tribunal under section 110(4) of the LRA 2002, to give effect to the estoppel by some remedy other than vesting the title in the squatter.

However flexible the doctrine may be, it has been developed in order to protect parties from unconscionable conduct, as the words of paragraph 5(2)(a) make clear. The Law

[43] C Harpum, S Bridge, M Dixon, *Megarry & Wade: The Law of Real Property*, 8th edn (London, Sweet & Maxwell, 2012) paras 16.001–16.033.

Commission report which preceded the LRA 2002 contains this example of the type of situation where the first condition would apply, namely:

> Where the squatter has built on the registered proprietor's land in the mistaken belief that he or she was the owner of it, and the proprietor has knowingly acquiesced in his or her mistake. The squatter eventually discovers the true facts and applies to be registered after 10 years.[44]

This example might of course overlap with the third condition—reasonable belief as to ownership of adjacent land on a boundary—since in the circumstances described, the squatter's belief would appear to be reasonable, given the expenditure of money and the lack of action by the registered owner. However, there may be technical reasons why the third condition might not apply—the land in question may not lie on a boundary between the squatter's and registered proprietor's land, for instance—in which case, it will be essential for the squatter to satisfy the first condition.

There have been few decided cases on this condition. In two decisions of the Tribunal in which it has been relied upon, the Tribunal has rejected the claim.[45]

B. The Second Condition: 'Any Other Reason'

The 'second condition' which allows a squatter to defeat the registered proprietor's counter-notice arises when the applicant is for some other reason entitled to be registered as the proprietor of the estate'.[46] According to the Law Commission:

> This exception is more straightforward. From time to time there may be cases where the squatter has some other right to the land that would entitle him or her to be registered as proprietor irrespective of any period of adverse possession. Two examples may be given by way of illustration.
>
> (1) The claimant is entitled to the land under the will or intestacy of the deceased proprietor.
> (2) The claimant contracted to buy the land and paid the purchase price, but the legal estate was never transferred to him or her. In a case of this kind, the squatter-buyer is a beneficiary under a bare trust, and, as such, can be in adverse possession.[47]

There have been very few cases in which this condition has been relied on.

One decision worthy of mention is *Cooper v Gick*.[48] A squatter had been in adverse possession of the disputed land for more than 12 years prior to first registration. However, the squatter's application was made in Form ADV1 under schedule 6, on the basis of 10 years' adverse possession prior to the date of the application. The squatter had relied on the third condition—reasonable belief as to ownership of adjacent land. However, this was unavailable, because the land had not been registered for a year prior to the date of the application, as the third condition required. The Deputy Adjudicator held as follows:

> The application I am dealing with under [s]chedule 6. If my preliminary decision was incorrect and paragraph 5 of [s]chedule 6 is engaged I must consider whether the Applicants have satisfied

[44] Law Com No 271 (n 1) para 14.42.
[45] *Tarr v Ahmed* [2009] EWLandRA 2008_1085; *Tomlinson v Foster* [2012] EWLandRA 2011_1049.
[46] LRA 2002, sch 6, para 5(3).
[47] Law Com No 271 (n 1) para 14.43 (footnotes omitted).
[48] *Cooper* (n 42).

> one of the conditions. It was effectively and correctly conceded that they cannot rely on the third condition because although the Verge was now registered over a year ago it was not as of the date of the application which is the relevant point of reference for paragraph 5(4)(d). However, having concluded that I am permitted to consider whether any of the conditions are satisfied I have considered whether any other condition applies. The second condition is whether the Applicants are entitled to be registered for some other reason. Having been in adverse possession for over 12 years while the Verge was unregistered with the result that the paper title was extinguished, aside from any entitlement under the Schedule 6 regime they are entitled and could have applied to alter the register pursuant to Schedule 4 and for first registration in their own name on the basis of 12 years' adverse possession of unregistered land. I have concluded they are entitled to be registered for some other reason namely 12 years' adverse possession of unregistered land rather than 10 years adverse possession of registered land and the satisfaction of a condition.[49]

Morgan J in *Balevents v Sartori* has also held that the second condition would apply in such circumstances.[50]

C. The Third Condition: 'Reasonable Belief' as to Ownership of Adjacent Land

Paragraph 5(4) provides that the 'third condition' is met when:

> (a) the land to which the application relates is adjacent to land belonging to the applicant,
> (b) the exact line of the boundary between the two has not been determined under rules under section 60,
> (c) for at least ten years of the period of adverse possession ending on the date of the application, the applicant (or any predecessor in title) reasonably believed that the land to which the application relates belonged to him, and
> (d) the estate to which the application relates was registered more than one year prior to the date of the application.

Sub-conditions (a), (b) and (d) are straightforward. Sub-condition (c) has, however, given rise to certain difficulties, given the potentially ambiguous meaning of the phrase 'for at least ten years of the period of adverse possession ending on the date of the application'. For what period of time must the reasonable belief be held? Is it sufficient to have the belief for a total period of 10 years that might have come to an end prior to the date of the application? Or must the belief be retained up to the actual date of the application?

The Law Commission report that accompanied the Land Registration Bill clearly stated that to fall within the third condition, the squatter would have to prove that:

> (1) there has been a period of adverse possession of at least 10 years by the applicant or his or her predecessor in title ending on the date of the application; (2) for at least 10 years of the period, the applicant or his or her predecessor in title reasonably believed that the land to which the application relates belonged to him or her; and (3) the estate to which the land relates was registered more than one year prior to the date of the application.[51]

[49] *Cooper* (n 42) [33] (Brie Stevens-Hoare QC, sitting as Deputy Adjudicator).
[50] *Balevents* (n 41).
[51] Law Com No 271 (n 1) para 14.44.

The report goes on to point out that:

> at some point prior to making the application to be registered, the squatter will have become aware that he or she is not in fact the owner of the land in issue. It is likely to be this realisation that prompts the application. It follows that the period of adverse possession that will be needed will, in practice, be more (even if only marginally) than 10 years.[52]

It is apparent therefore that the Law Commission, the Land Registry (which co-authored the Law Commission report) and Parliament intended that the squatter might hold the reasonable belief for 10 years at any time during the period of adverse possession, but not necessarily up to the date of the application.[53]

Precisely this issue was considered in the Court of Appeal decision in *Zarb v Parry*.[54] The case was primarily concerned with an alleged interruption of the squatter's adverse possession. However, the Court of Appeal also considered whether the third condition under paragraph 5 had been satisfied by the squatter. Arden LJ said of the condition:

> [T]he necessary effect of the way that paragraph 5(4) is expressed is to make the unreasonable belief of the adverse possessor in the last ten years of his possession prior to the application for registration a potentially disqualifying factor even though his belief started out as reasonable but became unreasonable as a result of circumstances after the completion by him and/or his predecessor in title of a ten year period of possession. The consequence of that is that the paper title owner will have a last chance to recover the land if the adverse possessor did not have a reasonable belief during the last ten years. The moral is that, as soon as the adverse possessor learns facts which might make his belief in his own ownership unreasonable, he should take steps to secure registration as proprietor.[55]

Continuing, she said:

> The 2002 Act creates difficulties for proprietors with disputed boundaries. If a person discovers that his boundary is in fact on his neighbour's land and that he has been in possession for ten years, he can if he acts promptly apply to the Land Registry to be registered as proprietor of any land outside his title. The new provisions will, however, require the registrar to give notice of the application to the paper title owner of the land sought to be acquired. If the registered proprietor does not oppose the application, registration will follow. If the registered proprietor opposes the application, the adverse possessor may be unable to satisfy the third condition in paragraph 5 of schedule 6 to the 2002 Act, and will fail to secure registration save in the exceptional case where he can show that another condition is satisfied.[56]

Jackson LJ agreed with Arden LJ. Lord Neuberger MR gave a separate judgment, but did not in any way dissent from Arden LJ's views on the effect of the third condition.

These conclusions were expressed without any argument on the point, without reference being made to the Law Commission report, and without it in fact being necessary for its decision—because on the facts the squatters' reasonable belief had indeed continued until the date of the application. The result of that construction is, as the Court of Appeal itself appears to have realised, absurd. Even in the ordinary case, the squatter's entitlement to

[52] ibid.
[53] This view was reinforced in Law Com No 271 (n 1) paras 14.50–14.52.
[54] *Zarb v Parry* [2011] EWCA Civ 1306, [2012] 1 WLR 1240.
[55] ibid [17] (Arden LJ).
[56] ibid [55] (Arden LJ).

succeed under the third condition could depend on the quality of the arguments addressed by the registered proprietor or his solicitors to the squatter in possession. If the squatter is alerted, with convincing evidence, that he is in adverse possession of land on a boundary, then he may no longer have the relevant 'reasonable belief'; by contrast, if flimsy evidence is presented by the registered proprietor, the squatter's 'reasonable belief' might be more likely to continue. It is not apparent that such (relatively arbitrary) factors should determine the success or failure of the squatter's application for the title. The condition was introduced in order to allow 'deserving' squatters to be registered, and the right to be registered necessarily amounts to a proprietary right, as the Law Commission accepted. If the reasoning in *Zarb* is correct, the third condition would be rendered useless in any practical sense. It may be doubted whether the *Zarb* interpretation of paragraph 5 is compatible with Article 1 of the First Protocol of the European Convention of Human Rights, and compliant with the obligation under section 3(1) of the Human Rights Act 1998. It also overlooks that 'ten years of the period of adverse possession ending on the date of the application', badly drafted as it is, is susceptible to multiple interpretations: it can be read literally not only as having the meaning put on it by the Court of Appeal in *Zarb*, but also, and alternatively, as requiring reasonable belief for *any* ten years of the period of adverse possession leading up to the date of application, whether or not that belief continued up to that date. Had the Court of Appeal been aware of the clear understanding of the Law Commission, the Land Registry and Parliament, as demonstrated by the report and the wording of the Bill as included in that report, it must be doubted that it would have been so dogmatic in adopting an interpretation that would necessarily produce irrational and unfair results.

There has been at least one Tribunal decision which has departed from the *Zarb* approach,[57] and some critical discussion in another.[58] The difficulty posed by the *Zarb* construction of schedule 6, paragraph 5(4)(c) has also been recognised by the Law Commission in its recent Consultation Paper reviewing the LRA 2002.[59] The Law Commission has provisionally proposed that where an applicant relies on this condition, his reasonable belief that the land belonged to him must have ended not more than six months from the date of the application.[60] This would seem to be a pragmatic way of resolving the difficulty, reconciling the interests both of the registered proprietor and the applicant. The registered proprietor is protected by the long-stop date, while the six-month period of grace allows the applicant to evaluate the merits of the claim in the knowledge that his reasonable belief in ownership was mistaken.

Indeed, in an earlier case before the Adjudicator, *Davies v John Wood Property Ltd*,[61] the condition was construed as having the meaning seemingly intended by the Law Commission. Furthermore, in a subsequent Tribunal decision, *McLeod v Brown*,[62] it was also held that the reasonable belief did not have to be held up to the date of the application, since such a construction would have perverse results. *Zarb v Parry* was not, however, cited, and is not mentioned in the *McLeod* decision.

[57] *Crew v London & Continental Ltd* [2017] UKFTT 0047 (PC) [30].

[58] *Mendoza* (n 24) [38]–[40].

[59] See Law Commission, *Updating the Land Registration Act 2002—A Consultation Paper* (Law Com CP No 227, 2016).

[60] Ibid, para 17.47.

[61] *Davies v John Wood* (n 40).

[62] *McLeod v Brown* [2014] EWLandRA 2013_0833.

The other element of the condition that has given rise to some difficulty is the requirement that the applicant 'reasonably believed' that the land to which the application relates belonged to him. If the third condition merely required the applicant to believe that he owned the disputed land, the test would be entirely subjective. He could have a firm and settled belief which, on examination, was entirely irrational. The requirement that the applicant's belief must be 'reasonable' necessarily introduces an objective element into the test. Inevitably, however, the factors that will render a squatter's belief reasonable or unreasonable will vary from case to case.

In *Zarb v Parry* itself it was argued that it was unreasonable for the Parrys (the squatters) to have ignored a solicitors' letter from the registered proprietors (the Zarbs), in which a detailed explanation was given for their contention that the Parrys did not have legal title to the disputed land. There had been an earlier dispute concerning the boundary between the Zarbs and the Parrys' predecessors in title, the Ceens. That dispute had been dormant for some five years and the Ceens (and their purchasers, the Parrys) believed that it had been resolved. Arden LJ decided[63] that, in the circumstances, the Parrys' continuing belief that they did own the land was reasonable. Among the relevant factors considered by the Court was the fact that, after the dispute had arisen, a boundary surveyor had advised the Parrys that they did own the disputed land by reference to the title plans.

Since all registered titles have a filed plan annexed, the question often arises whether an applicant whose belief is based on an incorrect interpretation of the plan, can be regarded as holding a reasonable belief. It has been held that the belief should be treated as the belief of a lay person,[64] not a lawyer or surveyor. Accordingly, a failure to realise that the land possessed by the applicant was not included within the registered boundary is not an unreasonable belief for a lay person to hold—only a person with specialised knowledge of registered boundaries would have realised that the land was excluded. This may suggest that the test would indeed be differently applied if the applicant did have specialised knowledge. Further, there may be cases where the title plan is sufficiently clear that even a superficial examination would reveal that the land was excluded from his title. This was the case in *Lory v Harpserve*[65] in which a total of six factors were identified which rendered the applicant's belief in ownership unreasonable.

The significance of plans was also considered in *Howell v Shoreham Port Authority*.[66] The factors which rendered the belief reasonable were identified in the following passage:

> The title plans for WSX31653 and WSX151717 show the southern boundary as a straight line, which line continues towards the east. A person having knowledge of Ordnance Survey practice would note that the solid line marked on the plan by the Ordnance Survey must be a wall and not a line where the surface material changes. However, the title plan does only show the general boundary and could be interpreted as being either the wall of the buildings or the edge of the road. I accept Mr Howell's evidence that he did believe the Strip belonged to him. I also consider that this belief was reasonable. It was a reasonable belief for the following reasons.
>
> (1) The title plan shows a general boundary which is capable of being interpreted as the southern edge of the Strip.

[63] ibid [49]–[51].
[64] *McLeod v Brown* [2015] UKFTT 0310 (PC).
[65] [2009] EWLandRA 2008_1530.
[66] [2015] UKFTT 0522 (PC).

(2) When Mr Howell acquired 4&5 Nicholsons Wharf, there were containers at each end of the Strip, being the container sited on the Strip itself at its western end and a second container sited on land immediately to the east of the Strip. Those containers appeared to demarcate the Strip as being something apart from the road.

(3) The presence of the container on the western end of the Strip, the chimney overhanging the eastern part of the Strip, the manhole and sceptic tank in the Strip and the doors hinging out over the Strip are all relevant factors. Those factors taken together would lead a reasonable man when considering the location of the boundary and looking at the ground with a copy of the plan showing the general boundary to conclude that the Strip formed part of the land in his title.

The issue of the applicant's 'reasonable belief' has been the subject of a number of other Tribunal decisions,[67] a study of which demonstrates the variety of different circumstances that can affect the outcome of this question.

VII. The Conundrum of *Parshall v Hackney*[68]—Double Registration and Adverse Possession

Parshall v Hackney is not a schedule 6 case, being a case decided under the jurisdiction to alter or rectify the Register. It nevertheless raises issues which may apply equally to a claim under the LRA 2002.

The facts were unusual, but by no means unprecedented. The appellants' title—No 29 Milner St, in South West London—had been first registered in 1904, and (correctly) included a small triangle of paved land in front ('the disputed land'). 31 Milner Street ('No 31') was first registered in 1980, and by a mistake, the Land Registry included the disputed land within this title, thus creating a double registration. In July 1988, the owners of No 31 fixed a chain and metal eye (or hook) into a concrete bollard to demarcate the disputed land as a parking space, which had been used, and was used thereafter, exclusively by the owners of No 31. In 2000, the Land Registry revised the title plan, and compounded the mistake by omitting the disputed land from the appellants' title to No 29. The proprietors of No 29 made an application to the Land Registry in August 2008 to rectify the Register by excluding the disputed land from the title plan to No 31, and to add it to the title plan of number 29.[69] They recognised that the owners of No 31 were registered proprietors of the disputed land and had been in possession of it for many years, and that these facts prima facie afforded the No 31 owners a defence to the rectification claim. However, they argued that this defence was defeated on the statutory ground that it would be unjust *not* to allow rectification on the facts.[70] The proprietor of No 31 resisted the application for rectification, primarily on the ground that the title to the disputed land which had been part of

[67] See *Griffin v Crown Mill (1993) Management* [2016] UKFTT 0711 (PC); *Crew v London & Continental Ltd* [2017] UKFTT 0047 (PC); *Holroyd v Gething* [2017] UKFTT 0048 (PC); and *Blanchard v Basingstoke & Deane DC* [2017] UKFTT 0522 (PC).

[68] *Parshall v Hackney* [2013] EWCA Civ 240, [2013] Ch 568.

[69] LRA 2002, s 65 and sch 4.

[70] LRA 2002, s 65 and sch 4, para 6(2).

No 29 had been barred by operation of the adverse possession provisions in the Limitation Act 1980, prior to the coming into force of the LRA 2002. The argument succeeded before the Deputy Adjudicator, who also said that, but for the adverse possession point, he would have rectified the register against the owners of No 31. There was an unsuccessful first appeal to the Chancery Division.[71] However, permission was given for a second appeal, which was heard by the Court of Appeal. Mummery LJ gave the leading judgment, with which the other judges agreed.

According to Mummery LJ: 'The appeal thus turns on whether the owners of No 29 were dispossessed of the disputed land in July 1988 and whether the owners of No 31 were in adverse possession of it throughout the period down to 2003'.[72] It had been found as a fact that the owners of No 31 had physically demarcated the disputed land in July 1988, and had been in exclusive possession and control of the land ever since, using it as a parking space. Since they used it to the exclusion of the owners and occupiers of No 29—who were unable to obtain access or to use the land due to the physical barriers erected—it might be thought that the owners of No 29 had indeed been adversely dispossessed. However, Mummery LJ came to a different conclusion. He noted that Slade LJ had previously discussed the requirements of adverse possession in *Buckinghamshire County Council v Moran* in the following terms:

> Possession is never "adverse" within the meaning of the Act of 1980 if it is enjoyed under a lawful title. If, therefore, a person occupies or uses land by licence of the owner with the paper title and his licence has not been duly determined, he cannot be treated as having been in "adverse possession" as against the owner with the paper title.[73]

Mummery LJ applied this dictum to the facts in *Parshall*, as follows:

> There was no dispossession in July 1988, because the taking of possession of the disputed land was not unlawful. It was lawful for the owners of No 31 to take and remain in possession of the disputed land, because they had a registered title to it. As long as they remained registered proprietors of the disputed land, that possession would be lawful and could not be adverse to the owners of No 29.[74]

Accordingly, he held that since the owners of No 31 were the registered proprietors of the disputed strip, it was not possible for them to be in 'adverse' possession as against the owners of No 29. It followed that time never started to run against the owners of No 29 under the Limitation Act 1980.

With the greatest deference to a very distinguished property lawyer, this reasoning is difficult to follow. It is of course true that (per Slade LJ in *Moran*), where a person is in possession with the consent of the true owner, such possession is not *adverse* possession at all. Since the occupier is present with the consent of the true owner, no cause of action to recover possession can arise. It would be necessary to determine the licence, and only then is possession adverse. However, this analysis cannot sensibly apply to a case of double registration such as in *Parshall v Hackney*. In such a case, *both* registered proprietors have a legal title conferred by what is now section 58 of the LRA 2002, formerly section 69(1) of

[71] *Parshall v Hackney (sub nom Parshall v Bryans)* [2012] EWHC 665 (Ch).
[72] *Parshall* (CA) (n 68) [85] (Mummery LJ).
[73] *Buckinghamshire CC v Moran* [1990] 1 Ch 623, 636 (Slade J), cited in *Parshall* (CA) (n 68) [87].
[74] *Parshall* (CA) (n 68) [87] (Mummery LJ).

the LRA 1925. Mummery LJ seemed to have some problem with this concept, as this passage demonstrates:

> The problem is that, as a matter of law, the disputed land is owned either by the appellant or by the respondent. They cannot both be owners of a fee simple in the same piece of land.[75]

Even as a matter of unregistered conveyancing, this statement is questionable, given that different fee simples may co-exist simultaneously in the same land.[76] This statement ignores the doctrine of relativity of title.[77] On any footing, the reasoning could not apply to the registered titles in this case, since upon registration the registered freehold proprietor of land is deemed to have vested in him, without any conveyance, the legal estate in fee simple in possession.[78] A transferee under a forged disposition would not, as a matter of unregistered title, obtain any interest in the subject land. However, if he succeeds in becoming registered, he will be deemed to have a legal title by virtue of LRA 2002, section 58 (and its statutory predecessor). Accordingly, the registered proprietors of No 29 retained their registered legal title to the disputed land at the date (in July 1988) when they were physically dispossessed by the owners of No 31. Their names remained on the proprietorship register, and the entry into physical possession by the owners of No 31 had no legal effect as regards their registered title.

The relevant provisions of section 15 of the Limitation Act 1980 are as follows:

> (1) No action shall be brought by any person to recover any land after the expiration of twelve years from the date on which the right of action accrued to him or, if it first accrued to some person through whom he claims, to that person.
>
> (6) Part I of Schedule 1 to this Act contains provisions for determining the date of accrual of rights of action to recover land in the cases there mentioned.

Schedule 1 provides:

> 1. Where the person bringing an action to recover land, or some person through whom he claims, has been in possession of the land, and has while entitled to the land been dispossessed or discontinued his possession, the right of action shall be treated as having accrued on the date of dispossession or the discontinuance.
>
> 8.(1) No right of action to recover land shall be treated as accruing unless the land is in the possession of some person in whose favour the period of limitation can run (referred to below in this paragraph as 'adverse possession'); and where under the preceding provisions of this Schedule any such right of action is treated as accruing on a certain date and no person is in adverse possession on that date the right of action shall not be treated as accruing unless and until adverse possession is taken of the land.

It is hard to see how it could be argued that the registered proprietors of the disputed land—the owners of No 29—did not fall within the terms of Schedule 1, paragraph 1. As registered proprietors, they were physically excluded, or dispossessed. At that point, they were manifestly entitled to bring proceedings for possession against their dispossessors. It matters not that the occupiers could have defended the proceedings on the grounds that

[75] *Parshall* (CA) (n 68) [9] (Mummery LJ).
[76] See, eg, the discussion in this chapter at section II(B)(ii) ('The Second Interpretation').
[77] A point made by the respondents—see *Parshall* (CA) (n 68) [14].
[78] LRA 1925, s 69(1).

they also had a registered title. The accrual of the cause of action does not anticipate what defences may be run by the occupier. Any number of defences, from permission to estoppel, could exist. However, the critical factor is the existence of the right to sue for possession, an entirely separate question from the possible defences. At paragraph 87 of his judgment, Mummery LJ demonstrates the fallacy inherent in the decision: 'As long as they remained registered proprietors of the disputed land, that possession would be lawful and could not be adverse to the owners of No 29'. The notion of their occupation being 'lawful' and therefore not 'adverse' confuses the title of the owners of No 29 with that of No 31. Clearly, the possession of the disputed land by the owners of No 31 could not be adverse to their own title—they have their own permission to be there. However, it can certainly be adverse to the other title to which the land belongs, namely No 29.

The result of this decision, therefore, was to deprive the owners of No 31 of their title to the disputed land, and further to deprive them of the ability to claim a title by adverse possession. The owners of No 29, who had been out of possession of the disputed land for some 20 years, succeeded in their claim for rectification. Having found against the respondents on the adverse possession argument, the Court of Appeal was not prepared to interfere with the decision of the Deputy Adjudicator to the effect that he would have rectified the register, had the claim to adverse possession not succeeded. In the words of Mummery LJ:

> There are no grounds for interfering with the decision of the Deputy Adjudicator as to how he would have exercised his discretion to rectify, but for the possessory title point. The points forcefully advanced by Mr Rodger QC against rectification could not disguise the plain unvarnished fact that his client is seeking to take the benefit of a mistake by the Land Registry, which had occurred through no fault on the appellants' side and which it would be unjust not to correct.[79]

Under LRA 2002, schedule 4, a registered proprietor in possession will not be subject to rectification unless 'it would for any other reason be unjust for the alteration not to be made'.[80] I would suggest that it was manifestly more unjust to rectify the register against the parties in possession than it was to refuse rectification in favour of the appellants. The appellants had been out of possession of the disputed land for 20 years, and had taken no steps to recover it during that period. It had been enjoyed as part and parcel of the respondents' title for the same period. It is difficult to see why the interests of the appellants should have been preferred to the interests of the respondents, bearing in mind that the burden was on the applicants to demonstrate that a refusal to alter the register would amount to injustice. There is perhaps a sense in which the decision reflects a lack of judicial enthusiasm for the position of the squatter.

VIII. Endnote

It is some 12 years since the new adverse possession regime came into force. Inevitably, there have been teething troubles, and difficulties have emerged in the process which were perhaps not foreseen by the draftsmen of the LRA 2002. By and large these difficulties

[79] *Parshall* (CA) (n 68) [97] (Mummery LJ).
[80] LRA 2002, sch 4, para 3(2)(b).

have been satisfactorily resolved by sensible judicial interpretation. However, a number of issues remain. Fortunately, the Law Commission has carried out[81] a comprehensive 10-year review of the workings of the LRA 2002, and has made a number of sensible proposals for reform. At some future date, therefore, it is likely that at least some of the specific problems identified in this chapter will have been resolved by amendments to the Act.

[81] See Law Com CP No 227 (n 59).

6

The Continuing Relevance of Relativity of Title Under the Land Registration Act 2002

AMY GOYMOUR AND ROBIN HICKEY*

I. Introduction

A. The Nature of the Inquiry

Section 58(1) of the Land Registration Act ('LRA') 2002 provides for the conclusiveness of the Register, in the following terms:

> If, on the entry of a person in the register as the proprietor of a legal estate, the legal estate would not otherwise be vested in him, it shall be deemed to be vested in him as a result of the registration.[1]

There are some well-known qualifications to this provision. Most obviously, the conclusive and constitutive effect of section 58(1) is subject to: (a) the Act's schedule 4 alteration provisions (as broadly interpreted by the courts);[2] and (b) the express proviso in section 58(2), which prevents section 58(1) applying where a 'registration requirement remains to be met'.[3] Generally, however, section 58 sits comfortably with a view that emphasises the peremptory character of the Register in determining matters of title in

* We would like to express our thanks to Elizabeth Cooke and Stephen Watterson for their helpful comments on previous drafts of this chapter. All errors remain our own.

[1] Note that the LRA 2002, s 58, applies to any 'legal estate' that is registered. LRA 2002, s 132 defines 'legal estate' by reference to the Law of Property Act ('LPA') 1925, s 205(1)(x) of which provides (with implicit reference back to s 1) that '"legal estates" means the estates, interests and charges in or over land (subsisting or created at law) which are by this Act authorised to subsist or to be created as legal estates'. As such, s 58 applies not only to freeholds and leaseholds, but also to dependent interests, eg, easements and charges. Note too that the effect of the registration of charges is supplemented by the LRA 2002, s 51.

[2] See, eg, *Ajibade v Bank of Scotland plc* [2008] EWLandRA 2006_0163; *Knights Construction (March) Ltd v Roberto Mac Ltd* [2011] EWLandRA 2009_1459, [2011] 2 EGLR 123; *Barclays Bank v Guy (No 2)* [2010] EWCA Civ 1396, [2011] 1 WLR 681; *MacLeod v Gold Harp Properties Ltd* [2014] EWCA Civ 1084, [2015] 1 WLR 1249. Note that the decision in *Fitzwilliam v Richall Holdings Services Ltd* [2013] EWHC 86 (Ch), [2013] 1 P & CR 19, which limited the constitutive effect of s 58 to the bare *legal* title (as opposed to any associated beneficial rights), has since been discredited: *Swift 1st Ltd v Chief Land Registrar* [2015] EWCA Civ 330, [2015] Ch 602.

[3] Note the (probably incorrect) concession in *Gelley v Shephard* [2013] EWCA Civ 1172, which gave the LRA 2002, s 58(2), a broad meaning. See further ch 16 of this book, section III(A)(i).

respect of registered land. On this view, it is 'the fact of registration and registration alone that confers title'.[4] Outwardly at least this principle—that *registration 'alone'* creates title—seems to stand in stark contrast to the principles that underlie general property law (and which continue to govern unregistered conveyancing)—whereby *possession* is the ultimate root of title. In the general law system—where possession is a source of title—it is possible for multiple, *relative* titles to coexist over the same physical plot of land. For example, A might be the first possessor of Greenacre. His possession confers a title—a common law fee simple. If A is dispossessed by B, B also acquires a title by taking possession—a new, *original* common law fee simple, which is not *derivative* of A's title. As such, there are two fees simple over Greenacre, which are ranked *relative* to one another according to a basic common law rule which ranks titles according to their date of creation—the first having priority. As with any title to land, both fees simple can be conveyed to others.

This chapter is not concerned with the inroads made into the conclusive effect of section 58 of the LRA 2002 by the two qualifications identified at the start—those in sections 58(1), and those resulting from the schedule 4 alteration regime. Instead, it investigates broad questions as to the nature of the title which *is* conferred by section 58. Has the LRA 2002 regime created a unitary, absolutist concept of title, which ousts the general law doctrine of title relativity? Or does the title relativity doctrine continue to have a role within—or perhaps alongside—the Act? More fundamentally, we ask whether the idea of title relativity sits comfortably with the policy ambitions of our land registration system, and therefore whether title relativity *ought* to have any continuing role.

B. The Perception that Relativity of Title is Fading under the LRA 2002

There is a general perception in the academic literature that, under the LRA 2002, the doctrine of relativity of title is fading. Arguments have been put forward in recent property law scholarship to suggest that: (a) the LRA 2002 represents a shift away from title relativity towards a system of absolute ownership; and/or (b) that such a shift is, or would be, desirable. Seeds for this idea were sown by the Law Commission's statement that the LRA 2002 was to be a system where '*[t]he* basis of title should… be the register' (emphasis added)[5]—which hints that title to land is singular and absolute, and derives exclusively from the Register.[6]

[4] Law Commission, *Land Registration for the Twenty-First Century—A Conveyancing Revolution* (Law Com No 271, 2001) para 1.10. See also Law Commission, *Land Registration for the Twenty-First Century: A Consultative Document* (Law Com No 254, 1998) para 10.43, which stated '[i]n making our proposals for reform we have two objectives. The first is to accept that the system of land registration is "not a system of registration of title but a system of title by registration". The basis of title should therefore be the Register'. Note also the discussion in F Burns, 'Adverse Possession and Title-By-Registration Systems in Australia and England' [2012] *Melbourne Univ L Rev* 773.

[5] Law Com No 254 (n 4) para 10.43.

[6] This theme was picked up by Ouseley J in *Best v Chief Land Registrar* [2014] EWHC 1370 (Admin), [2014] 3 All ER 637 [9], where he stated that 'the register and not possession is the root of title to registered land'. This statement may be viewed in two ways: (1) it merely states that one only acquires title to a *registered* estate if one is registered as owner (in which case the statement is tautologous); or (2) *any* title over land which is registered can *only* be acquired through registration—thereby excluding any notion of relative titles relating to land that has been registered. Ouseley J further stated, at [18], that '[t]itle to registered land does not go with possession as such; superior possessory title does not extinguish the registered proprietor's title. The register entry confers title. By contrast with unregistered land, the registered proprietor's title is not extinguished by the requisite period of adverse possession. The passage of that period gave no automatic right thereafter to be registered, nor did it define the relevant period for an application to be registered; that was the ten years preceding the application'.

Scholars have developed this theme, expressing doubts about the long-term survival of title relativity.[7]

Many of these observations have been expressed in the context of the LRA 2002's provisions relating to adverse possession. That the discussion should arise in this context is not surprising: adverse possession claims—where the 'real owner' and the adversely possessing 'squatter' each claim to be entitled to the relevant land—offer the paradigm form of (relative) title dispute. The gist of the arguments that title relativity is fading is that: (i) schedule 6 of the LRA 2002 institutes a regime whereby squatters may apply to acquire the registered title;[8] (ii) if successful, the squatter's own fee simple is extinguished, and he becomes the registered proprietor;[9] and therefore (iii) it is no longer possible for a squatter's possessory common law fee simple to mature into a right resembling ownership, conferring rights good against the world—and for this reason it makes no sense to continue to regard that possessory title as a significant interest.[10] In a chapter entitled 'Whatever Happened to Relativity of Title?', Elizabeth Cooke has explained that the changes made to adverse possession in the LRA 2002 mean that, in substance (even if not in form), a squatter has few rights unless and until registered via schedule 6's provisions. She has written:

> Legal ownership is by registration alone. Although, technically, a squatter can still be growing a fee simple by adverse possession, that fee simple will never, by itself, mature into true ownership and so it is not a significant interest. [...] Now that, in the vast majority of cases, the squatter's interest in the land can no longer turn into true/sole ownership, it may be that we shall in time cease to regard it as a fee simple (since most land law concepts have been defined by reference to their practical effects).[11]

Such perceptions of the decreasing significance of the adverse possessor's common law title are thought to reflect a broader change wrought by the LRA 2002—a shift from possession to registration as the basis of title. Along these lines, Simon Gardner has observed that the LRA 2002's adverse possession reforms 'involved eradicating ... the idea that possession

[7] See, eg, 'relativity of title ... used to be an important concept, but is no longer' (E Cooke, *Land Law*, 2nd edn (Oxford, OUP, 2013) 243); '[I]t was inevitable that the impact of relativity of title, whilst not eliminated from the law of registered land, should be greatly curtailed' (K Gray and SF Gray, *Elements of Land Law*, 5th edn (Oxford, OUP, 2009) 183). See also C Jessel 'Concurrent Fees Simple and the Land Registration Act 2002' (2014) 130 *LQR* 587, 606, which states '[t]he general rule is that there is only one legal estate in fee simple and only one registrable freehold in any piece of land and the two are the same. Where the convolutions of the law have led to a different understanding, it would be best to provide and define new rights to serve a clear modern purpose free from the obscurities of ancient law'.

[8] LRA 2002, sch 6, para 1.

[9] LRA 2002, sch 6, para 9.

[10] Not everyone agrees with this last step in the reasoning. For example, Ben McFarlane, Nicholas Hopkins and Sarah Nield recognise that the adverse possession provisions of the LRA 2002 'provide a significant departure from the previous law', but continue to acknowledge 'that adverse possession confers an independent freehold title from the moment at which possession begins', albeit a title that is rendered 'ghostly' by its significant vulnerability to the superior registered title: B McFarlane, N Hopkins and S Nield, *Land Law: Text, Cases and Materials*, 3rd edn (Oxford, OUP, 2015) 252, 282. In a similar vein, Aruna Nair treats the title of an adverse possessor as 'highly watered-down', but one which nevertheless 'exists on a continuum with the rules that generate ... more powerful rights and cannot be understood except in the context of a system in which possession generates rights': A Nair, 'Morality and the Mirror: the Normative Limits of the Principles of Land Registration' in S Bright (ed), *Modern Studies in Property Law, Volume 6* (Oxford, Hart, 2011) 263.

[11] Cooke, *Land Law* (n 7) 243–44. Cooke does note that any change to the nature of the adverse possessor's common law interest would require 'legislative redefinition', which seems to suggest that, as things stand, an adverse possessor continues to acquire an unregistered fee simple in respect of registered land notwithstanding the enactment of the relevant provisions of the LRA 2002.

in itself gives someone a title to the land';[12] likewise, Kevin Gray and Susan-Francis Gray have opined that that the 'quaintly medieval notion that unchallenged possession generates a presumptive form of estate ownership' has yielded to the reality of a 'state-regulated bureaucratic fact'.[13] The Grays' view also includes the broader argument that, within the LRA 2002, concepts of *title* and *registered estates* are becoming fused, leaving no room for relative titles—under the Act, '"title" is no more and no less than the Register entry which records proprietorship of the relevant estate'.[14] As such, they suggest that English law is moving towards a concept of absolute title to land that itself approaches Roman *dominium*:

> No longer can 'title' be detached from the 'estate' ... The overall effect is to weld concepts of 'title', 'estate' and 'proprietor' into a form of statutory ownership of land which begins to resemble the civilian model of proprietorship ... A new *in rem* quality has been conferred on estate proprietorship (and particularly on ownership of the fee simple estate). The titles maintained by Land Registry are beginning to evince a more 'absolute' quality than they have ever previously enjoyed, thereby demonstrating, in effect, an inexorable drift towards the hitherto alien continental concept of *dominium*.[15]

C. Challenging the Perception that Title Relativity is Fading

This chapter will examine whether the LRA 2002's land registration regime inevitably entails this kind of change in English law's perception of title—whether we are necessarily drifting from a system premised on notions of relative titles towards one in which title is more absolute. We address two main concerns.

First, working on the assumption that section 58 does as it says, and confers *a* title to a 'legal estate' in land, we argue that the doctrine of relativity of title nonetheless remains relevant where a title to land is registered. Nothing in the LRA 2002 expressly ousts the relativity doctrine and, indeed, several provisions go further and assume—more or less explicitly—the presence of relative titles in the context of registered land. The existence of a registered title does not necessarily preclude the existence of *other*, relatively inferior or superior, titles to or interests over that same piece of land. As such, in certain circumstances, whilst the registered title to an estate confers *a* title to that estate, other lesser titles may exist in a relative 'underworld', below the surface of registered titles; in other circumstances, the converse may arise—the registered title might itself exist in a relative 'underworld', being inferior to other relatively superior titles.

Secondly, this chapter questions whether it is appropriate or desirable, as a matter of policy, for title relativity—an inherently common law doctrine which predates notions of title registration—to have this kind of continuing role in a registration regime. For example, can we justify a system that contemplates that RP, a registered proprietor with absolute freehold title, might discover that someone else, O, in fact has an unregistered freehold

[12] S Gardner with E MacKenzie, *An Introduction to Land Law*, 4th edn (Oxford, Hart, 2015) 135.

[13] Gray and Gray (n 7) 180.

[14] ibid, 182. See also *Secretary of State for Transport v Quest Maidstone Ltd* [2011] EWLandRA 2010_0210 [40] (Judge Rhys); and *Pilling PC v Wells* [2008] EWHC 556 (Ch), [2008] 2 EGLR 29 [7] (Lewison J).

[15] ibid, 183. See also *Pilling PC v Wells* (n 14) [7]–[8] (Lewison J) and *Quest Maidstone* (n 14) [40] (Judge Rhys). See also Burns, 'Adverse Possession' (n 4) 792–93 and 807.

which is relatively superior to RP's registered title? Conversely, can we justify someone, S, claiming to have an unregistered freehold title which is relatively *inferior* to RP's registered freehold title?

The question as to the continuing desirability of recognising title relativity necessarily taps into a broader issue that pervades land registration scholarship. This concerns the extent to which the statutory registration regime operates as a closed, autonomous and self-sufficient system, and/or whether external general property law rules (which pertain to unregistered land) should continue to play a part in determining rights relating to registered land. Our conclusions on title relativity are context-specific.

On the one hand, in certain contexts, title relativity is consistent with the LRA 2002's fundamental ambitions—offering certainty and stability to those who deal with registered land—and its continuing existence need not be understood as undermining those underlying principles. Indeed, we go further and argue that the subsistence of relativity of title in such circumstances is important and desirable.[16] The title relativity doctrine has useful explanatory force—it provides a structured and coherent set of rules with which to respond to cases, involving registered titles, that would otherwise be difficult to decide or explain. To this extent, the LRA 2002, rather than imposing a radically different, self-contained system of rules for registered land, seems to tap into and/or work alongside the traditional general property law principle of title relativity. Thus, it seems that there might be greater conceptual unity between the rules governing titles to unregistered and registered land than has hitherto been acknowledged.

On the other hand, we must not be blinded by the potential compatibility, in some contexts, of the LRA 2002 regime with title relativity. There are some other important contexts in which the relativity doctrine may disrupt—and even wholly undermine—the fundamental policy ambitions of the LRA 2002 registration regime. Going forwards, it is crucial to identify those situations where the title relativity doctrine would make unwanted intrusions, and that measures are put in place to guard against this happening.

II. A Preliminary Point: What is 'Title Relativity'?

As a preliminary matter, it is important to acknowledge at the outset that the notion of 'title'—and therefore 'title relativity'—is itself a contested concept. Doubts exist about its meaning and contours. Analysed carefully, the law and surrounding commentary use the terms 'title' and 'title relativity' to express three subtly different concepts.

[16] Recognising that relativity of title persists may also, in certain circumstances, contribute to our understanding of the substantive position of a particular party under the law. For example, in a case of adverse possession, recognition that a squatter continues to acquire an unregistered title on the basis of possession contributes to the view that he should be able to sue for trespass during the currency of the qualifying period. We do not pursue this line of inquiry in this chapter, save for some brief comments on this adverse possession scenario, at text to n 43 below. The reason for not pursuing it here is that there is no necessary conceptual reason to treat acquisition of a fee simple as the basis on which trespass is allowed—the squatter's right to sue for trespass could be achieved (as it was once) by recognising that he could sue on the basis of possession alone; that is, that he acquired a personal right to restrain interference with his possession. As Cooke observes: '[a]ll the rigmarole about his ability to evict later trespassers is scarcely necessary; he need not be regarded as having a property right during this period': Cooke, *Land Law* (n 7) 254.

A. Co-existing *Substantive* Freehold/Possessory Titles ('View 1')

First, 'title' most frequently denotes a *substantive freehold proprietary right in land.* This seems to be the meaning given to 'title' in the academic works discussed in section I(B) above.

With 'title' understood in this sense, a dispute concerning 'relative titles' would typically arise between freehold 'owners' and squatters. In such circumstances, there are two competing freehold titles. One title (the 'owner's') is typically (but not necessarily) *derivative*, having derived from the previous freehold 'owner'; the other freehold title (the squatter's) is *original*: as soon as the squatter takes adverse possession of the land he acquires, from the inception of that possession, his own *independent* freehold estate.[17] Furthermore, were a second squatter to take possession adversely from the first squatter, he too would acquire an original possessory freehold, leading to the coexistence of three rival concurrent freeholds.

Thus, on this view, 'title relativity' disputes involve a priority contest between competing *substantive* rights to possession/freeholds of land. As every land lawyer knows, English law ordinarily resolves such disputes via a straightforward 'first-in-time' rule: the owner has priority over the squatter (unless and until his title is compromised by any relevant adverse possession legislation),[18] because the owner's freehold title arose first.

B. Multiple *Claims* to a Single Freehold Estate ('View 2')

A second interpretation equates 'title' not with the acquisition of a *substantive* estate or interest, but with the ability to make a *claim* to a singular, substantive interest. It used to be orthodoxy—even up to the dawn of the twentieth century—that only *one* fee simple estate could exist in respect of given land.[19] The language of relative 'titles' to a fee simple was therefore a reference not to multiple co-existing titles, but to multiple opposing *claims* to a single fee simple, with rival parties leading evidence that they were *the* freehold owner—whether on the basis of a conveyance, succession or by taking possession. On this view, 'title' denoted a conceptual space between the facts on the ground and the resultant legal rights. This second, and older, interpretation of 'title' generally has now yielded to the other two views, and is not addressed further in this chapter.

C. *Entitlements* to Competing Derivative Interests in Land ('View 3')

According to Views 1 and 2, 'title' is necessarily bound up with the notion of a 'freehold estate'—'title' meaning either a *substantive* freehold right (View 1) or a *claim* to a freehold

[17] See, eg, C Harpum, S Bridge and M Dixon, *Megarry & Wade—The Law of Real Property*, 8th edn (London, Sweet and Maxwell, 2012) paras 4.008–4.009; *Asher v Whitlock* (1865–66) LR 1 QB 1; *Turner v Chief Land Registrar* [2013] EWHC 1382 (Ch), [2013] 2 P & CR 12; *Harepath LLP v Care and Skill Pest Control Ltd* [2016] EWLandRA 2015_0739 [29]–[30] (Judge McAllister).

[18] Via the Limitation Act 1980, ss 15 and 17 (where the relevant 'owner's' title is unregistered); or via the LRA 2002, ss 96–97 and sch 6 (where the relevant 'owner's' title is registered).

[19] See, eg, the observations of A Hargreaves, 'Terminology and Title in Ejectment' (1940) 56 *LQR* 376.

(View 2). The third view, advocated by David Fox,[20] severs the link between 'title' and 'freehold', and instead equates 'title' to one's '*entitlement*' to *a particular interest, whatever that interest may be.*

On this view, disputes between owners of *freehold titles*—typified by disputes between a 'real owner' and a 'squatter', which are the focus of View 1—represent merely *one* manifestation of title relativity. View 3 ascribes to title relativity a wider explanatory remit. It posits that title relativity may also explain the existence of inconsistent and competing titles to interests *other than freeholds*. It therefore embraces, eg: competing leasehold estates in the same land (as where Y freehold owner has granted two mutually inconsistent leases to X and Z tenants respectively, as occurred in *MacLeod v Gold Harp Properties Ltd*)[21]; or two competing and inconsistent easements; or competing and inconsistent easements and leaseholds. In these sorts of scenarios, the competing titles tend to be derivative, rather than original. Both derive from the same owner/interest-holder, as where Y freeholder grants an lease to X, and subsequently a lease to Z over the same title. They are not original titles, arising afresh, from the act of taking possession alone.[22]

It is clearly necessary for the law to rank the two competing and inconsistent incompatible interests—to determine which is *relatively* superior to the other. This is the function of the law's priority rules. As we discuss below, sections 28 and 29 of the LRA 2002 are the primary determinants of priority in the registered land context.[23]

It might be noted that View 3 is not substantively inconsistent with View 1: both views accept that disputes between competing freehold title holders involve relative titles. View 3 parts company with View 1 via its suggestion that title relativity has *wider* explanatory force—it explains the incidence of *any* competing titles or interests over a plot of land.

The third view of 'title'—as an *entitlement* to an *interest*, of whatever type, in land—presents the most cogent challenge to the academic view, noted in section I(B) above, that concepts of *title* and *registered estates* are being fused by the provisions of the LRA 2002.[24] Such a fusion is intrinsically impossible under the third view, for the Act expressly acknowledges that entitlements to certain types of interest can subsist without being registered—eg, short leases, and inherently equitable interests, such as beneficial interests under trusts of land and restrictive covenants.[25]

D. This Chapter's Focus: Views 1 and 3

Given their continuing modern relevance, this chapter engages with Views 1 and 3. However, it has a particular focus on View 1, since it represents the prevailing academic interpretation of the meaning of 'title'.

[20] D Fox, 'Relativity of Title at Law and in Equity' [2006] *CLJ* 330.

[21] *MacLeod v Gold Harp Properties* [2014] EWCA Civ 1084, [2015] 1 WLR 1249.

[22] Note that even *prescriptive* easements, which might look as though they are created by the effluxion of time itself, are actually conceived as derivative interests: they rest on a fictional grant by the relevant freehold owner. See A Goymour, 'The Creation of Rights in Property by the Effluxion of Time', in E Cooke (ed), *Modern Studies in Property Law, Volume IV* (Oxford, Hart, 2007).

[23] Note also LRA 2002, s 30—a priority rule which, being concerned with dispositions *by registered chargees of their charge*, necessarily has a narrow focus, and is not analysed further in this chapter.

[24] Gray and Gray (n 7) 182–83.

[25] LRA 2002, ss 2 and 27.

III. Relativity of Title under the LRA 2002 Registration Regime

This section considers the operation of the LRA 2002. It demonstrates that, in a broad range of situations, the Act's provisions and its associated case law are at least consistent with the common law's doctrine of relativity of title. Indeed, many provisions go further and offer express or implied support for the subsistence of title relativity—with 'title' being understood according to either View 1 or View 3 above. We discuss seven such situations, which include: the treatment of adverse possessors; the express recognition of different classes of registered title; the ordering of titles in cases of double-registration; the reconciliation of two equal but inconsistent registered leases; and the Act's general 'priority' rules.

The LRA 2002's provisions are not always entirely clear or unequivocal (see, eg, the discussion of schedule 6 below). Even so, this section demonstrates that, in general, the Act is at least internally consistent with the doctrine of relativity of title. Furthermore, contrary to the prevailing academic accounts, the new registration regime will not, as a matter of legal doctrine, inevitably result in title relativity withering or fading away.

Although the persistence of title relativity was unanticipated by many academics, its continued relevance is, in many contexts, not only *consistent* with the principles underlying the LRA 2002 registration regime, but is also a *desirable* explanatory doctrine. Nevertheless, as we demonstrate in this section, there is a real risk that if the relativity of title doctrine is given a free rein and is left to roam in an unbridled fashion, then it may in certain contexts drag a metaphorical coach and horses through the LRA 2002's provisions—thereby thwarting the Act's policy ambitions. Care must be taken to work out exactly where the title relativity doctrine ought—or ought not—to have any role to play.

A. The LRA 2002's Treatment of Bankruptcy of the Registered Proprietor

We begin with a straightforward example of the continuing relevance of title relativity within the registration regime, which concerns the consequences of a registered proprietor becoming bankrupt. The LRA 2002 and the Insolvency Act 1986, which together govern a registered proprietor's bankruptcy, provide that as soon as a trustee in bankruptcy is appointed, that trustee acquires 'the bankrupt's estate'[26] (labelled a 'title' in the LRA 2002)[27]—eg, the bankrupt's freehold. This is so notwithstanding that the bankrupt remains the registered proprietor unless and until the trustee in bankruptcy applies to have the Register altered.[28] As such, prior to the Register being altered, there appear to be two titles to the land: (a) the registered title belonging to the bankrupt, which he inevitably retains by virtue of his remaining on the Register;[29] and (b) the trustee in bankruptcy's unregistered title, conferred by the Insolvency Act.

[26] Insolvency Act 1986, s 306.

[27] LRA 2002, s 86(5).

[28] The relevant ground of alteration would be to bring the Register up to date: LRA 2002, sch 4, para 2(1)(b). See Law Com No 271 (n 4) para 4.19.

[29] LRA 2002, s 58. Indeed, it is implicit in s 86(5) that the bankrupt registered proprietor may subsequently deal with his registered estate.

Although it may initially appear puzzling that two equal and inconsistent freehold estates may co-exist over the same land, the title relativity doctrine offers a straightforward explanation: both freeholds subsist, but one is *relatively* superior to the other. Here, it is implicit in the legislation that, as between the bankrupt and his trustee in bankruptcy, the latter has the better title.[30]

B. Adverse Possession Against an Already-Registered Estate

Our second context concerns adverse possession against an already-registered estate. According to the orthodox modern view of the common law title relativity doctrine, a squatter who adversely possesses against an *unregistered* estate acquires a relative original common law fee simple, at the inception of his adversely taking possession of the land—an understanding which is consistent with Views 1 and 3 of title relativity.[31] The argument here is that, notwithstanding certain judicial suggestions to the contrary,[32] this seems to remain the case where the squatter goes into adverse possession against a *registered* superior estate. Nothing in the LRA 2002 expressly alters the legal status of a squatter on going into possession; indeed, certain key provisions actually recognise the squatter's (necessarily inferior) 'title'.

i. Express/Implied Statutory Acknowledgements of Title Relativity

Express acknowledgements of the squatter's relative (and, by implication, inferior) estate are found in schedule 6 of the LRA 2002, which governs adverse possession of registered land. Paragraph 9(1), in particular, confirms that when a squatter successfully applies for registration under schedule 6 after accrual of the relevant period of adverse possession, 'the *title* by virtue of adverse possession which he had *at the time of the application* is extinguished' (emphasis added). This recognises that, during the period when the squatter is a mere (unregistered) adverse possessor, he nonetheless has a 'title' which exists concurrently with, and is necessarily inferior to, the registered proprietor's superior registered title. Similarly, where a subsequent squatter, S2, takes a transfer from a previous squatter, S1—prior to either S1 or S2 being registered as proprietor via schedule 6—the transferee squatter, S2, is described by the schedule 6, paragraph 11(2)(a) of the Act as a 'successor in *title*' (emphasis added).

Schedule 6 also acknowledges the continuing relevance of title relativity indirectly, via its provisions which determine how a squatter who is adversely possessing against a registered title might accrue the necessary time in 'adverse possession' for making a schedule 6 application. Schedule 6, paragraph 11(2)(b) provides that where an applying squatter, S1, entered into adverse possession against a registered proprietor, and was himself subsequently adversely possessed against by another squatter, S2, then S1 may tack S2's

30 See the Insolvency Act 1986, s 306(1); LRA 2002, s 86(5). The latter provides for exceptional situations where a disponee from the bankrupt might take free of the trustee in bankruptcy's title. It is implicit that the default rule is that the bankrupt and his disponees are bound by the trustee's title, which must inevitably rank higher than the bankrupt's title.

31 See, eg, Law Com No 254 (n 4) paras 10.21–10.24; *Turner* (n 17).

32 See, eg, *Quest Maidstone* (n 14) [40] (Judge Rhys).

period of adverse possession onto his own when making a schedule 6 application, provided that S2's possession is sandwiched between two periods of the applicant's (S1's) own periods of possession. Implicit in this is an assumption that S1 is *entitled* to recover the land from S2—in order to avail himself of the paragraph 11(2)(b) 'sandwich' rule—and therefore that S1, by virtue of his taking adverse possession of registered land, obtains a 'title' which trumps S2's later-acquired title.[33] As such, this provision indirectly seems to recognise that S1, by virtue of his taking possession against a registered freehold estate, acquires a relative title to that land.

As such, a squatter, upon going into adverse possession of registered land, seems to obtain a legal fee simple estate in the land, which, *inter alia*, he can assert against third parties (other than the superior registered proprietor) and/or choose to alienate. The squatter's freehold is necessarily *unregistered*[34] and is therefore governed by the rules pertaining to unregistered land, including those rendering an unregistered estate vulnerable to extinction via the provisions of the Limitation Act 1980. This would be so where, for example, a subsequent squatter, S2, adversely possesses against the S1's (unregistered) title for 12 years.[35]

ii. Statutory Provisions which are Ambivalent about Title Relativity

However, schedule 6 of the LRA 2002 does not deliver a consistent story. There are features that are ambivalent towards, or fail to consider, the notion that a squatter possessing land, title to which is registered, might have a relative fee simple estate. Nonetheless, none of these ambivalent provisions offers a fatal blow to the continuing relevance of title relativity.

One such ambivalent provision is schedule 6, paragraph 5(4), which relates to adverse possession of land on boundaries. To rely on this provision, adjacent land must 'belong to' the claimant squatter, and said squatter must reasonably believe that the disputed boundary land 'belong[ed] to' him. What does 'belonging to' mean in this context? The answer seems to depend on whether title relativity survives the LRA 2002's registration regime, which is not answered by the provision itself. On a non-relativist view (which rejects the continuing relevance of title relativity), the legislation might require the claimant squatter to be the paramount 'owner' of the neighbouring estate—in effect meaning that the claimant squatter must be the registered proprietor, if the land is registered; or the superior fee simple owner, if the adjacent land is currently unregistered. In contrast, on a relativist view, it might be sufficient for the claimant squatter to be in *adverse possession* of that neighbouring estate, such that paragraph 5(4) can operate where merely a relatively inferior fee simple 'belong[s] to him'. Early signs in the case law indicate a preference for the latter interpretation, thereby supporting the continuing relevance of title relativity.[36]

[33] As explained in section III(A) above, S2 him/herself has a possessory freehold title.

[34] *Best* (n 6) [14] (Ouseley J). For a contrary view, see *Moore v Buxton* [2009] EWLandRA 2007_1216 [27] (Judge Rhys).

[35] Limitation Act 1980, ss 15 and 17. The idea that titles which are unregistered, but which exist in relation to land to which *a title* is registered, are governed by the 1980 Act provisions was confirmed by Judge Rhys in *Sexton v Gill* [2015] EWLandRA 2013_0472_0473, reversing his own earlier statements to the contrary in *Sexton v Gill* [2014] EWLandRA 2013_0472.

[36] In *Crosdil v Hodder* [2011] EWLandRA 2009_1177 [33], Judge McAllister interpreted another reference to 'belonging to' in the same statutory provision (whereby the claimant squatter must in good faith mistakenly believe the land he is claiming 'belonged' to him for the requisite period) as including ownership of a mere possessory title. She stated: '[i]t seems to me clear that "belonging" (which is not defined in the Act) includes ownership

Similarly ambiguous is section 98 of the LRA 2002, which provides that, when faced with an action for possession, a squatter may plead schedule 6 by way of a 'defence', in certain circumstances where the squatter would have been entitled to make a schedule 6 application to acquire the registered title. It is clear that a squatter may invoke section 98 (whether successfully or not) by way of a defence in the straightforward scenario where the current *registered proprietor* seeks possession of the land. The provision is, however, ill-equipped to deal with certain other factual scenarios that might arise if—as this chapter argues—title relativity survives under the LRA 2002. It is, for example, unclear whether a second squatter, S2, can rely on section 98 when facing a possession claim by a previous squatter, S1, whom S2 has dispossessed, but who has a superior, albeit unregistered, title. Although it might be argued that the legislature, by not providing a ready-answer to this scenario, intended to oust title relativity, it is more likely that point was not considered.

In short, despite the presence of the legislative ambiguities just discussed, schedule 6 is not inconsistent with the proposition that a squatter acquires an original and relatively inferior unregistered freehold estate as a consequence of his adverse possession of a registered estate.

iii. The LRA 2002's Broad Effect of Reducing the Likelihood of Squatters Acquiring an Indefeasible Title

Whilst schedule 6 does not *technically* oust title relativity from the land registration regime, it is arguable that the schedule's *broad functional effect*—in greatly reducing the possibility that a squatter will ultimately acquire an indefeasible title—might, via a side-blow, result in the *practical* demise of the notion of title relativity.

The weakening of the squatter's position follows plainly from the LRA 2002's disapplication of the Limitation Act 1980's provisions[37]—which formerly applied to both unregistered and registered land; and the simultaneous creation of the new schedule 6 application procedure for squatters.[38] Only in certain narrow circumstances, set out in schedule 6, will a squatter succeed in defeating the former registered proprietor's rights, and become the registered proprietor.

The much-diminished possibility that a squatter will become indefeasibly entitled to a registered estate is a major premise in those academic views and predictions—set out in section I(B) above—that relativity of title will fade or die. As Cooke has said, now that in most cases the squatter's interest 'can no longer turn into true/sole ownership, it may be that we shall in time cease to regard it as a fee simple'.[39] However, this assumption—that the principal practical effect of the law recognising a possessor's fee simple is that it has the potential to ripen into an indefeasible title—is not without its difficulties. As a matter of authority, doctrine and policy, it is important that the squatter continues to be regarded as holding a relative freehold notwithstanding that he may never become the paramount owner.

of a possessory title: a possessory title is a class of freehold title: see section 9(1)(c) of the 2002 Act'. See also *Gill v McCarthy* [2016] UKFTT 0019 (PC) [104], where the claimant squatter was a tenant of the adjacent land; his rights as tenant were seemingly accepted as satisfying the 'belonging to' requirement notwithstanding that he was not *the freehold* owner.

[37] LRA 2002, s 96.

[38] Sch 6 is incorporated via LRA 2002, s 97.

[39] Cooke, *Land Law* (n 7) 243.

First, as a matter of authority, it is notable that the potential for a squatter's title to become indefeasible was not material in the key cases taken to establish that a squatter acquires an original fee simple. *Asher v Whitlock* held that an adverse possessor's title was capable of devolving to his heir before expiry of limitation period,[40] and *Rosenberg v Cook* held that a possessor's title passes on conveyance notwithstanding that it is a title 'liable to be defeated' by the paramount claim of an owner.[41] These cases establish broad propositions about a squatter's entitlement to transmit his holding and to exploit the capital that it represents. As such, they establish that the squatter's holding exhibits core proprietary qualities:[42] it is in substance a valuable property right—a freehold estate—even though it is, and may continue to be, relatively inferior to a superior title before the expiry of the limitation period (where land is unregistered), or in the absence of the squatter making a successful schedule 6 application (where land is registered).

Secondly, there are important reasons of doctrine and policy why adverse possession should continue to be regarded as generating an independent title, even if that title is unlikely ever to become indefeasible. A first point is that human rights concerns relating to Article 1 of the First Protocol to the European Convention on Human Rights, which protects the enjoyment of one's possessions, might materialise if the LRA 2002 were interpreted—without explicit justification—to deny the acquisitive effects of a squatter going into adverse possession.

A second point relates to the adverse possessor's standing to bring an action for the recovery of the land[43]—and incidentally to sue in nuisance and trespass—during the period when he is a 'mere' adverse possessor, and before he becomes owner (if indeed he ever becomes owner).[44] A possessor's ability to recover the land from those who subsequently dispossess him might be viewed as a foundational common law right.[45] Focusing on potential future indefeasibility as the touchstone of a squatter's legal position may obscure the conceptual and practical significance of a squatter, from the inception of his taking possession, being able to protect the land against interferences by third parties (other than the paramount owner) and bring actions to recover possession from unlawful dispossessors. There are good reasons why possessors should be able to protect their rights in this way. As has long been recognised in the chattels context, it is in the interests of preserving a peaceful society that possession—however obtained and even where the possessor is not the

[40] *Asher v Whitlock* (1865–66) 1 LR QB 1.

[41] *Rosenberg v Cook* (1881) 8 QBD 162, 165.

[42] See, eg, A Honoré, 'Ownership', in A Guest (ed), *Oxford Essays in Jurisprudence* (Oxford, OUP, 1961).

[43] Procedurally, the action for the recovery of land is exercised by bringing a 'possession claim' within Part 55 of the Civil Procedure Rules (CPR). 'Recovery' actions and 'possession claims' are seemingly one and the same thing: the CPR is merely a procedural framework for the underlying common law action. See further A Goymour, 'Remedies for Vindicating Ownership Rights in Real Property', in G Virgo and S Worthington (eds), *Commercial Remedies: Resolving Controversies* (Cambridge, CUP, 2017).

[44] The prevailing academic view is that the action to recover land depends on the relevant claimant having a possessory *title*, and does not require proof of wrongdoing, such as trespass or nuisance, for which claims title is not a pre-requisite (see *Manchester Airport plc v Dutton* [2000] QB 133 (CA)). For support for this view, see *Secretary of State for the Environment, Food and Rural Affairs v Meier* [2009] UKSC 11, [2009] 1 WLR 2780, [60]–[78] (Lord Neuberger). For the contrary view, see B McFarlane, *The Structure of Property Law* (Oxford, Hart, 2008) 358. For further discussion, see Goymour, 'Remedies' (n 43).

[45] This is possibly clearer in the case of trespass, in respect of which the courts' jurisdiction was originally anchored in broader constitutional concerns about breach of the peace: D Ibbetson, *A Historical Introduction to the Law of Obligations* (Oxford, OUP, 1999) 39.

true owner—is safeguarded against the unauthorised incursions of strangers. Were this not the case, strangers could lawfully take property from any non-owning possessor, potentially leading to a 'free-for-all' between non-owners—a situation which should be neither encouraged nor permitted.[46] If the legislation was intended to remove a squatter's ability to protect his possession of the land against strangers, one would expect substantial discussion of the point, and sound reasons offered for any such change. A squatter's rights should not be regarded as being swept aside, in a side-wind, by the title-stabilising provisions of the LRA 2002.

It follows from these arguments that, in appraising the continued relevance of title relativity, care should be taken not to conflate 'title' with 'indefeasible title'. The fact that under the LRA 2002, the only way that a squatter might rely on his adverse possession to acquire an indefeasible title is via schedule 6, does not inevitably commit English law to the proposition that this is the only way to acquire a title to that land. Indeed, there are sound reasons of substantive law and policy for recognising the continued existence of the squatter's independent relative title, notwithstanding the decreasing likelihood that he will successfully oust the registered proprietor of the estate.

iv. Evaluating the Persistence of Title Relativity in this Context

In conclusion, there is a strong case for the persistence of title relativity in this context—for three key reasons.

First, it is doctrinally *possible* for an adverse possessor to acquire an *unregistered* relative fee simple, upon going into possession against a registered estate. Nothing in the LRA 2002 ousts this possibility; and certain provisions go further, and even assume the existence of a squatter's relative title. Secondly, not only is the recognition of a relative title *possible* within the terms of the LRA 2002; it is also *desirable* for a mere possessor to acquire a title enforceable against third-party strangers.[47] Thirdly and importantly, the squatter's title, being inferior, in no way threatens the integrity of the registered proprietor's superior

[46] See, eg, *Jeffries v Great Western Railway Co* (1856) 5 El & Bl 802, 119 ER 680, and, generally, Fox 'Relativity' (n 20) 338. See also the protection given to possessors via the possessory interdicts in Roman Law. See, eg, W Buckland, *A Textbook of Roman Law*, 2nd edn (Cambridge, CUP, 1932) 732–36, and the discussions in R Hickey, '*Armory v Delamirie* (1722): Possession, Obligation, and the Evolution of Relative Title to Goods' and A Goymour, '*Bruton v London & Quadrant Housing Trust* [2000]: Relativity of Title, and the Regulation of the "Proprietary Underworld"', both in S Douglas, R Hickey and E Waring (eds), *Landmark Cases in Property Law* (Oxford, Hart, 2015).

[47] Furthermore, our argument that the squatter has a freehold on the inception of his possession might add weight to the criticism of the new offence of squatting in a residential building provided by s 144 of the Legal Aid, Sentencing and Punishment of Offenders Act 2012. Section 144 provides that 'a person commits an offence if (a) she is in a residential building as a trespasser having entered it as a trespasser; (b) knows or ought to know that she is a trespasser, and (c) is living in the building or intends to live there for any period'. It has been decided by the Court of Appeal in *Best v Chief Land Registrar* [2015] EWCA Civ 17, [2016] QB 23 that the new criminal sanctions for residential squatters do not impact on the squatter's ability to make a sch 6 application after 10 years' adverse possession, even if he has committed the new criminal squatting offence. However, it is not entirely clear that it is satisfactory to impose a criminal sanction at the entry point to adverse possession, particularly if it provides a further incentive for squatters to conceal their activities. Acknowledging that a squatter acquires an independent relative title from the inception of his adverse possession may provide some support for those who would resist the policy underlying s 144 (for criticism of the provisions, see, eg, <http://www.squashcampaign.org/docs/SQUASH-Campaign-Case-Against-Section-144.pdf>). Understood in this context, s 144 criminalises conduct sufficient to generate property rights at common law, resulting in the troubling general position that criminal law and property law take radically different views on the significance of living in a residential building as a trespasser.

title—nor the reliability of the Register more generally. The registered proprietor's title is only threatened by the squatter's presence *if* the squatter fulfils the stringent requirements of schedule 6—which is a transparent and integral component of the LRA 2002 regime. It is not open to the squatter to challenge the registered proprietor's title via any off-Register, and less-transparent, route.

Notwithstanding the overwhelming case for recognising the squatter's inferior fee simple, one practical niggle remains concerning the *registrability* of the squatter's inferior freehold under the LRA 2002. As we discuss in section III(D) below, section 9 of the Act recognises three 'classes' of registered freehold title: 'qualified', 'possessory, and 'absolute'. A difficult question arises as to whether a squatter, upon going into possession and acquiring his common law freehold estate, might be registered with 'possessory title', concurrently with the true owner's 'absolute' registered title. There seems no reason—of law or policy—why this should not be possible. As a matter of law, the squatter seems eligible within the legislation to be so registered—he fits the section 9(5) criteria (a) that he is 'in actual possession of the land ... by virtue of the estate', and (b) that there 'is no other class of title with which he may be registered'. Secondly, as a matter of policy, the co-existence of two concurrently-registered titles—one absolute title, one possessory title—would not undermine the reliability of the Register. Looking at the Register, everyone would be able to see which is the superior, and which the inferior title.

However, the Land Registry has hitherto taken the view (which has been supported by associated case law) that squatters—whether in adverse possession of unregistered or registered land—must be in possession for 12 years before they are eligible to be registered with possessory title.[48] This position appears surprising given the section 9(5) criteria for registration. A possible explanation for the Registry's stance might lie in the practical difficulties that might otherwise ensue in the light of a further problematic provision—LRA 2002, section 62(4)—which provides that after 12 years on the Register, a 'possessory title' 'may' be upgraded to 'absolute' by the Registrar. Were a squatter to be registered with 'possessory title' in year 0, upon going into adverse possession against an 'absolute' registered title, the Registrar might seem to be empowered by section 62(4) to upgrade the title to 'absolute' in year 12—resulting in two concurrent 'absolute' registered freehold titles to the same land. This could be an unpalatable consequence—particularly if the Register does not reveal to those who rely on it which 'absolute' title is the superior and reliable one.

The Registry's 'solution' for avoiding this problem has been to interpret section 9(5) narrowly—with the result that many squatters have been prevented from registering their relative freehold titles with possessory title. This 'solution', however, is inconsistent with both the express wording of section 9(5)[49] and the fact that the Act, via its other provisions, recognises the squatter's possessory freehold title. An alternative—and in our view preferable—'solution' to the problem is to give a purposive construction to the Registrar's

[48] *Phillips v Vaughan* [2016] EWLandRA 2014_0497; *Harber v London Borough of Havering* [2015] UKFTT 0621 (PC). See also discussion of the point in *Scott v Akram* REF/2013/1088 (24 September 2014, First-tier Tribunal (PC)) [21] (Judge Tozer); *Tickle v Admiral Taverns Ltd* [2013] EWLandRA 2012_0122; *Lynn Lewis Ltd v The Environment Agency* [2007] EWLandRA 2005_1068 [63]–[65] (Judge Rhys). But cf *Crescent Farming Co Ltd v Bellway (Builders) Ltd* [2009] EWLandRA 2007_0978 [22] (Judge Michell).

[49] Note the observation to this effect in *Crescent v Bellway* (n 48) [22] (Judge Michell), and the arguments of counsel (Mr Harpum) for the applicant possessor in *Botes v Binks* [2005] EWLandRA 2004_0903.

power to upgrade titles in section 62(4). The notion that a title 'may' be upgraded from 'possessory' to 'absolute' after 12 years reflects the 12-year adverse possession period that applies to unregistered titles under the Limitation Act 1980. As such, the upgrading of a squatter's 'possessory title' to 'absolute' is apt in those cases where the real owner's title is *unregistered*: except in some exceptional cases (eg, where the property is held on trust, or by the Crown) the squatter *will* automatically become the indefeasible owner after 12 years of adverse possession, and so the Register title upgrade will appropriately reflect this.[50] In contrast, the year-12 upgrade seems wholly *inappropriate* where the squatter possesses against a *registered* title: the Limitation Act 1980's 12-year limitation period does not run against such titles, and has been replaced by the schedule 6 application regime. To reflect the difference between adverse possession against unregistered and registered titles, it would be preferable for the Registrar to take account of the underlying applicable adverse possession regime, when exercising his section 62(4) upgrade power—and only upgrade where the real owner's title has actually been effectively compromised by the applicable adverse possession rules. Adopting such a construction would lead to the desirable conclusion that squatters' relative titles could indeed be registered (as 'possessory' titles)—leading to a more informative (and accurate) Register—without running the risk of having two 'absolute' freehold titles on the Register after 12 years.[51]

C. Adverse Possession and First Registration

A third scenario in which the relevance—or irrelevance—of title relativity assumes importance involves adverse possession by a squatter where the 'true owner's' title is initially unregistered, and is subsequently registered for the first time. The following scenario presents particular difficulties:

(i) a squatter, S, goes into adverse possession of land belonging to A, the unregistered superior freehold owner;
(ii) S remains in adverse possession for 12 years—resulting in A's title being (automatically) extinguished by the Limitation Act 1980; and
(iii) subsequently, A successfully applies to the Registry for first registration as freehold proprietor with absolute title—ignorant of the fact that his title has already been extinguished, and S's title has thereby become paramount.

Here, it is uncontroversial that the title relativity doctrine explains the relative positions of A and S at least up to the point of A's registration: from the inception of his adverse

[50] Note, however, the problem inherent in the (problematic) decision in *Parshall v Hackney* [2013] EWCA Civ 240, [2013] Ch 568 discussed in the text to n 81 below, which considered that possession by someone with a registered title is legitimate and therefore not 'adverse' for the purpose of accruing time in adverse possession. See further Law Commission, *Updating the Land Registration Act 2002—A Consultation Paper* (Law Com CP No 227, 2016) para 17.66.

[51] Note further that after 12 years' adverse possession against an unregistered title, the squatter's title is generally paramount—the unregistered title having been extinguished under the Limitation Act 1980. As such, the squatter ought to qualify for registration with '*absolute*' title, and not merely a 'possessory' title (as recognised in, eg, *The Trustees for Methodist Church Purposes v Child* [2006] EWLandRA 2005_1604). This observation casts further doubt on the current practice that squatters must wait 12 years for registration with *possessory* title.

possession, S enjoyed a possessory fee simple, which was *inferior* to S's superior fee simple. After 12 years' adverse possession by S, A's superior fee simple is extinguished, leaving S with the sole, and therefore by default the paramount, fee simple. However, ascertaining the effect of A's subsequent registration (of his now-non-existent title) on S's status is more difficult—and raises some tricky title relativity dilemmas.

Assuming that A acquires *a* title upon registration—via section 58's conclusive title effect—we must turn to section 11 to ascertain which pre-existing rights burden A's registered estate at first registration. Relevantly, section 11(4) provides that A's estate will be bound by S's prior right if either S is in actual occupation of the land at the registration date;[52] or A had 'notice' of S's prior right—being an 'interest acquired under the Limitation Act 1980'.[53]

If either of these conditions is satisfied, S's right survives first registration, and binds A's registered estate. Although not articulated by the LRA 2002, the only plausible explanation of the nature of S's surviving right is that it is the *unregistered possessory freehold* he acquired upon initially going into adverse possession. Seen in this light, section 11 offers another blow to the argument that title relativity is fading under the LRA 2002. The provision, via its recognition of the superiority of a prior squatter's title over a registered title, countenances—or even confirms—that relative titles might exist in relation to registered land. Here, there are two titles: A's 'absolute' registered freehold—arising from registration, via section 58; and S's unregistered freehold (which is *superior* under section 11)—arising from the initial act of taking possession. Henceforth, S would be entitled (although there is no obligation) to seek a schedule 4 alteration of the Register—by arguing that he should replace A as the proprietor of the registered absolute freehold, in order to more accurately reflect the paramount status of S's title.[54]

Trickier problems arise in those cases where S fails to meet either of the section 11 conditions—ie where S is out of possession, and the existence of S's superior right is unknown to A, when A is first registered.[55] It seems clear that the immediate effect of section 11 is to 'clear' A's registered title from the prior title held by S—meaning that S can no longer immediately vindicate the paramount title he once enjoyed, via an action for the recovery of the land.[56] However, it is far from clear whether this 'clearing' effect is *permanent*, or merely *temporary*. Can A—who, remember, had *no title* at all at the time of seeking registration—really argue that he has acquired an unchallengeable registered title as a result of section 11? There are two plausible, and diametrically opposed, outcomes.

On the one hand, section 11, taken in isolation, seems to have a conclusive and enduring 'clearing effect'—giving A an indefeasible fee simple, and clearing away

[52] LRA 2002, s 11(4)(b) and sch 1, para 2. See, by analogy, *Davies v John Wood Property Ltd* [2010] EWLandRA 2008_0528, concerning sch 3, para 2.

[53] LRA 2002, s 11(4)(c). Note that, although the sense is clear, one might raise a question as to the technical correctness of this provision. It suggests that a squatter's rights are *acquired under* the Limitation Act 1980, whereas in truth the rights are acquired by virtue of the squatter *going into possession*. The 1980 Act does not confer rights on the squatter; it merely has the *effect* of upgrading the relative priority of his existing possessory fee simple, by extinguishing the real owner's superior title.

[54] See Law Com CP No 227 (n 50) para 17.57, which suggests that the relevant alteration 'ground' might be that of giving effect to a 'right excepted from effect of registration' (sch 4 para 2(1)(c)). Alternatively, the Register might be altered on the ground of 'bringing [it] up to date' (sch 4, para 2(1)(b)).

[55] As noted in Law Com CP No 227 (n 50) para 17.51, as far as is known, no such cases have yet arisen. See also ch 17 of this book, section II(B)(iii).

[56] See *Moore v Buxton* (n 34) [26] (Judge Rhys).

S's formerly-superior estate indefinitely, with no possibility of any Register-alteration or Registry-indemnity award for S. On the other hand, section 11's immediate clearing effect might be susceptible to reversal via the LRA 2002 schedule 4 alteration regime—with the result that S would become registered as proprietor in A's place. On this latter analysis, S would argue that A's registration constituted a 'mistake' by the Registry which required alteration within schedule 4, because A—once his title had been extinguished under the Limitation Act 1980—had no entitlement to be registered as proprietor. Any consequent change to the Register would necessarily be 'prejudicial' to A's currently-registered title, which was at least temporarily cleared by section 11 of S's better claim to the land, and so A would qualify for a Registry indemnity.[57]

The Law Commission's 2001 Report suggests that schedule 4 cannot be used to 'undo' the clearing effect of section 11—at least in the context where, following extinction of A's title by adverse possession, A sells his 'paper title' to B and B (rather than A) becomes the first registered proprietor. In the Commission's view,

> [S] will not be able to seek alteration of the register because [B] is not bound by [S's] rights and there is, therefore, no mistake in the register that requires correction.[58]

With respect, this view suffers from the vice of circularity. It underestimates both the reach of schedule 4's alteration provisions, and also the significance that title relativity might continue to have within the registration regime—with the effect that the Law Commission's policy ambition (to insulate B's title from S's claim) seems to be thwarted.

Whilst the Commission's statement that 'B is not bound by S's rights' is an accurate reflection of section 11's *immediate* effect, its subsequent statement—'therefore [there is] no mistake in the register that requires correction'—is a *non-sequitur*. In particular, the fact that section 11 *immediately* clears B's title from S's prior right does not compel the conclusion that *B's registration* was not itself mistaken, and therefore susceptible to removal from the Register via a schedule 4 correction. The title relativity doctrine tells us that, at the time of B's registration, the 'paper title' (which originally belonged to A and then B) had been extinguished and that S's title had become paramount. As such, B's registration should be regarded as mistaken—and therefore rectifiable within schedule 4.[59] Once removed from the Register, B can, of course, no longer rely on section 11—which is a provision that clears prior rights from *registered* titles—and S can then seek to register his paramount title.

In 2016, the Law Commission rightly recognised that the view it took in 2001 has become unsustainable—and that S can indeed probably seek rectification of the Register against A/B.[60] It has, in effect, been compelled to abandon its 2001 ambition to protect

[57] LRA 2002, sch 4, para 1; sch 8, para 8 and para 1(1)(a). Note that Law Com CP No 227 (n 50) paras 7.58–7.59 raises the possibility that this might be a *mere* alteration (and therefore not indemnity-justifying), but that is difficult to conclude given the immediate effect of LRA 2002, s 11. Note also that some cases contemplate that S might be able to bring a sch 6 claim—relying on the second condition in para 5(3) to justify registration after 10 years' adverse possession—'the applicant is for some other reason entitled to be registered as the proprietor': *Cooper and Cooper v Gick* [2008] EWLandRA 2007_0103 [33] (Judge Stevens-Hoare); and *Pawson v Vaines* [2016] EWLandRA 2015_0339. This interpretation is, however, puzzling: the squatter is *not* entitled to be owner *until* the Regsiter has been altered; if he could secure registration via sch 6, he would, effectively bypass the sch 4 alteration regime. For further discussion, see ch 17 of this book, section II(B)(iii).

[58] Law Com No 271 (n 4) para 3.47.

[59] *Cooper v Gick* (n 57). See also *The Council of the City and County of Swansea v Tennant* [2008] EWLandRA 2007_0327 and *Crosdil v Hopper* (n 36).

[60] Law Com CP No 227 (n 50) para 17.58.

A/B against S, and instead to cede to the combined force of schedule 4's alteration regime and the title relativity doctrine. Whilst the 2016 Law Commission now accepts that there are policy reasons why it might be desirable to prefer S over A/B, the fact remains that the 2001 Law Commission's original ambitions—to prefer A/B over S—were thwarted, in part owing to its failure to appreciate the continuing significance of, and threat posed by, the title relativity doctrine.

A lesson may have been learned for the future—that unless the relativity doctrine is expressly excluded by the Act's provisions, there is a danger that it could interfere with the intended functioning of the registration regime.

D. The LRA 2002's Express Recognition of Different Classes of Title

A fourth indication that relativity of title has survived the LRA 2002's enactment lies somewhat outside the adverse possession context, in the Act's provisions which expressly recognise different classes of freehold (or leasehold) title. Thus, section 9 provides that freeholds may be registered with: (a) absolute, (b) qualified, or (c) possessory title (and section 10 creates an equivalent title structure for leaseholds). Qualified registered titles are 'extremely rare'[61] and are not considered further in this chapter; but it is instructive to observe the consequences of registration with either possessory or absolute title—both of which raise tricky title-relativity issues.

i. Registration with Possessory Freehold Title

Registration with *possessory* title presupposes that the applicant does not meet the criteria for registration with an *absolute* title and therefore that some other person may have a better title to the land.[62] Crucially, the LRA 2002 provides that the status of any superior title is not destroyed by the registration with possessory title of any inferior title.[63] As such, the relevant legislation seems to expressly recognise title relativity, in that more than one title may co-exist over registered land. Despite the apparent clarity of the relevant provisions, various unanticipated niggles have arisen, which concern the manner in which the relativity doctrine relates to the registration regime.

The first problem concerns timing: *when* is someone who has acquired a title *by possession* (eg an adverse possessor) entitled to seek *registration* of that possessory title within section 11? There are two sub-issues. First, as we discussed in section III(B)(iv) above, the Land Registry and associated case-law have decided—wrongly in our view—that the possessor must wait 12 years before qualifying for registration with a possessory title. As we argued above, the 12-year qualifying period is inconsistent with both the express terms of the LRA 2002 and the title relativity doctrine. Secondly, whilst it is uncontroversial that a squatter might seek registration with a possessory title where someone else has a superior *unregistered* freehold, a question arises as to whether he might secure such registration

[61] Law Com No 271 (n 4) 470.

[62] LRA 2002, s 9(5).

[63] See LRA 2002, s 11(7); *Thompson v Hatherton Marina Ltd* [2007] EWLandRA 2004_0765 [74] (Judge Cousins).

where the superior title is *registered (with an absolute title)*. The 2016 Law Commission Consultation Paper, agreeing with current Land Registry practice, suggests not—and that the squatter should be compelled to route his registration application via schedule 6 instead.[64] The Commission was particularly concerned that if the squatter could register with a possessory freehold, that title would benefit, pursuant to section 62(4), from an 'automatic' upgrade to 'absolute' status after 12 years—which would effectively permit the squatter to circumvent the conditions of schedule 6. With respect, we disagree. As we have demonstrated in section III(B)(iv) above, there is nothing 'automatic' about the 12-year upgrade possibility; the better view is that a squatter who does not satisfy the schedule 6 criteria should not benefit from such an upgrade. Furthermore, nothing in section 9 precludes registration with possessory title in such circumstances. As such, it seems plausible that two *registered, relative* titles to the same plot of land might co-exist on the Register—clear evidence of the persistence of title relativity within the registration regime. Here, we might note that the title relativity doctrine aligns with, rather than threatens, the reliability of the Register: it would be clear from the Register to any observer that the adverse possessor's title, being graded merely 'possessory', is not necessarily secure and reliable.

A second problem concerns the particular status of a squatter who is registered with possessory title, vis-à-vis a paramount unregistered owner. Two questions have troubled the courts: (i) whether a squatter, once registered with possessory title, continues to be in *adverse* (as opposed to non-adverse) possession against the true owner; and (ii) if he does continue in adverse possession post-registration, which adverse possession rules apply—the LRA 2002's schedule 6 regime, or the provisions of the Limitation Act 1980?

Stepping back, there seems to be no compelling reason as a matter of policy why the squatter's registration with possessory title should prevent his accruing time against the unregistered owner under the Limitation Act 1980: the squatter should not be *worse off* as a result of registering his possessory title; and neither should the unregistered owner—who has failed to register his own title—*benefit* from the squatter's incidental registration.[65] The early case law adopted a troubling position on both issues, favouring the unregistered owner. Thus: (i) there were suggestions that once the squatter is registered, his registration renders his possession legitimate, and so not 'adverse';[66] and (ii) some cases decided that the squatter's registration pushed *any* dispute involving that land into the clutches of the LRA 2002's registration regime, including schedule 6—and away from the provisions of the Limitation Act 1980.[67]

Both conclusions can be readily avoided—and a more desirable outcome reached—if the LRA 2002's provisions are interpreted in the light of the title relativity doctrine. Once it is acknowledged that *both* the unregistered owner *and* the (registered) squatter have relative freehold titles, it becomes apparent that the squatter's registration does *not* legitimise his

[64] Law Com CP No 227 (n 50) paras 17.63–17.81.

[65] Indeed, it is clear from Law Com No 254 (n 4) para 10.19 (which preceded the LRA 2002) that the disapplication of the limitation period in relation to registered land should serve as an 'incentive' for unregistered owners to register their titles. It would therefore be oddly perverse if an unregistered owner could acquire this benefit as a result of the *squatter* registering his title.

[66] See *Parshall v Hackey* (n 50) (although in a different context). And see the discussion in Law Com CP No 227 (n 50) para 17.66.

[67] *Quest Maidstone* (n 14); *Joslin v Hipgrave* [2015] UKFTT 0497 (PC); *Moore v Buxton* (n 34).

possession vis-à-vis anyone with a superior-ranking title (ie the unregistered owner), against whom his possession *is* adverse. Furthermore, only *one* of the two freeholds is registered, meaning that the LRA 2002 applies to disputes concerning the *registered* title, whilst the general law applies to the *unregistered* title. As such, the squatter *will be* in *adverse* possession against the *unregistered* superior title, and his dispute with the holder of that superior title engages the Limitation Act 1980's provisions. It is encouraging that this conclusion—which relies on title relativity to make sense of the relevant statutory provisions—has now received express judicial support from Judge Rhys in *Sexton v Gill*.[68] We might therefore conclude that, in this context, the recognition of relative titles poses no threat to the ambitions of the registration regime. Title relativity is, in fact, an integral implicit component of the relevant provisions.

ii. Registration with Absolute Freehold Title

Secondly, we must also query the continuing relevance of title relativity once someone is registered with *absolute* title to the land. Does registration with absolute title necessarily preclude the possibility that there might be *other* inferior or superior registered titles to the same land? The absolutist language of 'absolute title' might appear to suggest that it does—that an absolute title is a singular, exclusive, and unitary form of ownership. However, closer analysis reveals that this is not the case.

First, it is of course possible for a registered absolute title to exist concurrently with an *inferior* possessory freehold—as where a squatter goes into adverse possession of registered land. As we discussed in section III(B) above, the recognition of an *inferior* relative (possessory) freehold title poses no threat to the reliability of the Register.[69]

Secondly, a more difficult question arises as to whether registration with absolute title precludes the possible coexistence of a *superior* relative freehold title. This question might arise in practice if B successfully applies to become (first) registered proprietor of some land (with 'absolute' title) in circumstances where A was in fact the unregistered 'paper owner'. Whilst it will be rare for someone with a non-paramount right to be registered with absolute title, it is certainly possible within the terms of the LRA 2002. This is because, in order to achieve registration with absolute title, there is no need for the applicant (here B) to prove absolute ownership; rather he need only convince the Registrar 'that [his] title to the estate is such as a willing buyer could properly be advised by a competent professional adviser to accept'.[70] Thus, the Registrar may register a defective title as absolute if he merely 'considers that the defect will not cause the holding under the title to be disturbed'.[71] This raises the possibility (albeit a slim one) that B is registered as absolute owner when, unbeknownst to B or the Registrar, A was actually the superior owner.

[68] *Sexton v Gill* [2015] EWLandRA 2013_0472_0473, especially [19]. Note that in this case, Judge Rhys moved away from his earlier decisions on the point (in, eg, *Moore v Buxton* (n 34)). See too the Law Commission's discussion in 2016, in Law Com CP No 227 (n 50) paras 17.72–17.79.

[69] As we have discussed in sections III(B) and III(D)(i), it remains unclear whether the squatter may *register* this relatively inferior possessory title—so that the squatter's registered possessory title exists concurrently with the superior owner's registered absolute title. Nevertheless, this uncertainty does not undermine the possible coexistence of multiple fees simple in this context.

[70] LRA 2002, s 9(2).

[71] Law Com No 271 (n 4) 470.

The key question is whether B's registration extinguishes A's pre-existing superior title. As we discuss in section III(C) above, the answer depends on the effect of section 11(4)—and whether A's superior title is preserved by either B having 'notice' of A's prior right, or by A being in 'actual occupation' of the land at the time of B's registration. In both of these cases, there will be two concurrent relative fees simple over the land—again proving the continuing relevance of title relativity, in this case as a result of the legislation's terms.[72]

E. Cases of Double Registration with Absolute Freehold Title

A fifth context in which tricky title relativity issues may arise is where two independent parties are concurrently registered as absolute freehold proprietors of the same plot. There are two key situations in which double-registration might occur. They raise distinct problems.

i. Enlargement of Leaseholds into Freeholds

First, according to current Land Registry practice, two freeholds may be concurrently registered in those situations where a long leasehold interest is 'enlarged' into a freehold title. Such enlargements are permitted by section 153 of the Law of Property Act ('LPA') 1925, under certain conditions (including requirements that the original leasehold term must have been for at least 300 years, that at least 200 years remain at the point of enlargement, and that no rent (or a merely nominal rent) is payable by the lessee). Views differ as to the effect of such leasehold enlargements under the general law and, in particular, whether the former landlord's freehold disappears (leaving the former leaseholder with the sole freehold),[73] or persists (such that it exists concurrently with the former leaseholder's new freehold).[74] The divergence in views reflects a more fundamental dispute as to whether more than one freehold estate can subsist in relation to land more generally, and therefore whether title relativity has any role. As we have demonstrated above, in our view, title relativity is unambiguously accepted by, and is an integral part of, the *general law*. Hence, it is not *impossible* for two fees simple to exist in relation to the same land, if that outcome is consistent with the language of section 153 of the LPA 1925.

Given the divergence of views on the effect of leasehold enlargement under the LPA 1925, the Land Registry has adopted an (appropriately) conservative approach to registration. Its Practice Guide 26 states:

> The effect of enlargement on the former landlord's legal estate is unclear. Accordingly, if the landlord's title is registered it will not be closed. This means there will be more than one registered freehold estate in the same piece of land.[75]

[72] And even if the facts fall outwith these two conditions, there is a possibility that A might seek the reversal of B's 'mistaken' registration via a claim to rectify the Register. See section III(C) above.

[73] See, esp Jessel, 'Concurrent Fees Simple' (n 7). See also the *obiter* comments to this effect in *Earl Cadogan v Panagopoulos* [2010] EWHC 422 (Ch), [2010] 3 WLR 1125 [38] (Roth J).

[74] Law Com CP No 227 (n 50) para 3.5.

[75] HM Land Registry, *Practice Guide 26: Leases—Determination*, para 12. Note that this practice was adopted in March 2013, prior to which date the landlord's freehold had been removed from the Register on enlargement of the tenant's estate into a freehold: Law Com CP No 227 (n 50) paras 3.1–3.2.

The 2016 Law Commission Consultation Paper has expressed support for this practice.[76]

As both registered freehold titles are deemed conclusive by section 58 of the LRA 2002, it becomes necessary to work out how they relate to one another. As we have seen, relative freeholds typically rank in order of their creation, as where a squatter goes into adverse possession against an earlier—therefore superior—fee simple estate. However, this basic 'first in time' rule should be regarded merely as a default ranking rule, which is susceptible to displacement by inconsistent legislation. As such, the way in which the two freeholds which result from leasehold enlargement rank *inter se* should be regarded as a function of section 153 of the LPA 1925. The broad effect of section 153 is *not* to produce a binary ranking, like that encountered in adverse possession cases (one title being wholly better than the other). Instead, the legislation creates a more complex relationship between the two (relative) titles: the former leaseholder is entitled to possession as against the former landlord, and yet remains bound by the former leasehold covenants.

Crucially, we must ask whether the coexistence of two relative registered (potentially 'absolute') freehold titles is consistent with the broader aims of the registration system. In theory, there is a risk that the Register might give the impression that both freehold titles are wholly 'absolute' and unencumbered, when of course they are not: the former landlord's title, for example, confers no right to possession. As such, the reliability of the Register might seem to be threatened. Thankfully, this risk is averted by the Land Registry's (sensible) practice of ensuring that the two registered titles cross-refer to one another, in order to reduce the incidence of confusion and/or fraud.

ii. Mistaken Double Registrations

Secondly, two independent parties may have been registered with an absolute freehold title to the same land as a result of a mistake—a case of so-called 'double registration'. Where this occurs, the starting point is that section 58 of the LRA 2002 seems to work its 'statutory magic'[77] on both titles—thereby deeming both parties to be the lawful proprietor. But what does this mean in this context? Are they both *equal* owners and, if so, how would this work? Or can we draw upon the title relativity doctrine, such that the two registered titles are ranked relatively *inter se*—one superior to the other?

Double registration occurred recently in *Parshall v Hackney*,[78] a Court of Appeal decision in which part of a London parking space was concurrently registered with two different parties. Although the case was decided under the former LRA 1925, it raises a tricky conundrum which is useful to explore under the LRA 2002, whose provisions are materially the same for these purposes.[79]

Much simplified, *Parshall* turned on the relative status of A, the rightful registered proprietor since 1904, and B, who was subsequently mistakenly and concurrently registered as proprietor in 1980. B started possessing the land in 1988. To add salt to A's wounds,[80]

[76] Law Com CP No 227 (n 50) paras 3.2–3.14.

[77] See, eg, *Knights Construction* (n 2); *Odogwu v Vastguide Ltd* [2008] EWHC 3565 (Ch) [3]; *Lloyds TSB Bank Plc v Markandan & Uddin (A Firm)* [2012] EWCA Civ 65, [2012] 2 All ER 884 [51]; Law Commission, *Making Land Work: Easements, Covenants and Profits à Prendre* (Law Com No 327, 2011) para 4.12.

[78] *Pashall v Hackney* [2013] EWCA Civ 240, [2013] Ch 568.

[79] See Kester Lees, who opines that the same principles would apply under both the LRA 1925 and the LRA 2002: K Lees, '*Parshall v Hackney*: A Tale of Two Titles' [2013] *Conv* 222.

[80] Or rather, on the facts, the wounds of A's successors in title.

A's title was mistakenly removed from the Register in 2000, when the Register was digitised, leaving B as the sole registered proprietor from then onwards. In the ensuing litigation, A sought alteration of the Register, to reveal himself (A) as the sole registered proprietor. Prima facie, this was assumed to be straightforward, given that B's title emanated from a mistaken registration. However, B argued that he had been in adverse possession against A between 1988 and 2000—during which 12-year period A and B were concurrently registered—thereby extinguishing, under the Limitation Act 1980,[81] any rights that A may have had, and entitling B to remain on the Register as the rightful proprietor.

The Court of Appeal, led by Mummery LJ, decided in A's favour, according to the following analysis.

His Lordship's starting point was that during their concurrent registration (between 1980 and 2000) A and B had 'two parallel legal estates in the same land':[82] there was '*equality* of registered titles, rather than the normal case of *relativity* of titles'.[83]

Secondly, Mummery LJ rightly recognised that 'equality' between two parties who expect from the Register to have exclusive rights in the same land is unsustainable, and that there is a practical need to break the 'deadlock'[84] that would otherwise persist between the two co-owners. He said:

> The problem is that, as a matter of law, the disputed land is owned *either* by the appellant *or* by the respondent. They cannot both be owners of a fee simple in the same piece of land. They are not co-owners with beneficial shares in the disputed land. The court has to perform the delicate task of sorting out a muddle.

Thirdly, his Lordship opined that the only way to untangle the 'muddle' was via the LRA 1925's alteration provisions, and confirmed that, unless and until the Register was altered, A's and B's titles remained equal.[85] This had the consequence that during the period of concurrent registration, B could in no sense adversely possess against A. In the first place, no-one with a registered (and therefore lawful) title could be in 'adverse' possession; secondly, because A's entitlement to the land was no better than B's, B had failed to meet a fundamental requirement of the Limitation Act 1980—ie infringement of the real owner's right to recover possession from him.

Fourthly, in conclusion, the failure of B's adverse possession argument meant, by default, that A's claim to rectification should succeed.

The Court of Appeal's reasoning raises some important questions. In particular, is it really true—and is it satisfactory—that unless and until one title is removed from the Register, two concurrently registered titles confer absolutely identical and equally-ranked rights—ie, that both proprietors have concurrent rights to possess the land? Might it be possible and/or desirable to draw on the title relativity doctrine, in order to rank the concurrently registered fees simple *inter se* in the period prior to rectification of the Register?[86]

As we explain in the next section, there is an argument (premised on both doctrine and policy) for importing the title relativity doctrine to deal with these cases. Nevertheless, we

[81] The Limitation Act 1980 applied to adverse possession against both registered and unregistered titles prior to the coming into force of the LRA 2002 which disapplied the 1980 Act in relation to registered titles.

[82] *Parshall* (n 78) [33].

[83] ibid [89].

[84] ibid [81].

[85] ibid [89].

[86] See further Lees, '*Parshall v Hackey*' (n 79). See also ch 16, section III(C)(i)(b).

ultimately explain in a later section that this is narrowly outweighed by the threat which the title relativity doctrine would pose in this context to the general reliability of the Register. On balance, the temptation to import the title relativity doctrine to deal with these cases should be resisted.

iii. Arguments for Importing the Title Relativity Doctrine

There are three key reasons why it might be desirable to draw on the title relativity doctrine in mistaken double-registration cases.

First, for reasons of pure legal logic, it might be desirable to rank concurrent registered freeholds inter se: it is conceptually impossible for two independent parties both to have *exclusive* rights over the same land at the same time. For the law to permit the impossible seems incoherent.[87]

Secondly, related to this, but from a more practical perspective, what happens where both parties wish to occupy the land exclusively as against the other? One, or both, may bring against the other an action for the recovery of the land. There is a strong argument that the law should offer an *immediate* answer as to who may possess the land,[88] without compelling the parties to await the outcome of possibly lengthy alteration/rectification litigation.

Finally, the outcome of any rectification claim arguably depends on which party has the 'better' title in the first place. Thus, despite Mummery LJ's assertion that the relative ranking of rights *follows* from rectification,[89] it is at least arguable, as counsel for B in *Parshall* had suggested, that rights require ranking *prior* to rectification, in order for the rectification claim to be resolved.[90]

If the argument that title relativity should play a role is accepted, then the concurrent registered fees simple need to be ranked *inter se* (notwithstanding any later claim for Register alteration)—the law must provide rules for determining which fee simple is superior. There are two plausible sources of ranking rules, both of which would rank A's title ahead of B's. First, it is possible that the rules for ranking A's and B's concurrently registered fees simple lie outwith the confines of the LRA 2002, within the general law. Here, A's registered title would be superior to B's, simply by virtue of having arisen first. Alternatively, we might call upon the LRA 2002's internal priority rules: sections 28 and 29. These provisions would rank A's first-registered freehold ahead of B's second-registered freehold, on the basis that: (a) A's title, being first in time, binds B under section 28, and (b) being registered, A's title would be immune from 'postpone[ment]' to B's title under section 29.[91] Both sets of ranking rules are consistent with the notion that A's and B's registered titles exist *relative* to one another; the ranking rules merely determine which is the superior title.

[87] See ibid; also McFarlane, Hopkins and Nield (n 10) 251.

[88] Note that if B possessed to the exclusion of A, where A had the relatively superior title, B would prima facie be a trespasser against A. Despite this, it is possible that the law of tort might afford B a defence of justification where he trespassed under the colour of a lawful registered title.

[89] *Parshall* (n 78) [89].

[90] ibid [82]. The counterargument to the view posited in the main text is that the LRA 2002's alteration rules exclusively provide an answer as to how the Register should be altered, and that these do not necessarily require a prior determination of which right is superior.

[91] Furthermore, it is unlikely in double registration cases that s 29 is engaged at all. Section 29 is only engaged by 'registrable dispositions', which may not include void dispositions. Thus, where B has derived a title to some land from a legitimate source, but the Land Registry mistakenly included A's land (x) as an addition to B's title, there is no valid underlying disposition of x land to B. For discussion of this, see ch 17 of this book, section III(D)(i)(a).

iv. Problems Associated with Importing the Title Relativity Doctrine

Notwithstanding these arguments, there are problems associated with importing the title relativity doctrine in this manner. In particular, if the titles are ranked relative to one another, *whilst they are both registered with absolute title,* then any subsequent claim by A, as the higher-ranked proprietor, to alter the Register to reflect the existing paramountcy of his title,[92] would not cause any 'prejudicial' loss to B. The lower-ranked title was, from its inception, *subject to* the superior title, and so any Register-change to 'bring the Register up to date' will merely reflect the existing state of affairs.[93] As such, the Register-alteration against B will not qualify as a 'rectification', and no Registry-indemnity will be payable to B.[94]

The conclusion that the lower-ranked registered proprietor will lose his title without any compensation from the Registry is potentially problematic as a matter of policy. B will have conducted his affairs in reliance on what the Register told him—that he was proprietor of an absolute freehold title. Furthermore, B may have conveyed the property onwards to a purchaser, C, who also understandably relied on the Register for proof of B's 'absolute title'. The idea that B (or C) might lose their titles, without any Registry-indemnity for the loss they might suffer as a result of the Register's misleading them, seems hard to justify—and may ultimately undermine the public's confidence in the Register.

We might avoid this undesirable conclusion if we resist the temptation to rank the two registered titles *inter se*, and instead interpret the parties' rights according to what the Register appears to say: that both 'absolute' titles are of equivalent and paramount standing—neither being superior to the other—unless and until the deadlock is broken by an alteration to the Register. On this view, the party who was *correctly* registered as proprietor, A, can seek alteration of the Register against the party who was *mistakenly* registered, B (or, if relevant, B's successor in title, C). This time, B (or C) *will* be 'prejudiced' by the Register-alteration: he will lose what was once a good paramount title, and as a result will *prima facie* qualify for a Registry-indemnity.[95]

There is, however, an obvious downside to this approach. Prior to rectification, it will be impossible to know which of the two parties, with equally-ranked registered titles, is entitled to use the land. But, this problem will only ever be temporary in any given case, and is a small price to pay for adopting an approach that maintains the Register's reliability.

The problem of mistaken double-registrations teaches an important lesson—that, whilst the relativity doctrine might be useful in some contexts, it may threaten the reliability of our registration system in other contexts. We must take care to impose proper limits on the relativity doctrine, where appropriate.

F. The Co-Existence of Two Equal-Length But Inconsistent Registered Leases

The previous section examined title relativity in the event of a mistaken double-registration of *freehold* interests, where an argument was made to restrain our reliance on the relativity

[92] ie by either removing the lower-ranked title belonging to B from the Register, or having it downgraded to a lower class of title.

[93] LRA 2002, sch 4, para 2(1)(b).

[94] LRA 2002, sch 4, para 1; sch 8, para 1(1)(a). See ch 16 of this book, section III(C)(i)(b).

[95] ibid.

doctrine, and instead to channel any resolution of the problem via the LRA 2002's rectification/alteration regime.

In this section, we examine the possibility that a registered freehold proprietor might grant identical registered leases (with terms expiring on the same day) over the same plot of land, to two different leaseholders. Nothing in the Act prevents the grant (and consequent registration) of two such identical leases.

What happens where one leaseholder asserts superiority over the other? Here, unlike the cases discussed above of mistaken double-registrations of freeholds, there is no 'mistake' on the Register which requires correction: both leases were validly created and registered. As such, any dispute between the two leaseholders—in terms of who has the right to *use* the land in practice—cannot be resolved by appealing to the schedule 4 alteration/rectification regime. Instead, we must ascertain what it means to have two equal and inconsistent leases on the Register. Is one to be treated as void, and the other valid? Or are they both valid, but ranked *inter se*? The title relativity doctrine enables us to adopt the latter interpretation—that both titles are valid, but relatively ranked. Here, we must rely on View 3's vision of title relativity—that it involves titles to competing *derivative* interests in land.[96]

Our argument that the relativity doctrine is not only a *plausible* explanation of the parties' rights, but also a *desirable* one can be illustrated by the recent Court of Appeal decision in *MacLeod v Gold Harp Properties Ltd*.[97]

Much simplified, Lease 1 in *Gold Harp* belonged to X, and was mistakenly deleted from the Land Register following misconduct by the registered freeholder. Subsequently, the freeholder created an identical lease, Lease 2, in Z's favour, which was registered. The question for the Court of Appeal was whether X had a right under the LRA 2002's alteration provisions[98] for Lease 1 to be reinstated on the Register, with priority over Z's title (Lease 2). The Court of Appeal found for X, ordering—crucially—that Lease 1, belonging to X, should be re-registered *in addition to*,[99] and *with priority over* Lease 2, belonging to Z.[100]

At first glance, it might seem odd that our registration system countenances the simultaneous registration of two materially identical and yet mutually incompatible leases. However, this apparent oddity is readily explained by the relativity of title doctrine, which permits two identical titles to co-exist, so long as they are ranked *inter se*. It is notable that Underhill LJ, giving the main judgment, effectively adopted this relativity explanation, expressly observing that one registered leasehold title (Lease 2, on the facts) would be necessarily inferior to the other (Lease 1), rather than void.[101] Practically, this meant that any right to enjoy possession pursuant to the inferior title was suppressed unless and until the superior title terminated prematurely (eg via forfeiture, surrender, etc).

[96] See section II(C) above.

[97] *MacLeod v Gold Harp Properties Ltd* [2014] EWCA Civ 1084, [2015] 1 WLR 1249.

[98] LRA 2002, sch 4.

[99] Note that Z's Lease 2 had not been registered in error, and so there was no ground for removing it from the Register. This was because, even if X's lease (Lease 1) remained on the Register throughout, the LRA 2002 nonetheless gave the registered freeholder the power (relying on LRA 2002 ss 23–26) to validly create further registrable interests over the land. Thus, the freeholder undoubtedly had the power to create a second lease (Lease 2) over the land in Z's favour, even though Z's lease was identical to X's, and was due to expire on exactly the same date. As such, there was nothing mistaken about the registration of Z's lease. What X rightly sought was not the deletion of Z's lease from the Register, but the reinstatement of their own, with priority over Z's.

[100] According to LRA 2002, sch 4, para 8, X's lease was afforded priority prospectively, from the date of the Register being altered.

[101] See further A Goymour, 'Resolving The Tension Between The Land Registration Act 2002's "Priority" And "Alteration" Provisions' [2015] *Conv* 253.

The doctrine of title relativity is crucial for understanding the outcome in *Gold Harp*. The practical result would have been subtly different in a world without title relativity. In such a world, there appear to be two alternative ways of dealing with the *Gold Harp* facts—both of which lead to problematic and undesirable conclusions. On the one hand, both leases might be treated as *equal*—and, as such, it would be impossible to resolve the conundrum regarding which leaseholder could *use* the land at any given time. Secondly, and alternatively, a world devoid of title relativity might conclude that only one lease could be valid (say, Lease 1), and so the other (say, Lease 2) would necessarily be void. As such, if Lease 1 were to end prematurely, the right to possession would revert to the *freeholder*, rather than the proprietor of Lease 2. Stepping back, this result looks odd, and is inconsistent with that contemplated by *Gold Harp*. The freeholder burdened his estate for x years, by granting equivalent leasehold titles to two parties. As such, it is not obvious that he deserves to find that his estate is *unencumbered by either lease*, in the event of one of the leases ending prematurely. The relativity doctrine allows us to avoid this unpalatable conclusion, by recognising that *both* leases, ranked *inter se*, bind the freehold title.

G. The LRA 2002's 'Priority Rules'

The LRA 2002's priority rules (contained in sections 28–30) offer a seventh manifestation of the continuing relevance of title relativity in registered land. These rules determine the relative priority of two or more competing interests that are both derived from the same registered estate—eg where the registered freehold proprietor: (a) first declares that he holds his estate on trust for A, and then grants a 10-year lease to B; or (b) grants an easement to A, and then transfers the freehold to B; or (c) grants A and B identical, and therefore incompatible, leases.

In all such situations, the Act's priority rules determine whether the first-created right is 'protected' against or 'postponed' to the second-created interest.[102] In either case, it is important to recognise that *both* interests—whether protected or postponed—seem to subsist: neither is rendered void under the Act.[103] This outwardly-peculiar state of affairs can, once again, be readily and usefully explained by the doctrine of relativity of title, as it applies to competing *derivative* titles emanating from a common owner.[104] It means that, to the extent that the higher-ranked interest is *inconsistent* with the existence of the lower-ranked interest, the former can be enjoyed to the exclusion of the latter.

In particular, the relativity analysis permits a more precise understanding of the consequences of 'postponement' and 'protection' under the LRA 2002's priority provisions. Take example (a) above as an illustration, where the registered proprietor declares that he holds his estate on trust for A, and then grants a 10-year registered lease to B. Unless A's interest is protected as an overriding interest, it will be postponed to B's lease under the Act's priority rules.[105] 'Postpon[ement]' is left undefined by the Act, but it makes sense when seen

[102] The first interest is generally postponed if: (a) section 29 is engaged by the disposition to the second interest-holder (this is the case where there is a registrable disposition for valuable consideration, which is completed by registration); and (b) the first interest is neither protected on the Register nor overriding within LRA 2002, sch 3.

[103] See *Rosefair Ltd v Butler* [2015] UKFTT 0395 (PC).

[104] The analysis here relies on the understanding of title relativity advocated by Fox, 'Relativity' (n 20), and discussed above as View 3, in section II(C) of this chapter.

[105] Land Registration Act 2002, ss 29 and Schedule 3.

as a concept concerning relativity of title: A's 'postponed' trust interest is not void; rather it continues to subsist, albeit at a relatively inferior level to B's lease.[106] Practically, this means that A cannot enjoy his right whilst B's lease subsists. Crucially, however, A's right will 'resurface' once B's lease ends, at which point it can be fully enjoyed. The doctrine of title relativity is central to explaining the survival of A's interest in this manner.

The reverse is true where A's interest is not 'postponed' to B's interest, but is 'protected' by the LRA 2002's priority rules. Here, A's interest, rather than B's, takes priority, meaning that B's interest subsists, but can only be enjoyed if and when A's interest comes to an end.

IV. Conclusions: The Future of Title Relativity

Section III has sought to show that relativity of title is not inconsistent with the LRA 2002. While the position is not completely unequivocal, in general, and across a broad range of situations, the provisions of the Act provide both express and implied support for the possibility that title relativity continues to subsist in the context of registered land. Prima facie, then, the existence of a registered title does not necessarily preclude the existence of other, relatively inferior/superior, titles to or interests over that same piece of land.

In fact, the point can be put more strongly. The continued recognition of principles of title relativity in the registered land context brings substantial advantages to English land law, and it is desirable that these principles should be acknowledged and maintained—at least to the extent that they are consistent with the registered land regime. Section III has shown that, in many important situations, the title relativity doctrine continues to provide a convincing and structured basis on which to approach matters that would otherwise would be difficult to resolve or reconcile. Sometimes this will be because a case presents a conceptual difficultly that is quickly and coherently dissolved by an application of relativity of title principles—as where a squatter seeks registration of a possessory title under section 9,[107] or where section 11 must be applied to ascertain whether a first-registered proprietor's title is burdened by a previously completed period of adverse possession against the unregistered title.[108] At other times, as in a case like *Gold Harp*, the title relativity doctrine is worth serious consideration because the outcome of a case would necessarily be different in a world without title relativity.[109]

To the extent that relativity of title retains such a useful and persuasive function in dispute resolution, it seems desirable to regard the doctrine as subsisting in the context of registered land, and correlatively disadvantageous to regard it as fading or withered. This is so notwithstanding that the paradigm case of a squatter acquiring an indefeasible title to

[106] See further *Halifax Plc v Curry Popeck (A Firm)* [2008] EWHC 1692 (Ch); M Dixon 'Priorities under the Land Registration Act 2002' (2009) 124 *LQR* 401.

[107] See section III(D) above.

[108] See sections III(C) and III(D)(ii) above.

[109] See sections III(F) above.

a registered estate is unlikely to materialise under the provisions of LRA 2002.[110] Indeed, it is arguable that a skewed impression of the declining significance of this paradigm has exerted too heavy an influence on commentators, and has led them to conclude, too swiftly, that title relativity is something of the past. As we have argued, it is important not to equate the existence of relative titles with the likelihood of a squatter's acquisition of an *indefeasible* title, and it would be an overreaction to allow the attenuation of the significance of adverse possession by schedule 6 of the LRA 2002 to dictate the broader status and availability of arguments about title relativity.

It follows that we must treat with caution the view that principles of land registration in general, and the LRA 2002 in particular, have committed English law to a Roman-style concept of *dominium*, or absolute ownership, of land. Nothing about the existing law inexorably entails this view. Instead, we would do better to replace broad assertions of the dominance of registration principles in title matters with careful contextual analysis of the possible impact of title relativity reasoning. This does not mean that all title disputes must be informed or governed by title relativity principles—sometimes this will not be appropriate or desirable, even when superficially attractive, as our discussion of *Parshall v Hackney* has shown.[111] However, it is important that courts and commentators at least consider the possible impact of title relativity reasoning in undertaking their analysis. This more than anything serves to confirm its standing as a cardinal principle of English land law.

In short, the LRA 2002 does not require us to accept that the Register is *the* basis of title. It is *a* basis of title—we can even fairly say of a particularly strong title—but it is not necessarily the *only* basis.

[110] See section III(B)(iii) above.

[111] See section III(E)(ii)–(iv) above.

B

Alteration and Indemnity

7

Guaranteed Title: No Title, Guaranteed

EMMA LEES

I. Introduction

The degree to which title to land is guaranteed by the Land Registration Act ('LRA') 2002 is contested: this issue is both widely discussed in the academic literature,[1] and is the subject of multiple judicial decisions. It has now also been the subject of a Law Commission Consultation.[2] However, this chapter will demonstrate that the proliferation of case law and commentary, far from simplifying the issues, has merely highlighted that the problem of what registration actually means is far more complex than the simple question, 'Does the Register guarantee title?', makes it seem. Furthermore, the complexity which this chapter discussed is not solved by the Law Commission's proposals.

Whilst the current legal position (following, in particular, *Gold Harp v McLeod*[3] and *Swift 1st v Chief Land Registrar*)[4] represents a clear, and welcome, interpretation of the particular statutory provisions which were relevant to the cases before the courts, what remains is a sense that there is no overall harmony in these interpretations. Neither is there harmony in the prevailing academic approaches.[5] Thus, this chapter seeks to analyse not the judicial

[1] See M Dixon, 'What Sort of Land Registration System?' [2002] *Conv* 349; E Cooke, 'Land Registration: Void and Voidable Titles—a Discussion of the Scottish Law Commission's Paper' [2004] *Conv* 482; E Cooke, 'The Register's Guarantee of Title' [2013] *Conv* 344; S Cooper, 'Regulating Fallibility in Registered Land Titles' [2013] *CLJ* 341; M Dixon, 'A Not So Conclusive Title Register?' (2013) 129 *LQR* 320; M Dixon, 'The Past, the Present, and the Future of Land Registration' [2013] *Conv* 463; A Goymour, 'Mistaken Registrations of Land: Exploding the Myth of "Title by Registration"' [2013] *CLJ* 617; E Lees, 'Title by Registration—Rectification, Indemnity and Mistake and the Land Registration Act 2002' (2013) 76 *MLR* 62; E Lees, '*Richall Holdings v Fitzwilliam: Malory v Cheshire Homes* and the LRA 2002' (2013) 76 *MLR* 924; E Lees, 'State Guaranteed Title: The Land Registration Act 2002', in A Apers, S Bouly, E Dewitte and D Gruyaert (eds), *Property Law Perspectives III* (Cambridge, Intersentia, 2013); E Lees, 'Indemnity and the Land Registration Act 2002' [2014] *CLJ* 25; S Cooper, 'Resolving Title Conflicts in Registered Land' (2015) 131 *LQR* 108; E Lees 'Rectification of the Register—Prospective or Retrospective? (2015) 78 *MLR* 361; S Cooper, 'Registered Title and the Assurance of Reliability' in *Modern Studies in Property Law, Volume 6* (Oxford, Hart Publishing, 2015); E Lees, 'Registration Make-Believe and Forgery—Swift 1st v Chief Land Registrar' (2015) 131 *LQR* 515; S Cooper, 'Removing Title Blemishes as a Function of Registration' in A Wudarski (ed), *Functions of Land Registers in a European Comparative Law Perspective* (Berlin, Duncker Humblot 2016); and E Lees, 'The Public Face of the Register: Confidence in the Land Registration Act 2002' in Wudarski (ed) (ibid).

[2] Law Commission, *Updating the Land Registration Act 2002—A Consultation Paper* (Law Com CP No 227, 2016).

[3] *Gold Harp Properties Ltd v MacLeod* [2014] EWCA Civ 1084, [2015] 1 WLR 1249.

[4] *Swift 1st v Chief Land Registrar* [2015] EWCA Civ 330, [2015] Ch 602.

[5] Contrast, eg, Lees, 'Rectification, Indemnity and Mistake' (n 1), Goymour, 'Mistaken Registrations of Land' (n 1) and Cooper, 'Resolving Title Conflicts in Registered Land' (n 1).

decisions themselves, but rather the interaction between these decisions in the context of the statutory provisions in the LRA 2002—sections 58, Schedule 4, and Schedule 8—to give some sense of the overall picture for guaranteed title. It seeks in essence to take a step back, to review these decisions as a single whole, and to examine the problems which emerge when these perfectly sensible individual pieces of statutory interpretation are combined. It becomes apparent, through this analysis, that the case law does not speak with one voice. There is, in fact, no coherent whole. Rather, in places 'title is guaranteed'; in others, not, and there is no clear justification for these divergences, nor for the divergences in terms of indemnity which result.

Most importantly, it will be argued, there is a failure in the system to recognise that the existence of a guaranteed title should, if the logic of land registration is pursued, mean that there is a concomitant guarantee that there are no other superior titles to the land which are not present on the Register nor protected as an overriding interest. By considering the land registration question from this perspective, the inconsistencies which have emerged, and therefore the problems which the Law Commission ought to have, but arguably did not, solve, become clear. Following this line of analysis, this chapter then concludes by considering whether the lack of coherence is the fault of the case law failing to take a step back to consider the broader picture, or whether it is a result of the statutory provisions themselves. It will become clear that the case law has taken us as far as it can in developing a coherent whole, and that reform is required even if not along the lines currently proposed.

II. Background

There is a considerable amount of academic commentary on the position of guaranteed title under the Land Registration Act 2002; this chapter does not seek to analyse it again. Both Cooper[6] and Goymour[7] have suggested that routes can and should be found within this legislation, the case law, and the policy goals surrounding land registration, to ensure a consistent, 'middle ground' approach—one which neither focuses solely on the merit of registration, nor gives too much weight to the 'off-Register' position. Indeed, they argue that the case law as it stands is travelling in that direction.[8] It is the purpose of this chapter to examine whether the existing case law and legislation is indeed susceptible to an interpretation which gives rise to a single, unified approach to the weight of the guarantee of title, and as to the considerations which ought to be taken into account when assessing changes to the Register. Thus, this chapter takes a somewhat different approach to much of the existing literature. Its aim is not to examine what the law is by reference to some fixed policy goal, but rather whether—perhaps more prosaically—there is a consistent set

[6] Cooper, 'Resolving Title Conflicts in Registered Land' (n 1) 109: 'registered land titles should be made less secure by an expansive interpretation of the rectification power. It recommends that a former proprietor who has been wrongly ousted by a mistaken register change should not necessarily have the claim guillotined upon the intervention of a purchaser but should be given a forum in which to put the case for recovery'.

[7] Goymour, 'Mistaken Registrations of Land' (n 1) 650: '[t]he third–and preferable–option is to devise a system that integrates the best parts, and avoids the pitfalls, of both the "title by registration" and general property law schemes'.

[8] Ibid, 646–47.

of rules which can be discerned from that existing law. In attempting to discern this, it is necessary to engage not only with the outcomes of the various authorities, but also with the mechanics by which those outcomes are achieved. It is in these mechanics, as will be seen, that divergences emerge.

The starting point is to recognise that not all land registration problems which might occur have currently been considered by the courts. Rather, there is a whole range of different issues which might arise following (broadly) 'wrongful' registration, and a whole range of different issues involved in the modification of (or the refusal to modify) the Register in response to that wrongful registration. The language used here is deliberately neutral. The aim of this chapter is not to limit its enquiry to situations of mistake *stricto sensu*, but to consider, broadly, what happens now when something goes wrong, and to ask whether these solutions speak with one voice.

III. The Case Law

There have been, since the LRA 2002 came into force, a number of decisions of the Court of Appeal, of the High Court, and of the First-tier Tribunal (Property Chamber) (formerly the Adjudicator to HM Land Registry). Of these, only the first is strictly binding upon other courts. It is with the Court of Appeal decisions therefore that we begin our enquiry. These decisions are: *Gold Harp v McLeod*;[9] *Swift 1st v Chief Land Registrar*;[10] *Walker v Burton*;[11] *Parshall v Hackney*;[12] and *Barclays Bank v Guy No 1*[13] and *No 2*.[14] Of these, the litigation in *Barclays Bank* can be discounted on the basis that the hearings were permission to appeal hearings, and then a practice direction; they do not, as a result, have the force of precedent and are not binding on lower courts. We are therefore left with a 'quartet' of leading cases. In addition to these, there are some other significant decisions worthy of mention. In particular, the decision of the Adjudicator to HM Land Registry in *Knights Construction v Roberto Mac*[15]—a decision now widely considered to be the leading authority on the meaning of mistake, albeit that in terms of authority the position is still very much up for grabs[16]—is central to the current operation of the land registration scheme. Each of these decisions will be briefly outlined, before the overall picture is analysed.

[9] *Gold Harp* (n 3). For further discussion of the case, see C Harpum, 'Can Rectification be Retrospective?', ch 8 of this book. See also M Dixon, 'Rectification and Priority: Further Skirmishes in the Land Registration War' (2015) 131 *LQR* 207; A Goymour, 'Resolving the Tension between the Land Registration Act 2002's "Priority" and "Alteration" provisions' [2015] *Conv* 235; E Lees, 'Rectification of the Register—Prospective or Retrospective?' (2015) 78 *MLR* 361; and R Smith, 'Land Registration: Rectification and Purchasers' [2015] *CLJ* 10.

[10] *Swift 1st* (n 4).

[11] *Walker v Burton* [2013] EWCA Civ 1228, [2014] 1 P & CR 9.

[12] *Parshall v Hackney* [2013] EWCA Civ 240, [2013] Ch 568. Strictly speaking, this case is decided under the provisions of the Land Registration Act 1925, but the reasoning applies equally to the LRA 2002, and there are no relevant differences in the statutory provisions to justify taking a different approach in relation to the later Act.

[13] *Barclays Bank v Guy* [2008] EWCA Civ 452, [2008] 2 EGLR 74.

[14] *Barclays Bank v Guy* [2010] EWCA Civ 1396, [2011] 1 WLR 681.

[15] *Knights Construction v Roberto Mac* [2011] EWLandRA 2009_1459, [2011] 2 EGLR 123.

[16] *Gold Harp* (n 3) [81] (Underhill LJ).

A. *Gold Harp v McLeod*

In *Gold Harp*, the Court of Appeal was required to assess whether a lease, mistakenly removed from the Register, was required to be re-registered *as if* it had never been removed, or, alternatively, whether its removal and later re-registration would involve its losing priority to any subsequently registered interests. We can represent this thus:

(i) A (freeholder) grants lease to B, which is duly registered.
(ii) B's lease is mistakenly de-registered.
(iii) A grants a lease to C, which is duly registered.
(iv) B discovers the mistake and wishes to be re-registered.

Question: Does B have priority over C, or vice-versa?

The court concluded that B ought to be re-registered so as to have priority over C.[17] This conclusion was reached on the basis of an interpretation of schedule 4, paragraph 8 which states that: '[t]he powers under this Schedule to alter the register, so far as relating to rectification, extend to changing for the future the priority of any interest affecting the registered estate or charge concerned'. 'Change for the future' was held to mean that the court could give B the priority which they ought to have had if no mistake had been made, but only for the future, such that C would not be liable in trespass or for mesne profits if C used the land prior to the date of the change made to the Register.[18]

B. *Swift 1st v Chief Land Registrar*

In *Swift 1st*, the Court of Appeal was largely concerned to address the decision in *Fitzwilliam v Richall*,[19] and its predecessor, the Court of Appeal decision in *Malory Enterprises v Cheshire Homes*,[20] as to whether a trust arises in favour of the original proprietor following a void, yet registered, onward transaction. Again, much has been written on this line of case law, and it is not the aim of this chapter to replicate that.[21] Rather, the goal is to distill the basic conclusion from this case, such that its interaction with the rest of the case law can be examined.

In *Swift 1st*, Mrs Rani, the registered proprietor, was the victim of a fraud such that a void mortgage was granted to Swift 1st. The mortgage was registered. Mrs Rani applied to have the mortgage removed from the Register. It was accepted that she would be able to do this. The difficulty was whether this would allow the bank, the registered charge-holder, to obtain an indemnity to cover its loss.

[17] ibid [96] (Underhill LJ).
[18] ibid.
[19] *Fitzwilliam v Richall* [2013] EWHC 86 (Ch), [2013] 1 P & CR 19.
[20] *Malory Enterprises v Cheshire Homes* [2002] EWCA Civ 151, [2002] Ch 216.
[21] R Smith, 'Forgeries and Indemnity in Land Registration' [2015] *CLJ* 401; P Milne, 'Guarantee of Title and Void Dispositions: Work in Progress' [2015] *Conv* 356; and E Lees, 'Registration Make-Believe and Forgery' (n 1).

Again, we can represent this set of facts as follows:

(i) A is registered proprietor.
(ii) B obtains a registered mortgage which is void as a forgery.
(iii) B's mortgage is removed from the Register.

Question: Can B obtain an indemnity?

The Court of Appeal concluded that the Bank (B) would be able to obtain an indemnity on the basis that schedule 8, paragraph 1(2)(b) of the LRA 2002 states that where a registration is obtained as a result of forgery, as here, for the purposes of calculating the indemnified-against loss, it ought to be assumed that the disposition was valid.[22] Thus, the 'worthless' charge granted to Swift 1st—worthless, due to A's right to rectify taking priority over the charge thanks to A's actual occupation at the time of the grant of the charge, or, possibly, worthless due simply to the void conveyance[23]—was deemed to be worth something such that the lender was entitled to an indemnity from the Land Registry. The statutory fiction therefore gave value to a right which was valueless given the precise mechanics of its creation.

C. *Walker v Burton*

In *Walker v Burton*, the Court of Appeal assessed whether in cases of mistaken registration, where the 'true' owner was not actively claiming the land, it would be right to rectify against a registered proprietor in possession. In this case, the Burtons had acquired a property near Ireby Fell. They believed, and it had been accepted by the Land Registry, that the property came with entitlement to a Lordship and, with this Lordship, came title to the Fell. The Burtons were duly registered as the first registered proprietors of the Fell land and went into possession of it. The residents of the local village took exception to this and discovered that in fact the Lordship had fallen into abeyance, and that the 'true' owner of the Fell was therefore either the Duchy of Lancaster or the Crown. The residents of the village then applied for rectification of the Register against the Burtons.

The facts can be represented thus:

(i) A is registered as proprietor.
(ii) A goes into possession of the land.
(iii) It comes to light that A's registration was mistaken.

Question: Ought the Register to be rectified against A?

The Court of Appeal held that in these circumstances, rectification should be refused. This conclusion was reached on the basis that the statutory provisions in schedule 4 presume

[22] *Swift 1st* (n 4) [51] (Patten LJ).

[23] There is a lot of controversy as to whether the 'right to rectify' argument which allows the former proprietor to rely on the priority rules is correct, and even if it is, it seems inappropriate as a mechanism by which an immediate disponee would be bound. For a full discussion of this please see S Cooper and E Lees, 'Interests, Powers and Mere Equities in Modern Land Law' (2017) 37 *OJLS* 235, which argues that the best explanation of the current law is the right to rectify the Register can be binding against a remote disponee (although not an immediate disponee) *but* that this result gives rise to some practical problems.

that there will be no rectification against a proprietor in possession unless it would be unjust not to rectify.[24] In the circumstances of the case, it was held not to be unjust not to rectify, and so the Burtons retained their title.[25]

D. *Parshall v Hackney*

The question in *Parshall v Hackney*, the final Court of Appeal authority, was whether, in cases where two persons are registered independently as sole proprietor of the same piece of land, it could be said that either was in adverse possession against the other, and whether the solution was to be found in the presumption in favour of the proprietor in possession, or in the 'off-Register' position. The facts were relatively simple. Both parties had been registered as owners of the same parcel of land, under different title numbers. The 'true' owner requested that the other proprietor be removed from the Register. The other proprietor, who had been in possession, argued that they had been in adverse possession and so were entitled to be registered.

Thus:

(i) A and B are both (independently) registered as proprietors of the same piece of land.
(ii) A claims that B should be removed from the Register.
(iii) B claims that they (ie B) have been in adverse possession and so are now the 'correct' registered proprietor.

Question: Can the problem be solved through the rules of adverse possession and, if not, how is it solved?

Mummery LJ, giving judgment for the Court of Appeal, held that there was certainly no adverse possession by B on these facts.[26] He stated that it was not a question of relativity of titles, but of two equally valid titles.[27] Thus, neither party could be in adverse possession of land to which they had registered title.[28] Therefore, the position was to be solved through rectifying the Register and in this case it should be done on the basis of the 'off-Register' position, ie, the person who ought to have been registered should be registered.[29] This gives little weight to the presumption against rectification against a proprietor in possession, but looks instead to the position in terms of the off-Register conveyances which had taken place.

E. *Knights Construction v Roberto Mac*

In this final case, a decision of the Adjudicator to HM Land Registry, land was registered pursuant to a first registration in the name of the Salvation Army. However, this was

24 *Walker v Burton* (n 11) [39] (Mummery LJ).
25 ibid [102]–[106] (Mummery LJ).
26 *Parshall v Hackney* (n 12) [89] (Mummery LJ).
27 ibid.
28 ibid [90] (Mummery LJ).
29 ibid [95] (Mummery LJ).

a mistake. The land had never belonged to the Salvation Army. The chain of conveyance demonstrated that the 'true' owner was Knights Construction. Before this had come to light, however, the Salvation Army had sold the disputed land to Roberto Mac Ltd, which had duly become registered proprietor. The question in the case was whether the registration of Roberto Mac was a 'mistake' such that either they could be removed from the Register and obtain an indemnity, or, if appropriate, they would remain on the Register but Knights Construction would be entitled to the indemnity.

Thus:

(i) B is mistakenly registered. A is the 'true owner'.
(ii) B transfers land to C under a valid disposition.

Questions: Can C be removed from the Register; and who is entitled to an indemnity and under what circumstances?

The Adjudicator held that Roberto Mac's title could be removed, either because it was a mistake in and of itself, or because it was the consequence of a mistake such that in order to 'correct' the original mistake of registering the Salvation Army, Roberto Mac too would need to be removed from the Register.[30] Although this is a controversial decision in terms of the meaning of mistake, it is now widely assumed that this represents the correct solution to the most simple of the so-called A-B-C problems, that is, the situation where title has been further transferred to a remote disponee.

IV. Conclusions from the Case Law

Having considered the relevant case law, we can begin to draw out some relevant conclusions from it. First, from considering the results in the case law, the cases show—although not consistently—a general preference for the 'off-Register' position, at least where the person 'most' entitled under that position is themselves seeking to benefit from a change in the Register. In so doing, they therefore, to a certain extent, retain many of the policies represented by the rules relating to unregistered land. Secondly, the courts are now, albeit inconsistently, displaying a preference for solving problems of subsequent registrations/registered charges (ie, the A-B-C-etc situation) which were mistaken—or if not themselves a mistake, the consequence of a mistake—by removing the mistaken registration and remedying all those 'down the chain' with an indemnity. The courts are willing to manipulate the statutory provisions to ensure an indemnity is available in such circumstances even where, on its face, they appear not to be warranted under the precise terms of schedule 8 given the courts' reasoning. Thirdly, the courts do not, for the most part, engage with *why* a transaction has gone wrong—ie what the precise flaw in the transaction might be—unless such is required to ensure that an indemnity is available. The mechanics of the faulty registration are given less focus than the fact of its existing, the subsequent need for it to be corrected, and the route through the statutory provisions which are able to achieve this outcome. As a result, little attention is paid to the relative responsibilities within the chain.

[30] *Knights Construction v Roberto Mac* (n 15) [132] (Michael Mark).

A. Weak and Fluctuating Preference for the Off-Register Position

We can examine these conclusions in more detail, to demonstrate how far consistency exists in this regard. First, as to the question of the preference for the 'off-Register' position, it is clear that the courts prefer to 'return' land to someone who has lost it through no fault of their own, in preference to protecting the sort of dynamic security concerns represented by 'immediate' or 'qualified indefeasibility of title'. By 'preference for the off-Register position', it is meant that, for the most part, the courts appear to wish to undo mistakes (broadly-defined), whether or not the mistake is the result of fraud, so as to put the parties into the position that they would have been in had no mistake occurred. It is important to consider, however, the extent to which the courts are utilising this off-Register position as a guide to what ought to happen—and, as corollary to this, whether the merits of the off-Register position are determined solely by the rules relating to unregistered land; by policy considerations (including the respective desires for land or indemnity and the needs of the parties); or by both of these.

By displaying this preference, the courts do not provide for either immediate or deferred indefeasibility of title—notwithstanding the dicta in *Gold Harp* that, '[t]he system of land registration thus provides only for qualified indefeasibility of registered title'[31]—since there is no 'cut-off' point at which the courts would refuse to rectify against a registered proprietor who obtained title under a faulty chain. Rather, the goal is to unpick a chain of conveyance as far as is required to put the parties into the position dictated to the courts by the unregistered land principles.

This can be seen most clearly in *Gold Harp*. In this case, the goal of the court was, from the outset, to put the parties into the position that they would have been in had there been no mistake.[32] On the facts of the case this was made relatively more palatable by the fact that Gold Harp (the subsequent lessee) was connected to the freeholder;[33] was complicit in the freeholder's dubious behaviour;[34] and had provided no consideration for their lease.[35] However, the fact that Gold Harp was a volunteer does not appear to have been central to the court's approach.[36] Rather, the primary goal was seen to be aligning the Register with the off-Register conveyancing position, giving effect, primarily, to the substantive law of property, rather than the registration provisions *per se*.[37] Furthermore, the goal of putting the claimants into this position did not explicitly involve consideration as to the merits of the various parties—suggesting that the 'off-Register' position, and thus the justice considerations encapsulated in the presumption in favour of the proprietor in possession in schedule 4, are determined solely by the rules of unregistered conveyancing.

Such an approach can also be seen in *Parshall v Hackney*, which, whilst recognising the power of the Register to confer two equally-valid titles simultaneously, seeks to

[31] *Gold Harp* (n 3) [23] (Underhill LJ).
[32] ibid [94] (Underhill LJ).
[33] ibid [9] (Underhill LJ).
[34] This is implied in ibid [10] (Underhill LJ).
[35] ibid [18] (Underhill LJ).
[36] ibid [34] (Underhill LJ).
[37] ibid [99] (Underhill LJ).

resolve the resulting title conflict by reference to the off-Register position. The attitude of Mummery LJ to the question is not, however, entirely clear. Thus, he reasons:

> The land register is a system of state-guaranteed registered title. Mistakes may be made. If they are, the legislation caters for that by providing machinery for their correction and for indemnification with safeguards to protect the interests of the proprietor in possession and to prevent injustice. That is the machinery which has to be used to establish the true title to registered land before any question arises of establishing possessory title to registered land.[38]

This approach would seem to give priority to the proprietor in possession rather than the position in unregistered land. However, elsewhere in the judgment, his Lordship reasons that:

> The determination of the question of rectification is logically prior to the determination of the question of possessory title. It has to be decided *who was entitled to be registered* as proprietor of the disputed land before it can be decided whether the right of the proprietor to recover the disputed land is statute barred.[39]

This approach seems much more to be a question of unregistered conveyancing. Nowhere in this case, however, is there any open discussion as to the relative needs, responsibilities etc of the two parties, such that it appears that the off-Register position is simply a question of conveyancing rules, rather than a merits or policy-based assessment. This can be contrasted to *Walker*, which is discussed below.

On this point, therefore, two weak and rebuttable preferences emerge from the case law: firstly, that land should be returned to the person 'most deserving of it' when the off-Register position is considered—and that it should be so returned unburdened by any subsequent rights (as confirmed in *Knights Construction*)[40]; and secondly, that the question as to who 'most deserves' title is determined by the rules of unregistered conveyancing. There is, therefore, a limited general consensus. Whilst it is this author's view that this is a misinterpretation of the original intention of the Law Commission's report and the statutory provisions,[41] it is to be preferred at least that some consistency exists, in whatever direction.

However, there are cases which point to inconsistency in this approach. The different tentacles of land registration have not all preferred the off-Register position. We can see the effects of this in *Swift 1st*, which clearly prioritises the information provided *on* the Register for the purposes of valuing indemnity awards. As far as the removal of the charge was concerned, the off-Register and registration-focused results would be the same. The conveyance granting the charge was void at law, and the registration was a mistake, on the grounds that the registration was effected pursuant to a forgery. Removing the charge is not in the least bit controversial. However, the court's calculation, and eventual conclusion, as to the *value* of that charge is ambiguous in this regard, and requires further examination.

The court concluded that, in essence, an interest registered on the basis of a void transaction caused by forgery (we do not know what happens in relation to other types of void transaction, nor for voidable transactions, nor, indeed, for purely administrative

[38] *Parshall v Hackney* (n 12) [95] (Mummery LJ).
[39] ibid [89] (Mummery LJ).
[40] *Knights Construction v Roberto Mac* (n 15) [131] (Michael Mark).
[41] Lees, 'Rectification, Indemnity and Mistake' (n 1).

mistakes where there is no conveyance at all), is an interest of no value. It was always susceptible to the superior right of the registered proprietor to have that interest removed if the registered proprietor is in actual occupation at the time of the transfer (this is a controversial caveat, discussed elsewhere in this chapter).[42] This implies that, following the creation of the charge, the registered proprietor has two rights: first, they retain their freehold title to land; and secondly, they obtain an additional right to have the Register rectified to remove the forged charge.[43] We might wonder at the need for the additional right—given that the charge was void, and there was no onwards disposition of the charge—but this does appear to be the reasoning of the court. As a result, the court was only able to give Swift 1st an indemnity by invoking a statutory fiction as to the value of forged conveyances. In so doing, it may be argued, the court is relying entirely on the off-Register position.

However, this would be incorrect. The court, instead, is relying very heavily on the existence of the Register to justify giving the void charge some value. The off-Register position is not only that the charge is valueless; it is that it does not exist. The court, by giving the charge value due to its registration (along with its mode of creation in the form of the forgery as a result of schedule 8, paragraph 1(2)(b)) is giving it a value which is present *because* it is registered. The registration of the right is not, in this sense, purely a formality. Registered estates have a value because they are registered and because, in so being, the proprietor of that estate has bought into the insurance that the Register is supposed to provide.

What does this mean for the weak preference for the 'off-Register' position? It means that this preference is confused by our refusal to abandon the guarantee of title altogether. Registration still has significant legal consequences, and not only in cases where there is onward transfer, even if it can be very easily undone. There is no criticism intended here; this ambivalence is entirely natural given the wording of the provisions. The clear justice in 'returning' land unscathed to someone who has lost it, and the desire to protect those who have in all good faith acquired something which they believe to be valid (and the validity of which the state assures them), are both of value. The criticism lies in the resulting confusion, not in the motivation which drives it.

Furthermore, it is debatable whether the 'justice' referred to in the schedule is fully encapsulated by considering only the chain of conveyance. There is more to the question of 'justice' than simply what has occurred in terms of the conveyancing process. This is very clearly shown by the decision in *Walker v Burton*, where the fact that the 'true' owner was not hugely desirous of having their land returned to them was a very relevant factor in the court's eventual decision not to rectify the Register.[44] The issue of third party rights in relation to the land is also relevant according to *Knights Construction*, where the Adjudicator considered whether the position of tenants of the mistakenly-registered proprietor should be taken into account when altering the Register.[45]

Thus, to summarise, there is, in practice, a weak presumption in favour of the 'true' proprietor, a presumption which is at odds with the language of the statute (which has an

[42] See n 23 above, and Part V below.

[43] The court expresses this as being a question of priority, but this does not make sense given that Mrs Rani's right (to rectify) can only have arisen *after* the registration of the charge. Nevertheless, the idea of rights being always subject to a prior claim—the essence of *Swift 1st*—still requires analysis notwithstanding the difficulty with expressing this in terms of *priority*.

[44] LRA 2002, sch 4, para 3(2)(b).

[45] *Knights Construction v Roberto Mac* (n 15) [133]–[138] (Michael Mark).

explicit presumption in favour of the proprietor in possession),[46] and which is unevenly applied. However, in achieving this position—which relies on giving primary weight to the off-Register position—a potentially unpalatable situation is produced whereby subsequently registered interests are rendered worthless by the existence of the power to rectify.[47] This is itself a position which the courts appear unable to tolerate, so these valueless subsequently-registered rights are given some value, in some circumstances—ie, where there is a forgery involved—although perhaps not in others. The position, in short, is inconsistent in two ways: first, as to the strength and content of the presumption in favour of the off-Register position; and secondly therefore, as to the value of interests which are registered by mistake in the face of a desire to return to the position which would exist but for the existence of the mistake.

Why does this ambiguity exist? It is argued that it exists because of the wording of the test in schedule 4, paragraph 3(2)(b) regarding the presumption against rectification against a proprietor in possession. The provision states that:

> (2) If alteration affects the title of the proprietor of a registered estate in land, no order may be made under paragraph 2 without the proprietor's consent in relation to land in his possession unless—
>
> ...
>
> (b) it would for any other reason be unjust for the alteration not to be made.

The test is that such proprietors in possession should not be rectified against—one assumes, whatever the off-Register position—unless a failure to rectify would be unjust. This test, on its face, seems to provide a strong degree of protection for the current registered proprietor where he is in possession, and thus, one can assume, where he at least has some strong practical connection with the land, and usually would believe that he was entitled to that land (unless himself a fraudster)[48] and that the land would 'remain' with him. However, in practice, except in cases such as *Walker v Burton* where the 'true' owner is not themselves interested in recovering the land, it appears that it will always be unjust not to rectify since this represents a removal of the 'true' owner's property without their consent.[49] Furthermore, even in cases like *Walker*, because the Duchy of Lancaster/Crown were not fully involved in the decision, and thus the weighing of the justice of refusing to rectify was not as fully explored as it might have been if they were interested in the land, we can probably say that the matter is not *res judicata* as far as the Duchy or Crown later bringing its own action for rectification of the Register,[50] in which they very well may succeed. Such an action, if successful, would leave the Burtons' title potentially precarious.[51] This is all caused by a failure to define 'unjust not to rectify'.

[46] LRA 2002, sch 4, para 3(2).

[47] As in *Swift 1st* (n 4) [51] (Patten LJ), thanks to the authority in *Re Chowood, Chowood Ltd v Lyall (No 2)* [1930] 2 Ch 156.

[48] In which case, the exception to the presumption in LRA 2002, sch 4, para 3(2)(a) would apply, allowing rectification against a proprietor in possession where the loss is caused by his own fraud or lack of proper care.

[49] As the courts have indicated, such a result would be a potential breach of the proprietor's rights arising from the European Convention on Human Rights, art 1 of the First Protocol. See *Knights Construction v Roberto Mac* (n 15) [61], [96] and [131] (Michael Mark). See also *Baxter v Mannion* [2011] EWCA Civ 120, [2011] 1 WLR 1594 [34] (Jacob LJ).

[50] *Walker v Burton* (n 11) [92] (Mummery LJ).

[51] *Derbyshire CC v Fallon* [2007] EWHC 1326 (Ch), [2007] 3 EGLR 44.

There is no guide as to what in fact constitutes 'justice' or 'injustice' in this context: what, if anything, apart from the off-Register position, would justify the exercise of the power to rectify against a registered proprietor in possession? The statute does not outline what is fair or 'just' in such circumstances, and in failing to do so, we are left with some ambivalence as to what might be the overall policy aim of the statute in this particular context. Thus, the wording of the statute, and its failure to articulate what constitutes justice in relation to rectification, results in a great deal of flexibility as to the weight to be given to the status of registered proprietor in possession, and therefore to the status and importance of the registered proprietor in general—producing an uneven and unpredictable guarantee of title.

The courts have therefore shown, for the most part, a desire to prioritise the 'off-Register' position where possible, by manipulating the terms of the statute to achieve that outcome. But this happens inconsistently, and there is a clear sense, both in cases where the 'true' owner is not seeking return of the land, and for the purposes of calculating an indemnity, that registration having taken place does matter. What is less clear is how much it matters, and why. This, then, can be taken to be the first defining characteristic of the relevant case law. It is argued, however, that the case law has taken analysing these matters as far as it can without a clear steer as to the policies behind these provisions, as well as a definition of 'unjust', and some statement as to how and when the off-Register position (whatever that may be) is relevant. The Law Commission consultation does not provide such a statement. The closest that it gets is to highlight a few important features of possession which may be helpful to the courts: that 'possession often reflects where land is most valued or needed';[52] and that the presumption in favour of a proprietor in possession may be 'particularly useful where possession has been for a very short time, or has fluctuated over time so that the registered proprietor is in possession almost by chance'.[53] These statements suggest that the Law Commission at least sees more than the off-Register *conveyancing* position to be critical to the exercise of the discretion, but no precise definition is provided.

B. Reliance on Indemnity to Achieve 'Overall Fairness'

We can now turn to our second general trend in the case law: a general reliance on the indemnity provisions to achieve 'overall fairness' and to compensate those who lose what appears to be a guaranteed interest, through no fault of their own. This is, in essence, the reverse of the point discussed in subsection A above. Allowing modifications of the Register based upon a broad definition of 'mistake' allows for most modifications to fall into the sub-category of 'rectifications'. This is important, for only rectifications trigger the indemnity provisions.[54] This perfectly understandable desire is, however, achieved uncertainly—through

[52] Law Com CP No 227 (n 2) para 13.104.

[53] Law Com CP No 227 (n 2) para 13.117.

[54] If, however, a narrow interpretation of mistake is adopted, then an indemnity will not be available. This is a consequence of the language in LRA 2002, sch 8, which states, in para 1(1)(a) and (b) that, 'A person is entitled to be indemnified by the registrar if he suffers loss by reason of—(a) rectification of the register, [or] (b) a mistake whose correction would involve rectification of the register'.

reliance on a very broad conception of 'mistake', through a broad conception of 'correcting',[55] or simply through manipulation of statutory provisions.[56]

The clearest examples of this are the decisions in *Swift 1st*, and in *Knights Construction*. In both cases we can see the courts using the indemnity solution as a way to mollify the 'losing' proprietor. In *Knights Construction*, the Adjudicator was aware that a failure to interpret the rectification provisions in schedule 4 in the way suggested to him by counsel for Knights Construction (the rectification claimant) would also result in the denial of an indemnity for Knights Construction, such that '[a]ny other result would fall foul of Article 1 of Protocol 1 of the Human Rights Convention unless the provisions of Schedule 8 were construed in a manner which would stretch them almost to breaking point'.[57] In other words, the availability of an indemnity was central to the approach of the Adjudicator to the question of the availability of rectification. In *Gold Harp*, too, the relevance of the availability of an indemnity to the court's general approach to the interpretation of the rectification provisions was clear. Underhill LJ reasoned that:

> The carefully structured provisions of [LRA 2002, schedule 4] paragraphs 2 and 3 (and their equivalents in the case of rectification by the Registrar), with the special protection given to a proprietor in possession, allow a fair balance between the competing interests to be struck in any particular case; and Schedule 8 gives the loser the right to an indemnity.[58]

It seems clear from these approaches that part of the reasoning in each case is that any potential unfairness caused by a willingness to allow rectification can always be remedied by the availability of an indemnity. The motivation for the courts to take this approach is clear, and the tying together of the possibility of rectification and indemnity in schedules 4 and 8 makes consideration of the availability of indemnity when assessing the possibility of rectification a natural consequence.[59] However, except in *Swift 1st*, the statement that an indemnity is available is not accompanied by any assessment as to the mechanics by which such an indemnity would be granted. The possibility of an indemnity is, in all other cases, merely assumed, rather than explored. This means that if the overriding interest approach from *Swift 1st* is adopted wholesale, the possibility of an indemnity may not be as universal as is assumed in some of the judgments—in cases where there was no forgery, for example.

C. Neglecting the Mechanics of the Transfer

The final trend which we can discern from these cases is perhaps the most important one for the problem identified here. It is that the courts, in achieving their two central policy goals—preference for the off-Register position, and use of indemnity to produce an overall 'fair' outcome—pay scant attention to the precise mechanics as to why and how a transaction has gone wrong, and why this might matter. The courts' approach is a generally broad one.

[55] *Knights Construction v Roberto Mac* (n 15) [132] (Michael Mark) and *Ajibade v Bank of Scotland plc* [2008] EWLanRA 2006_0163.

[56] *Swift 1st* (n 4) [47] (Patten LJ).

[57] *Knights Construction v Roberto Mac* (n 15) [131] (Michael Mark).

[58] *Gold Harp* (n 3) [98] (Underhill LJ).

[59] See also on this point S Cooper, 'Lack of Proper Care', ch 11 of this book.

However, it is argued here that, given the weak commitment shown to the Register, the precise mechanics as to why there is an error on the Register, and what this means in terms of the off-Register position, are critical. These mechanics explain what 'exists' or does not exist off the Register, and it is these mechanics which will also explain when an indemnity will be available.

We can see this failure to fully address the mechanics behind the decision in *Gold Harp*. Here, the court alludes to the possibility of an interest in the shape of the claimants' de-registered leases which would take priority over Gold Harp's lease,[60] but does not go into the issue in more detail given that it was not fully argued before the court.[61] In particular, there is no explanation as to *what right* the claimants would have had: some form of equitable lease arising on the de-registration of their legal lease, or a 'right to rectify' the Register as in *Swift 1st*. Although this would not have mattered in the instant case given that Gold Harp did not provide consideration for their own lease, it would be very important in other cases given the judicial discretion to rectify or not. There is no criticism of the court here—courts can only deal with the issues before them—but it is nevertheless unfortunate that more attention was not paid to this argument, not least because it would be very helpful to know what exactly the claimants had after their legal leases had been de-registered.

To conclude therefore, the courts are demonstrating three trends in their decision-making: (i) favouring the off-Register position (largely characterised by the unregistered land conveyancing rules); (ii) taking into account the possibility of an indemnity to justify their decisions; and (iii) neglecting the mechanics of the error on the Register. When these three trends are combined however, an obvious danger emerges: the courts justify their approach to rectification on the basis of the availability of an indemnity; and yet, if *Swift 1st* is correct, in many cases where it is assumed that an indemnity is so available, the claimants would have suffered no substantive loss. A failure to consider exactly what has gone wrong, what rights (if any) have arisen subsequent to the error and why, and how these rights interact with the rectification provisions, means that we have no clear judicial articulation of this potential danger.

V. Consequences of the Three Characteristics of Decision Making

There are three key areas where the characteristics identified in section IV manifest themselves in practical uncertainties: (i) in relation to the right to rectify (its status, when it would arise etc); (ii) in relation to the question of indemnity (who is entitled to an indemnity, and, importantly, for what reason); and finally (iii) in relation to the value or otherwise of an estate which is registered as part of a 'faulty' chain. Behind all of this lies the continuing failure of the case law to define 'mistake' for the purposes of rectification, despite continual calls from the academic community for a definition to be adopted. These three areas of uncertainty—which, it is suggested, are a direct result of the judicial

[60] *Gold Harp* (n 3) [34]: 'I would suppose, the result of the basic rule is that the Claimants' leases enjoy priority irrespective of the Judge's order, simply by being prior in time' (Underhill LJ).

[61] ibid.

approach outlined above (albeit an approach arguably caused in part by failures in the statutory provisions)—will be considered in turn.

A. Rights to Rectify and Overriding Interests

Whilst this is not the place to discuss the meaning and nature of the right to rectify in detail,[62] what can be said at this point is that there is undoubted inconsistency on this point in the case law, and that this inconsistency causes serious problems in practice in terms of assessing: (a) when the Register will be rectified, and (b) what the value of a right which is registered by mistake might be, for the purposes of assessing loss for an indemnity award. Underhill LJ in *Gold Harp* expresses himself to be somewhat uncomfortable with the idea that the issue of changes (alterations and rectifications) to the Register can be resolved by simply relying on the priority rules.[63] Furthermore, in his analysis, he appears to be of the view that the relevant right which would take priority would be the claimants' leases themselves[64] not some other right in the nature of a right to rectify, thus muddying further the position in relation to such rights. However, in *Swift 1st*, the question emerged whether it was correct to state that:

> Swift's registered charge therefore took effect subject to any overriding interest which Mrs Rani could assert against its title. The Registrar's position is that this would include her right to have the charge removed from the register as a void disposition by reason of the forgery. On this basis Swift's charge, although substantively registered, was always liable to be defeated by a claim brought by Mrs Rani and was never therefore de facto enforceable against the registered title to the Property at least so long as she remained its owner.[65]

Thus, the issue was not whether the charge could be removed or a question of priority *per se*—that was clear on the basis that the transfer granting the charge was itself void—but rather whether the charge was always subject to a prior right of the registered owner to remove the charge on the basis of actual occupation, such that it was valueless. The logic of this position is doubtful, but in *Swift 1st* the court does reason that the 'right to rectify' approach was the correct one, albeit that the court then utilised the statutory fiction[66] to give the charge value once more—thereby meaning that strictly speaking, the conclusions on the right to rectify are *obiter* (the statutory fiction would have applied either way, since there was a forgery). However, on a fair reading of *Swift 1st*, the possibility of an overriding proprietary interest taking priority over a forged charge, such that the charge is always subject to the ability of the true registered proprietor to remove the charge, is accepted. This tension—which concerns whether the right to rectify is a property interest which is capable of binding a subsequent disponee within sections 28–30 of the LRA 2002—is a matter of inconsistency in the case law which cannot be resolved here. In particular, it is not entirely clear how a right to rectify could be relevant in *priority* terms as against the immediate transferee given that any such right could only arise *after* the disputed disposition. On this point, the Law Commission has

[62] Cooper and Lees (n 23).

[63] *Gold Harp* (n 3) [34] (Underhill LJ).

[64] ibid.

[65] *Swift 1st* (n 4) [10] (Patten LJ).

[66] That forged dispositions should be treated as valid dispositions for the purpose of calculating loss—see LRA 2002, sch 8, para (1)(2)(b).

recommended that any right to rectify which arises should not have the ability to override.[67] They do not however resolve the fundamental controversy as to whether it does arise in the first place, and so do not provide a full solution to this problem.[68] What, however, can be said, is that the presence of this inconsistency demonstrates that there is no clear understanding of the precise mechanics as to what rights arise, and why, and when, when there is a mistaken registration, and under what circumstances these rights can be defeated by a later registered proprietor. That this question has never been resolved is symptomatic of the fact that the courts' tendency has, quite understandably, been to focus on the particular question before them and designing a bespoke response to that outcome, without direct reference to solutions to different, but related, questions.

B. Questions of Indemnity

A further difficulty relates to the question of indemnity. The question as to who is entitled to an indemnity, and under what circumstances, is a matter of great uncertainty. In part, as has been discussed elsewhere, the difficulty in determining the answer is a reflection of the fact that there has been no commitment to any one definition of 'mistake'. Without a clear definition of mistake, it is of course impossible to have a consistent approach to indemnity, since indemnity is premised on the correction of a mistake (or a court's decision to decline to correct a mistake). There are, however, further difficulties, not least the difficulty outlined immediately above in relation to *Swift 1st*. Where registration is mistaken, and the Register is rectified, the person who 'loses' their registered estate/interest in land as a result of that rectification ought to be entitled to an indemnity if it cannot be shown that they contributed to their own loss by fraud or lack of proper care.[69] However, *Swift 1st* indicates that, except in cases of forgery—where the statutory fiction of a deemed 'loss' can be employed—there is likely to be no indemnity thanks to the existence of an overriding interest. This raises the odd spectre of having indemnity unavailable in lots of cases even where rectification takes place because there is a 'prior interest' (although, logically, it could only have arisen after the disputed disposition) which takes priority. The prior interest, in such cases, would be relevant only to questions of indemnity, and not to the availability of rectification per se, since that will depend upon the presumptions in schedule 4 (albeit that these presumptions seem to operate in such a way that they are determined by the hypothetical existence of any off-Register 'rights' which would have existed had the situation arisen in relation to unregistered land).

Thus, for example, where a freehold title is registered pursuant to a forged transfer, whether or not the court will rectify the Register depends, as in *Walker v Burton*, first, on whether the registered proprietor is in possession, and therefore whether the presumption against rectification applies, and secondly, if so, whether it would be unjust not to rectify etc. However, the availability of an indemnity for the person who thereby loses out depends not upon these factors as such, but on whether they have lost anything as a result of the twin combination of the actual occupation of the previous proprietor, and the statutory fiction applying to forgery.

[67] Law Com CP No 227 (n 2) para 13.60 ff.

[68] For a full analysis of the limitations of the Law Commission's proposals on this point, see Cooper and Lees (n 23).

[69] LRA 2002, sch 8, para 5.

To make matters more complex, if we consider a 'down the chain' conveyance, so that the registration of the transfer from A to B is mistaken (be that due to forgery, or an administrative mistake) and then B conveys to C, then a multitude of options emerges. First, following *Knights Construction v Roberto Mac* and its endorsement in *Gold Harp*, the registration of C can be undone, even though it is not itself a mistake, as part of the process of 'correcting the mistake'. However, C may not be entitled to an indemnity even on this position, if the approach in *Swift 1st* is followed, because the transfer to C is not a forgery, and therefore C cannot take advantage of the statutory fiction benefiting those who take 'under' a forged disposition, if the 'true' owner (A) happened to be in actual occupation at the time of the registration such that they had an interest which could override the disposition. In such a situation, C would be removed from the Register as part of the consequences of the original mistake, but not being able to rely on *Swift 1st*, where A is in actual occupation at the time of C's transfer, so that C would have lost nothing of value. However, if the court concluded that it would not rectify against the proprietor in possession, C (were C to be in possession), then C would be able to retain the entire value of the right, whether or not A had in fact been in actual occupation at the time of the transfer.

Whilst these outcomes are not in direct conflict with one another, they can hardly represent a satisfactory series of outcomes demonstrating a consistency of treatment and principle. By treating the rights of the original proprietor as being capable of overriding for the purposes of calculating an indemnity, but not seeing these currently as determinative to the question of *rectification* of the Register, the strange outcome can emerge whereby the decision facing the court, where A is in actual occupation, is between: (a) leaving C on the Register, thereby leaving C with the full value of the right, or (b) removing C from the Register, whilst at the same time stating that C has lost nothing of value because there was a prior interest (ie A's interest) which took priority.

A second, more obvious, potential inconsistency is the inconsistency which emerges where there is no forgery. As has been considered elsewhere, we ought to consider why forgery is treated differently from all other causes of a void transaction.[70] Thus, '[*Swift 1st*] means that the proprietor registered because of a non-forged, but nevertheless mistaken conveyance, would not be entitled to an indemnity, whereas his lucky compatriot whose loss arose from forgery, rather than mistake, would be so entitled'.[71] Such an outcome is made particularly problematic when we consider it against the background of decisions such as *Knights Construction v Roberto Mac*, where the very justification for the ability of the court to return parties to the position they would have been in had no mistake been made is premised upon the availability of an indemnity, *whether or not* there is a forgery, and regardless of the actual occupation of the wronged proprietor.

However, these are not the only difficulties which may be encountered by utilising indemnity solutions 'down the chain'. A further difficulty may emerge in relation to the existence or otherwise of a duty to mitigate loss. There is, for example, no duty in relation to land registration, to pursue other possible sources of indemnity before pursuing the Land Registry itself. In effect, the Land Registry 'takes over' the ability to sue third parties in relation to the faulty registration. However, where there is some doubt as to the scope of a potential indemnity claim due to the current inconsistency in the case law, and the

[70] E Lees, 'Registration Make-Believe and Forgery' (n 1) 517–18.
[71] ibid.

problematic interaction between leading decisions, it is far from clear what losses will in fact be compensated by the Land Registry, thus motivating those who lose out as a result of land registration problems to pursue other avenues first. We may not conclude that this is a position to be avoided: the Land Registry is, for the moment, a public body after all. However, it is not perhaps what was intended by the land registration system and it does not represent anything approaching the insurance model which the rhetoric of the Law Commission report, which led to the LRA 2002, at least implies.[72]

In short, therefore, the prevailing approach in the courts, characterised by a narrow focus on an individual issue, produces inconsistencies, both in terms of when an indemnity is available, and in terms of how that indemnity is calculated. The result of this is likely to be an incentive to avoid pursuing indemnity claims where other more certain claims may be available. This is to be regretted in a system which claimed to be premised on making titles simpler and more secure, and may result in the need to take a 'title insurance' style approach, despite the difficulties that such an approach causes elsewhere.

C. Chains of Conveyance

Finally, there appears to be inconsistency and uncertainty in the position of the person who takes a registered title under a flawed chain of conveyance. Although the conveyance to them (and consequent registration) was perfectly valid on its own terms, if there was a flaw in the chain of conveyance somewhere in the past, it may be necessary to remove the current registered proprietor's title from the Register, in order to correct an earlier mistake. Clarity as to whether this is possible is obviously essential. Prior to the coming into force of the LRA 2002's provisions relating to adverse possession, 'chains of conveyance' problems would be fixed, eventually, by the automatic vesting of title. Where a flawed (ie, non-consensual) purported disposition between A and B was followed by an unbroken period of 12 years in which the land was possessed by either the original non-consensual transferee (B), or subsequent consensual transferees from B (ie, to C, and then D, etc), the flaw from A to B would no longer be of relevance.[73] However, under the new law in the LRA 2002, where adverse possession does not happen in this way, there can be no such 'fixing' of the flaw in the title.[74] Thus, it becomes necessary to make a direct policy choice about the position of a registered proprietor who obtains title through such a chain of conveyance, and it becomes necessary to do so for chains of conveyances from the commencement of compulsory registration of title onwards, since the statute contains no time limit for rectification claims. As a result, when *Knights Construction v Roberto Mac* speaks of needing to travel steps down the chain in order to 'correct the [earlier] mistake', it becomes necessary to ask how far down this chain a rectification claim extends, if, as appears clear from *Gold Harp*, the Register does not in fact impose a sort of deferred indefeasibility; rather, it confers a discretionary indefeasibility.

In particular, we might validly ask in this regard, whether the question of 'unjust not to rectify', and therefore the position of the proprietor in possession in schedule 4, is at all

[72] Law Commission, *Land Registration for the Twenty First-Century: A Conveyancing Revolution* (Law Com No 271, 2001) para 1.7.

[73] Limitation Act 1980, ss 15 and 17.

[74] LRA 2002, ss 96–97 and sch 6.

affected by the length of the chain of conveyance, and any delay in seeking rectification. As outlined above, there appears to be a weak consensus that the reference in the statutory provisions to 'unjust' is a reference to what the position would have been in unregistered land, rather than a tool to allow the courts to make a merits-based assessment as to who deserves title the most, and why. However, it could validly be argued that part of this assessment ought to be some consideration as to how far down the chain of conveyance it would be 'just' to rectify the Register. The Law Commission response to this is simply to institute a time-based cut off (10 years).[75] This is a pragmatic solution, but as with the other issues raised in this paper, the pragmatic solution, in a sense, merely papers over the more conceptual difficulties.

VI. A Change of Perspective or a Change to the Statute: Guarantee of Title, or Guarantee that no Other Title Exists?

From assessing the existing case law, and some of the characteristics of this case law, as well as the uncertainties to which these lead, it is possible to discern some essential elements which are absent from the current statutory provisions, and which are required if we are to make progress in providing a land registration system which operates not only in a consistent manner, but also in such a way as to meet its policy goals. These are, first, that either through statutory reform, or through case law, we must develop a consistent approach as to what constitutes 'unjust' circumstances and therefore, we must decide precisely what the relationship is between the rules of conveyancing for unregistered land, and the land registration system. The Law Commission does not achieve this.[76] Secondly, there needs to be a clear commitment to what substantive rights arise, if any, following mistakes on the Register (eg, a right to rectify). Again, whilst *one* aspect of this would be resolved by the Law Commission proposal, the fundamental and conceptual issues are not addressed. Finally, there needs to be some explicit assessment of how far down a 'chain of conveyance' rectification and indemnity are allowed, and if all the way down that chain, how losses are calculated down the chain and where any duty to mitigate loss might fit into this process. The existing reliance on indemnity as central to the fair operation of the system means that commitment is required as to exactly when and how much indemnity is permitted. Here, the Law Commission does provide some assistance with the ten-year long stop cut-off—at which point title becomes indefeasible—but the indemnity issues are not resolved.

The precise scope of these problems is not immediately clear, however, and this may account for the failure in solving them to date. It is suggested that such problems are much clearer if we focus on the question 'what does the Register guarantee/promise *not* to exist?', rather than the question 'what does the Register guarantee/promise *does* exist?'. When looked at from this perspective, it becomes much clearer that a solution to these problems is required, and therefore this perspective can provide a useful 'cross-check' in the reform procedure. By way of example, we could argue that where there is a guaranteed title, there must also be a corresponding guarantee that no other titles to the land exist.

[75] Law Com CP No 227 (n 2), paras 13.124–13.125.
[76] Law Com CP No 227 (n 2).

If the only way that title is conferred is by registration, then no other title should exist but for registration. But we know this not to be true (not least because not all leasehold titles must be registered under sections 4 and 27 of the LRA 2002), and so instead we need to have a more nuanced explanation of what the Register guarantees does not exist. We can split this into three further sub-questions: first, when a person is mistakenly de-registered, what do they have? We know that a conveyance to them cannot be of effect at law until such times as the conveyance is *completed by registration*. What happens where the conveyance was completed by registration, but the registration has now been reversed, ie the title has been de-registered? Does this give rise to any rights on the part of the now de-registered 'proprietor'? If so, the registration system does not guarantee that any former proprietors have 'lost' their title to land even though they no longer appear on the Register. Secondly, does the Register provide by its guarantee of title that no better proprietary interest or administrative power in the land exist which will justify the removal of the registered proprietor? Again, we know the answer to this is 'no', but we must nevertheless ask *how far* that answer is 'no' and in particular we need to know whether all such proprietary interests are governed by the priority rules in sections 28–30 of the LRA 2002, or whether they are subject to some other regime. Finally, where a person relies on the Register to ascertain whether they are safe in, for example, purchasing a leasehold estate or registered charge in a registered estate held by X, does the Register both guarantee that X *does* hold an estate in the land, and that *no other person does* (or at least that no other person does which will have priority over the potential purchaser)? Again, we know the answer to this is 'no'.

By considering the question of what the Register guarantees from this perspective, it becomes clear just how much we do not know. There is a growing practical consensus that the question of section 58, the meaning of mistake, and the availability of an indemnity are becoming increasingly settled. This could not be further from the truth. Rather, it is very clear that the multiplicity of case law which decides only one small point, without ever openly considering both the result and obiter comments of other, related cases, has produced a situation which is replete with implicit inconsistencies, and explicit uncertainties.

There is, in short, no consistent approach to the question of what registration actually guarantees. The characteristics of the judicial approach discussed here—weak but inconsistent preference for the off-Register position without any consistent explanation as to what is relevant about that position and why; a preference to manipulate indemnity provisions to produce a 'fair' outcome even where the statutory provisions do not naturally provide for it; and the failure to articulate what the mechanics of faulty registrations are—are causes of this uncertainty. However, it is argued here that, more fundamentally, they are symptoms of a failure in the statutory provisions to articulate answers to two fundamental questions: first, when is registration mistaken; and secondly, what does the Register guarantee *does exist* and what does it guarantee *does not* exist. Until the statutory provisions answer these key questions, the small uncertainties that exist now will continue to multiply and pose difficulties in practice.

8

Can Rectification be Retrospective?

CHARLES HARPUM

I. Introduction

The titles to the vast majority of properties in England and Wales are now registered. Every day, solicitors, conveyancers, barristers, and no doubt many other professionals, refer to and examine registered titles to properties. This examination will often precede a transaction and it will form the basis for an evaluation of the title. Sometimes, the examination will be conducted because something has gone wrong. Whatever the reason for perusing the Register, a decision will commonly be taken in reliance upon the information that it provides. In other words, money will often be spent or lent in consequence of the evaluation of the title as it is disclosed in the Register.

In the joint report of the Law Commission and the Land Registry which accompanied the draft Bill that was subsequently enacted as the Land Registration Act ('LRA') 2002, Law Commission, *Land Registration for the Twenty-First Century: A Conveyancing Revolution* (Law Com No 271, 2011) ('LC 271'), it was stated that:

> The fundamental objective of the Bill is that, under the system of electronic dealing with land that it seeks to create, the register should be a complete and accurate reflection of the state of the title of the land at any given time, so that it is possible to investigate title to land on line, with the absolute minimum of additional inquiries and inspections.[1]

The importance of that passage has not escaped judicial attention.[2]

Although the system of electronic conveyancing that was created by the LRA 2002 will not now be implemented in the form enacted, the fundamental objective that was set out by the Law Commission and the Land Registry in LC 271, in the paragraph quoted above, was in fact an acknowledgment of the practical reality. The Register *is* constantly relied upon and conveyancing would not operate smoothly if it was not. While mistakes in the Register are made, and everyone knows that they are, the correction of those mistakes by alteration of the Register within the framework provided by the LRA 2002 should reflect the 'fundamental objective' set out in LC 271. As this article explains, that is what the Law

[1] Law Commission, *Land Registration for the Twenty-First Century: A Conveyancing Revolution* (Law Com No 271, 2001) para 1.5.

[2] See the remarks of Lewison LJ in *Cherry Tree Investments Ltd v Landmain Ltd* [2012] EWCA Civ 736, [2013] Ch 305 [105] ff.

Commission and the Land Registry had intended. Until recently, the provisions were interpreted in accordance with that intention. That is no longer the case.

The provisions for the alteration and rectification of the Register are found in schedule 4 of the LRA 2002. The question addressed in this chapter is whether rectification—that is to say the alteration of the Register to correct a mistake that prejudicially affects the title of a registered proprietor—can have retrospective effect. The answer to that question must turn on the true meaning of schedule 4, paragraph 8 of the LRA 2002, which provides that:

> The powers under this Schedule to alter the register, so far as relating to rectification, extend to changing for the future the priority of any interest affecting the registered estate or charge concerned.

This question whether rectification of the Register can be retrospective has been the subject of a recent decision of the Court of Appeal in *Gold Harp Properties Ltd v MacLeod* ('*Gold Harp*').[3] The court comprised Richards, Sullivan and Underhill LJJ.[4] The sole reasoned judgment was given by Underhill LJ.

II. The Facts of *Gold Harp*

The facts of the case were striking and, in the light of them, there was a very short answer to the case as I shall explain; but although Underhill LJ appreciated the point, the case had not been argued on the basis of that very short answer.

The case concerned a three storey building near Ladbroke Grove. Originally the whole house had been owned by the claimants—who were a group of school teachers—but in due course, the freehold and possession of the first and second floors were acquired by a company that was owned by Mr Grahame Ralph ('GR'). Long leases of the two flats on the top floor were granted in 2000 for terms of 135 years from 27 July 1988,[5] in favour of the claimants. Nobody lived on the top floor. The claimant teachers went to work in Africa.

GR wanted to acquire the top floor and develop the property, but he did not want to pay the claimants for their leases. The following events occurred, all of which were orchestrated by GR:

(i) The freehold was vested in GR's son.

(ii) In 2009, there was a delay by the claimants in paying the ground rent. The landlord could only forfeit the leases if that delay exceeded three months.

(iii) Before the three months had elapsed, GR's son purported to forfeit the leases by peaceable re-entry.

(iv) Shortly afterwards, and again before the expiry of the three month period, the arrears of rent were sent to GR, as the claimants had not been told of the change in the freeholder.

[3] [2014] EWCA Civ 1084, [2015] 1 WLR 1249.

[4] No member of the court had a Chancery background.

[5] The exact date does not appear from the report, but is present in the Register of title.

(v) In those circumstances, the trial judge found that the purported forfeiture of the leases was ineffective. That decision was not challenged on appeal.
(vi) GR's son applied to the Land Registry to have the registered titles to the two leases closed and for the notices of the leases on the freehold title to be cancelled. The Land Registry obliged. Because the leases were in fact still on foot, these changes to the Registers were a mistake for the purposes of the rectification provisions in schedule 4 of the LRA 2002.
(vii) GR's son then granted a new lease of the top floor to a company owned by an associate for 135 years from 27 July 1988.[6] This was said to be for a premium. That lease was duly registered and then assigned, first to one of GR's companies, and then to Gold Harp Properties Limited ('Gold Harp'), which was another of GR's companies.
(viii) Although both the grant of the lease and the two successive assignments were stated to have been made for valuable consideration, the trial judge found that no consideration had in fact been paid.

When these facts came to light, the claimants sought to have their leases reinstated in the Register with priority over the lease held by Gold Harp. On those facts, it is difficult not to be very sympathetic to the claimants. The trial judge granted the relief they sought and Gold Harp unsuccessfully appealed to the Court of Appeal.

III. The Issues

In this chapter, the *Gold Harp* case is considered under the following headings:

(i) Was there a short answer on the facts of the case?
(ii) The principal issue.
(iii) What were the consequences of dismissing of the appeal?
(iv) What would the consequences have been if the appeal had been allowed?
(v) What are the wider consequences of the case?

It is the thesis of this chapter that this is an example of a hard case making bad law, though it need not have been so. The appellant—in substance GR, acting through companies he controlled—was wholly devoid of merit and had behaved in an appalling manner and deserved no sympathy. Few, if any, would cavil at the outcome, but it is the argument of this chapter that the route that led to the result was achieved by a misinterpretation of the LRA 2002.

IV. Was there a Short Answer on the Facts of the Case?

On the facts, there clearly was a short answer to the case. Although the registered titles to the claimants' leases had been wrongly closed, so that they ceased to be legal estates, they

[6] This does not appear from the report but, again, is present in the Register of title.

still subsisted in equity (that must follow as a correlative from section 27(1) of the LRA 2002).[7] As both the grant and transfers of the new lease had not been made for valuable consideration, the claimants' equitable leases would have had priority over the new lease under the basic rule of priority in section 28 of the LRA 2002, by which (in essence) the first interest in time of creation prevails. Gold Harp could not avail itself of the protection of section 29 of the LRA 2002, because the grant and transfers of the new lease were not made for valuable consideration as section 29 requires. Accordingly, the absence of any protective notices in the Register was irrelevant. Underhill LJ drew attention to this point,[8] but, because there was no respondent's notice taking it, the Court of Appeal considered that it could not decide the case on that basis. This is unfortunate, because it was the true answer to the case. By not resolving the case on that basis, the Court of Appeal had to proceed on the basis of an assumption that was not factually correct—namely, that Gold Harp was not bound by the interests of the claimants under the priority provisions of the LRA 2002, even though it was not a purchaser for valuable consideration.

V. The Principal Issue

The principal issue in the case—and the only one that is relevant to this paper—was whether the Register of the freehold title should be rectified retrospectively when reinstating the registration of the leases, so that those leases had priority over the subsequent lease held by Gold Harp. That in turn depended, as explained above, on the interpretation of schedule 4, paragraph 8 of the LRA 2002, and in particular, on the words 'for the future'.

It is of course true that the decision of the Court of Appeal will stand unless and until it is reversed by the Supreme Court. Cases before the Supreme Court on conveyancing matters are rare and there is in practice little prospect of the matter coming before the highest tribunal. However, given the importance of the point in the scheme of the land registration, it merits a careful analysis. It is also right that the Law Commission's clear intentions at the time of the LRA 2002—which are explained below—should be flagged.[9] A decision will have to be taken as part of the review of the LRA 2002 that the Law Commission is presently undertaking, whether the interpretation originally intended by the Law Commission should be reinstated, or whether the interpretation in *Gold Harp* should be accepted and perhaps ameliorated in other ways.

In his judgment, Underhill LJ undertook a lengthy analysis of the legislative history of schedule 4, paragraph 8 of the LRA 2002. For the purposes of this paper it is unnecessary to

[7] LRA 2002, s 27(1) provides that, 'If a disposition of a registered estate or registered charge is required to be completed by registration, it does not operate at law until the relevant registration requirements are met'.

[8] *Gold Harp* (n 3) [34].

[9] The reform of land registration at the Law Commission was a tortuous and at times acrimonious process. The matter was neutrally summarised at Law Commission, *Land Registration for the Twenty-First Century—A Consultative Document* (Law Com No 254, 1988) paras 1.7–1.9.

dissect that analysis. What is important for present purposes is that Underhill LJ concluded, after that analysis, that the words 'for the future' in paragraph 8 meant that:

(i) rectification could be retrospective; but
(ii) the person who sought rectification and who was the beneficiary of the change in priority could only exercise his rights as owner of that interest, to the exclusion of the rights of the owner of the competing interest, from the moment that the order for rectification was made.[10] Accordingly, that person could not, for example, sue for trespass for the period prior to the court order.

It is explained below that that was certainly *not* what schedule 4, paragraph 8 of the LRA 2002, was intended to do—or at least it was only part of what paragraph 8 was meant to do.

The fundamental question in *Gold Harp* was whether schedule 4, paragraph 8 of the LRA 2002 had been intended to change the law from what it had been under the Land Registration Act ('LRA') 1925. The relevant provision of the LRA 1925 was section 82(2), which provided that:

> The register may be rectified under this section, notwithstanding that the rectification may affect any estates, rights, charges, or interests acquired or protected by registration, or by any entry on the register, or otherwise.

There were two decisions under the LRA 1925 in which it was held that rectification took effect only from the date specified by the court in its order and that rectification could not be retrospective. These cases were *Freer v Unwins Ltd* ('*Freer*')[11] and *Clark v Chief Land Registrar* at first instance ('*Clark*').[12]

In simplified summary, what happened in *Freer* was that when the freehold title of a shop was first registered, a restrictive covenant, previously protected as a land charge, was not entered on the charges register of the freehold title. The freeholder then granted a lease (which was for 21 years and not therefore registrable). Following an assignment of the lease, the assignee traded in breach of the restrictive covenant of which he was oblivious. The Register of the freehold title was then rectified and the question arose as to whether the lessee was bound by the rectification. Walton J held that he was not. This was because, when the lessee took the assignment, the restrictive covenant was not entered in the Register of the freehold title. Unfortunately, nobody cited section 82(2) of the LRA 1925 to Walton J. However, Walton J made it clear that, if the lease had been registrable, he would not have exercised his discretion to rectify it on the facts before him.[13]

Freer was followed by Ferris J in *Clark* at first instance.[14] It is unnecessary to go into the facts of the case, but it arose out of the Land Registry's failure to act upon an entry in the Register (a caution). After reviewing *Freer*, Ferris J expressed his doubts as to whether he

[10] *Gold Harp* (n 3) [96].
[11] *Freer v Unwins Ltd* [1976] Ch 288 (Ch).
[12] *Clark v Chief Land Registrar* [1993] Ch 294 (Ch).
[13] *Freer* (n 11) 299.
[14] *Clark* (n 12).

had any power to order retrospective rectification, because there was no express power to do so in the LRA 1925.[15] However, he said:

> even if the court has the power I consider that it would not be right to exercise it in this way in the circumstances of this case, particularly when this too would merely substitute the second defendant for the plaintiffs as a claimant to an indemnity.[16]

As in *Freer*, section 82(2) of the LRA 1925 was not cited to Ferris J. On appeal, the Court of Appeal in *Clark* said that there was no doubt that Ferris J had been correct in his decision on rectification.[17] Once again, however, section 82(2) was not cited to the court.

Both *Freer* and *Clark* could be regarded as incorrect because they were decided *per incuriam* without consideration of section 82(2) of the LRA 1925. In the Law Commission's 1998 Consultative Document, *Land Registration for the Twenty-First Century*,[18] doubts were expressed about the correctness of the two decisions precisely because they did not refer to section 82(2).[19] The inference from that paragraph was that section 82(2) would be re-enacted as it was in any new Land Registration Act. But, as anyone who has worked at the Law Commission knows, views change between consultation and final report. Opinions are expressed on consultation that must be carefully and fully considered. A very great deal evolves and develops following such consultation. The structure of a draft Bill emerges and very detailed instructions to Parliamentary Counsel are prepared. The proposals are then subjected to intense and highly critical scrutiny by Parliamentary Counsel. There are frequently second thoughts in the light of such scrutiny. The draft Bill and draft report are then subject to further critical analysis by the other Commissioners. Those criticisms are often telling and have to be met. In short, it is the final report that accompanies the draft Bill that matters, not the preceding consultations or (in this case) any earlier reports. It is only that final report that contains the concluded views of the Commissioners.

What changed after the 1998 Consultative Report was a realisation that *Freer* and *Clark* did in fact embody a principle that was fundamental to the Bill that was being prepared. That principle, mentioned above, was that a person should be entitled to rely on the correctness of the Register at any given time.[20] Of course that principle was subject to the countervailing principles of alteration and rectification that the Bill was to embody, but the Bill restricted the ambit of rectification much as did the considerably enhanced protection against rectification given to proprietors in possession.[21]

[15] ibid, 317–18.

[16] ibid, 318.

[17] *Clark v Chief Land Registrar* [1994] Ch 370 (CA) 385.

[18] Law Com No 254 (n 9) para 8.33.

[19] Similar doubts had been expressed by the Law Commission in its earlier reports on land registration. However, in the draft Bill that was produced at that stage—see the *Fourth Report on Land Registration* (Law Com No 173, 1988)—cl 44(2) provided (with emphasis added): 'A register may be rectified under this section, notwithstanding that the rectification may affect any registered, protected, overriding or minor interest; and an entry giving effect to a rectification under this section shall have effect, or be deemed to have had effect, *from such date as may be specified in the entry*.' In other words, the court would have been given a discretion as to the date from which rectification was to take effect as well as whether to rectify. That was not a straight re-enactment of the LRA 1925, s 82(2). It was thought to be necessary to make express provision as to when rectification should take effect.

[20] Law Com No 271 (n 1) para 1.5. This principle was particularly important because of the proposals for the introduction of electronic conveyancing under which transactions would be made and simultaneously registered.

[21] It should also be noted that in *unregistered* conveyancing, in the equivalent situation where a land charge—say a restrictive covenant—was not disclosed on an official search, a purchaser of a legal estate for money or money's worth would take free of the interest because of the conclusive effect of a certificate of search: that is the effect of Land Charges Act 1972, ss 4(6) and 10(4) when read together. That is the same result as in *Freer* and *Clark*.

The matter was set out as follows in the final joint report of the Law Commission and the Land Registry that accompanied the draft Land Registration Bill (with the footnotes as in the original), at paragraph 10.8:[22]

The Bill makes it clear that

(1) rectification of the register, whether by order of the court or by the register can (as now)[23] affect derivative interests; but
(2) any such changes are prospective only,[24] which accords with the manner in which the analogous provisions of the Land Registration Act 1925 have been interpreted.[25]

The hubristic nature of the word 'clear' in that passage has now become apparent.

In *Gold Harp*, Underhill LJ commented on that paragraph from where he said 'is not entirely easy to reconcile with the references to *Freer* in the earlier reports, but there is no discussion of the specific proposition in it which was being endorsed'.[26]

The *reasons* for a change of direction may not have been spelt out in the Law Commission/Land Registry joint report, but what paragraph 10.8 made clear was that there had been such a change. The intention of schedule 4, paragraph 8, as set out in the joint report, was to codify the law as it stood at the date of the Act, so that it both:

(i) Carried forward the principle in section 82(2) of the LRA 1925 that derivative interests could be rectified; and
(ii) Added the gloss in *Freer* and *Clark*, that any such rectification was only prospective in effect.

Whatever the references may have been to *Freer* in earlier reports of the Law Commission, paragraph 10.8 of the joint report was clear and unequivocal. There was no accidental overlooking of the position adopted in the 1998 Consultative Document,[27] but a deliberate and considered decision to codify *Freer*. Furthermore, that interpretation much more naturally explains the wording of schedule 4, paragraph 8 of the LRA 2002, than the interpretation adopted by the Court of Appeal. Underhill LJ's conclusion that 'there is nothing in the drafting of the bill or its exposition in the 2001 report to suggest any change from the thinking in the 1998 consultation paper'[28] is, with respect, factually incorrect. There was an explicit statement that a different view was being taken in paragraph 10.8 of the 2001 joint report.[29] It has been explained above why changes often occur in the process of preparing a Law Commission Bill.

In preparing this chapter, I have re-read the Instructions to Parliamentary Counsel on what became schedule 4, paragraph 8[30] of the LRA 2002, and it is from those Instructions

[22] Law Com No 271 (n 1) para 10.8.
[23] See Land Registration Act 1925, s 82(2).
[24] See sch 4, para 8.
[25] The Land Registration Act 1925 is not explicit on this point: see *Freer* (n 11) 296.
[26] *Gold Harp* (n 3) [64].
[27] Law Com No 254 (n 9).
[28] *Gold Harp* (n 3) [65].
[29] Law Com No 271 (n 1).
[30] The Instructions were drafted by a senior Land Registry lawyer in conjunction with one of the Law Commission's Government Legal Service lawyers and myself. I handled the subsequent exchanges with Parliamentary Counsel in close consultation with the Solicitor to the Land Registry.

that I have been able to summarise the position above. Those Instructions explicitly stated that the substance of section 82(2) of the LRA 1925 was to be retained. However, Parliamentary Counsel was also instructed to give effect in the Bill to the objective that 'any rectification of the register shall not have retrospective effect'. The Instructions contained a full consideration of the law and a discussion of both *Freer* and *Clark*. Of course, such matters are not admissible in interpreting a statute that enacted a Law Commission Bill, but paragraph 10.8 of the 2001 joint report *was* plainly admissible—and was considered by the Court of Appeal—and that paragraph reflected the Instructions to Parliamentary Counsel. It should be noted that the intended interpretation of schedule 4, paragraph 8, was accepted on two occasions in proceedings before a Deputy Adjudicator to the Land Registry.[31]

In the *Gold Harp* case, the principal interpretative justification that was given by the Court of Appeal for its decision is found in Underhill LJ's judgment.[32] The argument put to the court was that 'an alteration to a priority which already exists cannot be described as an alteration "for the future"'. Underhill LJ's response to that was that:

> if that is right then their effect [that is the words 'for the future'] is to prevent the Court from changing priorities in the very situation which paragraph 8 is intended to address. There is no problem of competing priorities once the rectification has been achieved. The only priorities that could be changed relate, necessarily, to interests which have already been created.

On the face of it that is a very compelling argument, but on closer analysis it will not, with respect, bear scrutiny. The matter can be tested this way. Suppose that schedule 4, paragraph 8 did not contain the words 'for the future', but read as follows:

> The powers under this Schedule to alter the register, so far as relating to rectification, extend to changing the priority of any interest affecting the registered estate or charge concerned.

Anyone reading that provision would immediately ask the question: 'from what date is rectification to take effect?'. They would particularly ask that question because, when a *document* is rectified, rectification is retrospective in its effect. Paragraph 8 answers that question by providing that priorities are to be changed 'for the future'. Those priorities are therefore *not* to be changed retrospectively to the time of the mistake.

VI. What were the Consequences of Dismissing the Appeal?

Because of the rather obvious merits, the Court of Appeal was no doubt determined to find a way of rectifying the Register in such a way that the claimants recovered their leases in possession. The court wished to ensure they were not left merely with an indemnity from the Land Registry.

[31] See *Piper Trust Ltd v Caruso (UK) Ltd* [2010] EWLandRA 2009_0623 (Land Registry Adjudicator); *DB UK Bank Ltd v Santander UK plc* [2012] EWLandRA 2011_1169 (Land Registry Adjudicator). The present writer argued the point successfully as counsel for Santander UK plc in the latter case.

[32] *Gold Harp* (n 3) [94].

The consequences of dismissing the appeal were as follows:

(i) The claimants were entitled to their leases in possession.
(ii) Gold Harp held a lease of the reversion on the claimants' two leases.
(iii) Gold Harp's lease was for an identical term to those two leases and all that it entitled Gold Harp to receive were the payments of ground rent from the claimants and possibly other payments that may have been due under those leases.
(iv) Such a lease of the reversion would have very little value and would certainly be far less valuable than a lease in possession, especially as such a lease in possession would have enabled GR to carry out a development of the property.
(v) Gold Harp would be entitled to *claim* indemnity for loss caused by the rectification from the Land Registry under schedule 8, paragraph 1(1)(a) of the LRA 2002.
(vi) Whether Gold Harp would in fact *recover* any indemnity is a question that cannot be answered without a much fuller knowledge of the facts. However, it is highly likely that any such claim would be vigorously resisted by the Land Registry under the provisions of schedule 8, paragraph 5 of the LRA 2002. Under that paragraph, no indemnity is payable in cases of fraud or where the loss is caused wholly by the applicant's lack of care, and there is also reduction for contributory negligence.

VII. What Would the Consequences have been if the Appeal had been Allowed?

While it is impossible not to sympathise with the distaste that the Court of Appeal rightly felt at the appalling behaviour of the appellants, it is respectfully suggested that the appeal should have been allowed on the retrospectivity point. If that had happened the consequences would have been as follows:

(i) Gold Harp's lease would have remained in possession.
(ii) The claimants' leases would have taken effect in reversion and they would have been entitled to such rent, if any, as was due under Gold Harp's lease.
(iii) As the claimants' leases were rendered effectively worthless, they would have been entitled to an indemnity for the value of their leases from the Land Registry under schedule 8, paragraphs 1(1)(b) and (3) of the LRA 2002. Quantum would have been determined under schedule 8, paragraph 6(b), according to the value of the leases when the mistake was made in 2009, but with the payment of interest and consequential losses.
(iv) The Land Registry would almost certainly have had rights of recourse to recover the sums paid as indemnity against GR and possibly Gold Harp, under their very wide powers in schedule 8, paragraph 10.

That outcome is not particularly shocking. The claimants had not lived on the upper floor of the property.[33] Their loss was financial and it could be compensated by payment of an

[33] If they had, they would have enjoyed other forms of protection under LRA 2002, sch 4: see paras 3 and 6.

indemnity. GR would not escape the consequences of his nefarious conduct because of the sweeping rights of recourse which the Land Registry has (and, in practice, uses). Furthermore, it would have been open to the Court of Appeal to require Gold Harp to pay the costs of the appeal, even though the appeal was allowed in part.

VIII. What are the Wider Consequences of the *Gold Harp* Case?

The day-to-day consequences of *Gold Harp* may not be very great, mainly because of the very wide protection against rectification that is given to proprietors in physical possession by the LRA 2002. If the facts of *Freer* were to recur under the LRA 2002, and there was an attempt to rectify the Registers of title of the freehold and of the lessee's registered lease, the provisions of schedule 4, paragraphs 3[34] or 6[35] of the LRA 2002, coupled with the wide definition of proprietors in possession found in section 131 of the LRA 2002, would bar the rectification of both the freehold and leasehold titles unless it would be unjust not to make the alteration. There are however, a number of points about the *Gold Harp* case that cause disquiet.

First, the *Gold Harp* case appears to be unique amongst reported cases, because the Court of Appeal did not interpret the LRA 2002 in the manner that was set out in the Law Commission/Land Registry 2001 joint report.[36] Of course, a court is in no sense bound to adopt the Law Commission's own view of what it intended to do. That has been clear at least since *Yaxley v Gotts*,[37] where the Court of Appeal considered what weight should be given to Law Commission reports where legislation enacted the Law Commission's recommendations. While that is plainly correct in principle, *Gold Harp* is already causing difficulties in practice, an example of which is given below.

Secondly, these difficulties stem from the rather cavalier treatment in *Gold Harp* of the principle of the sanctity of the Register. The principal concern about the case at the Property Bar is indeed that it partially undermines the fundamental principle that a purchaser should be able to rely on the Register, which was the single most important objective of the LRA 2002. As explained above, that principle was set out in the Law Commission/Land Registry 2001 joint report,[38] which was actually quoted by Underhill LJ in *Gold Harp*.[39] He described it as being 'very general in character' and so it is, but it underlies much that is in the LRA 2002.

Thirdly, an example of those difficulties that has occurred in practice is as follows. A landowner entered into a deed by which it covenanted that 'no transfer or disposition of

[34] Rectification by the court.
[35] Rectification by the Registrar.
[36] Law Com No 271 (n 1). In most of the cases in which a point of principle on the LRA 2002 has arisen, the court has considered what was said in Law Com No 271.
[37] [2000] Ch 162 (CA).
[38] Law Com No 271 (n 1) para 1.5.
[39] *Gold Harp* (n 3) [78].

the property' was to be made without the disponee first entering into a covenant in a particular form with X. The deed was duly submitted to the Land Registry, with an application for the entry of a restriction to reflect the precise terms of that covenant. Unfortunately, the restriction that was entered was not in the form requested. By reason of the Land Registry's mistake, the obligation to certify that a disponee had entered into a covenant with X was limited merely to *transfers* of the registered estate and did not include charges. The landowner charged the land by way of a registered charge. The chargee did not enter into a direct covenant with X but the charge was duly registered because it was not caught by the terms of the restriction.

If the Register was rectified retrospectively to correct the mistake in the wording of the restriction, what would be the effect on the legal charge that was registered without any covenant with X? Would the charge be invalidated? Would the chargee have to enter into a covenant with X? If so, what if either X or the chargee refused to do so? The answers are not obvious. However, the matter is made more complicated because the LRA 2002 contains provisions by which a registered proprietor is deemed to have 'owner's powers' in favour of a disponee: see sections 23–26 of the LRA 2002. That means that in the absence of any entry in the Register, the registered proprietor has the power to make any disposition under the general law, subject to exceptions that are presently immaterial. The purpose of these provisions was to protect disponees of registered land from registered proprietors whose powers were limited in some way, but where that limitation was not reflected by any entry in the Register.[40] The present writer's view is that those 'owner's powers' provisions must prevent any retrospective rectification on the facts set out above, but the point will no doubt have to be tested in litigation. It was not an issue that was considered by the Law Commission and the Land Registry when the LRA 2002 was being drafted, because—as has been explained—it was thought that rectification would only be prospective in effect.

Fourthly, while no one disputes that the LRA 2002 embodies a principle of qualified and not absolute indefeasibility, the extent to which that indefeasibility is qualified was substantially reduced by the LRA 2002 through the enhanced protection given to the registered proprietor in possession. There were quite a number of other strategies embodied in the LRA 2002 that were also designed to make the Register more conclusive, such as the reduction in the number and effect of overriding interests. The intended consequence of all those strategies was that it should lead to cheaper and quicker conveyancing and the reduction in the risk that a buyer might be bound by an undisclosed encumbrance. *Gold Harp* has damaged that strategy.

The world will not come to an end as a result of the *Gold Harp* decision. However, it is unfortunate that the Court of Appeal has chosen to ignore the stated views of the Law Commission as to the purposes of schedule 8, paragraph 4 of the LRA 2002, and in so doing has reached a conclusion that damages one of the cornerstones of the Act.[41]

[40] See LRA 2002, s 26.

[41] The Law Commission has provisionally proposed the retention of the *Gold Harp* decision: see Law Commission, *Updating the Land Registration Act 2002—A Consultation Paper* (Law Com CP No 227, 2016) paras 13.189–13.197. The present writer has responded critically to those proposals: <www.falcon-chambers.com/publications/articles/P10>, paras 120 ff.

9

Assessing Rectification and Indemnity: After *Gold Harp* and *Swift 1st*

ROGER SMITH

I. Introduction

This chapter sets out to evaluate the state of the law on rectification and indemnity. It first sets the scene by identifying the central statutory provisions and describing the facts and issues in the two recent Court of Appeal decisions: *MacLeod v Gold Harp Properties Ltd*,[1] and *Swift 1st Ltd v Chief Land Registrar*.[2] Thereafter, the need for reform of the law relating rectification and indemnity will be investigated. Very recently, in 2016, the Law Commission published a consultation paper[3] reviewing certain aspects of the Land Registration Act ('LRA') 2002; these include rectification and indemnity. This chapter does not set out to analyse the consultation paper, but will mention those proposals relating to the issues considered below.

One aspect of the Law Commission's recent proposals is worth a brief mention, as it is rather different from the present rules. It is suggested that there be long stop after ten years, such that rectification will not be available more than ten years after a mistaken registration.[4] The long stop would not operate if the claimant is in possession, or if the proprietor is guilty of fraud or lack of proper care. It may be anticipated that this proposal, whilst seeming to be soundly based on the principle of providing finality for registered titles, will have limited effect.[5]

[1] *MacLeod v Gold Harp Properties Ltd* [2014] EWCA Civ 1084, [2015] 1 WLR 1249.

[2] *Swift 1st Ltd v Chief Land Registrar* [2015] EWCA Civ 330, [2015] Ch 602.

[3] Law Commission, *Updating the Land Registration Act 2002—A Consultation Paper* (Law Com CP No 227, 2016) chs 13 and 14.

[4] ibid, paras 13.100 ff.

[5] Though the much criticised *Parshall* v *Hackney* [2013] EWCA Civ 240, [2013] Ch 568 would be differently decided: Law Com CP No 227 (n 3) para 13.145.

II. The Background: Statutory Provisions

Schedule 4 of the LRA 2002 regulates rectification. The schedule provides for 'alteration' in a range of cases. Most straightforward is bringing the Register up to date and reflecting existing legal rights. Of greater interest is 'rectification'—which is defined as an alteration which 'involves the correction of a mistake' and 'prejudicially affects the title of a registered proprietor'.[6] It is the latter element that distinguishes rectification from other alterations, but the scope of the concept of 'mistake' is crucial in determining when rectification is available. The protection of proprietors in possession against rectification is also of great importance: rectification is not allowed unless: (a) there is fraud or lack of proper care, or (b) it would be unjust not to rectify.[7] The operation of this protection will not be studied in detail in this chapter. In summary, the cases show that a purchaser who buys land in the normal way has little to fear.[8] The great majority of registered proprietors will be proprietors 'in possession', as the LRA 2002 allows landlords, mortgagors, licensors and trustees to be in possession where the corresponding party (tenant, mortgagee, licensee, beneficiary) possesses.[9] There will be no registered proprietor 'in possession' if the land is completely vacant or is occupied by the person claiming rectification. A registered chargee also cannot claim that protected status—it is limited to the proprietor of a registered *estate*, which is defined to exclude a registered charge.[10] Absent possession, rectification will be ordered unless there are 'exceptional circumstances'.[11]

On occasion, as in *Gold Harp*, there will be a mistake in the registration of one person, who then creates a derivative interest (such as a lease or charge) in favour of a second person. When that derivative interest is registered, can there be rectification affecting that second person? Paragraph 8 of schedule 4 provides that the powers 'so far as relating to rectification, extend to changing for the future the priority of any interest affecting the registered estate'.

Indemnity is governed by schedule 8 of the LRA 2002. Its availability is tied very closely to the ideas and language just discussed. Leaving aside numerous forms of administrative error, schedule 8 provides for an indemnity to be payable by the Land Registry where there is rectification (and not merely alteration),[12] or where a mistake has been made which would require correction by rectification.[13] Suppose that the wrong person (B) is registered as proprietor of A's land; prima facie A loses the land. Should A's rectification claim succeed, then A will recover the land, but B will be compensated for the losses consequent on rectification being ordered. Conversely, if A fails to obtain rectification—perhaps because B is a proprietor in possession—then A will be compensated for the losses consequent on the mistake.

Two points may be stressed at this stage. The first is that liability to rectification is not a financial disaster. Though the land is lost, compensation will usually be payable.

6 LRA 2002, sch 4, para 1.

7 LRA 2002, sch 4, paras 3(2), 6(2).

8 See, eg, *Walker v Burton* [2013] EWCA Civ 1228, [2014] 1 P & CR 116 (whether lack of care); *Hounslow LBC v Hare* (1990) 24 HLR 9, especially at 27 (whether unjust not to rectify).

9 LRA 2002, s 131(2).

10 LRA 2002, s 132(1): 'a legal estate the title to which is entered in the register, other than a registered charge'.

11 LRA 2002, sch 4, paras 3(3), 5(3).

12 LRA 2002, sch 8, para 1(1)(a), read with para 11(2).

13 LRA 2002, sch 8, para 1(1)(b).

Obviously, many people prefer keeping the land to receiving money, but the legislation makes some allowance for this in protecting a registered proprietor against rectification where there is possession.[14] The second point is that rectification and indemnity are closely connected. Those who wish to limit the meaning of 'mistake' in order to protect registered proprietors against rectification have to recognise that—within the LRA 2002 framework, as currently drafted—this limits the availability of indemnity. If limiting rectification were to result in a significant restriction of rights to indemnity, then it might be questioned whether the link with rectification should be severed.

A well-recognised principle is that no indemnity is payable where rectification gives effect to an overriding interest. This principle goes back as far as the 1933 decision in *Re Chowood's Registered Land*.[15] The reasoning was devastatingly simple. Although the registered proprietor had suffered loss, this was not a result of rectification of the Register—he was bound by the claim (as an overriding interest) prior to rectification, and the rectification itself made him no worse off. The LRA 2002 confirms this result, because in these circumstances there is no rectification as defined by schedule 8—merely alteration. The reasoning of course is very similar to that in *Chowood's*: the proprietor is not 'materially prejudiced' by the alteration. We shall see later that overriding interests played an important part in the analysis in *Swift 1st*.

A final observation is that schedule 8 makes specific provision for forgery. The early decision in *Attorney-General v Odell*[16] had held that a good title was not obtained by registration of a forgery, and that no indemnity was payable when the title of the registered proprietor was, as a result, rectified. This applied even though the registered proprietor was not the forger and was in good faith. The statutory response in the LRA 1925 was to provide for indemnity in cases of forgery. This provision is repeated as paragraph 1(2)(b) of schedule 8: such a proprietor 'is, where the register is rectified, to be regarded as having suffered loss by reason of such rectification'. It follows that, although the registered proprietor may have a 'bad' title, indemnity is still payable. Further analysis of this point will be delayed until *Swift 1st* is studied, later in this chapter.

III. The Decisions in *Gold Harp* and *Swift 1st*

A. *Macleod v Gold Harp Properties Ltd*

The facts in *Gold Harp* were striking.[17] The proprietor of land (B) persuaded the Land Registry to remove A's lease from the Register, quite unjustifiably. There was no difficulty in saying that this was a mistake, such that rectification could be ordered. However, the

[14] Although A Goymour, 'Mistaken Registrations of Land: Exploding the Myth of "Title by Registration"' [2013] *CLJ* 617 argues convincingly that rectification (alongside other elements) denies any absolute concept of indefeasibility of registered titles, she may be thought to exaggerate the actual effect of rectification as defeating expectations of keeping the land itself.

[15] *Re Chowood's Registered Land* [1933] Ch 574 (Clauson J).

[16] *Attorney-General v Odell* [1906] 2 Ch 47.

[17] It has generally been welcomed by commentators: see notes by M Dixon (2015) 131 *LQR* 207; A Goymour [2015] *Conv* 253; E Lees (2015) 78 *MLR* 361 (but arguing that purchasers deserve more protection); R Smith [2015] *CLJ* 10.

complication was that B had subsequently granted a lease (the 'new lease'), which was itself registered. This lease had then been assigned to C. Given that both the new lessee and C were companies controlled by B or his business associate, it is easy to see the lease as a ploy to thwart rectification—the merits were all on the side of A.

A background point concerns the relationship between rectification and indemnity. As discussed in the preceding section, indemnity depends upon there being rectification or a power to rectify. A very real problem is therefore that, if rectification is unavailable against C, then A might both lose the land and be refused indemnity. It might be thought that the mistake in B's registration would be enough to ensure indemnity. However, the facts may be such as to ensure that B is bound by A's claim. In turn, that means that no loss is caused to A at that stage (such that there would be alteration, rather than rectification, of B's registered title). If there is then a registered disposition in favour of C, any claim to indemnity would have to concentrate on the registration of C. In the absence of a right to rectify C's title, there is a real risk that A will not be entitled to indemnity. A might have a personal claim against B, but that would be worthless if B has disappeared or become insolvent. Few would dissent from the proposition that a system that denies A's title without compensation is incredibly harsh; indeed, it might well be inconsistent with human rights principles. Unless the indemnity provisions can be made to work in this scenario,[18] this provides a strong case for allowing rectification against C.

There are, perhaps, two central questions to ask about this sort of situation. The first is whether the registration of C is itself a mistake. Given that B as registered proprietor had full powers of leasing,[19] it is easy to see the argument that there is no new mistake in registering C's lease.[20] This is discussed in the following section.

The second question is whether rectification in respect of C's registered leasehold title may follow from rectification of B's registered fee simple title. At this point, things become complex. There are at least four potential strands of reasoning. Two were mooted by Lord Neuberger MR in *Barclays Bank plc v Guy (No 2)*:[21] first, that the rectification of B's title may require rectification of C's title in order to be effective; and secondly, that the subsequent registration may be seen as 'part and parcel' of the mistaken registration—the latter approach coming close in practice to saying that the registration of the lease constitutes a mistake. Thirdly, there has also been discussion whether rectification can be retrospective, in the sense of affecting interests created prior to the rectification. This idea may be especially useful where the later interest is an overriding interest (so that there is no *registered* derivative interest that can itself be rectified).[22] The balance of authority may have been hostile to this,[23] though it was never settled. The fourth argument is that rectification

[18] For possibilities, see E Lees, 'Title by Registration: Rectification, Indemnity and Mistake and the Land Registration Act 2002' (2013) 76 *MLR* 62.

[19] LRA 2002, s 23.

[20] *Norwich and Peterborough BS v Steed (No 2)* [1993] Ch 116 and *Barclays Bank plc v Guy* [2008] EWCA Civ 452, [2008] 2 EGLR 74; see sections IV(C) and V below. On the facts of *Gold Harp* (n 1), this is strengthened by the observation that C's lease was not inconsistent with A's lease: the question was which had priority.

[21] *Barclays Bank plc v Guy (No 2)* [2010] EWCA Civ 1396, [2011] 1 WLR 681 (an unsuccessful attempt to re-open the initial 2008 rejection of leave to appeal).

[22] As in *Freer v Unwins Ltd* [1976] Ch 288.

[23] The cases are discussed in *Gold Harp* (n 1). Differing views had been expressed in the one preceding Court of Appeal decision: *Malory Enterprises Ltd v Cheshire Homes (UK) Ltd* [2002] EWCA Civ 151, [2002] Ch 216 [79], [87], [89].

may affect C by virtue of schedule 4, paragraph 8 of the LRA 2002 (quoted above). Its predecessor provision, section 82(2) of the LRA 1925, was differently expressed: it did not include the words 'for the future'. The relationship between these strands of reasoning was never made clear in the earlier cases, nor is it discussed in *Gold Harp*.

In *Gold Harp*, the Court of Appeal concluded that C's lease should be rectified, so as to ensure that A's lease had priority over it. This was based almost entirely upon paragraph 8 of schedule 4, though there was extensive discussion of the earlier material and especially retrospective rectification. Cases and the textbook analyses were discussed, the court noting that both had taken very different approaches. Quite a lot of stress was placed upon the Court of Appeal decision in *Argyle BS v Hammond*[24] that rectification against a chargee, C, was available where the prior registration of B had been consequent upon a void transfer (an alleged forgery). Reliance was also placed on the Law Commission's 1998 Consultative Document,[25] though the court underplayed the point that there appears to have been a change of heart in the Commission's 2001 Report.[26]

The Court of Appeal regarded the clinching argument as being that the paragraph 8 powers make sense only if subsequent interests can be affected. The limiting words 'for the future' can readily be given effect by stressing that no liability can be incurred by C for pre-rectification events. Suppose, for example, that C had been in possession prior to rectification of the new lease:[27] there would be no possibility of this making C liable for trespass. Only continued possession after rectification could give rise to a trespass claim.

Overall, the result looks to be correct: it will be observed later that it is supported by the Law Commission's 2016 Consultation Paper.[28] Though the earlier cases provide only limited support, the conclusion follows from the natural reading of paragraph 8. The extent to which it fits the policy underlying the legislation necessarily depends upon the reader's perception as to the role of registration.[29] It is understandable that we should be wary of enabling an attack to be made on a bona fide purchaser who has little choice but to rely upon the Register. However, *Gold Harp* stresses that C, if in possession, will be protected by paragraphs 3 and 6 of schedule 4 of the LRA 2002. This confirmation that the protection of proprietors in possession applies in the paragraph 8 context is to be applauded—it goes a long way to allay concerns that paragraph 8 could unfairly prejudice those who have relied upon the Register. Consequently, the protection of possessors can operate at multiple stages. Take an example where B is mistakenly registered as the freehold owner, following a forged disposition of A's registered freehold title and where B subsequently leases to C.

[24] *Argyle BS v Hammond* (1985) 49 P & CR 148; see further at section IV(B) below.

[25] Law Commission, *Land Registration for the Twenty-First Century—A Consultative Document* (Law Com No 254, 1998) para 8.33.

[26] *Gold Harp* (n 1) [64]. It is noted that the Law Commission was critical of *Freer v Unwins* (n 22) in its 1998 consultative document for failing to consider LRA 1925, s 82(2) (Law Com No 254, 1998 (n 25) para 8.33), but that the Law Commission's 2001 report had cited the same case with apparent approval (Law Commission, *Land Registration for the Twenty-First Century: A Conveyancing Revolution* (Law Com No 271, 2001) para 10.8).

[27] In *Gold Harp* (n 1), the new lessee (C) was not in possession.

[28] Law Com CP No 227 (n 3), discussed further in section V(B) below. The Law Commission acknowledges, at para 13.195, that the views expressed in Law Com No 271 (n 26) were rather different, but does not think this sufficient to call into question the outcome in *Gold Harp*.

[29] S Cooper, 'Resolving Title Conflicts in Registered Land' (2015) 131 *LQR* 108 argues persuasively that we should not automatically protect the purchaser, taking into account economic aspects of land purchase. Some of that analysis might support a wide meaning of mistake in contexts other than that of subsequent purchasers such as C, but this raises really difficult issues.

Here, there is the possibility of a rectification claim by A against both B's and C's registered interests. The success of either of these independent claims depends on whether the particular defendant (B or C) can rely on the possession defence. It is quite possible that A's claim might succeed against one of B or C, and not the other, if only one of the parties satisfies the elements of the defence.

Further, C may be protected by indemnity if rectification is ordered. A most welcome consequence of *Gold Harp* is that it removes the risk (described above) that inability to rectify against C might mean that A loses the land without any right to rectification or indemnity. Can A claim indemnity if, despite paragraph 8, rectification of C's title is refused on the facts (perhaps because C is in possession, and can therefore rely on the possession defence)? It does appear that indemnity is payable: in the language of the legislation, there is a mistake (the registration of B) the correction of which requires rectification (of C's title).

This chapter will say no more about the merits of the conclusion in *Gold Harp*, but some of the reasoning and, in particular, the scope of application of paragraph 8, will be studied in more detail in subsequent sections.

B. *Swift 1st Properties v Chief Land Registrar*

Though several significant legal issues were presented by *Swift 1st*, the facts were straightforward. A fraudster forged a charge in favour of the innocent claimant; the charge was registered. After the facts came to light, the Register was rectified so as to remove the charge. Rectification was unchallenged—inevitably, given that registered chargees cannot use the proprietor in possession defence, and that the proprietor of the freehold estate was in actual occupation. The only viable remedy for the chargee was to seek indemnity.

The indemnity claim raised three primary issues. The first concerned the effect of registration of the forged charge: did this confer a good title on the chargee (prior to rectification)? The much criticised[30] decisions of the Court of Appeal in *Malory Enterprises Ltd v Cheshire Homes (UK) Ltd*[31] and of Newey J in *Fitzwilliam v Richall Holding Services Ltd*[32] held that registration of a forged disposition does *not* confer good beneficial title (section 58 clearly confers legal title). *Swift 1st* decided not to follow *Malory*. It seems likely that this aspect of the decision will be well received.[33] However, it is curious that it was decided on the basis that *Malory* was decided as being per incuriam section 114 of the LRA 1925—a provision that was repealed by the LRA 2002, and was not relied upon by any of the critics of *Malory*! Nevertheless, the practical outcome is welcome. One reason for this is that, *even if* registration of a forgery does confer good beneficial title, the defrauded proprietor may still be able to recover the land, via rectification. If the registered disponee,

[30] C Harpum, 'Registered Land—A Law Unto Itself?' in J Getzler (ed), *Rationalizing Property, Equity and Trusts* (Oxford, Oxford University Press, 2003) 197–202; E Cooke, 'Land Registration: Void and Voidable Titles—a Discussion of the Scottish Law Commission's Paper' [2004] *Conv* 482, 485–486; A Hill-Smith, 'Forgery and Land Registration: The Decision in *Malory Investments v Cheshire Homes*' [2009] *Conv* 127; M Dixon (2013) 129 *LQR* 320.

[31] *Malory* (n 23) [65].

[32] *Fitzwilliam v Richall Holdings Services Ltd* [2013] EWHC 86 (Ch), [2013] 1 P & CR 19.

[33] See E Lees (2015) 131 *LQR* 515; R Smith [2015] *CLJ* 401; P Milne [2015] *Conv* 356.

taking under the forged disposition, is not in possession (remembering that chargees do not qualify for this protection), then rectification will nearly always follow—as in *Swift 1st* itself. In any event, the losing party will be paid indemnity (absent fault). The forgery aspect of the case is a very important one, but it will not be discussed further—it is tangential to our concern with rectification and indemnity.

The second and third issues will be discussed further below, with a very brief summary at this stage. These issues relate to overriding interests and indemnity. It has already been observed that a purchaser who is bound by an overriding interest suffers no loss as a result of alteration of the Register and accordingly is not entitled to indemnity. On the facts of *Swift 1st*, the proprietor of the freehold estate was in actual occupation.

The second issue concerned the nature of the proprietor's overriding interest—it was held that her right to rectify the Register was an overriding interest (adopting reasoning in *Malory* on this point). The third issue was whether this precluded indemnity. The court held that indemnity was payable, despite the overriding interest. This was not based on the special nature of the right to rectify, but on the statutory deeming of loss in schedule 8, paragraph 1(2)(b) of the LRA 2002.

IV. Rectification—the Meaning of Mistake

A. General Considerations

In this section, we investigate the general meaning of mistake. It may be observed that mistake is not defined by the legislation, nor is it explained by the Law Commission.[34] Our investigation will include the meaning of mistake in the context of subsequent registrations, though this section goes well beyond that issue.

A quite convincing analysis of mistake is provided by *Ruoff & Roper*—arguing that an entry constitutes a mistake if the Registrar would not have made the entry if aware of the true facts.[35] This obviously covers registration of a forged transfer, the unauthorised removal of a non-forfeited lease in *Gold Harp*, the mistaken acceptance of the adverse possession claim in *Baxter v Mannion*,[36] and the first registration of a person who is in fact not entitled to the fee simple.[37] *Ruoff & Roper* proceed to argue that registration of a voidable transfer is not a mistake (a question discussed below). Nevertheless, a voidable transfer almost inevitably involves a claim being available against the transferee and this will justify alteration, on the ground of 'bringing the register up to date' (not amounting to rectification).

[34] S Cooper, 'Regulating Fallibility in Registered Land' [2013] *CLJ* 341, 343–344, has a useful discussion of mistake, criticising the use of this undefined test.

[35] *Ruoff & Roper: Registered Conveyancing* (London, Sweet & Maxwell, 2003–) (looseleaf) para 46.009. A rather similar analysis is employed by C Harpum, S Bridge and M Dixon, *Megarry & Wade: The Law of Real Property* 8th edn (London, Sweet & Maxwell, 2012) para 7.133. S Cooper [2013] *CLJ* 341, 355 ff supports the similar idea of 'mandate'.

[36] *Baxter v Mannion* [2011] EWCA Civ 120, [2011] 1 WLR 1594.

[37] See, eg, *Sainsbury's Supermarkets Ltd v Olympia Homes Ltd* [2005] EWHC 1235 (Ch), [2006] 1 P & CR 17, [84]. Failure to enter a notice of a claim to an adverse interest on first registration (as in *Freer v Unwins* (n 22)) would also seem to be covered.

Though the *Ruoff & Roper* analysis of mistake is helpful, it is not necessarily the only approach. Its weakness may be that it places too much stress on the role of the Registrar. Thus, they argue that, where there is a voidable transfer, there is no mistake in the entry in the Register.[38] Yet the 2002 Act makes no reference to 'entry in the Register'—it simply requires a mistake. In contrast, Emmet and Farrand[39] are fiercely critical of any distinction between void and voidable transfers, observing that the mistake need not mean a mistake in the Register. Perhaps it is justifiable to read in the words 'in the Register'—after all, it is the Register itself that is being rectified. However, their criticism stands as a reminder that different approaches could be taken as to the meaning of mistake. This is enhanced by obiter dicta of Jacob LJ in *Baxter v Mannion*,[40] in which he doubts the void/voidable distinction.

Unfortunately, Jacob LJ fails to tell us what the meaning of mistake is. Indeed, I struggle to get a sense of exactly what is supported by Emmett and Farrand—save that it is wider than the *Ruoff & Roper* analysis. Perhaps the principal rival idea is that the Register fails to record the position that would have existed in unregistered land.[41] Though such an idea is anathema to the Law Commission,[42] there is an argument that there is a mistake when—following rescission of the voidable disposition—the Register fails to reflect the rights of the disponor. This highlights, of course, the question whether the mistake must be *in the entry* on the Register. Many will have sympathy for the proposition that we should not treat unregistered land as the holy grail of what is obviously correct (such that anything else constitutes a mistake). Nevertheless, the failure to define mistake opens up this sort of argument.

B. Void and Voidable Transfers

The above discussion reveals a dispute as to the application of the LRA 2002's concept of mistake to void and voidable transfers. Alongside subsequent dispositions, this is the main area in which the meaning of mistake has, so far, been considered. It is relatively straightforward to assert that registration of a void transfer (or other disposition) is a mistake. More problematic is the registration of a voidable disposition. The issue comes to the fore when there is a subsequent registered disposition by the new registered proprietor and the claim is to rectify that registered disposition.

That differences may exist between void and voidable dispositions is highlighted[43] by two pre-2002 Court of Appeal decisions in the same litigation: *Argyle BS v Hammond*[44] and *Norwich and Peterborough BS v Steed*.[45] *Argyle* involved an assumed forgery of a

[38] *Ruoff & Roper* (n 35) para 46.009.

[39] *Emmet on Title*, 9th edn (London, Longman, 1986–) (looseleaf) paras 9.027–9.028. Note also the balanced analysis of E Lees (2013) 76 *MLR* 62, 71–72.

[40] *Baxton v Mannion* (n 36) [31].

[41] See S Gardner, 'The Land Registration Act 2002—the Show on the Road' (2014) 77 *MLR* 763, 771–773.

[42] Law Com No 254 (n 25) para 8.19 is most explicit.

[43] Litigation on voidable dispositions goes back to *Re Leighton's Conveyance* [1936] 1 All ER 667 (Luxmoore J) (reversed on other grounds, [1937] Ch 149).

[44] *Argyle BS v Hammond* (n 24)

[45] *Steed* (n 20).

transfer of the freehold. The new proprietor then executed a charge which was registered. That the original proprietor could recover the freehold was not in doubt, but the question was whether the registered charge could be rectified so as to ensure that it did not affect the original proprietor. The court held that rectification of the freehold could affect a registered charge. The reasoning was partly based upon section 82(2) of the LRA 1925, the forerunner of schedule 4, paragraph 8 of the LRA 2002: 'The register may be rectified under this section notwithstanding that the rectification may affect any estates, rights, charges, or interests acquired or protected by registration, or by any entry on the register, or otherwise'. Following *Argyle*, the question whether there was in fact a forgery (coupled with the application of the rectification rules) had to be settled. In *Steed*, it transpired that the transfer of the freehold had not been forged, but had been induced by fraud. It was held that the subsequent registered charge could not be affected by rectification, as the registration of the charge did not fall within any of the grounds for rectification.

These two decisions pose numerous problems. Turning first to *Argyle*, a point of central importance, though it is not mentioned in *Gold Harp*, is that section 82(1)(g) of the LRA 1925 permitted rectification where 'a legal estate has been registered in the name of a person who if the land had not been registered would not have been the estate owner'. Because the common law rule is that no rights can be acquired under a forgery, even following a subsequent disposition, this wording would clearly apply to the registered charge in *Argyle*.[46] It follows that section 82 provided a direct right to rectify the charge, separate from the right to rectify the freehold. It was easy to argue that there was jurisdiction to rectify, without any need to rely upon section 82(2) of the LRA 1925. Section 82(1)(g) does not apply to voidable transfers, as title can pass at common law under a merely voidable transfer. Accordingly, the *Argyle* basis for a right to rectify did not apply in *Steed*.

Although section 82(1)(g) was sufficient to provide a right to rectify in *Argyle*, the court did place some reliance on section 82(2). That reliance on section 82(2) was to be given prominence in *Gold Harp*.[47] It is odd that the reliance in *Argyle* on section 82(2) was not mentioned in *Steed*: the outcome in *Argyle* is supported by the application of section 82(1). Though the application of section 82(1) might indeed distinguish between void and voidable transfers, the same is not true of section 82(2).

It has been observed that the distinction between void and voidable dispositions has been important when there has been a subsequent registered disposition. It is noticeable that few pre-2002 cases deal with subsequent dispositions: section 82(2) is stressed in some of them, but ignored in others. The explanation of this may lie in the history of section 82(2). Brickdale and Stewart-Wallace[48] explain that, before 1925, rectification did not give rise to indemnity and this led to limits on when rectification (adversely affecting the registered title) was available.[49] The main purpose of section 82(2) was to ensure that rectification

[46] The reference in LRA 1925, s 82(1)(g) to 'estates' included charges: LRA 1925, s 3(xi). LRA 2002, s 132(1), defines 'estates' so as to exclude charges.

[47] *Gold Harp* (n 1) esp [54].

[48] C Brickdale and JS Stewart-Wallace, *The Land Registration Act, 1925*, 4th edn (London, Stevens, 1939) 217.

[49] See also *Re 139 Deptford High Street* [1951] Ch 884, 888.

really did affect the registered title in question (the freehold estate in *Argyle*)—a proposition that modern lawyers would take for granted. This may explain why section 82(2) was often overlooked, perhaps until *Argyle* itself.

It was noted earlier that *Ruoff & Roper* contend that 'mistake' does not include registration of a voidable transfer, though rescission will result in alteration of the Register.[50] The position of the proprietor taking directly under the voidable transfer appears to be the same whether or not we extend mistake to voidable transfers—alteration of the Register can be supported, even if it does not also amount to 'rectification'.[51] But what as regards subsequent registrations? Can it be argued that there is no longer any distinction between void and voidable dispositions, given: (i) that the LRA 2002 contains no equivalent to section 82(1)(g) of the LRA 1925, and (ii) the *Gold Harp* clarification that subsequent registrations can be affected by rectification? There is nothing in schedule 4 of the LRA 2002 explicitly pointing towards such a distinction. Provided that paragraph 8 is not limited to situations in which the alteration of the registered voidable transfer amounts to rectification (an issue discussed below),[52] then the subsequent registration can itself be rectified. That analysis operates whether the disposition is void or voidable, without needing to determine the meaning of mistake.

Should paragraph 8 should not operate in that fashion, it would be necessary to consider other ways of obtaining rectification of the subsequent registered disposition. This might be by finding other routes (mentioned above in describing *Gold Harp*) whereby the initial alteration may be made effective regarding subsequent registered dispositions. However, of greater interest within the present section would be the question whether the registration of the subsequent disposition (whether before or after the voidable transfer is avoided) constitutes a mistake within the meaning of schedule 4 of the LRA 2002.[53]

This takes us back, of course, to the earlier discussion as to the meaning of mistake. Given the lack of statutory definition, there is a risk of its being interpreted as covering the situation where the position as it would be in unregistered land is different from what appears on the Register. This may be described as a 'risk' because it raises the possibility of the priority rules for unregistered land being imported into the registration system—this could really compromise the success of the system.[54] This was the effect of section 82(1)(g) of the LRA 1925, but that was a provision with a specific and limited effect. One might here make a plea to have statutory guidance as to the scope of mistake, even if it is no more than a confirmation of the *Ruoff & Roper* analysis.

What legal policies are involved in this area? This is a question that should, perhaps, have been raised much earlier. Emmet and Farrand are, of course, very hostile to any distinction between void and voidable titles. Yet this distinction has operated

[50] See section IV(A) above. Note that *NRAM Ltd v Evans* [2017] EWCA Civ 1013, which was decided after this chapter was submitted, adopts the *Ruoff & Roper* analysis, and appears to settle the issue discussed in this section.

[51] In addition, the transferee will not receive indemnity even if there is a mistake: loss is caused by the rescission rather than by alteration of the Register.

[52] See section V(A) below.

[53] Simply rejecting the *Ruoff & Roper* analysis and saying that the initial registration of the voidable transfer was a mistake would not suffice: correcting that mistake would constitute alteration rather than rectification.

[54] This argument is developed by S Cooper, 'Regulating Fallibility in Registered Land Titles' [2013] *CLJ* 341, 347–350.

outside the registration system for a very long time: lawyers are very familiar with the proposition that a claim to rescind a transaction can fail once a third party has taken an interest. Why should it be different in registered land? Nevertheless, the Emmet and Farrand argument appears compelling when looking at the distinction from the perspective of the subsequent registered proprietor. That proprietor's position arguably should be the same whether the 'fault' made an earlier disposition void or voidable. Whilst it is true that in unregistered land the subsequent disponee's position is crucially dependent upon that distinction, in registered land the subsequent disponee relies upon the Register and not the dispositions which led to current state of the Register. From that perspective, we might agree with Emmet and Farrand that the distinction looks dubious. This is supported by the factors that, first, the subsequent disponee may have the defence of proprietor in possession and, secondly, that indemnity will normally be payable. This permits a more nuanced outcome than available under the void/voidable distinction.

C. Mistakes and Subsequent Dispositions

Prior to *Gold Harp*, there was considerable debate as to whether the registration of a subsequent disposition constitutes an independent mistake such as might justify rectification directly against the later purchaser, lessee or chargee. The application of paragraph 8 schedule 4 of the LRA 2002 in *Gold Harp* removes much of the significance of this question. However, it will be seen in the following section that there may be limits to the paragraph 8 analysis—any limit would return this debate to prominence.

In principle, it is difficult to see how the registration of such a subsequent disposition by a registered proprietor can be a mistake, given the combined effect of sections 58 and 23 of the LRA 2002. This was the conclusion of Lloyd LJ in *Barclays Bank plc v Guy*.[55] On the other hand, this assumes that we look for a mistake in the entry in the Register—the *Ruoff & Roper* analysis discussed above. Should we adopt a broader meaning of mistake, then it might well apply to the subsequent registration.

D. Recent Law Commission Proposals

Although the Law Commission notes that there have been calls for mistake to be defined, no reform is proposed. Whilst it may be thought that this is a missed opportunity, the Law Commission is surely justified in thinking it inappropriate to list situations in which rectification is available: definition is difficult and could produce unfortunate results.[56] Further, it may be thought encouraging that the Law Commission supports the approach adopted by *Ruoff & Roper* and *Megarry & Wade*. This limits the risk of an unacceptably wide meaning of mistake emerging.

[55] *Barclays Bank plc v Guy* (n 20) (though the stress on the relevance of knowledge of the title defect is awkward). It is also supported, under the previous law, by *Steed* (n 20).

[56] Law Com CP No 227 (n 3), paras 13.79 ff.

V. Rectification and Subsequent Registrations

A. The *Gold Harp* Decision and the Role of Schedule 4, Paragraph 8

It has been seen that *Gold Harp* relied upon paragraph 8, schedule 4 of the LRA 2002, to order rectification of a subsequent registered lease. It appears from *Gold Harp* that paragraph 8 is treated as providing a separate (and seemingly sole) justification for rectifying a subsequent registered disposition. Although the contrary has been suggested,[57] it appears that paragraph 8 is treated as doing more than merely limiting a right that already exists.[58] This does not rely on treating the registration of the new lease as a separate mistake. If it were, there would appear to be no need to rely upon paragraph 8.

The important question now to be asked is whether there are circumstances in which paragraph 8 will not apply and will therefore not provide a basis for altering the Register. If so, then we might need to have recourse to other ideas discussed by the Court of Appeal, mentioned above in the earlier summary of the decision.[59] These include treating the subsequent registration as a mistake.

We will start by identifying two problems, though there may well be more. The first builds upon a question raised by Lees.[60] Accepting that a rectification may affect other holders of registered interests, does this apply only where the original registration (perhaps of a void transfer) is still on the Register? Suppose that registration of X as freehold proprietor is mistaken and X leases to Y for 10 years; Y's lease is registered. *Gold Harp* provides authority that removal of the lease may be ordered. Is it different if, instead, X transfers the fee simple to Z? We will assume that the registration of Z is not, by itself, a mistake. When paragraph 8 refers to 'any interest affecting the registered estate' it is questionable whether 'any interest' applies to the estate itself. It is too late to rectify X's title, as that no longer exists. But failure to apply paragraph 8 to Z's title would constitute a serious restriction on its utility. And standing back from the technicalities, it is difficult to understand why a tenant (especially of a long lease) should be more at risk of rectification than a purchaser of the fee simple.

The second problem arises from the wording of paragraph 8: it was spotted by Emmet and Farrand.[61] Paragraph 8 applies specifically to rectification: 'so far as relating to rectification'. Suppose, then, that X's title is altered rather than rectified. This would nearly always be because X was inherently bound by the rights of the person claiming rectification (R).[62] Does this mean that paragraph 8 does not apply and so cannot be used to justify rectification as against Z? At least from some points of view, that would be a strange limitation. It might mean that the worse that X's conduct is (leading to his being inherently bound by R's rights), then the less likely it becomes that rectification is available against a subsequent disponee. Perhaps this dilemma might be avoided by saying that paragraph 8 refers to rectification of

[57] A Goymour [2015] *Conv* 253.

[58] *Gold Harp* (n 1) [91]–[92].

[59] See section III(A) above.

[60] E Lees (2013) 76 *MLR* 62, 74. A similar analysis is seen in A Goymour [2015] *Conv* 253.

[61] *Emmet & Farrand on Title* (n 39) para 9.029.

[62] There could be many reasons for this, including X's being bound by an overriding interest (relevant where Z is not so bound).

the *subsequent* title (ie, Z's title), though that is not a natural construction. More convincing is the response that the facts of *Gold Harp* involved a question whether the equivalent to X was bound before the subsequent transaction. That question was not decided,[63] but there is no suggestion that it is relevant to the application of paragraph 8.

This second problem becomes of particular importance when voidable transfers are considered—alluded to in the above discussion of void and voidable transfers. Suppose that X obtains a transfer by a fraudulent misrepresentation (a classic example of a voidable transfer) and then leases the land to Y (who is acting in good faith) for 10 years. There are two hurdles to be surmounted before the original proprietor, R, can seek rectification of Y's registration by virtue of paragraph 8. The first is that there must be a mistake so far as X is concerned (given that paragraph 8 depends upon rectification against X being ordered and that in turn requires a mistake in the registration of X). The *Ruoff & Roper* analysis would deny that, but it may be possible to argue that the Register does contain a mistake once the fraudulent transfer is avoided. If that is possible, the second hurdle is that altering X's title does not cause any new loss to X, and if so, there is technically no 'rectification' as the alteration is not prejudicial to X. This then raises the question whether paragraph 8 operates when X's title has been altered rather than rectified.

An alternative way to surmount the first hurdle—that there should be a mistake in the registration of X—could be that X's title may be altered without there being a mistake.[64] But this analysis is far from comfortable. If, on this analysis, rectification of Y's lease is refused on the facts—most obviously because Y is in possession—then no indemnity is payable to R, since there is no mistake as required by schedule 8, paragraph 1(1)(b). The normal link between rectification and indemnity has been broken.

Suppose that one or both of these problems with paragraph 8 is recognised as valid. The absence of a remedy against Y could be highly problematic. In summarising *Gold Harp*, it was observed that a powerful argument in its favour is that it removes the risk of the original victim (here R) being left without either rectification or indemnity. The problems just identified with paragraph 8 could restore that risk. Commentators and judges have viewed that risk as unacceptable, and it is likely that a court would seek an alternative route to permit rectification to be sought against Y.

This takes us to the question whether the pre-*Gold Harp* analyses[65] continue to operate as alternatives to paragraph 8. This is not clear from *Gold Harp* itself. The reliance on *Argyle* is explicable, as that case was based on section 82(2) of the LRA 1925—the origin of paragraph 8. It is possible that the views expressed by Lord Neuberger in *Guy* might apply, though neither that approach nor the idea of retrospective rectification would clearly overcome the first problem—of the initial mistaken registration (of X) no longer being on the Register. If we could say that the subsequent registration (of Y) is a separate mistake (perhaps the most difficult possibility to pursue), then that would solve both the problems.

A rather different point concerns the manner in which a paragraph 8 decision to affect a subsequent registration (or other disposition) will be made. Much of this debate at earlier times revolved around the question whether rectification could be made

[63] *Gold Harp* (n 1) [34]. *Swift 1st* (n 2) displays a similar reluctance to construe rectification too narrowly in the indemnity context (LRA 2002, sch 8, para 1(2)(b)).

[64] LRA 2002, sch 4, para 2(1)(b): 'bringing the register up to date'.

[65] See section III(A) above.

retrospective—an issue extensively discussed in *Gold Harp*. That debate appears to assume that, if retrospective rectification is possible, then the court would exercise a discretion. What discretion operates when paragraph 8 applies? Save for confirming that the purchaser in possession protection can apply, *Gold Harp* does not provide useful guidance on this. The circumstances were such that the merits appeared entirely in favour of rectification.

Some discretion will apply where, as will be common, the subsequent interest holder is a proprietor in possession so that paragraph 3(2) or paragraph 6(2) of schedule 4 applies. What happens in other cases? These will include cases where a proprietor is not in possession (as in *Gold Harp*) and where there is an overriding interest lease (as in *Freer v Unwins Ltd*).[66] We must, of course, look to the wording of paragraph 8: 'The powers … extend to changing for the future …'. That might indicate that changing the priority is not automatic—it is simply one of the consequences the court may choose to order. However, this needs to be considered alongside paragraph 3(3) of schedule 4 (paragraph 6(3) for alterations by the Registrar), which requires alteration to be ordered unless there are exceptional circumstances. Those provisions appear to mean that the court or Registrar must normally order that subsequent interests are affected by rectification.[67] It might be noted that rectification takes effect under paragraph 2 (rather than paragraph 8 standing by itself)—that was assumed by *Gold Harp* in recognising the protection of the proprietor in possession.

Finally, does the court possess any discretion when deciding whether or not to rectify the title of a subsequent proprietor where there has been a voidable disposition (assuming that paragraph 8 can apply in such cases)? Any court will appreciate the unregistered land principle that a person subsequently acquiring an interest from a party holding title pursuant to a voidable disposition is not to be affected, without more, by the defect (it is otherwise for void dispositions, of course). How does that protection apply within the rectification proceedings? Doubtless it is easy to favour the subsequent proprietor who is in possession, but what about other cases? Apparently, only the 'exceptional circumstances' provision provides a way out—but this looks less generous to the subsequent proprietor than the unregistered land principle. This example would provide a nice test of the strength of unregistered land principles within the registration system.

B. Recent Law Commission Proposals

The Law Commission[68] accepts the outcome in *Gold Harp*. It is interesting that it is equated with retrospective rectification, though it is not clear that the cases discussing retrospective rectification (mentioned in *Gold Harp*) were dealing with paragraph 8 (or its LRA 1925 predecessor). It is to be presumed that there is no unqualified right to retrospective rectification: at the very least, it has been seen that *Gold Harp* enables the subsequent proprietor to rely on the proprietor in possession defence.

What is most interesting is that *Gold Harp* is dealt with in the specific context of competing derivative interests—the two leases in *Gold Harp* itself. Where the subsequent

[66] *Freer v Unwins* (n 22); the protection of proprietors in possession is inapplicable to overriding interests.
[67] Supported by dicta in *Gold Harp* (n 1) [95].
[68] Law Com CP No 227 (n 3) para 13.195.

proprietor is instead a purchaser of the registered freehold estate (as where a forged transfer of a freehold estate is registered and then the freehold estate is transferred to a purchaser), then a rather different analysis is taken. Instead of using paragraph 8, the Law Commission accepts that the subsequent registration is a mistake, paving the way for rectification.[69] Little authority is provided to support this conclusion,[70] though (as discussed in section III(A) above) the availability of rectification may be applauded. A similar approach is adopted by the Law Commission in cases where rectification is sought to place a derivative interest on the Register.[71]

What is striking is that the Law Commission clearly places rectification at the forefront in settling indefeasibility disputes. Instead of deciding cases according to relatively inflexible rules, the Law Commission suggests that it is preferable that they should be channelled through rectification. This both allows the facts of the individual case to be considered (most obviously, the fact of possession) and ensures that indemnity is available for the losing party. This is manifested in contexts beyond subsequent registrations. Thus, the Law Commission both supports the *Swift 1st* rejection of the *Malory* forgery analysis and also seeks to limit the resolution of disputes by the use of overriding interests (when that might give priority to the original registered proprietor). Though it lacks certainty of outcome, this approach is to be welcomed as providing very desirable flexibility.

VI. The Right to Rectify as an Overriding Interest

In *Swift 1st*, the Court of Appeal accepted that the actual occupation overriding interest includes a statutory right to rectify the Register. This section will investigate the nature of this overriding interest, the authority supporting it, and its proper role in our system of land registration. Its significance in the context of indemnity claims—and specifically, the application of paragraph 1(2)(b)—will be considered later.

One introductory observation is that this overriding interest analysis is not limited to the forgery context of *Swift 1st*. It will apply whenever a person is registered as proprietor as a result of a mistake. A very simple example would be where the wrong person is mistakenly registered as first proprietor of land.

A. The Origins of the Analysis

The analysis first surfaced in *Blacklocks v JB Developments (Godalming) Ltd*.[72] It was argued by counsel, though there is doubt regarding the true basis for the decision of Judge Mervyn

69 ibid, paras 13.29, 13.73.

70 *Knights Construction (March) Ltd v Roberto Mac Ltd* [2011] EWLandRA 2009_1459, [2011] 2 EGLR 123 is very fairly relied upon. However, that case also employs alternative analyses (see [131]) and most other cases use different analyses. The Law Commission also relies upon the fact that rectification would have been available under the LRA 1925, and Law Com No 254 (n 25) para 8.43, which indicates that mistake is intended to encompass the old grounds, though this does not sit easily with what the same report also stated at paras 8.38 and 8.40.

71 Law Com CP No 227 (n 3) para 13.162.

72 *Blacklocks v JB Developments (Godalming) Ltd* [1982] Ch 183.

Davies. There is much to be said for the view of Farrand[73] that the judgment is based upon the equitable right to rectify documents, rather than the statutory right to rectify the Register. Barnsley[74] was sharply critical of the statutory right being treated as an overriding interest, claiming that it 'by-passes the statutory code … and produces a result capable of working injustice in certain situations'. It might be added that any doubt regarding the proprietary status of the equitable right to rectify documents has been laid to rest by section 116 of the LRA 2002, but there is no indication that section 116 could apply to the *statutory* right to rectify.[75]

B. Recognition of the Analysis in *Malory* and *Swift 1st*

Despite this inauspicious start, Arden LJ accepted in *Malory Enterprises Ltd v Cheshire Homes (UK) Ltd*[76] that the statutory right to rectify the Register could be an overriding interest—at that time, under the old section 70(1)(g) of the LRA 1925—when coupled with actual occupation. It appears to be assumed that the right to rectify the Register gains proprietary status as a consequence of the status of the equitable right to rectify documents. In truth, this merely begs the question of proprietary status. It fails to engage with the reality that the equitable and statutory rights have different origins and can apply in different situations, even though there are occasions (most notably *Blacklocks*) when they may overlap. Nor is there any attempt to consider the consequences of proprietary status.

Malory concerned a forged transfer. The question was whether the innocent transferee could be bound by an overriding interest consisting of the right to rectify. One specific argument put to the court[77] was that this right arose *after* registration. Arden LJ treated registration and the right as arising at the same time, such that registration does not predate the right. There is some merit in this—it is redolent of the rejection of the scintilla temporis analysis by the House of Lord in *Abbey National BS v Cann*.[78] However, the legislation requires '[a]n interest belonging at the time of the disposition …'.[79] It is very difficult to say that the right to rectify exists at that stage.[80]

Although the overriding interest point was central to *Swift 1st*, little was said about it. Patten LJ observed[81] that:

> the court's determination [in *Malory*] that the right … to obtain rectification of the register was capable of taking effect as an overriding interest has generally escaped criticism and is not challenged on this appeal …

[73] JT Farrand [1983] *Conv* 169, 257.

[74] DG Barnsley, 'Rectification, Trusts and Overriding Interests' [1983] *Conv* 361, 366. Barnsley believes that the judgment was based on the statutory right to rectify.

[75] See Law Com No 271 (n 26) paras 5.32 ff.

[76] *Malory* (n 23) [66]–[70].

[77] ibid [69].

[78] *Abbey National BS v Cann* [1991] 1 AC 56 (HL).

[79] LRA 2002, sch 3, para 2.

[80] See P Milne [2015] *Conv* 356, 363. In contrast, *Blacklocks* involved the assertion of a right to rectify against a subsequent transferee. There would, of course, be no difficulty in saying that a statutory right to rectify exists at the time of that subsequent transfer.

[81] [2015] EWCA Civ 330, [2015] Ch 602, [37].

This may be unduly optimistic. Though Harpum[82] and Fox[83] were supportive of the *Malory* dicta on this point, Cooke[84] and Milne[85] have been distinctly hostile and Goymour[86] somewhat sceptical about the point. Though it is certainly correct that other aspects of *Malory* have attracted far more criticism, there had not been consistent support for the overriding interest analysis.

C. Consequences of Overriding Interest Status

As stated by Lord Denning MR in *Strand Securities Ltd v Caswell*,[87] overriding interests are intended 'to protect a person in actual occupation of land from having his rights lost in the welter of registration … No one can buy the land over his head and thereby take away or diminish his rights'.

It is easy to see how this might operate on the facts of *Blacklocks*.[88] A transfer of land by the claimant to G mistakenly included an unintended area. G subsequently sold the land to the defendant, though the claimant had remained in actual occupation of the excess area. The status of the claimant's interest as an overriding interest protected the claimant against the normal effects of registration of the defendant as proprietor. This applies whether the case involved the equitable right to rectify documents as an overriding interest or the statutory right to rectify as an overriding interest.

However, the status of the statutory right as an overriding interest remains open to objection. It can be argued that it is quite different from normal proprietary interests (including the equitable right to rectify documents)—remembering that *National Provincial Bank Ltd v Ainsworth*[89] limited actual occupation overriding interests to 'rights in reference to land which have the quality of being capable of enduring through different ownerships of the land, according to normal conceptions of title to real property'. It is certainly arguable that schedule 4 constitutes an exhaustive code regarding rectification of the Register—and that affording overriding status to the statutory right to rectify is an unintended and disruptive complication.

The overriding interest analysis, based upon the statutory right to rectify, is more curious on the facts of *Malory*. Normally, overriding interests operate so as to bind subsequent purchasers, such as the defendant in *Blacklocks*. To apply it against the initial transferee in *Malory* is equivalent to applying it against G in *Blacklocks*. Regardless of the overriding interest, there is already a right to rectify the title of the initial transferee in *Malory* (and that of G in *Blacklocks*). Taking *Malory* as an example, the registration of the forged transfer

[82] Harpum, 'Registered Land—A Law Unto Itself?' (n 30) 197–198.

[83] D Fox, 'Forgery and Alteration of the Register under the Land Registration Act 2002' in E Cooke (ed), *Modern Studies in Property Law, Volume 3* (Oxford, Hart Publishing, 2005) 30.

[84] E Cooke [2004] *Conv* 482, 486.

[85] P Milne [2015] *Conv* 356, 361 ff.

[86] Goymour, 'Mistaken Registrations of Land' (n 14) 640.

[87] *Strand Securities Ltd v Caswell* [1965] Ch 958, 979, recently quoted by Lord Collins in *Southern Pacific Mortgages Ltd v Scott* [2014] UKSC 52, [2015] AC 385 [34].

[88] *Blacklocks* (n 72).

[89] *National Provincial Bank Ltd v Ainsworth* [1965] AC 1175, 1226, 1228, 1240, 1262, approving Russell LJ in the Court of Appeal, [1964] Ch 665, 696.

was clearly a mistake for the purposes of schedule 4. The same would be true in non-forgery cases, as where the wrong person is registered as proprietor. When there is a right to rectify the initial transferee's title, why should it be relevant that this right to rectify also amounts to an overriding interest?

A role for an overriding interest analysis might be found if it means that rectification is, in practical terms, automatic.[90] This is only likely to be relevant in the quite rare[91] situation where the transferee has the protection of a proprietor in possession.[92] Where there is no possession, alteration has to be ordered unless there are 'exceptional circumstances'—this seems to apply whether or not there is an overriding interest. However, Dixon[93] has argued persuasively that it is inappropriate to treat a claim to rectify as an entitlement to rectification—there is never a right to rectification or automatic rectification.

Overall, it may be thought that there is no role (and nor should there be) for the statutory right to rectify as an overriding interest as regards the initial transferee.

D. A Useful Role in the Modern Law?

This section considers whether the right to rectify as an overriding interest plays a useful role today. In doing so, we will return to the two situations just discussed, regarding subsequent purchasers (*Blacklocks* style cases) and proprietors taking directly under the mistake (*Malory* and *Swift 1st* style cases).

As regards the first situation (the three-party scenario), the simple point can be made that *Gold Harp* permits rectification against the subsequent proprietor. There is no need to rely on an overriding interest analysis—it may be noted that there was no actual occupation in *Gold Harp*. This argument is subject to an important caveat. As we have seen, there might be situations in which the *Gold Harp* paragraph 8 analysis does not apply, especially if it is limited to derivative interests. There could be a role for overriding interests in such situations, at least if no other methods of affecting subsequent proprietors can be made to work.

Turning to the second situation (the two-party scenario), it has already been seen that the overriding interest is largely redundant: rectification is already available.

E. Alternative Ideas

In the case of a mistaken registration (such as of the forged charge in *Swift 1st*), could it be argued that the original owner has a proprietary interest, other than the right to rectify? This proprietary interest might take the form of a legal or equitable fee simple.

[90] It was common ground in *Malory* that there should be rectification (*Malory* (n 23) [66]) and in *Swift 1st* rectification had taken place unopposed (*Swift 1st* (n 2) [5]).

[91] It will be rare because actual occupation will normally preclude possession by the transferee—unless the actual occupation is given up before the rectification proceedings.

[92] Technically, the overriding interest would mean that no loss is caused by the alteration, as assumed in *Swift 1st* (n 2). In those circumstances the alteration would not amount to rectification and the proprietor in possession protection would not apply.

[93] M Dixon, 'Rectifying the Register under the LRA 2002: The *Malory 2* Non-Problem' [2016] *Conv* 382.

Swift 1st holds that a transferee taking under a forged transfer has a good legal and equitable title. That proposition is fully accepted, but might the original proprietor, who has remained in actual occupation, claim a possessory fee simple which has the status of an overriding interest? No such argument featured in *Swift 1st* and the Court of Appeal apparently assumes that there is no such overriding interest—otherwise there would have been no need to rely upon the right to rectify as an overriding interest. Accordingly, the following discussion flies in the face of orthodoxy, as expressed in *Swift 1st*.

When discussing whether the right to rectify could be an overriding interest, a distinction was drawn between situations in which it binds the immediate registered disponee (whose registration was a mistake) and those in which it binds a subsequent disponee. In the present discussion, we will concentrate upon the position of the immediate disponee—as did *Swift 1st*. We will start by asking whether the original proprietor can claim an *equitable* fee simple by way of overriding interest. This has been the basis upon which most discussion of the position has proceeded. It is uncontroversial that section 58 of the LRA 2002 confers the legal estate upon the transferee. This makes it difficult (but perhaps not impossible, as discussed later in this section) to argue that the original proprietor could argue a legal fee simple by way of overriding interest.

Most of the following discussion is based upon the supposition that the disposition takes the form of a transfer of the registered freehold estate. However, there might be a mistaken registration of a lease or (as in *Swift 1st*) a charge. In these situations, the original proprietor has the legal fee simple both before and after the mistaken registration. Towards the end of this section, it will be asked whether this might affect the analysis.

Where there is mistaken registration of a transfer of a registered estate (forgeries provide the best example), two arguments may be advanced *against* the recognition that the original proprietor, if in actual occupation, may have a freehold title that could be an overriding interest. The first is that section 58 of the LRA 2002 confers both legal and beneficial ownership,[94] such as to preclude the assertion of equitable ownership by the original proprietor. An argument as wide as this is unacceptable—the *Williams & Glyn's Bank Ltd v Boland*[95] line of cases demonstrates that beneficial rights can be overriding interests. More credible is the second argument that, prior to the mistaken or forged transfer, the original proprietor does not have any equitable estate[96]—it is widely considered that it is fallacious to assert that a beneficial legal owner has both legal and equitable titles. Rather, there is legal ownership with no equitable claim by another person as beneficiary. This is a formidable argument, though Gardner has responded that finding an equitable interest is 'both intelligible and juridically supported', being based on the lack of intention on the part of the original proprietor to transfer title.[97]

[94] Harpum, 'Registered Land—A Law Unto Itself?' (n 30) 197–202, supported by E Cooke [2004] *Conv* 482, 485–486. The contrary view is taken by A Hill-Smith [2009] *Conv* 127, 133–135 and S Gardner [2013] *Conv* 530, 535.

[95] *Williams & Glyn's Bank Ltd v Boland* [1981] AC 487.

[96] E Cooke [2013] *Conv* 344, 349; A Goymour [2013] *CLJ* 616, 643–644. *Boland* (n 95) is different, as the occupier never had anything other than an equitable interest.

[97] S Gardner [2013] *Conv* 530, especially at 533.

Perhaps the fullest judicial consideration of the point is that of Newey J in *Fitzwilliam v Richall Holdings Services Ltd*.[98] Although he did not need to decide whether the original registered proprietor could claim a fee simple as an overriding interest, Newey J described as 'unattractive' the proposition that the only person with an interest in land who cannot claim an actual occupation overriding interest is the original registered proprietor. Indeed, one might suppose that such a person has the best claim to protection! The original proprietor in actual occupation would readily be awarded rectification against a person whose disposition was mistakenly registered. Nevertheless, there remains the problem that the effect of *Swift 1st* is that the transferee is the legal and beneficial owner of the property until rectification. This provides entitlement to occupation and rents (where there is a tenant) for the intervening period.[99]

In response to the analysis of Newey J, it can be argued that the actual occupation analysis does not work well where the purchaser is dealing (innocently) with a forger, who forges the signature of the original proprietor. The normal conveyancing consequence of actual occupation is that the purchaser makes enquiries of the occupier—the legislation protects the purchaser if the occupier unreasonably fails to disclose the claim.[100] This is nonsensical in the forgery context as described above, as the purchaser believes that the apparent vendor (the forger) is the person in actual occupation—the person whose signature is forged. Asking the vendor whether they have claims to the land is clearly superfluous.[101] So if we are serious about protecting transferees taking under forgeries, as evidenced by schedule 8, paragraph 1(2)(b), and *Swift 1st*, then it may be queried whether it makes sense to accept that the original registered proprietor in actual occupation has an overriding interest. Nevertheless, it remains an open question whether these arguments are sufficiently convincing to defeat the claim of the original proprietor.

A rather different, if unconventional, point is that the original registered proprietor may be able to assert *legal* ownership as an overriding interest. Though section 58 confers legal title on the new proprietor, it does not in terms defeat any rival legal claim.[102] In other words, the original registered proprietor may retain a legal fee simple despite the loss of the registered title.[103] Furthermore, the Law Commission[104] earlier accepted the argument that there can be more than one legal fee simple in registered land—strong support for the point here proposed. A possible objection might be that the occupier's legal estate disappears once the registration removes their name from the Register, as in *Malory*. However, it is not obvious that their title depends solely upon the Register.

Finally, is the position different if the mistaken registration is of a lease or charge, so that the original proprietor, who is in actual occupation, also remains throughout the registered

[98] *Fitzwilliam v Richall* (n 32) [89]–[92]. The finding as to the effect of forgery must be treated as being overruled by *Swift 1st* (n 2), but that is not the identical issue. The approach of Newey J appears to have been assumed by Wilberforce J in *Re Boyle's Claim* [1961] 1 WLR 339.

[99] This sort of point was raised in *Malory* (n 23) [45], [65]. It was held that the original proprietor could sue in trespass, but that was on the now discredited ground that registration of a forged transfer did not confer good equitable title.

[100] LRA 2002, sch 3, para 2(b).

[101] This argument was seen and adopted by Law Com CP No 227 (n 3) para 13.63.

[102] Rival claims would be defeated by LRA 2002, ss 11 (first registrations) and 29 (registered dispositions), but those provisions are subject to overriding interests.

[103] See also Goymour and Hickey, ch 6 above.

[104] Law Com No 254 (n 25) para 10.27, in the adverse possession context.

proprietor? This was the position in *Swift 1st*, which involved a forged charge. Here, it seems easier to argue that the original proprietor has a legal fee simple, which may be an overriding interest. It might appear odd that a registered estate could be overriding in this way,[105] but (as stressed by Newey J in *Fitzwilliam*) we are used to protecting occupiers' rights.

What conclusions may be drawn? It has to be recognised that *Swift 1st* is inconsistent with any argument that there is an overriding interest in the form of a legal or equitable fee simple, although the court did not explicitly address the point. Leaving that on one side, there are respectable arguments in favour of an equitable fee simple or (at least in mistaken registrations of leases and charges) a legal fee simple. There are, of course, difficulties with these arguments; as a matter of principle, the status of such overriding interests cannot be said to be beyond argument.

F. Conclusions and Recent Law Commission Proposals

If the original proprietor can claim an overriding interest as legal or equitable owner, then it is plainly superfluous to recognise the statutory right to rectify as an overriding interest in cases such as *Malory* and *Swift 1st*. Now that *Gold Harp* has shown rectification may be sought against subsequent purchasers, the law has no need for such a new and arguably unprincipled form of proprietary right as an overriding interest. It is difficult to avoid the conclusion that it was because both the equitable right and the statutory right refer to 'rectification' that the jump between them was made. One wonders whether the law would have developed in the same fashion if the LRA 1925 had used the language of 'alteration' or 'amendment' rather than 'rectification'. Bearing in mind the relatively weak support for the statutory right to rectify as an overriding interest,[106] it may be concluded that it should be rejected.

The Law Commission considers these questions in its 2016 Consultation Paper. After a fairly brief analysis, it concludes that the statutory right to rectify should not be recognised as an overriding interest.[107] This is partly because of doubts about whether the nature of the right is sufficiently proprietary, and partly because an overriding interest usually precludes indemnity.[108]

The Law Commission also discusses whether the original proprietor could have an equitable fee simple by way of overriding interest. The firm conclusion is reached that there should be no such right.[109] This is based partly on the difficulty in finding a separate equitable right prior to the mistaken transfer, and partly because the recognition of such a right would bypass rectification and not allow for indemnity. The latter point follows because the alteration of the Register would not cause further prejudice to the proprietor whose title is altered and hence not count as rectification within schedules 4 and 8.

105 LRA 2002, sch 3 is headed 'Unregistered interests …', but the only explicit exclusion is that of interests protected by notice (s 29(3)).

106 See sections VI(A) and VI(B) above.

107 Law Com CP No 227 (n 3) paras 13.84–13.87. Dixon (n 93) argues that the limits on how the right operates as an overriding interest are such that statutory reform is not needed.

108 ibid paras 13.60–13.63

109 ibid paras 13.44 ff.

VII. Indemnity—General Considerations

The recent Law Commission's 2016 Consultation Paper contains a chapter on indemnity.[110] However, the issues there addressed do not include the matters discussed in this section.

It has been seen that indemnity may be payable if there is: (i) rectification, or (ii) a mistake in circumstances where rectification is not ordered.[111] It follows that the scope of mistake is crucial for these purposes. A narrow meaning of mistake will restrict rectification (which some commentators would regard as a good thing), but at the same time, will greatly restrict the scope for indemnity to be paid.

This link between indemnity and rectification came to the fore in some of the analyses (judicial and academic)[112] relating to the position of subsequent registered dispositions. The original mistaken registration might not cause loss where the new proprietor had not obtained a good title.[113] If there is a subsequent registered disposition, this may (without rectification) take priority over the original proprietor. This would, of course, cause loss to the original proprietor. Unless there could be rectification of that subsequent registration, the spectre arose of a situation in which the original proprietor could obtain neither rectification nor indemnity. As has been observed, it is almost impossible to justify that outcome and it which might well contravene human rights principles. Fortunately, *Gold Harp* employs paragraph 8 of schedule 4 to ensure that rectification is possible against the subsequent proprietor. This, combined with the Law Commission's support for rectification being available against the titles of subsequent proprietors, means that the most pressing concerns are allayed.

However, in contexts other than subsequent proprietors, it remains correct that a narrow scope for rectification (following from a narrow reading of mistake) entails a narrow scope for indemnity.

Prior to *Gold Harp*, there was a persuasive argument that the link between rectification and indemnity should be reviewed,[114] in order to permit a wider scope for indemnity. An existing example of this wider scope is provided by paragraph 1(2)(b) of schedule 8. This provision, discussed below, enables indemnity to be paid to a registered disponee taking in good faith under a forged disposition—even if the alteration of their title causes no new loss.

However, this would require a complete rethink of the principles and rules underpinning indemnity.[115] Given the use of paragraph 8 of schedule 4 in *Gold Harp*, the case for radical reform looks relatively weak today.

[110] Law Com CP No 227 (n 3) ch 14.

[111] See text to n 12 and n 13 above. Various administrative errors also give rise to indemnity, but these lie outside our present analysis.

[112] Examples are *Knights Construction* (n 70) [126]–[129], [131] (referred to with apparent approval in *Gold Harp* (n 1)) and S Cooper, 'Regulating Fallibility in Registered Land Titles' [2013] *CLJ* 341, 364.

[113] This was commonly discussed in the context of forgery, though this is redundant after *Swift 1st* (n 2). There are, however, other situations in which the problem can arise—as where the original registration (but not the subsequent registration) is bound by an overriding interest.

[114] In one minor context, this link would be broken by the Law Commission (Law Com CP No 227 (n 3) para 13.176): when rectification removes protection on first registration against an unprotected derivative interest (protection deriving from LRA 2002, s 11(4)). This is a curious proposal, given that there is priority prior to rectification and that rectification which deletes the new title will continue to give rise to indemnity.

[115] Any such reform would need to avoid open-ended liability. This risk torpedoed earlier proposals to indemnify purchasers bound by overriding interests: Law Com No 254 (n 25) para 4.19.

VIII. Forged Transfers and Schedule 8, Paragraph 1(2)(b)

It will be recalled that the LRA 2002, schedule 8, paragraph 1(2)(b), contains a special rule allowing an indemnity for a registered proprietor who innocently takes under a forged disposition. Whether or not registration provides a good title as against the original proprietor, they are financially protected if their title is rectified. It was common ground in *Swift 1st* that the purpose of paragraph 1(2)(b), in its earlier incarnation in the LRA 1925, was to reverse the effect of *Attorney-General v Odell.*[116] In that case, a purchaser's title had been rectified so as to restore the original registered proprietor. The Court of Appeal denied indemnity to the purchaser.

A very simple starting point is to ask whether paragraph 1(2)(b) is redundant today. Now that *Swift 1st* establishes that the legislation confers good legal and beneficial title, despite the forgery, on the purchaser upon his registration, the *Odell* problem has disappeared. If the new proprietor does have a good title, then rectification will cause loss: in the language of the LRA 2002, it 'prejudicially affects the title'.

It is not, unfortunately, quite as simple as that. What happens if the original registered proprietor has an overriding interest? The normal principle is that an alteration of the Register to give effect to an overriding interest simply reflects the existing legal position. It causes no (new) loss to the new registered proprietor and, accordingly, no indemnity is payable. We can reason either that the rectification causes no loss[117] or, under the LRA 2002, that there is alteration but not rectification in such circumstances.[118] It should be noted that these problems can arise whatever the nature of the overriding interest. In *Swift 1st*, it was a right to rectify, but a more conventional proprietary interest with the status of an overriding interest could give rise to almost identical issues.

A. The Construction of Paragraph 1(2)(b) Regarding Overriding Interests

Though there is no evidence that schedule 8, paragraph 1(2)(b), was drafted with overriding interests in mind, there is nothing in its wording which prevents it from applying where the original registered proprietor, whose signature was forged, has an overriding interest. It will be recalled that paragraph 1(2)(b) provides that the proprietor 'is ... to be regarded as having suffered loss by reason of such rectification'. This deeming of loss appears to apply regardless of whether there is an overriding interest. It was largely on this basis that the Court of Appeal in *Swift 1st* held that the provision applied, with the result that indemnity was payable.

Nevertheless, there is a problem in the wording of the provision: it applies only where there is rectification. If no loss is caused by the rectification, because the title of the proprietor was already subject to the rival claim, it simply is not rectification in the first place—it is merely alteration. However, as was most clearly pointed out at first instance in *Swift 1st*,[119]

[116] *Odell* (n 16).
[117] *Re Chowood's* (n 15).
[118] See LRA 2002, sch 8, para 11(2) (coupled with para 1(1)(a)).
[119] 31 January 2014, [35] (Richard Sheldon QC).

this would prevent paragraph 1(2)(b) from ever having any effect; that is unacceptable. The problem arises only as a consequence of the contrast between alteration and rectification introduced by the LRA 2002. There is absolutely no evidence that this change was intended to alter the operation of paragraph 1(2)(b), as compared to the corresponding provision previously found in the LRA 1925.

Patten LJ explicitly treated the issue as a difficult one. He accepted that paragraph 1(2)(b) was not designed to deal with overriding interests—overriding interests formed no part of *Odell*. However, he decided in favour of the claimant on the basis that the wording of the paragraph could not sensibly be limited: for an exception for overriding interests to exist 'some much clearer indication would ... be necessary in the language of the statute'.[120] Under the pre-LRA 2002 law, Hayton[121] had noted that indemnity would be payable and, as Patten LJ stressed, there is no indication that the Law Commission intended to limit the effect of the paragraph.

A consequential question is raised by Milne.[122] Insofar as paragraph 1(2)(b) gives protection where there is an overriding interest, does this apply also to a subsequent registered purchaser? At first sight, it appears curious if such persons were not to be indemnified. However, it is mentioned below[123] that one can justify indemnity for the person taking under the forged disposition where the vendor (in fact the forger) is thought to be the same person as the person in actual occupation (whose signature is forged). This is not the case as regards a subsequent purchaser: it is clear to that purchaser that the occupier (still the person whose signature was forged) is not the vendor in the subsequent purchase.

B. Special Characteristics of the Right to Rectify as an Overriding Interest

Swift 1st involved a statutory right to rectify as an overriding interest. In this section, we investigate whether that right possesses special characteristics such that it is not necessary to rely on schedule 8, paragraph 1(2)(b). This will be vitally important for indemnity claims where the mistake is something other than forgery, so that the paragraph is inapplicable; it would also reduce the significance of paragraph 1(2)(b) where there is forgery.

Why might the right to rectify lie outside the normal rules applying to overriding interests? With other overriding interests, it is clear that the alteration of the Register, to give effect to the interest, does not cause any loss—and that for that reason, the 'alteration' is not an indemnity-triggering 'rectification'. However, with the right to rectify, there is a danger of circularity. Absent any overriding interest, we would not dream of suggesting that rectification causes no loss simply because there is a right to rectify. Take the following example. By mistake, P is registered as a chargee of land owned by L. L had earlier leased the land to T, receiving the rent. In this example, L is not in actual occupation[124] and P appears

[120] *Swift 1st* (n 2) [51].

[121] DJ Hayton, *Registered Land*, 2nd edn (London, Sweet and Maxwell, 1981) 185.

[122] P Milne [2015] *Conv* 356, 364. The question is whether that the subsequent proprietor claims 'under a forged disposition'. Though it might be thought that the wording does not naturally apply, one might contrast the wording used in the rectification context in the LRA 1925, when it was intended that later purchasers should not be covered: 'immediate disposition to him was void' (LRA 1925, s 82(3)(b)).

[123] See text to n 133.

[124] It was otherwise prior to the LRA 2002.

not to be in possession. Rectification will almost certainly be ordered,[125] as there are no 'exceptional circumstances'[126] to deny it. It is plain that indemnity will be paid: it cannot be argued that P's title was always subject to L's right to rectify.

If the likelihood of rectification has no effect on an indemnity claim, why should it be different if there is an overriding interest consisting of the right to rectify? This is, perhaps, most problematic if there is an overriding interest binding a subsequent proprietor: the *Blacklocks* scenario. Suppose that in the above example P subsequently sells the charge to Q; at the time of Q's registration as the new registered chargee, the lease has ended and L is in actual occupation. Is it rational that P should receive indemnity if there had been no transfer to Q, but that Q could not receive an indemnity after the charge had been transferred to him? After all, it is the same right to rectify that affects P that is binding on Q. A possible response is that Q could have discovered the true position by making enquiries of L. However, that can be taken into account under paragraph 5 of schedule 8: lack of proper care may deny or reduce indemnity.

Malory and *Swift 1st* both involved the initial mistaken transfer being affected by the overriding interest. For similar reasons, it can be argued that there is little justification for denying indemnity in such cases—indeed, it might be argued that denial of indemnity would be the principal effect of recognising the right to rectify as an overriding interest. This further supports the earlier criticism of the right to rectify as an overriding interest.

There has been little discussion of the question whether the statutory right to rectify, assuming it has the status of an overriding interest, might be outside the *Chowood* limits on indemnity.[127] It is fair to say that most academic discussion of the area assumes that *Chowood* applies,[128] such that the overriding interest means that no loss is caused by alteration and so no indemnity is payable. It was also assumed in *Swift 1st*. However, those who have discussed the point have been inclined not to apply *Chowood*.[129] It is suggested that these last commentators are well justified in taking that position.

C. Should Paragraph 1(2)(b) be Retained?

In *Swift 1st*, Patten LJ found the interpretation of schedule 8, paragraph 1(2)(b), difficult and deserving of review by the Law Commission. There are two inter-related questions to ask. The first is whether it should apply to overriding interests. The second is whether it should simply be repealed.

Apart from the overriding interest point, it is difficult to see any role for the provision. This is because *Swift 1st* decided that a good title is given by the registration of a forged transfer, as a result of section 58 of the LRA 2002. Loss is today caused by the rectification (if rectification is ordered):[130] no special rule is required to enable the transferee to claim indemnity.

[125] As in *Swift 1st* (n 2), though that case also involved an overriding interest.

[126] LRA 2002, sch 4, paras 3(3), 6(3).

[127] For discussion of *Chowood* see text to n 15 above.

[128] DG Barnsley [1983] *Conv* 361, 364 provides an early example. See also Harpum, 'Registered Land—A Law Unto Itself?' (n 30) 198.

[129] Fox, 'Forgery and Alteration of the Register under the Land Registration Act 2002' (n 83) 31–32; E Lees (2015) 131 *LQR* 515, 518 (see also [2014] *CLJ* 250, 252); P Milne [2015] *Conv* 356, 360.

[130] If rectification is refused (most likely because the transferee is in possession) then the original proprietor is clearly entitled to indemnity.

Accordingly, the application of paragraph 1(2)(b) to cases where the title of the party against whom rectification is sought is affected by an overriding interest, forms its sole role today. Can it be justified? The technical wording of the provision is not here in issue: we are concerned with legal policy issues. Though its application to overriding interests is an unintended effect of paragraph 1(2)(b), it does not necessarily follow that it is inappropriate. More important, perhaps, is whether forgery is justified as the sole exceptional situation in which an overriding interest does not preclude indemnity.

It is important to remember that paragraph 1(2)(b) applies to all overriding interests—not just rights to rectify.[131] Take the following example. H and W are registered proprietors, holding as trustees for themselves as beneficial tenants in common. H forges W's signature on a charge, which is registered. It is clear that W's beneficial interest is an overriding interest binding the chargee (assuming that W is relevantly in actual occupation).[132] If the charge is deleted from the Register, should the chargee be entitled to indemnity?

At least at first sight, such entitlement appears dubious. Being bound by an overriding interest is one of the risks inherent in transactions involving the purchasing or charging of land: a purchaser or chargee should take steps to discover overriding interests. Whilst a few overriding interests will exist where there has been a forgery, the majority will not.

However, it can be argued that there are good reasons to protect the purchaser. This can be seen as part of the general rationale behind singling out forgery in paragraph 1(2)(b)—even before *Swift 1st*, there was a perception that a purchaser who is taken in by a forgery and is registered (the Registrar having been similarly taken in) is deserving of protection. There is, indeed, a good reason to single out forgery. In nearly all other situations, the person in actual occupation will be somebody other than the proprietor—an enquiry of that person is obviously required in such cases. However, in the case of a forged transfer of land, the purchaser believes that the person in actual occupation is the person who is transferring the land—the purchaser will understandably think it pointless and nonsensical to make enquiry of the occupier/vendor.[133] Of course, we might seek to criticise the purchaser for being taken in by the forgery and not insisting upon proper proof of identity. However, that argument is valid as regards any forgery, regardless of actual occupation. The key point is that the added element of actual occupation does not seem to be a conclusive reason against paying indemnity.

On the other hand, paragraph 1(2)(b) may also operate where the overriding interest is held by a third party, rather than (as in *Swift 1st*) the purported vendor. This may be illustrated as follows. Suppose that O holds on a constructive trust for herself and her partner, M. F forges O's signature in a transfer to P. P is registered as proprietor, but that title is altered so as to restore O (in actual occupation) as proprietor. It seems clear that paragraph 1(2)(b) operates to support an indemnity for P to the extent of O's beneficial interest, applying *Swift 1st*. But does it mean that P can claim indemnity in relation to

[131] But many overriding interests will not involve forgeries and will thus be outside the scope of LRA 2002, para 1(2)(b); *Re Chowood's* (n 15) itself provides an example.

[132] This appears to have been conceded in *Mortgage Corpn v Shaire* [2001] Ch 743, 756 and assumed in *Abbey National plc v Moss* (1994) 26 HLR 249. It is unaffected by *Swift 1st* (n 2), given that W has an equitable interest predating the forgery.

[133] See also text to nn 100–101, in the context of overriding interests where there has been a forgery.

M's claim, notwithstanding M's overriding interest? There is nothing in its wording that restricts its operation in these circumstances. Yet it would be wholly irrational to indemnify P in respect of M's claim, as a trust beneficiary, when P purchases under a forgery, but not if P had in fact purchased from O (the archetypal *Boland* scenario). Even if paragraph 1(2)(b) is retained, this situation would benefit from statutory clarification.

Overall, a case can be made for maintaining the paragraph 1(2)(b) protection of the purchaser, perhaps contrary to what might be expected. This is supported by the point made above that any lack of proper care will deny or limit indemnity. But is this sufficient to repel the arguments that the rather specialised context of overriding interests is insufficient to justify maintaining a special rule, and that singling out forgery is anomalous?[134] There may be defects in transfers other than forgery (*non est factum* springs to mind)[135] where a similar case could be made for paying indemnity to the purchaser. This makes it more difficult to justify retaining a special rule limited to forgery. In any event, the significance of paragraph 1(2)(b) is diminished if the overriding interest is a right to rectify and the law is developed, as proposed above, so that this rectification does cause loss.[136] Certainly, it would be difficult to justify inserting a provision like paragraph 1(2)(b) if it did not already exist. Though the arguments are finely balanced, it is suggested that it should be repealed.

[134] See E Lees (2015) 131 *LQR* 515, 518.

[135] Other examples may be lack of capacity or where the transfer can be challenged for undue influence or some similar invalidating conduct.

[136] This would allow indemnity on the facts of *Swift 1st* (n 2), assuming that the right to rectify is the only overriding interest that can be claimed.

10

De-throning King Midas: The New Law of Land Registration in Scotland

KENNETH GC REID

I. Introduction

A. Looking to England

Until little more than a century ago, a lawyer from Scotland who chose to examine the state of land registration south of the border would return with his sense of national superiority agreeably renewed. For if nations, like people, were good at different things, then the Scots were good at land registration and the English, quite frankly, were not:

> [A]s some Sciences, Trades and Inventions flourish more, because more cultivat in one Nation than another, humane nature allowing no universal excellency, and God designing thus to gratifie every Countrey that he hath created; So Scotland hath above all other Nations, by a serious and long experience, obviated most happily all frauds, by their publick Registers.[1]

In the pamphlet from which that quotation is taken, written in the third quarter of the seventeenth century, Sir George Mackenzie—Lord Advocate, man of letters, and persecutor of the Covenanters[2]—was responding to a view expressed in English legal circles that there was no need for registration of land. In the eyes of Mackenzie, the desirability of a system of registration was a self-evident truth:

> [I]f any man in England can for a Crown, know in the space of a day, the condition of these from whom he purchases, then Registers are not necessary, but if otherwise, they are: If any Lawyer in England can assure his Client, that the purchase he makes is secure above all hazard, then Registers are not necessary; but if they cannot, then Registers are necessary.[3]

[1] G Mackenzie, 'An Answer to some Reasons printed in England, against the overture of bringing into that Kingdom, such Registers as are used in Scotland' in G Mackenzie, *Pleadings in some Remarkable Cases Before the Supreme Courts of Scotland Since the Year 1661, To which, the Decisions are Subjoyn'd* (Edinburgh, George Swintoun, James Glen and Thomas Brown, 1673) 221, 222.

[2] For an account of Mackenzie's remarkable career, see A Lang, *Sir George Mackenzie* (London, Longmans, Green & Co, 1909); C Jackson, 'Mackenzie, Sir George, of Rosehaugh (1636/1638–1691)' in *Oxford Dictionary of National Biography* (2004) vol 35, 580.

[3] Mackenzie, 'An Answer to some Reasons printed in England' (n 1) 226.

In short, Mackenzie concluded, since:

> Registers have been found so advantageous, and that experience hath herein seconded reason, it is humbly conceived, that Scotland is much to be magnified for their Registers; And that England may, without disparagement, introduce this new amongst their old Statutes.[4]

England, needless to say, was unpersuaded.

By the time Mackenzie was writing, the system he extolled was already more than half a century old.[5] Established by statute in 1617,[6] the Register of Sasines was a public register of deeds; and if not the oldest land register in Europe, it may have been the first to operate on a national, rather than merely a local, basis. After 1617 registration was an indispensable requirement for the transfer of land, and potential acquirers thus had the reassurance of protection against latent and unregistered deeds. One result is that today there is virtually no unregistered land in Scotland, if by this is understood land in respect of which deeds are registered in the Register of Sasines.

Thus matters stood for 300 years. But by the start of the twentieth century, an uneasy feeling began to find expression that other countries had drawn level with Scotland in matters of land registration, or had even overtaken it. It was true that, in England and Wales, the first tentative steps towards a national system of registration dated only from the 1860s.[7] Yet, while slow to begin, England had the advantage of the late starter in having available as models the systems of land registration in other countries, and particularly those of Germany and the Hapsburg Empire.[8] With the legislation of 1897,[9] and especially that of 1925,[10] England seemed to have opened up a decisive lead over Scotland. By comparison with the system of registration of title in England, Scotland's system of registration of deeds, efficient as it was, was beginning to look distinctly old-fashioned. And so it was that traditional Scottish condescension towards the position in England gave way, first, to admiration and, in the course of time, to imitation.

B. Registration of Title and the Act of 1979

For Scotland, registration of title was always a more natural 'fit' than it had ever been for England. Not only is Scotland's land law simpler than that of England—there are no equitable rights, hardly any rights created off-Register, and, after 2004, no feudal system—but Scotland has the system of absolute (as opposed to relative) title that registration of

[4] ibid, 232.

[5] For the history of land registration in Scotland, see especially: L Ockrent, *Land Rights: An Enquiry into the History of Registration for Publication in Scotland* (Edinburgh, William Hodge, 1942); KGC Reid and GL Gretton, *Land Registration* (Edinburgh, Avizandum Publishing Ltd, 2017) ch 1.

[6] Registration Act 1617, APS iv 545 c 16, RPS 1617/5/30.

[7] For the history of land registration in England and Wales, see S Anderson, 'Property' in *The Oxford History of the Laws of England* vol XII (Oxford, Oxford University Press, 2010) 3, 213–31; E Cooke, *The New Law of Land Registration* (Oxford, Hart Publishing, 2003) 15–34.

[8] See in particular the report to Parliament by C Fortescue-Brickdale, the Assistant Registrar of the (English) Land Registry: *Registration of Title to Land: General and Detailed Reports of the Assistant Registrar of the Land Registry on the Systems of Registration of Title now in operation in Germany and Austria-Hungary* (1896, C 8139).

[9] Land Transfer Act 1897.

[10] Land Registration Act 1925.

title more or less presupposes. Once, therefore, the idea began to be advocated, at the beginning of the 20th century, it was not surprising that it should in the end be adopted.[11] Initially, however, there was a natural reluctance to abandon the system which had served well for more than 300 years. A Royal Commission which reported in 1910 was unable to reach agreement as to whether to support registration of title, and the matter lapsed for half a century.[12] When it revived, the view taken was largely positive. In 1963 a committee under the chairmanship of Lord Reid recommended that registration of title should be introduced,[13] a second committee was then established to consider a series of technical issues,[14] and legislation—the Land Registration (Scotland) Act—was passed in 1979 (the '1979 Act').

Following the passage of the Act, registration of title was phased in, county by county, over a period of 20 years. Once a county was 'operational' for the new system, any transfer for value triggered registration in the new Land Register. The first titles were registered in 1981; by 2014, 58% of all titles, representing 26% of the country's land mass, had migrated from the Register of Sasines to the Land Register.[15] The current target is to complete the migration by 2024, with the help of voluntary registration and, where necessary, registration carried out by officials at the Register without the participation of the owner.[16]

The actual legislation, however, proved less successful. In seeking to introduce registration of title, the Reid Committee had available to it three main models: the system in England, the Torrens systems in Australia and elsewhere, and the systems found in Germany and central Europe. With the parochialism of the time, only the first of these was given serious consideration, and the 1979 Act turned out to be a close (if much simplified) copy of the English Act of 1925.[17] The three structural pillars of the latter—registration, rectification, and indemnity—all found their way into the Scottish legislation; and, crucially, registration, as well as being a necessary condition for the acquisition of property rights, as had been the case in Scotland since 1617, became a sufficient condition as well. As in England, therefore, the system of registration of title adopted in Scotland was one of title by registration.

It was not to prosper. Misgivings as to the 1979 legislation were quick to emerge. As early as the mid-1980s some harsh things were being said about the new system,[18] and many of these (and other) criticisms appeared to be borne out by subsequent experience as well as by court decisions. The government's response was to refer the matter to the Scottish Law Commission; and beginning in 2003 the Commission engaged in an intensive review

[11] For details, see Reid and Gretton (n 5) paras 1.13–1.17.

[12] *Reports by the Royal Commission on Registration of Title in Scotland* (Cd 5316, 1910).

[13] *Registration of Title to Land in Scotland: Report by a Committee appointed by the Secretary of State for Scotland* (Cmnd 2032, 1963) ('Reid Report').

[14] *Scheme for the Introduction and Operation of Registration of Title to Land in Scotland: Report by a Committee appointed by the Secretary of State for Scotland* (Cmnd 4137, 1969).

[15] Registers of Scotland, *Completion of the Land Register: Public Consultation* (2014), paras 4, 16 and 17.

[16] Reid and Gretton (n 5), ch 7. Provision for registration by officials at the Register is made by s 29 of the Land Registration etc (Scotland) Act 2012 ('2012 Act').

[17] Reid Report (n 13) para 66: 'We ... received some evidence about the South African system, but conditions there are so different that we have not thought it necessary to consider that system in detail. For the same reason we have not investigated the Torrens system or any of the systems in use in Europe'.

[18] See in particular the series of articles by the present writer published in (1984) 29 *Journal of the Law Society of Scotland* 171, 212, and 260.

of land registration.[19] The Commission's final report, published in 2010,[20] was swiftly followed by legislation, the Land Registration etc (Scotland) Act 2012 ('2012 Act'), which came into force on 8 December 2014.[21]

The 2012 Act marks a decisive break with title by registration and with a number of other features of the (English) Land Registration Act 1925, and now of the Land Registration Act ('LRA') 2002. Little more than 30 years after joining, the Scots have deserted the English camp. This chapter considers why.

C. Protection: Who? and How?

If all titles were good, the type of system of land registration would hardly matter. But in cases where titles are not good—where a person seeking to sell or burden land is not the land's owner or where the implementing deed is defective in some way—two difficult choices fall to be made by the law. One is *who* to protect; the other is *how* to protect. And while the questions are different and distinct, the answer to the one is likely to influence the answer to the other, making it of particular importance to determine the order in which the questions are answered. The choice of who to protect is a choice between the person seeking to acquire the property right and the person who owns the land; the choice of how to protect lies between protection which is automatic but defeasible and protection which is indefeasible but must be earned. Since the first is a matter of policy and the second, largely, one of technique, it seems obvious that technique should serve policy and not the other way around. In this chapter, therefore, I begin with the question of policy before moving on to consider the question of technique.

II. The Question of Policy: Who is to be Protected?

A. Security of Ownership or Facility of Transfer?

Who, when things go wrong, is to be protected—the person who is seeking to acquire the property right, or the person who is the property's owner? The traditional answer is not in doubt. A transfer which is radically defective is no transfer at all. Ownership, therefore, remains where it was, and the would-be acquirer must go without. That was the rule for unregistered conveyancing in England and Wales. It was equally the rule for transfers registered in the Register of Sasines in Scotland.

[19] The Scottish Law Commission issued three Discussion Papers for comment, namely: *Land Registration: Void and Voidable Titles* (DP No 125, 2004); *Land Registration: Registration, Rectification and Indemnity* (Scot Law Com DP No 128, 2005); *Land Registration: Miscellaneous Issues* (Scot Law Com DP No 130, 2005). All publications of the Scottish Law Commission are available at www.scotlawcom.gov.uk. I was the Law Commissioner in charge of the project, and the author of the papers.

[20] Scottish Law Commission, *Report on Land Registration* (Scot Law Com No 222, 2010). My successor as Law Commissioner, Professor George Gretton, was responsible for the Report.

[21] For a study of the 2012 Act, see Reid and Gretton (n 5). The Act makes many changes which cannot be touched on in this chapter.

Registration of title cannot take this approach. Its very essence is that acquirers can rely on what they see, or do not see, on the register; and on this 'curtain principle'[22]—this assurance that nothing beyond the register need be consulted—depends the facility of transfer, and hence the reduced transaction costs, which form a large part of the system's attraction.[23] So if the register shows Robert as owner of Blackmains, the acquirer must be able to proceed on the basis that Robert is indeed the owner. Or if Blackmains is shown as unencumbered by charges or other burdens, that too must, so far as the acquirer is concerned, be treated as true. Registration of title thus offers both a positive and a negative warranty to acquirers—a warranty, positively, that what is stated on the register is true, and a warranty, negatively, that nothing which should be on the register has been omitted.[24] There is, of course, one pre-condition. An acquirer who knows the register to be wrong is not able to rely on its protection.[25] But subject to this requirement of good faith—or, in the negative (and by no means identical)[26] formulation often favoured by legislation, this requirement of absence of fraud—what acquirers see is also what they will get.

A move, then, from registration of deeds (or no registration at all) to registration of title is, necessarily, a move from protecting owners to protecting acquirers or, as it is sometimes put, from static security to dynamic security.[27] Yet the extent of the move is subject to a degree of choice. How complete should it be? If the old system protected owners always and acquirers never, should the new system give unqualified protection to acquirers (at least in the absence of fraud)? Some versions of the Torrens system come close to achieving this result. It has the attractions of simplicity and certainty. Yet it is neither fair to the owner nor as advantageous to the acquirer as first appears.

The unfairness to owners is self-evident. We do not need the European Convention on Human Rights ('ECHR') to remind us that confiscation of property requires strong justification, such as public benefit (as with compulsory purchase) or the owner's own long neglect (as with acquisitive prescription or adverse possession).[28] Viewed in this light, the convenience of acquirers might not be enough, or at least enough in all cases, to justify the act of confiscation.

[22] This term is widely used in the international literature on registration of title. It seems to have been coined by Theodore Ruoff, the Chief Land Registrar in England and Wales: see T Ruoff, 'An Englishman looks at the Torrens System' (1952) 26 *Australian Law Journal* 162 (reprinted, with other papers on land registration, in T Ruoff, *An Englishman Looks at the Torrens System: Being some Provocative Essays on the Operation of the System after One Hundred Years* (Sydney, Law Book of Australasia Pty, 1957)).

[23] The potential saving in transaction costs was a key argument for the introduction of registration of title in Scotland: see, eg, 'Land transfer reform in Scotland' (1904) 16 *Juridical Review* 316, 317–18; Reid Report (n 13) paras 60–63.

[24] For this terminology, see JE Hogg, *Registration of Title to Land Throughout the Empire* (Sydney, Law Book Co, 1920) 96–7. Hogg prefers 'affirmative' to 'positive'.

[25] One should perhaps say *should not* be able so to rely. In Scotland one of the defects of the 1979 Act was that, because only fraud or carelessness could remove an acquirer's protection, acquirers were protected against errors already present on the Register even if they knew the errors to exist: see *Dougbar Properties Ltd v Keeper of the Registers of Scotland* 1999 SC 513 (OH).

[26] As to which see Scottish Law Commission, DP No 125 (n 19) paras 7.1–7.7

[27] This terminology was first used in the context of land registration by Pamela O'Connor: see, eg, P O'Connor, 'Registration of Title in England and Australia: A Theoretical and Comparative Analysis' in E Cooke (ed), *Modern Studies in Property Law, Volume 2* (Oxford, Hart Publishing, 2003) 81, 85–6.

[28] The interaction of adverse possession with art 1 Protocol 1 of the ECHR was considered in the celebrated case of *JA Pye (Oxford) Ltd v United Kingdom* (2008) 46 EHRR 45. I do not, however, seek to argue that the confiscatory nature of registration of title is contrary to the ECHR; in this connection the compensation arrangements (discussed at section II(B) below) are of critical importance.

But acquirers too are made vulnerable by a rule cast in so uncompromising a form. They acquire a good title, of course, at the expense of the property's owner. But as owners in turn, they are vulnerable to the loss of ownership by the same means in the future. In an important insight, the American scholar, Thomas W Mapp, pointed out that: 'To whatever extent ... [a person] can acquire an interest from a predecessor through error, he is vulnerable to losing that interest through the same error repeated after his registration'. 'Easy come' (the ready acquisition of the property) leads inexorably to 'easy go' (the possibility of its subsequent loss to a future acquirer).[29] To make life easy for acquirers is also to make titles to land less secure.

B. Money or Mud?

It is too crude, then, to replace a rule of 'owners always win' with one of 'acquirers always win'. Under registration of title, acquirers must often prevail over owners, it is true; but they need not, indeed should not, always do so. The difficulty lies in deciding when.[30]

Fortunately, money eases the choice. In England, and hence in Scotland also, all parties receive prizes, so that the person who is denied the property—the 'mud' in Thomas Mapp's terminology[31]—is bought off by being given the 'money', that is to say, the value of the property that has been lost. Such generous arrangements are not an inevitable accompaniment of registration of title. In the Torrens systems, compensation is more limited; in the systems of Continental Europe, it is unknown. But in Scotland and England the loss of title is, with some obvious exceptions,[32] salved by the balm of money. If the acquirer is awarded the 'mud', the (now former) owner receives the 'money'; if the owner retains the 'mud', it is the (failed) acquirer who receives the 'money'.[33] No doubt both parties would often prefer the 'mud'; but the availability of the 'money'—of the second prize—reduces the importance of the choice.

Choice, however, there still must be. In Scotland, the 1979 Act, on the English model, made the choice largely on the basis of the state of possession. The problems with this approach, and the possible alternatives to it, are the subject of the rest of this section.

C. The 1979 Act: The Criterion of Possession

Under the 1979 Act, title conflicts were resolved largely on the basis of possession. If possession was with the acquirer, the acquirer was awarded the 'mud' and the owner the 'money'; if the owner, or someone else, was in possession, the distribution of prizes was

[29] TW Mapp, *Torrens' Elusive Title: Basic Legal Principles of an Efficient Torrens System* (Edmonton, University of Alberta, Faculty of Law, 1978) paras 3.13 and 4.26.

[30] For an analysis of this choice, see M Harding and R Hickey, 'Bijural Ambiguity and Values in Land Registration Systems' in S Bright (ed), *Modern Studies in Property Law, Volume 6* (Oxford, Hart Publishing, 2011) 285. The authors argue that the values underlying static and dynamic security are 'largely incommensurable' so that it is not possible to say that one is right and the other wrong.

[31] Mapp, *Torrens' Elusive Title* (n 29) para 4.24.

[32] As where the loss was caused by the claimant.

[33] 2012 Act, ss 73 and 77 (compensation to acquirer) and s 94 (compensation to owner).

reversed. More precisely, the rule was that no 'inaccuracy'[34] on the Register could be rectified to the prejudice of a proprietor in possession; instead the inaccuracy would remain in place, to the acquirer's benefit, and the former owner (or other right-holder) would be paid indemnity.[35] To this rule there were a few exceptions, of which the most important was where the inaccuracy had been caused by the acquirer's own fraud or carelessness.[36] Otherwise possession was determinative. Possession included indirect possession, such as possession through a tenant.[37]

This rule, of course, was taken from the corresponding legislation in England and Wales.[38] Its justification lay in the view that the person in possession had the stronger tie to the land, and hence the more compelling claim to the 'mud'. In Scotland, however, that view soon came under challenge.[39] To qualify as a proprietor in possession was not very exacting. There was no requirement of possession for a prescribed period. The law asked for no more than possession at the time when the decision as to rectification was being taken.[40] Historic possession was irrelevant. So land which had been in the same family since the reign of Mary, Queen of Scots could be lost, on being mistakenly allocated to a neighbour on first registration, if the neighbour chanced to possess at the right time.[41] More prosaically, the same might be true in a dispute between any two neighbours one of whom had a registered title and the other of whom did not. Momentary possession, in short, was an uncertain way of calibrating a person's tie to the land.

Furthermore, experience showed that possession might be seized precisely to obtain, or to withhold from others, the status of proprietor in possession. For where the allocation of entitlements depended on possession in the future and not on possession in the past (or on something else), then the temptation to take the law into one's own hands might prove irresistible. In *Kaur v Singh*,[42] a flat was acquired on the basis of a deed of transfer which, unknown to the acquirer, had been forged. The acquirer moved into the flat. Two months later the 'true' owner, returning from an extensive trip abroad, broke into the flat, changed the locks, and resumed possession. Later, the acquirer retaliated in kind. Whether the acquirer was protected as a proprietor in possession depended on the precise point of time at which the question was asked. Similar issues arose in

[34] The Scottish equivalent of 'mistake'.

[35] 1979 Act, s 9(3)(a).

[36] 1979 Act, s 9(3)(a)(iii).

[37] In England this is the subject of express enactment (LRA 2002, s 131(2)). In Scotland, the 1979 Act was silent as to whether such 'civil' possession counted, but the courts decided that it did: see especially *Kaur v Singh* 1999 SC 180 (IH) 191G (Lord President Rodger).

[38] Reid Report (n 13) para 115. The current English provisions can be found in the LRA 2002, sch 4 paras 3(2) and 6(2).

[39] Scottish Law Commission, DP No 125 (n 19) paras 4.22–4.28.

[40] Or perhaps—the position was never entirely clear—at the time of the application: see *Burr v Keeper of the Registers of Scotland* (Lands Tribunal for Scotland, 12 November 2010) [27].

[41] Just as I was completing this chapter I received an email from a member of the public headed 'Land Registration—Devastating Impact'. The email explained that a strip of coastal land of hers, held on a Sasine title, had in 2011 been included within the registered title of a development company. Previously, the family had used this area 'for drying washing, drying nets and fish, and a play area for the children for at least 4 generations'. Yet it was now the property of the development company and could not be retrieved. 'In our opinion, and from a layman's understanding of the land registration system, it feels as if it is promoting Land Grab by failing to rectify clear errors.' Some of the cases listed in note 67 below tell a similar story.

[42] *Kaur v Singh* 1999 SC 180 (IH).

Safeway Stores plc v Tesco Stores Ltd,[43] where Tesco used a crane to place marker posts on a disputed section of riverbed, complete with notices which read: 'Private property of Tesco Stores Ltd. Unauthorised access prohibited'. In due course the poles were removed by Safeway. Events of this kind were good for locksmiths and crane-operators but not, perhaps, for the orderly and principled resolution of title disputes. In George Gretton's caustic observation, it was 'ironic that a supposedly sophisticated system seems to have revived the priority rules of the Stone Age'.[44] On the eve of the Act's replacement, courts were showing signs of disregarding the more blatant examples of possession and counter-possession,[45] but it was too late to save the reputation of the rule.

There were other difficulties with the 1979 Act's rule as well. As, typically, acquirers were in possession and owners were not, an allocation of entitlements based on possession was strongly skewed in favour of acquirers. Further, even if the rule had worked better in respect of the acquisition of rights, or in other words in respect of the system's positive warranty, it seemed quite out of place in respect of the negative warranty.[46] It was not obvious, for example, why the state of possession should determine the validity of a security (mortgage) which had been omitted from the Register by mistake. The logic of registration of title was that acquirers should *always* take free of omitted burdens;[47] the effect of a possession-based rule was otherwise.

Yet the intuition that possession should play some part in the choice between acquirer and owner was not wholly misplaced. If the difficulties just described could be overcome, there might still be a role for possession. This is a subject to which we must return.[48]

D. Alternatives to Possession

If the allocation of 'money' and 'mud' is not to depend on whether the acquirer is in possession, some other criterion or criteria must be found in its place. In formulating proposals for reform of the 1979 Act, the Scottish Law Commission identified three: the type of error; the type of right being acquired; and past possession.[49] Only the last was novel. The second was already a feature of the 1979 Act, while the first was found in the Torrens systems and, especially, in the systems of Germany and central Europe. The Commission conceived these criteria, not as alternatives, but as cumulative requirements. In other words, for acquirers to receive the 'mud' and not the 'money', they must satisfy all three. As we will see, that was also the approach to be adopted by the Land Registration etc (Scotland) Act 2012.[50]

It is necessary to say more about each criterion.

[43] *Safeway Stores plc v Tesco Stores Ltd* 2004 SC 29 (IH).

[44] George Gretton, commentary on *Kaur v Singh* at 1998 SCLR 863.

[45] Which were characterised as a mere 'tennis match': see, eg, *Nicol v Keeper of the Registers of Scotland* 2013 SLT (Lands Tr) 56, [26]; *Burton v Keeper of the Registers of Scotland* 2014 SLT (Lands Tr) 69, [61].

[46] For this terminology, see section II(A) above.

[47] As is now provided for by s 91 of the 2012 Act. This is because acquirers need to be able to rely on the Register. See section II(H) below.

[48] See section II(G) below.

[49] Scottish Law Commission, DP No 125 (n 19) paras 4.37 ff.

[50] For a full account of the 2012 Act's provisions, see Reid and Gretton (n 5) ch 12.

E. The First Criterion: Type of Error

The errors that might affect an acquirer's title can be divided into two groups. There are 'old' errors, already present on the Register before the current transaction begins; and there are 'new' errors which arise as part of the current transaction. In the terminology adopted by the Scottish Law Commission, there are thus both 'Register errors' and 'transactional errors'.[51] Examples of the former are where the Register is mistaken as to the proprietor or the property or as to the burdens to which the property is subject. Examples of the latter are where the new deed is blundered or the person granting the deed lacks legal capacity or where the person's signature is forged.

That acquirers must be protected against Register error is beyond dispute. The curtain principle demands as much. In order for acquirers to be relieved of the need to go behind the Register, they must be able to rely on what the Register says, or does not say. Pre-existing errors on the Register cannot, therefore, be allowed to affect acquirers in good faith. That is a non-negotiable feature of registration of title.

Transactional errors are different. The Register has not misled the acquirer. Rather, something has gone wrong with the acquirer's own transaction during its pre-registration phase. Often it will be possible to sort the difficulty out. But where this cannot be done, the question arises as to whether the acquirer should nevertheless receive a good title on registration. Ordinary property law would say 'no'. Should registration law—*need* registration law—arrive at a different result? German registration law declines to intervene.[52] In Torrens systems, the matter is contested, with some countries opting for the protection of acquirers and others not.[53]

To law reformers in Scotland, the arguments seemed clear-cut.[54] To give the property to the acquirer is, necessarily, to take it away from the owner. Protection of the one thus presupposes expropriation of the other. Expropriation, however, requires strong justification.[55] The owner should be sacrificed only where the logic of registration of title leaves no choice; otherwise an owner's registered title should be left undisturbed. Protection against Register error is a matter of necessity for registration of title; protection against transactional error is not.

There are other arguments as well.[56] In choosing to enter into the transaction, the acquirer assumes the risk of things going wrong, or at any rate is in the best position to

[51] Scottish Law Commission, DP No 125 (n 19) paras 3.15–3.18.

[52] BGB § 892(1): 'Zugunsten desjenigen, welcher ein Recht an einem Grundstück oder ein Recht an einem solchen Recht durch Rechtsgeschäft erwirbt, gilt der Inhalt des Grundbuchs als richtig, es sei denn, dass ein Widerspruch gegen die Richtigkeit eingetragen oder die Unrichtigkeit dem Erwerber bekannt ist'. [In favour of the person who acquires a right in a plot of land or a right in such a right by legal transaction, the contents of the Land Register are presumed to be correct, unless an objection to the accuracy is registered or the inaccuracy is known to the acquirer.] This only protects acquirers against Register error (errors in respect of the 'Inhalt des Grundbuchs').

[53] P O'Connor, 'Registration of Invalid Dispositions: Who Gets the Property?' in E Cooke (ed), *Modern Studies in Property Law, Volume 3* (Oxford, Hart Publishing, 2005) 45, 53–9; P O'Connor, 'Deferred and Immediate Indefeasibility: Bijural Ambiguity' (2009) 13 *Edinburgh Law Review* 194. This is the dispute between 'immediate indefeasibility' (which protects acquirers against transactional error), and 'deferred indefeasibility' (which does not).

[54] Scottish Law Commission, DP No 125 (n 19) paras 4.44 and 4.45.

[55] See also section II(A) above.

[56] See also O'Connor, 'Registration of Invalid Dispositions' (n 53) 60 ff.

detect and avoid error. In a question between owner and acquirer, in respect of transactional error, it is reasonable that the owner should be preferred. Indeed, to do otherwise is to remove the acquirer's incentive to take care with the conveyancing. In most cases such a result will also be economically efficient in the sense of allocating the property to the person who values it most highly.

The acquirer is not, of course, left bereft. The type of error is simply a means of allocating the prizes. Although the acquirer is not to receive the 'mud', in respect of transactional error, he will be compensated with the 'money'. That is a substantial improvement on the position under Sasine (or unregistered) conveyancing. Furthermore, unless the owner gets round to asserting his title, what was a transactional error in respect of the first transaction will become a Register error in respect of the next. Indefeasibility of title will therefore come; it is simply that, in the language of Torrens scholars, it is 'deferred' and not 'immediate'.[57] Take the case of identity theft. Anne is the registered owner of land. Barbara, stealing Anne's identity, sells the land to Colin and forges Anne's signature in the deed of transfer. Colin, in good faith, presents the deed for registration and is entered on the Register as proprietor. As the error (ie, the forged deed) is transactional in nature, Colin's title is defeasible. Indefeasibility is thus 'deferred'. If the error comes to light, Anne can procure rectification of the Register, whereupon Colin will receive compensation from the Registrar for his loss.[58] But if the error does not come to light, and Colin later transfers the land to David, David is able to rely on the Register's statement that Colin is the proprietor. What was a transactional error with respect to Colin becomes a Register error in respect of David. On registration, therefore, David will receive an indefeasible title, and it is Anne who will be compensated by the Registrar.[59]

F. The Second Criterion: Type of Right

It is only in respect of certain types of right that the acquirer will want the 'mud'; for others, receipt of the 'money' is a satisfactory, or even a desirable, outcome. To the criterion of type of error, therefore, can be added the criterion of type of right.

The 1979 Act restricted the 'mud' to those seeking to acquire the rights of ownership or lease.[60] The 2012 Act, more or less, does the same.[61] The policy choice seems uncontroversial. Faced with an invalid security (mortgage) deed, for example, a bank will be satisfied by repayment of the loan and has no need of a property right. In respect of subordinate property rights such as these, it will usually be better to free the owner of the burden and to pay compensation to the would-be acquirer.

[57] For this terminology, see, eg, O'Connor, 'Registration of Invalid Dispositions' (n 53) 53–4.

[58] 2012 Act, ss 73, 77 and 80, In Scottish terminology the Registrar is 'the Keeper of the Registers of Scotland' or, for short, 'the Keeper'.

[59] 2012 Act, ss 86 and 94.

[60] In other words, only those acquiring ownership or lease were eligible for protection against rectification. This was achieved by restricting the meaning of 'proprietor'.

[61] But not quite. Assignees of leases are eligible for the 'mud' but not the initial grantee. Further, the 'mud' is also extended to the grantees of servitudes. The relevant provisions of the 2012 Act are ss 86–90.

G. The Third Criterion: Past Possession

Finally, and perhaps unexpectedly, the Scottish Law Commission found a role for possession. But this is not the post-transaction possession on which protection under the 1979 Act turned and which was subject to severe criticism.[62] What is required under the 2012 Act, rather, is pre-transaction possession. A rule of buyer in possession has been replaced by one of seller in possession.

So far as I know, no other country has added a requirement of possession to what is, in essence, a system of deferred indefeasibility. There is none in the German system, which in many respects was the model for the Scottish reform. Nor is it found in the Torrens systems. Its role in the 2012 Act is to counter what was seen as a structural weakness in the model.[63] In systems of deferred indefeasibility, the 'true' owner's entitlement survives the first transaction but not the second. If this entitlement is to be realised, therefore, the 'true' owner must rectify the Register before a second transaction can take place. In the example involving identity theft given earlier,[64] Anne must rectify before Colin, the registered proprietor, can transfer to David. But how is Anne to know about Colin's hostile title, and hence of the need for rectification? The answer, in the 2012 Act, is that for David to receive an unassailable title from Colin, Colin must first have taken possession of the land; and furthermore, and by contrast to the 1979 Act, that possession must have been held for a year, either by Colin alone, or by Colin followed by David.[65] Anne's ownership cannot be lost, therefore, without Anne first losing possession for a year; and in that loss of possession there is notice that something may be amiss with her title.

This approach can be criticised as impeding facility of transfer. It is not enough for acquirers to examine the Register; they must also have regard to the state of possession. To be sure of an indefeasible title, David must check, not only that Colin is named on the Register as proprietor, but that Colin has been in possession for a year. Admittedly, the second check will usually be perfunctory, for if Colin is in current possession and has owned for a year or more, it can be assumed that he has possessed for a year.[66] But the fact that the check is necessary at all may seem a disproportionate response to what may only be an occasional problem. Time will tell. Early indications are of a surprisingly large number of cases where, on first registration, the proprietor was mistakenly awarded part of a neighbour's property and where, without the possessory requirement, the neighbour's title would be at serious risk.[67]

[62] As to which see section II(C) above.

[63] Scottish Law Commission, DP No 125 (n 19) paras 4.46–4.52.

[64] At section II(E) above.

[65] 2012 Act, s 86(1)(b), (3)(a).

[66] If Colin has owned for less than a year, the 'missing' period of possession can be completed by David. Until that has been done, David is at the (slight) risk of a challenge to his title by Anne. In the event of such a challenge he would finish up with the 'money' rather than with the 'mud'.

[67] This is brought out in the case law. See: *Nicol v Keeper of the Registers of Scotland* 2013 SLT (Lands Tr) 56; *Burton v Keeper of the Registers of Scotland* 2014 SLT (Lands Tr) 69; *Gray v Keeper of the Registers of Scotland* 2014 SLT (Lands Tr) 117; *Van Eck v Keeper of the Registers of Scotland* 2014 SLT (Lands Tr) 92; *Pattie v Keeper of the Registers of Scotland* 2014 SLT (Lands Tr) 28; *Mathers v Keeper of the Registers of Scotland* 2015 SLT (Lands Tr) 109; *Rivendale v Keeper of the Registers of Scotland* [2015] CSIH 27, 2015 SC 558.

H. The Negative Warranty

The 2012 Act gives effect to the positive warranty, as we have just seen. But it is no less assiduous in its attention to the negative warranty.[68] No person acquiring ownership or a lease is affected by a burden which was mistakenly omitted from the Register.[69] The burden is extinguished by the very act of the acquirer's registration; its former holder receives compensation from the Registrar.[70] The acquirer must be in good faith, of course, but the state of possession is irrelevant, as surely it ought to be.[71] In respect of omissions, therefore, as much as of commissions, acquirers can rely on the contents of the Register. The curtain principle is scrupulously observed.

III. The Question of Technique: How is Protection to be Conferred?

A. 'Title If' or 'Title Always'?

Under the Scottish reform, then, the position of good-faith acquirers depends on the type of right and on the type of error. Acquirers of ownership and lease take free from Register error[72] though not from transactional error; acquirers of other property rights[73] take free from neither. In the first case, there is deferred indefeasibility; in the second, indefeasibility is withheld permanently and the acquirer is compensated by the 'money'.

How is this policy to be given effect as a matter of technique? In particular, what is the acquirer to receive by way of title at the moment of registration? One possibility would be to give different answers for different cases. But if what is sought is a general rule, then the choice lies between a rule of 'title if' and one of 'title always'. The former confers title at the moment of registration if the acquirer qualifies for it; the latter confers title at the moment of registration whether the acquirer qualifies or not. The former withholds title from those who, under the policy rules just described, are not to receive it; the latter gives title now but allows it to be taken away later.[74]

The 1979 Act, on the English model, employed a rule of 'title now' or, as it is often expressed, of 'title by registration'.[75] This, however, was widely criticised in Scotland, and the 2012 Act has reverted to a rule of 'title if'. In the eyes of the Scottish Law Commission, and others, there were four key objections to a rule of title by registration.[76] It put the title in

[68] For this terminology, see section II(A) above.

[69] 2012 Act, ss 91 and 92.

[70] 2012 Act, s 94.

[71] Compare here the rule under the 1979 Act where the enforceability of the burden was determined by the state of possession: see section II(C) above.

[72] Assuming possession for a year on the part of the person granting the deed: see section II(G) above.

[73] Except for servitudes: see 2012 Act, s 90.

[74] ie, by rectification of the Register.

[75] Land Registration (Scotland) Act 1979, s 3(1).

[76] Scottish Law Commission, DP No 125 (n 19) paras 5.14–5.39.

the wrong place; it was indiscriminate; it was complex; and it was uncertain. Each objection merits more detailed consideration.

B. The First Objection: Title in the Wrong Place

To the extent that the law chooses not to protect acquirers, a rule of title by registration puts the title in the wrong place; for if someone is to be given a title only to have it taken away again later, it would have been better not to have given the title in the first place. Under title by registration, a person who is mistakenly registered as owner *is* the owner, with all the rights and obligations that ownership carries, until such time as he is removed from the Register by rectification; for rectification is not, and should not be, retrospective.[77] Conversely, the 'true' owner is, for the same period, deprived of his rights.

Admittedly, the objection is weaker in systems where acquirers are nearly always protected. Title by registration thus works better with immediate defeasibility than with deferred indefeasibility. But unless indefeasibility is also to extend to the lesser property rights, such as securities (mortgages), the objection remains a serious one.

C. The Second Objection: King Midas and the Problem of Indiscriminate Title

In Greek mythology, everything that King Midas touched turned to gold. There is much to be said for such a power, of course. Yet there are some things which must be touched but which should not be gold. King Midas's food was one; his daughter was another. The trouble with the Midas touch is that it is indiscriminate: it applies to *everything*. Title by registration, the Scottish Law Commission observed, is no less indiscriminate. It is a form of Midas touch, for everything that is registered is turned to valid.[78] If that result is sometimes unacceptable, the Registrar, like King Midas, is powerless to prevent it.[79] Suppose that I forge a deed of transfer in respect of land which belongs to you. On registration, the land becomes mine and ceases to be yours. The Midas touch rewards forgers and penalises the innocent. Of course, in the end my forgery will be my undoing, if you are alert enough to notice. You can have the Register rectified and so be restored to ownership. But unless or until you do so, the land is mine and not yours.

The Midas touch can also extinguish rights as well as create them. In *Santander UK plc v Keeper of the Registers of Scotland*,[80] the purchase of a flat was financed by a substantial loan in respect of which a standard security (mortgage) was registered in favour of the lender, Santander. After six months, the borrower forged a discharge of the security and presented

[77] *Stevenson-Hamilton's Exrs v McStay* 1999 SLT 1175 (OH); *Keeper of the Registers of Scotland v MRS Hamilton Ltd* 2000 SC 271 (IH).

[78] Scottish Law Commission, DP No 125 (n 19) para 5.34. The terminology has stuck, and has even found its way into discussions of English law: see A Goymour, 'Mistaken Registrations of Land: Exploding the Myth of "Title by Registration"' [2013] *CLJ* 617, 626.

[79] Unless, of course, the Registrar happens to detect the error and refuses registration.

[80] *Santander UK plc v Keeper of the Registers of Scotland* [2013] CSOH 24, 2013 SLT 362.

it for registration, whereupon the security was removed from the Register. More money was then borrowed, this time from the Bank of Scotland, and a new security was registered. Later, when the fraud was discovered, Santander had the Register rectified and its security restored. The case was decided under the 1979 Act. Although the discharge was forged, therefore, the Midas touch gave it legal effect on registration and the security was extinguished. When it later revived, as a result of rectification, this was not with retrospective effect; and by that time a prior-ranking security, in favour of the Bank of Scotland, was in place.[81] The flat was sold for less than the sums owed to the Bank of Scotland. Santander received nothing, not even compensation from the Registrar.[82] If the case had been decided under the 2012 Act, without Midas, the result would have been different and, in policy terms, far preferable. The forged discharge would have had no effect, and Santander's security would have been undisturbed by its temporary disappearance from the Register. The Bank of Scotland security would have ranked second and not first. Santander would have recovered its loan from the sale of the flat;[83] the Bank of Scotland, misled by the temporary omission of Santander's security from the Register, would have recovered its loan from the Registrar.[84]

D. The Third Objection: Complexity

To work well, law reform should, ideally, build on existing rules. Title by registration, however, is a radical departure from everything that went before. Worse still, the previous rules are suppressed rather than replaced, and reappear unpredictably when the system is under stress. The result is not one set of rules but two, each complete in itself and yet prone to chaotic interaction. This 'bijuralism' can be seen at work in the provisions for rectification.[85]

In the event that the Register contained an 'inaccuracy', the 1979 Act provided for its rectification (subject to the protection mentioned earlier for proprietors in possession).[86] But in this idea of 'inaccuracy' lay a puzzle. If the Midas touch turned everything to valid, how could an 'inaccuracy' ever occur? If the Register was correct, how could it also be wrong? The Act itself gave no clue as to the answer, and it took the courts some years to find one. In the end it was accepted that 'inaccuracy' fell to be judged, not by the rules of land registration law, as might have been expected, but by the ordinary rules of the law of property which land registration law was intended to replace.[87]

[81] Compare the decision of the English Court of Appeal in respect of the similar fact-pattern in *MacLeod v Gold Harp Properties* [2014] EWCA 1084, [2015] 1 WLR 1249. Rectification was held to have retrospective effect.

[82] Indemnity was not due under the 1979 Act, s 12(1) because rectification was granted rather than refused. Santander attempted to recover on the basis of common-law negligence, but that too failed. For a discussion of the decision, see KGC Reid and GL Gretton, *Conveyancing 2013* (Edinburgh, Avizandum Publishing Ltd, 2014) 178–82.

[83] Assuming a sufficient sale price.

[84] 2012 Act, s 73(1)(b).

[85] 'Bijuralism' was first used in this sense in Scottish Law Commission, DP No 125 (n 19) paras 1.11 and 5.15–5.22. Since then the term has been taken up by some of those writing about land registration in other jurisdictions.

[86] 1979 Act, s 9(1). For proprietors in possession, see section II(C) above.

[87] See, eg, *Short's Tr v Keeper of the Registers of Scotland* 1994 SC 122 (IH) 140F (Lord President Hope).

Take the example of identity theft mentioned earlier.[88] Anne is the registered owner of land. Barbara, stealing Anne's identity, sells the land to Colin and forges Anne's signature in the deed of transfer. Colin presents the deed for registration. The effect of registration of Colin's deed is for Colin to become owner instead of Anne: that is the unavoidable effect of the Midas touch. Judged by the rules of land registration, therefore, the Register is perfectly accurate in showing Colin as owner. But if the facts are re-run under ordinary property law, the owner would be Anne and not Colin, for no title can pass under a forged deed. To the question, 'who is owner?', the two systems of law give different answers. The result is for the Register to be 'inaccurate' in the sense meant by the 1979 Act. But this is a 'bijural' rather than an 'actual' inaccuracy;[89] the owner is Colin, according to one set of rules, but should be Anne, according to another. And it is the existence of the 'should-be' owner which reveals the existence of the inaccuracy.

Bijuralism, moreover, is not confined to cases involving error; it applies to all registrations. Take an ordinary and blameless case of transfer. Margaret owns land. She sells to Neil. A deed of transfer is drawn up and signed by Margaret. It complies with the law with respect to content. It complies equally with the law in respect of formalities of authentication. This perfect deed is presented for registration and, on registration, Neil becomes owner. But Neil's acquisition of ownership was not caused by the perfect deed; his title comes from the act of registration alone. If the deed had been blundered, the result would have been the same.[90] In a sense, therefore, the care in drawing up the deed is a charade, a sentimental harking-back to the days when title really did pass by the parties' consensual act. Yet if the perfect deed is not needed by the rules of land registration, it is indispensable according to the rules of ordinary property law. Without it, Neil would still be owner, but the entry on the Register would be (bijurally) inaccurate.

Bijuralism seems more of an improvisation than a coherent and thought-through system. It is complex and clumsy. It tempts courts to play up the rules of property law, with which they are comfortable and familiar, at the expense of the rules of land registration law, with which often they are not.[91] And, as we will see in the next section, bijuralism gives rise to uncertainty.

E. The Fourth Objection: Uncertainty

A difficulty with bijuralism is to know how, precisely, the two sets of rules interact. Consider, for one last time, the case of identity theft.[92] Colin has become registered as owner on the basis of a forged deed of transfer. Land registration law says that he is owner; ordinary property law says that he is not, and that ownership remains with Anne, the victim of the forgery. The Register is thus (bijurally) accurate and can be rectified by Anne. But now extend the example. Before Anne can take steps to procure rectification,

[88] See section II(E) above.

[89] For the difference, see Scottish Law Commission, DP No 125 (n 19) paras 2.11–2.15

[90] Of course, if the blunder is obvious, the deed will be rejected by the Registrar and no registration will take place.

[91] This topic is explored, in the context of English law, in Goymour (n 78).

[92] See section II(E) above.

Colin conveys to David, who is registered as owner in Colin's place. David is in good faith. Is the Register still inaccurate? That depends on the reach of bijuralism. Ordinary property law would deny a title to David for the same reason that it would deny a title to Colin: for if Colin would not have become owner, no right of ownership could be passed on by Colin to David. But perhaps it is wrong to apply property law in this cumulative manner. Perhaps it is only the current transaction—the transfer to David—which is to be evaluated by reference to property law and, for the rest, we must accept the verdict of the law of land registration. In other words, perhaps the starting-point for a property-law analysis is with the proposition that Colin was owner of the land. If so, there is no inaccuracy, because property law, like land registration law, would then acknowledge David as the owner. Which approach is correct? There is nothing in the 1979 Act, or in the nature of bijuralism, to provide an answer. The best that can be said is that the indemnity provisions in the Act may support a continuing inaccuracy; for if there is no inaccuracy, there is no ground for paying indemnity to Anne, and it seems wrong that she should lose her property without compensation.[93] Now that the 1979 Act has been repealed it is unlikely that we will ever know the answer.[94]

This example raises another difficulty with title by registration, at least in its 1979 Act version. For how long is the title of acquirers, and their successors, vulnerable to challenge? At what point is the original error cured? Or is there no cure, so that a Midas title is always an insecure title? In cases where legal policy determines that acquirers are to be given the 'mud', this should, as the Scottish Law Commission observed, be 'real mud'—an unchallengeable title—and not merely 'quasi-mud', the future status of which is worryingly uncertain.[95] At some point matters are likely to be settled by prescription or its equivalents, which will either fortify the title of the acquirer[96] or extinguish the right of the challenger.[97] But a clear rule might be expected from the law of land registration itself. There is none in the 1979 Act.

The 2012 Act offers 'real mud', like any system of 'title if'. Thus, if the conditions for acquisition of title are satisfied, David's title as owner is indefeasible; if they are not satisfied, David does not become owner at all and receives compensation instead. The choice is thus between 'real mud' and 'money': the 2012 Act does not trade in 'quasi-mud'. Which would David receive in the above example? This is a case of Register error and not of transactional error, and David is entitled to rely on the Register. Provided, therefore, that Colin has possessed for a year, the error is cured, forever, and David's title is indefeasible.[98]

[93] Under the 1979 Act, s 12(1), indemnity was tied to rectification or its refusal, and if there was no inaccuracy the question of rectification did not arise.

[94] This issue has also caused trouble in England: see E Lees, 'Title by Registration: Rectification, Indemnity and Mistake' (2013) 76 *MLR* 62.

[95] Scottish Law Commission, Report No 222 (n 20) para 21.36.

[96] ie, by acquisitive prescription (or adverse possession). However, acquisitive prescription did not normally run in respect of 1979 Act titles.

[97] ie, by extinctive prescription (or limitation). The relevant period of extinctive prescription in Scotland is 20 years: see Prescription and Limitation (Scotland) Act 1973, s 7.

[98] 2012 Act, s 86. See also section II(G) above.

F. De-throning King Midas: The 2012 Act

At the time of writing, the 2012 Act had been in force for a little over a year.[99] Experience, no doubt, will expose its imperfections. But by discarding 'title always' in favour of 'title if'—by abandoning title by registration and dethroning King Midas—it at least avoids the difficulties just described. To this promising beginning the 2012 Act adds some solid virtues. It works within the grain of property law. It eschews novelty. And it achieves its main policy objective by a simple and familiar device, namely the conferral of good title on *bona fide* acquirers. This is section 25 of the Sale of Goods Act 1979 as applied to the transfer of land.[100] What could be less threatening than that?

IV. Concluding Remarks

I close, as I began, with some words of Sir George Mackenzie on land registration: 'since I only design to defend our own Law, and not to impugn theirs'—that is, the law of England—'it were impertinent for me to recommend too zealously, that wherein I am not much concerned'.[101] In England and Wales, the Law Commission is, once again, engaged on a review of land registration.[102] No doubt it will be of interest to look at the recent changes in Scotland. But, like Mackenzie, I will avoid the impertinence of zealous recommendation.[103]

[99] It came into force on 8 December 2014.
[100] For discussion of this analogy, see Scottish Law Commission, DP No 125 (n 19) para 5.27.
[101] Mackenzie (n 1) 226.
[102] See Law Commission, *Updating the Land Registration Act 2002—A Consultation Paper* (Law Com CP No 227, 2016).
[103] See, however, the zealous recommendation in Goymour (n 78) 650.

11

Lack of Proper Care

SIMON COOPER

I. Introduction

The rigid structures of land registration, its formal communication methods, its bureaucratic administration and its bright-line rules, all combine to render it easily portrayed as mechanistic, simplistic, formulaic and routine. It has been depicted as highly abstract and devoid of features which enable it to recognise the complexity of human interactions: Gray and Gray[1] castigated it as 'non-Atkinian' in reference to its dissociation from Lord Atkins' ideal duty of care between neighbours in law.[2] This chapter seeks to contest those characterisations, to redress the balance by demonstrating the significant legal role that is played by 'care' in human interactions concerning title and registration, and to put forward a structured basis for understanding and applying care as a concept in registered land.

Central to understanding any registration system is the degree to which the Register is determinative of title. In England, the Register is qualified by the power to rectify, whose exercise may be affected by a 'lack of proper care' by one or more of the parties. A requirement to take care is therefore an integral component of the registration system, and one which is practically important to all participants, yet the High Court has found it 'curiously void of discussion or consideration in the authorities and textbooks'.[3] That omission is remedied here.

The aim of this chapter is to bring order to the requirement of care in the context of registration. It does so in two stages: concept-building and normative evaluation. The first stage—concept-building—begins in section II by showing the statutory channels through which care may be relevant to the resolution of disputes about rectification of the Register and claims to indemnity. Section III then puts forward the foundational concept in land registration law of a care requirement which occurs as a feature of the relationship that exists between certain participants in registration processes. It argues that the care requirements introduced through the various statutory channels can only be understood by reference to a particular relationship involving a requirement on one person to act or forbear from acting

[1] K Gray and S Gray, 'The Rhetoric of Realty' in J Getzler (ed), *Rationalizing Property, Equity and Trusts* (London, Butterworths, 2003).

[2] *Donoghue v Stevenson* [1932] AC 562, 580.

[3] *Sainsbury's Supermarkets Ltd v Olympia Homes Ltd* [2005] EWHC 1235 (Ch), [2006] 1 P & CR 17 [87] (Mann J). See also *Mann v Dingley* [2011] EWLandRA 2010_0582 [37] (Michael Michell).

in certain ways so as to protect the interests of another. It categorises the relevant relationships and identifies the interests which are protected within those relationships.

The conceptual structure created in the first stage paves the way for the second stage of the chapter which asks what conduct should be expected of the participants. It advances some pivotal normative propositions and justifies them by reference to the protected interests within the relevant relationships. The propositions are arranged according to the different relationship settings in which they arise. Section IV deals with the position of acquirers towards owners; section V deals with the position of owners towards acquirers; and section VI deals with the position of both owners and acquirers towards those responsible for providing an indemnity. Collectively, they give substance to the nature and content of the care requirement and provide guidance on a crucial but neglected element influencing the indefeasibility of titles.

The analysis in this chapter relies on an existing tradition in scholarly literature which re-conceives the events that generate title disputes and priority disputes as 'accidents' insofar as they are the occasion for the recognition of a loss.[4] The loss must be allocated to a losing party and so property law can be understood as carrying out a function which resembles a function of tort law—although, unlike accidents, priority disputes also allocate a corresponding gain of the entitlement to the winning party. In developing some of its techniques, the chapter accordingly draws inspiration from tort law, such as the duty of care and the reasonableness criterion. In particular, in the course of discussing the possible ways to interpret and apply the legislative rules, it considers a party's potential opportunities to take cost-effective precautions that might prevent such disputes from arising, and whether the failure to do so should have negative repercussions for his entitlements to property or compensation in rectification or indemnity proceedings.

II. Legal Background: The Statutory Framework

If the Register were only ever changed so as to allocate rights in accordance with a legal entitlement to procure such a change, such as a valid conveyance from the true owner, then there would be no occasion for inquiring, more generally, into participants' behaviour. But when a Register change has been effected by mistake, further provisions come into play: the correction power becomes available to determine who acquires or retains the land,[5] and in some cases also the statutory indemnity provisions determine any entitlement to a state monetary award.[6] Claims under these provisions are the occasions when participants' lack of care may be scrutinised.

[4] D Baird and T Jackson, 'Information, Uncertainty and the Transfer of Property' (1984) 13 *JLS* 299; D Baird, 'Notice Filing and the Problem of Ostensible Ownership' (1983) 12 *JLS* 53; T J Miceli et al, 'Title Systems and Land Values' (2002) 45 *JLE* 565; B Arrunada and N Garoupa, 'The Choice of Titling System in Land' (2005) 48 *JLE* 709; S Sterk, 'Property Rules, Liability Rules, and Uncertainty about Property Rights' (2008) 106 *Mich LR* 1285; M Mautner, 'The Eternal Triangles of the Law: Toward a Theory of Priorities in Conflicts Involving Remote Parties' (1991) 90 *Mich LR* 95; G Calabresi, 'Transaction Costs, Resource Allocation and Liability Rules' (1968) 11 *JLE* 67; S Levmore, 'Variety and Uniformity in the Treatment of the Good Faith Purchaser' (1987) 16 *JLS* 43; B Medina, 'Augmenting the Value of Ownership by Protecting It Only Partially' (2003) 19 *JLEO* 343.

[5] LRA 2002, sch 4, para 2(1)(a).

[6] LRA 2002, sch 8, para 1(1)(a), (b).

The correction power is available to resolve entitlements to the land itself following a mistaken change to the Register. The relevant provision blandly states, '[t]he court may make an order for alteration of the register for the purpose of—(a) correcting a mistake …'.[7] When this correction power is available it must be exercised unless there are 'exceptional circumstances'.[8] If the proposed correction would prejudicially affect the title of the proprietor of a registered estate in land, the situation is known as 'rectification' and special consequences follow. Generally, no correction order may be made in relation to land in the registered proprietor's possession.[9] That is the strongest form of protection against correction that a registered title receives under the Land Registration Act ('LRA') 2002. But that protection is specifically excluded by a pair of provisos which apply where the proprietor 'has by fraud or lack of proper care caused or substantially contributed to the mistake'[10] or where it would for any other reason be 'unjust for the alteration not to be made.'[11] If either is present, then the power is restored and must once again be exercised unless there are exceptional circumstances.[12]

The legislation makes express reference to lack of proper care in only one of these provisos. But the open texture of the words used in the other provisions suggests that, when a claim is brought under the correction power, there may be further channels through which the degree of care by participants in registration processes could be a relevant factor. In relation to correction proceedings, this chapter identifies three statutory channels by which the determination of entitlements may be influenced by participants' lack of care. They are:

(i) Channel 1: 'the exceptional circumstances test' which denies correction to a claimant on grounds amounting to exceptional circumstances.
(ii) Channel 2: 'the lack of care proviso' which removes the protection against rectification for a proprietor in possession on grounds of his lack of proper care which substantially contributed to the mistake.
(iii) Channel 3: 'the injustice proviso' which removes the protection against rectification for a proprietor in possession on grounds that it would be unjust not to rectify.

Turning now to the state compensation provisions, there are further occasions when participants' care may be taken into account. Whenever correction amounts to 'rectification', the power is supplemented by an indemnity for the loss caused to whichever party suffers from the adverse exercise of discretion, whether the entry is rectified or allowed to stand.[13] That indemnity, however, is excluded[14] in cases where the loss is suffered by the indemnity claimant wholly as a result of his own lack of proper care, and it is reduced proportionately[15]

[7] LRA 2002, sch 4, para 2(1)(a). A similar power is conferred on the Registrar by para 5(a).

[8] For court proceedings: LRA 2002, sch 4, para 3(3) (rectification) and Land Registration Rules 2003, r 126 (correction) (the 'exceptional circumstances test'). For proceedings in the First-Tier Tribunal: LRA 2002, sch 4, para 6(3) (rectification); there is 'nothing wrong' with applying the same approach to correction: *Derbyshire County Council v Fallon* [2007] EWHC 1326 (Ch) [28] (Mr C Nugee QC).

[9] LRA 2002, sch 4, para 3(2).

[10] LRA 2002, sch 4, para 3(2)(a) (the 'lack of care proviso').

[11] LRA 2002, sch 4, para 3(2)(b) (the 'injustice proviso').

[12] LRA 2002, sch 4, para 3(3); Law Commission & HM Land Registry, *Land Registration for the Twenty-First Century: A Conveyancing Revolution* (Law Com No 271, 2001) para 10.18, n 79.

[13] LRA 2002, sch 8, para 1(1)(a), (b).

[14] LRA 2002, sch 8, para 5(1)(b).

[15] LRA 2002, sch 8, para 5(2).

where the loss is suffered by the claimant partly as a result of his own lack of proper care.[16] These instances may be grouped together as representing a fourth situation in which participants' care will influence entitlements, this time pertaining not to recovery of the land itself, but to the compensatory award:

(iv) Channel 4: 'the lack of care defence to indemnity' which removes or reduces in quantum the entitlement to state compensation for loss suffered by rectification on grounds of lack of proper care.

Those, then, are the four channels which this chapter identifies as the means through which participants' care might intrude into judicial decision making concerning entitlements in registered land. The next part will establish the conceptual tools for use in understanding those provisions.

III. Conceptual Foundations: The Care Requirement and Relationship Settings

This part proposes an autonomous concept of a 'care requirement' which will be of value in understanding the commonalities across all four of the channels mentioned above, and which will be used as the basis for making recommendations about the interpretation and application of the correction and indemnity provisions. For this purpose, a 'care requirement' exists where, within the registration system, a rule or principle has the effect of prejudicing the entitlement (whether to the land itself or to indemnity) of a person who failed to meet some standard of behaviour, where that standard of behaviour required the person to act or forbear from acting in a certain manner so as to protect the interests of another.

The concept of the care requirement possesses its own internal coherence and is capable of tying together important aspects of decision-making across all four channels. Imagine A is the true owner of land. B, an applicant for registration on the ground of long adverse possession,[17] lodges an inaccurate statutory declaration which is accepted at face value by the Registry. A is notified of it but neglects to act, and B is registered as proprietor. To the extent that B has not reached a certain minimum standard of behaviour to protect A from loss of title, B has failed to meet the care requirement which, as elaborated later, applies to a party in his position. This could have a variety of consequences. B's lack of care in causing the mistaken entry could remove his protection as proprietor in possession through either the lack of care proviso or the injustice proviso. On the other hand, to the extent that A has not reached a certain minimum basic standard of behaviour to protect B from future disputes, A too has failed to meet the care requirement which, as elaborated later, applies to a party in his position. In correction proceedings, the court may form the opinion that A's conduct is sufficiently crass and sufficiently relevant to refusing relief that it counterbalances the factors which might otherwise have satisfied the injustice proviso, or

[16] Note that lack of care on the part of a person from whom the claimant derives title (otherwise than under a disposition for valuable consideration which is registered or protected by an entry in the Register) is to be treated as if it were fraud or lack of care on the part of the claimant: LRA 2002, sch 8, para 5(3).

[17] See LRA 2002, s 97 and sch 6.

it may deny correction on the basis of 'exceptional circumstances'. Whichever party loses in the correction proceedings might then also find that indemnity is denied or reduced by reason of their lack of care.

The concept of the care requirement supposes a relationship between two parties which establishes a legal requirement that one must act in a certain manner for the benefit of the other. That the legal response is founded on a particular relationship has been forcefully made in another regime which determines liabilities as between the true owners and certain converters of cheques,[18] where a care requirement is expressed in terms of the converter's negligence: '[t]here can be no negligence without neglect of some duty'.[19] The negligence contemplated by the provision is a failure to take 'such reasonable precautions as ought to be taken with reference to the interests of the [true owner]'.[20] The requirement is a 'purely statutory one imposed on [the converter] in favour of the true owner, and the negligence consists in the disregard of his interests ... It is from the standpoint, then, of the true owner that all questions of negligence under this section must be viewed'.[21] It is this concept of a relationship, pursuant to which one must have regard to the interests of the other, which underlies the care requirement in relation not only to cheques but also, it is submitted, in relation to the LRA 2002.

Although it is possible to portray the care requirement as a 'duty' in a loose sense, it does not connote a freestanding duty enforceable through an action in tort for damages.[22] There is no necessity to establish independently any tortious duty of care between acquirer and owner through rules of proximity and foreseeability. The care requirement does not give rise to a duty in Hohfeld's terminology, but only removes the new acquirer's immunity from rectification, or leads to the dismissal of the ousted owner's claim to rectify; it is therefore accurately if cumbrously described as the forfeiture of legal power to recover title or the susceptibility to loss of title.

The final concept used in this analysis is the categorisation of participants as either owners or acquirers. This is necessary in order to determine who are the parties to the relationship that carries the care requirement. Every rectification claim, by definition, must involve a mistake whose correction would prejudicially affect the title of a registered proprietor. Given that registration as a proprietor confers title,[23] and assuming all land to have been in the ownership of someone, it follows that every rectification claim must involve two persons: the owner of a right[24] who has been ousted[25] by a mistaken change to the Register,

[18] Cheques Act 1957, s 4, and its predecessors. The provision would prevent a defendant bank from relying on the statutory defence to liability for conversion when collecting on a cheque for someone other than the true ower unless it did so 'without negligence'.

[19] *Patent Safety Gun Cotton Co v Wilson* (1880) 49 LJ QB 713; *Bissell & Co v Fox Bros Co* (1884) 51 LT 663 (QB), (1885) 53 LT 193 (CA).

[20] *Bissell & Co v Fox Bros Co* (1884) 51 LT 663 (QB).

[21] *Marfani v Midland Bank Ltd* [1964] 1 WLR 956 (CA) 964–65.

[22] cf the Registrar's right to recover under LRA 2002, sch 8, para 10(1).

[23] LRA 2002, s 58(1).

[24] In some cases, the ousted owner is deregistered and loses a registered interest by the mistake; in others, the ousted owner is the holder of a pre-registration title which has been overridden by a later mistaken Register entry.

[25] The owner may be ousted wholly or partly. The ousted owner may actually continue to appear on the Register despite the mistaken change to the Register, as where the mistake is the entry of an acquirer with a lesser interest, or the opening of a separate but conflicting register.

and the new acquirer of a competing registered right taking directly or indirectly under the mistake.[26] This yields the characterisation of parties as either owner or acquirer. They are the two fundamentally different statuses by which the parties in the care relationship are to be categorised, although of course one individual will occupy the two roles at different times as his efforts to acquire come to fruition and he makes the transition from acquirer to owner. The two roles will be used to create the foundation for building the distinctive content of their respective care requirements.

Using those concepts, the care requirement imposed on the new acquirer may be fleshed out. Due to the vesting effect of registration, an application for registration by the acquirer will harm the owner's interests if it results in their acquiring title without authorisation. That is the loss against which the acquirer should take care. In this first relationship, the care requirement ought to be that a prospective acquirer act carefully during the course of acquisition. It exists to safeguard the owner of the property.

A corresponding approach can also be taken towards owners. The care requirement imposed on an owner requires a consideration of the loss that might be caused by an owner through his conduct relating to title. The owner's failure to warn prospective acquirers about the owner's rights might result in an acquirer squandering resources in attempting to acquire title from a non-owner, becoming caught up in a priority dispute, and suffering losses as a result of his reliance on an expectation of gaining title. That is the loss against which the owner should arguably take care. In this second relationship, the care requirement ought to be the requirement that an owner act carefully to warn others of his ownership. It exists to safeguard persons who are contemplating acquisition.

Those are the distinct care requirements imposed respectively on acquirers and owners which pursue the policy of encouraging care so as to reduce the incidence of mistaken changes to the Register that may harm the other affected party. Further care requirements are imposed by the LRA 2002. In particular, there is the lack of care defence to indemnity which applies when loss occurs due to mistake.[27] A successful claimant against the Indemnity Fund depletes the fund and casts a burden on those who pay. That suggests a separate relationship of care between all participants in land registration processes and those responsible for the fund. In this third relationship, the care requirement ought to be that anyone who is liable to make an indemnity claim, whether owner or acquirer, act carefully in order to safeguard the interests of those who endow it.

The care requirement in the three relationship settings will be used as the conceptual foundation for the work undertaken in the remainder of this chapter. The relationships each carry distinct ramifications for the content of the care requirement which will now be explored separately. Section IV deals with the acquirer's care requirement towards the owner; section V deals with the owner's care requirement towards acquirers; and section VI deals with both owners' and acquirers' care requirements towards the funders of indemnity. These parts involve a significant change of tack as they turn to making prescriptive arguments about the content of the care requirement within those relationship settings.

[26] Claims involving correction that do not amount to rectification do not follow the pattern of ousted owner and new acquirer since they do not involve or affect a proprietor with guaranteed title. Nor can they engage the second, third or fourth channels for introducing the care requirement, but are regulated only by the exceptional circumstances test. They are not considered further.

[27] LRA 2002, sch 8, para 5.

IV. Care and Alteration Claims: What Should be Required of Acquirers of Land?

Having identified the channels through which care requirements might influence decisions about entitlements, and having developed concepts for the purpose of analysing care issues, the chapter now moves to examine what standards ought to be expected from participants in registration processes by way of the care requirement. It does so by proposing various principles about how the scope and content of the care requirement should be regulated and demonstrating why those principles are justified by context and policy. It is intended throughout that the principles offered are compatible with the statutory provisions and underlying policy concerns, so that the care requirements can properly find legal expression via the statutory channels identified above, and thereby influence the success of rectification or indemnity claims. Relevant case law will be drawn upon to provide useful scenarios for practical illustration of the points being made, and in order to point out where decisions conform to or depart from the propositions presented here.

This part is concerned with the care requirement that should be recognised as imposed upon an acquirer to protect the interests of an owner. It is assumed that the acquirer obtained an interest in land pursuant to a mistaken entry and that rectification proceedings have been initiated; the concern is not, however, with the conduct of the acquirer in the rectification litigation, but instead with the steps he should have taken in the stages leading up to the acquisition of the interest, particularly when putting forward his application for registration. The starting point is that the care requirement in this first setting demands that the acquirer disclose defects or weaknesses (representing a potential outstanding owner's claim) in his submission to the owner or Registry, and thereby provide an opportunity for them to address the matter and to object before the acquirer gains title by registration. There are many different contexts in which an acquirer might submit an application: it might be at first registration; it might relate to a title which has arisen by operation of law that does not derive from a registered proprietor; or it might relate to a derivative title obtained by purchase from from a registered proprietor. It will be argued that in some of these contexts any care requirement ought to be entirely excluded from the legal equation, and in other contexts, where a care requirement should apply, arguments are put forward about factors that should assist in setting the standard of care at a suitable level.

A. Carve-Out from the Care Requirement to Avoid Undermining the Register

Registration of title is about convenience and reliability of the information sources and the cheapness of acquiring that information. To superimpose a care requirement is to introduce a concession to other values, such as morality and cost-efficient loss avoidance. Nevertheless, it is argued that there are places in which the primary statutory objectives of reliability and cheapness must be protected from erosion through the imposition of a particular care requirement. The first of these relates to defects arising not from the events by which the acquirer claims to have obtained title, but from events which already affected the registered title of the owner from whom title was obtained—flaws, that is, in the 'root of title'. The second relates to the capacity of the owner to deal with the property, where any defects in his capacity are not apparent from the Register.

If an acquirer takes a transfer of registered land, the vendor having been registered pursuant to a mistake, then there must be no scope for care requirements to play a part in penalising the acquirer simply on the ground that he ought to have known of the mistake. It is imperative that care requirements should give way to certainty of title in these circumstances. The reason is that the introduction of a care requirement here would undermine reliability of the Register. It might encourage conveyancers to seek out potential mistakes or rectification claims. That would reintroduce all of the disadvantages of wide-ranging, costly and inconclusive investigations associated with the doctrine of constructive notice. The registration system would have failed to achieve its basic purpose. It is therefore submitted that an applicant for registration who takes a derivative grant comes under no requirement to alert the Registry or the owner to any defects in the registered root of title. Fortunately, there is no judicial support for it, except an isolated interlocutory reference to 'turning a blind eye'[28] towards such a matter.

In addition to excluding from care requirements any investigation into possible defects into the registered root of title, the same arguments apply to defects in the capacity of the registered proprietor to make a disposition. A proprietor's capacity is presumptively confirmed by the Register unless a restriction is entered,[29] and so proper care must not require investigations into unregistered limits on capacity.

While any equivalent to the old doctrine of constructive notice of defects in the Register must be eliminated from the remit of the acquirer's care requirement, the matter is not so compelling in relation to actual notice of defects in the registered root of title or capacity to grant. The possibility of actual notice resurfacing through a care requirement was recognised in *Odogwu v Vastguide Ltd*[30] which represents the high water-mark of the acquirer's obligations in the case law. Odogwu was the registered proprietor, an imposter granted a registered charge to a lender, and the lender sold to Vastguide. Vastguide had been alerted before completion to the fraud. Upon Vastguide's registration, Odogwu sought rectification and it was held that Vastguide's actual knowledge of the fraud at the time it took the transfer constituted a lack of proper care.[31]

Nevertheless, it is argued that, on balance, actual notice of defects in the root of title or the capacity to grant should be excluded from the care requirement. An approach to rectification proceedings which penalises those who acquired with awareness of a defect in the Register introduces the same problems suffered by the concept of 'actual notice' as employed in the equitable doctrine of notice. It is deeply unsatisfactory for its indeterminacy and its likely practical effects. It would, in particular, tend to encourage litigation that probes the borderline of subjective awareness,[32] and the problems of such litigation are magnified when the alleged owner's information is uncorroborated and self-serving. The problems are illustrated by the facts of *Odogwu*. The ousted owner had not lodged a

[28] *Barclays Bank v Guy* [2008] EWCA Civ 452, [2008] 2 EGLR 74 [23] (Lloyd LJ); not taken further in *Fye v High Grange Developments Ltd* [2015] UKFTT 0437 (Property Chamber) [31] (Judge Owen Rhys). See also *Iqbal v Najeeb* [2011] EWLandRA 2009_1234 [37].

[29] LRA 2002, ss 23–26.

[30] *Odogwu v Vastguide Ltd* [2008] EWHC 3565 (Ch).

[31] ibid [64] (Sir Donald Rattee). See the text to n 58 below where the implications of this finding are discussed.

[32] cf *Midland Bank Trust Co Ltd v Green (No 1)* [1981] AC 513 (HL) 530 (Lord Wilberforce).

restriction, had not had his claim filtered by the Registry, and offered no supporting affidavit or undertaking in damages. The information suggestive of a defect in the Register came to light only after contracts had been exchanged between the selling lender and Vastguide, forcing the new acquirer into the difficult position of having to make a decision about the quality of the information under time pressure from the vendor, and knowing that a breach of contract action could result from delay or withdrawal. Upholding the reliability of the Register would avoid these practical quandaries and the particularly troublesome litigation over states of mind which they generate.

The conclusions that might be drawn from these pragmatic arguments—that an acquirer's actual awareness of such root or capacity defects should be disregarded—might be reinforced by the LRA 2002's terms. The lack of proper care proviso, which defeats a possessing registered proprietor's defence to a rectification claim, operates when the acquirer has 'caused or substantially contributed to the mistake'.[33] This rule would be a potent source of purchaser protection if the 'mistake' referred to is limited to the *original* mistake which first led to the ousted owner's right to rectify. As stated in *Epps*:[34]

> [i]f the proprietor [that is, the new acquirer] is not the first registered proprietor but is a subsequent transferee [of an already-registered title] he will not normally be responsible for the mistake in registration in any way at all.[35]

Adopting this interpretation, the relevant question (for the purpose of interpreting the lack of care proviso) is whether the acquirer has contributed, through lack of care, to the mistaken registration of the vendor. Where the acquirer's involvement with the property arises only *after* the vendor has been mistakenly registered, he will not have caused—whether through lack of care or otherwise—the relevant mistake. This interpretation of the causation issue would generally eradicate any requirement on an acquirer to attend to mistakes already in the Register. It appears to have been confirmed by Sir Christopher Slade in *Kingsalton Ltd v Thames Water Developments Ltd*.[36] His Lordship regarded the acquirers as entitled to assume that their registered title would be afforded the normal protection of registration despite their actual knowledge of the ownership dispute pre-dating first registration which had led to a mistake in the registered title: '[t]he very purpose of registration was to resolve such doubts'.[37] Those two cases were decided under the LRA 1925 but the same interpretation has been reiterated under the LRA 2002 by *Fye v High Grange Ltd*[38] which denied 'any basis in law for requiring [the acquirer] to go behind the register, and satisfy itself that the earlier transaction was bona fide.[39]

The position under the LRA 2002 has, however, been complicated by the answer that recent cases have given to the question whether the registration of a transferee of a mistaken

[33] LRA 2002, sch 4, para 3(2)(a). It is not enough to show there was lack of care by a predecessor in title: *Paton v Todd* [2012] EWHC 1248, [2012] 2 EGLR 19 [62] (Morgan J); see also *Kingsalton Ltd v Thames Water Developments Ltd* [2001] EWCA Civ 20, [2002] 1 P & CR 15 [25] (Peter Gibson LJ).

[34] *Epps v Esso Petroleum Ltd* [1971] 1 WLR 1071 (Ch).

[35] ibid, 1079D.

[36] *Kingsalton* (n 33).

[37] ibid [56] (Sir Christopher Slade; Arden LJ concurring).

[38] *Fye* (n 28) (obiter as the proprietor was not in possession).

[39] ibid [24] (Judge Owen Rhys). See also *Wheeler v Patnaik* [2015] EWLandRA 2014_0519 [52] (Judge McAllister).

title was rectifiable as a mistake in itself or was rectifiable merely to correct the consequences of the earlier mistake.[40] *Odogwu v Vastguide Ltd*[41] accepted that there was a mistake in entering the acquirer as successor to the mistaken entry—albeit on the basis of issue estoppel—and proceeded to make striking comments against the protection of acquirers from defects in the registered root of title. The acquirer was denied the possession defence against rectification on the ground that it chose to 'compound the effect of the fraud'[42] by taking the transfer knowing that it was able to do so only because of that fraud. The case represents a clear conflict with the principle outlined above. Even if the care requirement were to take account only of actual awareness of an existing right to rectify, and not constructive notice, it would still engender a risk that the Register becomes perceived as having impaired reliability; defensive investigative practices might in turn ensue, along with litigation over the requisite mental state.

It is submitted that the preferable approach involves the provision of a safe harbour for acquirers through the no-causation analysis illustrated by *Epps*, so that actual notice of defects in the registered root of title is disregarded when applying the care requirement. Although that proposition was developed in the context of the lack of care proviso, it concerns the content of the acquirer's care requirement generally and so should apply uniformly to that care requirement, independently of the particular channel under which it is considered. As such, it must be equally inappropriate to smuggle the same factor into decision making either through the 'injustice proviso', as was suggested as an alternative route in *Odogwu*,[43] or through the 'exceptional circumstances' test, as was done in *Kingsalton* and *Barwell*.[44] Those cases should all fall together.

B. Care Requirements Not Undermining the Register

There are occasions when a potential care requirement might suggest that investigations should properly be undertaken by an acquirer into matters other than the validity of Register information. As such, they would not undermine the Register, and there is no objection on that ground to imposing a care requirement—which might, as explained above, carry adverse consequences in rectification or indemnity proceedings. The following paragraphs explain three factual contexts. Subsection C then explores how any care requirement ought to be fulfilled in each.

The first context involves defects in the immediate disposition to the acquirer. If the acquirer is aware of such a defect, then there is no reason to resist the recognition of a requirement to raise the matter with the Registry or the owner, so as to afford the opportunity to object. Such a requirement would not encourage conveyancers to undertake undesirable investigations. The case law has recognised a care requirement—correctly on the arguments presented here—when the acquirer submits a transfer containing a defect

[40] The point was recognised in *Fye* (n 28).

[41] *Odogwu* (n 29).

[42] ibid [68] (Sir Donald Rattee).

[43] ibid [68] (Sir Donald Rattee).

[44] *Kingsalton* (n 33) [27] (Peter Gibson LJ); *Barwell v Skinner* [2011] EWLandRA 2010_0982 [126] (Mr Simon Brilliant).

which is not apparent on its face, and does not draw the defect to the attention of the Registry or owner. Examples include execution under a revoked power of attorney,[45] attestation by an absent witness,[46] and an interpolated execution page.[47]

The second context in which a care requirement would not compel investigations behind the Register concerns adverse possession applications and other modes of acquisition without consent. Such circumstances show clearly the nature of the obligation on the acquirer: it requires some communication from the acquirer to the Registry or owner which discloses potential defects and affords the owner an opportunity to object. A compelling account of that reasoning is found in *Balevents Ltd v Sartori*[48] in which Sartori secured registration as freehold proprietor on the basis of his false statutory declaration as to the nature and duration of his adverse possession against its owner. Balevents Ltd, which had previous connections with Sartori, then sought rectification against him on the basis either that Sartori's possession enured to the benefit of Balevents Ltd, or that Sartori held the title on constructive trust for Balevents Ltd, or that neither had any title. Balevents Ltd argued that Sartori was prevented from relying on his possession as a defence to rectification, owing to the lack of proper care in his application for registration.

The court's decision was that the acquirer in this case—Sartori—had not exercised proper care, and was therefore unable to resist the rectification claim on the ground of being in possession. The importance of the case lies in the court's explanation of why the false statement in Sartori's application should have amounted to lack of proper care. The court found lack of proper care on the basis that: (i) the false assertion was effective to persuade the Registry not to serve a notice on a potential rival claimant who knew of the history and would have effectively opposed the application, and (ii) the false allegation also led to the Registry being dismissive of the objections put forward by the true owner.[49] Such reasoning demonstrates that truthful communication to the Registry of the facts about possession are required and that misleading statements of fact in statutory declarations can be penalised through the lack of care proviso.[50] But most importantly, it confirms that this is required in order that the Registry might then be equipped to alert interested parties and make an informed decision, and thus implies that this is a care requirement designed to the protect the interests of owners.

The third context involves the care requirement in applications for first registration—which by definition cannot involve inquiry behind any Register entries. The case law recognises the potential relevance of the care requirement in this context, typically in the submission of ambiguous or imprecise plans or parcel descriptions,[51] and confirms that the care requirement is satisfied through communicating in a way that enables opposition to

[45] *Iqbal* (n 28).
[46] *Xu v Guo* [2015] UKFTT 0525 (Property Chamber).
[47] *Garguilo v Gershinson* [2012] EWLandRA 2011_0377.
[48] *Balevents Ltd v Sartori* [2014] EWHC 1164 (Ch).
[49] ibid [174] (Morgan J).
[50] *Balevents* (n 48); *Wheeler v Patnaik* (n 39); *Wilson v Grainger* [2009] EWHC 3145 (Ch); *Thompson v Hatherton Marina Ltd* [2007] EWLandRA 2004_0765; *Khalifa Holdings Aktiengesellschaft v Way* [2010] EWLandRA 2008_1438; *Baxter v Mannion* [2011] EWCA Civ 120, [2011] 1 WLR 1594; *Chapman v Godinn Properties Ltd* [2005] EWCA Civ 941 [20] (Chadwick LJ).
[51] *Epps* (n 34); *Mann* (n 3); *Barwell* (n 44); *Facey v Bedford BC* [2014] EWLandRA 2014_0022.

the application. It is submitted that this is the correct approach to take. In *Saxon v Moore*[52] and *Mann v Dingley*,[53] the prospective acquirer was found to have lacked proper care when he was well aware of the existing dispute over ownership but had nevertheless applied for first registration without making disclosure in a way that would have prompted Registry inquiries which in turn would have given the owner an opportunity to object. When the putative owner sought rectification of the Register, the judge noted that:

> Mr Dingley [the acquirer who successfully applied for first registration] was under a duty to bring the fact that there was a dispute about the land which had been the subject of correspondence with HM Land Registry to the attention of the Registry. It might have been different had he warned Mrs Mann [who claimed to be true owner under a prior unregistered title] that he was going to make the application so that she could have make representations to the Registry herself.[54]

The principles embodied in that passage are unassailable. The acquirer's lack of proper care resulted in his being denied the possession defence to the owner's rectification claim. On the facts, however, the decision is somewhat unsatisfactory. Mr Dingley had failed to make frank disclosure and thus lost protection against rectification, yet Mrs Mann failed at trial to substantiate her assertion of prior ownership, and so—incongruously—the case effectively imposes on the acquirer a requirement to protect the interests of someone who turned out not to have been the owner.[55] That approach appears to create a concept of care in the abstract and misses the point that a care requirement makes practical sense only when understood in terms of a particular relationship setting. The court should not have stigmatised Dingley's conduct as careless and should have declined rectification: rectification exists to protect private interests rather than to police careful behaviour for its own sake. For that reason, the same criticism applies to cases in which an acquirer is penalised for failing to take care when an action is brought by a concerned member of the public.

The facts of *Sainsbury's Supermarkets Ltd v Olympia Homes Ltd*[56] demonstrate the converse position. The acquirer's solicitor had previously held discussions with the Registry concerning an anticipated title problem—admittedly on a narrow point about the title to be conveyed—but the discussions still had the effect of drawing to the Registry's attention the broader problem which indicated the existence of a mistake. Against that background, the court thought the acquirer's solicitor:

> should [not] have been expected to do anything more than submit the title documents with which he had been supplied so that the Registry could make up its own mind on what sort of title they entitled his client to.[57]

That approach is supported on the ground that the acquirer had discharged the care requirement by acting (whether consciously or not) in a way that drew at least an aspect of the issue to the attention of the Registry.

[52] *Saxon v Moore* [2005] EWHC 27 (Ch).
[53] *Mann* (n 3).
[54] ibid [40] (Judge McCahill QC). See *Saxon* (n 52) [92], point 2 (Judge Behrens).
[55] The same criticism applies to *Walker v Burton* [2013] EWCA Civ 1228, [2014] 1 P & CR 9.
[56] *Sainsbury's Supermarkets Ltd v Olympia Homes Ltd* [2005] EWHC 1235 (Ch), [2006] 1 P & CR 17.
[57] ibid [87] (Mann J). See also *Walker v Burton* [2012] EWHC 978 (Ch) [99] (Jeremy Cousins QC).

C. Fulfilling the Care Requirement

Having addressed certain conditions in which the acquirer should and should not be burdened by the care requirement, it now remains to consider some important dimensions in the application of the care requirement.

i. A Requirement to Communicate or a Requirement to Desist from Seeking Registration?

The preceding sections have argued that the primary responsibility of the acquirer in fulfilling any care requirement is one of communication with the owner or the Registry to draw attention to facts which are potentially indicative that the proposed acquisition could create a mistake in the Register. But it must also be questioned whether the care requirement may demand more than mere communication. The court in *Odogwu v Vastguide Ltd*[58] appears to go further. The judgment can be interpreted as extending the acquirer's care requirement (in the context of the lack of care proviso) to include a requirement to desist from proceeding with an application to register.

Recall that Odogwu was registered proprietor of the fee simple. A fraudster, impersonating Odogwu, executed a registered charge in favour of Credit & Mercantile. The latter negotiated a sale to Vastguide, the acquirer. Before the exchange of contracts for sale, Vastguide was informed by Odogwu's solicitor that the charge had been executed by an imposter; the police confirmed the fraud in a letter received by Vastguide between contract and transfer. Thereafter—and before taking the transfer—Vastguide's solicitor had corresponded with Odogwu's solicitor; he had stated that Vastguide had contracted to buy, he had invited Odogwu to initiate proceedings before completion of the purchase, he had telephoned to inquire what Odogwu planned to do, and he had later offered a very short delay in completion to permit an emergency injunction application. In the absence of a reply, Vastguide completed the purchase and was registered as proprietor. Thus presented, the facts showed a concern by the potential acquirer (Vastguide) to disclose its acquisition plans fully to the ousted owner (Odogwu) and to give the ousted owner an opportunity to object. It is difficult to see what further level of communication could have been offered by or demanded from the acquirer on these facts. Despite this, it was held that Vastguide came within the lack of care proviso, meaning it was denied the defence against the owner's rectification claim, which would ordinarily be available to a possessor. The court did not describe what more it expected of the acquirer, but there is one crucial allusion: Vastguide 'apparently did not think fit to ask Credit & Mercantile to release it from its contract ... once it had knowledge of the fraud'.[59] That establishes an innovation that goes far beyond all other reported cases: a requirement to desist from applying for registration, even if the acquirer had already contracted to buy and had paid over the price to the vendor (in this case, Credit & Mercantile).

It is submitted that a requirement to desist from seeking registration should be rejected as it leads to an unacceptable allocation of responsibilities. First, by deterring prospective

[58] *Odogwu* (n 30).
[59] ibid [64] (Sir Donald Rattee).

purchasers, it would detract from the right of the vendor (Credit & Mercantile) to dispose of its property. Secondly, the requirement to desist would mean that the prospective acquirer would not proceed; and the vendor would meanwhile expect the former owner to commence proceedings for rectification of his title. Because the vendor cannot claim a statutory indemnity until the rectification question has been resolved,[60] the vendor's desire to avoid the alteration litigation might provide an undesirable incentive for the vendor to sell to another without disclosing the problem, thereby throwing the risk of that lawsuit onto a third party. Thirdly, it would put an unfair risk of delay on the acquirer who must wait for the ousted owner to take action and yet there is no limitation period for the owner's rectification proceedings.

Those arguments would be relevant in a case such as *Odogwu*, where the acquirer had notice of an alleged flaw affecting the seller's registered title—ie, of a defect 'behind' the Register. But even if the acquirer's care requirement does not extend to such defects, as proposed above, then the point remains valid that acquirers should not be required to desist from registering. That would remain relevant in cases where the acquirer sought registration under an entitlement by operation of law or at first registration. In those circumstances, a requirement to desist from seeking registration would involve unnecessary paternalism towards owners. There is no basis for treating owners as unduly vulnerable and they have various registration facilities available to protect their position. A better balance would be struck between the interests of the acquirer and the ousted owner if the law accepted that the acquirer will discharge his responsibility by disclosing and giving the opportunity to object. Consequently, the acquirer's care requirement should be satisfied merely by making suitable disclosure on or before applying to be registered, and should not demand that acquirers desist from seeking registration altogether.

ii. Standard of Care: Subjective Awareness and Constructive Notice

So far it has been argued that the acquirer's care requirement ought to apply only in relation to matters which do not lie behind the Register, and that it extends only to appropriate communication with the Registry or the owner. It is now possible to move on to consider the standard of care within those parameters.

Standards of care have long been managed in the tort of negligence through a framework of factors that have universal applicability.[61] The factors, bearing on what 'reasonable care' requires, traditionally dwell on the four matters indicated in these extracts:

> not only [1] how remote is the chance that a person might [suffer harm] but also [2] how serious the consequences are likely to be.[62]

Furthermore,

> [i]t is well settled that in measuring due care [3] you must balance the risk against the measures necessary to eliminate the risk. To that proposition there ought to be added this: [4] you must balance the risk against the end to be achieved.[63]

60 LRA 2002, sch 8, para 1(3).
61 *Bamford v Turnley* (1860) 3 B&S 62; 122 ER 25, *United States v Carroll Towing Co* (1947) 159 F 2d 169.
62 *Bolton v Stone* [1951] AC 850 (HL), 867 (Lord Reid).
63 *Watt v Hertfordshire CC* [1954] 1 WLR 835 (CA) 838 (Denning LJ).

Those factors also serve well in the land registration context. The harm is constant in taking one of two forms—it equates to the ousted owner's loss of title or the acquirer's squandered efforts to acquire good title—so attention focuses on the foreseeability of those two harms, the practicability of precautions, and the social desirability of reducing the precautionary measures needed to be taken by owners or the investigatory measures taken by acquirers. When it comes to applying these factors, there is a difficult balance to be struck if expropriation via a mistaken registration is to be combatted while avoiding costly investigations that impede the acquisition of rights. The following paragraphs will focus on one particular controversy: how the factors just identified relate to an acquirer's actual and constructive notice of facts which indicate that a mistake will arise by the acquirer's entry as registered proprietor. It will be argued that an acquirer's subjective awareness of a competing claim, if not appropriately communicated, will amount to a breach of the acquirer's care requirement. Beyond this, there will also be circumstances in which the care requirement is more stringent, in as much as it might penalise an acquirer for conduct which falls below an *objective* standard, even in the absence of subjective awareness of a competing claim. In effect, this may involve attaching legal consequences to a failure to observe a limited objective duty of inquiry in certain circumstances.

It is contended here that legal significance should be attached to the acquirer's actual notice or subjective awareness of an outstanding claim derogating from the title with which he seeks to be registered, or of a flaw in his application which could represent an outstanding claim, coupled with lack of candid disclosure. The importance of subjective awareness in the standard of care is twofold. First, it operates as a distinctive moral element that serves to penalise an acquirer who conceals another's claim for the purpose of advancing his own application to register. Secondly, the use of subjective awareness does not imply any obligation to make unprompted inquiries in the field. That is significant to the test of reasonableness found in tort law, which has traditionally considered the cost of precautions. In the context of information about rival claims, the cost of precautions must equate to the costs of detection. If an outstanding ownership claim could be detected in the course of other endeavours without any cost, and disclosure would be equally costless, that is likely to tip the scales of reasonableness, especially if the information appears reliable and thereby raises the foreseeability or probability of the risk materialising. In these circumstances of low-cost protection of the owner's rights, the acquirer should be expected to act.

This approach does not appear to require any departure from the existing case law. Subjective awareness certainly figures in the cases, although it has not been explicitly tied to the reasonableness factors noted above. It has been emphasised in relation to an acquirer's awareness of facts indicating defects in the immediate transfer. Examples include acquirers seeking to register transfers known to be executed under a revoked power of attorney,[64] executed improperly[65] or attested by an absent witness.[66] It also makes an appearance in first registration applications. *Epps v Esso Petroleum Ltd*[67] is an early case which broadly attaches significance to an acquirer's awareness of a defect concerning a boundary at first

[64] *Iqbal* (n 28) [34]–[35] (Michael Mark) (obiter).
[65] *Garguilo v Gershinon* (n 45) [82] (Ann McAllister).
[66] *Xu* (n 46) [16] (Judge Owen Rhys).
[67] *Epps* (n 34).

registration. The acquirers who sought first registration 'were taking a gamble … [They] must have realised that there might be some difficulty over the boundary',[68] yet did not communicate their doubts. That was held to engage the injustice proviso, although the facts and reasoning could have equally support analysis under the lack of care proviso as the Law Commission has recognised.[69] Further, subjective awareness has been considered relevant in claims to acquire registered land by adverse possession. The failure to disclose an ongoing dispute of which the acquirer was all too aware has also been held sufficient to invoke the injustice proviso against the acquirer, when facing a rectification claim by the owner.[70]

These common case references are consistent with the argument that *subjective* awareness or actual notice of a defect which the acquirer does not disclose may indicate unreasonable conduct and thus fail the acquirer's care requirement. However, the cases mentioned do not indicate what place (if any) *objective* tests of knowledge have in determining standards of care. In particular, it is not clear whether subjective awareness was a redundant feature in those cases, whether standards of care are assessed by an objective test, or whether they operate in tandem so that an acquirer may satisfy an objective standard yet fail overall to show proper care due to his subjective awareness of a problem.

The importation of an objective element may be less welcome. It has associations with the taboo of constructive notice[71] that traditionally raises fears of unpalatable vagueness, adjudication with the benefit of hindsight, and excessively onerous expectations in investigating title, collectively tending to increase cost and unpredictability for acquirers.

Despite those reservations, objective standards should have a place in the application of the standard of care required by the provisions of the LRA 2002. Apart from the objective connotations of the phrase 'proper care',[72] which suggests action and not passively waiting to see if information finds its way to one's attention, there are substantial policy considerations in favour of objective minimum standards. They ensure predictable minimum protections for owners, they deter acquirers from consciously avoiding cheap and convenient investigations, they ensure there is background information which equips the acquirer to recognise subsequent warning signs that may suggest defects, and they avoid problems in attributing subjective mental states to corporations.[73] To resurrect some features of constructive notice in the present context would not infringe the paramount principle that Register entries must not be questioned, since the present context is restricted to occasions such as first registrations and disposition defects where that principle has traditionally had no application. Nevertheless, it is also submitted that in applying any care requirement one should heed the reservations noted above and be alert to the danger of escalating conveyancing costs and unnecessarily hampering the formal acquisition of rights. The terminology of constructive notice may be avoided by reframing the objective care requirement in tortious

[68] ibid, 1080–81 (Templeman J).

[69] Law Commission, *Third Report on Land Registration* (Law Com No 158, 1987) para 3.14, n 36.

[70] *Andrews v Tonks* [2013] EWLandRA 2012_0518 [41] (Judge Michell).

[71] See R Smith, *Property Law*, 8th edn (Harlow, Pearson Longman, 2014) 280. See also Law Commission, *Third Report on Land Registration* (Law Com No 158, 1987) paras 3.14–3.15 and Law Commission, *Land Registration for the Twenty-First Century—A Consultative Document* (Law Com No 254, 1998) paras 3.44–3.49.

[72] LRA 2002, sch 4, para 3(2)(a); also, in a different relationship setting, LRA 2002, sch 8, para 5(2).

[73] On attribution to corporations: see *Facey v Bedford Borough Council* REF/2014/22 (11 Sept 2014) and (17 Nov 2014).

terms: unreasonably taking foreseeable risks in circumstances of heightened probability of error where precautionary investigative costs are low.

That principle probably cannot be broken down further to provide more concrete guidance in any universal formula. But further assistance is to be gained from taking separately the diverse types of situation in which the care requirement may be applied. Four key illustrations can be considered in turn.

First, when applied to the acquirer's conduct at first registration, it is submitted that an objective standard of care is not merely desirable, but vital to the working of land registration under the English model. It ensures that the enduring record of title is compiled from information generated by a minimum level of inquiry in a regime where the Registry places reliance on the conveyancer's work. That approach necessarily assumes a reasonable conveyancer rather than a reasonable lay person. However, it is not unduly onerous as the Registry adopts the standard that would typically be used by conveyancers acting for willing purchasers, namely what might be called a 'safe holding title'[74] as opposed to 'good marketable title'.[75] The starting point for the proposed objective standard of care should, therefore, simply track the obligations owed by a solicitor to a client in relation to investigating title,[76] as qualified by the requirements of the LRA 2002, the Land Registration Rules ('LRR') 2003,[77] and professional standards developed in response to published Registry guidance.[78]

That approach seems compatible with the case law. In *Johnson v Shaw*,[79] there was recognition of an objective standard in that the acquirer knew 'or ought to have known'[80] that she had no entitlement, a matter that was relevant in deciding whether to order rectification under the unregulated discretionary test as it stood before the exceptional circumstances test was introduced.[81] The point has since been made fully and forcefully in *Walker v Burton*[82] where an objective test was explicitly argued. While the Court of Appeal did not categorically confirm the point, it did refer to the 'reasonableness' of the acquisitive conduct[83] and generally approved the High Court's approach which had clearly applied objective standards of proper care[84]—although its precedential value is somewhat weakened by the procedural failure to plead lack of proper care in registering the relevant *wasteland* (the object of the claim) as opposed to the *manor* (which was not the object of the claim), and by the fact that the acquirer's solicitors had been subjectively aware of the limitations of their title investigations. The adoption of an objective standard may be evident in the court's acknowledgement that 'issues of proportionality of costs to the subject matter have to be kept in mind'.[85] In these circumstances, the investigations should not be treated in isolation

[74] Land Transfer Act 1875, s 17(3), now embodied in LRA 2002, s 9(2) and (3). See *Report of the Royal Commissioners Appointed to Inquire into the Operation of the Land Transfer Act* (1870, c 20) para 77; *Royal Commission on the Land Transfer Acts: Second and Final Report of the Commissioners* (Cmd 5483, 1911) para 59.

[75] Formerly required by Land Registry Act 1862, s 5.

[76] *Prestige Properties Ltd v Scottish Provident Institution* [2002] EWHC 330 (Ch), [2003] Ch 1 [36] (Lightman J); *Walker v Burton* [2013] EWCA Civ 1228, [2014] 1 P & CR 9 [97] (Mummery LJ).

[77] eg, LRA 2002, s 71; Land Registration Rules ('LRR') 2003, SI 2003/1417, rr 24, 28 and 30.

[78] eg, Land Registry, *Practice Guide 1: First Registrations* (Feb 2017).

[79] *Johnson v Shaw* [2003] EWCA Civ 894, [2004] 1 P & CR 10.

[80] ibid [48] (Peter Gibson LJ).

[81] LRA 1925, s 82(1).

[82] *Walker v Burton* (CA) (n 76).

[83] ibid [98].

[84] *Walker v Burton* [2012] EWHC 978 (Ch) [88] (Mr Jeremy Cousins QC).

[85] ibid [88].

from the communications to the Registry. While the acquirer's conveyancers had probably not undertaken investigations that would satisfy the traditional unregistered conveyancing standard, they had deduced documentary evidence back to 1836 and pointed out to the Registry that they declined to certify title in the usual way. That was perfectly acceptable as it would have been 'unrealistic'[86] to require the acquirer to undertake the factual and legal research necessary to resolve the title issues (which related to the devolution of a manor from a charter of 1254) and in circumstances where the only other rival claimants had been identified and dealt with directly,[87] and there had been no public suggestion for over a century that anyone else claimed superior title. The court's approach in *Walker* is conceptually and practically sound: it sets an objective threshold based on reasonableness and proportionality for acquirers at first registration according to the principles proposed here.

Secondly, a comparable approach should be applied when dealing with registered land that is being conveyed through intermediate instruments as yet unregistered. When, for example, land of a deceased registered proprietor is sold by executors to a developer, who resells before making a registered entry, the ultimate acquirer should be expected to take reasonable steps to ensure that all intermediate instruments are effective before lodging an application for registration. The task requires a review of parcels clauses, proper execution, and so on, to ensure that there is nothing on the face of the instruments to suggest invalidity. Similar considerations should always apply to the immediate instrument under which the acquirer takes the entitlement to become registered even if there have been no other intermediate transactions.

Thirdly, there are problems concerning identity verification. The Register does not, of course, guarantee that the identity of a particular vendor matches the registered proprietor. This too should be a matter for an objective standard on account of the general advantages put forward above. In relation to identity theft, the case of *Swift 1st* has already considered the possibility of lack of care in the practice of commercial lenders when confirming a mortgagee's identity. In *Swift 1st*, the court examined the lender's standard routines in a way that suggests it was those processes that were assessed, rather than any subjective awareness of the identity fraud, to determine whether the minimum level of care had been reached.[88] It is submitted that is the correct attitude to the matter of an acquirer's investigation into a vendor's identity for the purpose of the care requirement. *Swift 1st* itself concerned the 'lack of care' defence to indemnity, but because the lender's investigation into the mortgagor's identity is the very conduct whose omission could cause expropriation of the true owner, the same stance should also be taken respecting the acquirer's care requirement vis-à-vis the owner.[89] How might proper care be demonstrated? For some acquirers, such as regulated

[86] ibid [88].

[87] *Burton v Walker* [2010] EWLandRA 2007_1124 [112] (Mr Donachie) and [116] (Mr & Mrs Brown).

[88] *Swift 1st Ltd v Chief Land Registrar* [2014] EWHC 4866 (Ch) [61] (Richard Sheldon QC). See also the hypothetical reference to reckless lending policies in *English v English* [2010] EWHC 2058 (Ch) [60] (HHJ David Cooke).

[89] While the principle generally holds good, the specific context of identity deception by mortgagors is unlikely in practice to generate judicial consideration of the care requirement imposed on mortgage acquirers towards the true owners if the legislation denies mortgagees protection against rectification through restrictive definitions of 'proprietor in possession' (LRA 2002, s 131(2)) or proprietors of 'estates' (LRA 2002, sch 4, para 3(2) and s 132(1)); the only remaining channel is the 'exceptional circumstances' test, but it is inconceivable that the mortgagee's lack of care would justify refusing the defrauded owner's claim to correction.

lenders obtaining mortgages from their clients, there are some obvious sources of guidance to help determine the range of investigations into identity that are required to fulfil the basic objective threshold: they will comprise professional duties as understood in the light of regulatory guidance, money laundering controls, emerging information sources and risk assessments. For acquirers acting through conveyancers, some similar types of sources might be relevant, but the obvious difference from mortgage lending is that the transferor is not the acquirer's client; where the transferor is legally represented, a test of reasonableness might suggest that the acquirer's conveyancer should generally be permitted to rely on the identity verification undertaken by their opposite number. In other situations, few such advance guidelines are likely to be available and generalisations are difficult; it may even be reasonable to rely on the transferor's own assertion of identity if the transaction is one in which the circumstances strongly militate against any likelihood of deception.

Fourthly and finally, when applying the standard in relation to adverse possession and other unilateral acquisitions where an entitlement is claimed by operation of law, the position is again made complex by the absence of any existing legal or regulatory standards by reference to which the appropriate investigations can be determined. The factual context also takes it out of the normal market conditions in which standards have developed for other legal purposes. Unilateral acquisitions involve an informational asymmetry that favours the acquirer and an absence of transactional deadlines; both of these may influence the application of the reasonableness factors and suggest that the acquirer should be required to take steps to verify the assertions he makes when seeking registration. Such a requirement has the advantage of offsetting the temptation to overstate claims which might influence certain acquirers who see a chance to gain without paying and for whom the penalties for false declarations may be an insufficient deterrent. Any counter-argument that the truth will ultimately emerge from the owner's opposition fails to acknowledge the many reasons that might explain an owner's failure to object.

Implementing the recommended proposal for an objective standard in these unilateral claims would not require any departure from existing case law, but would simply make explicit what seems already to be a theme in the case law. For example, in *Thompson v Hatherton Marina Ltd*,[90] the existence of an error in the acquirer's statutory declaration would have engaged the lack of care proviso or the injustice proviso as it was 'something which proper care could have established'[91] implying the applicant should have investigated further. In *Khalifa Holdings Aktiengesellschaft v Way*,[92] an adverse possession claimant omitted to mention that her occupation had been under licence, a matter that engaged the lack of care proviso as it 'amounts to, at best, a lack of proper care',[93] again suggesting an objective standard since it presumably implies lesser blameworthiness than deliberate concealment.[94] In *Balevents Ltd v Sartori*,[95] it was indicated that the acquirer, if he

[90] *Thompson v Hatherton Marina* (n 49).
[91] ibid [81] (Mr Cousins).
[92] *Khalifa Holdings* (n 49).
[93] ibid [24] (Michael Michell).
[94] See also *Wilson v Grainger* (n 49) [37] (Vos J), commentating on the Deputy Adjudicator's finding of lack of care on grounds that the applicants 'ought to have known' of rival claim.
[95] *Balevents Ltd v Sartori* (n 47) [174] (Morgan J).

was unsure about possession, could have 'investigated the facts rather than making up the assertions' to avoid the application of the lack of care proviso.

This chapter has proposed both a potential subjective test of general application and an objective test in relation to certain unilateral acquisitions. Their simultaneous existence requires reconciliation. The solution is simply that the subjective awareness of material facts always justifies a requirement to disclose to the owner or to the Registry; and that for acquisitions by operation of law, in circumstances where the Registry must rely on the acquirer propounding a version of events that is not supported by the former owner's consensual disposition, a minimum objective threshold should be set that requires certain pre-emptive investigations and disclosures, with the standard varying according to the strength of the policy of facilitating unilateral acquisitions.

V. Care and Alteration Claims: What Should be Required of Existing Owners?

The second relationship setting for the imposition of a care requirement exists between the same participants—acquirer and owner—but operates in reverse. It relates to an owner's conduct in protecting a prospective acquirer from loss. This loss could comprise the wasted expense incurred by the acquirer in dealing with a third person whom the acquirer wrongly believed to have title; alternatively, where the acquirer succeeds in taking title by virtue of registration, it might comprise expenses incurred in defending rectification proceedings and, if unsuccessful in that defence, any wasted expenditure incurred in reliance on his expectation of ownership according to the Register. The owner could help to reduce the incidence of such expenses by taking steps in advance to communicate the existence of the owner's rights and disabuse the acquirer of any false expectations over who has title. In the light of this, this section argues that it is appropriate to impose a care requirement on the owner to alert acquirers to the owner's interest.

It is uncontroversial that the LRA 2002 prescribes a means for the owner to warn others via a Register entry and, as against a purchaser for value of the relevant estate, penalises failure to do so through its provisions on priority.[96] These provisions represent the central core of the owner's care requirement—to alert acquirers by means of an entry in the Register, whether as registered proprietor or via the entry of a notice or restriction. As reflected in these provisions, this duty is strict and not cast in terms of 'taking care': an owner is either entered in the Register (and therefore protected) or not entered (and therefore vulnerable to subsequent registered dispositions). Nevertheless, this section argues that this core duty to register does not exclude the possibility that the requirement of care in using the registration system might have a wider scope, which augments the strict duty of registration expressed through the priority rules, and which may assume relevance in the various channels that penalise lack of care. The following subheadings explore the potential scope and content of the care requirement that should be acknowledged through those channels.

[96] LRA 2002, ss 29 and 30.

A. Use of Warning Facilities

There are occasions when an owner's use of the Register as a warning facility is mishandled. The classic example occurs upon first registrations which follow a sale of part. A, owner of unregistered Blackacre, conveys part of Blackacre to S1, who becomes first registered proprietor of the severed part. The retained part of Blackacre undergoes first registration and the registered proprietor is R1. It transpires that S1 became registered with either too much or too little land because his registration either went beyond or fell short of what was covered by the conveyance to S1. That error then influences the registration of R1, who becomes registered with correspondingly less or more land than he should have been.

This is a context where care is potentially relevant. Had S1 taken greater care at first registration to ensure the accuracy of his Register entry, the issue would have been caught and resolved before R1 became registered proprietor. Once R1 becomes registered, the issue must be resolved through rectification proceedings to make adjustments to the relevant registered plan or plans. The situation is therefore one in which S1's defective registration resulted in R1 becoming embroiled in rectification litigation. This may justify consideration being given to S1's potential breach of care requirement towards R1 in any alteration proceedings brought by R1. There is some evidence in the cases that courts may indeed stigmatise such failures. In *Kingsalton*,[97] for example, S1's conduct was branded as 'carelessness',[98] although it was not apparently relied on in deciding the outcome. For the reasons given here, this attitude is fully justified.

Taking the illustration one stage further, it should also be noted that R1 might be guilty of a similar neglect. Had R1 taken greater care at his own first registration to ensure the accuracy of his Register entry, the issue would have been spotted and resolved at that point. That would be of benefit to any person to whom S1 subsequently transfers the severed part—S2. The situation is therefore one in which R1's defective registration could result in S2 becoming embroiled in rectification litigation. This may justify consideration being given to R1's potential breach of care requirement towards S2 in any alteration proceedings between them. Such a scenario occurred in *Barwell v Skinner*,[99] where it was said that there was 'weight' in the contention that R1 was 'culpable'[100] when considering the exceptional circumstances test.

The care requirement in these circumstances would typically require acquirers to take the practical step of checking that the eventual registered entry reflects their entitlements under the conveyance that was lodged for registration. However, there is no reason to restrict the precautionary steps to the registration context; the same penalty for failing in the care requirement is capable of extending even to neglected pre-registration conduct, such as failing to warn others by indorsing a sale of part on the vendor's deeds.[101] Whatever the context, the standard expected should be sensitive to the cost, time and effort involved in the detection of possible mistakes, in line with the factors identified in section IV as

[97] *Kingsalton* (n 33).

[98] ibid [25] (Peter Gibson LJ).

[99] *Barwell* (n 44).

[100] ibid [125] (Simon Brilliant).

[101] cf *Re Sea View Gardens* [1967] 1 WLR 134 (ChD) where non-indorsement was the origin of the problem, although not attributed with any legal significance on the facts.

material to determinations of what reasonable care requires. It would ordinarily be reasonable to require an owner to inspect the Register to ensure the accuracy of his own warning entry; conversely, it would hardly be reasonable to go significantly further, and require an owner to seek out possible conflicting entries elsewhere, or to cross-check all corresponding entries for easements or covenants in a subdivided estate involving many separate registers.

Where the owner has a right in unregistered land and the duty to apply for first registration has not been activated, there are still facilities for the owner to warn others. The safest option for the owner might be voluntary first registration, or a caution against first registration, if permissible.[102] Failure to employ these voluntary protective measures should not typically be stigmatised as failing the care requirement.[103] Ultimately, the requirement's demands in these circumstances are heavily fact-dependent. The owner of the right may not even have been informed of the availability of those facilities; in particular, an owner may have acquired the right in circumstances where there was no solicitor advising, or long ago when the introduction of compulsory registration to the district was a remote prospect and thus the solicitor gave no advice that it might be desirable to invoke the voluntary measures as protection against another's application for first registration.

B. Requirement to Communicate or Requirement to Resist the Acquirer's Attempts to Register?

The preceding section argued that the primary responsibility of an owner is to alert acquirers to the owner's entitlement. In the light of recent case law, it must be questioned whether the care requirement should demand something more than mere communication.

Case law has generally taken a stance against recognising that an owner might be responsible for refreshing any warnings or actively resisting an acquirer's manoeuvres. In *Facey v Bedford CC*,[104] there was no hint of criticism of the owner who had ceased answering the acquirer's direct correspondence and who had merely requested the Registry not to register the acquirer without offering the owner an opportunity to object. In *Mann v Dingley*,[105] where the owner failed to take court proceedings to resolve the dispute after having threatened to do so, this was not to be held against her as she had beforehand vigorously communicated her objections to the acquirer's claims. The courts have even accepted that, in circumstances where a statute sets a deadline before which the owner must object, it is not fatal to any subsequent rectification claim by the owner that he might have missed this deadline. In particular, in the context of decisions concerning whether the injustice proviso should be invoked, such delay was belittled as not 'very telling' in *Sainsbury's Supermarkets*[106] and as mere 'thistledown' in *Baxter v Mannion*.[107] There is nothing here to

[102] LRA 2002, s 16(3).

[103] Cases such as *Horrill v Cooper* (2000) 80 P & CR D16 (CA) and *Rees v Peters* [2011] EWCA Civ 836, [2011] 2 P & CR 18, in which ousted owners incurred no criticism for failing to lodge cautions against first registration, are of little value here as the owners of the right had given warning through the Land Charges Register.

[104] *Facey v Bedford Borough Council* REF/2014/22 (17 Nov 2014).

[105] *Mann v Dingley* (n 3) [35] (Michael Michell).

[106] *Sainsbury's Supermarkets* (n 3) [92] (Mann J).

[107] *Baxter v Mannion* (n 50) [42] (Jacob LJ).

suggest that the owner's communication alone is insufficient and that the owner must go further and actively contest an acquirer's efforts.

In contrast, *Johnson v Shaw*[108] accepted that the owner's failure to act on a Registry letter proposing a solution to the dispute was a discretionary factor in favour of the acquirer, even though the owner had already communicated his objections to the acquirer and the Registry prior to the letter. Demanding more of owners than communication of the basis for objection could yield some advantages. To require an owner to answer Registry letters might cheaply and simply avert an acquirer's foreseeable loss; and to require an owner actively to controvert the acquirer's claim would help quieten titles. But such advantages pale in comparison to the cost, time and effort of defending or recovering one's title, perhaps repeatedly, against successive acquirers. Furthermore, the owner's warning should be enough to empower the acquirer to make a decision; acquirers as a class are not so vulnerable that owners should protect them against their own poor decision to press ahead with acquisition. For those reasons, the better approach is to reject the extension of the care requirement to active resistance, and adopt the owners' and acquirers' reciprocal communication requirements of warning and disclosure as the basic institutions of careful registration practice.

C. Additional Care Requirements when Communication Procedures are Known to be Bypassed

The care requirement has great flexibility. It was argued in section IV that, in relation to acquirers, subjective awareness of a high risk of a particular flaw in the title which the acquirer propounds to the Registry should impose on him responsibilities to take steps to communicate the problem. The same is true in relation to owners. An owner should bear extra responsibility when, despite having used the registration system to warn the world of his rights, he is aware that the acquirer is nonetheless proceeding with an acquisition. This may occur when the owner becomes aware of someone who has the ability or desire to create a mistaken Register entry—a typical example occurs when an owner suspects that a stranger is planning an identity theft or that the owner's own agent is no longer to be trusted. These cases are unique because the owner foresees that the defect in the acquirer's application to the Registry will not be disclosed, with the result that the Registry's notification processes will not be invoked and the owner's opportunity to object will be bypassed. In these circumstances, the owner must anticipate that his warning by registration will be ineffective. His subjective awareness of this problem justifies imposing a further responsibility on him to take action to counteract the risk of a mistaken Register entry and of the land being transferred to an innocent buyer who will be caught in a rectification dispute.

One precautionary mechanism available to an owner which might forestall this type of harm is the entry of a restriction.[109] It is likely for it to be reasonable (in the light of the

[108] *Johnson v Shaw* (n 79) [49] (Peter Gibson LJ).

[109] LRA 2002, s 42(1). The appropriate restriction might be a restriction in Form RQ requiring the owner's conveyancer to confirm the genuineness of the owner's signature as a protection against identity theft.

reasonableness factors discussed in section IV) to require an owner to utilise this mechanism. The owner's position of knowledge, the expected likelihood of risk materialising, the owner's capacity to take a cheap precaution that will efficiently prevent loss, and the purchaser's assumed powerlessness as a victim of misapprehension, all point towards imposing such a requirement on the owner once the suspicious behaviour has been brought to his attention.

Of course, a fact-sensitive approach must be taken when applying this care requirement. The most difficult are cases where, in the period before there is a mistaken entry in the Register, the owner merely *suspects* that a mistake might occur in the future, eg due to identity theft or agent misconduct. A court would need to consider, amongst other factors, the degree of confidence that the owner had in his suspicions of the acquirer's intentions, how the owner perceived the likelihood of those suspected intentions being put into practice, whether the owner had embarked on steps to investigate the matter, and so on. Employing that approach does not appear to require any substantial departure from the case law,[110] but it is likely to result in challenging litigation involving issues of fact and inference so troublesome that they might call into question the desirability of treating such suspicion as potential failure of care. In contrast, once the suspected unauthorised entry becomes a reality and the owner becomes aware of the fraud or error, the position changes dramatically. Suspicion is then replaced by a certainty, and thereafter owners should receive clear censure for failing to protect further potential acquirers by decisive action, such as seeking a protective entry, claiming rectification, or initiating court proceedings to block further transfer.[111]

Following a mistaken registration, the owner's care requirement should remain one of warning potential future acquirers of the danger of becoming caught up in rectification proceedings. But that warning should be regarded as a good discharge of the owner's responsibility only if it is mediated through the Register by way of a protective entry such as a notice or restriction. It was argued in section IV that an acquirer should not be prejudiced through any of the legal channels simply for having gained actual notice of a defect in the root of title from some source outside the Register; and if the acquirer should not be deterred by notice outside the Register, then it follows that it would make no sense to require the owner to give such notice to the acquirer since it would have no impact on the acquirer's legal position. Were the owner permitted to give such informal notice in fulfilment of the care requirement, it would allow personal correspondence from the owner to undermine the reliability of the Register. It would force the purchaser to take difficult decisions about the veracity of the allegations made by the alleged ousted owner at the purchaser while under pressure from the vendor to complete. A policy-led approach should accordingly recognise that in relation to Register mistakes the requirement on the owner is to communicate *via the Register* with its built-in safeguards.[112]

[110] See *Iqbal* (n 28) [36] (Michael Mark); *Nouri v Marvi* [2005] EWHC 2996 (Ch), [2006] 1 EGLR 71 [49] (Judge Rich QC). See also *Andrews v Tonks* (n 69) [40] (Judge Michell) (delay in bringing rectification proceedings was not an exceptional circumstance).

[111] *Odogwu* (n 30) [64] (Sir Donald Rattee); *Iqbal* (n 28) (Michael Mark) [36]–[37] (exceptional circumstance denying rectification); *Nouri* (n 110) [49] and [51] (Judge Rich QC) (lack of care proviso applied).

[112] eg, duty not to lodge notices, restrictions or objections without reasonable grounds: LRA 2002, s 77. Consider also an action by a seller against an ownership claimant for slander of title.

D. Proactive Monitoring

From the discussion above it is clear that the owner's responsibility to warn acquirers should not necessarily be discharged once and for all by making a warning entry. In cases where the owner actually suspects an unauthorised removal of the warning from the Register, for example, the care requirement should demand further action. But the discovery of the information which generates the suspicion may be entirely serendipitous. This raises the question whether the owner should be required to gather information proactively, by regularly reviewing the Register, observing activity on the ground, monitoring agents and so on, in order to build an information base which would facilitate the detection of suspicious behaviour.

While agencies now offer the service of regularly checking the Register for unauthorised alterations, it is submitted that the law should not require this in fulfilment of the owner's care requirement. There are various arguments against this step. First, there is a broad argument of cost and benefit. Imposing monitoring requirements would exceed reasonable precautions: given the still relatively low likelihood of fraud and error, the limited capacity to prevent loss once a problem is detected, and the integral scheme of indemnity designed to spread the losses, it would be a disproportionate social cost to require every landowner to order office copies at frequent intervals for every parcel. Secondly, there is an argument from convenience that restricting the owner's obligation to communication of actual suspicion of mistake would draw a relatively clear line for future guidance, whereas the introduction of any further general requirement to monitor frequently would open entirely new arenas for dispute over the required extent of precautionary acts.[113]

Further questions might arise where private agents are acting for an owner. Does a care requirement under the LRA 2002 imply a duty to monitor such agents? There is a case to be made for extending an owner's care requirement beyond monitoring the Registry to include systematic monitoring of private agents. The Registry is a statutory body charged with the constitutional function of administering registration, and it would seem appropriate to allow citizens to repose confidence in its actions without requiring on-going supervision. No such argument is available in respect of private agents. Nevertheless, on balance, it is suggested that the difficulty in fixing a suitable standard for the infinitely variable circumstances of agency makes it appropriate to require actual suspicion of agent misconduct before an owner can be accused of falling below the standard of care required. That appears to be in line with the case law which has made no reference to any requirement to monitor the donee of a power of attorney[114] or a family friend acting as informal agent.[115]

Keeping apprised of events on the ground constitutes a further potential opportunity for monitoring. However, it is doubtful that failure to monitor events on the land should ever prejudice an owner's position in alteration proceedings, despite the existence of doctrines elsewhere in land law—such as adverse possession—which imply that it is good practice to

[113] eg, lodging the restriction in Form RQ (requiring confirmation of the owner's conveyancer as a protection against identity theft) when aware of heightened risk factors.

[114] *Iqbal* (n 28).

[115] *Nouri* (n 110).

monitor one's land. It is a mistake to draw an analogy from the doctrine of adverse possession which is designed to protect the acquirer's long use of land and to penalise the owner's long non-use. It is not a doctrine concerned with the protection of titles from the consequences of misappropriation and is therefore unhelpful in discussions of the care required for the purpose of denying rectification claims by an owner. As there appears to be little else to justify special and onerous monitoring obligations in respect of land, it is submitted that there should be no unprompted requirement to monitor the land.[116]

VI. Care and Indemnity Claims

The third and final care requirement arises between a participant—whether owner or acquirer of land—and those responsible for making or funding indemnity awards. A care requirement is implicit in the statutory rule which denies or reduces an indemnity payment where the loss is suffered as a result of the indemnity claimant's lack of proper care.[117] In this setting, the owner or acquirer's responsibility for taking proper care is given legal expression through the claimant's susceptibility to losing the entitlement to compensation in full or in part. It is argued that this care requirement serves to protect the following bodies: (i) the Land Registry, as the entity which owns the Indemnity Fund[118] (albeit that it should not deliberately aim to build up a surplus)[119] and as the entity which bears the immediate burden of replenishing it; (ii) central government, as the entity which guarantees the solvency of the Indemnity Fund and to which the Fund's surpluses may be transferred;[120] and also, in an indirect sense, (iii) future taxpayers, whose burden will ultimately increase if the actuarial calculations require greater public contribution to the Fund.

It is submitted that the care requirement in this setting has two constituent limbs. The first constituent is simply parasitic on the communication responsibilities, discussed in sections IV and V, which owners and acquirers owe each other to prevent the other suffering by reason of a mistake in the Register. Those care requirements affect not only the availability of rectification but also indemnity; they recognise the interests of the Land Registry, central government and taxpayers in discouraging avoidable conduct that contributes to Register mistakes, which may result in indemnity payments. Similar reasons also justify a second constituent limb to the care requirement: to avoid any unreasonable escalation in the burden on the Fund. This implies a requirement on owners and acquirers to avoid magnifying the extent of their own losses beyond the loss of the land itself, and consequently it is not restricted to a contribution to the mistake in the Register.

[116] A reference in *Fye* (n 28) [33] (Judge Owen Rhys) to the owner's neglect of the land for 30 years, and then a further 11 years after the fraud, must be taken not as a failure to monitor but as delay in bringing proceedings and a general lack of interest in enjoying the land in specie.

[117] LRA 2002, sch 8, para 5(1) and (2).

[118] The Indemnity Fund is calculated on an actuarial basis. Indemnity claims are, in the first instance, charged against the Fund.

[119] HM Treasury, 'Guide to the Establishment and Operation of Trading Funds' (May 2004) paras 8.2.2–8.2.3.

[120] Government Trading Funds Act 1973, s 4.

A. Magnifying One's Own Loss

The advantage of dividing up the care requirement into the two constituent limbs is that it reveals an important difference in the legal significance of failing to take suitable steps to protect oneself from any losses going beyond the loss of the land itself. On the one hand, a failure to minimise harm to oneself should have no role in rectification decisions as it does not affect the balance of equities between the rival parties' claims to the land itself. On the other hand, such failure should be an important constituent of the care requirement in the indemnity context in order to protect the Fund from avoidable loss. The requirement to minimise loss to oneself is therefore unique to the indemnity context and has no counterpart in the care requirement existing as between owner and acquirer.

To illustrate the proposition that carelessly exacerbating loss to oneself should be an irrelevance in proceedings for rectification, take *Rees v National Trust*.[121] Rees built a lengthy fence over difficult terrain, presumably at substantial cost, on land claimed by him but of which the National Trust was mistakenly registered as proprietor. The fact that an ousted owner had undertaken such work when unaware of a rival claim might normally be a factor supporting an order for rectification in his favour. However, because Rees had been well aware that his claim to the land was contested, the works were held not to count positively in his favour when considering the application of the injustice proviso in rectification proceedings.[122] Equally, there was no basis to hold the expenditure against him. That reasoning is impeccable. Rees may have exacerbated his own loss by his expenditure on the fence, but that fact alone could not inflict any loss on the National Trust, assuming that the fence did not devalue the land.[123] It could not, therefore, constitute a breach of his care requirement towards the National Trust, and should not be treated as lack of care in the context of altering the Register. This decision appears to recognise that a disregard for one's own interests is pertinent to rectification proceedings in only one way—it negates the force which expenditure might otherwise have had in the balance of equities between the parties for the purpose of determining their respective claims to the land within alteration proceedings.

Another case, in contrast, appears to have taken a conflicting position. In *Saxon v Moore*,[124] the court held it to be a relevant factor supporting an order for rectification in the owner's favour that the acquirer had erected a fence and installed utilities in full knowledge of the dispute and in the teeth of objections.[125] This approach suggests that the acquirer was required not to magnify his own potential losses. However, that cannot

[121] *Rees v National Trust* [2007] EWLandRA 2005_1838.

[122] ibid [48]–[50] (Simon Brilliant).

[123] While one party's exacerbation of his own loss could not by itself affect the other, that is not to imply that his expenditure could have no bearing on their respective positions. If the acquirer had performed works that led to the land possessing significantly greater value to the acquirer than to the ousted owner, the court might be prepared to look upon such *ex post facto* considerations as exceptional circumstances justifying the refusal of rectification. But they would be unrelated to any care requirement.

[124] *Saxon* (n 52).

[125] ibid [92] (Judge Behrens).

be right in the context of rectification: the ousted owner has no interest in being protected from the acquirer's failure to mitigate the acquirer's own losses. Whether the ousted owner wins or loses the rectification proceedings, such losses have no bearing on him. Only the acquirer himself and the Indemnity Fund are concerned with those losses, so the extent of those losses should not have been raised in relation to the rectification issue. On that basis, it is argued that the reasoning in the case should not be followed.

In direct contrast, indemnity claims should certainly take account of any exacerbation of one's own loss. The concept of 'a duty to oneself' occasionally makes an appearance in the case law, but it does not make sense unless restated in terms of a requirement to minimise the burden on the Indemnity Fund. It is submitted that such a requirement underlies the comment in *Prestige Properties Ltd v Scottish Provident Institution*, that a lack of care for indemnity purposes would embrace a claimant's lack of proper care 'in respect both of the occurrence and quantum of loss'.[126]

It might be noted, however, that this is not universally accepted: there is an ambiguous comment in *Dean v Dean*[127] to the effect that a dereliction of duty to oneself is irrelevant to indemnity.[128] In *Dean*, a house was purchased by Dean and the registered title was vested in a Gibraltar company, Honeysuckle Ltd, which he owned and which was serviced by corporate directors and a corporate secretary. Dean's wife and others fraudulently caused the corporate secretary to deregister Honeysuckle Ltd from the Companies Register and then arranged for the registration of a new company with the same name, under the fraudsters' control, through which they fraudulently sold the house. It was seven years before Dean discovered that the original Honeysuckle Ltd had been removed from the Companies Register. When Dean sought an indemnity, the Land Registrar argued that it was a dereliction of duty to himself that Dean should have done nothing about Honeysuckle Ltd. The court, however, ultimately held that his inaction was not relevant to the availability of an indemnity.[129]

In the light of the arguments presented above and the decision in *Prestige*, it is impossible to support any general proposition that a dereliction of duty to oneself is irrelevant to the availability of indemnity. On the contrary, as a general rule, one does owe a duty to oneself in this context. The view expressed in *Dean* is acceptable only if it is read subject to some implied qualification reflecting a particular feature of the case. For instance, it could be construed in context to refer to a dereliction of duty specifically in respect of superintending the company's affairs. Recast in those terms, it would be a perfectly tenable proposition, affirming that owners have no responsibility to the Registry to undertake any pre-emptive monitoring of property holdings in the absence of suspicion, just as they have no such responsibility to potential acquirers to do so.

[126] *Prestige Properties Ltd v Scottish Provident Institution* [2002] EWHC 330 (Ch), [2003] Ch 1 [36] point (g) (Lightman J). Whether the claimant's losses had been magnified by its contractual arrangements was not raised properly on the pleadings. See also *Swift 1st Ltd v Chief Land Registrar* [2014] EWHC 4866 (Ch) [61]–[64] (Richard Sheldon QC).

[127] *Dean v Dean* (2000) 80 P & CR 457 (CA).

[128] ibid, 463 (Gibson LJ).

[129] ibid, 463 (Gibson LJ).

B. Relationship between Care in Rectification and Care in Indemnity

The arguments put forward above propose a distinction between the content of the care requirement as it is used in the rectification context and its content as it is used in the indemnity context. Although the same words in a statute are generally to be interpreted alike, the context justifies interpreting the phrase 'lack of proper care' as bearing different content according to the rule in which it is employed; it is an example of the maxim that in a single scenario the attribution of cause and blame may vary with the purpose of the inquiry.[130] Since rectification determines land title allocation between rival parties, whereas indemnity determines broader wealth allocation through state involvement, the two bodies of rules have quite different functions.

Differentiating the care requirements assists in determining the relevance of indemnity as a factor in rectification proceedings, a matter on which judicial views have spanned the entire spectrum.[131] It was argued earlier that a requirement not to magnify one's own loss should be relevant only in the setting of the relationship between a party and the Indemnity Fund, and irrelevant in determining rectification claims. If the court were to anticipate the outcome of the future indemnity claim and take that into account as a factor in rectification proceedings, then matters pertinent to indemnity would be brought into rectification. In particular, a party's failure to fulfil a care requirement towards the Indemnity Fund, such as a failure to mitigate, might obliquely influence the outcome of rectification proceedings. That result is undesirable: one party's care requirement towards the Indemnity Fund has no bearing on the other party, and consequently should have no significance in regulating the allocation of title between the owner and the acquirer.

In the light of that argument, one case is open to criticism. In *Nouri v Marvi*,[132] an ousted owner's loss of title had been caused in part by his own lack of proper care. In his rectification proceedings against the acquirer, the court regarded the anticipated indemnity position as a primary reason to decline rectification. The court anticipated that any indemnity for the ousted owner would be reduced due to his lack of care, but commented that it would be perverse to regard the reduction of indemnity as a reason for restoring the land to the ousted owner; on the contrary, it was perceived as a reason to refuse rectification and 'avoid relieving the [ousted owner] of the consequences of his own disregard for his own interests'.[133] Such reasoning is unsatisfactory. Rather than anticipating the determination of a future indemnity claim, the court should have placed reliance solely on the ousted owner's failure to take the necessary care to protect the interests of the acquirer. That approach would keep attention focused on the relations between the owner and acquirer, without

[130] *Environment Agency v Empress Car Co (Abertillery) Ltd* [1999] 2 AC 22 (HL) 29 (Lord Hoffmann).

[131] *Nouri* (n 110) [51] (Judge Rich QC); *Pinto v Lim* [2005] EWHC 630 (Ch) [99] and [102] (Blackburne J); *Malory Enterprises Ltd v Cheshire Homes (UK) Ltd* [2002] EWCA Civ 151, [2002] Ch 216 [15] (Arden LJ); *Kingsalton* (n 33) [27] (Peter Gibson LJ); *Fye* (n 28) [32] (Judge Owen Rhys); *Epps* (n 34) 1082–83 (Templeman J); *Ijacic v Game Developments Ltd* [2009] EWLandRA 2008_1081 and 1083 [71]–[76] (Simon Brilliant); *Paton* (n 33) [84] (Morgan J); *Wheeler v Patnaik* (n 39) [57] (Judge McAllister).

[132] *Nouri* (n 110) [51] (Judge Rich QC).

[133] ibid [51] (Judge Rich QC).

introducing the extraneous relationship with the Indemnity Fund and would preserve the value of rectification proceedings as a forum for a wide ranging, merit-based assessment of the parties' relative positions.

VII. Conclusion

A minimum requirement of care is inherent in every registration system, if only in respect of the owner's core responsibility to warn others by making a Register entry on pain of losing title or ceding priority. It has been submitted here that the English system goes very much further, as its rectification scheme, and thus indefeasibility generally, are structured around a web of implicit and sometimes explicit care requirements that take a central role in the event of an unauthorised change to the Register. In particular it was proposed that owners have distinctive responsibilities to acquirers; acquirers have distinctive responsibilities to owners; and both have responsibilities to the indemnity provider.

The analysis offered in this chapter, through its elaboration of the care requirement and the identification of the key relationship settings, is able to bring structure to a legislative system which must regulate conduct in circumstances of immense factual variety. It organises the field using the concept of relationships and reveals how the application of the care requirement differs between them. It exposes the care requirements that lie concealed within the injustice proviso and the exceptional circumstances test. It facilitates the determination of the factors which should influence the setting of the standards of care. It explains why the care requirement must show a significant divergence as between the rectification and indemnity provisions. The structured environment created by the care requirement analysis can also be put to use in appraising case law. It equipped this chapter with the tools to challenge existing jurisprudence, including the acquirer's supposed duty to desist from acquiring, the owner's supposed duty to resist acquisition by another, the supposed duties to mitigate owed by owners and acquirers to each other, the supposed irrelevance to indemnity of 'dereliction of duty to oneself', and the over-reliance on indemnity as a factor in rectification.

Further areas are ripe for examination using this structure. In particular, more is needed to unravel situations where interactions have involved lack of care by multiple parties. How do the care requirements of owner and acquirer interact when both have been careless towards each other? That requires a debate on the merits of compelling owners to take greater responsibility for safeguarding their own property as opposed to requiring greater rigour from acquirers in investigating the basis for their own application to become registered and in communicating to the Registry their knowledge of possible outstanding ownership claims. That complexity is exacerbated when the Registry itself fails to take care towards owners and acquirers. Where the Registry is at fault, the impact on what is expected from owners and acquirers is far from clear and leads to difficult questions of comparative fault and causative potency. If e-conveyancing and operational reforms bring a more passive role for the Registry, with a wholesale shifting of responsibility onto the parties and their conveyancers, then the existence and content of these and perhaps other care requirements can be expected to assume a very much heightened importance.

12

Reforming the Indemnity Scheme

NICHOLAS HOPKINS[1]

I. Introduction

In March 2016, the Law Commission published its Consultation Paper, *Updating the Land Registration Act 2002*. The Paper includes a wide-ranging examination of the indemnity provisions in the Act. It does not question the basic principle that land registration should be underpinned by an indemnity scheme through which the Land Registry incurs liability as an insurer of first resort.[2] The consultation does, however, raise significant questions about how the indemnity scheme that operates in relation to registered land in England and Wales might be reformed.

The purpose of this chapter is twofold. The first is to increase awareness, and encourage debate, of the distinct policy issues raised by the indemnity provisions of the Land Registration Act ('LRA') 2002. In the academic literature, indemnity appears to have become the 'ugly step-sister' to rectification's 'Cinderella'. Rectification has increasingly attracted attention[3] as the nature of the guarantee of title now contained in section 58 of the LRA 2002 has been scrutinised in a series of cases.[4] Indemnity, in contrast, has attracted relatively little comment.[5] Yet the operation of indemnity—even when paid as a consequence of a decision to rectify the Register—raises distinct policy questions. In this chapter, three policy questions are considered: first, the extent to which the indemnity scheme should seek to ensure that losses lie with a party who is at fault, in those cases where

[1] Law Commissioner, Law Commission for England and Wales. I am indebted to Samihah El-Gindy and Elizabeth Welch for their contributions to this chapter.

[2] Law Commission, *Updating the Land Registration Act 2002—A Consultation Paper* (Law Com CP No 227, 2016) para 14.11.

[3] See, eg, A Goymour, 'Mistaken Registrations of Land: Exploding the Myth of "Title by Registration"' [2013] *CLJ* 617; E Lees, 'Title by Registration: Rectification, Indemnity and Mistake and the Land Registration Act 2002' (2013) 76 *MLR* 62; S Cooper, 'Regulating Fallibility in Registered Land Titles' [2013] *CLJ* 341; A Goymour, 'Resolving the Tension Between the Land Registration Act 2002's 'Priority' and 'Alteration' Provisions' [2015] *Conv* 235.

[4] *Malory Enterprises Ltd v Cheshire Homes (UK) Ltd* [2002] EWCA Civ 151, [2002] Ch 216; *Barclays Bank plc v Guy* [2008] EWCA Civ 452, [2008] 2 EGLR 74; *Knights Construction (March) Ltd v Roberto Mac Ltd* [2011] EWLandRA 2009_1459, [2011] 2 EGLR 123; *Fitzwilliam v Richall Holding Services Ltd* [2013] EWHC 86 (Ch), [2013] 1 P & CR 19; *Parshall v Hackney* [2013] EWCA Civ 240, [2013] Ch 568; *Gold Harp Properties Ltd v MacLeod* [2014] EWCA Civ 1084, [2015] 1 WLR 1249; *Swift 1st Ltd v Chief Land Registrar* [2015] EWCA Civ 330, [2015] Ch 602.

[5] For an exception, see S Cooper, 'The Versatility of State Indemnity Provisions' in M Dixon (ed), *Modern Studies in Property Law, Volume 5* (Oxford, Hart Publishing, 2009) ch 2.

fault is present; secondly whether indemnity should operate as a universal scheme; and thirdly the relationship between the state indemnity scheme and private title insurance.

The second purpose of this chapter is to assess the options for reform identified by the Law Commission against the purposes of the indemnity scheme. The chapter argues that the options for reform highlighted by the Law Commission's 2016 Consultation Paper are consistent with the fundamental constitutional objective that underpins the indemnity scheme. The chapter does not, however, seek to speculate on what reforms (if any) the Law Commission may or should recommend in its final Report. Consistency with the purposes of the indemnity scheme gives legitimacy to the options under consideration, but it does not mean that any or all of them should be taken forward.

As a preliminary issue, this chapter first addresses the impact of the government's consultation on privatisation on the approach adopted to reform of indemnity by the Law Commission. The chapter then outlines the scope of the indemnity scheme and the purposes that it performs, and explains the reasons for the Law Commission's current review. It concludes by addressing the three key policy questions identified above.

II. The Indemnity Scheme and Privatisation

The Law Commission's 2016 Consultation Paper was written at a time of uncertainty as to whether the Land Registry would remain a state entity. The government had previously consulted on a proposal to develop a new service delivery company to have responsibility for processes relating to land registration. The government's conclusion was equivocal, with no decision taken to change the Land Registry's model, whilst noting that further consideration of the proposal would be valuable.[6] Subsequently, it was announced by the Chancellor in the 2015 Autumn Statement and 2016 Budget that a consultation would take place on options to move Land Registry operations into the private sector.[7] In the event, the government's consultation on the issue was published one week prior to the Law Commission's own Consultation Paper.[8] The government's consultation on privatisation offered some reassurance in respect of the continued operation of the indemnity scheme. The paper noted:[9]

> This [the State-backed guarantee of ownership] is something we believe is very important to the smooth functioning of the property market in England and Wales and reduces the cost of transactions. Under these proposals, the principle of no fault indemnity would continue unaffected.

Notwithstanding, attitudes towards any proposed changes to the indemnity scheme are likely to be coloured, at least to an extent, on whether Land Registry operations are being conducted by the state or by a private entity. The Law Commission's Consultation Paper was therefore confined to asking open questions about possible reform, rather than identifying a provisional policy. Confirmation of the government's plans came in the Chancellor's 2016

[6] Law Com CP No 227 (n 2) para 1.30.

[7] ibid, para 1.31.

[8] Department for Business, Innovation and Skills, *Consultation on Moving Land Registry Operations to the Private Sector* (March 2016).

[9] ibid, para 49.

Autumn Statement, in which it was announced that 'the government has decided that HM Land Registry should focus on becoming a more digital data-driven registration business, and to do this will remain in the public sector'.[10] The announcement enables policy to be formulated with certainty as to the environment in which the indemnity scheme will operate.

III. Land Registration's 'Insurance' Principle

A. The 'Insurance Principle' and the LRA 2002

Ruoff famously described the indemnity scheme as land registration's 'insurance principle'. In his terms:[11]

> The true (insurance) principle is this, that the mirror that is the register is deemed to give an absolutely correct reflection of title but if, through human frailty, a flaw appears, anyone who thereby suffers loss must be put in the same position, as far as money can do it, as if the reflection were a true one. A lost right is converted into hard cash.

Ruoff's insurance metaphor has stood the test of time, even if his reference to 'human frailty' does not reflect the full scope of the indemnity, insofar as it may indicate that to attract an indemnity, a flaw must be the result of fault. Any error in the Register ultimately lies in the act or omission of a person, whether through malice, negligence, or other fault or innocent accident. The Land Registry carries the risk in all circumstances as insurer of first resort, though as explored below, the LRA 2002 also reflects a principle that loss should ultimately lie with the party at fault, where fault is present.

The LRA 2002 provides eight grounds on which an applicant is entitled to an indemnity.[12] Where it is provided for, the indemnity is payable as a matter of entitlement. It is necessary only for the applicant to establish that his or her claim falls within one of the specified grounds. In some of the circumstances in which an indemnity is payable, it is inherent in the ground of the claim that there has been some 'fault' on the part of the Land Registry, though *proof* of negligence or other fault is not required. For example, an indemnity is paid to a person who suffers loss as a result of a mistake in an official search,[13] or as a result of the loss or destruction of a document lodged at the Registry for inspection or safe custody.[14] In one instance—failure by the Registrar to perform his duty to give notice of the creation of a statutory charge[15]—the indemnity is triggered by a breach of statutory duty by the Registrar.

[10] HM Treasury, *Autumn Statement 2016* (November 2016) para 1.66.

[11] TBF Ruoff, *An Englishman Looks at the Torrens System* (Sydney, Law Book Co of Australasia, 1957) 13.

[12] LRA 2002, sch 8, para 1, provides that a person is entitled to be indemnified if he or she 'suffers loss by reason of—(a) rectification of the register, (b) a mistake whose correction would involve rectification of the register, (c) a mistake in an official search, (d) a mistake in an official copy, (e) a mistake in a document kept by the registrar which is not an original and is referred to in the register, (f) the loss or destruction of a document lodged at the registry for inspection or safe custody, (g) a mistake in the cautions register, or (h) failure by the registrar to perform his duty under section 50'.

[13] LRA 2002, sch 8, para 1(1)(c).

[14] LRA 2002, sch 8, para 1(1)(f).

[15] LRA 2002, sch 8, para 1(1)(h). The Registrar's duty is contained in LRA 2002, s 50.

It should be apparent from this overview that, while the insurance principle has become a useful metaphor for provision of an indemnity, its availability may be explained as arising on one of two bases. In those instances where the applicant's entitlement is triggered by fault on the part of the Land Registry, the indemnity can be seen as compensation for a wrong. Such payments can therefore be rationalised without reference to the insurance principle. The insurance metaphor more accurately describes those situations in which an indemnity is payable despite the absence of any fault on the part of the Land Registry. Only through the Land Registry providing an indemnity in all cases—irrespective of fault—can indemnity achieve its constitutional function.[16]

The discussion of indemnity in the Law Commission's 2016 Consultation Paper is confined to two of the eight grounds on which an indemnity is payable: where the entitlement arises as a result of loss suffered by reason of 'rectification of the register'[17] or because of 'a mistake whose correction would involve rectification of the register'.[18] In the language of the LRA 2002, 'rectification' refers specifically to an alteration of the Register to correct a mistake in a manner that prejudicially affects the title of the registered proprietor.[19] These are the two grounds on which a claim to indemnity will arise—amongst other circumstances—following a fraudulent—and void—'transfer' of land, leading to a mistaken registration. For example, if A's registered title is, by fraud, transferred to B (both A and B being innocent parties to the fraud), then, once the fraud comes to light, one of the parties will be left with the land and the other will have (in Ruoff's words) his or her 'lost right [...] converted into hard cash' through an indemnity. If the Register is rectified to restore title to A, then B's entitlement to an indemnity is triggered by the rectification of the Register. If title is left with B, then A's entitlement to an indemnity arises through a mistake in the Register (the registration of B) 'whose correction would involve rectification'. The Land Registry's liability to indemnify in both of these instances is aptly described by the operation of the insurance principle: the mistake on the Register arises as the result of the fraud, not through any fault on the part of the Land Registry. In such cases, the Land Registry's liability to pay arises because the risks of a transaction have passed from the parties to the Land Registry.

The risk of a transaction passes to the Land Registry at the point at which the Land Registry registers a transaction. Therefore, there is a period of time between completion of the disposition as between the parties, and registration (the 'registration gap') when the risks remain with the transferee. The existence of the registration gap means that there is an element of chance as to whether the Land Registry or the transferee will bear losses arising through fraud. Where the loss falls on the transferee, in some (but not all) cases the transferee may have a cause of action against his or her conveyancer.

B. The Passing of Risk and the Registration Process

While the risk of a transaction passes by registration, there is no necessary connection between the fraud being discovered and the registration process. In the example of fraud

[16] See text to n 33 below.

[17] LRA 2002, sch 8, para 1(1)(a).

[18] LRA 2002, sch 8, para 1(1)(b).

[19] LRA 2002, sch 8, para 11(2). The definition of 'rectification' is also given in connection with rectification, rather than indemnity, in sch 4, para 1.

outlined immediately above, if the fraud was discovered by A and notified to the Land Registry before B's registration, then B suffers the loss. Once notified of the fraud, the Land Registry will not proceed with registration. If the fraud comes to light only after registration, then B is entitled to an indemnity. In both cases B is equally innocent of the fraud. Whether the fraud comes to light before or after acceptance of the transfer for registration by the Land Registry may be for reasons entirely unrelated to the registration process: for example, the fraud may have been perpetuated during a period of A's absence from the property and come to light on A's return.

The element of chance as to whether the Land Registry or the transferee bears the loss is not, however, arbitrary. In some instances, the fraud may be discovered through the registration process. In *Purrunsing v A'Court*,[20] a fraudster impersonating the registered proprietor purported to sell a house which he said he had received as a gift from his father. In the context of identity checks undertaken by the solicitor instructed by him, the fraudster produced (amongst other evidence) utility bills addressed to his current home, which did not appear on the Register as the address for the registered proprietor. The fraud was uncovered when the Land Registry contacted the true registered proprietor at an address recorded on the Register. The discovery of the fraud prior to registration meant that the risk remained with the purchaser.

C. Remaining Vulnerability of the Parties

Unless and until the risks of a transaction pass to the Land Registry, they remain with the transferee, who is vulnerable to the loss. Given appropriate facts, purchasers may sometimes be able to look to their conveyancers, with claims arising for negligence, breach of warranty of authority, or breach of trust. However, as these principles are based on the common law, the scope of liability under each of them changes—and may continue to change—over time, as courts respond to the facts of individual cases. As a result, the cases do not provide certainty for purchasers or conveyancers as to the parameters of conveyancers' potential liability. Further, each of the principles has developed separately from the others. Therefore, reliance on the principles does not permit an holistic assessment, as a matter of policy, of the circumstances in which it is appropriate for conveyancers to be held liable for the purchaser's loss. In *Purrunsing*, the purchaser was able to recover the amount of the purchase moneys paid from both his own and the fraudster's solicitors on the basis that the money had been paid to the fraudster in breach of trust. The court declined to give the solicitors relief from liability for breach of trust under section 61 of the Trustee Act 1925. Subsequently, in *P&P Property Ltd v Owen White & Catlin LLP*,[21] *Purrunsing* was distinguished. Judge Robin Dicker QC held that, as a result of the changes to the Law Society's Code for Completion by Post, the vendor's solicitors did not hold the purchase money on trust for the buyer's solicitor,[22] and were not otherwise liable for breach of trust where a genuine completion does not take place.[23] The judge noted that the facts of the

[20] *Purrunsing v A'Court & Co* [2016] EWHC 789 (Ch), [2016] 4 WLR 81.

[21] *P&P Property Ltd v Owen White & Catlin LLP* [2016] EWHC 2276 (Ch), [2017] PNLR 3.

[22] ibid [218].

[23] ibid [219]–[221].

case were broadly analogous to those in *Purrunsing*[24] and, as in that case, he would not have awarded relief under section 61 of the Trustee Act 1925, if a breach of trust had been established.[25] However, in the absence of a trust, or any other basis of liability, the loss remained with the purchaser.

The potential for liability for breach of warranty of authority became a cause for concern for solicitors following the decision in *Penn v Bristol and West Building Society*.[26] There, Mr Penn and his business partner had perpetrated a mortgage fraud by arranging for the transfer of a house jointly owned by Mr Penn and his wife to a purchaser (also party to the fraud), who raised money for the purchase through a mortgage. A solicitor who acted in the transaction mistakenly believed that he had been instructed by Mr and Mrs Penn and held himself out as such to the mortgage lender. In fact, however, Mrs Penn knew nothing of the transaction. When the fraud came to light, Mrs Penn was successful in having the mortgage set aside and the solicitor was held liable to the mortgagee for breach of warranty of authority. In particular, as liability for breach of warranty of authority is strict, the Law Society was concerned that the Land Registry would use its rights of recourse[27] to recover indemnity payments from solicitors who had acted innocently in transactions that transpired to be fraudulent. This concern led to assurances in Parliament during the passage of the Land Registration Act 1997[28] that it was neither 'the practice nor the intention of HM Land Registry to resort to its rights of recourse against those who are neither fraudulent nor negligent'.[29] In any event, the risks for conveyancers of such liability arising is further reduced in respect of identity fraud by *P&P Property Ltd*. There, the judge held that the solicitors had warranted only that they had authority to act for Mr Harper, the purported vendor, not that Mr Harper was the true owner of the property.[30]

IV. The Purposes of the Indemnity Scheme

The origins of the indemnity scheme contained in the LRA 2002 can be traced to the Land Transfer Act 1897 and coincided with the introduction of compulsory registration of title. Once registration became compulsory, dealings with land ceased to be the provenance of wholly 'private' transactions: the intervention of the state through the Land Registry became necessary to confer title. Writing in the 1930s, Stewart-Wallace placed the provision of an indemnity on a constitutional footing. He suggested that registration of title is an exercise by the state of sovereign authority and any exercise of sovereign power exposes subjects to danger.[31] Therefore, in his view, there must be provisions to safeguard landowners from the risk of the executive 'unjustly, illegally, mistakenly or tyrannically depriving them of

[24] ibid [222].
[25] ibid [248]–[279].
[26] *Penn v Bristol and West Building Society* [1997] 1 WLR 1356.
[27] See text to n 56 below.
[28] See text to n 44 below.
[29] Hansard (HL), 18 November 1996, vol 575, col 1166.
[30] *P&P Property Ltd* (n 21) [114]–[116]. Contrast, *LSC Finance Ltd v Abensons Law Ltd (t/a Abensons Solicitors)* [2015] EWHC 1163 (Ch).
[31] JS Stewart-Wallace, *Introduction to the Principles of Land Registration* (London, Stevens & Sons, 1937) 44.

their land by declaring itself or some other persons to have an absolute title to their land'.[32] Stewart-Wallace's work therefore reveals that the provision of an indemnity performs an important constitutional function in providing (financial) protection to individuals who are subject to an obligation, imposed by the state, to register title. Ruoff similarly linked his 'insurance principle'[33] to the fact that the state, rather than the parties, confers title, and the conclusive nature of registration means that the state can confer a better title than the transferor possessed. This link between the constitutional function of indemnity and the insurance principle is reinforced by the fact that the risk of a disposition passes to the Land Registry at the point that an application is accepted for registration: that is the point in time at which the transaction crosses from the private sphere of the parties' transaction to the public sphere of state involvement in conferring title. The involvement of the state in conferring title merits the parties being able to look to the state—and not merely to each other—when things go wrong. In turn, the constitutional function highlights the need for an indemnity to be payable even where the Land Registry, as an emanation of the state, is not at fault. The risk of loss to which landowners are exposed through the exercise of sovereign power is not dependent on any party being at fault.

At its highest, therefore, a title registration system's indemnity provisions perform, as Stewart-Wallace suggested,[34] a constitutional function. That function links directly with the need for parties to be able to rely on the Register when dealing with land. As the Register is conclusive,[35] the Register—rather than any underlying deeds—is the primary source of information on title. The need to rely on the Register is inherently connected with the underlying aim of registration of title. That aim, as explained by the 1857 Royal Commission, is to enable people 'to deal with land in as simple and easy a manner [...] as they can now deal with movable chattels or stock'.[36] In modern times, this same sentiment is reflected in the desire for easier, quicker and cheaper conveyancing.

Reform of indemnity in a manner that impinges on its constitutional function may undermine land registration, as it would prevent parties from being able to rely on the Register. That does not mean, however, that the constitutional function is the sole purpose of the indemnity, or that it should be used to define the scope of the indemnity scheme. The provision of an indemnity may also serve other purposes. Stewart-Wallace noted that provision of an indemnity enabled the Land Registry to take risks in individual cases and reduce the costs of investigation of title, building an indemnity fund for those instances where only impractically costly and stringent investigation of title might have revealed a flaw.[37] More broadly, Simon Cooper has highlighted the ability of the indemnity scheme to control the behaviour of those involved in the land transfer process.[38]

In its 2016 Consultation Paper, the Law Commission identifies three additional purposes served by the indemnity scheme contained in the LRA 2002. First, provision of indemnity is an integral aspect of security of a registered title. Parties can deal with the registered

[32] ibid.
[33] S Rowton Simpson, *Land Law and Registration* (Cambridge, CUP, 1976) 179.
[34] Stewart-Wallace, *Introduction to the Principles of Land Registration* (n 31) 44.
[35] LRA 2002, s 58.
[36] *Report of the Commissioners to Consider the Subject of Registration of Title with Reference to the Sale and Transfer of Land* (London, Eyre & Spottiswoode, 1857) 23.
[37] Stewart-Wallace, *Introduction to the Principles of Land Registration* (n 31) 44.
[38] S Cooper, 'The Versatility of State Indemnity Provisions' (n 5) 35.

proprietor in the knowledge that his or her title is backed-up by a state guarantee. This assurance, in turn, provides confidence in the property market.[39] As Simon Cooper has explained, even in the context of an established registration scheme, there is a risk of loss of confidence in the system if provision for indemnity was removed.[40] In this respect, provision of an indemnity may be particularly important in sustaining confidence in the system when significant changes are made—such as a move from paper to electronic conveyancing.[41] Secondly, the availability of an indemnity makes a registered title qualitatively superior to an unregistered title. That may in turn operate as an incentive for voluntary registration.[42] Thirdly, the indemnity provides for economic efficiency in conveyancing. Provision of title insurance through the indemnity is likely to be cheaper than a system in which those involved in land transactions protect themselves through private title insurance.[43]

V. Why Review the Indemnity Scheme?

The substance of the indemnity scheme contained in the LRA 2002 has not been changed since the Land Registration Act 1997; indeed, the origins of the reforms implemented at that time pre-date that Act by a decade. The Land Registration Act 1997 implemented recommendations made in the first report of a joint working group of the Law Commission, the Land Registry and the Lord Chancellor's Department.[44] Those recommendations, in turn, were drawn from the Law Commission's Third Report on Land Registration,[45] published in 1987, and a draft Bill contained in the Law Commission's Fourth Report[46] in the following year. The Consultation Paper that preceded the LRA 2002 was published in 1998.[47] Its proximity to the 1997 Act meant that the issue of indemnity was not reviewed.[48] The provisions on indemnity were 'completely recast' in accordance with the style of the LRA 2002,[49] but the substance of the provisions remained substantially unchanged. Hence the current scheme, though contained in the LRA 2002, is based on recommendations from 1987. And yet the landscape in which the indemnity scheme applies, particularly in respect of the incidence of fraud, has changed significantly since 1987.

In its Third Report, the Law Commission noted a 'development' in the indemnity scheme, whereby payments were now being made 'for matters which no traditional title

[39] Law Com CP No 227 (n 2) para 14.27.
[40] S Cooper, 'The Versatility of State Indemnity Provisions' (n 5) 37.
[41] AJ Bradbrook, SV MacCallum, AP Moore and S Grattan, *Australian Real Property Law*, 5th edn (Pyrmont, Thomson Reuters, 2011) s 4.430.
[42] Law Com CP No 227 (n 2) para 14.25.
[43] ibid, para 14.29.
[44] Law Commission, *Transfer of Land: Land Registration—First Joint Report of a Joint Working Group with HM Land Registry* (Law Com No 235, 1995).
[45] Law Commission, *Property Law: Third Report on Land Registration* (Law Com No 158, 1987).
[46] Law Commission, *Property Law: Fourth Report on Land Registration* (Law Com No 173, 1988).
[47] Law Commission, *Land Registration for the Twenty-First Century—A Consultative Document* (Law Commission CP No 254, 1998).
[48] ibid, para 2.42.
[49] Law Commission, *Land Registration for the Twenty-First Century—A Conveyancing Revolution* (Law Com 271, 2001) para 10.29.

investigation would have revealed, for example, a forged charge'.[50] What was a 'development' in 1987 has since become a focus of debate in respect of the indemnity scheme. In the 10 years immediately preceding publication of the Law Commission's 2016 Consultation Paper, fraud accounted for approximately 60% of the total paid out as an indemnity by the Land Registry, amounting to total payments of approximately £57.6m.[51]

These sums may appear relatively modest. Nevertheless, the incidence of registered title fraud revealed by them cannot be dismissed. The Land Registry itself funds indemnity payments through fees, and reports an annual surplus;[52] as such, the financial impact of fraud is effectively borne by the Land Registry's customers, who bear the cost of the indemnity, no matter how careful they have been in their own transactions. Furthermore, the rise in property values, even since 2002, means that the financial consequences of fraud are significantly greater now than they were at the time the LRA 2002 was enacted, let alone than they were in 1987, when the principles on which the scope of the scheme is based were devised.[53] There is also a risk of catastrophic loss, the costs of which would ultimately need to be covered through tax revenue if they could not be met by the Land Registry's resources.

As registered title fraud has increased, and no doubt become more sophisticated to adapt to online communication and vulnerabilities, it has also become apparent that the Land Registry is not necessarily best placed to detect and prevent fraudulent dispositions. For example, in respect of identity fraud, the Land Registry is dependent, to an extent, on checks undertaken by the parties' conveyancers. The fact that the risk lies with the Land Registry may mean that those who are dealing directly with the parties to a disposition and who may therefore be best placed to identify fraud, do not have an incentive to develop best practice. Existing rights of recourse[54] may enable indemnity payments to be recovered from the small minority of conveyancers whose conduct falls below the standard of a reasonable professional. However, the limited recovery made through rights of recourse in practice may be indicative of gaps in the scope of those rights.[55]

The absence of a review of indemnity in 2002, the increase in registered title fraud, and the change in the level of risk, might each justify a review of the indemnity scheme. Their collective effect makes the case for review compelling. The scheme of indemnity contained in the LRA 2002 was not devised to take into account modern incidents of registered title fraud, or the level of the financial risk involved in underwriting dispositions of land.

[50] Law Com No 158 (n 45) para 3.25.

[51] Collated from Table 1 in Law Com CP No 227 (n 2) para 14.34. Table 1 was compiled from the Land Registry's annual reports and accounts. Note that figures were rounded, which may result in variations from percentages recorded in the Land Registry's annual reports and accounts.

[52] See, most recently, HM Land Registry, *Annual Report and Accounts 2016/17* (July 2015) 37.

[53] By way of illustration, in 1987 the average UK house price (including Scotland) was £43,164.50; in 2015 the average UK house price had risen to £193.900.25 (including Scotland). The Office of National Statistics did not collect average house prices in 1987 and so figures have been collected from data supplied by the Nationwide Building Society. The Nationwide figures are used to supply the average 2015 house price in order to ensure a fair comparison. See Nationwide Building Society, *Regional Quarterly Indices (Post' 73)* (http://www.nationwide.co.uk/about/house-price-index/download-data#xtab:regional-quarterly-series-all-properties-data-available-from-1973-onwards).

[54] See text to n 56 below.

[55] In the ten years preceding the publication of the Law Commission's 2016 Consultation Paper, the proportion of indemnity payments made that were recovered ranged from 1% to 20%: see Law Com CP No 227 (n 2) para 14.51.

VI. Key Policy Questions for Law Reformers

Having set out the scope and purposes of the indemnity scheme and the reasons for conducting the current review, the remainder of this chapter discusses three key policy questions that underpin the options for reform being considered by the Law Commission.

A. Making Loss Lie with Fault?

i. The Current Position

The rights of recourse contained in the LRA 2002, schedule 8, paragraph 10, reflect a principle that, while the Land Registry acts as an insurer of first resort, loss should ultimately lie with the party at fault. These rights of recourse enable the Registrar to recoup indemnity payments, by allowing recovery of the amount paid from any person who has caused or substantially contributed to the loss by their fraud. The Registrar can also enforce any right of action that a claimant would have been entitled to enforce had the indemnity not been paid, or that a person in whose favour the Register has been rectified could have enforced if the Register had not been rectified.[56] The statutory rights of recourse are not intended to be exhaustive; paragraph 10(1) notes that the rights are 'without prejudice to any other rights [the Registrar] might have'.

In addition to not being exhaustive, the need for the recipient of the indemnity to have (or to have had, but for the indemnity) a cause of action, means that the rights of recourse are not comprehensive. For example, they do not enable recovery from a party who contributed to the loss through negligence if that party did not owe a duty of care to the recipient of the indemnity. In *Chief Land Registrar v Caffrey & Co*,[57] it was held that a solicitor who had forwarded a forged deed of discharge to the Land Registry, which resulted in a mortgage being wrongfully removed from the Register and the Land Registry indemnifying the bank, did not owe a duty of care to the bank to ensure that the discharge was not fraudulent. In turn, this meant the Registrar had no right of recourse against the solicitor. Although the Land Registry did have a right of recourse against the *fraudster*, in most cases it is unlikely to be of any practical value as the fraudster may not be discoverable or have sufficient assets to repay the sum procured.

However, in *Caffrey*, Master Matthews went on to hold that, as a matter of common law, the solicitors owed a duty of care to the Registrar in respect of the forged discharge provided to them by their clients. The decision in *Caffrey* sits logically within wider tort law principles. It has been held that a solicitor might owe a duty of care to a party other than his or her client if: (i) the solicitor and the third party have a sufficiently close and direct relationship, marked by the knowledge and intention that information given will be relied upon, (ii) the damage resulting from the misinformation is reasonably foreseeable, and (iii) it would be 'fair, just and reasonable' for a duty of care to be imposed.[58] A conveyancer knows and intends the

[56] HM Land Registry, *Land Registry Practice Guide 39: Rectification and Indemnity* (September 2016), para 10.

[57] *Chief Land Registrar v Caffrey & Co* [2016] EWHC 161 (Ch).

[58] *Gran Gelato Ltd v Richcliff (Group) Ltd* [1992] Ch 560, 569, citing *Caparo Industries Plc v Dickman* [1990] 2 AC 605.

Land Registry to rely on the applications he or she submits—for example, by acting to remove a charge from the Register. It is reasonably foreseeable that the Land Registry will suffer loss through payment of an indemnity if the discharge transpires to be a fraud.[59]

While a duty of care has therefore been found to exist at common law in certain circumstances, doubts remain as to its scope and utility in enabling the Land Registry to recover its losses. The losses suffered by the Land Registry in respect of indemnity payments are pure economic losses, which are not generally recoverable as a matter of tort law[60] except in cases of negligent misstatement.[61] Although the Land Registry was successful in *Caffrey*—which involved a negligent misrepresentation—the case is not a strong authority. The finding that the solicitor owed a duty of care to the Land Registry was qualified by the judge stating that he was only 'narrowly persuaded ... on the peculiar facts of [the] case'.[62] The solicitor did not appear before the court and the allegation that a negligent misrepresentation had been made to the Registrar was not defended. Further, there are other situations in which there may have been no misrepresentation by the conveyancing firm who, for example, failed to carry out checks to determine whether the fraudster was in fact a solicitor acting for the bank.

There is no doubt, as explained above, that in order for indemnity to perform its constitutional function, an applicant should be entitled to an indemnity regardless of whether a party involved in the transaction is at fault. Notwithstanding, it is legitimate within that constitutional function for provision to be made to enable recovery by the Land Registry from a party who is legally at fault, including a party who has acted negligently. The constitutional function reflects the fact that the transfer of title does not lie wholly in the private sphere, but requires state intervention. But that does not abrogate individual responsibility for the parts of the transaction that remain in the 'private' (law) sphere. In its 2016 Consultation Paper, the Law Commission therefore asks whether the existing common law duty of care could be made more effective, or should be supplemented by the introduction of a statutory duty of care.

ii. Could the Utility of the Common Law Duty of Care be Improved?

As previously explained, one of the difficulties of the common law duty of care is that it would generally enable the Land Registry to recover its economic losses only in situations where the breach of duty involves the making of a misstatement. Though this may cover many situations, it does not cover them all.

The Land Registry's forms are drafted such that they ensure in particular instances that certain statements are made. For example, on a sale of land, both the deed of transfer (Form TR1) and an application to change the Register (Form AP1) will be sent to the Land Registry. If one of the parties to the sale is not represented, then the conveyancer is required to verify that party's identity. Form AP1 requires the conveyancer to sign the following statement:

[59] Although the *Gran Gelato* case involved solicitors, Master Matthews commented in *Caffrey* that 'if solicitors owe a duty of care in what they tell the registry, so does anyone doing what they did'. As such, there is no reason to believe that a conveyancer who is not a solicitor would be considered any differently.

[60] See for example, *Spartan Steel & Alloys Ltd v Martin & Co (Contractors) Ltd* [1973] QB 27.

[61] *Hedley Byrne & Co Ltd v Heller & Partners Ltd* [1964] AC 465 and, notably, *Caffrey* (n 57) which involved negligent misrepresentation.

[62] *Caffrey* (n 57) [59].

'I confirm that I am satisfied that sufficient steps have been taken to verify the identity of [name] and that they are the registered proprietor or have the right to be registered as registered proprietor'.[63] This declaration has the effect of requiring a conveyancer to make a statement to the Land Registry that sufficient (reasonable) steps have been taken. If this is not in fact the case, then the conveyancer may be liable for making a negligent misstatement.

The efficacy of a common law duty of care could therefore be improved by amending the Land Registry's forms to require conveyancers to make further declarations—for example, that they have taken sufficient steps to satisfy themselves that documents relating to the application are genuine. The change would *not* necessarily mean that a conveyancer would be liable if it later transpired that a document had been forged or fraudulently presented to the conveyancer or the Land Registry. However, the change would ensure that where a conveyancer had not taken *reasonable* steps to ensure the validity of a document, then he or she could be liable to the Land Registry for negligent misstatement.

iii. Should a General Statutory Duty of Care be Imposed?

In Scotland, recommendations of the Scottish Law Commission have led to the introduction of a statutory duty of care.[64] This statutory duty lives alongside existing rights of recourse, which it is intended to supplement and not replace. It also operates as a supplement to any wider duty of care that that may exist under the common law.

Under section 111 of the Land Registration etc (Scotland) Act 2012 a duty is imposed on certain categories of persons to 'take reasonable care to ensure that the Keeper does not inadvertently make the register inaccurate'.[65] The duty is imposed on a person who is granting a deed intended to be registered or making an application for registration, and on his or her solicitor or legal advisor. The duty of care continues up until the point of application, but not beyond that time. This means that a conveyancer will not be held liable in respect of any facts that come to light after an application for registration has been made, even if registration itself has not yet taken place.[66] The extension of the duty of care to this period may have the unintentional but desirable effect of encouraging solicitors to expedite their post-completion paperwork.

In its 2010 report which lay behind the 2012 Act, the Scottish Law Commission emphasised that the duty is to take *reasonable* care. As such, it is clear that the imposition of the duty is not intended to raise the standard above what is already required of conveyancers, and that what is reasonable may change over time. Notably, section 111 does not require conveyancers to adopt 'best practice'.[67] The Scottish Law Commission also suggested that it would be unusual for lay persons or those not acting in a professional capacity when dealing with the Registers of Scotland to be found to be in breach of the statutory duty in the absence of actual dishonesty.[68]

The statutory duty of care in the 2012 Act plays two roles. First, it provides the Keeper with a direct right of action against a person who acts in breach of the statutory duty to

[63] Form AP1, Panel 13(2).

[64] Scottish Law Commission, *Report on Land Registration* (Scots Law Com No 222, 2010) paras 12.101–12.109; Land Registration etc (Scotland) Act 2012, s 111.

[65] Land Registration etc (Scotland) Act 2012, s 111(1), (3).

[66] Scots Law Com No 222 (n 64) para 12.105.

[67] ibid, para 12.103.

[68] ibid.

recover compensation 'for any loss suffered as a result of that breach', subject to remoteness and mitigation rules.[69] Secondly, the duty operates as a limitation on the availability of indemnity. No indemnity is payable to a claimant for inaccuracies in the Register attributable to a breach of duty by the claimant or his or her conveyancer.[70] Hence, if an individual suffers loss as a result of his or her conveyancer acting in breach of duty towards the Keeper, that person cannot recover those losses as an indemnity from the Keeper. The individual would need to rely on a cause of action against the conveyancer.

In the context of England and Wales, any new statutory duty of care could be introduced in the form of a new statutory tort. The tort would apply to persons executing a deed intended to be registered or making an application for registration; the primary intention being to impose the duty on conveyancers who are preparing these documents on behalf of their clients. Individuals would only be subject to the duty when acting otherwise than through a conveyancer and, as is the case in Scotland, it is unlikely any such individual would be found in breach of the statutory duty in the absence of actual dishonesty on his or her part. It would also be possible to go further than Scotland and exclude individuals from the scope of the new tort entirely.

A statutory tort could supplement rather than replace existing causes of action, both statutory and common law. The duty of care required under the statutory tort may, in some respects, be narrower than the common law duty of care; for example, it would apply only to those persons and to the transactions identified in the statute. However, in the circumstances in which it operates the statutory tort may go further than the common law, such as by enabling the Land Registry to recover for pure economic loss in situations in which recovery for such loss may not be possible under the general law. Under the LRA 2002, the quantum of an indemnity can already be reduced to take into account a lack of care on the part of the claimant.[71] It would be consistent with this general provision for any statutory tort to operate, as it does in Scotland, as a limit on the availability of indemnity. That would mean that an individual whose conveyancer acts in breach of the statutory duty is not entitled to an indemnity, but must seek to recover his or her losses directly from the conveyancer. An alternative approach, which is not specifically addressed in the Law Commission's 2016 Consultation Paper, would be to continue to enable individuals to claim an indemnity from the Land Registry, leaving the Land Registry to recover from the conveyancer for his or her breach of duty.

iv. Should There be a Specific Statutory Duty of Care in Respect of Identity?

Fraud is now the most significant context in which claims to an indemnity arise, and identity fraud is the most significant type of registered title fraud. In its Annual Report and Accounts 2014/15, the Land Registry noted that '[f]raud (usually by way of forgery) remains the single most significant cause of indemnity payments and this reflects the general trend over the past decade or so'.[72] The Law Commission's 2016 Consultation Paper therefore raises the possibility of imposing a statutory duty confined to verifying identity, as an alternative to a general statutory duty of care.

[69] Land Registration etc (Scotland) Act 2012, s 111(5), (6).
[70] ibid, s 78(c).
[71] LRA 2002, sch 8, para 5(1)(b).
[72] HM Land Registry, *Annual Report and Accounts 2014/15* (July 2015) 45.

The arguments as to whether any statutory tort that is introduced should be general, or should be confined to identity, are finely balanced. On the one hand, a duty in respect of identity is more focused on the specific problems arising in relation to the current law and may serve to focus attention on the practical importance of verifying identity. However, a statutory tort confined to identity may be seen as signalling that a duty of care is not owed in other respects where, in fact, a wider duty may still be owed under the common law.

A statutory tort in respect of identity checks could operate in the same way as the general statutory tort outlined above—namely, as a supplement to, and not a replacement for, existing statutory rights of recourse. Breach of the duty of care could give the Land Registry a cause of action against the party in breach, to recover an indemnity payment made but also operate as a limit on the availability of an indemnity. On that assumption, if an individual suffered loss as the result of a breach of the duty by his or her conveyancer, he or she would not be entitled to an indemnity and would need to bring a direct action against the conveyancer instead. Alternatively, the individual's ability to recover an indemnity from the Land Registry could be retained, leaving the Land Registry to recover from the conveyancer in breach.

Again, the threshold for liability would be based on taking reasonable steps to verify identity. In this respect, this option for reform should be considered alongside the discussion in the Law Commission's 2016 Consultation Paper of whether current identity requirements could usefully be rationalised, and whether the Land Registry's powers should be enhanced to enable it to formulate its own mandatory requirements in respect of identity verification.[73] A statutory duty of care, combined with guidance as to what is required to ensure that reasonable steps have been taken, could both help to reduce the incidence of registered title fraud and provide greater certainty to conveyancers as to what is expected of them.

v. *Duties of Care and Mortgagees*

A general statutory duty of care which applied to those executing a deed intended to be registered or making an application for registration, could in theory apply to mortgagees in respect of deeds executed and applications made to the Land Registry directly by mortgagees. However, in practice such a duty would have limited effect on mortgagees, since they would not usually execute deeds or make applications to the Land Registry directly; usually, conveyancers would make the relevant application. On that assumption, such a duty will not incentivise mortgagees to develop best practices in connection with the verification of the mortgagor's identity, even though mortgagees may be best placed to carry out such an exercise.

In the light of this, the Law Commission's 2016 Consultation Paper asks whether a specific statutory duty of care should be placed on mortgagees to take reasonable steps to verify the identity of mortgagors.[74] What would constitute 'reasonable steps' would either need to be established by a regulator, such as the Financial Conduct Authority, or—if the Land Registry's powers in respect of identity checks were enhanced as the Law Commission's 2016 Consultation Paper suggests[75]—by the Land Registry itself. If a mortgagee breached

[73] These options are explored further in Law Com CP No 227 (n 2) paras 14.87–14.101.

[74] ibid, para 14.123.

[75] ibid, paras 14.92–14.101.

this duty, and the registration of a charge was found to be a mistake, the Register would be rectified against the mortgagee without payment of an indemnity.

The majority of lenders already act reasonably. Nevertheless, imposing a specific duty of care on mortgagees to take reasonable steps to identity mortgagors' identities could be beneficial for two reasons. First, it would incentivise best practice in the prevention of fraudulent dispositions of land. Secondly, it would help to ensure that, in the minority of cases in which mortgagees' conduct does fall below a reasonable level, the financial consequences are borne by the party or parties whose failure to conduct business to a reasonable standard of care has caused the loss. As the next section explains, the imposition of a duty of care on mortgagees in relation to identity is a development that has already taken place across a number of other jurisdictions.

vi. Duties of Care and Mortgagees—A Comparative Perspective

Several Australian jurisdictions have imposed statutory duties on mortgagees to take reasonable steps (which may be prescribed in regulation) to confirm the identities of mortgagors, to ensure that they in fact are, or will become, the registered proprietor. If mortgagees fail to comply with this duty to take reasonable steps, then they are statute barred from claiming compensation.[76] Writing about Queensland's legislation, which was the first statute to impose a duty on mortgagees to take reasonable steps to check the identity of mortgagors, Pamela O'Connor explained, '[t]hese amendments provide the incentives for fraud avoidance that were lacking under the unconditional version of immediate indefeasibility'.[77]

The approach that has been applied in Australia reflects a view that lenders are best placed to prevent identity fraud. Victoria provides a recent example: in 2014, the Victorian government amended the Transfer of Land Act 1958 to impose a statutory duty on mortgagees to take reasonable steps to verify the authority and identity of a mortgagor at the time of the execution of the mortgage. Their respective statutory duties are laid out in section 87A, and they involve taking reasonable steps to ensure that the mortgagor is or will become the registered proprietor of the land, as determined in accordance with the requirements set by the Registrar or set out in the participation rules governing electronic conveyancing. Further, section 110(4)(c) limits indemnity in respect of fraud to mortgagees who suffered loss due to fraud despite their having complied with their statutory duties; mortgagees who do not comply with the statutory duties are liable to having their mortgage refused registration or removed from the Register, denying them indefeasibility and making the mortgage void.

Based on concerns about mortgage fraud, in 2010 the New Zealand Law Commission recommended amendments to the Land Transfer Act 1952. The New Zealand Law Commission explained:[78]

> We are therefore of the view that it is prudent to impose a legislative requirement on mortgagees to take reasonable steps to check that they are dealing with the actual registered proprietor and not

[76] See, eg, Real Property Act 1900 (New South Wales), ss 56C and 129(2)(j) (the bar on recovery is confined to losses arising as a result of their failure); Land Title Act 1994 (Queensland), ss 11A, 11B, 185(1A) and 189(1)(ab). See also Bradbrook et al, *Australian Real Property Law* (n 41) ss 4.225 and 4.470.

[77] P O'Connor, 'Deferred and Immediate Indefeasibility: Bijural Ambiguity in Registered Land Title Systems' (2009) 13 *Edinburgh Law Review* 194, 207.

[78] New Zealand Law Commission (in conjunction with Land Information New Zealand), *A New Land Transfer Act* (Report 116, 2010) para 2.20.

> with a fraudster. This may go some way towards preventing mortgage fraud becoming widespread. Mortgagees are also usually the 'cheaper cost avoider' and are usually in a better position to prevent fraud than is a registered owner. They can ensure that providing a loan is conditional upon proof of the borrower's identity. From the Bankers' Association submission it would seem that identity checks do not impose an additional onerous duty on banks.

The New Zealand Law Commission therefore recommended that mortgagees should be required to take reasonable steps to ensure that the person executing or transferring the mortgage is the actual registered owner of the property, or would become the actual registered owner. In order to do so, mortgagees would have to follow the reasonable steps for identification prescribed by the Registrar. If a mortgagee failed to take reasonable steps and the mortgagor was in fact a fraudster, the mortgagee would not gain indefeasible title by registration. They would also be prevented from claiming indemnity for any loss.[79]

However, the recommendations of the New Zealand Law Commission on this point do not appear to have been taken forward. The Law Commission's draft Bill was the foundation for the Land Transfer Act 2017. The Bill as originally introduced into the New Zealand Parliament on 11 February 2016 contained a duty on mortgagees to verify mortgagors' identities;[80] however, on 15 September 2016, the Government Administration Committee, after receiving submissions on the draft Bill, made recommendations which included omitting the sections imposing a duty on mortgagees to take reasonable steps to verify the identities of mortgagors.[81] It did so based on concerns that compliance with the requirements would impose significant costs on banks—costs which might in turn be imposed on customers. The Committee reported that it was widely believed that the existing verification of identity standards already provided sufficient protections from mortgage fraud, and that, moreover, mortgage fraud rarely occurs in New Zealand because of its sophisticated electronic conveyancing system. The costs of the identity requirements therefore outweighed the benefits.[82] Indeed, the New Zealand Law Society had noted that there had been only one known instance of attempted identity fraud in land transactions in New Zealand since the introduction of Landonline, its online conveyancing portal.[83]

B. A Universal Indemnity Scheme?

The indemnity scheme provided for in schedule 8 to the LRA 2002 is universal: it does not distinguish between different kinds of applicants. The Law Commission's 2016 Consultation Paper asks whether the indemnity scheme should continue to operate universally.

[79] NZLC Report No 116 (n 78) paras 2.20–2.21, and Part 2, Commentary on the Land Transfer Bill, 81–82 and 87.

[80] Land Transfer Bill 2016 (118-1) cls 54 and 61(1)(d).

[81] See NZ Parliament, Bills and Law, *Land Transfer Bill* (<https://www.parliament.nz/en/pb/bills-and-laws/bills-proposed-laws/document/00DBHOH_BILL68258_1/land-transfer-bill>).

[82] Land Transfer Bill 2016 (118-2) Commentary, 3.

[83] New Zealand Law Society, News & Communications, 'NZLS supports Land Transfer Bill, but urges fresh look at critical parts' (25 May 2016) <https://www.lawsociety.org.nz/news-and-communications/news/nzls-supports-land-transfer-bill,-but-urges-fresh-look-at-critical-parts>.

This question has already been addressed in a number of other jurisdictions. In Ontario, for example, the Land Titles Act 1990 distinguishes between registered owners and good faith purchasers of land used for residential purposes on one hand, and all other owners on the other. As the result of recent amendments, indemnity is provided as a first resort in respect of residential owners and purchasers, but not in respect of other categories of claimant.[84]

The Law Commission's 2016 Consultation Paper does not advocate distinguishing between residential and other registered proprietors of registered estates. However, as we have seen, a specific trend across a number of jurisdictions has been to operate their indemnity schemes differently in respect of mortgagees, through the imposition of a duty of care. In addition to considering whether a similar duty should be imposed on mortgagees in England and Wales, the Law Commission's 2016 Consultation Paper asks whether the circumstances in which mortgagees should be entitled to an indemnity should be narrowed. In doing so, the Paper questions whether the provision of an indemnity to mortgagees is explicable by reference to the purposes of the indemnity scheme.

i. Does the Application of the Indemnity to Mortgagees Fulfil the Purposes of the Scheme?

Some of the rationales for the provision of an indemnity scheme that were outlined in section IV above may apply equally to mortgagees. In both residential and commercial contexts, purchasers of land are often dependent on secured finance; therefore, lenders are an integral part of property transactions. If lenders did not have the same protection as borrowers, then they could pass the additional costs they incurred on to borrowers, undermining the aims of cheaper conveyancing and the economic efficiency of a state indemnity scheme. However, in other respects the position of mortgagees is different to that of a purchaser. Institutional lenders manage risk as an integral aspect of their business. To an institutional lender, a state-provided indemnity may play a significantly less important role than the lender's own risk management decisions. If so, then even the relevance of the constitutional function of the indemnity may be called into question in relation to mortgagees. As section IV has explained, the constitutional function is linked to the need for parties to be able to rely on the Register. Limiting protection for mortgagees would not offend the constitutional principle if, in fact, mortgagees are not placing reliance on the Register. This point is discussed further below.

It is possible, however, that in relation to mortgagees, the indemnity scheme is performing a different function: increasing lenders' willingness to lend. Lenders' willingness to lend is important, both as a means of financing business and as a means of providing access to home ownership. The availability of indemnity to mortgagees may therefore be performing a specific function of facilitating the operation of the mortgage market.

ii. Mortgagees and Reliance on the Register

The extent to which mortgagees may rely on the Register lies at the heart of one possible reform raised in the Law Commission's 2016 Consultation Paper. The Paper asks whether

[84] Land Titles Act 1990 (Ontario), s 57(4)(c), (4.1) and (4.2); Land Titles Act 1990 (Ontario), Regulation 690: Procedures and Records, reg 64(1). See also B Bucknall, 'Real Estate Fraud and Systems of Title Registration: The Paradox of Certainty' (2008) 47 *Canadian Business Law Journal* 1, 41.

the ability of mortgagees to claim an indemnity should be confined to situations in which a mortgage is granted on the basis of a pre-existing mistake in the Register, but not when the grant of the mortgage itself creates the mistake.[85]

Two contrasting scenarios illustrate the effect of this reform.[86] In the first ('A-B') scenario, where A's registered title is by fraud/forgery charged to a mortgagee B, then B would not be entitled to an indemnity: the grant of the mortgage has led to a mistake on the Register. This sort of 'A-B' scenario arose in *Swift 1st Ltd v Chief Land Registrar*.[87] The reform proposed would remove the mortgagee's (B's) entitlement to an indemnity that is currently available to a mortgagee in such a case. In the second ('A-B-C') scenario, where A's registered title is by fraud/forgery transferred to B, and B then grants a charge to C, C would remain entitled to claim an indemnity.

In the first scenario, the fraudster granting the mortgage is not the person (ie, the current registered proprietor, A) he or she is purporting to be. Arguably, the mortgagee is best placed to detect this sort of identity fraud. If the mortgagee uncovers the fraudster's true identity, then it will be apparent that he or she is not the registered proprietor; the mortgagee need not look behind the Register to reveal this fact, since the registered proprietor and mortgagor will simply be different people. However, in the second scenario, B is exactly who he or she purports to be: any checks the mortgagee undertakes will confirm that B is the current registered proprietor. In order to detect the fraud that tainted the transfer from A to B, the mortgagee would need to look behind the Register. On that basis, it may be considered consistent with the constitutional function of indemnity to deny a claim by a mortgagee B in the A-B scenario, but continue to provide an indemnity to a mortgagee C in the A-B-C scenario.

Such a reform would represent a policy decision to treat mortgagees differently for the purposes of the indemnity scheme. The Law Commission's 2016 Consultation Paper does not suggest that in the A-B scenario, an innocent purchaser B should be denied an indemnity. In one sense B—whether a purchaser or a mortgagee—relies on the Register to establish that A is the registered proprietor who can sell or mortgage the land. A decision to continue to provide an indemnity when B is a purchaser, but deny it when B is a mortgagee, would reflect a decision that a mortgagee can be expected to do more to establish whether it is actually dealing with A—as opposed to a fraudster impersonating A—than can be expected of a purchaser; or that as a matter of business practice, a mortgagee does not in fact rely on the Register in the same manner or extent as a purchaser.

iii. Mortgagees and Rectification

The discussion in the Law Commission's 2016 Consultation Paper of indemnity claims by mortgagees needs to be seen alongside a specific point that is raised in the Paper's review of rectification. Given that a mortgagee's interest in land is purely financial, the Paper suggests that if a mortgagee's title to a registered charge is registered by mistake, or is the result of a mistake, then the mortgagee should (only) be entitled to apply for an indemnity: the

[85] Law Com CP No 227 (n 2) paras 14.110–14.117.

[86] It is assumed in these examples that A, B and C are innocent victims of the fraud, and that the conveyancers and mortgagee have acted consistently with any duty of care.

[87] *Swift 1st Ltd v Chief Land Registrar* [2015] EWCA Civ 330, [2015] Ch 602.

mortgagee should not be able to oppose rectification so as to correct a mistake by removing its charge.[88]

This result would generally follow at present under the LRA 2002 because a registered chargee can never claim the special protection from rectification afforded to the 'proprietor in possession of a registered estate'.[89] However, there are situations under the current law where the registered chargee's position is not entirely clear. For example, in an 'A-B' or 'A-B-C' case where no-one is in possession, the Register will be rectified in A's favour absent exceptional circumstances. It is difficult to imagine exceptional circumstances where it would not be right to rectify in A's favour so as to remove the charge, but the Law Commission's provisional proposal—if adopted—would put the matter beyond doubt. However, it should be noted that taken together with the Law Commission's suggestion that mortgagees should not be able to oppose rectification, any change to the ability of a mortgagee to claim an indemnity would have a particular consequence. It would mean that in an 'A-B' case where A's registered title is by fraud/forgery charged to B, B would be unable to oppose A's application to rectify the Register (by removing the charge) even though it will not be entitled to an indemnity following the rectification. As the mortgagee, in practice, is unlikely ever successfully to oppose rectification under the current law, this consequence of the proposals may be considered unobjectionable. Indeed, if a policy decision is taken to reduce the circumstances in which a mortgagee can obtain an indemnity, it would be undesirable for that limitation to be circumvented by B opposing A's application for rectification, so that the charge remains registered and A is left to claim an indemnity; the funds from the claim being used to discharge B's registered charge. Further, it would be undesirable for the fact that A will be entitled to an indemnity and B would not be, to influence the court's decision whether rectification should be made.

C. The Relationship Between the State Indemnity and Private Insurance

The insurance metaphor reflects the fact that the indemnity scheme covers risks of a type that could, potentially, be met by the purchaser through private insurance. However, the purposes served by the indemnity scheme could not be replicated through reliance on private insurance without a significant risk to public trust and confidence in the Register. To hold out the Register as a guarantee of title, which can be relied upon for transactions with land, would have a hollow ring if coupled by the need, on every transaction, to purchase private insurance in the event that the Register is found to contain a mistake, Further, in its review of the Scottish legislation, the Scottish Law Commission reported that 'the economic evidence available to us suggests that title insurance as a standard feature for conveyancing transactions would not be cost-effective for titles in the Land Register, because the Keeper's indemnity … delivers comparable benefits at a much lower cost'.[90]

[88] Law Com CP No 227 (n 2) paras 13.91–13.97.

[89] LRA 2002, sch 4, paras 3(2) and 6(2).

[90] Scots Law Com No 222 (n 64) para 26.6. The report refers to work commissioned by the Keeper that revealed that property transaction costs in California, where private insurance is standard, are far higher than in Scotland and that this difference 'is due essentially to title insurance premiums'.

The Commission concluded that 'it would be unfortunate if [title insurance] came into routine use for ordinary titles'.[91]

Private insurance may have a role to play to provide protection against risks that are not covered by the indemnity scheme. Its role in this respect was noted by the Scottish Law Commission, which explained that it is used in 'non-standard cases' (or more complex cases) to cover risks that fall outside the scope of the indemnity scheme.[92] The New Zealand Law Commission considered whether the emergence of private insurance indicated deficiencies with the Torrens system. It concluded that this was not the case, and that '[i]f those dealing with land choose to take out insurance to cover situations that are excluded from cover under the Torrens compensation provisions ... this may complement the system'.[93] Private insurance plays the same role—acting as a complement to the indemnity scheme—in England and Wales and may be bought, for example, where the existence of a restrictive covenant affecting a title is apparent from the Register, but the scope of the covenant is not, or where possessory (rather than absolute) title is awarded.

However, some risks arise in every transaction—in particular, the risk that a transaction is fraudulent and that the fraud is discovered between completion and acceptance for registration. The benefits of economic efficiency would be lost if, to meet such risks, insurance were to be bought as a matter of course. Further, the development of private insurance may be used as an opportunity to reduce the scope of an indemnity scheme. In Ontario, the Land Titles Act 1990 allows residential owners and purchasers to claim against the indemnity fund (known as the 'Assurance Fund') as a first resort but only if their loss is not compensable through insurance.[94] Moreover, the 1990 Act may bar claims against the indemnity fund for all claimants who have private title insurance, since all claimants must demonstrate that they are 'unable ... to recover just compensation' to access the fund.[95] Under the Ontario regime, therefore, taking out private title insurance will disbar residential owners from applying to the indemnity fund as a first insurer, and may disbar all claimants from applying to the indemnity fund entirely. Title insurance in this context may be unnecessary and even unhelpful.[96]

In its 2016 Consultation Paper, the Law Commission asks whether the role of private insurance should be extended by placing a cap on the indemnity that could be paid to any party following a rectification of the Register (or where rectification is available but is not ordered).[97] Such a cap would mean that risks of a type generally covered by the indemnity scheme would be excluded where the financial risk of the particular transaction is exceptional. Where a disposition of land (or of a particular property right) is of exceptional value, parties would need to consider private insurance to cover their potential losses above the cap. A cap could therefore maintain the benefit of an indemnity scheme,

[91] ibid para 26.8.

[92] ibid.

[93] NZLC Report No 116 (n 78) para 4.35. The use of title insurance as a complement for the state guarantee is considered in P O'Connor, 'Double Indemnity—Title Insurance and the Torrens System' (2003) 3 *Queensland University of Technology Law and Justice Journal* 141.

[94] Land Titles Act 1990 (Ontario), Regulation 690: Procedures and Records, reg 64(1); Bucknall, 'Real Estate Fraud and Systems of Title Registration' (n 84) 42.

[95] Bucknall, 'Real Estate Fraud and Systems of Title Registration' (n 84) 42, citing Land Titles Act 1990 (Ontario), s 57(4)(c).

[96] Bucknall, 'Real Estate Fraud and Systems of Title Registration (n 84) 45–46.

[97] Law Com CP No 227 (n 2) paras 14.53–14.60.

whilst protecting the Land Registry from the risks of exceptional claims. No cap would apply where the indemnity claim arises through fault on the part of the Land Registry. In this respect, the cap would apply only where the provision of an indemnity could be rationalised in terms of the insurance principle, rather than reflecting a liability for fault on the part of the Land Registry.

Would the imposition of a cap be consistent with the constitutional function of indemnity? Arguments on this point may be finely balanced. The state's role in conferring title is the same, irrespective of the value of land held on that title. The purchaser of (for example) a major development must rely on the Register in the same way as the purchaser of a modest terraced house. But the extent of that reliance by a sophisticated purchaser may, as with a mortgagee, be different. However, even if removing wholly exceptional risks from the indemnity scheme is considered compatible with its constitutional function, the imposition of a cap would concede a significant point of principle that a registered title, having being conferred by the state, is then guaranteed by the state. The Law Commission's 2016 Consultation Paper therefore cautions against the imposition of a cap, without closing the door to the possibility.

VII. Conclusion

Provision of an indemnity is a hallmark of systems of registered title, but a comparative analysis demonstrates that there is no universally accepted 'blueprint' for the scope of the indemnity scheme. Ultimately, losses arising from mistakes on the Register will be borne by one of three parties: the state through its indemnity; conveyancers and other professionals; or the parties to a transaction. The distribution of losses between these parties requires policy choices that necessarily may vary between jurisdictions. This chapter has sought to encourage greater debate to assist in making those policy choices as part of the Law Commission's current review of the indemnity scheme contained in the LRA 2002. It has also argued that the options for reform identified by the Law Commission are consistent with the constitutional function of the indemnity. The Law Commission's work continues, with its final recommendations due to be published in spring 2018.

C

Priorities Between Competing Interests

13

Priority Contests Involving Registered Titles

MARTIN DIXON

I. Introduction

The Land Registration Act ('LRA') 2002, like its predecessor, has to grapple with a practical problem at the heart of our land law. In the common law system, nothing about land ownership or land rights is absolute. This is not a different way of making the obvious point that 'ownership' is about estates not dominium, or that all title is relative, but rather that our concept of proprietary rights, be they rights akin to ownership or more limited rights of enjoyment, positively encourages the distribution of the benefits of land use. A freeholder, their neighbour with an easement of way, the property developer with an option to purchase part of the property's large garden, the other neighbour with a covenant restrictive of building, the tenant holding a short-term tenancy and the lender who is securing an income stream via the freeholder's mortgage all have a real stake in the land. And, of course, the freeholder in principle is free to alienate their entire interest at any time, by gift or for value. In most cases, these interests co-exist without generating practical problems, largely because our insistence on certainty of creation for proprietary interests reduces the opportunities for surprises. However, land law needs a set of principles that can resolve disputes when the enjoyment of one person's rights over land potentially conflicts with another's. As the Law Commission puts it, '[p]riority is a central concept in land law'.[1]

One aim of the LRA 2002 was to introduce a 'clear statutory statement'[2] of priority, whilst avoiding any new elaborate scheme because this would be unnecessary given the intended introduction of electronic conveyancing.[3] In its 2016 Consultation Paper, the Law Commission put the matter slightly differently, reminding us that it is 'important in any system of land registration for there to be clear rules governing the relative priority of different interests'.[4] Maybe there is nothing in this small shift of emphasis, but after nearly

[1] Law Commission, *Updating the Land Registration Act 2002—A Consultation Paper* (Law Com CP No 227, 2016) para 2.56.

[2] Law Commission, *Land Registration for the Twenty-First Century—A Conveyancing Revolution* (Law Com No 271, 2001) para 5.1.

[3] Law Com No 271 (n 2) para 5.3.

[4] Law Com CP No 227 (n 1) para. 6.1.

15 years of the LRA 2002, perhaps the Commission recognise that while clarity is critical, there is nothing to be gained by a forced simplicity which underplays the complex nature of practical priority problems.

This chapter seeks to analyse how priority contests involving registered titles arise, and how they are resolved under the LRA 2002, but it does so bearing in mind that the Act was not intended to establish a comprehensive priority scheme. On close examination, the 'priority rules' of the LRA 2002 deal with different types of priority contests, and not all involve some kind of dealing with a registered title. However, the LRA 2002 is not the only statute that has something to say about priority. Nor is statute *per se* the only source of the relevant legal principles. This chapter's essential argument is, therefore, that while a case can be made that some aspects of the LRA 2002's priority rules should be modified, enhanced or clarified, this must be done holistically—recognising that priority contests can be multi-dimensional and, perhaps more importantly, can engage principles outside of the LRA 2002.

The following analysis proposes a four-fold categorisation of 'priority contests': (i) 'disposition priority contests'; (ii) '*inter se* priority contests'; (iii) 'mistake priority contests' (which can in turn be divided into 'alteration' and 'rectification' 'priority contests'); and (iv) 'adverse possession priority contests'. Sections II–V consider in turn how the LRA 2002 seeks to resolve them, bearing in mind that the provisions of the Act do not operate independently of other priority-type rules. Section VI offers some concluding thoughts.

II. Contests Between Registered Dispositions and Pre-Existing Proprietary Interests: 'Disposition Priority Contests'

The situation that may be most commonly thought of as a priority dispute involves what can be called a *disposition priority contest*—ie, a contest between a registered disposition of a registered title and a pre-existing interest that burdened the registered title immediately before the disposition. Such contests engage central provisions of the LRA 2002, as well as critical provisions of other statutes and general principles of the law of real property. In a typical case, a registered proprietor will transfer their title to another, or carve out a new registered title from their own (eg, a lease or mortgage), and the question arises whether any pre-existing rights that burdened the registered title will continue to 'bind' the new registered proprietor, lessee or mortgagee as the case may be.

The Land Registration Act ('LRA') 1925 dealt with these cases by stipulating that the new registered proprietor was vested with the relevant estate 'free from'[5] interests that were neither entered on the Register nor overriding.[6] It is clear that the LRA 2002 was not meant to change the law, but rather only to express the issue differently.[7] Importantly, the LRA 2002

[5] LRA 1925, s 20.
[6] With exceptions for leasehold covenants and dependent on the grade of title.
[7] Law Com No 271 (n 2) para 5.1.

did not propose to introduce a 'voidness' rule similar to that found in section 4 of the Land Charges Act 1972 in respect of conveyances of land of unregistered title.[8]

The current statutory rules regulating these disposition priority contests are found in sections 28 and 29, and schedule 3 of the LRA 2002. Importantly, however, the LRA 2002 does not—and is not meant to—answer all questions of priority in relation to registered dispositions. Consequently, consideration of sections 28 and 29 devoid of their wider context leads to a half-painted picture of the material priority rules, and might lead us to draw conclusions about their operation that are unwarranted.

A. Preliminaries

It is axiomatic, but not always remembered, that before a question of (registered) disposition priority becomes material, the earlier right alleged to have priority to the later disposition must actually be of a kind capable of binding the registered title immediately before the disposition under consideration. This is not simply a question of whether, on the facts, a recognised type of proprietary right exists.[9] It is also the question whether the alleged right is *capable* of being proprietary in the first place and whether, on the facts, there is anything that makes that right unenforceable, as against the registered title or the particular disponee, under the general law.

These issues necessarily arise before we even have to consider the specific priority rules found in sections 28 and 29 of the LRA 2002. The LRA 2002 partly helps to resolve them, precisely because of the need to bring certainty to disposition priority contests, by clarifying the status of rights of pre-emption, equities by estoppel and mere equities.[10] However, doubts persist in relation to the status of the alleged 'right' to rectify the Register in the event of a mistake. This 'right' can be critical in disposition priority contests—*if* this right is 'proprietary', and can have priority over a later registered disposition in accordance with the rule in section 29, the title guarantee embodied in section 58 of the LRA 2002 is potentially blown apart because the right's persistence may prevent the award of an indemnity to a later disponee whose title is altered to reflect it.[11] It is becoming apparent that the 'right's' status needs to be settled.[12] Further, having a right of proprietary character is only relevant if it is otherwise enforceable *immediately before* the disposition in question. So, questions of consent, undue influence, subrogation and the recent emergence of 'beneficiary authorisation'[13] are all relevant in disposition priority contests. These concern matters of general law, some of which are outside the realm of property law, let alone the LRA 2002.

[8] It is unclear whether the LRA 1925 postulated a voidness rule: 'free from' is perhaps stronger than 'priority' but weaker than 'void'.

[9] See, eg, the old but still relevant question of whether an occupation agreement gives rise to a lease or a licence—see recently *Camelot Properties v Roynon,* Bristol County Court, 25 February 2017 (judgment with author). See also *Southern Pacific Mortgages v Scott* [2014] UKSC 52, [2015] AC 385.

[10] See now the LRA 2002, ss 115 and 116, and *Mortgage Express v Lambert* [2016] EWCA Civ 555, [2017] Ch 93.

[11] See section IV below.

[12] See, eg, *Bakrania v Lloyds Bank plc* [2017] UKFTT 0364 (PC) and M Dixon [2017] *Conv* 161. See also S Cooper and E Lees, 'Interests, Powers and Mere Equities in Modern Land Law' (2017) 37 *OJLS* 435.

[13] *Wishart v Credit and Mercantile plc* [2015] EWCA Civ 655, [2015] P & CR 15.

We need to recognise the interplay between these preliminary issues and the disposition priority rules of the land registration regime. While the priority rules found in the LRA 2002 are designed to give clear outcomes,[14] an easy way to bypass them is to attack the prior interest-holder's apparent priority under these rules by other means. An example is *Wishart v Credit and Mercantile plc*,[15] where a single registered proprietor held the title on trust for a sole beneficiary, and where the section 29 rule would have led to the conclusion that a registered charge granted to the lender by the registered proprietor would be subject to the beneficiary's interest. The 'solution' to this inconvenient outcome (at least for the lender) was to challenge the continued enforceability of the beneficiary's interest under the general law. So, even if the disposition priority rules found in the LRA 2002 need very little amendment to clarify their effect,[16] we must consider how they work in practice when they dovetail with other rules of land law.

B. Overreaching

The availability of overreaching[17] might well be thought of as relating to questions of right enforceability—that is, whether the potentially overreached right has ceased to be enforceable under the general law, irrespective of the effect of the LRA 2002's disposition priority rules. However, it is unclear exactly *when* overreaching occurs.[18] Further, recent cases also clearly regard overreaching as an aspect of the disposition priority rules, as well as the rules relating to trustees' powers. In *Baker v Craggs*,[19] the High Court decided that the duly registered grant of an easement by joint registered proprietors was a conveyance of a *legal estate* sufficient to trigger overreaching. In *Mortgage Express v Lambert*,[20] the Court of Appeal determined that mere equities, and possibly equities by estoppel, were rights capable of being overreached on the grant of a registered mortgage. And in *Bakrania v Lloyds Bank*,[21] the First-tier Tribunal decided that the alleged 'right' to rectify the Register could be overreached, and, further, that it was immaterial that the title of the current (selling) registered proprietors had been obtained via a rectifiable mistake.[22] All three decisions came as something of a surprise, and while not being necessarily untenable, they certainly extend the horizon of overreaching. In all three cases, overreaching was effectively seen as an aspect of the disposition priority rule—the earlier right, if postponed via overreaching, could not

[14] Law Com No 271 (n 2) para 5.1 ff.

[15] *Wishart* (n 13).

[16] But see section VI below.

[17] Sometimes reference is made to the 'principle' or 'doctrine' of overreaching. This oversells it. It is simply a practical process designed to encourage alienability of land by ensuring that trustees have power to act and convey a clean title. It is not limited to trusts of land. See C Harpum, 'Overreaching, Trustees' Powers and the Reform of the 1925 Legislation' [1990] *CLJ* 277 and G Owen, 'A New Paradigm for Overreaching—Some Inspiration from Down Under' [2013] *Conv* 377.

[18] eg, is it on payment of the money or completion of the transaction? And if the latter, is it when the transaction is completed under the general law or when it is completed as a disposition of a legal estate by registration?

[19] *Baker v Craggs* [2016] EWHC 3250 (Ch), [2017] 2 WLR 1483. An application to appeal out of time has been granted.

[20] *Mortgage Express v Lambert* [2016] EWCA Civ 555, [2017] Ch 93.

[21] *Bakrania v Lloyds Bank plc* [2017] UKFTT 0364 (PC).

[22] This decision carries no precedential force. The current registered proprietors were not responsible for the mistake—a fraud was perpetrated by the persons they bought from.

re-gain priority via the application of the LRA 2002's specific priority provisions.[23] The importance of considering overreaching in the context of disposition priority rules, and perhaps clarifying its reach, is apparent from these cases. So too, and conversely, we should learn from *AIB Group (UK) plc v Turner*,[24] where a lengthy analysis of whether the claimant was in 'actual' occupation sufficient to trigger an overriding interest under the LRA 2002, schedule 3, paragraph 2, was in fact wholly unnecessary given that the mortgage had been executed by two trustees of land sufficient to overreach under *City of London Building Society v Flegg*.[25]

C. Sections 28 and 29 of the LRA 2002

Assuming that the holder of a prior interest can overcome the hurdles identified above, sections 28 and 29 come into play.

As is well known, section 28 operates in respect of all dispositions of a registered title, whether registered or not,[26] save where the relevant disposition is a registered disposition for 'valuable consideration' which attracts the special priority rule in section 29. Section 28's effect is that in relation to such dispositions, all pre-existing proprietary rights have priority over the interest of the later disponee.[27] As such, the provision appears to reflect a 'first in time' rule, which can be regarded as the general law's default position when resolving priority disputes. However, section 28 is not entirely free from doubt for three key reasons.

First, section 28 does not actually state a disposition priority rule: it says negatively that priority is not affected by a disposition unless section 29 applies. It thereby incorporates the 'first in time' rule by reference and raises the possibility that it may be necessary to consider whether 'the equities are equal'—as is the case under the general law in the case of contests between competing equitable interests—when relying on section 28, despite the difficulties associated with this nebulous qualification.[28]

Secondly, section 28(1) establishes that 'the priority of an interest affecting a *registered* estate or charge is not affected by a disposition of the estate or charge', and then in section 28(2) that it 'makes no difference for the purposes of this section whether the interest or disposition is registered'. Presumably, this means that it does not matter whether the pre-existing interest whose priority is in question is entered in the Register *and* that it does not matter if the challenged subsequent disposition is substantively registered. However, the reference to the 'disposition' not needing to be registered is confusing, given that section 28(1) refers to a 'registered' estate or charge.

[23] In *Baker v Craggs* (n 19), there is a very useful account of the meaning of 'actual occupation' sufficient to trigger an overriding interest within the disposition priority rule, and in *Bakrania* (n 21) the Tribunal Judge determined that even if actual occupation existed, it was not 'discoverable' for the purposes of the LRA 2002, sch 3, para 2.

[24] *AIB Group (UK) plc v Turner* [2015] EWHC 3994 (Ch).

[25] *City of London Building Society v Flegg* [1988] AC 54 (HL).

[26] LRA 2002, s 28(2).

[27] See, eg, *Halifax plc v Curry Popeck* [2008] EWHC 1692 (Ch) and, on one view, *MacLeod v Gold Harp Properties Ltd* [2014] EWCA Civ 1084, [2015] 1 WLR 1249.

[28] In Law Com No 271 (n 2), the Law Commission appear to imply that section 28 was meant to stipulate an unqualified first in time rule, although that is not what it says in terms: see para 5.2.

Thirdly, section 28 establishes a priority rule in cases of a disposition of a registered title, but not as between interests where there is no registered disposition (or attempted registered disposition). So, section 28 *was* relevant in *Halifax plc v Curry Popeck*[29] because there was a disposition that was not registered, as per section 28(2). But it is *not* applicable in other types of 'inter se priority contests', which involve two interests affecting a registered title, neither of which is registered or capable of being registered—eg that between the holder of an option and the person entitled to enforce a restrictive covenant.[30] This does not matter if the priority rule incorporated by section 28 is the same 'first in time' rule as would govern these non-disposition inter se priority contests via the general law. But if the rule incorporated by section 28 is a 'pure' first in time rule, untainted by the 'equities being equal' qualification found in the general law's priority rules, we have a third rule in play in relation to registered land.

However, these concerns about section 28 are trivial compared to the uncertainty that infects section 29, a core provision of our land registration priority system. In practice, most dispositions of a registered estate in land are registered dispositions for value (sales, leases, mortgages and the like) and thus trigger section 29. The section establishes a special priority rule, reflecting the special protection given to purchasers of registered interests. Its effect is that a registered disposition[31] for value postpones the priority of all pre-existing proprietary interests (presumably the first in time priority given by section 28) to the interest acquired under the disposition, unless those pre-existing interests are entered on the Register or overriding within schedule 3. There are some obvious, and less obvious issues here.

First, given that section 29's special priority rule is at the heart of the land registration system, it is surprising that the LRA 2002 provides no positive definition of what amounts to 'valuable consideration'.[32] Perhaps the absence of reported litigation raising the issue indicates that this is not practical problem,[33] but the Law Commission's 2016 Consultation Paper certainly assumes that there is an issue here that requires attention.[34]

Secondly, section 29's rule must be read together with section 32. Even if an interest is 'the subject of a notice in the register',[35] it is clear that the pre-existing registered (or perhaps 'recorded')[36] interest will not in practice enjoy priority over a disposition that triggers section 29, unless the prior interest is actually 'valid'. Section 32(3) confirms that, unlike registered dispositions which are deemed to be conclusive under section 58 and benefit from the LRA 2002's title guarantee, the entry of a notice does not guarantee that the interest so recorded actually exists. This has allowed the Land Registry to enter notices with the

[29] *Curry Popeck* (n 27).

[30] See section III below on the impact in relation to 'inter se priority contests'.

[31] So, the relevant disposition must be *completed* by registration to trigger s 29 or be treated as such (see s 29(4)). Otherwise the attempted disposition is covered by s 28.

[32] LRA 2002, s 132(1) provides that valuable consideration 'does not include marriage consideration or a nominal consideration in money' but there is nothing about what it does include.

[33] Some cases ask whether the reported consideration actually was paid and thus whether the alleged 'sale' was a sham—see *Curry Popeck* (n 27) and *Gold Harp* (n 27)—but none consider the meaning of 'valuable' in this context.

[34] Law Com CP No 227 (n 1) para 7.8 ff.

[35] LRA 2002, s 29(2)(a)(i).

[36] Law Com CP No 227 (n 1) para 2.1. This terminology more accurately identifies the difference between interests that require registration for their existence and are guaranteed, and those where registration protects them but is not relevant to their existence.

minimum of enquiries *and* to shift responsibility for challenging the veracity of the notice application to the party whose title would be affected by the notice. More concerning, the Land Registry appear willing to do this in respect of an interest whose priority might already be thought to have been lost under the priority rules of the LRA 2002 itself.[37] This approach, which in fairness is facilitated by section 32, has permitted the Registry to move away from 'managing' the land registration system in order to achieve the system's goals, to simply administering it. It necessarily imports uncertainty and cost for the parties and anyone relying on the Register. It does, however, reduce Registry costs and makes it more profitable.

Thirdly, if an interest enjoys priority, it will do so only according to its inherent nature and terms. In the same way that loss of priority does not imply destruction of the interest,[38] gaining priority does not ensure enforceability for all purposes. An interest with priority does not somehow acquire an elevated status by reason of sections 28 and 29. For example, in *Southern Pacific Mortgages,*[39] even if Mrs Scott's interest had had priority, what would this have meant? If she had a lease, it would have taken priority according to its terms, and so may well have been determinable in due course. If she had an interest by estoppel, the satisfaction of the equity could have left her with no proprietary interest at all, or an interest that was time-limited or restricted in some other way. The priority of a right, and its substantive content and remedial enforceability, are different things.

Fourthly, and critically, the rule in section 29 merely *postpones* the priority of a pre-existing interest to the interest acquired via the later registered disposition. It does not render the pre-existing interest 'void': the interest does not cease to exist by reason of section 29's disposition priority rule.[40] The reasons for expressing the section 29 rule in terms of priority, rather than voidness, are well known. It means, for example, that even if a derivative registered interest (eg, a registered lease or mortgage carved out of a registered freehold) can claim priority over a pre-existing interest under the section 29 rule, the *superior* registered estate might still be subject to that interest: the interest does not cease to exist simply because it has lost priority to the derivative title.[41]

There are, nevertheless, some difficulties with the postponement strategy adopted by the LRA 2002. These concern, in particular, whether section 29 might be construed in such a way that a postponed interest may subsequently re-emerge and re-gain priority to a later disposition. Consider a case where X's interest burdens A's registered freehold estate. X's interest will lose priority pursuant to section 29 on subsequent sale of A's registered estate to B, if it is neither entered in the Register nor an overriding interest. However, if B, the new registered proprietor, subsequently *gifts* his registered estate to C, then section 29 will not be triggered in favour of C due to the absence of valuable consideration, and the statute might be interpreted to mean that X's previously-postponed interest can re-emerge to have priority over the disposition by B to C. A similar problem could arise even if B subsequently *sells* his registered estate to C, if before the sale has occurred, X's interest—which had been postponed to the registered disposition to B—is entered on the Register[42] or acquires

[37] ibid, para 8.22.

[38] See the text to n 41 et seq below.

[39] *Southern Pacific Mortgages* (n 9).

[40] See, eg, *Rosefair Ltd v Butler* [2015] UKFTT 0395 (PC).

[41] eg, the superior estate owner might have granted the interest.

[42] And it now appears that the Registry will make the entry of a Notice, leaving it to the registered proprietor to object when informed.

overriding status.[43] Could X's previously-postponed interest again re-emerge to have priority over the disposition by B to C?

Such outcomes are troubling, especially if they mean that a registered title effectively becomes encumbered for the purpose of subsequent dealings even if was unencumbered when the registered proprietor first acquired it. It is counter-intuitive to our understanding of title registration and contradicts essential policies of the LRA 2002. There are at least two ways of avoiding the problem. First, we could employ an inverse of the *nemo dat* rule—ie, a rule that a person with a registered title which has priority over pre-existing interests transfers that title *with its priority*.[44] This does not contradict the *Swift 1st* interpretation of section 58, but rather upholds it by ensuring that the title afforded to a registered disponee by section 58 remains completely guaranteed if it was enjoyed with priority over pre-existing interests. Secondly, the problem could be reduced if it became impossible to enter a notice in respect of an interest against a particular registered title where the Land Registry were clear that the interest had ceased to have priority over *that* registered title;[45] one could qualify overriding interests in the same way. However, the current Registry practice of not assessing whether an application to enter a notice is made in respect of an interest which *presently* encumbers and enjoys priority to the relevant registered title makes this difficult to achieve, even though it runs counter to our notion of what a land registration system should do. In fact, it reminds us more of the pre-registration 'private' conveyancing system of unregistered land where all matters of priority were left to the parties.

III. Proprietary Contests Between Competing Rights When They Do Not Affect a Registered Disposition: 'Inter Se Priority Contests'

As well as disputes when there is a registered disposition, for which the LRA 2002 makes specific provision, priority contests can arise between interests where neither is a registered disposition. These priority disputes—*inter se priority contests*—generally arise in two contexts.

A. An Attempted or Intended Registered Disposition, Which Does Not Occur

The first context in which an inter se priority context arises involves an attempted or intended registered disposition which fails to occur. These cases usually arise through some kind of error or miscalculation on the part of the transferee (usually by their legal advisers),

[43] eg, the interest-holder goes into actual occupation of the land.

[44] Perhaps s 62 of the Law of Property Act 1925 provides such an answer: 'A conveyance of land shall be deemed to include and shall by virtue of this Act operate to convey, with the land, all ... advantages whatsoever, appertaining or reputed to appertain to the land'.

[45] Thus, preserving the interest's priority over superior interests.

or perhaps as a result of deliberate fraud (as in *Curry Popeck*).[46] The relevance of this being a failed registered disposition is not only that the transferee for value cannot rely on section 29, but also that they will take only an equitable version of the interest intended to be transferred or created.[47] There is a further complication if the failed registered disposition is subsequently completed by a late registration which then triggers section 29, as in *Baker v Craggs*, especially if the competing interest arises in the 'registration gap'. The current law seems to generate the following three answers to this species of inter se priority contest.

First, if the intended registered disposition is never registered, the 'first in time rule' prevails because of section 28, which provides in section 28(2) that it does not matter whether the 'interest or disposition' is registered. As discussed above, this could be the first in time rule without the qualification of 'the equities being equal'.[48]

Secondly, if the disposition which was not initially registered is later registered, then section 29 kicks in and the matter turns into a disposition priority contest. This could be troublesome in a number of ways because the relevant time for assessing the priority of an interest for the purpose of the disposition priority rules is the time of *registration* of the disposition, subject to the qualification that actual occupation must also exist at the time the transaction was executed if this is the ground for finding that a pre-existing interest has priority.[49] So, a party might achieve priority by acquiring an interest *before* the late registration but *after* completion of the transaction, particularly if the interest is protected by means of a notice or overrides apart from paragraph 2 of schedule 3. Conversely, an interest holder with a long-enjoyed interest might lose priority—assuming that it is neither protected by notice or overriding[50]—because of the very late registration of a disposition of the affected registered title. The interest holder might then have to resort to an estoppel claim against the late registering disponee as the only way to defeat the priority given to the disponee by section 29.[51]

Thirdly, if the intended registered disposition is a *transfer* of the whole registered title to a claimant, then the equitable interest that the transferee obtains pending registration of the transfer is immediately vulnerable to a later properly-registered disposition by the still-registered original registered proprietor—as in *Baker v Craggs*.[52] In this situation, an inter se priority contest between the equitable transferee and the still registered transferor becomes a disposition priority contest between the equitable transferee and second registered transferee. Inevitably, it leads to disappointment for one of them depending on how section 29 applies.[53] One obvious mitigation of this last problem is, of course,

[46] *Curry Popeck* (n 27).

[47] LRA 2002, s 27.

[48] See section II above.

[49] LRA 2002, sch 3, para 2. See also *Thompson v Foy* [2009] EWHC 1076 (Ch), [2010] 1 P & CR 16; *Abbey National Building Society v Cann* [1991] AC 56; *Southern Pacific Mortgages* (n 9). In *Foy*, Lewison J indicated, obiter, that a person might also have to be in actual occupation at the time of registration as well as at completion of the transaction. This is contentious.

[50] Perhaps an unregistered freehold covenant.

[51] A 'standing by' estoppel would seem to offer the best chance of success.

[52] *Baker v Craggs* (n 19).

[53] It is not clear that there is a 'mistake' here sufficient to support an application to alter the Register/claim an indemnity. Is it a mistake within sch 4 to fail to register a disposition which should have been registered?

e-conveyancing as it was originally conceived—which would have eliminated the registration gap—but this now seems distant.

B. Contests Involving Interests, Neither Of Which Could Be Registered Dispositions

The second species of inter se priority contest arises where neither interest could amount to a registered disposition. An example would be where a registered proprietor has given a restrictive covenant to X, and an option to purchase to Y, and the priority contest arises between the interests of X and Y. In such cases, the protection of X's covenant and Y's option by notices against the registered title *does not affect their priority inter se*. As the Law Commission explain in their 2016 Consultation Paper, priority in these cases is determined by the order in which the interests are created.[54] This is not, technically, established by section 28, even though most commentators, including the present author, often note that it is. Section 28 says merely that priority is not affected by a disposition, whether registered or not. It does not tell us what the priority rule actually is when there is *not* something that could ever be a registered disposition. Thus, in these contests, if there is a rule that favours the first interest in time, it is a rule derived from the general law, rather than the LRA 2002, and specifically not section 28. Perhaps this is a mere technicality, except that if it is the *general law* that supplies the 'first in time' rule in this context, it might still matter whether 'the equities are equal'. It is likely that it was intended that all inter se priority contests would be governed by section 28 (if that even excludes the 'equities being equal' rule), but that is not what the section says.

The real issue caused by inter se priority contests of this second type is the potential inability of the parties to a transaction to know which interest has priority by simply looking at the Register. This is not so much a problem with the priority rules *per se*, but rather, a wider problem, of the parties not knowing that interests adverse to their own *actually exist*—if one knows that such a right exists, one knows that it may well have priority and can act accordingly. Indeed, there might be thought to be an inconsistency here, inherent in the priority scheme of the LRA 2002. Persons who acquire an interest via a registered disposition for valuable consideration are able to rely on the Register and achieve priority over pre-existing interests via section 29. However, persons granted other interests (eg covenants, options, rights of pre-emption and (rarely) equitable mortgages) are not similarly favoured—they receive no special protection from pre-existing competing interests that might have priority to the interest they have been granted.[55] Of course, the actual solution to this is simple: establish a new priority rule that says that interests not amounting to registered dispositions have priority according to the date they are entered on the Register (and optionally requiring also that they must have been acquired for valuable consideration to enjoy this priority). This would go a long way to solving this problem and establishing a more comprehensive registration scheme of priority. However, perhaps we should ask ourselves whether this is really a problem at all in practice. One has to imagine a

[54] Law Com CP No 227 (n 1) para 6.10 ff.

[55] They know, of course, that their interest is vulnerable to a *later* registered disposition if it is not adequately protected by a notice or as an overriding interest.

set of circumstances where (in my example) Y is about to be granted an interest by a registered proprietor that is not a registrable disposition (such as an option for value) and is not aware of the existence of any prior interests of persons such as X.[56] For sure, that awareness cannot be acquired conclusively by looking at the Register, particularly if the prior interest could not be entered in the Register (as per section 33) or would amount to an overriding interest, so that protection by registration is not needed. Nevertheless, it is not self-evident that we are dealing here with a serious practical problem given how conveyancing works and the enquiries that are made pre-contract. Actual cases are rare to non-existent, perhaps suggesting that parties' legal advisers are uncovering and dealing with any potential issues. Further, in reality, the problem that arises in these cases is no different from the priority problem which arises when a potentially registered disposition is not actually registered (the first species of inter se priority contest). While we might argue that in the second type of case, the person who loses is innocent, whereas in the the failed disposition cases, it is their own fault (eg in failing to ensure the disposition was registered), it is the latter case that causes more problems than the former. In other words, the rule in inter se priority contests could be tidied up, but it is not self-evident that it needs be.

IV. Priority Contests Following Mistakes: 'Mistake Priority Contests'

The Register is conclusive in respect of the substantive registration of dispositions of legal estates,[57] such as the transfer of freeholds, the grant and assignment of substantively registrable leases and mortgages.[58] This is the effect of the interpretation of section 58 of the LRA 2002 preferred by the Court of Appeal in *Swift 1st*, a decision which makes it clear that the previous registered proprietor retains no interest in the land even if the transfer to the disponee would have been void under the general law, eg for forgery. The LRA 2002, in this respect, knows no concept of *nemo dat*.[59] Nevertheless, necessarily, and properly, the Act recognises that some registered dispositions might be flawed and permits the Register to be altered in response to a mistake.[60] This is because, contrary to what seems to be a thread running through the Law Commission's 2016 Consultation Paper,[61] the LRA 2002 and its predecessor established a system of title *guarantee*, not title *indefeasibility*.[62] The LRA 2002

[56] This is because, if aware, a prudent grantee should be alerted to the need to check priority.

[57] The conclusiveness principle does not extend to protective registration of notices, see LRA 2002, s 32 as discussed above.

[58] LRA 2002, s 58. Query whether the entry of the grant of an easement is also conclusive, given that it has been held to be the grant of a legal 'estate': *Baker v Craggs* (n 19).

[59] Of course, this is not favoured by some, who point out that in terms section 58 could be said to apply to only 'legal' estates—but it is currently the law.

[60] LRA 2002, sch 4.

[61] See, eg, Law Com CP No 227 (n 1) para 13.98, in respect of removing mistaken mortgages from the Register.

[62] The difference is crucial. Title guarantee does not simply mean that the state underwrites the title, as is commonly believed. Title guarantee means that the current registered proprietor *is* the proprietor irrespective of matters leading to the registration; that people may deal with her safe in that knowledge; that she has power to deal with that title; and that the state will indemnify in the event of a mistake causing loss. This imports an element of title indefeasibility, but that is not the point of the system.

recognises that in some circumstances it is appropriate for mistakes in the Register to be undone—via alteration of the Register—but only as permitted by the Act itself. As a corollary, there is an indemnity for persons suffering loss by reason of certain types of alteration (ie, rectifications), or by a failure to rectify when that was possible.[63] The system is symmetric and self-contained.

The existence of a jurisdiction to alter the Register to correct mistakes, and the provision of indemnity for innocent parties suffering loss thereby, inevitably leads to a specific type of priority contest—the contest between the *original* registered proprietor who claims that they lost their title by mistake (eg, fraud of a third party) and the *current* registered proprietor who innocently obtained the registered title.[64] These *mistake priority contests* raise challenging questions. Whose title is it—the innocent original proprietor who lost it by reason of a mistake, or the innocent new proprietor? Who gets the land and who gets the indemnity? Or, as a variant illustrated by *Swift 1st*, where a third party's fraud results in the registration of a mortgage over a registered title, will the innocent registered proprietor retain title unencumbered by the mortgage, or is the innocent mortgagee able to exercise the remedies of a legal chargee?

The current law, found in schedule 4 of the LRA 2002, settles this type of priority contest in two ways. First, if the mistake does *not* prejudicially affect the title—in other words, it is trivial—then the Register is *altered* to correct the mistake, unless there are exceptional circumstances. These might be known as *alteration priority contests*.[65] Secondly, if the mistake does prejudicially affect the title—an alteration known as a *rectification*—then the mistake will not be corrected *if* the current registered proprietor is in possession of the land,[66] save only where the current registered proprietor consents to the correction, or by fraud or lack of proper care caused or substantially contributed to the mistake, or it would for any other reason be unjust not to rectify the Register. These might be known as *rectification priority contests*.[67]

It should be apparent that the LRA 2002 thus favours the original registered proprietor when there is no prejudicial effect or the new registered proprietor is not in possession, but otherwise favours the current registered proprietor in possession. The remarkable thing about these provisions is, in fact, their simplicity. They establish a self-contained code which divorces the workings of the land registration system from the general law of property—both personal property law and pre-registration real property law. They favour certainty, for even the safety-net that an alteration/rectification can be made against a registered proprietor in possession when it is 'unjust not to alter' is to be interpreted narrowly. Undoubtedly, though, the effect of these provisions is controversial—the workings of the Act in

[63] LRA 2002, sch 8.

[64] For example, *Patel v Freddy's Ltd* [2017] EWHC 73 (Ch) and *Bakrania* (n 21). A similar type of dispute concerns registered proprietors who find the title encumbered by a fraudulently-executed mortgage, as in *Swift 1st* itself.

[65] LRA 2002, sch 4, para 3(3). See *Paton v Todd* [2012] EWHC 1248 (Ch) for a discussion of the meaning of 'exceptional circumstances'.

[66] If they are not in possession, but it is still a 'rectification', the rectification must be made unless there are exceptional circumstances: LRA 2002, sch 4, para 3. However, in this case of non-possession rectification, even the existence of 'exceptional circumstances' does not bar rectification because those exceptional circumstances must be material: *Murphy v Lambeth LBC*, ChD (unreported, 19 February 2016).

[67] LRA 2002, sch 4, para 3(2); *Patel v Freddy's* (n 64).

mistake priority contests seem, at least to some, to run counter to notions of equity, and are certainly out of kilter with the wider law where void transactions carry no force. They also, at least for the Law Commission, compromise indefeasibility of title in the sense that there is no moment in time when a registered title cannot be the subject of an application to alter the Register. This is the origin of the 'long stop' proposal in the Law Commission's 2016 Consultation Paper, whereby an application to rectify could not be made after a set period had elapsed from the mistake.[68]

Of course, acceptance of the idea that an initial mistake makes all subsequent dealings with the registered title open to challenge under schedule 4[69] theoretically makes mistake priority contests open-ended—nevertheless, there is little actual evidence that this is so. Further, the in-built protection for an innocent proprietor in possession would make such a claim tenuous; the real issue is likely to be the availability of indemnity. After all, in these hypothetical cases, where the original mistaken registration occurred many years ago, there is little merit in allowing the original registered proprietor to recover title (even if schedule 4 allowed it) so long after they had lost it. A more significant issue, it is submitted, is the confusion between the two types of mistake priority contests identified above: *alteration* priority contests and *rectification* priority contests. They should be separate matters, the distinction between them being whether the *mistake* prejudicially affects the title of the current registered proprietor. Unfortunately, because of the clarity—or severity—of the alteration provisions of the LRA 2002, arguments have been made which blur this distinction by seeking to establish that the original registered proprietor retained an interest, and that the new registered proprietor's title was prejudicially affected by the persistence of that pre-existing interest—usually in accordance with the section 29 rule—and not the mistake. The result would be that what looked like a rectification priority contest could be treated as an alteration priority contest—and as such, likely to lead to the return of the title to the original proprietor. This clever use of what seems to be a disposition priority argument in mistake priority contests[70] disrupts the simplicity and clarity of the LRA 2002 scheme. The Court of Appeal's decision in *Swift 1st* dealt with this problem in part by denying that the defrauded original proprietor retained any substantive interest capable of binding in accordance with the section 29 rule (the so-called 'Malory 1' argument).[71] But there remains the 'Malory 2' argument, whereby an alleged 'right to rectify' the Register arises and can bind a transferee in accordance with the section 29 rule, causing the issue to be treated as an alteration priority contest.[72] While the present author thinks that the Malory 2 argument is as flawed as the Malory 1 argument, and that it deserves the same fate, it remains an open issue. This overcomplicates what should, in truth, be a straightforward matter of the application of a clear set of statutory principles in mistake priority contests.

[68] Law Com CP No 2016 (n 1) para 13.101.

[69] ie, that all dealings flowing from the mistaken one are themselves the product of a mistake. See *Gold Harp* (n 27), and the non-binding Adjudicator decisions in *Ajibade v Bank of Scotland plc* [2008] EWLandRA 2006_0163 and *Knights Construction v Roberto Mac* [2011] EWLandRA 2009_1459, [2011] 2 EGLR 123.

[70] See the argument by counsel in *Bakrania* (n 21).

[71] M Dixon, 'Rectifying the Register under the LRA 2002: the Malory 2 Non-Problem' [2016] *Conv* 382.

[72] This led to the complex argument in *Bakrania* (n 21), see M Dixon [2017] *Conv* 161.

V. Priority Contests When Use Challenges Entitlement: Adverse Possession Priority Contests

A main aim of the LRA 2002 was the effective emasculation of adverse possession in relation to registered titles. Portrayed in an exaggerated way as a necessary concomitant of the move to e-conveyancing, this has largely been achieved by the Act. Thus, claims to adverse possession in relation to registered title now concentrate on establishing either that the limitation period expired before the entry into force of the Act on 13 October 2003,[73] or that the claim falls within the exceptional situations identified in schedule 6 where adverse possession might still succeed.[74] Of these, the 'boundary' exception is perhaps the most likely to be in play, not least because of the uncertainty over the reach of the 'estoppel' and 'some other reason' exceptions. In these *adverse possession priority contests*, where the possessor of land challenges the title of the registered proprietor, it is clear that the LRA 2002 favours the priority of the formal owner, rather than the possessor. This is entirely consistent with the approach taken to section 58 in *Swift 1st* and is not inconsistent with the scheme adopted for resolving mistake priority contests.[75]

There are, inevitably, some worries over the way the LRA 2002 deals with adverse possession priority contests, but most of these concern questions of policy rather than how the law is shaped. There are, and always have been, powerful social and economic arguments supporting the transfer of titles from indolent owners to effective users, but the LRA 2002 prefers the certainty, stability and economic security which a *conclusive* title Register brings. The advent, or rather non-advent, of e-conveyancing weighs little in this policy balance. Of course, there are some uncertainties which might usefully be addressed. Apart from clarifying the meaning of the 'reasonable belief' criterion in the 'boundary exception' in paragraph 5 of schedule 6[76] and the role of the 'estoppel' and 'other reasons' exceptions, a lingering problem in adverse possession priority contests is the potential for protracted uncertainty. For claims falling under the LRA 2002, there is no limitation period: the adverse possessor may apply at any time after 10 years and, in essence, the registered proprietor usually gets a further two years to recover possession unless one of the exceptions applies. This has a double effect. First, there is an incentive for adverse possessors *not* to apply for registration because such application will often lead to their eviction. The Act thus actually encourages off-Register possession and the uncertainty this creates. Secondly, whereas the Law Commission think it wise to institute a 'long stop' in mistake priority contests, there is no similar proposal for adverse possession priority contests. An adverse possessor can possess the land for, say 30 years, but at no time are they secure in their possession. While it is a perfectly reasonable policy goal to favour the certainty of the Register against the uncertainty

[73] ie, that 12 years adverse possession had elapsed before that date, so entitling the possessor to title under the LRA 1925, s 75, and the LRA 2002, sch 12, para 18.

[74] LRA 2002, sch 6, para 5.

[75] Although in rectification priority contests, the LRA 2002 clearly favours the person in possession, this is coupled with their registration as proprietor.

[76] LRA 2002, para 5(4)(c); *Zarb v Parry* [2011] EWCA Civ 1306, [2012] 1 WLR 1240; *IAM Group plc v Chowdrey* [2012] EWCA Civ 505, [2012] 2 P & CR 13.

of adverse possession, the *reality* of how the provisions can work should inform the law. There is a risk, inherent in the way that the LRA 2002 currently resolves adverse possession priority contests, that the certainty that schedule 6 seeks to bring will be undermined by the failure to acknowledge—and address—the open-ended effect of its provisions.

VI. Food for Thought

The analysis in this chapter has sought to demonstrate that priority disputes involving registered titles are complex, multi-sided and raise questions of law beyond the interpretation of the LRA 2002. Of course, the Act does provide statutory solutions to certain types of priority contests. But, while it is clear that the Act does not intend to provide a comprehensive priority regime, it is not at all clear that it meets its goal of establishing a 'clear statutory statement'.[77] For this author, that is no surprise, for there is nothing simple about priority contests in relation to registered land and complex situations sometimes need complex rules. However, it should be possible to provide a set of priority rules that are broadly consistent in terms of principle[78] and broadly effective to meet those principles in the light of actual practice. Indeed, given that the LRA 2002 is due for a service, now is the time to consider whether any of the statute's priority rules need to be clarified. The following suggestions are offered as a basis for discussion, not prescription.

(1) It should be clarified whether section 28 incorporates an 'equities are equal' rule.
(2) It should be clarified whether section 28 applies to inter se priority contests which do *not* involve a registered disposition (or an attempted registered disposition).
(3) The effect of losing priority to a registered disposition, under the section 29 rule, should be clarified. A simple solution is to provide that a transfer of a registered title (and derivative interests carved out of it) carries with it the priority that the title enjoyed. This would preserve the effect of unprotected interests against superior titles, but solve the problems caused by the fact that an interest without priority vis-à-vis a registered title might re-emerge to bind a later disponee of that title.
(4) It should not be possible to register an interest, or enter any notice protecting an interest's priority on the Register, where the interest has already lost its priority to the registered title (or derivative interest carved out of it) against which the entry is sought to be made. Necessarily, this would require the Land Registry to investigate priority matters more fully and not to shift this responsibility to the party whose title would be affected by the entry. It would also encourage the Registry to be active in managing the land registration system in the way envisaged when it was first established.
(5) In the same way that interests once protected by a notice cannot re-emerge as overriding interests,[79] any interest which has lost its priority to a registered disposition

[77] Law Com No 271 (n 2) para 5.1.
[78] I am not arguing for any particular type of principled approach, just that whatever principles the system is built on, should be reflected consistently in the priority rules.
[79] LRA 2002, s 29(3).

should not be able to re-emerge as an overriding interest against the registered title acquired pursuant to that disposition (or any derivative estate or interest) on a subsequent disposition—even if that subsequent disposition is not for valuable consideration.

(6) Should priority *inter se* for recorded interests be governed by the date they are entered on the Register by a notice, or is this more of a theoretical rather than a practical problem?

(7) Interests protected by a notice may more properly be regarded as being 'recorded' as indicated by the Law Commission in its 2016 Consultation Paper. But should they also be regarded as valid when so recorded? Should a 'registration guarantee' extend to them?

(8) The meaning of valuable consideration, in the context of the section 29 rule, should be clarified.

(9) The extent of overreaching should be clarified, and in particular, whether two registered proprietors who have been registered by mistake may still effect an overreaching transaction. Consideration might also be given to amending section 2 of the Law of Property Act 1925 to bring more clarity to what type of rights may actually be overreached.

(10) If there is to be a long stop for alteration claims under schedule 4 in favour of the current registered proprietor, should there also be a long stop in favour of the possessor for adverse possession claims under schedule 6? If the goal is title certainty, both would seem appropriate.

(11) The status of the alleged 'right to rectify' should be settled.

(12) The interpretative uncertainties surrounding the 'boundary exception' and the impact of 'reasonable belief' in paragraph 5 of schedule 6 should be resolved.

14

Subrogation, Priority Disputes and Rectification: Mapping a Route Through the Thicket

STEPHEN WATTERSON

I. Introduction

This chapter examines the operation of subrogation within a registered title system, focusing on the concept of 'subrogation to another's *extinguished* rights'.[1] It therefore concerns a substantial body of authorities that exhibit the following general pattern: (1) C-claimant is responsible for discharging a liability owed by D-debtor to X-creditor; and (2) C-claimant is held to be 'subrogated' to X-creditor's rights against D-debtor, including any security that X-creditor held for D's debt. Commonly, C is a disappointed lender, who advanced money to finance a property purchase or refinance existing borrowing, but failed to obtain security of the nature that it required as a condition for its advance. To rescue itself from this dilemma, C may argue that it is entitled in equity, by 'subrogation', to security equivalent to that previously held by X, the earlier creditor paid off via C's advance.

The English courts have proved remarkably generous in assisting C in such circumstances. Previously, the courts might invoke a presumption that C intended to 'keep alive' the prior security interest for its own benefit.[2] However, the landmark decision in the *Banque Financière* case[3] has brought a revolution in our understanding. This new orthodoxy holds that such subrogation is a restitutionary remedy, afforded to reverse the unjust enrichment that would otherwise result, at C's expense, to D-debtor and others from the release of X-creditor's security.

This chapter seeks to shed further light on the operation of such subrogation entitlements *within a registered title system*, and in particular, the system created by the Land Registration Act ('LRA') 2002. What exactly does C acquire, when subrogated to a paid-off creditor's security interest? And, parasitic on the answer to that question, how are priority

[1] See C Mitchell and S Watterson, *Subrogation: Law and Practice* (Oxford, OUP, 2007) ch 1.

[2] eg, *Ghana Commercial Bank v Chandiram* [1960] AC 732 (PC).

[3] *Banque Financière de la Cité v Parc (Battersea) Ltd* [1999] 1 AC 221 (HL); see further *Menelaou v Bank of Cyprus (UK) Ltd* [2015] UKSC 66, [2016] AC 176. Cf *Swynson Ltd v Lowick Rose LLP* [2017] UKSC 32, [2017] 2 WLR 1161 (which did not involve subrogation to a security interest).

disputes involving such subrogation entitlements resolved? Although these are general questions, they present peculiar problems within registered title systems. This chapter's working premise is that two guiding principles should shape the law's development. Subrogation entitlements must arise and operate within the LRA 2002 system in a manner which is: (1) consistent with how they arise and operate more generally, *outside* the LRA 2002 setting; and (2) compatible with, and does not undermine, the LRA 2002's framework and its underpinning policies.

Have the courts or the Land Registry infringed either principle? Not necessarily, but there are risks that they might, if some troublesome lines of analysis are given unwarranted credence. This chapter attempts to chart a course through the thicket that can avoid these pitfalls. To that end, it examines four key questions:

(1) How far would the recognition of subrogation entitlements subvert the LRA 2002's underlying policies?
(2) What is the nature of the entitlement that C acquires, if C is subrogated to a paid-off creditor's security interest?
(3) How are priority disputes between a subrogation entitlement and third party interests to be resolved?
(4) What is the role for alteration/rectification of the Land Register, in the process of effectuating subrogation entitlements?

II. Will Subrogation Subvert the LRA 2002's Framework?

A. Two Potential Pitfalls

Subrogation might be accused of subverting the LRA 2002's framework or underlying policies in two key ways.

i. Undermining the LRA 2002's Ordering of Competing Interests

The first problem is general. It exists to the extent that subrogation entitlements arise and operate in a manner that undermines the LRA 2002's ordering of competing interests affecting registered titles. Subrogation affords C rights affecting a registered title, in the nature of a security interest, *by operation of law*. This is not necessarily incompatible with the LRA 2002's framework. Nevertheless, problems would arise if these rights bound third parties in circumstances that unjustifiably undermined the 'priority promise'[4] embodied in LRA 2002, section 29—whereby prior rights affecting a registered title, which are neither entered in the Register nor 'overriding interests', are postponed to a registered disposition made for valuable consideration. The extent of this risk depends upon the basis on which priority disputes involving subrogation entitlements are resolved.

[4] For this terminology, see A Goymour, 'Resolving the Tension Between the Land Registration Act's "Priority" and "Alteration" Provisions' [2015] *Conv* 253, 254; see further chs 15 and 17 of this book.

ii. Rescuing Parties from Non-Compliance with the LRA 2002's Demands

The second problem is more limited. It is potentially present if C invokes subrogation to relieve itself from the consequences of its own failure to do what the LRA 2002 framework requires.

This problem is most likely in a subset of defective financing transactions, where C-lender advances money to D-borrower to fund the acquisition of property or refinance existing secured borrowing, and does not obtain security of the nature bargained-for. C-lender's expectations of security may be materially disappointed for many different reasons. In almost all instances,[5] the English courts have been willing to assist C-lender, by finding that C-lender is subrogated to X-creditor's security, which was discharged using the loan-monies. However, what if C's expectations of security are disappointed because of the failure of C (or C's agents) to take steps necessary, under the LRA 2002 framework, to ensure that C obtains security of the nature bargained-for?

Imagine that a charge is executed in an appropriate form by D-registered proprietor in favour of C-lender, but that the charge is not submitted by C-lender for registration. This will not cause problems for C, if circumstances do not change before the omission is noticed and registration belatedly occurs. However, what if transactions occur in the meantime, which result in third parties acquiring interests that affect D's registered title, and which (applying the LRA 2002's priority rules) have priority to C's unregistered charge? Can C argue that its failure to obtain security of the nature specified as a condition of its advance, justifies its being subrogated to X-creditor's security, with priority to such later interests?

Anfield (UK) Ltd v Bank of Scotland plc,[6] raised exactly this problem. Applying the *Banque Financière* unjust enrichment analysis, Proudman J concluded that C, the disappointed lender, could make out a subrogation claim: C's failure to register its security interest gave rise to a restitution/subrogation-triggering 'failure of basis', notwithstanding that C had acted negligently. In isolation, this was not *necessarily* a false step in the judge's reasoning. Neither the LRA 2002's underlying policies, nor any other public policy, clearly requires that a 'failure of basis'—caused by C's negligence, or otherwise—should *never* justify C's obtaining a subrogation remedy. The bigger problem is that Proudman J proceeded to afford C's subrogation entitlement a priority status that looks contrary to the LRA 2002's ordering of competing interests. Her decision requires extended analysis.

B. The Difficult Case of *Anfield (UK) Ltd v Bank of Scotland*[7]

i. Background

In 2006, Bank of Scotland (BOS) loaned money to D, a registered proprietor, to redeem a registered charge held by Halifax Building Society, intending to obtain a new first-ranking registered charge as security. BOS received an executed charge from D which was *capable*

[5] cf where C's expectation is defeated by its failure to secure timely registration in the Company Charges Register: *Burston Finance Ltd v Speirway Ltd* [1974] 1 WLR 1648 (Ch); *Smith (Administrator of Cosslett (Contractors) Ltd) v Bridgend CBC* [2001] UKHL 58, [2002] 1 AC 336; Mitchell and Watterson (n 1) paras 7.113–7.115.

[6] *Anfield (UK) Ltd v Bank of Scotland plc* [2010] EWHC 2375 (Ch), [2011] 1 WLR 2414.

[7] ibid.

of being registered as a legal charge. Unfortunately, an oversight meant that BOS failed immediately to procure its registration, and its charge remained equitable. Before the error was noticed and BOS could take steps to rectify the problem, third parties had acquired competing claims to D's registered title. In 2007, LSFL was registered as proprietor of a registered legal charge; and in 2008, Anfield acquired an equitable charge via a charging order which was duly noted in the Register.

D's subsequent bankruptcy made the relative rankings of these security interests crucial. If left to rely on its unregistered equitable charge, BOS would have faced difficulties. *Anfield's* equitable charge might well rank after BOS's prior equitable charge (applying section 28 of the LRA 2002); but BOS's charge would be postponed to LSFL's subsequent registered charge (applying section 29 of the LRA 2002). BOS therefore argued that it was subrogated to Halifax's first-ranking registered charge and on that basis, had priority over *both* LSFL *and* Anfield. The County Court judge, in a decision upheld by Proudman J, held that BOS was entitled to this priority by subrogation. Indeed, the judge apparently proceeded to give effect to this conclusion by ordering that BOS *should be registered as holder of Halifax's first-ranking registered charge*, which formally remained on the Register.

The dynamics of the *Anfield* litigation require comment. Anfield had initiated the proceedings to establish that its equitable charge had priority over BOS's prior unregistered equitable charge. This was destined to fail: section 28 of the LRA 2002 would give BOS's charge priority. Nevertheless, Anfield's claim seemingly caused BOS to respond that it had priority, via subrogation, *over both Anfield and LSFL*. LSFL was then joined as third party. Following BOS's success in the County Court, however, only Anfield appealed. Proudman J was therefore faced with an unmeritorious appellant, and denied the benefit of argument from LSFL, the later *registered* chargee, who had the strongest claim to resist BOS's claim.

ii. Proudman J's Reasoning

How did Proudman J reach her conclusion that BOS was subrogated to Halifax's first-ranking charge? Proudman J took seriously *Banque Financière*'s re-rationalisation of subrogation as a 'restitutionary remedy' afforded by the law to reverse 'unjust enrichment'. As such, she explicitly justified the remedy's availability using the analytical framework and principles of the law of unjust enrichment.

Central to this exercise was Proudman J's identification of the relevant 'unjust factor': a form of 'failure of basis'.[8] She explained that:

> the factor that rendered the enrichment … unjust [was] the non-fulfilment of [BOS's expectation as to] the security [which had formed] the basis [of its decision to advance funds][9]

And more fully, that:

> [t]he enrichment [was] unjust because [BOS] funded the repayment of the Halifax charge on the basis that it would obtain a legal charge. Because of the failure to register under the Land Registration Act it obtained only a subsequent equitable charge.[10]

[8] See esp C Mitchell, P Mitchell and S Watterson, *Goff & Jones—The Law of Unjust Enrichment*, 9th edn (London, Sweet & Maxwell, 2016) ch 12.

[9] *Anfield* (n 6) [34].

[10] ibid [36].

It did not matter that the borrower had performed the terms of the bargain with the lender, as regards the execution of a valid charge in BOS's favour;[11] nor that the only reason why BOS's security expectations were disappointed was BOS's negligent failure to procure registration of its security.[12] A lender's negligence in relation to obtaining the hoped-for security was not, by itself, fatal:

> The court is required ... simply to look at the question of the justice of the enrichment of the defendant[;] [y]ou do not lose your right to resist an unjust enrichment gained at your expense simply because you have been careless in relation to the security.[13]

A sufficient 'failure of basis' was shown merely by proving that BOS did not obtain the expected security, even though this 'failure' was caused by *BOS's* negligent conduct.

So far, Proudman J's reasoning represented a relatively orthodox application of the general law of unjust enrichment. It is generally accepted: (1) that restitution for mistake is not barred merely because the relevant mistaken belief was carelessly formed/held;[14] and (2) that restitution may be available for failure of basis, even where the failure is claimant-precipitated, if the risk of failure occurring for the relevant reason was not a risk which the claimant was meant to bear.[15] Were there nevertheless any special reasons why this particular form of claimant-precipitated failure should not trigger subrogation rights?

An argument along this lines was indeed presented in *Anfield*. Anfield argued that to allow subrogation would 'subvert the policy of the 2002 Act'. Proudman J thought this 'boiled down to [a submission] that the Act forms some sort of conclusive code, enabling those who lend to rely on the position on the face of the register'. She was emphatic in rejecting the argument:

> If that was correct, it would be difficult to claim subrogation in any case of registered land. ... In my judgment the policy of the Act does not encroach on the principle of unjust enrichment. ... [A]ny unfair consequences of subrogation can be dealt with by way of a defence founded on change of position. This is quite different from the cases about moneylenders where subrogation was denied on public policy grounds[.][16]

This reasoning needs careful unpacking.

iii. Would Subrogation Subvert the Policies of the LRA 2002?

When determining whether subrogation would subvert the LRA 2002 in *Anfield*-like circumstances, two questions must be kept separate.

[11] ibid [36].

[12] ibid [29]–[31], relying on statements in *Banque Financière* (n 3).

[13] ibid [30].

[14] eg, *Kelly v Solari* (1841) 9 M & W 54, 152 ER 24; *RE Jones Ltd v Waring & Gillow Ltd* [1926] AC 670 (HL) 688–89; *Barclays Bank Ltd v WJ Simms Son & Cooke (Southern) Ltd* [1980] QB 677, 686–87; *Banque Financière* (n 3) 227, 235, 242–43; *Dextra Bank & Trust Co Ltd v Bank of Jamaica* [2002] 1 All ER (Comm) 193 (PC) [45]. Cf HW Tang, 'The Role of Negligence and Non-Financial Detriment in the Law of Unjust Enrichment' [2006] *RLR* 55. For earlier subrogation decisions consistent with this position, see Mitchell and Watterson (n 1) para 6.64.

[15] See, eg, *Dies v British & International Mining & Finance Corp Ltd* [1939] 1 KB 724; *Rover International Ltd v Cannon Film Sales Ltd (No 3)* [1989] 1 WLR 912 (CA), allowing restitution of advance payments, not construed as deposits, made by a claimant whose breach of contract precipitates termination of the contract by the other contracting party. For earlier subrogation decisions consistent with this position, see Mitchell and Watterson (n 1) paras 6.87–6.90.

[16] *Anfield* (n 6) [38].

The first question is whether there is any necessary incompatibility between the LRA 2002 framework and subrogation rights, such that a lender should *never* be afforded subrogation rights where its expectations of security are disappointed. Authority and principle suggest there is no such necessary incompatibility. It is not even obvious that C's own *negligent* failure to protect its interest, as in *Anfield*, should *automatically* prevent C establishing subrogation rights, based upon its disappointed expectations of security; the contrary view seems unjustifiably penal in effect.

The second question is whether subrogation rights are being recognised in a manner which is inconsistent with the LRA 2002, and in particular, which fails to respect the LRA 2002's mandated priority-ordering. This is the real worry raised by *Anfield*. The main objection was not that the facts should not have triggered subrogation rights at all, but that BOS was claiming an *unjustified priority* for them, given the registered land context. BOS wished to be subrogated to Halifax's first-ranking registered charge, to achieve priority over competing interests *subsequently* acquired by LSFL and Anfield. Priority over Anfield is readily justified. But *LSFL*—as a later *registered* chargee—arguably stood in a different position. Unfortunately, Proudman J's failure to analyse the applicable priority principles yielded a conclusion that, if generalised, seriously threatens the integrity of the LRA 2002 regime.

a BOS's Position *Without* Subrogation

BOS's unregistered charge was an equitable charge. As it was not protected by any entry in the Register at the relevant times, the interests of BOS, LSFL and Anfield would rank as follows:

(i) LSFL's registered charge;
(ii) BOS's unregistered, equitable charge;
(iii) Anfield's equitable charge.

Section 29 of the LRA 2002 would give LSFL's registered charge priority over BOS's charge. In contrast, BOS's charge would have priority over Anfield's later equitable charge via section 28 of the LRA 2002's first-in-time rule.

b. BOS's Position *Assuming* Subrogation: (1) 'Conventional' Analysis

How might subrogation change matters? This is where there is a risk of error, if the rights afforded via subrogation are not well-understood.

The best view[17] is that where C is subrogated to X's security interest, C is not entitled to X's security interest, by transfer or otherwise. Rather, C acquires *new* rights in equity, which presumptively replicate X's rights, as a mechanism for reversing the unjust enrichment that would otherwise accrue to D (the discharged debtor) and relevant others (typically, existing junior creditors and other subordinate incumbrancers) from their release from X's rights.[18] It is controversial whether C immediately acquires an equitable replica of X's security interest, or whether D and others merely become liable in equity to be subject, via a later court order, to legal relations mirroring those that previously existed.[19] Either way, C typically

[17] See section III(A) below.
[18] See esp *Day v Tiuta International* [2014] EWCA Civ 1246 [43]; Mitchell and Watterson (n 1) ch 8.
[19] See section III(A)(iii)(a) below.

acquires an equitable entitlement *in rem*, from the time of the subrogation-justifying facts, whose capacity to affect later parties turns on the priority principles that generally determine the priority-ordering of interests of the relevant kind, in the relevant subject-matter.

In any particular case, this conventional approach requires careful identification of the point in time at which C's entitlement first arose. In *Anfield*, this was not precisely analysed by Proudman J. Assuming that C's entitlement would date from the point when the subrogation-justifying 'failure of basis' occurred, there are two major possibilities, consistent with Proudman J's characterisation of the 'unjust factor' in play.[20] Whichever is assumed, the conventional approach suggests that BOS should not obviously have been any better off via subrogation.

Early Failure, Owing to Non-Registration of BOS's Charge

The first possibility is that the 'failure' occurred at an early stage, simply because of BOS's failure to procure registration of its charge, shortly after it had been executed—an omission which rendered its security, as an unregistered equitable charge, susceptible to future subordination on later dispositions of the affected title by the registered proprietor. Even if, *from that time*, BOS was entitled in equity to a security interest replicating Halifax's security interest, BOS would be no better off. The LRA 2002's priority provisions would arguably yield the same priority-ranking:

(i) LSFL's registered charge.
(ii) BOS's subrogation-based equitable charge.
(iii) Anfield's equitable charge.

For priority purposes, BOS's subrogation-based charge would rank as a new equitable entitlement, dating from the subrogation-justifying facts. This interest, not being protected by any relevant entry in the Register, would be postponed via section 29 of the LRA 2002 to LSFL's later registered charge. However, being earlier in time, it would retain priority via section 28 of the LRA 2002 over Anfield's later equitable charge.

Later Failure, on Later Subordination of BOS's Charge

The second possibility is that the 'failure' only occurred at a subsequent stage, when that risk became a reality—when LSFL obtained a registered charge which took priority to BOS's still-unregistered charge as a result of section 29 of the LRA 2002. In this case, the conventional approach might look even more adverse to BOS. If BOS's subrogation entitlement only arose on LSFL's later acquisition of a superior charge, then it might appear to post-date LSFL's interest—even if only by a split second. LSFL's interest might then take priority in any event under section 28 of the LRA 2002's first-in-time rule.

c. BOS's Position *Assuming* Subrogation: (2) Proudman J's Analysis

Proudman J reached a different conclusion. She seemed to assume that if BOS was subrogated to Halifax's first-ranking charge, then BOS would *necessarily* have priority to Anfield's

[20] See text at nn 8–15 above.

equitable charge *and to LSFL's registered charge.*[21] This is difficult to comprehend, for three reasons—even on the view most favourable to BOS, that it acquired a subrogation entitlement that *pre-dated* LSFL's charge.

First, her conclusions are hard to square with the LRA 2002's priority provisions and with section 29's 'priority promise'. Even if BOS's subrogation entitlement did pre-date LSFL's charge,[22] LSFL could rely on section 29 to establish priority for its subsequent registered charge over any competing earlier interest, unless that earlier interest was an overriding interest or entered in the Register at the relevant time. BOS's subrogation-based entitlement was not an overriding interest. Nor was it protected by entry in the Register. At best, all that relevantly appeared in the Register when LSFL registered its charge was *Halifax's* still-registered charge—an empty shell[23] that fortuitously remained only because BOS had failed to procure its removal and replacement with BOS's newly-registered charge. Prima facie, therefore, there was no basis *within the terms of section 29* for preserving the priority of BOS's subrogation-based entitlement over LSFL's registered charge.

Secondly, Proudman J's general understanding of subrogation, unless treated with caution, risks subverting the LRA 2002 framework. A subrogation claimant should not obtain priority over later interests *merely* because it has been responsible for discharging an earlier, first-ranking registered charge. Priority should only be afforded insofar as the LRA 2002 framework allows for it. Otherwise, the LRA 2002's 'priority promise', and the ability of later parties to rely on the Register, could be unjustifiably undermined. Anfield's counsel raised exactly this objection.[24] Unfortunately, the problem which Anfield faced was that the LRA 2002 framework does not embody any *universal* policy of the sort argued for. Only a subset, albeit a large subset, of parties are currently peculiarly favoured: those, like LSFL, who acquire an interest under a registered disposition for valuable consideration, and can rely on section 29 of the LRA 2002 to establish priority over earlier interests. Otherwise, the logic of the LRA 2002's priority provisions is that later parties like Anfield act at their peril: an earlier unprotected interest, not visible from the Register, prevails.

Thirdly, although there *are* ways of explaining Proudman J's conclusion that LSFL's registered charge was subject to BOS's subrogation entitlement, *despite* the apparent effect of section 29 of the LRA 2002, each raises difficulties.

The Absence of Prejudice, Given Halifax's Subsisting Registered Charge

One 'gut instinct' response is that LSFL suffered no real prejudice *on the facts.* When LSFL acquired its registered charge, a Register search would have revealed Halifax's still-registered charge. In truth, Halifax's charge was an empty shell. Nevertheless, if LSFL was willing to take what *appeared* to be a second-ranking charge, ranking after Halifax's charge, what injustice would be caused by holding LSFL bound by BOS's subrogation-based entitlement, even if it was not discoverable in the Register? LSFL could not have thought that D-borrower had an unencumbered title. Unfortunately, gut instincts do not, without more, constitute a basis for principled judicial determinations. Indeed, the assumption that LSFL

[21] *Anfield* (n 6).

[22] See the text following n 20 above.

[23] The liabilities owed to Halifax were discharged; there was no outstanding liability owed to Halifax which the charge secured.

[24] See section II(B)(ii) above, text following n 15.

was not prejudiced might not be correct. LSFL might have inquired of Halifax/the registered proprietor as to the outstanding indebtedness secured by Halifax's subsisting charge, and been given the answer that there was none.

Parasitic Protection for BOS's claim, via Halifax's Subsisting Registered Charge

A second explanation achieves at least formal consistency with the LRA 2002 framework. On this view, BOS's subrogation-based entitlement would *not* be postponed to LSFL's registered charge via section 29 of the LRA 2002, because the priority of BOS's interest would be deemed to be protected by an entry in the Register in respect of Halifax's subsisting registered charge—a 'parasitic' form of priority protection. In *Bank of Scotland plc v Joseph*,[25] the Court of Appeal recently held that a notice which a lender had entered in respect of an equitable charge could preserve the priority of the subrogation-based entitlement that arose as a result of the charge's invalidity. However, an equivalent argument in *Anfield* requires a greater leap of reasoning. The existing protective entry would be in the name of a *different party* (Halifax)—ie, not that of the subrogation claimant (BOS).

Subrogation Operates via Exact Replication of the Paid-Off Creditor's Priority Position

A third explanation involves an unconventional analysis of how subrogation works, whereby C steps into X-creditor's shoes *in all respects*. Accordingly, if C discharges X-creditor's first-ranking registered legal charge, C occupies exactly the same position via subrogation. C's priority position vis-à-vis subsequent incumbrancers is determined *as if C had a pre-existing first-ranking registered legal charge*. C's subrogation-based entitlement then necessarily prevails over all later parties. Proudman J's decision may implicitly involve such a premise. She suggested that '[i]ntermediate lenders are necessarily enriched by the discharge of a prior security',[26] implying an assumption that C's priority vis-à-vis those parties is necessary to prevent/reverse *their* unjust enrichment. Put differently, the implicit assumption might be that:

(i) if X's charge had subsisted, the third parties *would have been affected by it*;
(ii) the discharge of X's charge has accordingly 'enriched' them, insofar as they are not bound by an interest that would otherwise have affected them;
(iii) to prevent/reverse that 'enrichment', C's subrogation-based charge must have *exactly the same priority as X's charge would otherwise have had*.

There are two possible objections. First, on conventional accounts, subrogation does not work like this. Subrogation-generating facts trigger an immediate equitable replica of X's charge, or a liability in equity to be subject by court order to such a charge. This is the law's response to the enrichment that immediately results from the 'unjust release' of X's charge, to D (the discharged debtor) and relevant others (existing junior incumbrancers). However, C's position vis-à-vis *subsequent* incumbrancers is resolved on the different assumption, that C has a pre-existing equitable entitlement *in rem*, whose priority is determined on conventional principles. Secondly, this unconventional analysis threatens the LRA 2002's

[25] *Bank of Scotland plc v Joseph* [2014] EWCA Civ 28, [2014] 1 P & CR 18.
[26] *Anfield* (n 6) [11].

mandated priority-ordering. Following the analysis to its logical conclusion, if C discharged X's registered charge, a party in LSFL's position might be affected by C's subrogation-based charge even though, when it acquired its own registered charge, *there was no entry affecting the registered title*, in favour of either C or X. That is hard to defend.

Subrogation Affects Third Parties Via 'In Personam', 'Direct Rights'

The last explanation attempts a different reconciliation with the LRA 2002. On this view, the reason why BOS could claim priority vis-à-vis LSFL was not that BOS had an entitlement *in rem*, affecting BOS on conventional priority principles, but that BOS could establish a direct *in personam* right against LSFL, to be treated as if it was the holder of Halifax's first-ranking registered charge, in order to prevent the unjust enrichment that would otherwise accrue *to LSFL* from the release of Halifax's security. The LRA 2002's priority provisions do not rule out *in personam* claims: they determine the priority ordering of *in rem* entitlements. Nevertheless, this analysis looks fragile. It requires an assumption that subrogation works in a dramatically *in personam* fashion—such that, if we wanted to ascertain whether any subsequent party, like LSFL, may be subject to BOS's subrogation claim, we would ask directly whether it is necessary to regulate BOS's position *vis-à-vis that particular defendant* as if BOS was effectively an assignee of Halifax's security, in order to prevent *that particular defendant's* unjust enrichment. However, as Part IV explains, this is an unstable approach, which does not offer a tolerable explanation of how the remedy of subrogation to extinguished rights works.[27] And it might not, in any event, yield the conclusion reached in *Anfield*. Was LSFL really *unjustly* enriched by the release of Halifax's security, at BOS's expense, *if section 29 of the LRA 2002 provided for LSFL's registered charge to have priority?*

d. Wider Implications

The *Anfield* decision involves under-analysed and arguably faulty assumptions. It reached the wrong result, or the right result by a flawed process of reasoning which, if generalised, could seriously undermine the LRA 2002's priority framework. This is not inevitable: subrogation entitlements can arise and operate consistently with the LRA 2002. Nonetheless, for this to be possible, the courts require a clear and stable understanding of the rights that subrogation affords, and of the principles that determine their priority vis-à-vis competing interests.

III. What Rights Does Subrogation Afford?

A. General Principles

A necessary first step for understanding how subrogation operates *within* the LRA 2002 setting must be to understand the rights that subrogation affords under the general law. This is often misperceived.

[27] See further section IV(A)(ii)(c) below, text following n 62.

i. C Does Not Actually Acquire X-Creditor's Rights

First, when C discharges X-creditor's security interest, in circumstances that justify C being subrogated to X-creditor's rights, C does not obtain X-creditor's actual rights, or the benefit of X-creditor's actual rights, by transfer or otherwise.[28] The discharge of X-creditor's rights is a *pre-condition* for the subrogation remedy.[29] As such, 'subrogation to *extinguished* rights' is unlike the more familiar species of subrogation, encountered in indemnity insurance, where an indemnity insurer, having indemnified its insured, is entitled to bring proceedings, in the insured's name, to enforce the insured's *subsisting* rights against third parties.

ii. C is Afforded New and Independent Rights, Replicating X-Creditor's Rights

Secondly, properly understood, the subrogation remedy affords C *new* rights that prima facie replicate the characteristics and content of X-creditor's rights. Previously, courts might talk of X-creditor's security being 'kept alive' in equity for C's benefit,[30] or of C being akin to an 'equitable assignee' of X-creditor's security.[31] However, such statements are at best metaphors, and not literal truths. X-creditor's rights are not actually 'kept alive' for C's benefit.[32] Where such subrogation operates, equity operates on the facts to afford C *new* rights that prima facie replicate the rights which X-creditor previously held, against D and others, and which C's payment extinguished.[33] This is a restitutionary mechanism, which reverses *in specie* the unjust enrichment that would otherwise result, to D and others, from the release.[34]

iii. The Quality of C's Rights

a. An *Equitable* Entitlement Arising Out of Court

Thirdly, the weight of authority suggests that, *from the time of the subrogation-justifying facts*, C has an *equitable* entitlement, ordinarily effective *in rem*, even when X-creditor's rights were *legal* in quality. This was a truth conveyed in older cases via the language that X-creditor's rights were 'kept alive' 'in equity' for C's benefit.[35] If C discharged X's legal charge/mortgage, C was entitled *in equity* to be treated as if it occupied X's position. This did not *technically* mean that C had, or would obtain, a *legal* charge/mortgage. In none of the relevant cases did the court state that C actually had a legal charge/mortgage, or that C was entitled to have such security, by subrogation. Equity apparently regulated C's relations with others *as if* C had such security, even though, in truth, C did not. This was an

[28] esp *Banque Financière* (n 3) 236–37; *Filby v Mortgage Express (No 2) Ltd* [2004] EWCA Civ 755; *Day* (n 18) [43].

[29] *Boscawen v Bajwa* [1996] 1 WLR 328 (CA) 340. See also *Banque Financière* (n 3) 236.

[30] eg, *Chetwynd v Allen* [1899] 1 Ch 353 (Ch) 357; *Butler v Rice* [1910] 2 Ch 277 (Ch) 282; *Chandiram* (n 2) 745; *Western Trust & Savings Ltd v Rock* [1993] NPC 89 (CA).

[31] eg, *Burston* (n 5) 1652; *Western Trust* (n 30).

[32] esp *Banque Financière* (n 3) 236–37.

[33] See esp *Filby* (n 28) [63]; *Day* (n 18) [43], relying on Mitchell and Watterson (n 1) ch 8.

[34] See further S Watterson, 'Modelling Subrogation as an "Equitable Remedy"' (2016) 2(2) *Canadian Journal of Comparative and Contemporary Law* 609, esp Part II, unpacking the *Banque Financière* orthodoxy.

[35] See the cases cited in n 30.

oblique way of expressing the truth that C was afforded *new* rights, *in equity*, which replicated those previously held by X-creditor.[36]

The exact quality of C's equitable entitlement has not been well-analysed. The cases arguably waver between two models of how the subrogation remedy works.[37] The *strong institutional model* suggests that C obtains a fully-formed, vested equitable replica of X-creditor's rights, independently of any court order, either automatically from the time of the subrogation-justifying facts,[38] or on C's exercising a 'power *in rem*', which arose *ab initio*, to bring such rights into being. This has been said to follow from C's entitlement 'in equity' to be treated as if it held the paid-off security.[39] In contrast, the *liability model* assumes that a court's order is necessary for the final crystallisation of C's rights. Subrogation-justifying facts trigger a *liability*, on D and relevant others, to be subjected by court order to legal relations equivalent to those that previously existed, when this is appropriate to reverse the unjust enrichment that resulted from their release. C has a concomitant entitlement to bring proceedings to obtain such an order, but will not acquire enforceable replicas of X-creditor's rights *until* a court determination. Nevertheless, in the meantime, this *liability* to have the court recognise legal relations in relation to D's asset, equivalent to those that previously existed, has effect *in rem*, and renders C's concomitant entitlement a species of equitable *in rem* entitlement, insofar as it can affect third parties who subsequently acquire competing claims to the same subject-matter.[40]

b. The Role of the Court in Subrogated Proceedings

Uncertainty concerning the nature of C's pre-court entitlement is mirrored by uncertainty about the court's role in effectuating C's claim. Two types of order are routinely granted to subrogation claimants. Their effect and significance varies according to the correct model of the remedy.

First, subrogation claimants routinely obtain *declaratory orders*,[41] which declare that they have become entitled to be subrogated to some paid-off security interest, typically dating back to the time it was discharged. The strong institutional model suggests that such orders are merely affirmatory. They are not *necessary* for the creation of C's rights, which pre-date any court's order. They merely confirm that C has previously become entitled in equity to rights replicating X-creditor's rights. In contrast, the liability model suggests that the court's declaration has an essential constitutive effect, in *finally crystallising C's rights*. It transforms

[36] This is not inevitable: the law *could* have developed otherwise, such that C would/could have rights by subrogation of *precisely the same quality*, legal or equitable.

[37] For full discussion, see generally Watterson 'Modelling Subrogation' (n 34) esp Part IV. Note the further question, inadequately addressed in the authorities, whether the nature of the entitlement that C acquires under either of the models discussed here is ever 'power-contingent', in the sense that its existence/crystallisation/enforceability may be contingent on the exercise of some relevant power by C (eg, to rescind a defective transaction under which money is paid, or to obtain rights to some asset consequent upon a tracing exercise): ibid, 653–64. The answer given to this question may affect the *dating* of C's entitlement, and its *quality*—there would be stronger case for regarding C's interest, pending exercise of such a power, as a 'mere equity'.

[38] As assumed in *Halifax plc v Omar* [2002] EWCA Civ 121, [2002] 2 P & CR 26.

[39] ibid.

[40] cf occasional statements that C has an 'equity', or 'equitable property right', which is 'satisfied'/'enforced'/ 'vindicated' by the court's later 'order' for subrogation: in particular, *Boscawen* (n 29) 335, 342; and cf also subsequently, *Omar* (n 38) [81], [82]; *Eagle Star v Karasiewicz* [2002] EWCA Civ 940 [19]; *Day* (n 18) [42].

[41] See Watterson 'Modelling Subrogation' (n 34) Part III.A and Part V.A.1.

C's nascent subrogation entitlement into an enforceable equivalent of X-creditor's rights. C's ultimate position should not, however, differ under the two competing models. Either immediately from the operative facts, or the court's later crystallising order, C is entitled *in equity* to be treated as if it held rights equivalent to those previously held by X-creditor.

Secondly, subrogation claimants also routinely seek *consequential enforcement orders.*[42] These are conventional orders available to holders of standard security interests, according to the bundle of rights/powers conferred by security of that nature, and the ordinary mode(s) of its enforcement (eg, orders for possession, the appointment of receiver, or sale). There is a consistent and uncontested practice that the orders available to subrogation claimants *are those, but only those, available in respect of the discharged security.* This means, on the one hand, that C cannot assert rights/obtain an order that would not be available in respect of security of the nature discharged. For example, if C is subrogated to an unpaid vendor's lien, the available orders are only those ordinarily available to a lien-holder.[43] On the other hand, C can assert rights/obtain any order that would be available in respect of security of the nature discharged, even though such a right/order may not be available as an ordinary incident of an equitable security interest.[44] An equitable charge/mortgage does not characteristically bring a *right* to possession, enforceable out of court or by a court order for possession. Nevertheless, if C discharged another's legal charge/mortgage, which conferred such a right, C may be equivalently-placed, by virtue of subrogation. It is not necessary, to explain that outcome, to assume that C actually holds a legal charge. It is sufficient that equity would regulate C's relations, with D and relevant others, *as if* C had equivalent rights.

B. The Nature of Subrogation Rights Within the LRA 2002 Regime

Must this analysis change within the LRA 2002's registered title system? It is not obvious that C's position should be any different. Nevertheless, some courts have instinctively, without discussion or argument, proceeded differently—granting orders to subrogation claimants that *transform* their subrogation entitlements into something that, in cases *outside* the LRA 2002 framework, C would not have. Is that a false step?

Imagine that X held a security interest which encumbered D's registered title, and which C discharged in circumstances that would justify C's being subrogated to X's position. Imagine further that X's security interest was, alternatively:

(i) an equitable charge;
(ii) a registered legal charge, which was fully paid off and removed from the Register;

[42] ibid, Part V.A.2.

[43] eg, *Thurstan v Nottingam Permanent Building Society* [1902] 1 Ch 1 (CA) 14 (Romer LJ) ('The defendant society, having only an equitable charge, was not entitled to take possession of the mortgaged property. The proper remedy of the society was to obtain a receiver.').

[44] eg, *Western Trust* (n 30); *Castle Phillips Finance Co Ltd v Piddington* (1995) 70 P & CR 592 (CA); *Halifax Mortgage Services Ltd v Muirhead* (1998) 78 P & CR 418 (CA); *Karasiewicz* (n 40); *UCB Group Ltd v Hedworth (No 2)* [2003] EWCA Civ 1717, [2003] 3 FCR 739. Each of these cases seems to manifest an unexamined assumption that C-lender, being subrogated to an earlier paid-off legal charge, was entitled to an order for possession (subject to the normal restrictions).

(iii) a registered legal charge, which was fully paid off but formally remains on the Register; or

(iv) a registered legal charge, which was only partly paid off and formally remains on the Register.

Does the quality of C's subrogation entitlement vary as between these four situations? In particular, in cases (ii), (iii) or (iv), will C's entitlement encompass an entitlement *to a registered (legal) charge*? Three different analyses vie for recognition.

i. C Can Never Become a New Registered Charge-Holder, by Subrogation

The first analysis, most faithful to historic and modern understandings of the remedy, is that C's entitlement is the same *in every case*. Regardless of whether X's interest was an equitable charge or a registered legal charge, and, if a registered legal charge, whether it has been removed from the Register, or formally remains, the nature of C's entitlement is the same. C is not entitled to X's actual rights, or the benefit of X's actual rights: the very assumption on which C becomes entitled to the subrogation remedy is that these rights have, so far as relevant, been extinguished. Instead, by virtue of equity's operation on the facts, or a court's subsequent crystallising order, C acquires a new and independent equitable security interest, which prima facie replicates that previously held by X. This reflects the basic premise on which the subrogation remedy is understood to operate: C is entitled in equity to be treated as if it holds a security interest which replicates the paid-off creditor's. On this view, even when X's charge was a registered legal charge, C's interest is not technically a registered charge, and C has no right to such a registered charge by subrogation. Furthermore, C's interest cannot be converted, by any order of the court, *into* such a charge—whether for the future, or a fortiori, for the past. Within the unregistered title regime, C would not be entitled, via subrogation, to a *legal* charge. The nature of C's entitlement should not be transformed, merely by its translation into the registered title/LRA 2002 regime.

Some cases nevertheless cast doubt on this understanding. Without analysis, they assume that even where C has fully paid off X's registered charge, the court might order that C be registered *as proprietor of that charge*.[45] This has apparently occurred, without comment (1) where fortuitously, X's charge was never formally vacated from the Register;[46] but also (2) where X's charge had been removed from the Register.[47] One example is *Castle Phillips Finance Co Ltd v Piddington*,[48] where C-lender was *sub*-subrogated[49] to an earlier lender's registered charge. The Court of Appeal ordered the Register to be rectified, seemingly to show C as proprietor of the earlier lender's registered charge, *which had been vacated from the Register many years earlier*. Another example is *Cheltenham & Gloucester*

[45] *Piddington* (n 44); *Cheltenham & Gloucester plc v Appleyard* [2004] EWCA Civ 291; *Primlake Ltd v Matthews Associates* [2009] EWHC 2776 (Ch); *Anfield* (n 6). Cf Mitchell and Watterson (n 1) paras 8.113–8.123.

[46] eg, *Appleyard* (n 45); *Anfield* (n 6).

[47] *Piddington* (n 44).

[48] ibid.

[49] For discussion of the concept of 'sub-subrogation', see Mitchell & Watterson (n 1) paras 9.16–9.17; Watterson 'Modelling Subrogation' (n 34) Part III.E.

plc v Appleyard,[50] where C-lender, C&G, was subrogated to B&B's first registered charge, which C&G had paid off. On an application by C&G following a first instance judgment in its favour, the Registrar seems to have rectified the Register to show C&G as proprietor of the B&B charge.

These decisions look surprising. They are susceptible to two different readings.

ii. C Can Be Registered as Holder of X's Charge

One analysis is that the courts really have thought that they can effectuate C's subrogation entitlement by ordering the re-registration of X's charge, in favour of C (if it had been vacated), or its transfer to C (if it subsisted). However, this would be inconsistent with the modern 'orthodoxy', that C does not actually acquire X's rights, or the benefit of X's rights, by subrogation. The subrogation remedy does not 'reverse' unjust enrichment by affording C the actual rights/the benefit of the actual rights that X has/had. As Lord Hoffmann stated in *Banque Financiere*, where a secured debt is repaid, 'the charge is not kept alive at all … [it] is discharged and ceases to exist'.[51] The subrogation remedy does not directly contradict this—literally preserving or bringing back to life X's rights. Equity affords C *new* rights, which prima facie replicate X's rghts, only to the extent that X's rights were extinguished.

Consistently with this, *outside* the registered title/LRA 2002 setting, a court would not have made an order that would have invested C with the legal mortgage/charge previously held by X.[52] A court would just have found that C was entitled in equity to be treated *as if* it had the rights that were discharged. Why should the court's role, and the nature of C's resulting entitlement, be transformed *merely* because the case arises in the registered title/LRA 2002 setting? Whatever should be occurring, it certainly should not be the registration of C as holder of X's registered charge. And it should not matter whether X's charge: (1) had previously been removed from the Register, or (2) was fully paid off but not removed from the Register, or (3) was partly paid off and remained on the Register to secure D's outstanding liabilities to X. In each case, the quality of C's right is the same: a *new* and *independent* right that only arises *to the extent that* the liabilities secured by X's charge were paid off.

iii. C Can Be Registered as Holder of a New Registered Charge, Replicating X's Charge

A less dramatic analysis is that the courts in cases like *Piddington* did not *really* mean that C can be registered as proprietor of *X's* charge. Instead, what they actually meant was that C was entitled in equity to equivalent rights to those previously held by X, and that a court could legitimately give further effect to C's entitlement, *by elevating it to the formal status of a (new) registered charge*. That is, a court might further effectuate C's entitlement to be

[50] *Appleyard* (n 45).

[51] *Banque Financière* (n 3) 234.

[52] cf the Mercantile Law Amendment Act 1856, s 5, which pre-dates modern developments, and which might work on a different premise, out of line with the wider judicially-developed law.

treated in equity as having rights equivalent to X's, by transforming the right, at least for the future, into what, within the LRA 2002 framework, is actually a registered (legal) charge. Whilst the Land Registry might seem to record C as holding *X's* charge, this was not what was intended. It is just a misleading shorthand for the truth: C is entitled, by subrogation, to a *new* registered charge that replicates X's paid off charge.

This alternative analysis looks less obviously wrong. It merely involves the court giving full(er) effect to the entitlement that C is assumed to have: a *new* right, replicating X's. Nevertheless, there are reasons for caution.

Above all, there is little evidence that the courts did/could have achieved a similar transformation of C's rights into a *real* legal charge within the unregistered title system. The courts *might* have decided that C would, by subrogation, obtain a real legal charge/mortgage, or have a right to call on D or the court to grant C a legal charge/mortgage replicating X's charge. However, as already indicated, that was not the basis on which the courts appear to have proceeded. C was treated *in equity, as if* it had an equivalent charge—a process of reasoning that assumes that C does not, actually. If so, and if C would not have—and could not ask the court to grant/order the granting of—an unregistered legal charge within the old unregistered title system, why should matters look different within the LRA 2002's registered title system? Why should the court/Land Registry be able to transform or elevate C's subrogation entitlement into something that C would not otherwise have—a real legal charge?

Three other points might be noted. First, it may not strictly be necessary to transform C's rights in this way. C is entitled in equity to be treated as if it holds a security interest that replicates the paid-off creditor's, vis-à-vis D-discharged debtor, and relevant others. Vis-à-vis *those* parties, C can seemingly rely on the ordinary incidents/advantages characteristic of the security interest paid off.[53] If that is correct, then C may not suffer any significant prejudice because C does not *technically* have a registered charge. Secondly, if transformation is tolerated, there is a risk that the courts/Registry may confuse the process involved—lapsing into the flawed theory that C is *actually taking over* X's rights, and deriving from that unwarranted implications. Thirdly, if C's subrogation-based entitlement is afforded the status of a *registered* charge—a state-guaranteed[54] form of interest—it may thereby obtain greater validity than its juristic origins warrant. C's subrogation entitlement, a remedy afforded to reverse unjust enrichment, may justifiably exhibit greater fragility than a conventional, consensually-acquired charge. A preferable approach, respectful of those origins, is to accept that C's entitlement is an off-Register interest, arising by operation of law, whose priority is merely *protected* by a notice in the Register. Such an entry does not enhance the interest's validity: notice protection does not guarantee an interest's inherent integrity/validity.[55]

[53] See section III (A)(ii) and (iii)(b) above.

[54] For the distinction between 'registrable interests' (whose validity is 'guaranteed') and rights that are merely 'recorded' in the register (whose priority is thereby protected, but whose validity is not thereby 'guaranteed'), see, eg, Law Commission, *Updating the Land Registration Act 2002—A Consultation Paper* (Law Com CP No 227, 2016) paras 2.27–2.31. The precise nature of the 'guarantee' depends upon the extent to which a registered interest is susceptible to removal/qualification by alteration/rectification of the Register (via LRA 2002, sch 4), and the availability of an indemnity for loss suffered in that event (via LRA 2002, sch 8).

[55] LRA 2002, s 32(3).

IV. How are Priority Disputes Resolved?

A. The General Problem

i. Priority Dimensions

Where C discharges D's liabilities to X-creditor, which were secured by a security interest over D's title, there are three categories of third party whose status/priority vis-à-vis C's subrogation-entitlement must be understood. First, immediately before X-creditor's security interest was paid-off, and C's subrogation-entitlement arose, third parties may have held interests that also encumbered D's title: *pre-existing incumbrancers*. These may be other creditors with security interests, or non-creditors with another form of interest (eg a merely equitable/beneficial co-owner). Their interests may have been subject to X-creditor's security interest, or have had priority over it. Secondly, where D's liabilities to X-creditor are not completely discharged, X-creditor remains in the picture: its original security interest will subsist as security for D's outstanding liabilities. Thirdly, other parties may acquire interests affecting D's title *after* X-creditor's security interest was paid off, and C's subrogation-entitlement arose: *subsequent incumbrancers*. They may be, eg, later transferees of D's freehold or leasehold title, or lessees, or other creditors who acquire some form of security over D's title, by grant or otherwise.

ii. Resolving these Problems

How are these problems resolved? Crucially, there is no single, simple answer. Each situation requires a different solution.

a. Pre-Existing Third Party Incumbrancers

This first problem is susceptible to simplest solution, on the authorities and in principle. Where C discharges X's security interest, in circumstances justifying the subrogation remedy, C is ordinarily entitled to be placed in an equivalent position, for the purpose of reversing the unjust enrichment that would otherwise arise, at that time, from the release of X's security, to D and others. As such, C is ordinarily entitled to be treated, from the time of the subrogation-justifying facts, as holding a security interest that inherits the priority-ranking of X's security vis-à-vis pre-existing incumbrances.[56] C's subrogation-based security will therefore be *subject to* pre-existing interests to which X's security was subject (eg, a pre-existing first-ranking charge, where X's security was a second-ranking charge). Conversely, it will have *priority to* pre-existing interests that were subject to X's security (eg, a pre-existing second-ranking charge which ranked behind X's first-ranking charge, or the interest of a beneficial co-owner which was subject to X's charge). This is all that the remedy's rationale requires. The release of X's security improves the position of pre-existing subordinate

[56] eg, *Mortgage Express Ltd v McDonnell* [2001] EWCA Civ 887, [2002] 1 FCR 162; *Karasiewicz* (n 40); *Appleyard* (n 45); *National Westminster Bank plc v Mayfair Estates Property Investments Ltd* [2007] EWHC 287 (Ch); *Kali v Chawla* [2007] EWHC 2357 (Ch), [2008] BIPR 415; *Barons Finance Ltd v Kensington Mortgage Co* [2011] EWCA Civ 1592.

interests—a form of 'secondary' enrichment. Affording C security with priority vis-à-vis those interests is a tailored way of reversing that unjust secondary enrichment *in specie*.[57]

b. X, the Paid-Off Creditor

The second problem, arising where X creditor is only partly paid-off, needs more sensitive treatment.[58] It is sometimes assumed that C can acquire no subrogation entitlement, or no immediately enforceable subrogation entitlement, here, at least before X has been fully paid. However, there is no satisfactory basis in principle for any universal proposition to that effect. Sometimes, it will be inconsistent with a contract between C and X for C to claim subrogation rights at least before X is fully paid. Otherwise, bold statements that C can have *no* subrogation rights until X is fully paid involve a disproportionate response to an understandable concern: that C's subrogation rights might unduly prejudice X's ability to obtain satisfaction for its outstanding claims.

If C indeed obtained, by subrogation, an entitlement to take over X's actual, subsisting security interest, this might seem a real risk: any attempt by C to enforce that security would appear necessarily to compete with, and detract from, X's enforcement ability. However, *Banque Financière* confirms that this is not how this species of subrogation works: C does not acquire X's rights, or the benefit of X's rights; C acquires *new* rights in equity to the extent that X's rights have been diminished.[59] As such, there is no conceptual objection to C's acquiring a security interest, by subrogation, whilst X's security interest subsists. Furthermore, C's new entitlement can be recognised in a form which *does not prejudice X's position*. It is only necessary to assume that C is entitled to a *new* security, which ranks immediately *after* X's security interest, but otherwise replicates the priority-ranking that X's interest had vis-à-vis pre-existing third party interests. There is old authority for this solution,[60] but it also has the support of modern cases.[61] It should, in principle, be preferred.

c. Subsequent Third Party Incumbrancers

The third problem is more resistant to easy resolution. It brings the greatest potential for misunderstanding, and, depending on its solution, the greatest risk of conflict with the LRA 2002 framework. In unpacking the law's approach, one is forced to confront a basic controversy about how subrogation *really* works—a controversy fuelled by Lord Hoffmann's explanation for the remedy's operation in *Banque Financière*:

> [S]ubrogation [...] [is] an equitable remedy against a party who would otherwise be unjustly enriched. It is a means by which the court regulates the legal relationships between a plaintiff and a defendant or defendants in order to prevent unjust enrichment. When judges say that the charge is 'kept alive' for the benefit of the plaintiff, what they mean is that his legal relations with a defendant who would otherwise be unjustly enriched are regulated *as if* the benefit of the charge had been

[57] See further *Goff & Jones* (n 8) paras 39.61, 39.21–39.23; cf previously, Mitchell and Watterson (n 1) paras 8.68, 4.03–4.22.

[58] For full discussion of the dilemmas that arise where X-creditor's secured debts are only partly discharged, see Mitchell and Watterson (n 1) paras 9.50–9.101, 8.80–8.89; and more briefly, *Goff & Jones* (n 8) paras 39.62–39.68.

[59] See esp *Banque Financière* (n 3) 236 (Lord Hoffmann).

[60] eg, *Chetwynd v Allen* (n 30); similarly, *Gedye v Matson* (1858) 25 Beav 310, 312, 53 ER 655, 656 (Romilly MR).

[61] See esp *Banque Financière* (n 3) 235–36 (Lord Hoffmann), and 243–45 (Lord Hutton), where the approach adopted in *Chetwynd v Allen* (n 30) is treated as correct.

> assigned to him. It does not [...] follow that the plaintiff must for all purposes be treated as an actual assignee of the benefit of the charge and, in particular, that he would be so treated in relation to someone who would not be unjustly enriched.[62]

Assuming that subrogation is a remedy that reverses the unjust enrichment that would otherwise result from the release of another's security, what exactly does this mean? Three interpretations, with very different implications, compete for recognition.

An Open-Ended, In Personam Remedial Inquiry

The most radical approach assumes that subrogation works in a dramatically open-ended, *in personam* fashion: to ascertain whether a later party is affected by C's subrogation claim, one asks directly whether, if that party were not so affected, it would be unjustly enriched at C's expense. Followed strictly, this analysis appears disturbingly unstable. C will never acquire what is a conventional right '*in rem*', mirroring X's entitlement. Whether and how far C should be treated as equivalently-placed to X would fall to be decided by the answer to an open-ended, *in personam* inquiry: is it necessary in the circumstances to regulate C's position vis-à-vis *this particular defendant*, as if C were an assignee of X's security, to prevent this particular defendant's unjust enrichment? It seems very unlikely that this really was what Lord Hoffmann meant. It is inconsistent with long-standing authority and numerous post-*Banque Financière* cases, which proceed on the assumption that C acquires a real entitlement *in rem*, in the nature of a fully-fledged security interest, by subrogation.

An Entitlement in Rem; Complete Replication of X's Priority Position

The second approach assumes, more conventionally, that C is entitled to a security interest by subrogation. However, it then also takes the bold further step of assuming that the priority position of C's interest should replicate the priority position of X's interest *in all respects*. As such, C's interest will not only inherit X's priority-ranking vis-à-vis pre-existing incumbrancers, which were subject to X's interest at the time of its discharge. C can *also* claim the same priority vis-à-vis later interests *as X's interest would have had, if it had not been discharged*. Followed strictly, this approach has dramatic implications. X's charge is typically a registered charge. Being registered, it would ordinarily prevail, pursuant to sections 28 and 29 of the LRA 2002, against *any* interest subsequently acquired over the relevant registered title. The logic of this second approach suggests that C would claim *the same priority* for its subrogation-based charge.

This is one way of rationalising Proudman J's approach in the *Anfield* case, where BOS, which was subrogated to Halifax's first-ranking registered charge, was thought to be entitled to priority vis-à-vis LSFL, a later registered charge-holder. Proudman J assumed that BOS could claim the same priority as Halifax had, seemingly on the basis that, subject to LSFL showing that it suffered prejudice amounting to a change of position defence, this priority was necessary to reverse the 'unjust enrichment' that would otherwise accrue to intervening incumbrancers, including LSFL, from the release of Halifax's prior charge. But for its release, Halifax's charge would have continued as a first-ranking registered charge. Any later party—including a party who, like LSFL, could rely on section 29 of the LRA 2002—would

[62] *Banque Financière* (n 3) 236.

have been subject to it. To negate, inter alia, the advantage that LSFL would otherwise obtain, if its charge prevailed, BOS's subrogation-based charge would have exactly the same priority as Halifax's security would have had, but for its discharge.

This analysis cannot be accepted, except at the cost of subverting the LRA 2002's priority framework. Generalised, it means that C can assert its subrogation-based charge, which was not the subject of any entry on the Register, vis-à-vis any later party who would have been subject to X's security, *if* it had remained in existence on the Register—even though the LRA 2002's priority framework would suggest that any entitlement that C might have, being *actually* not on the Register at the relevant time, should be postponed. This would seriously undermine the Register's reliability. It is also difficult to see how this theory works, even when judged within its own terms. A third party, like LSFL, would otherwise take title clear of an interest like that of C—which was neither entered in the Register nor an overriding interest—via section 29 of the LRA 2002. How can this outcome—which is specifically mandated by the LRA 2002 to ensure the reliability of the Register and the security of registered dispositions—involve an *unjust* enrichment to the later party?

A New Equitable Entitlement in Rem; Priorities Independently Determined

A third approach should ultimately prevail. It resolves C's position vis-à-vis later third-party incumbrancers on a more conventional, property law basis. As such, the courts should proceed on the basis that C acquires a *new* equitable entitlement *in rem* as the subrogation-justifying facts occur, and that the priority of that entitlement falls to be determined on that basis, according to conventional property law principles: ie, using the principles that are conventionally used to determine the relative priorities of rights of the relevant quality, affecting that particular subject-matter. This allows C's position to be ascertained on a stable basis, compatible with prevailing priority frameworks.

This third approach is the approach which is overwhelmingly supported by authority.[63] There is, however, some room for disagreement about the exact nature of this equitable entitlement '*in rem*', reflecting a larger theoretical disagreement about the operation of the subrogation remedy, discussed above.[64]

One analysis, clearly evident in *Halifax plc v Omar*,[65] reflects a *strong institutional model*: C is assumed to acquire a fully-formed equitable replica of X's rights from the time of the subrogation-justifying facts. On that basis, C is assumed to have a full equitable interest, and not anything less. In contrast, the alternative *liability model* assumes that as subrogation-justifying facts occur, D (the discharged debtor) and others (eg existing junior incumbrancers) only come under a liability, enforceable by C, to be subject by court order to legal relations replicating those that previously existed. Adopting this view, a court order is *necessary* for the final crystallisation of that nascent entitlement into a fully-formed equitable replica of X's rights. What is C's priority position in the intervening period? The cases suggest that the liability to the remedy exists *in rem*, insofar as it can affect third parties who subsequently acquire competing interests in the same subject-matter. However, the law faces a choice, as regards whether this liability *in rem*—and therefore

[63] See esp *Chandiram* (n 2); *Boscawen* (n 29); *Omar* (n 38); *Appleyard* (n 45) [44]; *Joseph* (n 25).
[64] See section III(A)(iii)(a) above, and Watterson 'Modelling Subrogation' (n 34) esp section IV.B.
[65] *Omar* (n 38).

C's concomitant *in rem* entitlement—affords C a full equitable interest, or only a lesser mere equity. There is no pre-ordained, logically correct answer. Happily, for the purposes of this chapter, any uncertainty about what model operates, and its implications, has limited importance. C holds either a full equitable interest or a mere equity, out of court, from the time of the subrogation-justifying facts.[66] Even if C's pre-court entitlement was a mere equity, it would still qualify as an 'interest capable of binding successors in title', and be subjected by the LRA 2002 to the same priority framework as a full equitable interest.[67]

How might this third approach work in practice?

B. Resolving Disputes with Subsequent Interest-Holders

i. Introduction

The parameters of the priority problems raised by subrogation claims should now be clearer. The first stage is always to ascertain whether facts have occurred that justify C's being subrogated to X's security interest. Where this is the case, C ordinarily has some species of equitable entitlement *in rem*, dating from the subrogation-justifying facts. The second stage is to then determine the priority implications of that starting-point. This requires the application of conventional property law principles: identifying and applying the priority rules conventionally used to resolve a competition between interests of the relevant quality, affecting the relevant subject-matter. Where the competing interests affect a *registered* title to land, the primary reference-point is the LRA 2002's priority regime, contained in sections 28 and 29. However, a closer inquiry reveals some hidden complexities.

ii. Achieving Priority For C's Entitlement Over Later Interests

Applying section 28 of the LRA 2002, C's interest, created first in time, will presumptively prevail over *any* later interest. Nevertheless, C's interest is clearly vulnerable to later dealings with the registered title that attract the application of section 29 of the LRA 2002—namely registr*able*, and subsequently register*ed*, dispositions made for valuable consideration. The activation of section 29 may lead to the postponement of C's interest to the later registered disposition. On what assumption might the priority of C's interest be protected vis-à-vis such transactions that activate section 29?

a. Direct Protection

C can certainly protect its subrogation-based interest via a notice in the Register. This should ensure priority against any later interests, including later registered dispositions of the relevant title.

[66] Note also what is said in n 37 above about the under-examined possibility that the interest that C acquires via either model may sometimes be 'power-contingent', such that its existence/crystallisation, or at least enforceability, may be contingent on the exercise of some relevant power by C (eg, to rescind a defective transaction under which money is paid, or to obtain rights consequent upon a tracing exercise). This answer given to this question may affect the *dating* of C's entitlement, and its *quality*—there would be stronger case for regarding C's interest, pending exercise of the power, as a 'mere equity'.

[67] LRA 2002, s 116; Law Commission, *Land Registration for the Twenty-First Century—A Conveyancing Revolution* (Law Com No 271, 2001) paras 5.32–5.36.

Such priority is wholly consistent with the LRA 2002 framework. However, some cases go further than this, and generously permit C a form of *parasitic* priority protection. Here, C's priority is not protected by an entry *specifically* designed to protect the priority of C's subrogation-based interest. Instead, C's priority is protected parasitically, because it is treated as preserved vis-à-vis later registered dispositions *by some other entry in the Register.*[68] Whether this is proper ultimately depends on whether the decision to afford C's interest priority over the third party's interest illegitimately contradicts the priority promise which the LRA 2002's main body offers via section 29. Several different forms of parasitic protection require consideration.

b. Parasitic Protection: Entry of Notice by C in Respect of a Defective Charge

First, C might enter a notice in respect of an equitable charge which C *believed* was valid, but which is actually invalid. This deficiency may in turn justify C being subrogated to an earlier paid-off creditor's security. Unfortunately, if unaware of the problem, C will not enter a notice *specifically* to protect the priority of its subrogation-based interest. Will it therefore be postponed to an intervening registered disposition by section 29 of the LRA 2002? Or can C rely on the notice entry in respect of the defective charge, to gain 'parasitic' priority protection for the subrogation-based interest, which arose because of the deficiency in the charge which C intended that notice to protect? The Court of Appeal's recent decision in *Bank of Scotland plc v Joseph*[69] suggests that C can do so. Is this justified? This reading certainly erodes the extent of the immunity afforded by section 29 of the LRA 2002 to registered disponees, and it subjects them to C's subrogation-based charge, without the benefit of an indemnity. But perhaps the third party cannot really complain, insofar as: (i) a Register-search would have suggested that there was a prior charge held by C; and (ii) C's subrogation-based charge would certainly not exceed, in nature and quantum, what C had bargained-for and believed it had obtained.

c. Parasitic Protection: Registration of a Charge by C, Which Proves Defective[70]

Secondly, more commonly, C will obtain a *registered* charge which subsequently proves to be defective. If the charge had been valid, any intervening party would have taken subject to the charge by virtue of its registration. But what if the charge is invalid, in circumstances that entitle C to be subrogated to an earlier creditor's security. Can a later registered disponee argue that, whilst it would be subject to C's *registered* charge, if valid, it will *take free* of C's 'unprotected' subrogation-based entitlement?

No case has yet directly addressed this problem, but it could have arisen in *Filby v Mortgage Express (No 2) Ltd.*[71] ME advanced money to Mr and Mrs Filby, to discharge an existing first registered charge over their co-owned home, on the condition of its acquiring a new first registered charge. The earlier charge was discharged, and ME was registered as proprietor of a new registered charge. Later, HSBC obtained a second registered charge over

[68] *Joseph* (n 25) (notice protecting ineffective charge). Cf *Filby* (n 28) (ineffective registered charge). See further Mitchell and Watterson (n 1) paras 8.124–8.128.

[69] *Joseph* (n 25).

[70] cf Mitchell and Watterson (n 1) paras 8.124–8.128.

[71] *Filby* (n 28).

the property, for the couple's valid debts. After default on ME's loan, it was realised that Mrs Filby's consent to ME's loan/charge had been forged. This could present the following conundrum. HSBC, as a later registered chargee, would take its interest subject to ME's forgery-tainted first registered charge. However, an application by Mrs Filby, to have the Register rectified to cancel ME's charge, would almost certainly succeed. The same circumstances might entitle ME to a charge by subrogation to the earlier, paid-off creditor's valid registered charge, effective against Mr and Mrs Filby; but this subrogation-based charge would not have been directly protected by any entry on the Register when HSBC's charge was registered. Could HSBC rely on section 29 of the LRA 2002, to take free of ME's unprotected subrogation-based interest?

That would appear a rather unmeritorious argument. In taking its registered charge, HSBC cannot have assumed that the couple's title was unencumbered: the Register would show ME as first-ranking registered chargee. Allowing HSBC priority would look even more objectionable, if HSBC was only able to acquire its own registered charge because, without any intention to cede priority, ME had consented to its creation/registration.[72] There are several possible ways of avoiding this unappetising conclusion. First, and most straightforwardly, the courts might allow the entry in respect of C's (here ME's) defective registered charge to afford parasitic protection to the subrogation-based right that arose because of its unknown invalidity. This would follow from *Joseph*,[73] extended to include (defective) registered charges, and not only notices relating to (defective) equitable charges. Secondly, to similar general effect, the courts might adopt a principle that where a later incumbrancer would have taken subject to C's security, if valid, it is estopped from denying priority to any subrogation-based charge that was triggered by the unknown ineffectiveness of C's security. Thirdly, more narrowly, if the later incumbrancer's security only achieved its status as a registered charge because C had consented to its registration[74] under the mistaken assumption that it would be subordinate to C's registered charge—and therefore without any intention to cede priority—priority for C's security might perhaps be justified as a way of reversing the later incumbrancer's unjust enrichment at C's expense. Fourthly, C might seek similar priority by the more indirect route of rectification, relying on the Registrar's/court's jurisdiction to 'correct' a 'mistake'.[75]

d. Parasitic Protection: Continuation of X's Charge's Entry in the Register

A final situation, which effectively arose in the *Anfield* case,[76] is even more challenging. Imagine that C is subrogated to X's registered charge, which was paid off but not formally cancelled from the Register. There is no entry in the Register *in C's* name, which protects the priority of any interest C might have vis-à-vis later registered disponees. However, does

[72] This situation could in theory arise if the underlying registered title, subject to ME's charge, had been subject to a 'restriction' (see LRA 2002, ss 40–47), which purported to prevent the registration of any dealing by the registered proprietor, without the consent of ME, as charge-holder.

[73] *Joseph* (n 25).

[74] For explanation of this possibility, see n 72 above. Cf the unsuccessful argument, based upon a mistaken consent to registration by the holder of an equitable charge 'protected' by a restriction, in the more complex factual configuration involved in *Barons Finance* (n 56).

[75] See further section V(D) below.

[76] *Anfield* (n 6).

the fortuitous continuance of the entry in respect of *X's* charge, *in X's name*, change the equities? Intuitively, one might think that there could be a difference. A later registered disponee could not have legitimately assumed, based upon any inspection of the Register, that the property was unencumbered: a Register-search would have disclosed that a charge subsisted. Unless the later disponee had inquired of X, the registered charge-holder, and was led to believe that it was an empty shell, it is not obvious that a later registered disponee would be seriously prejudiced, if it were subject to C's interest. The relevant title *appeared* to be encumbered, and if the later disponee indeed proceeded without inquiry, it arguably accepted the risk that it might have a subordinate interest.

How might this conclusion be reached, if desired? One obvious option is to argue for 'parastic protection', by analogy to that allowed in *Joseph*: the priority of C's interest is protected *parasitically on the enduring registered status of X-creditor's right*. Would this nevertheless be a step too far? The subsisting entry here is not in C's name. As such, and unlike the entry in *Joseph*, it would not direct a person searching the Register *to the person claiming the relevant, parasitically-protected right*.

One advantage of this solution to *Anfield*-like facts is that it meets the justice of the case, without requiring any blanket recognition that C's subrogation-based interest has identical priority *in all respects* to X's charge—ie, as if X's registered charge remained, even where it did not. It only involves recognising the reality that where X's empty charge fortuitously remains on the Register, a third party's legitimate expectations may not be substantially defeated if C's subrogation-based right, which arose from the discharge of X's charge, is afforded parasitic priority protection. The equities look rather different if X's registered charge *had been de-registered*, after X was paid off, and before any later registered disposition in favour of a third party. There would then be no Register-entry suggesting that the relevant title was encumbered, in favour of X or C. As a result, there would be no obvious basis for finding that a later registered disponee, who could rely on section 29 of the LRA 2002, should be subject to C's subrogation-based right. To enhance its priority position, C would need to rely on some highly-contestable arguments grounded on the Registrar's/court's jurisdiction to alter/rectify the Register.[77]

V. What is the Role for Alteration/Rectification?

A. Introduction

The final task for this chapter is to examine the role for alteration/rectification of the Register in effectuating subrogation rights.[78] What might C subrogation claimant stand to gain from an application to have the Register altered/rectified to reflect—or give further

[77] See further section V(D) below.

[78] Contrast cases where alteration/rectification of the Register may be a *trigger* for subrogation, because it is the event that defeats the lender's security-expectation—eg, if rectification of a forged disposition to B leads to cancellation of B's registered title, and the further consequence that the registered charge granted by B to C, to secure borrowing from C, falls away: cf *Nouri v Marvi* [2005] EWHC 2996 (Ch), [2006] 1 EGLR 71.

effect to—its subrogation entitlement? This area is littered with potential traps.[79] In the absence of reasoned decisions, it is necessary to return to first principles. Two basic situations require exploration: where X's charge was a merely equitable charge; and where X's charge was a *registered (legal)* charge. What might be achieved, in either case, within the LRA 2002's jurisdictional parameters of 'bringing the register up-to-date' or 'correcting a mistake'?[80] The best answer is 'relatively little', and certainly less than the courts sometimes seem, without analysis, to have assumed.

B. The Origin and Nature of C's Interest

Where C has paid off an earlier *equitable* charge affecting D's registered title, in circumstances triggering subrogation, C may be entitled to an equivalent charge by subrogation. No Register entry is required to bring C's interest into being. It would arise in accordance with general principles of law and subsist 'off-Register'.

Less obviously, the position is no different, where C paid off an earlier *registered* charge affecting D's registered title. C's subrogation entitlement is the result of *equity's* intervention. Equity treats C *as if* C held X's paid-off charge, although C does not. As such, C has a new and independent equitable charge that prima facie replicates X's paid-off charge. This is so even when X's paid-off charge was a registered charge, and irrespective of whether X's paid-off charge has been de-registered or formally remains. Following this line of analysis, as where X's paid-off charge was a merely equitable charge, no entry in the Register is required to bring C's subrogation entitlement into being. It arises and subsists *independently* of the Register. Furthermore, the better analysis is that C cannot obtain a registered charge by this process of subrogation—neither X's previous registered charge, nor any new registered charge, replicating X's charge. C's only entitlement is to be treated *in equity as if* C held an equivalent charge.

If these suggestions are correct, then some courts have erred in assuming that they can order C to be recorded as holder of a registered charge—and *a fortiori* of X's registered charge—pursuant to C's subrogation entitlement. That cannot be justified in order to 'bring the register up to date': that would require the false assumption that *C had become entitled to a registered charge.* It also could not be justified on the basis that it is required to 'correct' any 'mistake' by the Land Registry.[81]

[79] cf Mitchell and Watterson (n 1) paras 8.115–8.123.

[80] LRA 2002, sch 4, paras 2(1)(a), (b) (alteration pursuant to a court order) and 5(a), (b) (alteration otherwise than pursuant to a court order). For extended general discussion of the proper interpretation of these provisions, see *Ruoff and Roper: Registered Conveyancing* (London, Sweet and Maxwell, looseleaf) ch 46, and the growing academic literature, including E Lees, 'Title by Registration: Rectification, Indemnity and Mistake and the Land Registration Act 2002' (2013) 76 *MLR* 62; S Cooper, 'Regulating Fallibility in Registered Land Titles' [2013] *CLJ* 341; A Goymour, 'Mistaken Registrations of Land: Exploding the Myth of "Title by Registration"' [2013] *CLJ* 617; S Cooper, 'Resolving Title Conflicts in Registered Land' (2015) 131 *LQR* 108.

[81] See, eg, *Ruoff & Roper* (n 80) para 46.009, which adopts the commonly-held view that the statutorily-undefined ground of 'correcting' a 'mistake' in sch 4, LRA 2002, requires a mistake by the Land Registry, and that this might exist where the Registrar: makes an entry in the Register that he would not have made; makes an entry in the Register that would not have been made in the form in which it was made; fails to make an entry in the Register that he would otherwise have made; or deletes an entry that he would not have deleted, had he known the true state of affairs at the time of the entry or deletion.

One variety of 'mistake' that has recently been recognised as potentially rectification-justifying under schedule 4 is the Land Registry's 'mistake' in de-registering an existing registered interest (eg a freehold/leasehold estate).[82] Consistently with this, one can imagine an argument being advanced in a subrogation case that the Land Registry may have made a 'mistake' in de-registering X-creditor's registered charge, which should instead have been 'kept alive' for C's benefit, and that this justifies C becoming registered as holder of X's charge. The flaws in this reasoning may be obvious. It is difficult to see how X's de-registration is a 'mistake', and *a fortiori*, a 'mistake' that should be corrected by recording *someone else* as holder of the relevant charge. X, the paid-off creditor, received funds in discharge of liabilities owed to it by D. As between X and D, this discharge was intended and effective. Indeed, the discharge of X's rights is the very thing that justifies the generation of *new* rights in favour of C, the subrogation claimant.

C. The Priority of C's Interest Vis-à-Vis Pre-Existing Interests

There is also no material distinction, when it comes to the priority of C's interest vis-à-vis pre-existing interests, according to whether X's charge was a merely equitable charge or a registered charge. In either case, no entry in the Register is required to ensure that C's interest is effective vis-à-vis D-discharged debtor and/or subordinate incumbrancers, who held subordinate interests at the time X-creditor's charge was discharged.

In principle, C's ability to assert rights against *those* parties does not depend on C's interest being a proprietary interest, which affects them in accordance with ordinary priority principles. It depends on the circumstances: (i) that those parties were previously affected by X's charge, as debtor/chargee and/or junior incumbrancer; and (ii) that, as a result of paying off X's charge, C has obtained new rights against them, as a remedy to reverse their unjust (primary and secondary) enrichments. These new rights comprise a charge, prima facie inheriting the priorities of the old, and are effective vis-à-vis those parties *without entry in the Register*. It is not strictly necessary, therefore, in order to secure C's position vis-à-vis those parties, for C to have the Register altered to note the existence of its subrogation-based charge as adversely affecting the debtor/chargor's registered title and as having priority over the junior incumbrancers. At best, C might seek such alteration, if possible, in the interests of *transparency*. This would 'bring the register up to date' to reflect *off-Register events*—ensuring that the Register accurately reflects subsequent circumstances that have adversely affected the interests of the relevant parties. Several further consequences would quite properly follow. Alteration would have to be ordered unless exceptional circumstances justified not making the alteration;[83] there would be no special protection for any registered proprietor in possession;[84] and no indemnity would

[82] See, in particular, *Barclays Bank v Guy (No 2)* [2010] EWCA Civ 1396, [2011] 1 WLR 681; *MacLeod v Gold Harp Properties Ltd* [2014] EWCA Civ 1084, [2015] 1 WLR 1249.

[83] Land Registration Rules 2003, r 126(1), (2).

[84] cf LRA 2002, sch 4, para 3(2) (court order), para 6(2) (Registrar order), a restriction which applies only to instances of 'rectification', a species of 'alteration' that involves the 'correction' of a 'mistake' in a manner that prejudicially affects the title of a registered proprietor: LRA 2002, sch 4, para 1.

be available under schedule 8 to the debtor/chargor and junior incumbrancer, who are adversely affected.[85]

D. The Priority of C's Interest Vis-à-Vis Intervening Interests

There is also, finally, no material distinction to be drawn, when it comes to the priority of C's interest vis-à-vis intervening interests arising *after* X's charge was discharged, according to whether X's charge was a merely equitable charge or a registered charge. In either case, C's position would be decided according to the same basic priority premises, elaborated earlier.[86] They can be summarised as follows.

Analysis should proceed on the basis that C acquired a form of equitable entitlement *in rem* as the relevant subrogation-justifying facts occurred. C's priority vis-à-vis later interests is determined by applying the general priority rules of the LRA 2002 regime, on that assumption. As such, C's interest should have prima facie priority vis-à-vis later interests via section 28 of the LRA 2002, but it would be postponed to a later registered disposition that triggered section 29 of the LRA 2002, unless it was relevantly 'protected' at the appropriate time. In principle, the priority of C's interest can be protected directly, for the future, via a notice entered against D's registered title. Beyond this, courts may find the priority of C's interest to be protectable *indirectly*, via a form of 'parasitic' protection, based upon some other entry in the Register, as discussed above.[87] It is unclear how far they will go in this regard. Insofar as parasitic protection is recognised, it would certainly seem appropriate to allow 'alteration' of the Register to reflect the 'truth' and bring the Register 'up to date'. This might involve replacing the entry that affords parasitic protection, with a notice that directly refers to and protects C's *subrogation* entitlement—eg, amending a relevant notice to refer to C's *subrogation*-based interest, rather than any interest which was previously directly protected in that manner.

Ultimately, the most difficult question is whether C could ever achieve, via alteration/rectification of the Register, *priority which C could not otherwise claim* in accordance with the general priority rules of the LRA 2002 regime, or other principles of law (eg, some priority arrangement with D's other creditors). In particular, could C, via the court's/Registrar's jurisdiction to alter/rectify the Register, obtain priority vis-à-vis an intervening interest to which C's interest would otherwise be subject?

In practice, this would probably involve C seeking 'rectification' to achieve priority over a later party who seeks to rely on section 29 of the LRA 2002's priority promise. Any amendment with that effect would almost certainly need to be justified as a form of 'rectification', appropriate to 'correct' a 'mistake' in the Register. It would also raise the thorny question, addressed in *MacLeod v Gold Harp Properties Ltd*,[88] whether rectification can re-order

[85] See LRA 2002, sch 8, para 1(1)(a), (b), which provides for an indemnity if a person suffers loss by reason of 'rectification' of the Register, or by reason of a mistake whose correction would involve 'rectification' of the Register. An alteration that merely brings the Register up to date, and does not amount to 'rectification' (see n 84 above), does not trigger this right to an indemnity: eg, *Ruoff & Roper* (n 80) para 46.006.

[86] See section IV(B)(i) and (ii) above.

[87] See section IV(B)(ii)(b), (c), and (d) above.

[88] *Gold Harp* (n 82).

priorities retrospectively, or at least prospectively from the date of any rectification order. It is impossible at this stage to predict the exact form in which such an argument might be raised. But some testing examples can be contemplated.

A simple configuration would be where C sought a notice to protect the priority of its subrogation entitlement, and the Land Registry entered the notice against the wrong title. C could no doubt seek alteration of the Register, to correct this error—removing the notice from the wrong title, and entering it against the correct title. Greater difficulty might arise if, prior to this correction in the Register, there was an intervening registered disposition in favour of a third party which attracted section 29 of the LRA 2002. Prima facie, the interest created by that registered disposition would be free of C's interest, which at the relevant time, was not relevantly protected in the Register or otherwise overriding. However, the *Gold Harp*[89] case recently suggests that a court might, as part of the process of 'correcting' the mistake, effectively re-order priorities—at least prospectively, from the date of the court order. On that controversial assumption, C might seek an adjustment to the Register that would afford its entitlement priority vis-à-vis the later registered disposition.

More complex configurations can be envisaged. For example, imagine that C has been granted a forged charge, which is registered, and that the money C has loaned has been used to pay off X-creditor's secured loan. It later turns out that C's charge is ineffective. The Registrar should not have registered the forged charge; the appropriate entry would instead be a notice to protect C's subrogation-based entitlement, generated in the same circumstances. It is harder here to say that the Registry has made a 'mistake' in *omitting* to make an alternative notice entry in respect of the subrogation-based charge, which might be appropriately 'corrected' by making such an entry.[90] However, even if—which seems unlikely—that leap could be made, difficult questions would then arise if there was an intervening registered disposition that attracted section 29 of the LRA 2002. How might that situation be resolved? One solution would be to say that in this case, the priority of C's subrogation-based entitlement is protected parasitically, via the entry in respect of its forged charge—a solution that does not require any strained reading of the rectification jurisdiction, but that would deny the third party the benefit of any indemnity. An alternative would be to follow *Gold Harp*, and allow for the possibility that rectification might be ordered to enter a notice of C's subrogation-based entitlement against D's registered title, and in a manner that gives C's entitlement, at least for the future, priority over the intervening third party disposition.

Some of this reasoning is clearly strained. Furthermore, it will only sporadically improve C's priority position. Its viability requires a relevant qualifying act/omission of the Land Registry, presumably in response to an application made to it, which can be regarded as 'mistaken'. The examples already given are easy illustrations. In each case, the *Registry* made

[89] ibid. For analysis, see, eg, Goymour, 'Resolving the Tension' (n 4); E Lees, 'Rectification of the Register—Prospective or Retrospective' (2015) 78 *MLR* 361.

[90] It would require a rather expansive reading of sch 4 to say that there may be a qualifying 'mistake', in failing to enter such a notice, either: (a) at the the time when the forged charge was first registered, or (b) at any later point when the previously-registered forged charge is deleted from the Register. It would require an assumption that the Registrar at either point, without any request/application, and potentially without sufficient information as to the underlying facts, should then have entered a notice to protect the resulting equitable subrogation-based entitlement.

an inappropriate entry—registering a notice against the wrong title, or registering a forged charge when it should have made an entry in respect of the subrogation-entitlement that arose on the same facts. Other problematic financing transactions will not exhibit this feature. Often, C is granted an interest that is, at least at the time of registration, a duly-registered charge. The only problem is that C receives something other than C expected, from the point of view of priority—eg, because C finds its charge is encumbered by a pre-existing beneficial interest, whose priority is protected by the occupation of the interest-holder.[91]

One last point needs to be made. One possible benefit of an expansive view of rectification as a mechanism for improving C's priority position—relative to other mechanisms such as 'parasitic protection'—is that if C's enhanced priority vis-à-vis later interests can be attributed to the rectification process, this can trigger an indemnity for those adversely affected by rectification.[92] C might then obtain priority, and the Land Registry would foot the bill for the prejudice that results to third parties, except insofar as the third party was fraudulent or carelessly responsible for the problem.[93]

VI. Conclusions

Close analysis of the operation of subrogation rights within the LRA 2002 regime reveals three problems that future courts will need to be careful to avoid.

First, the courts, and potentially the Land Registry, run the risk of unthinkingly affording subrogation-claimants rights that may be *unjustified*—being more extensive than are strictly warranted, once the jurisdictional basis of subrogation is understood. We may not recognise the difference if the paid-off security interest is equitable (an equitable charge/unpaid vendor's lien). But we may potentially notice a difference, if the paid-off security interest is legal (a registered legal charge). Courts seem persistently to misunderstand, or under-analyse, what the claimant's rights should be in this setting.

Secondly, and relatedly, the proper resolution of priority disputes has been inadequately analysed. The preferable approach, which is justifiable in terms of the *Banque Financière* analysis and does least violence to the integrity of the LRA 2002 framework, involves the assumption that one must distinguish two key priority questions—the status of C's subrogation entitlement vis-à-vis pre-existing third party rights, that pre-dated the discharge of X-creditor's security, at C's expense; and the status of C's subrogation entitlement vis-à-vis subsequent third party rights, which arise only after that event. This analysis steers a mid-course between early decisions like *Omar*—which seemed to say that C's subrogation entitlement has nothing to do with unjust enrichment—and decisions like *Anfield*—which seem to imply that unjust enrichment has a role in explaining the priority that a subrogation claimant is afforded over all third party rights, whether pre-existing or subsequent. The key assumption is that a proprietary right/inchoate proprietary right, of equitable origin, is immediately generated to reverse unjust enrichment, but that after that, the relevant

[91] LRA 2002, sch 3, para 2; and see, eg, *Karasiewicz* (n 40) (involving equivalent provisions of the LRA 1925).
[92] LRA 2002, sch 8, para 1(1)(a).
[93] LRA 2002, sch 8, para 5.

rights *behave like standard property rights*—ie a third party who subsequently acquires an interest is affected *only* if that third party would be affected in accordance with the standard priority rules applicable to competitions between interests of the relevant quality, in the relevant subject-matter.

Thirdly, misunderstanding of these first two points can also produce some unwarranted conclusions when it comes to understanding the role for alteration or rectification. This is true whether C's subrogation entitlement relates to a previously vacated registered charge, or to a subsisting but still registered charge. In short, it threatens to muddy the answer to the question, what can an application for Register-alteration or -rectification achieve?

D

The Land Registration Regime and the General Law

15

A Tale of Three Promises: Setting the Scene

STEPHEN WATTERSON AND AMY GOYMOUR

I. Land Registration Regimes and the General Law

Land registration systems have long pedigrees, but they are not an innate feature of property law systems. Where they have been introduced in modern times, they are the product of legislative intervention, designed to achieve certain objectives that are at best imperfectly realised within the general law's framework.

In practice, no viable land registration system is, could, or should be a complete and fully autonomous regime—land registration systems are necessarily parasitic, in countless key respects, on established principles of property law. This is true of the Land Registration Act ('LRA') 2002, and of its predecessor statutes. Nevertheless, it is also evident that the ambitions of such systems can only be realised in practice via a framework that departs from the general law's operation in important respects. The exact nature and extent of this necessary departure depends on the legislature's ambitions for the regime. The issue was neatly captured by Lady Hale's discussion in *Southern Pacific Mortgages v Scott* as to whether it is general property law or the land registration regime which is in control in disputes concerning registered land. Opining that general property law should be the driver, and that the land registration regime was 'merely conveyancing machinery', her Ladyship warned against 'the danger of letting the land registration tail wag the land ownership dog'.[1]

We do not share Lady Hale's opinion. In the following three chapters, we argue that the aims of the LRA 2002 were intended to be realised via a combination of three fundamental 'promises'—'the title promise', 'the priority (or ordering) promise', and 'the empowerment promise'—and that each was intended, in varying degrees, to bring about a departure from the results that would pertain if general property law were the sole driver. We also suggest that the effective practical realisation of these three promises depends on their nature, extent and implications being made clear, and that in this respect, the Act has fallen short. Whilst the promises have a statutory foundation, each is afflicted by a myriad of interpretative uncertainties as regards both the intended scope and meaning of the rules explicitly posited by the Act, and the relationship between those statutory rules and the 'general law'.

[1] *Southern Pacific Mortgages v Scott* [2014] UKSC 52, [2015] AC 385 [96].

These uncertainties are pervasive, and the resulting interpretative leeway is regrettable. Above all, it allows the Act to be read and applied in a way that may frustrate the registration regime's intended objectives—or at least, fail fully to realise them. This is not a merely theoretical risk: it is borne out in a succession of knotty cases, involving disparate aspects of the LRA 2002's framework. Several are well-known, but these are only illustrations of what seems, on close scrutiny, to be an endemic problem.

Sound diagnosis is a necessary preliminary to effective cure. To that end, chapters sixteen, seventeen and eighteen undertake a 'risk assessment' exercise—seeking to identify the nature and extent of the present threat to the LRA 2002's objectives. In this chapter, we introduce the three promises and the rationale for their recognition within the LRA 2002's registration framework. The chapters that follow then subject each promise to systematic scrutiny. We investigate, in turn: the statutory basis of each promise; the interpretative controversies presented by the Act's drafting; and the ways in which each promise is qualified by design or is vulnerable to unwanted subversion by unexpected statutory interpretations or unplanned intrusions of the general law.

II. Three Fundamental Promises

Any system of land law faces a tension between the preservation of prior entitlements and the facilitation of land dealings. Land registration regimes—which have at their core a public register of land titles, appurtenant rights, and encumbrances—promise some very real benefits. Different legal systems' registration regimes certainly cannot be expected to be homogenous. Nevertheless, there are some endemic problems, associated with any system of *general property law* (ie, the property rules not relating to registration), that any registration regime can reasonably be expected to address.

The general law brings various well-documented vulnerabilities and uncertainties, both for those with prior entitlements over land, and conversely, for potential disponees. In particular, any rules which might call into question the validity and/or priority of a *disponee's* title will necessarily compel extensive and potentially expensive pre-conveyance investigations, private negotiation, and/or routine private insurance arrangements. The disponee's general law vulnerabilities stem from multiple sources.

First, any disponee will inevitably be concerned about immediate 'transactional' deficiencies—eg, problems of form, forgery, or the impairment of the disponor's consent by misrepresentation, duress or undue influence, that might render the immediate transaction (ie, the transaction from his immediate disponor) void, voidable or otherwise of compromised effect.

Secondly, beyond that, basic principles of the general law inevitably create further, significant traps for the disponee. These include the risks: that the disponor might not have had any title to convey; that the disponor's title was subject to some enduring 'defect' which might in turn render the disponee's title vulnerable to some better prior claim; that the disponor's title was subject to prior encumbrances that retained priority despite the later disposition, whether or not disclosed or discovered, and possibly even if not reasonably discoverable; and that the disponor's capacity or authority might have been limited, such that the purported disposition, if made beyond that capacity or authority, might be called into question.

A land registration system does not need to address all of these problems, but it will certainly need to address at least some of them. To borrow a phrase typically employed in accounts of trustee obligations, there may be an 'irreducible core' of features which must be present in order for a land registration system to be worth implementing and viable. Yet it is also evident that the LRA 2002's drafters sought to achieve a regime that went substantially beyond any minimum 'core'. If the promised benefits of electronic conveyancing were to be realised, it was thought necessary to maximise the reliability of the Register: the aim was that the Register should be as complete and accurate a picture of the state of title to land as possible, and that disponees could rely on it as such. As we see it, this ambition was more concretely realised via what we have styled three 'promises',[2] which collectively—if taken seriously—would force a significant deviation from the general law's position.

Taken at face-value, and subject to certain qualifications, these promises make the following bold assurances:

A. The Title Promise

According to the 'title promise', registration is a necessary—and constitutive—step in the acquisition of title to major interests in land. Once registered, the registered proprietor becomes the owner of that title, via section 58, whether or not he would have been so entitled under the general law. This registration-constituted title is 'guaranteed', such that even if it is subsequently removed or qualified in favour of a prior entitlement, the disappointed owner is ordinarily entitled to be indemnified from a Registry fund. As such, a disponee can obtain a title even when he might not under the general law, and even if that title is not impregnable, any deprivation of that title will prima facie be compensated.

B. The Priority Promise

The 'priority promise' (which might alternatively be labelled the 'ordering promise') offers preferential treatment, in terms of taking priority over others' prior entitlements, to those acquiring a registered interest. As regards first registration, section 11 prescribes which interests will and will not bind each particular grade of registered freehold title—absolute, possessory or qualified. More importantly, as regards subsequent dealings involving already-registered titles, section 29 provides a special priority rule that privileges registered dispositions for valuable consideration—affording them an immunity from prior interests which are not disclosed by an entry in the Register, subject to the limited but important exception of overriding interests.

[2] See further A Goymour, 'Resolving the Tension Between the Land Registration Act 2002's "Priority" and "Alteration" Provisions' [2015] *Conv* 253, where a distinction is drawn between the 'title' and 'priority' promises.

C. The Empowerment Promise

The 'empowerment promise', largely discernable from sections 23 to 26, assures a disponee that he can proceed on the basis that a registered disponor has all of the powers of disposition characteristic of an unencumbered owner. Even if the disponor's dispositional powers are in fact limited, the disponee should not be affected by any limitation—which might otherwise render the disposition ultra vires, and potentially invalid, under the general law—which is not reflected by the entry of a restriction in the Register.

III. Key Themes

Chapters sixteen, seventeen and eighteen explore the extent to which each of these three promises has been realised in practice, and whether each promise has brought about what we believe to be the legislature's intended departure from the general law. Close scrutiny reveals a variety of techniques, employed in the cases and/or the Act itself, via which each promise has been compromised or qualified, deliberately or otherwise. These include:

(i) restricting the circumstances in which the promise 'bites';
(ii) giving a restrictive interpretation to the content of the promise;
(iii) rendering what the promise delivers susceptible to reversal via the LRA 2002's 'alteration' provisions in schedule 4; and
(iv) neutralising the promise's effects via reliance on external general law principles.

Drawing attention to these three promises, and reflecting on when and to what extent they are justified, is the only rational basis on which we can bring some order to the current registered land regime. As chapters sixteen to eighteen reveal, unless we understand why the promises matter, and what is potentially at risk if they are not fulfilled, there is real risk that the courts may go astray when interpreting the registration legislation, and thereby undermine the very system they are seeking to apply.

More generally, the three promises provide useful lenses for engaging in a debate about what shape our registration system *ought* to take in future. Taken individually, each promise compels us to confront several key questions. Why is a particular promise offered? What shape should it take? Should it be qualified? Should it be susceptible to reversal? Who should it benefit? Furthermore, only by looking closely at each promise in isolation can we begin to tackle an even more difficult question—whether the three promises *should* align, or differ, in their key characteristics. Chapters sixteen to eighteen reveal that there are some significant differences between the three promises under the current law, whether as a result of legislative design or judicial interpretation. This realisation should pave the way for a rational future debate about whether these differences are indeed warranted.

16

A Tale of Three Promises: (1) The Title Promise

STEPHEN WATTERSON AND AMY GOYMOUR

I. Introduction

Within any system of land ownership, title questions assume paramount importance. By what mechanisms is title acquired? Does a particular person have title? If so, what is the nature and quality of that title? And is it vulnerable to being lost or trumped by some paramount claim, arising from a past or future event?

Under the general law—meaning for present purposes the property rules not relating to registration, which underpin the operation of unregistered conveyancing—most titles are acquired *derivatively*, via transfer from an earlier owner. And such derivative acquisition brings risks. Whether B can immediately obtain a good title by transfer from A[1] depends on whether A had a valid title to transfer, and whether there was a valid disposition of that title from A to B. This will in turn depend on whether A had the capacity/power to transfer, and whether, if A did, that capacity/power was validly exercised by A, in accordance with the general law's requirements of form and substance.

In theory, a registration system could operate simply as a publicising mechanism, layered onto the existing framework of conveyancing rules, but without changing them. However, in practice, it seems inevitable that a credible registration regime, if it is to achieve its objectives, must deliver at least some measure of security against some of the risks associated with derivative acquisition. These include, first and foremost, security against certain problems that might otherwise—under the general law—call into question the vesting of title in B, or the quality/security of the title thereby acquired.

The precise form of this security is not preordained. It might entail an immunity from the particular risk (the protection of the registered owner's *in specie* rights to the land—the so-called 'mud'),[2] or a monetary guarantee against its materialisation ('money' in lieu of 'mud'). Neither is it preordained what the precise extent of that security should be—ie, *what* risks are addressed.

[1] ie, as opposed to a 'good' original title based on long adverse possession.

[2] The mud/money metaphor can be traced to T Mapp, *Torrens' Elusive Title: Basic Legal Principles of an Efficient Torrens's System* (Edmonton, University of Alberta, 1978).

A credible registration regime will certainly need to provide some security from circumstances that would, under the general law, impair the validity or status of A's title: defects in the *root* of *A's* title. If it cannot, then a fundamental benefit of a registration regime is lost—ie, the elimination or reduction of the need for B to inquire into the transactional pre-history.

It is less obvious, although still conceivable, that a credible regime might additionally provide security from risks that relate only to whether A's title was *validly transferred* to B. Thus, it might well be thought desirable to offer B some assurance against the risk that A's *power or capacity* to transfer is limited in ways not made apparent in any title register—an 'empowerment promise'. However, it is less obvious that the system must offer B any assurance against the risk that the immediate *transaction*, via which B claims to have received A's title, may be void, voidable or otherwise of compromised effect—say, because of non-compliance with the general law's requirements of transactional form and substance. On a later disposition by B to C, this problem becomes a defect in the root of *B's* title, against which the system will certainly wish to offer some protection *to C*. Focusing only on the immediate disposition between A and B, however, the argument for insulating B from such 'transactional risks' is less clear.

II. Basis of the Title Promise

Within the LRA 2002, what we choose to call the 'title promise' is initially realised via section 58(1). Headed '[c]onclusiveness', this provides:

> If, on the entry of a person in the register as the proprietor of a legal estate, the legal estate would not otherwise be vested in him, it shall be deemed to be vested in him as a result of the registration.

Section 58 is a clear indicator of the basic orientation of the LRA 2002's registration regime—ie, it is a regime of title *by* registration, rather than a system of registration *of* title.[3] Registration as proprietor is of itself constitutive of title, even if under the general law—eg because of defects of substance or form—title would not otherwise vest in B. For this reason, section 58 empowers the Land Registrar with a metaphorical 'Midas touch'—everything that is registered turns into land law's equivalent of gold: a *legal* estate or interest. Although not immediately apparent, the ambit of this provision is extensive, in two key respects.

First, this transformative effect of section 58 applies both on first registration and on registration of subsequent dispositions by a registered proprietor. For these subsequent registered dispositions, subject to limited exceptions, registration is an essential step for such a disposition to be 'complete at law', such that it is only on registration that the relevant legal estate or interest is acquired.[4] What of *first* registration of a previously

[3] For judicial recognition, see, eg, *Wells v Pilling Parish Council* [2008] EWHC 556 (Ch), [2008] 2 EGLR 2 [7]–[8]. See also Law Commission, *Land Registration for the Twenty-First Century: A Consultative Document* (Law Com No 254, 1998) para 10.43.

[4] LRA 2002, s 27.

unregistered title? If voluntary, then the first registered proprietor will have previously acquired the *unregistered* legal estate under unregistered land rules.[5] This is equally true in cases where a transaction triggers compulsory first registration, with the difference that the initial vesting of the unregistered legal estate may be nullified if registration is not sought within the specified time-frame.[6] In both cases, registration is seemingly constitutive of a new (registered) title, which supplants the former unregistered title.[7]

The title conferred by registration—whether on first registration or pursuant to a later registered disposition—is a *new* title, whose substance and implications require statutory definition. Within the LRA 2002's framework, this is realised via a web of provisions. Central to this chapter is section 58, which achieves/confirms the *vesting* of title, and thus lies at the heart of the title promise. The *quality* and *priority* of this title are determined by sections 11–12 (relating to first registered titles) and sections 28–30 (for subsequent registered titles)—the legislative foundations of the regime's 'priority promise', discussed in chapter seventeen. The *dispositional capacities* associated with the registered title are defined by section 23—the lynchpin of the 'empowerment promise', examined in chapter eighteen.

Secondly, section 58 also operates expansively in favour of all those who obtain a 'registered interest', regardless of the type of interest so registered—including, eg, registered easements, leases, mortgages and freeholds. As long as the interest both qualifies for registration[8] and is in fact registered, it will benefit from the Registrar's Midas touch, and exist at law. Notably, any form of interest in land which is capable of existing at law qualifies for registration, with the exception of certain excluded interests.[9]

The ambit of section 58 is therefore extensive. Nonetheless, ambit does not equate to strength—like Goliath, something can be big but weak. Indeed, the title conferred through the Registrar's Midas touch is not as strong as it may initially appear. Once section 58 is situated within the wider framework of the LRA 2002, it becomes clear that the title acquired via a person's registration as proprietor is neither wholly irreversible, nor wholly absolute. The Act does not insulate the registered proprietor from all risks that might provide a ground for challenging his status as proprietor. Neither does it provide any complete monetary guarantee, in lieu, against the risks of this occurring. Much of this frailty is the result of deliberate design. But there are also several other ways in which the security which the Act was apparently designed to offer, via its title promise, can be and has been undermined

[5] LRA 2002, s 3.

[6] LRA 2002, ss 4–8.

[7] cf Law Commission, *Land Registration for the Twenty-First Century—A Conveyancing Revolution* (Law Com No 271, 2001) para 3.45; cf para 8.3.

[8] Most notably, leases of seven years or less are generally excluded from registration: LRA 2002, ss 3(3), 4(2)(b), and 27(2)(b).

[9] The LRA 2002 refers to a 'legal estate' as being registrable. This terminology encompasses *any* form of interest in land that is capable of existing as a legal interest—it is not limited to 'estates in land' as defined by the Law of Property Act ('LPA') 1925, and comprising leases (the 'term of years absolute') and the freehold estate (the 'fee simple absolute in possession'). See LRA 2002, s 132(1), incorporating the definition in the LPA 1925, s 1 (and in particular, s 1(4)), read with LRA 2002, s 2 (defining the scope of 'title' registration) and LRA 2002, sch 2 (defining the relevant registration requirements). Furthermore, the reference to registration '*as proprietor*' of the relevant 'legal estate' does not limit LRA 2002, s 58 to those interests that are independently registrable with their *own* registered title (eg, freehold estates, qualifying leases). It must be read in light of sch 2, which defines the relevant 'registration requirements' and provides for the appropriate mode of registration '*as proprietor*' for *all* forms of interests transferred or granted via a registrable disposition—including, eg, a registered charge, or an expressly-created easement (see, eg, sch 2, para 7, which would embrace easements).

via judicial interpretation—calling into question the ability of the registration framework to achieve the objectives of its authors.

III. Key Vulnerabilities

In this section, we identify five potential weaknesses in the title promise which, if inappropriately exploited, threaten to subvert—or at least significantly qualify—the ambit and effect of section 58's 'Midas touch'.

A. When is Section 58 Engaged?—Two Inherent Vulnerabilities

It is axiomatic that section 58 must be *engaged* in order for its conclusive effect to be realised. Close scrutiny reveals two inherent and explicit limitations affecting the circumstances in which the provision might bite, which concern respectively: (i) unsatisfied 'registration requirements', and (ii) boundary problems. These limitations may mean that a registered proprietor falls outside the ambit of the title promise, despite appearing to have a registered title. The likely upshot of failing to engage section 58 is that he is denied the assurance of retaining the 'mud', or of obtaining monetary compensation in lieu.

i. Unsatisfied 'Registration Requirements'

First, by section 58(2), section 58(1) will not deem the legal estate to be vested in the registered proprietor:

> [w]here the entry is made in pursuance of a registrable disposition in relation to which some other registration requirement remains to be met.

The intended effect of this provision should be clear. It is a very limited provision, intended to prevent circumvention of the requirements which the LRA 2002 *itself* prescribes, via section 27, for a registrable disposition to 'operate at law'.[10] As Newey J expressly recognised in *Fitzwilliam v Richall Holdings Services Ltd*:[11]

> The purpose of s 58(2) is to ensure that s 58 does not detract from the principle enunciated in s 27(1).[12]

The 'registration requirements' referred to in section 27(1) are detailed in schedule 2, and *only* schedule 2, and there is no reason to give them any wider meaning for the purpose of section 58(2).

The key to unlocking the function of section 58(2) is to appreciate that the registration of many types of 'registrable disposition' requires more than one form of 'entry' in the Register—eg, in the case of the grant of a registrable lease by a registered freehold proprietor,

[10] LRA 2002, s 27(1) and sch 2.

[11] *Fitzwilliam v Richall Holdings Services Ltd* [2013] EWHC 86 (Ch), [2013] 1 P & CR 19.

[12] ibid [81].

it is necessary both to: (i) register the grantee as proprietor of the lease, in a separate newly-opened title register, and to (ii) enter a notice in respect of the lease in the title register of the estate out of which the lease was granted.[13] Step (ii) is essential if the Register is reliably to indicate the interests that encumber registered titles. Section 58(2) ensures that section 58(1) does not operate only on completion of step (i); step (ii) must also be taken.[14]

An obvious corollary is that section 58(2) is not intended to undermine the vesting effect of section 58(1) where any other precondition for the validity of a disposition, imposed by the general law, has not been satisfied. This would include general transactional formality requirements, and in particular, the general requirement for a valid deed to grant or transfer a legal estate or interest in land.[15]

Consider *Bank of Scotland plc v Waugh*,[16] in which trustees purported to grant a registered charge in circumstances where the formalities were deficient—the necessary deed was not strictly present, because the relevant signatures were not duly attested.[17] Under the general law, since the charge was not validly executed by deed, it could not be effective as a legal charge. However, this changed on registration: the Registrar's Midas touch had the effect of creating a charge by way of legal mortgage. Judge Behrens attributed this to section 51, which provides that:

> On completion of the relevant registration requirements, a charge created by means of a registrable disposition of a registered estate has effect, if it would not otherwise do so, as a charge by deed by way of legal mortgage.

In fact, the creation of the legal mortgage in a case like *Waugh* ought to be attributed to the combined effect of sections 58 and 51. Section 51 *supplements* rather than replaces section 58, in relation to registered mortgages/charges. It is section 58, and not section 51, which governs the *vesting* of the legal charge, upon the chargee's registration as proprietor, despite the defect of form. Section 51 then builds on this, by clarifying the nature of the *powers* associated with that vesting, once it has occurred.[18] The point of section 51 is to confirm that the only *form* of mortgage/charge which can be created via registration under the LRA 2002 is a charge by deed by way of legal mortgage, and not any other form of mortgage/charge.[19]

The risk inherent in section 58(2) is that if its intended purpose is overlooked, and the relevant 'registration requirements' are interpreted more expansively, then section 58(1)'s ambit is unjustifiably narrowed. The knock-on consequence is that the LRA 2002's title promise is compromised, potentially seriously.

A recent illustration of this danger is *Gelley v Shephard*.[20] So far as relevant, this raised a question as to the effect of a transfer of registered land between two companies, A Co and B Co. A Co had been dissolved after being struck off the British Virgin Islands register

[13] LRA 2002, sch 2, para 3(2)(a), (b).

[14] For confirmation of this, see the Explanatory Notes to LRA 2002, s 58(2), quoted in *Fitzwilliam v Richall* (n 11) [81].

[15] LPA 1925, s 52(1) (subject to s 54(2)).

[16] *Bank of Scotland plc v Waugh* [2014] EWHC 2117 (Ch).

[17] Law of Property (Miscellaneous Provisions) Act 1989, s 1(3).

[18] See also the relevant headings in the LRA 2002: s 58 falls under the sub-Part headed 'Registration as proprietor'; s 51 falls under the sub-Part headed 'Powers as chargee'.

[19] Indeed, a charge by way of legal mortgage is the only form of legal charge/mortgage that can be created pursuant to the 'owner's powers' conferred by the LRA 2002, ss 23–24.

[20] *Gelley v Shephard* [2013] EWCA Civ 1172.

of companies. A fraudulent third party, acting without authority, nevertheless procured a transfer of the land to B Co, a newly incorporated company. Before registering B Co as proprietor, the Land Registry had required confirmation that A Co was an extant company; the evidence supplied in response to this request was, however, forged. In subsequent proceedings challenging B Co's registration, it was argued that section 58(1) vested title in B Co, notwithstanding that the transaction might be ineffective under the general law. At trial, counsel seems to have conceded that the requirement of the Land Registry that evidence be provided to prove that A Co was an extant company was a 'registration requirement' within the meaning of section 58(2), and that the provision of certificates of A Co's status that were forged, rather than genuine, meant that this registration requirement was not met, so that section 58(1) did not apply.[21] This seems clearly wrong, and represents an unwarranted over-expansion of the section 58(2) exception. It is regrettable that the Court of Appeal did not take the opportunity to decide as much. All that was relevantly said on the appeal was that the earlier concession could not now be withdrawn, and that it was no longer open to the parties to argue the contrary.[22]

ii. Boundary Problems

A second inherent qualification to the circumstances in which section 58(1) will be engaged follows from section 60, which establishes a default position that the boundary of a registered estate is a 'general boundary',[23] which 'does not determine the exact line of the boundary'.[24] The default position may be displaced following an application to the Registrar to determine the 'exact line' of the boundary.[25] However, it seems that in practice, such applications are unusual.

The fact that the registration regime's starting-point is the 'general boundaries' rule—and as a corollary, that the location of a registered estate's boundaries is not guaranteed—creates a significant risk for registered proprietors: they may suffer the uncompensated loss of what might be a substantial area of land, which they had believed was comprised in their registered title. This risk may eventually fall away after extended 'adverse possession' of the qualifying area. As is well known, when the boundaries are not conclusively settled by the Register, schedule 6 allows a registered proprietor, who has been in adverse possession for at least 10 years of an area of registered land adjacent to his own, in the mistaken belief that it belongs to him, to apply to be registered as proprietor of the boundary area.[26] Subject to that, however, a registered proprietor is vulnerable.

This vulnerability makes the appropriate classification of any dispute—as either a 'boundary dispute' or a 'property dispute'—crucial.[27]

If a dispute is classified as a 'property dispute', then the inclusion within a proprietor's registered title of any area of land that extends beyond what is found to be properly his, can

[21] ibid [76].
[22] ibid [77]–[81].
[23] LRA 2002, s 60(1).
[24] LRA 2002, s 60(2).
[25] Land Registration Rules ('LRR') 2003, rr 118–123.
[26] LRA 2002, sch 6, para 5(4).
[27] See further A Goymour 'Mistaken Registrations of Land: Exploding the Myth of "Title by Registration"' [2013] *CLJ* 617, 641–642.

be regarded as a 'mistake'. Since the correction of this 'mistake' will prejudicially affect the mistakenly registered proprietor's title, the correction will qualify as a 'rectification', with the further consequence that the relevant mistaken proprietor may be able to rely on the defence afforded to 'proprietors in possession', which enables them to resist rectification.[28] If this defence should prove unsuccessful, and rectification is ordered, then an indemnity is likely to be available to the disappointed party.[29]

In contrast, if the dispute is classified as a 'boundary dispute', greater problems will ensue. In this case, the real boundary can only be identified 'off-Register'. At any point, a relevant party may seek to 'determine' the exact boundary line, bringing the risk of thwarting the expectations of the registered proprietor who believed that he owned the relevant boundary area. 'Determination' of the boundary in a manner contrary to these expectations is likely to yield a change to the Register which is adverse to one of the relevant proprietors. Nevertheless, since any alteration to reflect this 'determination' would simply bring the Register up to date, the change would not prejudicially affect the disappointed registered proprietor's title—it would merely ensure that the Register reflected the true, off-Register state of affairs. Such an alteration would not qualify as a 'rectification', and the disappointed party would be denied both the mud and any monetary compensation in lieu from the Registry.

Does this matter? It can be argued that the risk presented by the general boundaries rule is tolerable, being consistent with the aims of land registration. A person who becomes registered as proprietor of an estate subject to the general boundaries rule does not benefit from any promise or guarantee of title *so far as it relates to the 'boundary' of his estate*. This is merely one matter in relation to which the Register is—by design—not reliable, and in relation to which registered proprietors' legitimate expectations must be appropriately reduced. Nevertheless, it might be argued against this that this position is only tolerable if a purchaser knows or should reasonably appreciate: (i) that the boundary is a general one, and (ii) the *extent* of his land that counts as relevant 'boundary' land for this purpose, and which is therefore vulnerable to *de facto* expropriation when the boundary is later determined. Unfortunately, such a purchaser cannot know for certain *what* land is non-guaranteed boundary land—as opposed to guaranteed non-boundary land—in the absence of a definition of the concept of a 'boundary'. The LRA 2002 provides no assistance in this respect. Whether litigation involves a 'property' or a 'boundary' dispute is therefore a matter left to courts' unguided interpretation. The further their definition of 'boundary' land veers from purchasers' reasonable expectations, the greater the risk that purchasers' confidence in the Register will be undermined, and that the land registration regime's aims are thwarted.

B. The Nature of Title on Registration

Assuming that section 58(1) is engaged by the registration of an interest, a crucial question then arises as to the *nature* of the title conferred by such registration. What is the extent of section 58(1)'s constitutive effect?

[28] LRA 2002, sch 4, paras 3(2), 6(2). And see *Salisbury v Calladine* [2016] EWLandRA 2015_0678.

[29] LRA 2002, sch 8, para 1(1)(a).

The view most favourable to the new registered proprietor is that section 58(1) confers a full beneficial title. On this view, whatever might be the position under the general law, the legal estate which is deemed to be vested in him by force of statute is vested in him *beneficially*—it is not a 'bare' or 'nominal' title only. That does not mean that he will remain irretrievably the beneficial legal owner—section 58 is at least subject to schedule 4's alteration regime. It does, however, make it more likely that if the Register should be altered against him, this will be prejudicial, causing him substantial (as opposed to nominal) loss, and thus amount to an indemnity-justifying 'rectification'.

As the following sections explain, the Court of Appeal in *Swift 1st Ltd v Chief Land Registrar*[30] has finally accepted this interpretation of section 58(1). Nevertheless, the assurance thereby given to the registered proprietor remains vulnerable to subversion, or at least partial circumvention, in other subtle ways.

i. A Discarded Heresy: Conclusiveness as to Legal Title Only

Prior to *Swift 1st*, a controversial line of authority had held that section 58(1) had a limited effect. Section 58(1) only guaranteed that the *bare legal estate* vested in the registered proprietor, via registration—even if it would not otherwise under the general law. By implication, the registered proprietor would only receive that estate *beneficially* insofar as the transaction pursuant to which he became registered as proprietor would have had that effect under the general law. If it would not have had that effect, then the new registered proprietor would only obtain the bare legal title, and would in substance be rendered a trustee for the former registered proprietor.

This analysis first emerged in the Court of Appeal's decision in *Malory Enterprises Ltd v Cheshire Homes (UK) Ltd*,[31] in the context of section 69 of the LRA 1925—the forerunner of section 58 of the LRA 2002. In that case, a stranger had been able, via fraud and without the knowledge or consent of the original registered proprietor, A, to 'sell' the registered title to B, who was thereupon registered as proprietor instead. Arden LJ considered that section 69 'deemed [B] to have vested in it' 'the legal estate in fee simple in possession'[32] and that, properly understood, section 69 'deal[t] only with the legal estate'.[33] Furthermore, as the forged transfer to B 'could not in law be of any effect in itself', it could not constitute a 'disposition' triggering section 20 of the LRA 1925, the forerunner of section 29 of the LRA 2002, which, *inter alia*, gave the holder of the disposed interest priority over certain pre-existing rights encumbering the registered title.[34] The result was that B's position as registered proprietor was 'subject to the rights of [A] as beneficial owner'.[35]

In *Fitzwilliam v Richall*,[36] on similar facts arising under the LRA 2002, Newey J noted that *Malory* had been widely criticised,[37] and found 'considerable force' in some of the

[30] *Swift 1st Ltd v Chief Land Registrar* [2015] EWCA Civ 330, [2015] Ch 602.

[31] *Malory Enterprises Ltd v Cheshire Homes (UK) Ltd* [2002] EWCA Civ 151, [2002] Ch 216.

[32] ibid [64].

[33] ibid [65]; see similarly [85] (Clarke LJ) and [89] (Schiemann LJ).

[34] ibid [65].

[35] ibid. On the facts, this finding did not affect A's ability to obtain rectification, but it was thought to enable A to sue B for trespass, and it prevented a claim by B for an indemnity.

[36] *Fitzwilliam v Richall* (n 11). See also subsequently, *Park Associated Developments Ltd v Kinnear* [2013] EWHC 3617 (Ch).

[37] ibid [75].

arguments made.[38] Nevertheless, Newey J felt bound to accept the *Malory* analysis,[39] and (in the absence of relevant distinctions between the provisions) to adopt the same interpretation of the equivalent provisions of the LRA 2002—ie, sections 58(1) and 29.[40] Accordingly, on the facts of *Fitzwilliam v Richall*, section 58(1) *only* operated to vest the legal estate, on registration, in B. A 'remained the beneficial owner', and since a 'void' disposition could not attract section 29, B's title would necessarily remain subject to A's prior right.

The *Fitzwilliam v Richall* reading of section 58, particularly when taken in conjunction with a narrow reading of section 29, was controversial for both conceptual and policy reasons. Conceptually, it might appear inconsistent with the view, preferred by Lord Browne-Wilkinson in *Westdeutsche Landesbank Girozentrale v Islington LBC*,[41] that a person (here A) cannot 'retain' the *equitable* beneficial title, if he was previously the unencumbered beneficial *legal* owner. He previously held no separate 'equitable title'; an 'equitable title' could only arise, if at all, anew, via what amounts to a form of imposed trust over B's legal title. This analysis would lead inexorably to the conclusion that, in the absence of any orthodox trust-generating event in *Fitzwilliam v Richall*, beneficial ownership should have followed legal ownership. Even more importantly, from the point of view of policy, the decision in *Fitzwilliam v Richall* also meant that that the general law remained vitally significant in determining the effect of registration. B's registration afforded only a bare legal title. Whether it also conferred a *beneficial* title depended on the legal effect of the underlying A–B disposition under the general law. Hence, if B became registered as proprietor, in circumstances in which he would have acquired no title from A under the general law—eg if his registration was the result of a forged disposition of A's title—section 58(1)'s only effect would be to vest the *bare* registered legal estate in B. The *beneficial* title would 'remain' with A, and would remain enforceable against B, subject to the possible effect of section 29 in 'clearing' B's title.[42]

This interpretation threatened to bring about various consequences which might have undermined the ambitions of the LRA 2002's drafters. First, in cases like *Malory* and *Fitzwilliam v Richall*, B's title was only a bare title, necessarily subject to A's beneficial interest. Second, reflecting this, if A sought to have the registered title restored to him, pursuant to his general law *Saunders v Vautier* rights, the Register alteration would not count as rectification—it would merely 'bring the Register up to date', and in any event, would not seem relevantly prejudicial to B, whose registered title was merely a bare legal title. Third, barring exceptional circumstances, A would almost certainly recover his title via alteration of the Register, even if B was 'in possession'—the 'proprietor in possession' defence applies only as a defence to 'prejudicial'/loss-causing 'rectifications' of the Register. Furthermore, B, even if innocent of fraud or negligence, and having purchased the registered title in good faith, would receive no indemnity. Fourth, the risk exposure of C, a later registered disponee of B's registered title, was also substantially increased. Even if C could rely on section 29's

[38] ibid [76].
[39] ibid [76].
[40] ibid [76]–[85].
[41] *Westdeutsche Landesbank Girozentrale v Islington LBC* [1996] AC 669 (HL) 706.
[42] In fact, for reasons that we explore in ch 17 of this book, we do not consider that s 29 of the LRA 2002 has any application in clearing B's title from interests that might arise only on or after B's registration, and which therefore do not encumber the title prior to B's acquisition.

priority promise, A's 'retained' beneficial interest might encumber C's title, if A had remained in 'actual occupation' and could therefore establish an overriding interest via schedule 3, paragraph 2. Once again, C would be exposed to a claim for Register-alteration, even if C were in possession—the proprietor in possession defence would not apply—and the alteration would not yield a Register indemnity.

English law has since been set on a different and to most eyes more satisfactory course following *Swift 1st*.[43] The Court of Appeal tackled head-on whether *Malory* had been decided in error in this respect.[44] Like Newey J, the Court of Appeal did not think that it was possible to distinguish *Malory* on the basis that it was confined to the LRA 1925: sections 58 and 29 of the LRA 2002 were not intended to effect any substantive change.[45] Thus, rather than distinguishing *Malory*, the Court of Appeal in *Swift 1st* decided that the *Malory* decision was *per incuriam* on both points, and therefore not authoritative on either point.

ii. Remaining Vulnerabilities

Nevertheless, all is not as it seems. At best, *Swift 1st* only confirms a negative: that section 58 does not have the '*bare*' vesting effect attributed to it by *Malory*. The *Swift 1st* decision did not go further and establish, more positively, the *strength* of B's title—it was unnecessary for the Court of Appeal to say more on the facts. On closer scrutiny, B's position as registered proprietor remains vulnerable in four key respects, summarised below. Taken together, these significantly impair B's position.

First, section 58 does not speak to the *strength* or *quality* of the title afforded via registration—and more specifically, whether it is paramount to other (inferior) titles, or conversely, subject to another (superior) title. Within the parameters of the LRA 2002 framework, this depends on the relevant grading of title. If the relevant registered title is an '*absolute*' title, then B—like A before him—has a guarantee against the existence of any better 'off-Register' title—eg, a concurrent fee simple, belonging to X, which prior to B's registration was relatively superior to the estate conveyed from A to B. But matters look otherwise if B's title is registered as *possessory* or *qualified*: the LRA 2002 provides that these lesser grade titles remain vulnerable to certain off-Register paramount titles or other rights. We examine this vulnerability in subsection C below.

Secondly, section 58 also does not speak to the *state* of B's registered title and, in particular, whether it is *encumbered* by interests that previously affected the estate. It is only concerned with the vesting of title, and not its priority vis-à-vis prior interests. Priority is a matter principally governed by the LRA 2002's priority provisions—found in sections 11–12 (where B is the first registered proprietor) and sections 28–30 (for subsequent registered dealings). These embody what we have called the Act's priority promise, which we examine at length in chapter seventeen.

Thirdly, even if B's registration is with absolute title, section 58 does not guarantee absolute security from problems that might affect the *root* of the registered title—whether these

[43] *Swift 1st* (n 30).

[44] ibid [1] ('[The case] raises the question whether the much-debated decision of this court in *Malory* … was decided *per incuriam* in so far as the court held that the innocent victim of a forged disposition acquired only the legal estate and not the benefcial ownership of the property'), [34]–[45].

[45] ibid [40].

problems affect the transaction (if any) from A to B that immediately preceded B's registration, or relate more remotely to the circumstances in which A himself, or even a predecessor of A, previously obtained title. This is because B's registration is subject to the court's/Registrar's jurisdiction to alter the Register, provided by the LRA 2002, schedule 4. In some instances, if B's title proves insecure, and is removed from the Register via alteration, B may benefit from the alternative protection of a monetary guarantee/indemnity. However, for reasons that we consider in subsection D below, this monetary guarantee is far from assured.

Fourthly, B's registration as proprietor does not afford B any automatic or general immunity from so-called 'direct rights' that arise under the general law in favour of another (X)—eg, in response to B's commission of a wrong against X, or B's making of a contract with X. As explored in subsection E below, and further in chapter seventeen, this is a potentially very significant incursion, with important ramifications for B, and potentially also for C, a subsequent disponee.

C. The Strength or Quality of Title on Registration

Accepting that B is registered as proprietor, and so benefits from section 58's vesting effect, the first remaining vulnerability relates to the strength or quality of the title which registration affords. Under the common law of real property as it applies to unregistered land, there may be two or more concurrent and valid freehold titles, which can and must be graded one against the other—the familiar phenomenon of 'relativity of title'. A fundamental question for any land registration regime in a common law system like ours is whether a registered proprietor's position would be illegimately compromised if the law were to recognise the continuing relevance of one or more competing concurrent freehold titles to the same plot. The problem has two main dimensions: (i) whether a registered proprietor's title is paramount vis-à-vis competing relative titles which pre-dated B's registration; and (ii) whether his registered title might be compromised by competing titles that might arise via post-registration events.

i. The Registered Proprietor's Security from Prior Competing Titles

In this section, we consider the extent to which the title promise made by section 58 encompasses a guarantee that B, upon registration, acquires a paramount title, enjoying priority over any competing titles which, prior to his registration, had been superior to his own. We argue that, if it is to be credible, the registration system established by the LRA 2002 must offer some guarantee of paramountcy to those afforded the highest grade of registered title ('absolute title')—via mud or money.

This proposition contains an important explicit caveat. Within the LRA 2002's framework, the strength or quality of title afforded by registration is not a corollary of section 58 alone, but of the relevant *grading* of title attached by the Land Registry. Under the LRA 2002, this is an exercise that occurs on first registration,[46] subject to any subsequent 'upgrading'.[47]

[46] LRA 2002, ss 9, 10.
[47] LRA 2002, ss 62–63.

Registration with the highest grade, of '*absolute*' title, means that A (the first registered proprietor), and by extension, B (the second registered proprietor), has a guarantee against the existence of any relatively superior 'off-Register' title. However, matters look otherwise insofar as the relevant grading of title is of some lesser grade—'*possessory*' or '*qualified*'—which in different ways expressly preserve A's vulnerability to some excepted prior paramount title or other right.[48] This vulnerability continues to affect any subsequent disponees—B, and subsequently C and D, etc—including a registered disponee who could otherwise rely on section 29's priority promise:[49] section 29 does not postpone an earlier interest which 'appears from the register to be excepted from the effect of registration'.[50] Neither A, nor any later disponee, obtains any immunity from such problems, or any monetary guarantee against them. In these instances where the title is graded as 'possessory' or 'qualified', the LRA 2002's title promise does not afford any assurance of paramountcy, *by deliberate design*.

From the perspective of the Register's reliability, the key question is whether any title promise which the Register *does* make—most crucially, to a person registered with 'absolute' title—is itself absolute and uncompromised. Does the LRA 2002 *really* deliver on its apparent promise, such that neither A, nor *a fortiori*, B, C, etc, can find their registered title disturbed by a relatively superior prior title? We explore three different contexts in which this problem may arise in the following three sections. Our conclusion in each case is that, to be credible, the LRA 2002's title promise must be interpreted robustly. As it applies to titles that are graded 'absolute', the promise is a promise of *paramount* title. This may not be realised in practice via *in specie* protection—retaining the mud—but this robust understanding of the promise's implications is crucial, for reasons that we explain below, in laying the foundations for a substantial monetary guarantee in lieu.

a. Vulnerability to a Paramount, Prior Unregistered Title

The first possible challenge to the paramountcy of a registered proprietor's (B's) absolute title exists where there may have been some prior unregistered title—belonging to X—which, at least up to the point of B's registration, had been superior. What change, if any, is wrought by B's registration?

The issues arising here can be illustrated by an example. A conveys his unregistered freehold title to B, who becomes the first registered proprietor. Unbeknown to B, A's title was not paramount: X, the earlier paper owner, retained paramount title. A had a valid freehold title by virtue of his adverse possession,[51] but X's superior title persisted at the time of the A–B conveyance because A had not yet accrued a sufficient period of adverse possession to extinguish X's better claim to the land.[52] Were this problem to be resolved solely by historic principles governing unregistered land, then any title that B could acquire pursuant to a transfer from A would, for the time being at least, remain an inherently inferior title. B (and indeed any successors in title) would have no defence to an action by X to recover

[48] LRA 2002, ss 11 (freehold), 12 (leasehold). There is a fourth grade of leasehold title: 'good leasehold'.
[49] See generally, ch 17 of this book, and in particular, section III.
[50] LRA 2002, s 29(2)(a)(iii).
[51] *Turner v Chief Land Registrar* [2013] EWHC 1382 (Ch), [2013] 2 P & CR 12.
[52] Limitation Act 1980, ss 15 and 17.

possession of the land; B would bear the risk of loss subject to the availability of private law claims against A, the seller, or B's legal adviser.

What difference would it make if, following the A–B conveyance, B is entered on the Register as first registered proprietor with 'absolute' title? And would it make any difference if B subsequently made a registered disposition to C?

Take first the title promise as it applies to C. A major purpose of the Register is to remove any routine need for intending disponees of an already-registered estate, like C, to investigate the pre-history of the title to B's registered estate. For this to be possible, the registration regime must generally immunise C from problems in the 'root' of title to B's registered estate; and where C is vulnerable, offer a money guarantee in lieu. Though nowhere stated, the integrity of the LRA 2002 framework thus probably demands that a registered title like C's must—whilst it subsists—ordinarily be treated as paramount, at least within the confines of the registration regime.

It is conceivable—though not essential—that a registration regime might confer a similar level of security on B, the first registered proprietor. B did not take a transfer of an already-registered estate, and hence B did not rely on the Register, pre-acquisition, to define the package of rights and burdens associated with his title. Nonetheless, reasons might be found to extend similar protections to first registered proprietors—eg that the promise of a degree of security may have the desirable effect of encouraging first registration, and may be deemed an appropriate *quid pro quo* for B's payment of the registration fee. Since the policy arguments for insulating B are more evenly-balanced than they are for C, the conceptual analysis which follows focuses on the position of C. However, it would be possible to apply the same analysis to B, if it were thought appropriate as a matter of policy for the title promise to be of equivalent strength for both categories of party. Nothing in the Act would prevent this.

What then should C's position be, as a registered proprietor with absolute title, as against competing unregistered titles, if the title promise, and its promise of paramount title, is to have real substance? C's position—which must be protected via either mud or money—can be analysed as follows.

First, C's title is 'paramount' solely within the parameters of the registration regime. There is nothing in the LRA 2002 to suggest that registration is now the *sole* source of title to land: title can, in particular, still be acquired under the general law via the taking of possession.[53] It follows that X's prior title may persist notwithstanding the registration with absolute title of B, and thereafter of C. Such registration does not seem to destroy X's prior unregistered title.

Secondly, it follows from this that both X and C might have credible claims to the mud. If we accept that X's prior right is not extinguished by B's/C's registration, then we must further accept: (a) that we must be able to rank X's and C's titles, one against the other; and (b)—to the extent that X's is regarded as superior—that X must have some mechanism for vindicating his superior claim to the land. However, finding resolutions to these problems

[53] This is clear, *inter alia*, from the LRA 2002, sch 6, para 9(1); see too Law Com No 271 (n 7) para 14.71. Note too that there are other events which may invest a legal title in certain categories of person by operation of law, without registration—eg, bankruptcy of the registered proprietor.

which are consistent with the principle that the title promise should guarantee C either mud or money, is difficult. There are three key routes via which this might be achieved, with radically different outcomes:

(i) X's superiority is unaffected by, and remains despite, B's/C's registration. Furthermore, X can immediately and directly vindicate his superior title directly via general law means—eg by an immediate action against C for the recovery of the land and/or for mesne profits for trespass. On this first view, it is not necessary, as a preliminary step, for X to make any application to the Land Registry to have the Register altered in his favour: notwithstanding C's registration, X has the paramount title. But X does of course have the option of seeking alteration to 'bring the register up to date'. This first solution effectively leaves the title promise without content: C will lose possession of the land via the general law vindicatory action. This solution would also deny C the possibility of a Registry indemnity: if X's title is indeed paramount and immediately-vindicatable, any consequential change to C's title in the Register would not seem to cause any indemnity-justifying loss to C.

(ii) As for option (i), the superiority of X's prior title persists despite B's/C's registration. However, as a necessary preliminary to the recovery of the land, X must first seek a change to the Register via the LRA 2002's alteration provisions: pending such alteration, C, the registered proprietor with absolute title, can point to his registered status as legitimising his continuing possession. On this second view, X is thus forced to mediate his claim via the provisions of the LRA 2002. Even so, this analysis does not significantly improve C's position. Once again, C is destined to lose the land without the assurance of an indemnity. An alteration to the Register would merely recognise X's enduring superior title, and would not seem to cause any substantial indemnity-justifying loss to C.[54]

(iii) The registration of B/C with absolute title affords a genuinely paramount right, which ranks ahead of X's formerly-paramount title. On this third view, the LRA 2002 embodies an implicit ranking rule, such that even a previously-paramount unregistered title is subordinated to a registered absolute title. The key corollary is that X cannot immediately vindicate his title vis-à-vis C via general law means. Whether X has any other form of recourse depends on the strength of the title promise made to C. On one view, C's registration with absolute title affords an *in specie* guarantee that he will retain the mud. As such, C is immune from any alteration claim which X might try to make: schedule 4 is inapplicable. The unappealing further corollary would be that the LRA 2002 renders C secure, but only at the cost of X having his own (previously paramount) title effectively extinguished, without any compensation. To avoid this unattractive conclusion, the better view may be that in this sort of situation, schedule 4 *can* be used by X to challenge the initial grading of title at 'first registration' as 'absolute'[55] (or any later upgrading to 'absolute').[56] If that is so, X may seek to have C's registered title cancelled, and possibly have a new title registered

[54] Similarly, C will not be able to avail himself of the possession defence against X's claim, which is reserved as a defence to claims amounting to loss-causing 'rectification': LRA 2002, sch 4, paras 3(2), 6(2).

[55] LRA 2002, ss 9, 10.

[56] LRA 2002, ss 62–63.

in his own name, on the basis that there has been a mistake in the Register: B/C were registered with the wrong grade of title. If X's alteration claim is successful, the alteration would qualify as an indemnity-justifying rectification: C was promised the 'absolute' title, and that promise has not been realised. Conversely, if the alteration claim fails, X may obtain an indemnity: his paramount title has been irreversibly subordinated to B's/C's registered title as a result of the Register mistake.

The LRA 2002 provides little or no explicit steer as to which of these three interpretations should be preferred. In choosing between them, guidance must therefore be found in the general aims and policies of the Act. Only the third solution endows the title promise, made to the proprietor of an absolute title, with any real content—C gets either the mud or money. This third solution also pays due regard to the continuing existence of X's relative freehold title—X's title will either re-gain superiority via rectification of the Register, or X will benefit from an indemnity payment. It is a solution which gains some support from the Law Commission's 2016 Consultation Paper, which assumes that sections 11–12 are subject to schedule 4, with the consequence that a mistaken grading at first registration[57] might be subject to rectification (or, if not, might support a Registry-indemnity for the deprived party).[58]

b. Vulnerability to a Concurrent Registered Title

The second context in which the title promise may come under strain, insofar as it is a promise of *absolute* title, is where the same area of land is mistakenly encompassed within two registered titles.[59] X and A may each be registered as freehold proprietor of Greenacre—eg following a double conveyance of the same land. Assuming that each registered title is nominally an absolute title, the question then arises as to whether and, if so, how these titles fall to be ranked *inter se*.

One possible view is that these titles are immediately rankable—ie, that the LRA 2002 framework implicitly incorporates a conception of relativity of (absolute) registered titles, equivalent to the idea of relativity that operates under the general law that pertains to unregistered land. As such, whilst both X and A are registered with absolute titles, those titles can be ordered—without resorting to the Act's alteration provisions—such that it is possible to say, eg, that one of the titles is the paramount title.[60] However, brief thought suggests that this approach might seriously threaten the integrity of the LRA 2002 framework: it would distort the operation of schedules 4 (alteration) and 8 (indemnity) in a manner that would be likely to nullify the title promise apparently made to the other registered

[57] Similarly, in the case of upgrading of title, via LRA 2002, s 62.

[58] See Law Commission, *Updating the Land Registration Act 2002—A Consultation Paper* (Law Com CP No 227, 2016) paras 13.171 ff. The 2001 Law Commission did not give a clear steer on the applicability of sch 4 to this situation, beyond making express provision for the availability of an indemnity to a person who suffered loss as a result of a title upgrading: LRA 2002, sch 8, para 1(2)(a). The 2001 Law Commission did not deal explicitly with the position of someone, like X, who suffered loss as a result of the *initial* title grading, leaving it unclear whether sch 4 might be used by someone with a paramount prior title to challenge the registration of B or C with absolute title.

[59] eg, *Parshall v Hackney* [2013] EWCA Civ 240, [2013] Ch 568. For extended discussion of the dilemmas by these cases, see ch 6 of this book, section III(E).

[60] See, eg, K Lees, '*Parshall v Hackney*: A Tale of Two Titles' [2013] *Conv* 222.

proprietor. Thus, for example, if A's registered title, whilst on the face of it absolute, were regarded as immediately (ie, presently) and inherently subordinate to X's registered title, several worrying consequences might follow:

(i) this vulnerability in A's title would not be visible on the face of the Register;
(ii) X's paramount title, and, in particular, his better right to immediate possession, would appear to be immediately vindicatable by general law means (eg, via a general law action to recover the land)—bringing the risk that A might be dispossessed without the protections that might be afforded via schedules 4 and 8; and
(iii) A would be similarly vulnerable if X sought to vindicate his rights via the alteration provisions in schedule 4 of the LRA 2002, as an alternative or as a preliminary step to bringing a general law claim, by requesting that the Register be brought up to date to reflect the paramountcy of his title—ie, by cancelling A's subordinate absolute registered title. Despite A's nominal registration with absolute title, his title would be *inherently subordinate*, and so any Register-amendment to reflect this would seem to be a claim for alteration merely (bringing the Register 'up to date'), rather than rectification. This would deny A the special defences available against rectification claims and the possibility of any Registry-indemnity award.

The better view, which has some support in the authorities,[61] is that the integrity of the registration regime requires that the LRA 2002 should *not* incorporate any concept of *implicit* relativity between registered titles of the same 'absolute' grade. Instead, whilst they subsist, the two 'absolute' titles can be regarded as of equal ranking. This means that neither registered proprietor can immediately resort to the *general law* to vindicate their paramount absolute title in a way that prejudices the position of the other. Instead, they can only do so consequent upon a successful application, via schedule 4, to have the other registered title cancelled. Crucially, if the regime recognises that these titles are not *inherently* ranked, then the double registration of A and X as absolute owners of the same land is necessarily mistaken.[62] This being so, any Register amendment to reverse the error can quality as 'rectification' and not mere 'alteration'—it involves the correction of a 'mistake' (there *should* be only one 'absolute' title), and this correction will prejudice the position of A, whose nominally 'absolute' title is cancelled. The defences available against rectification claims, and the possibility of a Registry-indemnity award for whichever of A or X loses his registered title via rectification, are thereby preserved. Only in this way can the title promise which is made to *both* registered proprietors be realised—in one case, *in specie* (retention of the mud), and in the other case, via the possibility of a Registry-indemnity award (money in lieu of the mud).

c. Vulnerability to an Earlier Registered Title-Holder

The third context in which the strength of the title promise might be tested is where A was the proprietor of a registered absolute freehold title, and where, without a valid disposition by A, B becomes the registered proprietor of the same estate in place of A. This is regrettably

[61] See, in particular, *Parshall* (n 59).
[62] The positions of A and X immediately before registration should reveal which of them deserved registration with the paramount 'absolute' title, and which was registered with this status in error.

a commonplace occurrence. For example, a fraudster may forge a conveyance of A's registered title to B, an unsuspecting purchaser, which is duly completed by registration.[63] In this situation, B's registered title is undoubtedly vulnerable, despite section 58, to a schedule 4 application by A to alter the Register. But on what assumption is this so?

Under the *general law* applicable to unregistered land, a forged disposition of A's unregistered title would have no effect on A's rights. B would obtain no more than an original and inferior common law title on his assumption of possession of the land. Furthermore, unless and until A's title was barred via B's adverse possession, A could directly vindicate his continuing title via appropriate general law means—eg via an action for the recovery of the land.

Is a different analysis required, where A's title is a registered title? It seems that it is, for the following reasons.

First, if we are to take seriously the idea that registration is *constitutive* of title, then there is no sense in which A—having ceased to be registered proprietor—could technically retain the *registered* title. Upon his de-registration, A loses that title, which then vests in B, on B's registration. Secondly, the better view is also that we cannot contemplate A's 'retaining', or having some other species of persisting title, which might remain paramount. After *Swift 1st*,[64] we know that A will not retain any paramount *equitable* title, in the face of section 58: B's registration as the new proprietor vests in him the *beneficial* legal estate. Equally, it cannot be right to say that A might retain any inherently superior *legal* estate—eg, derived from A's status as prior possessor. If the courts were to recognise either form of paramount title in A, then the effect would again be to disort the operation of schedules 4 and 8, at the risk of nullifying the title promise afforded to B (and potentially C, etc).

The upshot is that in such cases, A certainly has a good—and probably better—claim to the status of being registered proprietor. Nevertheless, a concern for the integrity of the LRA 2002 framework suggests that this claim should not be mediated via any assumption that A has throughout 'retained' a persisting 'superior' title. Instead, A's claim should be realised only via an application via schedule 4—reflecting the premise that B's registration as proprietor, and A's consequential de-registration, was a 'mistake', because it was not supported by any valid underlying A–B disposition. This analysis seems most likely to preserve the integrity of schedules 4 and 8, and will thereby render it more likely that the title promise made to B can be made good—if not *in specie* via retention of the mud, then at least via money in lieu (a Registry-indemnity), if A's application should succeed.

ii. Security from Subsequent Titles

As already observed, the major source of insecurity that a credible registration regime must endeavour to remove or reduce is the vulnerability of the registered proprietor, B, to another's paramount estate or interest that *pre-dates* his registration, over whose existence B has had little, if any, control. There is no obvious need for a registration system to go further, and offer any guarantee to B against *post*-registration events that may defeat or qualify his title as registered proprietor—whether as a result of B's own valid exercise of dispositional powers, or otherwise via the operation of law. These events might include,

63 eg, *Malory* (n 31); *Fitzwilliam v Richall* (n 11).
64 *Swift 1st* (n 30); see further section III(B)(i) above.

eg, a disposition of B's title to another, or the creation of an easement over B's title expressly or by operation of law.

This policy is largely reflected in the operation of the LRA 2002, which does not immunise B against loss caused by such post-registration events. Their effects would routinely be recorded in the Register, by way of an alteration to the Register to bring it up to date, with no possibility of a Registry-indemnity payment to B.

There is, of course, one important exception to this starting-point, clearly embedded in the LRA 2002 framework. Whilst the Act does not generally protect B against post-registration events that qualify or defeat his title, it does afford a degree of post-registration security in one key respect—ie, enhanced protection against loss of title to adverse possessors. As is well known, this represents a major departure from the old LRA 1925 land registration regime, under which a registered owner might automatically lose title after 12 years' continuous adverse possession by a squatter.[65] Nothing in the LRA 2002 prevents a person from subsequently taking adverse possession and from having, by virtue of this status, a common law possessory title—the Law Commission's 2001 Report[66] and the LRA 2002[67] each manifest a clear assumption that possession *remains* a source of title, even in relation to registered land. However, this possessory title is—necessarily—an inherently inferior title, and in contrast to the position for unregistered estates to which the Limitation Act 1980 remains applicable, it cannot become the paramount title merely by the effluxion of time.[68] Indeed, the only entitlement that arises from a qualifying period of adverse possession is a right to *apply* to replace the current registered proprietor[69]—an application which can only succeed in very narrowly-defined circumstances.[70] Whilst it is not strictly *necessary* for a credible registration regime to promise this degree of security against future adverse acquisition by squatters, it does make pragmatic sense in the short term, as an incentive for owners to register some areas of land that are not currently registered.

It may turn out that the 2001 Law Commission were rather too quick to reject the role for adverse possession within a registration regime. As the Law Commission itself recognised in its 1998 Consultative Document, the law of adverse possession, as it applied prior to the LRA 2002, had multiple functions.[71] It did not just facilitate the adverse acquisition of title by a knowing trespasser-squatter—a form of 'land theft' which the Law Commission were determined to eliminate.[72] Far more importantly, it had also permitted defective titles to be cured via the effluxion of time.[73]

This *curative* function of long adverse possession, which operates in the interests of the finality of transactions and titles, is overwhelmingly more salient in the context of *unregistered* conveyancing.[74] Nevertheless, there is no reason to suppose that this curative

[65] LRA 1925, s 75, which had the effect that the registered title would be held on a bare trust for the adverse possessor from the time when that title, *if it had been an unregistered title*, would have been extinguished by the Limitation Act 1980, s 17.

[66] See especially Law Com No 271 (n 7) para 14.71.

[67] LRA 2002, sch 6, para 9(1)—on registration of an adverse possessor as proprietor pursuant to an application under sch 6, 'the title by virtue of adverse possession which he had at the time of the application is extinguished'.

[68] LRA 2002, s 96.

[69] LRA 2002, sch 6, para 1.

[70] LRA 2002, sch 6, paras 3–6.

[71] Law Com No 254 (n 3) paras 10.4 ff.

[72] ibid, para 10.9.

[73] ibid, para 10.9.

[74] ibid, para 10.10, 10.18;

function is wholly incompatible with a registered title regime. Indeed, the Law Commission acknowledged that it should have a continuing role, even within the LRA 2002's registration regime, in those cases where the Register was not conclusive and there remained uncertainty as to land ownership—ie, in cases involving undetermined boundaries.[75] However, subsequent case law has arguably exposed a worrying further instability in registered titles which the doctrine of adverse possession—or some rule of equivalent effect—might be justifiably called on to cure.

As we explain below,[76] the schedule 4 alteration/rectification provisions have received an expansive interpretation. They are not time-limited, and they may in theory permit the adverse alteration of titles acquired pursuant to remoter transactions in a chain of conveyances. For example, if there is a forged disposition from A registered proprietor to B, who is duly registered as proprietor, the cases permit A to bring a rectification claim to recover his title not only against B, but also against remoter parties (eg C, D, etc) who may subsequently have derived a registered title/interest through B.

It may well be appropriate for a registration system—in the interests of finality—to provide some degree of protection for such remoter parties, who assume, relying on the Register, that they are acquiring a secure title. Schedule 4's alteration provisions build in some protections where the alteration process can be resisted: in particular, the so-called 'proprietor in possession' defence.[77] However, this defence is itself limited. It is only afforded in a narrow subset of cases—ie where there has been a Registry 'mistake', alteration would cause loss to the registered proprietor, and the registered proprietor did not by fault contribute to the Register mistake. Where the defence is inapplicable, the registered proprietor's title is potentially indefinitely at risk—there is a latent defect in his title which adverse possession cannot be relied upon to cure, given the highly-restricted ambit afforded to adverse possession under the LRA 2002. Happily, this threat to the security of registered titles has not gone unnoticed. In its 2016 Consultation Paper, the Law Commission has provisionally proposed that the problem might be resolved via the introduction of a 10-year long-stop for alteration claims.[78] This would go some way towards bringing finality to registered titles.

D. Non-Conclusiveness of Title-Vesting: Susceptibility to Schedule 4 Alteration

Even if section 58 is afforded a wide interpretation in terms of the *nature* and *strength* of the title which is *immediately* conferred by registration—such that the title is not only legal and beneficial, but also paramount—an important question remains as to the 'conclusiveness' or 'indefeasibility' of that registered title *going forwards*.

Significantly, registered titles remain expressly vulnerable, *post-registration*, to the possibility that they may be removed from the Register pursuant to the LRA 2002's schedule 4 'alteration' regime. Where this is the case, the registered proprietor, whose title had been vested in him by section 58, will subsequently be divested of that title.

[75] ibid, para 10.15; Law Com No 271 (n 7) paras 14.3, 14.33–14.52; LRA 2002, sch 6, para 5(4).
[76] See section III(D) below.
[77] LRA 2002, sch 4, paras 3(2), 6(2).
[78] Law Com CP No 227 (n 58) paras 13.115–13.126.

The possibility of such Register-alteration poses a very real threat to the strength of the Act's title promise. Clearly, there is little value in being promised something if, no sooner that the thing has been conferred, it is taken away. However, understanding the extent and potential illegitimacy of that threat is difficult, for two reasons.

First, in certain circumstances a Register-alteration will justify an indemnity being paid by the Registry to the losing party via schedule 8's indemnity provisions. This is so where the alteration specifically corrects a 'mistake', and causes 'prejudice' to the (former) registered proprietor.[79] In such cases, the title promise is weakened, but not wholly undermined—whilst the promise is not realised *in specie*, its beneficiary is at least afforded a money guarantee *in lieu*. Potentially more problematic are those situations where the registered proprietor loses his title, in circumstances which do not justify a Registry-indemnity; here, the title promise seems substantially empty.

Secondly, the presence of schedule 4's alteration provisions within the LRA 2002 means that *some* degree of Register-alteration was thought by the Act's architects to be consistent with the registration regime's ambitions. Nevertheless, if interpreted too widely—and particularly if no indemnity is available to compensate for the registered proprietor's loss of title via alteration—schedule 4's operation could come close to destroying the Act's title promise. This certainly was not intended, and would be unwarranted.

It follows that the title promise which is made to a registered proprietor might ultimately be realised (or not) in one of three ways:

(i) *in specie*—where the title is not susceptible to a Register-alteration at all, and the current registered proprietor therefore retains his title;
(ii) via money *in lieu*—where the Register is altered and yields a Registry-indemnity payment to the former registered proprietor; or
(iii) neither *in specie* nor via money *in lieu*—where the Register is altered in circumstances that do not justify a Registry-indemnity.

The overall coherence of our registration regime requires us to be able to justify the manner in which the title promise is realised in any given case. Which situations warrant *in specie* title protection? Which warrant a merely monetary guarantee? And which circumstances, if any, may justify the current registered proprietor losing his title without compensation? The terms of schedules 4 and 8 do not themselves supply clear and unambiguous answers—they are susceptible to differing interpretations. As such, we find a variety of approaches in the cases and associated academic literature. Some are broadly compatible with the land registration system's ambition for a reliable Register. Others are not, and pose an important threat to the integrity of the registration system.

Against that background, the following paragraphs evaluate the manner in which, in the light of the operation of schedules 4 and 8, the title promise is currently realised in two key scenarios. We call these, respectively, 'AB title cases' and 'ABC title cases'.

[79] In such circumstances, the 'alteration' amounts to a 'rectification': LRA 2002, sch 4, para 1. Crucially, only if the 'alteration' is a 'rectification' will the losing party qualify for a Registry-indemnity: sch 8 para 1(1)(a). Note, however, that the claimant's fraud or lack of care may result in the indemnity payment being reduced or denied: sch 8, para 5.

i. 'AB Title Cases'

Most straightforward and least problematic are 'AB title cases'. These arise where there is a 'flawed disposition' from a registered proprietor, A, to a disponee, B, who subsequently becomes registered as proprietor. The 'flaw' in the A–B disposition might be one that renders the disposition void under the general law (eg where the disposition is forged)[80] or merely voidable (eg, where the disposition is executed following a fraudulent misrepresentation).[81]

In such cases, the intended effect of the title promise made to B seems clear. Although B immediately acquires a title via section 58, he is not guaranteed to keep his title *as a matter of legislative design*. The vice in the A–B disposition will (indirectly) constitute one of the grounds set out in schedule 4 which justify the alteration of the Register—meaning that A can seek the reversal of B's registration. More particularly, where the A–B disposition is void under the general law, B's registration will constitute an alteration-justifying 'mistake';[82] conversely, where the disposition is voidable at the point of B's registration, but has since been validly avoided by A, A can seek to have the Register brought 'up to date'.[83]

In neither case, therefore, does the title promise guarantee that B can keep *the title*. Crucially, though, this outcome—a matter of conscious legislative design—should not undermine the public's confidence in the Register's correctness. Prior to the A–B conveyance, the Register was perfectly reliable in revealing A as owner of the relevant estate. The threat to B's title does not stem from *Register*-unreliability; rather, it is a product of the flawed status under the general law of the A–B *disposition*, over which B may have had some control.

Given that the source of B's misfortune is the flaw in the A–B *disposition*, and not the *registration regime*, there is no compelling reason why the *regime* should indemnify B for his loss of title. Nevertheless, the legislature has chosen to offer B an indemnity *in lieu* of retention of the registered title in *some* AB title cases—namely where the A–B disposition was void (eg, due to forgery or as a result of the *non est factum* doctrine),[84] rather than merely voidable (eg, if induced by a fraudulent misrepresentation),[85] except where B's fraud or carelessness contributed to the problem which led to his de-registration.[86] As such, in the former type of case (void dispositions), the title promise made to B is a promise of money *in lieu* of the title. In contrast, in the latter type of case (voidable dispositions), the promise may amount to nothing at all.

[80] See, eg, *Swift 1st* (n 30), where a fraudster forged the creation of a charge over A's title, in favour of B lender.

[81] See, eg, *Norwich and Peterborough Building Society v Steed* [1993] Ch 116 (CA).

[82] LRA 2002, sch 4, para 2(1)(a). The voidness of the A–B 'disposition' means B was not entitled to be registered as proprietor, and so the Registry is 'mistaken' in effecting B's registration. Note, however, that all alteration claims may be defeated by 'exceptional circumstances': sch 4, para 3(3). Further, where the claim constitutes a 'rectification claim' the current registered proprietor, B, may have a defence where he is in possession—unless B has fraudulently or carelessly caused the mistake, or it would be unjust not to alter the Register: sch 4 para 3(1), (2).

[83] LRA 2002, sch 4, para 2(1)(b). The alteration claim will succeed unless there are 'exceptional circumstances': sch 4, para 3(3).

[84] The availability of an indemnity is contingent on the alteration constituting a 'rectification' (LRA 2002, sch 8, para 1(1)(a)—which requires there to be a 'mistake', the correction of which would prejudice the current registered proprietor's title (LRA 2002, sch 4, para 1).

[85] Where the A-B disposition was merely voidable—and not avoided—at the time of B's registration, B was currently entitled to be registered, and so the Registry has not made an indemnity-justifying 'mistake'.

[86] LRA 2002, sch 8, para 5.

We are agnostic as to whether an indemnity *ought* to be payable in either case—a registration system will be well-functioning whether or not B receives money. Nonetheless, the legislature's policy decision to single out void disposition cases as indemnity-justifying might perhaps be explained by two factors. First, the Registry acts *correctly* when registering voidable dispositions, but *incorrectly* where the disposition is void and therefore non-existent—arguably the Registry should pay for its error. Secondly, B is likely to be at fault where the disposition is *voidable* (he may have fraudulently misled A into making the disposition) and hence undeserving of an indemnity; whereas there will be cases concerning *void* dispositions where B is completely ignorant (eg, where a third party has forged the A–B disposition) and more deserving of an indemnity.[87]

Whatever the merits (or otherwise) of the legislature's policy choices, the sharpness of the intended void/voidable distinction—and thus the availability of an indemnity in void disposition cases—has been threatened by the reasoning employed in some recent cases. Cases like *Swift 1st*[88] (an AB case concerning a forged charge) have seemingly accepted that B's registered title is, from the outset, *inherently* burdened by A's proprietary 'right' to seek a Register-alteration within schedule 4. This reasoning has been thought to bring the further consequence that B is not 'prejudiced' when A ultimately realises that right and, as such, will not qualify for an indemnity, for which 'prejudice' is a prerequisite.[89] This argument, in effect, erects a barrier between B and any indemnity award.

However, despite identifying the existence of this barrier, the *Swift 1st* Court of Appeal then proceeded to find a convoluted way around it. The Court noted that paragraph 1(2)(b) of schedule 8 deems there to be a 'loss' (and therefore 'prejudice') in cases where the registration of a '*forged*' disposition is reversed. As such, party B in *Swift 1st*, who held a forged and now de-registered charge, ultimately qualified for an indemnity. This was a neat way of side-stepping the barrier which the *Swift 1st* Court of Appeal had itself erected. However, the *Swift 1st* circumvention method, of deeming 'loss' to B via schedule 8, paragraph 1(2)(b), is inapplicable where the A–B disposition is void for reasons other than forgery—eg as a result of the *non est factum* doctrine, or the disponor's incapacity. In such cases, if the barrier erected by *Swift 1st* stays in place, B may end up with neither the title nor an indemnity—which seems flatly contrary to the legislature's intentions.[90]

ii. 'ABC Title Cases'

Even more problematic, and much more significant, are 'ABC title cases', which take the AB scenario one stage further. After A's *flawed* disposition to B (whether void or voidable) is registered, these 'ABC' cases involve B subsequently effecting a *valid* disposition to C, which is duly registered.

[87] Note, however, that in those cases where B is responsible for the forgery, he will be disqualified by his conduct from receiving a Registry-indemnity: LRA 2002, sch 8, para 5.

[88] *Swift 1st* (n 30), [45] and [51] (Patten LJ), drawing on *Malory* (n 31) (decided under the old LRA 1925). See also *Stewart v Lancashire Mortgage Corporation Ltd* [2010] EWLandRA 2009_0086 [37] (Judge Holland) and *Crawley v Gudipati* [2010] EWLandRA 2008_0602 [12] (Judge McAllister).

[89] LRA 2002, sch 4, para 1 and sch 8, para 1(1)(a).

[90] See the concerns expressed by E Cooke, 'The Register's Guarantee of Title' [2013] *Conv* 344 and M Dixon, *Modern Land Law*, 8th edn (Oxford, Routledge, 2012) 44, which were both acknowledged in *Swift 1st* (n 30) [37]–[38] (Patten LJ).

It is crucial here to ascertain what the title promise means for C. Does C receive a title which is guarantee *in specie*, or sometimes only an assurance of money *in lieu*, or does C have an assurance of nothing at all? Whilst the flaw in *B*'s registered title stemmed from the A–B *disposition*, any potential flaw in *C*'s registered title will not result from the B–C disposition—which was valid. C will have properly relied on the Register, which showed B as the lawful proprietor at the time when C acquired his interest. If we want a registration system in which potential disponees can place their confidence, it is vital that the title promise yields substantive benefits for people in C's position—whether the land itself, or money *in lieu*.[91]

This assumption, that a well-functioning registration system *must* offer substantive benefits for C, is largely borne out in practice—at least on an 'orthodox' interpretation of the LRA 2002's provisions.

a. A–B Disposition Voidable—Orthodox Approach

C receives the strongest form of protection—a guarantee that he can retain the title *in specie*—where the A–B disposition was merely *voidable*. Because B was *correctly* entered in the Register and B then *validly* conveyed to C, there is no general basis on which C's registered title can be called into question via schedule 4's alteration regime.[92]

b. A–B Disposition Void—Orthodox Approach

The position looks rather different, and has proved to be more controversial, where the initial A–B disposition is *void*. Many early academic accounts of schedule 4 preferred an interpretation which gave C a cast-iron guarantee of keeping his title *in specie*.[93] However, the current tenor of the case law is that C's registered title is vulnerable to a Register-alteration in favour of A, on the basis that C's registration resulted from a Registry 'mistake'.[94]

We do not intend to revisit the well-rehearsed debate as to whether it is appropriate, as a matter of policy, for the law to prefer A over C in a dispute concerning the *title*.[95] What matters for our purposes—and for ensuring the reliability of the Register—is that if C loses the *title*, he will at least qualify for a Registry-indemnity to compensate for his loss—unless

[91] At least where C is innocent, and has not fraudulently or carelessly caused the flaw in the A-B disposition.

[92] Notably, this outcome reflects the result that would have been reached under a straightforward application of the *general law*. See *Ruoff and Roper—Registered Conveyancing* (London, Sweet and Maxwell, looseleaf) paras 46.037–46.039 (August 2017 release). But note the important caveat registered in n 97 below, which arises from the fact that A's right/'equity' to rescind the disposition may be regarded as a proprietary interest (LRA 2002, s 116) which is capable of overriding the B–C disposition pursuant to LRA 2002, s 29 and sch 3, para 2.

[93] See esp E Cooke, *The New Law of Land Registration* (Oxford, Hart, 2003) 122–129; R Smith, *Property Law*, 4th ed (Harlow, Pearson, 2003) 260–262; *Ruoff & Roper* (n 92) paras 46.024–46.036 (September 2004 release); B McFarlane, N Hopkins and S Nield, *Land Law: Text, Cases and Materials* (Oxford, OUP, 2009) 533–534, 538–542; D Fox, 'Forgery and Alteration of the Register Under the Land Registration Act 2002' in E Cooke (ed), *Modern Studies in Property Law, Volume 3* (Oxford, Hart, 2005).

[94] See *Barclays Bank plc v Guy (No 2)* [2010] EWCA Civ 1396, [2011] 1 WLR 681 [35] (Lord Neuberger MR); see further, Goymour, 'Mistaken Registrations' (n 27) and Law Com CP No 227 (n 58) paras 13.64 ff.

[95] See, eg, S Cooper 'Regulating Fallibility in Registered Land Titles' [2013] *CLJ* 341; S Cooper 'Resolving Title Conflicts in Registered Land' (2015) 131 *LQR* 108; Goymour, 'Mistaken Registrations' (n 27); E Lees, 'Title by Registration: Rectification, Indemnity and Mistake and the Land Registration Act 2002' (2013) 76 *MLR* 62. We do, however, note that purchaser confidence in the regime may be enhanced by rules which, all things being equal, prioritise the disponee's *in specie* title, rather than awarding that disponee money in lieu.

he has carelessly or fraudulently caused the 'mistake'.[96] If that is the case, the title promise will still yield substantial benefits for C—he gets either the land, or money in lieu.

c. Threat to the Orthodox Approach

Looming large, however, is a differently-framed argument, which threatens to empty the title promise of any substantive content for C—whether the A–B disposition is voidable or void—and thereby undermine the Register's reliability.

Thus, it is conceivable that the argument accepted by the Court of Appeal in *Swift 1st*—ie, that A acquires a proprietary 'right' to seek a Register-alteration as soon as B is mistakenly registered—might be applied not only to 'AB' cases, but also to 'ABC' cases.[97] If that is allowed to happen, then A's alteration claim vis-à-vis B, having the quality of a proprietary 'right', may persist against C's title as an 'overriding interest', provided that A is relevantly in actual occupation of the land.[98] When A subsequently seeks to realise his alteration claim vis-à-vis C, C will thereby suffer no further prejudice or loss—he was bound by A's claim from the outset—and so may not qualify for a Registry indemnity.[99]

The dramatic effect of this extended *Swift 1st* argument cannot be underestimated. It fully negates the title promise for C—he will get neither the title nor money. In doing so, it risks shattering the public's confidence in the Register more generally.[100]

iii. A Way Forward?

If the title promise is to have teeth, the registration regime needs to ensure that where someone who has relied on the Register's correctness loses their title, they at minimum receive monetary compensation—at least in the absence of disqualifying fault. One solution may be to decouple the availability of a Registry-indemnity from notions of general law entitlement. This would mean that the LRA 2002's concepts of 'prejudice' and 'loss'—both of which are prerequisites for an indemnity award—would be defined by reference to what the disappointed registered proprietor has been *promised* by the registration regime, ie *a valid title*, and not (as is the current trend) by looking *outside* the Register at whatever the general law might say about that party's entitlements and vulnerabilities/liabilities. An indemnity regime which uses external doctrines as its reference point will forever be at the mercy of the general law and its developing understanding of the rights that prior parties might hold against a registered proprietor in the context of flawed dispositions. Only if we fully commit

[96] LRA 2002, sch 8, para 5.

[97] *Swift 1st* (n 30). Note that in ABC title cases where the A–B disposition is *voidable*, an alternative argument is plausible—that A's right to rescind *the disposition* is a (proprietary) 'equity' which is capable of overriding the B–C disposition. Similar problems ensue, in terms of Register-reliability, whether A is afforded a proprietary right via this analysis or via the *Swift 1st* analysis.

[98] LRA 2002, s 29 and sch 3, para 2.

[99] See *Swift 1st* (n 30) and Law Com CP No 227 (n 58) paras 13.61–13.62.

[100] It might be argued that C deserves this miserable fate as a matter of legislative design—he could have found out about A's overriding interest, by making relevant inquiries whilst A occupied the land (see further E Lees, 'Guaranteed Title: No Title, Guaranteed', ch 7 of this book). However, this argument is problematic as a matter of policy, and doctrinally circular: it makes an unfounded and probably incorrect assumption that the legislature contemplated that a sch 4 alteration claim would have proprietary status, and therefore might find its priority preserved against a registrable disposition by LRA 2002, sch 3, para 2. cf also Law Com CP No 227 (n 58), paras 13.62–13.63.

to the logic of the title promise in our interpretation of the alteration and indemnity provisions will we have a Register that is consistently and truly reliable.

E. Direct Liabilities

Any account of the title promise must also recognise that its practical effect may be substantially diluted via the imposition of so-called 'direct liabilities' on a registered proprietor, B. These direct liabilities are the product of a wide range of liability-generating rules whose sources lie outside the LRA 2002. They include: liability under contracts made by B; B's liability for wrongdoing, tortious or otherwise; and liability for B's unjust enrichment.

It is difficult to overstate the importance of the threat that these present to B, and also more generally to the integrity of any registration regime. Proper appreciation of the magnitude of this threat nevertheless requires some important distinctions to be drawn as regards the point in time when these direct liabilities arise. For reasons that we explain, no real threat arises from direct liabilities that are generated by *post*-registration events. In contrast, a very real threat is posed by direct liabilities that arise *before* or *at* registration—whether as a result of the immediate events by which B becomes registered proprietor, or of earlier conduct on B's part.

i. Direct Liability Arising From Post-Registration Events

As already noted,[101] a credible registration regime does not require B, or B's registered title, to be immune from liabilities arising from *post*-registration events, such as contracts made by B following his registration as proprietor.

A registration regime's principal aim is to secure the reliability of the Register for parties who *deal* with the registered proprietor—eg C, a prospective purchaser or mortgagee of B's registered title. The promises that it must afford and make good, via *in specie* immunity from challenge or money guarantee in lieu, amount to assurances as to the validity and priority of a present disposition, despite the existence of historic defects in the root of title, immediate transactional defects, or prior incumbrances not reflected in the Register at the time of the disposition by B.

By contrast, there is no compelling justification for any *continuing* assurance of immunity from *post*-registration events that might adversely affect B's legal position. Most obviously, B must be able to encumber his own title via the exercise of his dispositional 'owner's powers'.[102] Indeed, B's ability to do this is essential, if the registration regime is to make good its promise that future disponees—ie, C—can rely on B's registration and his accompanying owner's powers.[103] Equally, there is no good reason why B's status as a *registered* proprietor should afford him any peculiar immunity from the panoply of general law doctrines that might subject a proprietor to personal obligations, or generate rights affecting his title by operation of law—eg, via the mechanism of proprietary estoppel, or the imposition of a constructive trust.

[101] See section III(C)(ii) above.

[102] LRA 2002, s 23; see our discussion in ch 18 of this book.

[103] ie, the 'empowerment promise', which we outline in ch 15 of this book, and examine at length in ch 18.

ii. Direct Liability Arising From Pre-Registration Events

Pre-registration events inevitably pose more difficult problems. The problem comes in two different forms—what might be labelled: (1) *acquisition-related* direct rights, and (2) *pre-acquisition* direct rights.

First, it is sometimes arguable that, as result of the circumstances in which B has become registered as proprietor, B has come under some form of direct liability for the first time to another—whether a previous owner, A, or a third party, X.[104] This might be a personal liability arising from a contract made by B, liability for wrongful conduct (eg an economic tort, or an equitable wrong of dishonest participation in a breach of trust/knowing receipt), or possibly liability arising in unjust enrichment.[105] Alternatively, the relevant direct liability might involve the recognition that A or X has some form of *proprietary interest* affecting B's registered title—eg A might have an equity to rescind the transfer of title to B for fraudulent/innocent misrepresentation, duress, undue influence, or otherwise; or A or X might benefit from the imposition of a lien or constructive trust.

Secondly, it is also conceivable that at some earlier time *before* B became registered as proprietor, B was materially party to a transaction that justified the imposition of a personal liability on B, or the recognition of a right affecting the title of which B subsequently became registered as proprietor. This could easily occur in cases of voluntary first registration, as a result of events occurring whilst B owned the unregistered estate—eg, where B expressly created an easement over his unregistered estate prior to first registration. However, it could also occur in cases of compulsory first registration or subsequent registered dealings—eg, where rights affecting the registered estate arose whilst B was one of two joint registered proprietors, and where the registered estate was subsequently conveyed to B as sole proprietor.[106]

Accepting that B might incur liabilities of this sort under the general law if he had acquired an unregistered estate, does his status as a *registered* proprietor require the law to respond differently? In particular, does this status necessitate any immunity from these liabilities, which might otherwise be incurred?

a. A Preliminary Problem—The Uncertain Statutory Regulation of Direct Liabilities

An immediate problem, in attempting to answer this question within the LRA 2002, is that the issue of direct liabilities was barely touched on by the 2001 Law Commission, and, where it was, the treatment was only partial and susceptible to misunderstanding.

The better view is that the origination of direct rights against B, a registered proprietor—whether acquisition-related or pre-acquisition-related—is not something which is directly and expressly regulated by the LRA 2002. No express provision in the LRA 2002 immunises

[104] Such liabilities are discussed in, eg, E Cooke and P O'Connor, 'Purchaser Liability to Third Parties in the English Land Registration System: A Comparative Perspective' (2004) 120 *LQR* 640; B McFarlane, 'Constructive Trusts Arising on a Receipt of Property Sub Conditione' (2004) 120 *LQR* 664.

[105] A possibility examined in E Bant, 'Registration as a Defence to Claims in Unjust Enrichment: Australia and England Compared' [2011] *Conv* 309.

[106] cf *Halifax plc v Curry Popeck (A Firm)* [2008] EWHC 1692 (Ch), a case examined at length in ch 17 of this book, section III(D)(i)(c).

B from such liabilities, *as a general class*. In particular, neither section 58, nor the LRA 2002's priority provisions, has any such immunising effect.

Section 58's title-vesting effect—even if it affords B, the registered proprietor, a beneficial legal title—will not render him immune from direct liabilities. Its sole effect is to ensure that B obtains title upon registration, despite circumstances that might, under the general law, have prevented this. This is a rather limited curative effect, reflecting the legislature's intention that registration should be an original *source* of title. It will not immunise B from other problems that would not technically prevent his acquiring title, but would merely serve to impair his title's *quality* or *security*—eg the problem that B might validly obtain title, but that it is immediately subject under the general law to a trust, or to an equity to rescind that might lead to the title's subsequent divestment.

The key priority provisions of the LRA 2002, found in sections 11–12 and 28–30, are also of limited relevance in providing answers to the questions presented by direct liabilities. As we explain more fully in chapter seventeen,[107] these provisions—and particularly those found in sections 28–29—are true priority provisions, addressed narrowly to whether a third party's *pre-existing* proprietary interest, which encumbers an estate, should persist and retain priority in the face of a later disposition. They do not have any wider cleansing effect in immunising B from direct liabilities.

The inapplicability of the LRA 2002's priority rules seems particularly clear in cases of acquisition-related direct rights—ie, new rights, personal or proprietary, which are directly generated via the general law in favour of another, A or X, as a response to the circumstances in which B acquired his registered title. Logically, whether B's title is affected by A's/X's new direct right cannot be answered by the application of those priority rules—which concern *pre-existing* rights, not new ones—and is not otherwise expressly regulated by the LRA 2002. The Act's priority rules only become material on a later disposition by B—at which point the persistence of A's/X's direct right against the disponee can raise a priority problem.

This fundamental point has been misperceived in recent cases, some of which seem to treat section 29 as material *even* in cases involving only two parties—A and B. Thus, in *Swift 1st*,[108] where B had obtained a registered charge over A's registered estate as a result of a third party's forgery, the Court of Appeal's analysis of whether an indemnity was available to B was skewed by its underlying assumption that the removal of B's charge would prima facie entail no loss to B—B's charge was inherently subject to A's statutory right to alteration/rectification, which bound B in accordance with the Act's priority rules as an overriding interest, because A had remained in actual occupation. An equivalent assumption had previously been made in *Malory*[109] and in *Fitzwilliam v Richall*.[110] This analysis is impossible to accept. In a two-party case like *Swift 1st*, A's statutory right to alter/rectify B's title arises directly against B, whose title was registered as a result of a mistake. It is a *new* right which arises for the first time only on B's registration, and it is exigible against B without more, and without further qualification. Its exigibility against B does not depend

[107] See ch 17 of this book, section III(D)(ii).
[108] *Swift 1st* (n 30).
[109] *Malory* (n 31).
[110] *Fitzwilliam v Richall* (n 11).

on an application of the Act's priority provisions—sections 28 and 29—because it is not in the nature of a pre-existing interest, whose persistence depends on these priority rules.[111]

The applicability of the LRA 2002's priority provisions is trickier in relation to *pre-acquisition* direct rights, where B was a relevant participant in the events that generated the right. Consider, for example, a case where joint registered proprietors, A and B, together enter an option agreement with X, which is not protected by an entry on the Register. Subsequently, the registered title is conveyed for valuable consideration to B as sole registered proprietor. Can X still enforce his option agreement against B, following B's registration as sole owner? There are two dimensions that need to be unpacked here: (i) the status of X's claim as a pre-acquisition *property* right and (ii) the status of any continuing *personal* liability generated by the option contract.

It is axiomatic that the LRA 2002's priority rules, being concerned with the persistence of *property rights*, do not speak to the enforceability of *personal* liabilities that might have arisen before B became the sole registered proprietor. However, the application of the Act's priority provisions raises more difficult issues if B was implicated in events that generated a *property* right prior to his becoming sole registered proprietor—ie X's option, in our example. It has sometimes been assumed that section 11 (on first registration) and section 29 (on later registered dealings) might have an *extended* cleansing effect. In particular, they might clear B's registered title of X's pre-existing interest, which affected the estate before B's acquisition, even where B was a relevant participant in the events that had generated X's right—eg as co-grantor of X's option, in our example. For reasons that we explain in chapter seventeen,[112] this cannot be accepted without qualification. The 1998 Law Commission had in fact recommended an *explicit* proviso,[113] clarifying that what became section 29 would not affect the status of pre-existing rights to which B was party—a proposal which seems not to have been followed through by the 2001 Law Commission. However, even if the absence of such a proviso meant that the pre-existing interest *could* be subordinated via section 29, this should not preclude the recognition of a *new* right in response to a *continuing* obligation affecting B's own conscience—whether in the form of a property right affecting B's title, or a merely personal right arising against B.

As we explain in chapter seventeen, at some stage the courts must acknowledge that they have misunderstood and over-stated the significance of the LRA 2002 priority rules for direct rights.[114] Unless they do this, the nature of the risks presented by direct rights, and appropriate strategies for dealing with them, will be misperceived.

b. The Extent of the Direct Rights Incursion—An Open Tap, or Controlled Flow?

If the LRA 2002 implicitly allows for the imposition of *acquisition-related* direct rights upon B, a newly-registered proprietor—and possibly also, the persistence of *pre-acquisition* direct rights—there is a problem. In three ways, this form of liability might diminish the value of the title promise made by the Act.

[111] We discuss these points at greater length in ch 17 of this book, especially in section III(E), in the context of our discussion of the LRA 2002's priority promise.

[112] See ch 17 of this book, sections II(B)(i) and III(D)(ii).

[113] Law Com No 254 (n 3) paras 7.36–7.37.

[114] See ch 17 of this book, sections II(B)(i) and III(D)(ii).

First, such direct rights can substantially impair the quality and security of title which B obtains via his registration as proprietor. The creation/persistence of a direct right in A's/X's favour which is *proprietary* will impair B's ability to enjoy the land, and possibly deprive B of all rights to it, if enforcement of the direct right renders him vulnerable to losing his registered title—eg where a trust over B's title is collapsed in A's/X's favour pursuant to the *Saunders v Vautier* principle. Here, B would be unlikely to qualify for a Registry-indemnity: even if the recognition of A's/X's proprietary right results in an alteration that cancels B's title, any loss which results to B is caused by the creation of the direct right, and not by the consequent Register-amendment. Equally, even if the direct right merely comprises a *personal* liability owed by B to A/X—such that B's registered title is itself unburdened—B will be prejudiced by the imposition of a monetary liability. Indeed, B might find it necessary to sell his title in order to satisfy it. None of this means that the imposition of direct rights is inherently objectionable, but it does show that the grounds for their imposition need to be carefully managed, and kept within narrow bounds—ie, limited to cases where B's conduct is such that, given the policies that underlie the registration regime, he has no legitimate claim to a title which is secure, nor should he benefit from a state-indemnity against the risk of its loss.

Secondly, such direct rights do not just adversely affect B, against whom they immediately arise. If the relevant right is an interest that affects B's registered estate—eg via a constructive/resulting trust, an equity to rescind, or an estoppel equity in favour of X—then it will create risks for third parties, like C, who later deal with B. Such interests have the capacity to persist against such parties via the Act's priority provisions. Again, this is not inherently objectionable, *provided* that any priority promise made to these later parties, via section 29, is robust. This is discussed in chapter seventeen.[115]

Thirdly, underlying this is a deeper problem, which is that the LRA 2002 does not itself regulate the circumstances in which these disruptive direct rights can be imposed. Their existence and extent is left to the general, largely judge-made law—eg as to the circumstances in which constructive or resulting trusts may be imposed, or liability may arise for wrongdoing, unjust enrichment, etc. It follows that the LRA 2002 is not a self-contained and autonomous regime, which comprehensively accounts for all of the rights to which B is subject, on registration. That in turns poses a pressing problem: the tap is left open for direct rights to flood into the LRA 2002 framework, with no clear steer in either the LRA 2002 itself, or in associated law reform reports,[116] as to when it must be closed off.

There will certainly come a point at which direct rights are recognised in such wide circumstances by the general law that their imposition will illegitimately swamp and nullify the registration regime's intended effect. Unfortunately, lack of clarity about the Act's authors' ambitions—and divergent judicial reactions to similar facts—make it difficult to be sure about how, and when, that point should be identified.

A good illustration of this problem can be found in the recent First-tier Tribunal decision of *Phillips v Smith*.[117] Here, Smith (B) had become registered proprietor pursuant to a transfer ostensibly made by Phillips (A), and had subsequently mortgaged the property

[115] See ch 17 of this book, section III(D).

[116] cf the brief and inconclusive survey in Law Com No 254 (n 3) paras 3.48–3.49; even less attention was given to this issue in Law Com No 271 (n 7).

[117] *Phillips v Smith* [2017] UKFTT 0001 (PC).

to Nat West (C). In later proceedings by A to challenge the efficacy of these transactions, Judge Rhys held that the A–B transfer was not validly executed via a deed, and hence was a nullity—a conclusion which was thought to enable A to have the Register altered against B on the ground of mistake (ie, B's registration was effected on the basis of a defective transfer).[118] However, he also went on to find that A had 'retain[ed] the entire beneficial interest in the property', and that B therefore held the property on a bare trust for A, pending alteration of the Register.[119] This was a surprising conclusion, in the light of the Court of Appeal's decision in *Swift 1st*.[120] Judge Rhys reasoned that had the title been an unregistered title, the transfer 'would not have been effective to transfer the legal estate'.[121] B's present status as 'legal owner' was 'attributable only to the effect of section 58', and '[a]lthough [B] ha[d] the legal estate ... in view of the circumstances in which the Transfer was signed she never obtained [A's] beneficial interest in the Property'.[122] There was 'clearly no intention on [A's] part to give [B] her beneficial interest'. As such, 'the registration of the Transfer did not in any way affect the underlying beneficial ownership of the Property, which has always been that of [A]'.[123] *Swift 1st* was not cited by Judge Rhys. His conclusion, even if not his reasoning, can only be reconciled with the position taken by the *Swift 1st* Court of Appeal on the assumption that whilst section 58 ordinarily vests the beneficial legal estate in B, beneficial title was *restored* to A, via a trust imposed on B *immediately on B's acquisition*—reflecting A's lack of intention that B should obtain beneficial ownership. This is an explanation consistent with one vision of the basis on which resulting trusts arise[124]—indeed, A had argued that her beneficial interest arose via a resulting trust. Nonetheless, it must be accepted that if this is a tolerable explanation of the result in *Phillips*, then the tap is left wide open to the recognition of a direct right that directly negates the extensive title-vesting effect of section 58, as understood in *Swift 1st*.

IV. Future Challenges

The promise, embodied in section 58, that a registered proprietor acquires a 'title by registration' is often hailed in the literature as a headline feature of the LRA 2002's registration regime. The notion that registration not only *records*, but actually *constitutes* title, might be regarded as central to a register in which parties can place their absolute confidence when dealing with land.

However, as this chapter has demonstrated, the LRA 2002's title promise has not in practice yielded all of the bounties that it might, at first sight, appear to offer. Whether by deliberate legislative design, or as a result of judicial interpretation, several cracks have begun to

118 ibid [58].

119 ibid [62]. Judge Rhys saw that this conclusion would have implications for later dispositions by B, if A's continuing actual occupation meant that her beneficial interest, if not overreached, could have the status of an overriding interest under sch 3, para 2: ibid, [63].

120 *Swift 1st* (n 30), discussed in section III(B)(i) above.

121 *Phillips* (n 117) [62].

122 ibid.

123 ibid.

124 R Chambers, *Resulting Trusts* (Oxford, OUP, 2007).

emerge. From the perspective of those relying on the title promise, these vulnerabilities fall into two main categories.

The first and more benign type of vulnerability reflects the fact that the promise of '*title*' may in practice only be realised more weakly, by a monetary indemnity payment *in lieu* of the title, where the schedule 4 alteration regime, as generously interpreted by the relevant case law, allows a previous owner to obtain rectification of the Register against the current registered proprietor.[125] This 'crack' in the title promise alters the *nature* of the benefit afforded by the promise but not its *economic value*. If the promisee does not keep the land, he will at least recoup its value. To this extent, he can safely rely on the Register. It follows that we need not be excessively troubled by this sort of 'crack'—indeed, the presence of provisions that permit Register alterations within the registration regime is a realistic and necessary concession to the fact that, however undesirable they may be, Register mistakes and/or flawed dispositions occur in real life and should sometimes be unpicked. Provided the alteration provisions are applied in a cautious and disciplined way, the practical benefits which flow from them probably outweigh the relatively small 'crack' which they make in the title promise.

The second type of vulnerability is far more damaging to the purported promisee, and thus to Register-reliability more generally. It arises in cases where the title promise *appears* to have been made by the registration system, but actually yields no benefit at all to the registered proprietor—neither title nor money *in lieu*. In some cases, this might be readily justified—as where the registered proprietor has been fraudulent or careless. Yet even wholly blameless parties have sometimes been denied the benefit of the title promise. As this chapter has revealed, this second type of vulnerability has taken various forms, which—individually and collectively—pose a real threat to the Register's reliability.

First, section 58's title promise may be undermined *ab initio* by unwarranted expansive interpretations of the statutory exceptions as to when it bites—eg the meaning of 'registration requirements' in section 58(2).[126]

Secondly, even where section 58's title promise does bite, its effect can be diluted by incursions from sources of claim external to the Register—whether these are competing titles or direct rights.[127] Crucially, a registered proprietor whose title is considered to be burdened from its inception by a competing external title/right, will not qualify for a Registry-indemnity, and so the title promise is effectively negated.

Thirdly, a worrying trend is emerging in the case law in 'AB' and 'ABC title' cases, where the A–B disposition is flawed. As we have seen, the title promise is only minimally compromised if the Register is unwound in A's favour, but the losing registered proprietor (whether B or C) receives an indemnity *in lieu* of the title. However, recent case law has suggested that A's right to seek a Register-alteration might *inherently* burden B's and C's titles from the moment these titles are registered, in such a way that denies B or C an indemnity to compensate for their loss of title.[128] This is a problem, especially for C, who will have properly relied on the Register being correct.

[125] See section III(D).
[126] See section III(A).
[127] See sections III(C) and III(E).
[128] See section III(D)(ii)(c).

Being upfront about the significance of the title promise within the LRA 2002's regime throws into sharp focus the threats posed by judicial interpretations that deny promisees both title and money *in lieu*. Going forwards, it is vital that the title promise is properly understood, and that it serves as a compass for guiding future interpretations of the relevant legislative provisions. In particular, if deployed as a directional device, the title promise should hopefully divert the courts from problematic interpretative paths that threaten to deny all benefits in ABC title cases to C—who, of anyone, a credible registration regime must protect. If we approach C's position with a keen eye on the 'title by registration' mantra, it becomes clear that his registration is meant to confer substantive and valuable rights. This is so notwithstanding any general law vulnerabilities that might otherwise affect him. Approached in this way—ie, by reference to what the *registration regime* confers on him—C's removal from the Register is clearly 'prejudicial' to his registered title, and can appropriately trigger a Registry-indemnity for that 'loss'.[129] By this route, the title promise can be given the substantive content that it was meant to have.

[129] See section III(D)(iii).

17

A Tale of Three Promises: (2) The Priority Promise

STEPHEN WATTERSON AND AMY GOYMOUR

I. Introduction

This extended chapter examines the Land Registration Act ('LRA') 2002 regime's second key promise—what we have chosen to call the 'priority (or ordering) promise'. At the outset, it is important to see that priority disputes between competing interest-holders can take several different forms.

A. The Priority of Derivative Interests

The first and most familiar form of priority dispute concerns the priority or ordering of *derivative* interests that affect or arise out of the same registered title. Such disputes take two key forms. Each involves three parties—X, Y and Z—where X and Z compete for priority.

First are cases where the registered transferee of a registered title (eg, a registered freehold title) competes for priority with the holder of a lesser interest previously derived from that registered title (eg, an easement, a beneficial interest arising under a trust, a lease etc). For example, a registered freehold proprietor, Y, grants an easement to X, and subsequently transfers his registered freehold title to Z, leaving X and Z vying for priority (see Configuration 1, below).

Second are cases involving a priority contest between two lesser interests derived from the same registered estate. For example, a registered freehold proprietor, Y, grants an easement to X, and subsequently declares a trust of his registered estate for Z, leaving X and Z competing for the superiority of their interest as against the other (see Configuration 2, below).

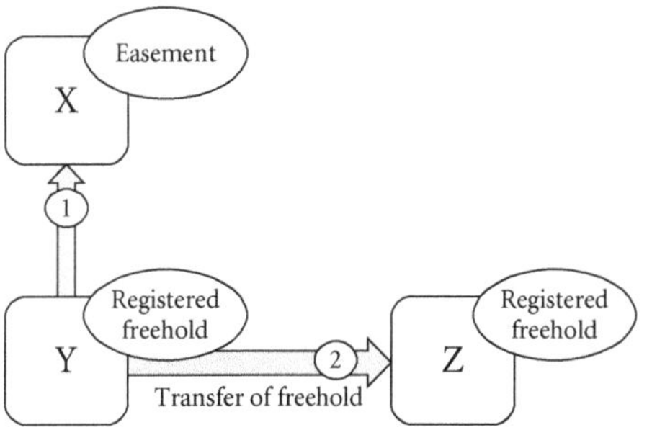

Configuration 1

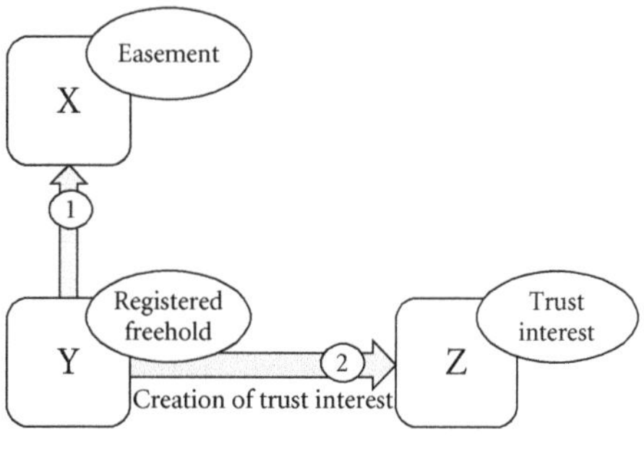

Configuration 2

Both types of factual scenario are governed by the same sets of rules. However, for good reason, these rules themselves differ according to whether a priority dispute arises at the point of *first* registration of the relevant title (when sections 11–12 of the LRA 2002 are governing), or on a *subsequent* disposition of an *already-registered* title (when sections 28–29 are governing). As we explain below, this difference is comprehensible given the likely ambitions of the LRA 2002.

At first registration, the key question concerns the priority of interests that *pre*-date the first registration. There is no compelling need for the registration framework, at the point of first registration, to *alter* the existing priorities that would pertain under general property law as it applies to unregistered land. If Z is the first registered proprietor, he has, by definition, not *previously* relied on the Register when taking his interest from Y, and so the reliability of the Register is not in issue.

The position is otherwise in cases involving *subsequent dealings* with an existing registered title—where Y was the registered proprietor before his disposition to Z. Here, it is a practical necessity for Z to be able to rely on the Register, and the applicable priority rules must be modified to support this reliance. Clearly, later parties dealing with a registered proprietor require some measure of immunity from pre-existing interests that affect the registered title but are not visible in the Register.

In this chapter, we examine priority problems arising at first registration in section II, and problems arising in the event of subsequent dispositions in section III, before offering some conclusions in section IV.

B. The Priority of Non-Derivative Interests

At the outset it is also important to note, for the sake of completeness, that priority disputes also arise in another context—where the dispute is between competing interests which are *not* derivative of the same registered title. For reasons of space, and because they have been examined in chapter sixteen, this chapter does not examine these problems. It is sufficient to note that such disputes between non-derivative interests take two forms. Neither is governed by specific express provisions of the LRA 2002.

i. Competing Registered and Unregistered Titles

The first dimension is where one interest is a registered interest, whilst the other derives from some other source. A key illustration is where there are apparently competing freehold titles: one title derived from registration, the other derived from another source—eg, an unregistered common law title based on the taking of possession, an original mode of acquisition. The LRA 2002 regime does not dictate that registration is the only possible source of title. Indeed, it is clear from schedule 6 of the LRA 2002 that such possession-based titles *do* persist.[1] However, the integrity of the LRA 2002 regime is likely, if only by

[1] As recognised by LRA 2002, sch 6, para 9(1); see further chs 6 and 16 (especially section III(C)(i)), of this book.

necessary implication, to require that the registered title—whilst it persists, and subject to rectification—should be treated as superior/paramount.[2]

ii. Competing Registered Titles

The second dimension is where each competing non-derivative interest is registered. This conundrum is illustrated by cases where, as the result of a mistake, the same area of land is subject to two 'absolute'-graded registered freehold titles. These present real dilemmas. What rights does each registered proprietor enjoy vis-à-vis the other, whilst both remain registered? Can their titles be ranked, or are they equally valid? If one is subservient to the other, or if one can be rendered subservient to the other via an amendment to the Register, what are the principles by which that can occur?[3] These are pressing questions that will require principled answers in the future.

II. Derivative Interests Affecting a Registered Title: First Registration

This section explores the nature, strength and vulnerabilities of the priority promise made by the LRA 2002 at first registration. Our concern is therefore with cases where: (i) X's interest binds Y's *unregistered* estate (eg, an unregistered freehold); (ii) the unregistered estate is subsequently registered—either by Y himself (via voluntary first registration), or by Z, a transferee from Y (in circumstances triggering compulsory first registration); and (iii) X subsequently claims priority for his interest against the registered estate (whether held by Y or Z). It will become apparent that the first registration priority promise is riddled with under-examined problems.

A. Basis and Ambitions of the Promise

The priority rules applicable at first registration have an explicit statutory basis in sections 11 (for freehold estates)[4] and 12 (for leasehold estates).[5] The nature and strength of the resulting promise can be sufficiently illustrated via the rules applicable to the most common and highest grade of title: an 'absolute' title to a *freehold* estate.[6] We focus on this in the following sections.

In general, it seems that the relevant rules are intended to be essentially *parasitic* and *neutral*. The *general law*—here, the law of unregistered conveyancing—is the primary

[2] For extended discussion, see chs 6 (especially sections III(C) and III(D)(ii)), and 16 (especially section III(C)(i)), of this book.

[3] For extended discussion, see ch 6 of this book, section III(E); and ch 16 of this book, section III(C)(i)(b).

[4] LRA 2002, s 11.

[5] LRA 2002, s 12.

[6] LRA 2002, s 11(2), (3)–(5).

reference-point for identifying which third party interests (held by X) are *capable* of burdening the relevant estate (held by Y or Z), and which *in fact* do so. Crucially, and self-evidently, the newly-registered proprietor has not, prior to registration, relied on the Register. It is only *after* first registration, upon subsequent dispositions of the registered estate, that it is strictly necessary to have autonomous priority rules for the registration regime to realise its ambitions. It is only then that disponees will rely on the Register's accuracy.

Where first registration of a legal estate is *voluntary*,[7] the relevant proprietor (Y) will have obtained his estate—perhaps some time ago—according to the rules of unregistered conveyancing. Where a disposition of an unregistered estate (eg, from Y to Z) triggers *compulsory* first registration, the legal estate is also immediately acquired in accordance with the rules of unregistered conveyancing—but its vesting in Z may subsequently be nullified if the registration requirement is not duly complied with,[8] in which case the estate must be re-conveyed by Y to Z in accordance with the same rules.[9] In either case, the priority of an interest belonging to X that affected the relevant estate (now belonging to Y or Z) before its registration, is intended to be determined, first and foremost, *in accordance with the rules of unregistered land*. Generally, the LRA 2002 does not mandate a different conclusion. Thus, according to Charles Harpum and Janet Bignall:

> As a general principle ... *first registration does not affect priorities but merely reflects priorities that have already been determined*. First registration may be voluntary so that there may have been no disposition to trigger registration. In any event, even where there is some disposition, that disposition precedes registration and any issue of competing priorities will be resolved at the time of that disposition. That resolution will depend upon the principles of unregistered conveyancing that necessarily apply to that disposition.[10]

In cases of first registration with *absolute* title to a freehold estate, the operative provision is section 11(4). This provides that such registration has the effect that:

> The estate is vested in the proprietor subject only to the following interests affecting the estate at the time of registration—
>
> (a) interests which are the subject of an entry in the register in relation to the estate,
> (b) unregistered interests which fall within any of the paragraphs of Schedule 1, and
> (c) interests acquired under the Limitation Act 1980 ... of which the proprietor has notice.[11]

The LRA 2002's strategy may not be immediately apparent here, since section 11(4) seems to incorporate two layers of condition. First, the relevant interest must have '*affected the estate at the time of registration*'. This is an implicit reference back to, and reliance on, the rules of unregistered land—was the estate encumbered by X's interest, in accordance with those rules, *at that time*?[12] However, section 11(4) also incorporates a second set of conditions which achieve a

[7] LRA 2002, s 3.

[8] LRA 2002, ss 6, 7.

[9] This is implicit in LRA 2002, s 8 (liability for the costs of having to re-transfer/re-grant/re-create a relevant legal estate).

[10] C Harpum and J Bignall, *Registered Land: Law and Practice under the Land Registration Act 2002* (Bristol, Jordans, 2004) para 4.1 (emphasis added).

[11] LRA 2002, s 11(4) (emphasis added). The corresponding provision for leasehold estates is LRA 2002, s 12(4).

[12] See, eg, *Ruoff & Roper—Registered Conveyancing* (London, Sweet & Maxwell, looseleaf) paras 6.002.01, 10.006 (August 2017 release).

further filtering effect. It is not sufficient that X's prior interest, if it to bind the first registered proprietor, '*affect[s] … the estate at the time of registration*'—a form of words which would be sufficient to transpose the pre-existing ranking of X's interest, on registration. The interest must also satisfy the further filtering conditions listed in sub-paragraphs (a), (b) or (c).

This second feature of section 11(4) initially makes it difficult to see how the first registration priority rules are not only *parasitic*, but also *neutral*. Neutrality would imply a simple transposition of the existing priorities. However, that is not, on the face of it, what the provision achieves: it appears to go further, clearing the estate of some existing encumbrances that *would* bind the estate under the rules of unregistered land. In so doing is not neutral.

One answer is that, despite appearances, the *general* objective of section 11(4)—evident from conditions (a) and (b)—is indeed a strategy of neutrality: ie, a strategy of replicating the priority conclusions that would be reached by the general law. These two conditions may reflect an implicit general assumption that, on first registration, the estate *should* remain subject to interests that previously affected the estate, but that this ambition should be realised via legal mechanisms that are consistent with, and necessarily employ the language of, the priority rules that will in future be governing (ie, those found in sections 28–29). Thus, pursuant to conditions (a) and (b), the pre-existing interest will affect the first registered title either if it is entered in the Register or because it is an overriding interest.[13]

The essential background point is that, in the run-up to first registration, the process of investigating and verifying title to the relevant estate includes a process of inquiry by the Land Registry into prior encumbrances belonging to parties like X. The Registry is expected to transpose and thus preserve the priority of such pre-existing interests, at first registration, via a Register entry;[14] and, in the absence of such an entry, the priority of X's interest may be ensured in any case, if the interest falls within schedule 1, as an 'unregistered interest which overrides first registration'. On this basis, all pre-existing interests which survive under the priority rules of the *general law* should *also* survive section 11(4)'s further filter—as being either entered on the Register, or overriding within schedule 1. It follows from this first view that the Registry *must* enter X's prior encumbrance on the Register at first registration if that encumbrance is susceptible to such entry,[15] so as to preserve the priority of X's prior right. The Registry has no power/mandate to elect *not* to do so, since failing to register X's right might downgrade its priority.

Unfortunately, this first view may be somewhat over-idealistic in its assumptions about Registry practice. It assumes that the Registry will *always* note registrable interests in the Register at first registration, in accordance with its duty. Yet Registry staff are, of course—like all of us—susceptible to making errors. Human nature is such that some registrable/recordable interests will inevitably be *omitted* from the Register, and as a result will fail to bind the first registered proprietor under the terms of section 11(4). Subscribers to this first view must therefore accept that, whilst the *theoretical aim* of section 11(4) might be neutrality, its effect *in practice* may fall somewhat short of that aim—at least unless the Register can be amended to correct the Registry's error.[16]

[13] There is an obvious echo here of the circumstances in which a *subsequent* registered disposition of a registered title, for valuable consideration, will be subject to a pre-existing interest: LRA 2002, s 29.

[14] See the Land Registration Rules ('LRR') 2003, r 35(1).

[15] cf LRA 2002, s 33 (interests not susceptible to notice-entry).

[16] See section II(B)(ii) and II(B)(iii) below.

A second answer is that, in the light of condition (c), section 11(4)'s operation is not wholly neutral, and indeed was not intended to be. The LRA 2002 embodies a deliberate strategy of *altering* the balance of the pre-existing law, at the point of first registration, in a way that will sometimes privilege the first registered proprietor. The scenario in question involves an unusual example of a competing *non-derivative* title, arising through adverse possession—a situation which, it will be recalled, is not the primary concern of this chapter.[17] Even though a squatter might have acquired the best freehold title to the relevant land via the Limitation Act 1980, the Law Commission apparently intended that the first registered proprietor should immediately acquire a good title free from the squatter's better title, unless the squatter met one of the conditions in section 11(4). It is certainly plausible, albeit rare, that a squatter might not meet any of the conditions, and will therefore find that his title is demoted at first registration—as where the squatter is not in actual occupation, and the first registered proprietor had no notice of his rights at the relevant time.[18]

Whichever of these two views is correct, neither in fact offers a complete picture of the priority of interests at first registration. The ultimate effect of section 11 cannot be understood in isolation from the possibility that the Register, and thus the ordering of interests achieved by section 11, might be vulnerable to subsequent *alteration* via the schedule 4 alteration provisions. This possibility is considered further below.[19]

B. The Nature, Strength and Limits of the First Registration Priority Promise

In terms, section 11(4) seems to assure a first registered proprietor, who is registered with absolute title to a freehold estate, that his estate is *only* subject to prior interests that meet conditions (a), (b), or (c). Nevertheless, viewed in isolation, section 11(4) does not unambiguously determine the nature and extent of that assurance.

The most testing cases will arise where X's interest, which affected the relevant estate at the time of first registration, is *neither* an overriding interest within schedule 1, *nor* subject to any Register entry that would be required to preserve its priority vis-à-vis the estate of the first registered proprietor ('RP1') on first registration. In that event, section 11(4) appears to have a '*filtering*' effect: X's prior interest, which would otherwise burden the estate under the general law, is cleared away.

Consider a case involving a restrictive freehold covenant, which restricts the use of the land in question, in favour of X. There are two ways in which a priority dispute might arise between X and the first registered proprietor of the potentially burdened freehold estate:

> **Scenario A—Direct Rights**: the covenant with X is directly entered into by Y, the unregistered freehold owner, who subsequently becomes RP1—giving rise to a potential priority contest between X (who holds a so-called '*direct right*') and Y/RP1.

[17] See section I(B) above.

[18] See the further discussion in section II(B)(iii) below. See also the fuller discussion in ch 6 of this book, section III(C). This non-neutral treatment of squatters could be regarded as consistent with the more general policy of the LRA 2002, and in particular, sch 6, which is much less generous towards squatters than was the former registration regime.

[19] See sections II(B)(ii) and II(B)(iii) below.

Scenario B—Pre-Existing Interests: the covenant with X might be entered into by Y, the unregistered freehold owner, who then conveys the freehold estate to Z, who duly becomes RP1. X's covenant might encumber the estate obtained by Z/RP1 under the rules of unregistered conveyancing because it is duly registered as a land charge in the Land Charges Register,[20] or even if not so registered, it might remain binding vis-à-vis Z/RP1 if Z/RP1 acquired his estate as a gift.[21]

If we assume that, in both scenarios, X's interest binds RP1 (Y in *Scenario A*, or Z in *Scenario B*) under the *general* law, it remains necessary to ascertain whether X's interest additionally survives first registration. This substantially depends on its being noted in the Register.[22] However, what if, in Scenario B, at the time of first registration, the Land Registry fails to transpose the registered covenant's entry in the Land Charges Register into the newly-opened title register in the Land Registry?[23] Alternatively, what if, in Scenario A the unregistered covenant is unnoticed or overlooked, such that there is no Register entry to preserve the covenant's prior status vis-à-vis RP1's title on first registration? In either case, the estate will be vested in RP1, by the express terms of section 11(4), free from X's covenant. The operative words '*subject only* ...' do not readily allow any other interpretation.

We might nevertheless query this outcome. As a matter of policy, it is not obvious that X's covenant—which may be strategically valuable to X, in terms of the particular use to which he puts his own land—should lose priority to the first registered proprietor. First, X may be entirely ignorant of the Registry's omission to note his covenant against RP1's newly-registered title. Secondly, this is not a situation where the beneficiary of section 11's filtering effect—RP1—has relied on the Land Register's correctness prior to acquiring his title, and where the integrity of the Register requires RP1 to be insulated from prior rights; indeed, by definition, there was no relevant registered title prior to RP1's first registration.

To meet these concerns, it is arguable that there should be some qualifications to section 11(4)'s seemingly rigid effect, although their precise status and ambit remains regrettably unclear. Similar issues arise in construing the priority promise that operates on *subsequent* dealings with an already-registered estate,[24] but the situations may not be identical. In short, it is likely to be less disruptive of the ambitions of the registration framework if the first registration priority promise is less absolute. Unlike the first registered proprietor, parties who later deal with the registered proprietor necessarily rely on the Register when acquiring their interests. This legitimate reliance is more obviously compromised, if the priority promise made to such parties is undermined.

In this section, we explore four potential sources of difficulty associated with the priority promise afforded at first registration by section 11(4).[25]

[20] LCA 1972, s 2(5)(ii) (Class D land charge).

[21] cf LCA 1972, s 4(6) (rendering an interest registrable as a Class D land charge, but not registered, void vis-à-vis a purchaser of a legal estate).

[22] Although factually unlikely, it is also possible for X's right to bind as an overriding interest, should X be in actual occupation of the burdened land: LRA 2002, sch 1, para 2.

[23] See LRR 2003, r 35(1).

[24] See section III(D) below.

[25] Note that on any view, the first registration priority promise only governs the effect of *existing* interests that affected the estate *at the time of registration*, and does not govern *subsequently-created* rights. By its express terms, LRA 2002, s 11(4) only cleanses RP1's registered estate of (*some* of) such interests. It does not afford any immunity from interests created by RP1 *after* registration. There is no legitimate reason for s 11(4) to speak to this issue. This is an obvious point which is correct as a matter of principle and policy. The effect of any later disposition by RP1 does not raise a 'priority' issue in its normal sense. Instead, it is a question of the dispositional powers of RP1

i. Direct Rights (Scenario A Cases)

First, how far does the clearing effect of section 11(4) prejudice the continuing status of what might be called 'direct rights'? This question relates to *Scenario A*, described immediately above[26]—where Y, as unregistered owner, creates a right in favour of X, and then Y himself becomes RP1. What exactly is Y/RP1 immunised from, via the provision that renders RP1's estate '*subject only*' to 'interests' of the specified nature? It is crucial in this context to distinguish between two different categories of case.

The first category involves purely *in personam* rights—rights against Y/RP1, and Y/RP1 only. These would include, inter alia, contractual rights relating to land created by a contract to which Y/RP1 is a party, which have no greater legal force than as 'mere' contractual rights—eg, a contractual licence or a positive freehold covenant. Rights of this sort, which do not afford the right-holder, X, any form of proprietary interest that might affect third parties, are very obviously not affected by section 11. Section 11 only speaks to the effect of 'interests' 'affecting the estate'. In context, this can only refer to interests capable of affecting successors in title—ie proprietary interests capable of existing as interests in land. The LRA 2002 does not, either at first registration or subsequently, purport to account for and order all rights that in a general sense *relate* to land—but only those rights that have a potentially enduring quality, as proprietary interests in land.

The second category involves rights which exist *in rem*—interests in land in the accepted sense—which arise for the first time *directly* against the party, Y, who becomes RP1. In some cases, Y/RP1 will have been responsible for the right's creation because it arose via an exercise of his dispositional powers as unregistered estate owner—eg via the grant of a lease, charge, easement or restrictive covenant. In other cases, the right might have arisen for the first time vis-à-vis him, by operation of law, for some other reason—eg via a constructive or resulting trust, or via an equitable lien, such as an unpaid vendor's lien. This sort of situation could easily arise in cases of voluntary first registration. However, it is also conceivable in cases of compulsory first registration—as where, simultaneously with the transfer or grant that triggers first registration, the transferee or grantee grants a charge over his estate.

The appropriate treatment of this second category—ie, direct *in rem* rights—is less clear. At first sight, the words of section 11(4) are apt to cover them, with the effect of prioritising Y/RP1's estate over X's interest, unless X's interest is protected by the terms of section 11—ie, unless it is noted in the Register or overriding. And yet cases involving these direct *in rem* rights are undoubtedly different in nature from the cases principally caught by section 11(4), which are typified by what we have labelled *Scenario B*[27]—where X's right derives from Y's unregistered estate, and then Y's estate is transferred to Z who duly becomes RP1. Strictly speaking, cases involving these direct *in rem* rights—whilst they concern interests in land—do not involve questions of 'priority' in the narrow sense at all. The capacity of

as estate owner, and RP1 has the same expansive dispositional 'owner's powers' as any later registered proprietor (RP2, etc): LRA 2002, ss 23–26; see ch 18 of this book. See also LRR 2003, r 38, which effectively extends the provisions that would apply to dealings with a registered estate, to pre-registration dealings with an unregistered estate which is subject to a compulsory registration requirement, during the period within which registration is required to occur.

[26] See introduction to section II(B) above.
[27] ibid.

such a direct right to bind the relevant estate would ordinarily be a corollary of the estate owner's *own* dispositional powers—eg, of whether a freehold owner (Y/RP1) can burden his estate by his *own* grant. Alternatively, it would be a corollary of the rules that govern the generation of rights that arise by operation of law directly against his estate—eg, whether in the circumstances the title of a freehold owner (Y/RP1) is subject to a new constructive or resulting trust. By nature, they are different from the classic priority cases typified by *Scenario B*, where Y's unregistered estate was encumbered by X's pre-existing interest prior to the estate's transfer to Z. Arguably, *Scenario A* cases raise a priority problem only by an artifice—ie, because the transition into the registration regime involves the replacement of Y/RP1's unregistered estate with a *new* 'registered' estate, thereby presenting the question whether that *new* estate should be subject to what *ex hypothesi* are then pre-existing interests. Furthermore, as a matter of policy, it is far from obvious that the event of first registration should be the occasion for clearing Y/RP1's title from interests that have arisen from Y/RP1's own pre-registration conduct—whether consensually or by operation of law.

The preferable view is that these direct rights should continue to bind Y/RP1 and his estate. However, the crucial question is whether this outcome can be achieved notwithstanding that section 11(4) appears, at first sight at least, to promise priority to RP1 against even direct *in rem* rights, except where those rights are overriding or noted on the Register.

In many *compulsory* registration situations, an answer can be found in a special provision of the Land Registration Rules 2003—rule 38(1).[28] This is addressed to dispositions that occur during the 'twilight period':[29] ie, the period, *starting* from the time of the transaction that triggers compulsory registration of an estate, and *continuing* either until registration occurs, or until the vesting of the unregistered estate is nullified upon expiry of the time period for first registration. Rule 38, which is headed 'Application of the Act to dealings prior to first registration' expressly provides:

> 38 (1) If, whilst a person is subject to a duty under section 6 of the [LRA 2002] to make an application to be registered as proprietor of a legal estate, there is a dealing with that estate, then the Act applies to that dealing as if the dealing had taken place after the date of first registration of that estate.

This provision is apt to apply to a purported disposition by RP1 to X, where RP1 had become first registered proprietor pursuant to a disposition to him that had triggered compulsory first registration.[30] If RP1, prior to first registration occurring, purported to create an interest over the estate in favour of X, at law or in equity, then rule 38(1) ensures that RP1's new registered estate is subject to that interest. The relevant 'dealing'—the grant of the interest to X—is treated for the purposes of the LRA 2002 *as if it had taken place after the date of first registration of the encumbered freehold estate*. As such, the status of X's interest vis-à-vis RP1's estate, on first registration, is not regulated by section 11. Rather, it is treated as a disposition by RP1, *as a registered proprietor*. It can be effective vis-à-vis RP1's estate in the ordinary way—ie, as an effective exercise of the 'owner's powers' conferred by sections 23–24.

[28] LRR 2003, r 38. For discussion, see *Ruoff & Roper* (n 12) para 8.014.03.

[29] For recent discussion of this, see Law Commission, *Updating the Land Registration Act 2002—A Consultation Paper* (Law Com CP No 227, 2016) paras 4.5–4.35.

[30] LRA 2002, s 4.

This is a neat (if rather roundabout) solution for *some* situations. Nevertheless, it cannot regulate all. For one thing, it does not readily accommodate dispositions by RP1 in the twilight period that cannot be characterised as 'dealings'. Read naturally, 'dealings' might imply a conscious exercise of dispositional powers by an owner, thereby excluding any interest that arises against an estate by operation of law. It also does not deal with situations of *voluntary* first registration: rule 38 bites only if an event has triggered compulsory first registration.

Accordingly, it seems impossible to avoid facing the question of section 11(4)'s impact on these 'directly arising' interests. Could RP1, on first registration, rely upon section 11(4)'s unqualified terms to argue that the estate which he acquires on first registration is cleared of the relevant interest? It is difficult to see why he should. What conceivable policy justification could there be for immunising RP1 from interests that *he was responsible for creating*, or which, for sound reasons, arose against him by operation of law?

There are various ways in which this dilemma could be avoided via recourse to one or more general law principles. For example, if X's interest has a foundation in a contract—whether or not it also serves to create a proprietary interest[31]—then RP1 should not be able to rely on section 11(4) to avoid the binding status of that contract *as a contract*. Beyond this, there is a possibility that RP1 might be estopped from denying the existence of the relevant right—eg, via some form of estoppel by deed or convention. Or, more narrowly, RP1 might be prevented from relying on section 11(4)'s clearing effect on the basis that it would enable statute to be used as an instrument of fraud—ie, as a means for the fraudulent avoidance of the consequences for RP1 of his own disposition. A further and attractive possibility is that, if X's prior interest is rendered effective in any of these ways, then X could make a schedule 4 application to bring the Register 'up to date'. This is an appealing argument because it provides a means for the Register to be adjusted to reflect the persistence of X's right against RP1's estate, more or less as a matter of right, and without triggering any indemnity for RP1—such an alteration would not be a loss-causing 'rectification' of the Register.[32]

If these suggestions are correct, then there may well be no real dilemma: one or more general law doctrines could achieve the necessary attenuation of section 11(4)'s literal effect on direct *in rem* rights. Nevertheless, it seems unfortunate that this problem is not explicitly resolved via the LRA 2002 itself. As we explain later,[33] in its 1998 Consultative Document,[34] the Law Commission had envisaged an *explicit* qualification to what became section 29, in order to avoid a similar problem arising in the context of subsequent registered dispositions (ie, from RP1 to RP2)—section 29 would not enable a registered disponee to claim priority, on registration, vis-à-vis interests that he had himself created/granted.[35] However, this proposal seems to have been shelved by the time of the 2001 Law Commission Report,

[31] See, eg, a lease granted by Y to X.

[32] It does not seem that the alteration could be characterised, in the alternative, as necessary to correct a 'mistake'. The relevant Register amendment would not prejudically affect RP1's title, since *ex hypothesi* the right independently binds RP1; as such, the other necessary condition for alteration to amount to 'rectification' would not be satisfied.

[33] See text to n 140 below.

[34] Law Commission, *Land Registration for the Twenty-First Century: A Consultative Document* (Law Com No 254, 1998).

[35] ibid, paras 7.36–7.37.

for no obviously good reason,[36] and the same idea was seemingly never considered in relation to section 11(4). Looking forwards, it would be desirable for the legislation to address the problem directly via an express qualification to section 11(4), such that it operates 'without prejudice to the continuing effect of interests previously created by, or arising directly against, the first registered proprietor'.

ii. Pre-Existing Interests Omitted from the Register (Scenario B Cases)

Many interests affecting an unregistered estate will not of course be in the nature of *direct rights*, arising immediately against the first registered proprietor, RP1. Rather, they will be pre-existing interests, held by X, which arose against the unregistered estate whilst that estate was held by Y, and which therefore *pre-date* the acquisition of the unregistered estate by Z, who becomes first registered proprietor, RP1, pursuant to a transfer from Y. This is *Scenario B*.[37] In such cases, the apparent effect of section 11(4), as previously explained, is that the persistence of X's pre-existing interest against Z/RP1's freehold estate will initially be determined via the unregistered conveyancing priority rules, but is then subject to the further filtering effect of section 11(4). Thus, first registration vests the freehold estate in RP1, '*subject only*' to pre-existing interests that satisfy conditions (a), (b) or (c)—and by necessary implication, the estate is 'cleared' of any interest that does not. The key issue which inevitably arises is whether this clearing is *final* or *irreversible*. This ultimately boils down to whether section 11(4)'s clearing operation is itself susceptible to correction via a Register-alteration pursuant to schedule 4. If available, such an alteration might take the form of a Registry entry noting X's interest against Z's registered title.

The availability of alteration in this context can only be determined in the light of the purposes of section 11(4) and schedule 4, viewed within the context of the wider policies of the LRA 2002. We examine this question below, but before we do so, two preliminary issues must be addressed.

First, before we can understand when a Register-amendment should be available, we must ascertain the effect of a Register-amendment on the rights of X and Z/RP1. It seems clear that, immediately upon first registration, section 11(4) clears Z/RP1's title of X's right if it was neither on the Register nor overriding within schedule 1. On that assumption, the subsequent entry of X's pre-existing but omitted interest against Z/RP1's registered estate would not be neutral/administrative in its effect—it would not merely bring the Register 'up to date'. Rather, the amendment would be 'prejudicial' to Z/RP1's title—it would substantively reverse the priority, conferred by section 11(4), which Z/RP1 had initially enjoyed against X.

Secondly, one must ask whether it is possible, within the confines of schedule 4, to amend the Register in this way. The original omission at first registration of a relevant entry in the Register relating to X's right would very likely qualify as a 'mistake' by the Registry which, being a ground for alteration in schedule 4, requires correction. In its 2001 Report, the Law Commission did not address this possibility.[38] However, in its 2016 Consultation Paper,

[36] Law Commission, *Land Registration for the Twenty-First Century—A Conveyancing Revolution* (Law Com No 271, 2001) para 5.10.

[37] See introduction to section II(B) above.

[38] cf Law Com No 271 (n 36) paras 9.28 and 10.31, dealing with the possibility of an indemnity in cases where title is upgraded by the Registrar in error, in a manner that adversely affects a prior right.

the Commission has recently conceded that section 11's operation should indeed be subject to schedule 4's alteration regime.[39] This chimes with the Commission's acceptance of the Court of Appeal's decision in *MacLeod v Gold Harp Properties Ltd*,[40] that the effect of the corresponding priority rules for subsequent registered dealings[41]—and in particular, section 29—might be adjusted via a Register-amendment.[42] Indeed, if section 29 is qualified by schedule 4, then it seems that section 11 must, *a fortiori*, also be. As we explain elsewhere, the priority promise made to subsequent registered disponees, who legitimately rely on the Register, can reasonably be expected to be stronger.[43]

Ultimately, the extent to which schedule 4's alteration jurisdiction can properly intrude in this setting requires an analysis of what ought to occur at first registration as a matter of policy, and of the justifications for section 11(4)'s clearing effect. Comparison with the position on subsequent registered dealings—which are governed by sections 28–29 and are explored at length in section III—may be instructive.

Where X acquires an interest affecting an already-registered estate, *after* first registration, the basic expectation—subject to the interest constituting an overriding interest within schedule 3—is that X will take steps to protect the priority of his interest. There is no expectation that the Registry should, of its own volition, identify and preserve the priority of such interests. On the contrary, the onus is on X interest-holder to do so, and he bears the risk of loss through his own failure to act—this can be regarded as an important disciplining incentive, to ensure the reliability of the Register.[44] As such, the mere absence of a notice in the Register cannot be regarded as a 'mistake' that requires correction—at least on the prevailing understanding of that concept, which requires some relevant erroneous act or omission on the part of the Land Registry.[45] There can only be a relevant mistake if the Registry has erroneously failed to act, where it *should* have acted—most likely, where it failed to enter a notice on an application made to it; or if the Registry has erroneously acted, where it *should not* have—most likely, where it wrongly removed an existing notice entry.[46]

Matters look quite different at first registration. The LRA 2002 certainly provides a facility, via the lodging of a caution against first registration,[47] for a party like X, who claims an interest that affects an unregistered estate, to be alerted of an application for first registration. This enables him to draw his claim to the Registrar's attention *before* first registration of Z/RP1's estate, and have its existence and priority resolved. This in turn makes it more likely that appropriate steps will be taken by the Registrar to ensure that the priority of X's interest is preserved on first registration by an appropriate Register entry. However, there is no indication within the LRA 2002 framework that parties like X are *expected* to lodge such cautions, and that they are to suffer the consequences if they do not. Nor, *a fortiori*,

[39] Law Com CP No 227 (n 29) paras 13.180–13.181.

[40] *MacLeod v Gold Harp Properties Ltd* [2014] EWCA Civ 1084, [2015] 1 WLR 1249.

[41] See section III(D)(iii) below.

[42] Law Com CP No 227 (n 29) paras 13.152–13.162; see also paras 13.189–13.196.

[43] See section I(A) and II(A), and text to n 24 above, and introduction to section III and text to n 49 below.

[44] This appears to have been a deliberate policy of the Law Commission, manifest, eg, in its narrowing of the category of easements that could have overriding status under what became sch 3, para 3, so as to exclude those *expressly* created: see Law Com No 254 (n 34) para 5.6 ff; Law Com No 271 (n 36) para 8.65 ff.

[45] This prevailing understanding is accepted in Law Com CP No 227 (n 29) para 13.79.

[46] cf the mistaken de-registration of the lease in *Gold Harp* (n 40).

[47] LRA 2002, ss 15–16.

are such parties *expected* to apply for the entry of a notice before first registration. Indeed, such a requirement would make no sense. As long as the relevant affected estate remains unregistered, X has a legitimate expectation that his interest has priority in accordance with the priority rules of *unregistered* conveyancing.[48] X cannot legitimately be required to be pro-active in anticipating the risk that the affected unregistered estate might in future become registered, and the consequential risk that his interest might be subordinated in the absence of an appropriate Register entry. In truth, responsibilities at first registration lie elsewhere—first and foremost, with the *Land Registry*. The onus is properly on the Registry to investigate, identify and appropriately protect any pre-existing interest, belonging to parties like X, that affects the estate, to ensure that the interest's priority is, so far as possible, *transposed* and *preserved* on first registration.

If this is correct, then the omission of a necessary notice on the Register in respect of X's interest may be readily attributed to a *Registry*-error which is potentially rectification-justifying—or if rectification is refused, which might support an indemnity award. This seems entirely appropriate in policy terms. If section 11(4) was absolute, such that its filtering effect was irreversible by a Register-amendment, then the event of first registration would risk destroying a pre-existing interest belonging to X *without* compensation, and without X having a realistic opportunity to prevent this occurrence. As far as X was concerned, his interest arose within a regime governed by the rules of *unregistered* conveyancing. There is no compelling justification for X to lose out as a result of the operation of *registered conveyancing's* rules. Furthermore, reading section 11(4) as absolute—ie, as immune from the effect of schedule 4—would perversely over-privilege the first registered proprietor relative to subsequent registered proprietors. The first registered proprietor cannot have relied on the Register's correctness when acquiring his title—there was no Register relating to his title at that time. In contrast, subsequent registered proprietors will legitimately rely on the Register's correctness, and yet the priority promise which is made to them via section 29 is—on recent authority—undoubtedly vulnerable to schedule 4.[49]

This still leaves the question: when exactly will there be a relevant qualifying 'mistake' that can be corrected?

The prevailing conception of mistake, which we also examine elsewhere,[50] is wide. It is not qualified by any requirement for Registry *fault*—eg, careless investigations which fail to reveal an interest, or careless conduct consequent on those investigations, which means that a protective entry is not effected.[51] Instead, according to the prevailing view there can be a qualifying 'mistake' where, regardless of Registry fault, an entry is omitted from

[48] eg, if X's interest is a legal estate or interest, then he can rely on its having priority, without more; if X's interest is an equitable interest which is registrable as a land charge, then he is assured of priority if he has duly registered his interest as such pursuant to the LCA 1972.

[49] See the discussion of *Gold Harp* (n 40) in section III(D)(iii) below.

[50] See ch 16 of this book, section III(D); and see also text to n 186 et seq.

[51] Thus, (i) there is nothing in the LRA 2002's words to suggest that 'mistake' must be qualified in this way; (ii) the authorities seem inconsistent with it (eg, in forgery cases, there is no suggestion that the identification of a mistake assumes that the Registrar has carelessly failed to spot the problem); (iii) it would result in a surprising risk-allocation (the indemnity fund would function as an insurance fund only against Registry negligence, leaving the risk of loss caused by fault short of this with the losing party); (iv) such fault qualifications would have capricious effects.

the Register which, had the Registrar been aware of all of the facts, *would* or *should* have been made.[52] Of course, inherent in this is still an inquiry into what the Registrar *would* or *should* have done. This will not always be obvious, but in the first registration context, the answer seems clear. It must be determined in the light of the foundational premise of neutrality, discussed above:[53] the premise that first registration is not generally meant to force a re-ordering of existing priorities, but merely, via appropriate means, to *preserve* them. If the priority of an interest can only be preserved on first registration via a notice entry, and yet no entry is made, then this neutrality is compromised—this holds true for interests which are capable of being protected on the Register[54] and which, if not entered onto the Register, do not otherwise override at first registration.[55] It follows that an appropriate mistake can be identified, within the meaning of schedule 4, *wherever the priority of an interest affecting the estate at the time of first registration, which is capable of being noted on the Register, is not transposed on first registration by an appropriate notice entry.*

A more difficult question is whether, if the Register *is* altered in X's favour under schedule 4, Z/RP1 might obtain an indemnity under schedule 8. This is not an easy question. Looking only to the terms of section 11(4), it may well be possible to identify a 'loss' that might be susceptible to indemnity: as a result of the alteration, Z/RP1's title is made subject to an interest that, under the terms of section 11(4), would not otherwise bind it.[56] On this understanding, section 11(4) *does* embody a priority promise to Z/RP1—ie, a promise that his estate is 'subject only' to the listed interests, on first registration. It is not a cast-iron guarantee of immunity from any other prior interests, insofar as Z/RP1 may find his title is made subject to X's right, despite section 11(4)'s terms, via a schedule 4 application. Nevertheless, the priority promise is still 'real', insofar as Z/RP1 can receive a money award in lieu that would not otherwise be available to him.

Yet can it really be right to afford Z/RP1 such a money guarantee? It seems to involve an over-expansion of the indemnity available at first registration which is not obviously required by the policy ambitions of the registration regime. Why should it be necessary or appropriate to indemnify a first registered proprietor against the fact that the Register may be altered to reflect the priority position that prevailed *pre*-registration, and which—had matters been properly perceived—would similarly have prevailed *on* registration? There is no need, in order to achieve the aims of Register-reliability, for the first registered proprietor to be guaranteed anything as regards priority against pre-existing interests—whether via irreversible priority or money in lieu of priority.

In truth, the section 11(4) priority rule might be better perceived *not* as a 'priority *promise*' at all, but simply as a 'real-time' picture of the ordering of interests, which can subsequently be redrawn if further evidence comes to light. Any such redrawing would not, contrary to

[52] See, eg, the interpretations offered in Law Com CP No 227 (n 29) para 13.77 ff; C Harpum, S Bridge and M Dixon, *Megarry & Wade—The Law of Real Property*, 8th edn (London, Sweet and Maxwell, 2012) para 7.133; *Ruoff & Roper* (n 12) para 46.009.

[53] See section II(A) above.

[54] cf LRA 2002, s 33, detailing the 'excluded interests' which are not protectable via a notice entry on the Register.

[55] LRA 2002, sch 1.

[56] As we have explained elsewhere, the effect of the LRA 2002's alteration and indemnity provisions is that the correction of a 'mistake' which causes loss by 'prejudicially affecting' the registered proprietor's title potentially yields an indemnity payout to the losing party. On this reading of the provisions, Z/RP1 would seem to qualify for an indemnity payment.

the analysis in the preceding paragraphs, constitute 'rectification', and thus would not result in any indemnity being payable to Z/RP1. However, without legislative amendment, it may be hard to avoid the alternative and unnecessarily generous conclusion that section 11(4) embodies a real 'promise' of priority for Z/RP1, and that Z/RP1 might indeed obtain an indemnity payment if it is not fulfilled.

iii. Existing Squatters' Rights

A third source of difficulty associated with section 11(4) concerns squatters' rights, and in particular the impact of section 11(4)(c). This provision is targeted at a rather narrow problem which arises where a squatter (S) has adversely possessed land for a period (typically 12 years)[57] sufficient to bar the paper owner's (O's) previously superior unregistered estate, but where, having regained possession, O has been able to obtain voluntary first registration with absolute title in his own name on the basis of documentary evidence (becoming O/RP1), or has been able to effect a conveyance to P which triggers compulsory registration and similarly results in first registration of P with absolute title (becoming P/RP1).

The intended effect of section 11(4)(c) is that first registration with absolute title will afford RP1 (whether O or P) a good title, freed from S's previously paramount title, unless either: (i) S remains in possession (in which case, S's title will remain paramount as an overriding interest by virtue of section 11(4)(b) and schedule 1), or (ii) RP1 has 'notice' of S's rights (as provided for by section 11(4)(c)). This is a very dramatic clearing rule—and a major departure from what might otherwise appear to be the basic *nemo dat quod non habet* principle. O, the relevant paper owner, would have had at best a subordinate common law possessory title, based upon his resumption of possession after his original title had been barred by the Limitation Act 1980. Nevertheless, he is enabled via the first registration provisions to effectively invest in himself (as O/RP1), or in his transferee (P/RP1), a registered title which is *paramount*. This filtering rule is not an accident. It was a deliberate design by the Law Commission to downgrade the rights of a squatter who has gone out of possession, and prioritise security of title for RP1 where he does not have notice of the squatter's paramount claim.[58]

How final is this filtering rule? There is certainly no wiggle room within section 11 itself. Might it nonetheless be possible for S to challenge the effect of section 11 indirectly, via schedule 4's alteration provisions? S might attempt to argue that RP1 (whether O or P) should never have been registered with absolute title: such registration was a Registry mistake, which can be corrected by rectification. The argument would presumably be that if the true facts had been known at the time of first registration, it would have been evident that RP1's title was not paramount—O/P should have been registered, if at all, with some lesser grade of possessory or qualified title, which would have operated without prejudice to the continuing paramount status of S's common law title.

The Law Commission's 2016 Consultation Paper seems receptive to such arguments.[59] It contemplates that S might indeed seek rectification under schedule 4 for the purpose of cancelling RP1's registered title or procuring its downgrading; and this would in turn

[57] Limitation Act 1980, ss 15, 17.

[58] Law Com No 271 (n 36) paras 3.45–3.47. For fuller discussion, see ch 6 of this book, section III(C).

[59] Law Com CP No 227 (n 29) paras 17.56–17.62.

raise the question whether RP1, if prejudiced by the downgrading, would be eligible for an indemnity. In isolation, it seems comprehensible that schedule 4 might apply. However, allowing such rectification would arguably stultify the very purpose of section 11(4)(c). The 2001 Law Commission's intention was seemingly that section 11(4)(c) should give RP1 *in specie* protection against squatters with superior titles who were out of possession, and of which RP1 did not have notice. Affording RP1 a monetary indemnity rather than the 'mud'—in the form of a permanently superior title—weakens section 11(4)(c)'s effect as a clearing/priority rule. The 2001 Law Commission's ambition for section 11(4)(c) may only be fully realised if section 11(4)(c)'s clearing effect is permanent and a schedule 4 challenge by S to RP1's title is impliedly excluded. Charles Harpum, the Law Commissioner responsible for the 2001 Report, has said as much in a scathing published response to the 2016 Law Commission Consultation Paper.[60]

There are nevertheless reasons to cast doubt on the policy balance struck by the 2001 Law Commission. This is especially so where it is O rather than P (a transferee from O) who becomes RP1—O being the very person whom S had dispossessed for 12 years, and against whom the Limitation Act 1980's provisions had most directly operated. It is dramatic for the LRA 2002 to permit P, an innocent transferee of O, to evade the effect of the Limitation Act 1980's extinction of O's unregistered title upon becoming RP1, but even more so to permit O himself to regain the paramount title upon first registration. Furthermore, it is often suggested that section 11(4)(c), which can bring the destruction on first registration of a squatter's previously-paramount title, may be vulnerable to challenge on human rights grounds.[61]

Drawing this discussion together, whatever the arguments may be for permitting first registration to downgrade S's previously-paramount title, the key point for present purposes is that if section 11(4)(c) achieves a result which is unwanted, it would be preferable to address this problem openly and directly by modifying the first registration priority rules in section 11(4)(c)—rather than by allowing the legislation's undoubted intention to be stifled via the schedule 4 sidewind.

iv. Existing Trusts

Section 11(5) contains one further 'filtering' rule, apparently carried over from the LRA 1925. This provision seems to clear RP1's estate, on first registration, of any pre-existing trust interest, belonging to X, that encumbered the estate, except insofar as RP1 has 'notice' of the interest:

> If the proprietor is not entitled to the estate for his own benefit, or not entitled solely for his own benefit, then, as between himself and the persons beneficially entitled to the estate, the estate is vested in him subject to such of their interests as he has notice of.

No reasons are offered in the Law Commission's 2001 Report for this provision, or for its continuation into the LRA 2002. *Ex hypothesi*, it is triggered only if, under the rules of unregistered conveyancing, the *unregistered* estate acquired by RP1 was itself subject to a trust for

[60] C Harpum, 'Response to Law Commission Consultation Paper No 227—Updating the Land Registration Act' <http://www.falcon-chambers.com/publications/articles> paras [166]–[169].

[61] eg, E Cooke, *The New Law of Land Registration* (Oxford, Hart, 2003) 88.

the benefit of X. A question then arises as to whether that trust survives *first registration*. It will certainly survive via section 11(4)(b) if X's trust interest qualifies as an overriding interest under schedule 1—as where the trust beneficiary is in actual occupation of the relevant land.[62] However, in cases where the trust interest does not override, section 11(5) introduces an additional filter—clearing the legal estate of the trust on first registration unless RP1 has 'notice' of the relevant interest.

On its face, section 11(5) has a wide ambit. No distinction is directly drawn according to whether the trust is express, constructive or resulting. Nor is there any distinction in the provision between:

(i) *new* trusts that arise for the first time upon RP1's acquisition of the unregistered estate (as where Y holds an unregistered title on trust for X, and then procures his own registration as RP1 (becoming Y/RP1)); and
(ii) *pre-existing* trusts that encumbered Y's unregistered estate, and would persist against that estate on its transfer to Z (who becomes first registered proprietor (Z/RP1)) under the rules of unregistered conveyancing. Under these unregistered conveyancing rules, X's *pre-existing* trust interest would remain enforceable against Z transferee if it is neither overreached, nor cleared via Z's taking as a bona fide purchaser without notice.

In which circumstances of first registration will section 11(5) clear the legal title, which would ordinarily be affected by X's trust interest under general property law? Four points need to be understood.

First, there will be cases where, on any view, RP1 cannot deny that he has 'notice' within section 11(5), and will therefore remain bound by X's trust interest. This is most obviously so where he (as Y/RP1) declared an express trust, or where the estate was conveyed to him (as Z/RP1) on the understanding that he would hold the property on express trusts declared by the previous owner.

Secondly, there will also be numerous situations in which it is less clear whether RP1 has relevant 'notice' for the purpose of section 11(5). This is particularly so where a resulting or constructive trust first arises directly against the party who himself becomes the first registered proprietor—as where a trust is imposed on Y in X's favour, and Y then becomes Y/RP1. One controversial view holds that some degree of notice is always a prerequisite for the finding that a trust has arisen. This was the view of Lord Browne-Wilkinson in *Westdeutsche Landesbank Girozentrale v Islington LBC*,[63] where his Lordship appeared to say that a new trust would be *imposed* on a potential trustee *only* if his 'conscience' was affected, and that this would require knowledge or actual notice of the trust-triggering facts. If that is right, then section 11(5) might only rarely downgrade trust interests on first registration—at least if the degree of notice required for the imposition of the trust also satisfied section 11(5). The *Westdeutsche* analysis is, however, contested. Many have argued that it is wrong, and that resulting or constructive trusts will arise even *before* a trustee's conscience is subjectively affected.[64] If this alternative view is right, then many more trusts may be at risk of downgrading via section 11(5) because of RP1's lack of relevant notice.

[62] LRA 2002, sch 1, para 2.
[63] *Westdeutsche Landesbank Girozentrale v Islington LBC* [1996] AC 669 (HL) 705–706.
[64] eg, R Chambers, *Resulting Trusts* (Oxford, OUP, 2007) 203 ff; S Worthington, *Proprietary Interests in Commercial Transactions* (Oxford, OUP, 1996) xiv–xvii.

Thirdly, notwithstanding these observations, there will be some scenarios where section 11(5) certainly can clear RP1's title of X's trust interest which would otherwise persist. This will be the case, for example, where Z/RP1 has acquired an unregistered estate from Y, which is subject to a pre-existing trust for X, as a gift rather than by purchase, and in circumstances where X was not occupying the land and Z had no form of notice of X's interest. Because of Z's status as a donee, Z's unregistered estate would continue to be encumbered by X's interest under the rules of unregistered conveyancing, regardless of Z's notice or its absence. However, section 11(5) would apparently clear Z/RP1's title of X's trust interest upon first registration.

Fourthly, where a beneficial interest is downgraded as a result of section 11(5), a key question is whether this downgrading is final or can be reversed via the alteration provisions of schedule 4. There are two dimensions to consider. First, as a matter of *mechanics*, it is not obvious how any amendment to the Register could have the effect of elevating the priority of X's beneficial interest. This is simply because there is no form of Register entry that could have been made, prior to or at first registration, which would have preserved the priority of X's trust interest against section 11(5)'s clearing effect: trust interests are expressly excluded from protection by the entry of a notice in the Register.[65] Second, what is the appropriate position as a matter of policy? If schedule 4 (and by association, schedule 8) are excluded, first registration may sometimes provide an occasion for the uncompensated destruction of X's beneficial interest, and a corresponding enrichment of RP1 which is arguably unmerited. The first registered proprietor, whether Y or Z, has not relied on the correctness of the Register when registering his title—and so cannot rely on this to justify his immunity from X's interest. Furthermore, the immunity afforded by section 11(5), which depends only on absence of notice and may work in favour of a mere donee, necessarily extends beyond the scope of the immunity available via the general law's plea of bona fide purchase. As such, it is far from obvious that all those who can rely on section 11(5)'s clearing effect deserve to do so.[66]

C. Conclusions on the Ambit of the Priority Promise at First Registration

When assessing the proper ambit of the priority promise made at first registration, due consideration must be given to its potential significance for all affected parties. It is insufficient to focus only on what the promise may offer to the first registered proprietor, RP1—though, self-evidently, this is important. It is also necessary to have regard to the impact that the realisation of any promise made to RP1 may have on pre-existing interest-holders who—prior to first registration—held interests that burdened the relevant estate.

[65] LRA 2002, s 33(a).

[66] Furthermore, without a compelling explanation for s 11(5)'s clearing effect in favour of RP1, one might also wonder whether it is also fertile territory for a challenge under the Human Rights Act 1998, as a rule which effectively expropriates X's trust interest for no compensation, and with no obvious justification. See the European Convention on Human Rights, Art 1, Protocol 1, and cf the reasoning of the European Court of Human Rights in *JA Pye (Oxford) Ltd v United Kingdom* (2006) 43 EHRR 3, (2008) 46 EHRR 3 (Grand Chamber).

A workable registration regime is certainly not *compelled* to do any more, at the point of first registration, than transpose—ie, preserve or continue—the existing priorities of such pre-existing interests. Such a regime would, in effect, be a regime that offered no first registration priority promise at all. However, as we have seen, under the LRA 2002 as drafted, first registration will have some filtering effect. In some instances, this is by deliberate design. More often, it will be the result of Land Registry oversight, which means that the appropriate steps have not been taken (via notice entry) to preserve a prior right's status. RP1 appears to benefit from an *in specie* immunity from some prior rights, or at least, a monetary indemnity in lieu.

The arguments for affording RP1 such a priority promise are finely balanced—it is not fundamental to the integrity of a registration regime. RP1 will not have relied on the *Register*, and what it revealed about encumbrances, when acquiring his estate: there was no relevant title register, prior to the event of first registration. There are, nevertheless, grounds on which such a promise *might* be supported: eg, as a *quid pro quo* for RP1's payment of the registration fee.

If such a promise *is* made and realised via an *in specie* immunity for RP1 from prior encumbrances, it is essential to see that this will come at a significant cost—the subordination, and potentially the practical negation, of those prior rights. The loss incidentally caused to those *individual* encumbrancers by the migration of unregistered estates into a registration regime, which is instituted in order to give the *public* confidence in land transactions, should be compensated. Unless the LRA 2002 regime allows such subordination to be reversed via a schedule 4 application, it is imperative that those encumbrancers should be able to obtain a Registry-indemnity in lieu. Careful interpretation of the LRA 2002 is needed to achieve this.

III. Derivative Interests Affecting a Registered Estate: Subsequent Registered Dispositions

Although the LRA 2002's first registration provisions are important, the enduring integrity and success of the Act's registration framework ultimately depends upon the priority promise which is made to *later* disponees of an already-registered estate. This promise becomes material when a registered estate owned by Y is burdened by an interest held by another, X, and Y subsequently effects a disposition of his registered estate in favour of a disponee, Z—whether by transferring his registered estate, or by creating some lesser interest over it. There are good reasons why the priority promise made upon such later dispositions must be particularly robust, and certainly at least as robust as the promise made at first registration. In simple terms, the reliability of the Register's depiction of the rights that encumber a registered title requires that *some* (even if not all) disponees must be privileged, via some assurance of immunity from rights that are not publicised by Register entry at the time of their disposition. Such disponees must be entitled to expect that their disposition will generally (if not always) be subject—and *subject only*—to pre-existing rights entered in the Register.

A. Basis of the Promise

Within the LRA 2002, the priority promise that applies to later dispositions derives from sections 29[67] and 30.[68] As these provisions are substantially identical in ambition and structure, our discussion focuses only on section 29, which governs dispositions involving registered estates and is by far the more significant in practice. Section 29(1) provides:

> If a registrable disposition of a registered estate is made for valuable consideration, completion of the disposition by registration has the effect of postponing to the interest under the disposition any interest affecting the estate immediately before the disposition whose priority is not protected at the time of registration.

On its face, section 29 embodies a special priority rule which privileges an important sub-set of dealings with a registered estate—'registrable dispositions',[69] made for 'valuable consideration', which are 'completed by registration'. This captures almost all dealings that would operate under the general law to transfer or create a legal estate or interest in land.[70] The section 29 rule, which necessarily operates at the expense of some pre-existing interests, has an absolutely pivotal role within the registration framework: it enables such privileged disponees to *rely* on the Register for its depiction of interests that encumber the relevant estate. Such dispositions have priority over any *earlier* interests affecting the estate—which are 'postponed'—unless they have been publicised by Register-entry, they appear from the Register to be 'excepted from the effect of registration', or they fall within a limited class of so-called 'overriding interests' listed in schedule 3. This last proviso is of course an important chink in the registration regime's armour—it means that such disponees cannot safely assume that they are free of *all* rights not disclosed by a Register entry. Nevertheless, the importance of the basic assurance that section 29 provides, in the context of already-registered estates, is manifest in the fact that the list of overriding interests is much shorter and narrower than the corresponding list in schedule 1 for first registration;[71] it is also evident in strategies introduced by the LRA 2002 to bring overriding interests onto the Register.[72]

Section 29's pivotal role is strongly reinforced by recent proposals of the Law Commission in its 2016 Consultation Paper.[73] These would extend the benefit of the section 29 rule to *any* disponee—not just disponees of *registrable* dispositions—for valuable consideration, who had sought and obtained a notice to protect their interest. This is an interesting proposal at a technical level, because it would fundamentally change the significance of notice entry within the registration framework. Hitherto, a notice has simply preserved the priority of the associated interest, if valid,[74] in the face of *later* dealings that trigger section 29.[75] However, in future—if the Law Commission's proposals were implemented—a notice entry

[67] LRA 2002, s 29 (for dispositions of registered estates).
[68] LRA 2002, s 30 (for dispositions of existing registered charges).
[69] See LRA 2002, s 27, for what qualifies as a 'registrable disposition'.
[70] The major exception is the grant/transfer of shorter legal leases (subject to limited exceptions, leases for 7 years or less).
[71] LRA 2002, sch 1; cf LRA 2002 sch 3.
[72] LRA 2002, ss 71 and 37, reinforced by s 29(3); see Law Com No 271 (n 36) paras 8.90–8.95.
[73] Law Com CP No 227 (n 29) paras 6.7 ff, and in particular, paras 6.29–6.30.
[74] LRA 2002, s 32(3).
[75] LRA 2002, s 29(2)(a)(i).

would have the further effect of affording the interest associated with the notice priority over *earlier* interests, via the operation of section 29. This would also be an important step in policy terms. By extending section 29 and the immunity it affords, a substantially wider category of parties would benefit from the priority promise and the assurance of Register-reliability. As such, the Law Commission's proposal signals an even stronger movement away from the general law's basic *nemo dat quod non habet* premise.

These recent law reform proposals make it all the more important to understand the nature and significance of the priority promise as it is currently embodied in section 29. As we explain fully below, all is not necessarily well. There are several risks of misinterpretation and misunderstanding which, if not clearly perceived, threaten the priority promise's integrity in one of two ways. First, there is a danger that the priority promise is wrongly *undermined*, directly or indirectly, through interpretations that limit its legitimate ambit of application and strength—a risk which, if realised, will reduce or negate the benefits that a reliable Register is meant to achieve. Secondly, there is the opposing danger that the priority promise is wrongly *over-extended* for the benefit those who should never be privileged by it—a risk which, if realised, may bring the registration system into disrepute, and force the courts into intricate legal acrobatics to avoid or mitigate the promise's unwanted effects.

B. The Relationship Between the Title and Priority Promises

As a preliminary point, it must be noted that, in very many cases, the LRA 2002's title and priority promises are concurrent: both promises are routinely made simultaneously to the same person. Thus, where Y sells his registered freehold estate to Z, Z's registration as proprietor will attract both the title promise (section 58) *and* the priority promise (section 29). Indeed, in a system committed to Register-reliability, it is crucial for Z to benefit from both promises. He needs both security against invisible flaws in the root of his title (section 58), *and* security against prior encumbrances which are undiscoverable—not being on the Register or otherwise 'overriding' (section 29).[76]

Nevertheless, the LRA 2002 does not completely follow this logic in at least two important respects. First, and most significantly, whilst section 58's title promise is afforded to all registered proprietors, only those who pay valuable consideration benefit from section 29's priority promise. It was manifestly a deliberate policy choice to restrict the latter promise to those in Z's position who, by paying for their interest, have a stronger claim to priority over prior interest-holders, like X. At one level, this position is not unattractive—why should X, an innocent pre-existing interest-holder, who may have paid for his own right, lose out to a later interest-holder, Z, who might not have paid anything? However, at another level, one might legitimately question whether this restriction on section 29's ambit is internally consistent with the statute's promise of title in section 58.

This problem is starkly illustrated by a comparison with section 58's application in so-called ABC title dispute cases. An example is where A begins as the registered freehold proprietor, a 'disposition' of A's title to B is forged, and B is registered as the new proprietor, before conveying to C, who is thereafter registered as proprietor. Section 58 vests title in

[76] See A Goymour, 'Resolving the Tension Between the Land Registration Act 2002's "Priority" and "Alteration" Provisions' [2015] *Conv* 253.

B and C in turn, notwithstanding the voidness of the A–B disposition, and even though neither B nor C may have paid valuable consideration. We might wonder why someone like C, in an ABC title dispute, deserves a good title as against a third party (here A) merely upon registration, without having to pay valuable consideration, whereas Z, in an XYZ priority dispute, must pay for the privilege of *priority* as against a third party (here X)? It is unfortunate that the 2016 Law Commission did not revisit the policy choices inherent in the LRA 2002.

C. The Role and Operation of Section 28's 'Basic Rule' of Priority

Before addressing the intricacies of section 29, it is important to say something about the 'basic rule' of priority established by section 28 of the LRA 2002, to which sections 29 (and 30) are the exception:

> 28 Basic rule
>
> (1) Except as provided by sections 29 and 30, the priority of an interest affecting a registered estate or charge is not affected by a disposition of the estate or charge.
> (2) It makes no difference for the purposes of this section whether the interest or disposition is registered.

Consistently with what is said in the Law Commission's 2001 Report, section 28 is generally assumed to embody a simple, general 'first-in-time' rule.[77] However, this conceals two significant controversies. One concerns the effect of the basic rule, and the second, its ambit.

i. First in Time: Absolute Rule, Qualified Rule or No Rule?

The most important issue concerns the sense in which it is correct to regard section 28 as establishing a first-in-time rule at all. Section 28 is in fact susceptible to three different interpretations.

a. No Rule—Parasitic Incorporation of the General Law's Ordering

The first reading would be that, counter-intuitively, section 28 establishes no 'rule' at all. Instead, it is a bare provision, which merely incorporates the priority rules and outcomes of the general law. As such, in stating that the interest's priority 'is not affected' by a disposition, section 28 means only: *the disposition will have no impact on the priority that would have pertained under the general law's principles.*

This reading must be immediately discounted. It is not easily reached via a natural reading of the statutory language. As importantly, it also seems unsustainable from the perspective of legislative intent. It would mean that, subject to the special rules in sections 29,

[77] Law Com No 271 (n 36) para 5.5; see too, eg, *Ruoff & Roper* (n 12) para 15.004. Note that in ch 13 of this book, Martin Dixon assumes that s 28 has a narrower range of application. He appears to assume that s 28 only lays down a rule in a case where the later disposition is at least in the nature of a 'registrable' disposition—whether or not in fact completed by registration. In our view, this is an unnaturally narrow reading of 'disposition' in the context of s 28. 'Disposition' has a wide meaning—to encompass the transfer or grant of *any* species of interest in land.

priority disputes would continue to be resolved by reference to historic rules, in all of their complexity. This would make little sense, and it was certainly not what the Law Commission intended. Its 2001 Report[78] indicates that the Commission wished to introduce a new basic rule, which was autonomous to the extent that it would not embody all of the nuances and variances found in the general law—eg, whereby the applicable principles vary according to the quality of the competing interests as legal estates or interests, equitable interests or mere equities.

b. Absolute Rule—An Autonomous and Unqualified Rule of Ordering by Time

The second reading, which lies at the other extreme, is that section 28 establishes an *unqualified* first-in-time rule—ie, it prescribes that an interest will have precedence over *any* subsequent disposition of the relevant registered estate or charge, *subject only* to the effect of sections 29 and 30. This would cast section 28 as an autonomous and unyielding absolute rule.

At first sight, this might seem to be exactly what the Law Commission intended. In its 2001 Report, the Commission noted that under the LRA 1925, and in the absence of any clear statutory rule, the courts had drawn on general law priority principles in ways that were apparently considered unsatisfactory. In particular, for competitions between two minor (equitable) interests, the courts had relied on the general rule that 'where the equities are equal, the first in time prevails'.[79] This is a default/presumptive rule of time-ordering, which is inherently subject to displacement by gross negligence or other culpable conduct of the holder of the first interest—nuances which the 2001 Law Commission apparently considered necessitated uncertain and difficult inquiries.[80] Similarly, the courts had historically treated mere equities as more fragile in priority disputes than equitable interests[81]—a distinction which the Law Commission also thought unjustified.[82] The Law Commission's solution was to confirm that mere equities were indeed interests 'capable of binding successors in title',[83] and to subject *all* interests—without differentiation—to the same 'basic' first-in-time rule.[84]

There is nevertheless a problem with this second reading of section 28, as an unqualified first-in-time rule. The Law Commission's reasoning can certainly support the adoption of a *common* first-in-time rule—'common' in the sense of *generally or universally applicable.* However, it requires a greater leap of reasoning, and is less obviously legitimate, to suppose that this *common* rule was also meant to be unqualified. The real thrust of the Law Commission's 2001 Report is that historic, jurisdictionally-coloured categorisations of interests in land should no longer be relevant to the applicable priority principles; for the future, there should be a *common* (universal) rule. The adoption of a *common* rule must necessarily involve the rejection of all of the historic variations that were peculiar to the type of interest

[78] Law Com No 271 (n 36) para 5.5; cf para 5.2.
[79] ibid, para 5.3.
[80] ibid.
[81] ie, a bona fide purchaser of *any* interest, legal *or* equitable, would take free of an equity, but not an equitable interest.
[82] Law Com No 271 (n 36) paras 5.32–5.36.
[83] LRA 2002, s 116.
[84] Law Com No 271 (n 36) para 5.36(2).

in issue. Furthermore, the *common* rule being preferred was manifestly that which was previously applicable to *legal* interests, where a basic first-in-time rule—and *nemo dat*—was the order of the day. However, that does not go to show that the resulting common rule is completely unqualified. The better view, indeed, is that it is not; a third reading should be preferred.

c. A Universal but Qualified Rule—Implicit Qualification by General Law Doctrines

The third reading assumes that section 28 embodies a common (universal) 'first-in-time' rule, which is nevertheless *qualified*. As such, where Y is proprietor of a registered estate, section 28 *generally* preserves the priority of any earlier interest belonging to X which encumbers the estate, vis-à-vis subsequent dispositions by Y to Z—whatever the nature of the respective interests of X and Z—subject to the effect of section 29. Nevertheless, it does not *guarantee* such priority. The general law recognises a number of additional rules or principles, of general application, which can affect priority and result in the postponement of an earlier interest to a later disposition. This third reading assumes that these general law principles are implicitly preserved by the LRA 2002—ie, section 28's basic first-in-time rule must be read as implicitly qualified by them. These principles include, in particular:

(i) general rules that determine the *time* of acquisition of interests;[85]
(ii) overreaching;[86]
(iii) consensual postponement/waiver of priority;[87]
(iv) estoppel.

This seems to be the only plausible analysis of section 28's operation. Furthermore, the provision is also susceptible to this reading, as a matter of language. In effect, its true meaning may involve an interpolation into section 28(1):

> … the priority of an interest affecting a registered estate or charge is not affected [merely] by a disposition of the estate or charge …

thereby leaving open the possibility that an interest's priority may be affected by additional circumstances, eg overreaching, waiver, etc.

There is no indication that the Law Commission intended that these additional doctrines should cease to be relevant under its newly-introduced basic rule. No justification was offered—the 2001 Report is silent on the point—and no justification is obviously available. Just as significantly, the *courts* have treated these general law principles as continuing to have a role within the LRA 2002 registration framework. In practice, such arguments are more often invoked to qualify the normal effect of *section 29*—and in particular, to explain why an earlier interest that might otherwise be an overriding interest, does not have

[85] eg, *Abbey National Building Society v Cann* [1991] 1 AC 56 (HL); *Southern Pacific Mortgages Ltd v Scott* [2014] UKSC 52, [2015] AC 385.

[86] See Law of Property Act ('LPA') 1925, s 2; *City of London Building Society v Flegg* [1988] AC 54 (HL); *State Bank of India v Sood* [1997] Ch 276 (CA); *Birmingham Midshires Mortgage Services Ltd v Sabherwal* (2000) 80 P & CR 256 (CA); *Mortgage Express v Lambert* [2016] EWCA Civ 555, [2017] Ch 93; *Baker v Craggs* [2015] EWHC 3250 (Ch), [2017] 2 WLR 1483. See further ch 18 of this book, sections III(C)(ii)(e) and III(C)(iii)(c).

[87] eg, *Paddington Building Society v Mendelsohn* (1985) 50 P & CR 244 (CA); *Credit & Mercantile plc v Kaymuu Ltd* [2015] EWCA Civ 655, [2015] 2 P & CR 15.

overriding status. Nevertheless, it would make no sense to limit their significance to that context. If these doctrines are relevant, then they should also in principle be available to undermine an attempt by an earlier interest-holder, X, to claim priority for his interest via section 28's basic rule. If X's priority is thereby lost to the later interest-holder, Z, there is no need for Z to rely on section 29's special priority rule at all.

d. Wider Implications

The third reading of section 28 has important wider ramifications. It makes it vital to know exactly *which* general law doctrines are allowed to infiltrate, and extend the circumstances in which an *earlier* interest might be postponed. Regrettably, this is not a question which the LRA 2002, or the Law Commission's 2001 Report which preceded it, provide any assistance in answering.

Does the answer matter? At first glance, it might seem that this uncertainty will not undermine the LRA 2002's central ambitions. The uncertainties directly infect the operation of section 28. They do not appear to undermine section 29, which embodies the priority promise that privileges later registered disponees, and is pivotal to the Register's reliability. Indeed, if allowed to operate, such general law postponement principles promise *further* benefits to parties who can rely on section 29—affording them priority in wider circumstances than those allowed for by that section's express terms.

On closer examination, though, this may be an unduly optimistic assessment. The LRA 2002 already ensures an important degree of security for those who can rely upon section 29, from undiscovered and undiscoverable prior rights. Importing additional general law postponement principles *further* privileges later disponees. To that extent, it might seem that the objective of the regime—to secure a reliable Register—is unharmed and, if anything, is enhanced. There is, nevertheless, a cost. *Any* principle that supplies a reason why a pre-existing right should be postponed will render such a right vulnerable—impairing or negating its value, potentially without compensation. The wider these principles are, the greater the vulnerability of prior interests. There will be a tipping-point at which it becomes too much—where prior interests are unduly destabilised. What this means is that the case for incorporating any general law postponement principle must be clear, and if incorporated, the relevant principles must be developed and applied with discipline, alive to the consequences. Past cases, decided under the LRA 1925 and LRA 2002, do not give much cause for confidence in this regard. In particular, the courts have not been at all slow to find reasons for subordinating an unregistered interest that might otherwise have overriding status.[88]

In fact, the problems could run even deeper. Conceivably, even the status of prior *registered* interests may be compromised by undisciplined incursions by these general law postponement principles. Consider, for example, a situation where Y's registered estate is encumbered by a *registered* interest held by X. If Y subsequently effects a disposition of his estate to Z, X's interest will seemingly take priority over Z's—as a result of either section 28 (if Z does not benefit from section 29's special priority rule) or section 29(2)(a)(i) (if he does—the status of X's interest as a *registered* interest means that it is protected against postponement). But is this the full story? There is nothing on the face of either section 28

[88] See the cases cited in nn 85–87 above, and in particular, the recent controversial decision in *Kaymuu* (n 87).

or section 29(2)(a)(i) that expressly immunises X's earlier registered interest from general law doctrines that might lead to its being subordinated to Z's later interest—eg, waiver of priority by X, etc.[89] Reliance on these general law principles to subordinate prior registered interests is not complete anathema to the integrity of the registration regime. Nevertheless, it is undoubtedly something that must be carefully watched: these general law priority-yielding doctrines, which are not obvious from the face of the LRA 2002, have the capacity to render prior *registered* interests, belonging to parties in X's position, less secure than they might otherwise appear to be. To make matters worse, their subordination to a later interest is unlikely to be compensated via a Registry indemnity award.[90]

ii. Competing Interests 'Affecting' a Registered Estate or Charge: Directly or Derivatively?

There is a second interpretative problem raised by section 28 which seems to have gone unnoticed, but remains of some considerable importance. Section 28 supplies a basic priority rule for competitions between interests that 'affect' a registered estate or charge. This clearly applies to competing interests that are *immediately* derived from a registered estate—eg, a lease or a charge granted by the registered freehold proprietor, RP. But what about competing interests that are more remotely derived, and are at one or more stages removed, from the registered estate or charge? Consider, for example, a case where RP grants an unregistered equitable charge to C, who thereafter executes competing unregistered subcharges (over his own charge) in favour of subchargees SC1 and SC2. Which rules determine the relative priority of SC1 and SC2?

The choice lies between applying the LRA 2002's priority provisions—here section 28—and resorting to the rules that would govern unregistered land.

The question whether section 28 is engaged turns on the breadth of the phrase 'affecting' the 'registered estate' in section 28(1). It clearly encompasses interests that *immediately* affect the registered estate—eg, C's unregistered charge over RP's registered estate. However, does it also extend to those interests—like the subcharges of SC1 and SC2—that might affect the registered estate, if at all, more indirectly, because they are derivative of an (unregistered) interest—ie, C's charge—which is itself derivative of RP's registered estate?

The widest reading is that the subcharges of SC1 and SC2 do indeed 'affect' RP's registered estate, because they are *ultimately* derived from the registered estate, even though they are not immediately created by RP. On this view, section 28 would govern the priority of the competing subcharges of SC1 and SC2.

On a narrower reading, section 28 would govern the priority of C's equitable charge vis-à-vis subsequent dispositions by RP of his registered estate, but it would have nothing to say about dispositions by *C*, relating to his (unregistered) equitable charge. Any priority contest

[89] See section III(C)(i)(c) above. Not all doctrines are equally relevant, of course, in relation to registered (legal) interests. In particular, overreaching will not be available to postpone such an interest to a later disposition; cf also LRA 2002, s 48, establishing a special regime for the ordering of registered charges, which is intended to enable the Register to reflect the existence of inter-creditor priority agreements that may vary the ordering that might otherwise follow from the registration regime's rules.

[90] ie, the insecurity derives from a general law postponement principle, whose application might support a Register 'alteration', and not from an amendment to the Register that could be characterised as 'rectification'; as a result, it would not be an indemnity-justifying event under sch 8.

between his subchargees—SC1 and SC2—would fall to be determined by the general law's default priority rules. If that is so, then there is effectively a 'proprietary underworld'[91] within the realm of registered land, which is ungoverned or incompletely-governed by the LRA 2002's priority framework, and which remains governed by the rules of unregistered land law—in all of their complexity—for the indefinite future.

The narrower reading seems to have been assumed by the reasoning of the Supreme Court in *Southern Pacific Mortgages Ltd v Scott*.[92] We are agnostic.

D. The Applicability and Effect of Section 29 in XYZ Priority Disputes

For disponees of an already-registered estate, section 29 assumes overwhelming significance as the legislative basis of the priority promise. This promise has equal significance, along with the title and empowerment promises, in ensuring the reliability of the Register. Where Y is the proprietor of a registered estate, section 29 offers a privileged subset of subsequent disponees, like Z, an assurance of immunity from prior interests encumbering the estate, held by X. Through this means, Z's interest may be afforded priority to X's earlier interest even in the absence of *general law* grounds justifying its postponement (eg, waiver, overreaching, etc). In the light of this, one would hope that section 29's applicability and effect was clear. Unfortunately, that is not the case: section 29 is afflicted by a surprising number of significant interpretative controversies. Uncertainty surrounds in particular:

(i) the triggering conditions for the prima facie application of section 29;
(ii) a disponee's vulnerability to direct rights, despite section 29's postponing effect;
(iii) the susceptibility of section 29's effect to reversal via the schedule 4 alteration provisions;
(iv) the interpretation of overriding interests; and
(v) supplementary general law grounds that might justify the postponement of X's earlier interest.

Individually, each type of uncertainty generates problems; but when considered as a whole, the picture begins to look even more chaotic. We explore these areas of uncertainty in the following pages. Our overarching aim—a necessary foundation for any future debate—is to identify their parameters and likely impact on the realisation of the registration regime's ambitions.

i. Triggering Conditions for the Application of Section 29

The first set of uncertainties concerns the triggers for the application/disapplication of section 29. By its express terms, the section 29 priority rule is triggered by a (1) 'registrable disposition' of (2) a 'registered' estate, for (3) 'valuable consideration', which is (4) 'completed by registration'. This raises at least two significant threshold questions, in cases where

[91] See A Goymour, '*Bruton v London & Quadrant Housing Trust* [2002]: Relativity of Title, and the Regulation of the "Proprietary Underworld"', ch 7 in S Douglas, R Hickey and E Waring (eds), *Landmark Cases in Property Law* (Oxford, Hart, 2015).

[92] *Southern Pacific Mortgages* (n 85).

Y's registered estate is encumbered by X's interest, and Y effects a disposition to Z disponee. Is section 29 triggered where the Y–Z disposition is void but Z is nonetheless registered as proprietor? And is it triggered where Z acts fraudulently?

a. 'Dispositions'—General Law Status as Valid/Void

First, does section 29 require that the 'registrable disposition' between Y and Z, which leads to Z's registration, be legally valid *under the general law* in order for Z to benefit from section 29's effect? Or is it sufficient that there is a *purported* disposition, which is legally effective (if at all) only upon its registration, owing to the constitutive effect of registration?[93]

This is best tested via facts involving an innocent disponee. Imagine that the registered proprietor, Y, is trustee of his estate for X, who is not in actual occupation. There is subsequently a forged 'transfer' of that title in favour of Z for valuable consideration, which is completed by Z's registration as the new proprietor. Z was unaware of the forgery. Under the general law, the forged 'transfer' is void. Despite this, as chapter sixteen has explained,[94] section 58 vests a valid title in Z upon his registration. This scenario is illustrated by the following diagram.

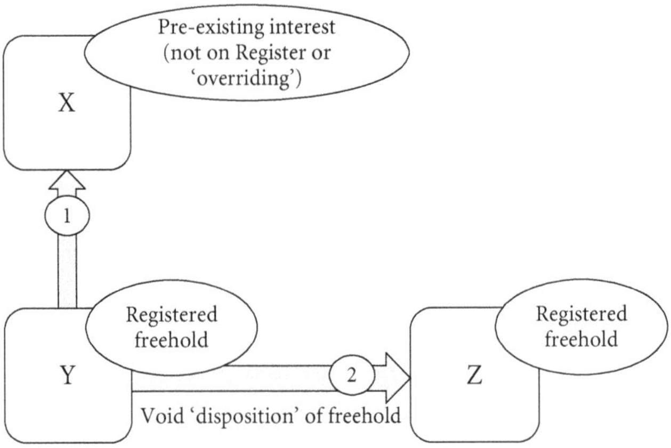

In this scenario, can Z rely on the special priority rule in section 29, on the basis that he acquired his interest via a 'registrable *disposition*'? The answer given to this question can have major ramifications.

On the one hand, if a *real* disposition were required, Z is vulnerable. Section 29 would not be triggered and Z's registered estate would be subject throughout to X's prior beneficial interest owing to section 28's first-in-time principle, even though X was not in actual occupation and Z was innocent, with no ready means of discovering X's interest. Indeed, to rub salt into Z's wounds, Y might seek and obtain alteration of the Register, in order to have the registered freehold re-vested in him, on the ground of correcting a 'mistake'.

[93] LRA 2002, s 58.
[94] See ch 16 of this book, sections I and III(B).

Z would thereby lose his registered title, with no likelihood of receiving any indemnity via schedule 8 to make up for the shattering of his expectation—engendered by his reliance on the Register and the section 29 rule—of taking free from X's trust interest. This is because, unless section 29 is triggered by a void disposition, the Register does not extend the priority promise to Z.[95]

On the other hand, if a valid underlying Y–Z disposition were *not* required, section 29 *would* be triggered and X's prior beneficial interest would be postponed to Z's registered interest. Y could nevertheless seek rectification of the Register. If granted, Y would then re-gain the registered freehold title, necessarily subject to the original trust for X. This time, Z *would* be entitled to an indemnity under schedule 8, since on this analysis the alteration *would* prejudicially affect Z's title, which section 29 had previously cleared of X's prior right.

Which is the best view? The most natural interpretation of the LRA 2002 is probably that 'disposition' should bear its ordinary meaning—a *real* disposition. Nevertheless, it is not evident that the Act's architects had this problem clearly in mind when they drafted the provision. Furthermore, as a matter of land registration policy, the competing arguments seem finely balanced. The question ultimately boils down to what kinds of promise the registration regime can be understood to be making to someone in Z's position—reflecting the nature of the reliance that he can legitimately place on the Register.

When assessing this, the principles that inform the operation and ambit of the LRA 2002's title promise, discussed in chapter sixteen, provide a useful starting-point, as well as a point of comparison. Take the familiar ABC scenario, where A begins as the registered freehold proprietor, a 'disposition' of A's title to B is forged (whether by B or by another), and B is registered as the new proprietor, before selling to C who is thereafter registered as proprietor. There are compelling reasons why a well-functioning registration system ought to guarantee *C* some protection against vices in his title—whether via 'mud' or 'money'.[96] C relied on B's having been *correctly entered on the Register* as proprietor when he took the conveyance from B, when in truth B had been mistakenly entered on the Register. Indeed, what is the point of a registration system, if not to offer those who rely on the Register's correctness, like C, at least some security of title? However, the same reasoning arguably cannot justify protecting *B* from vices in his registered title that reflect *flaws in the A–B transaction*: B's reliance on the *Register* has not been compromised. The Register has told B no lie: it correctly disclosed that A was the registered proprietor, and that A's title was a 'good' title. B's vulnerability, if any, did not stem from anything that the Register could or should have disclosed at the time of the purported A–B conveyance. It stemmed from a source that the Register does not speak to—ie, an 'off-Register' vice in the A–B 'transaction' that purported to convey A's registered title to B, and enabled B to apply to become the new registered proprietor.

In principle, therefore, the case for *immediate indefeasibility* (protection of B) is less obviously compelling than the case for *deferred indefeasibility* (protection of C). Despite this, the 2001 Law Commission seemingly took the position that the LRA 2002's title promise, as embodied in section 58 and fulfilled by either 'mud' or 'money', should extend to *both B and*

[95] Note that s 28 itself lays down a rule concerning the effect of a 'disposition' of a registered estate or charge, on the priority of an existing interest. If 'disposition' has the same narrow meaning here, then the s 28 rule speaks only to the effect of a valid disposition. Cf *Ruoff & Roper* (n 12) para 46.032.03.

[96] See ch 16 of this book, sections III(D)(i) and III(D)(ii).

C—thereby extending the title promise beyond what may be the 'irreducible core' requirements for a well-functioning registration system.

How might these observations inform the present debate about the proper ambit of the Act's *priority* promise in XYZ priority cases? Applying the same reasoning, we must first ascertain when, in principle, Z might be justified in relying on the Register's correctness (in terms of its non-disclosure of X's rights) when the Y–Z transaction is void. In contrast to ABC title cases, where it is clear that a well-functioning registration system must make some kind of title promise to C, the policy arguments bearing on whether Z should benefit from the priority promise are very finely balanced. In terms of desert, Z falls somewhere between B's and C's respective positions in the ABC scenario.

On the one hand, Z's position might be considered as materially analogous to C's. Thinking that he is acquiring Y's title, Z will place reliance on what the Register discloses about that title. Apart from overriding interests listed in schedule 3 (which of course bind despite their absence from the Register), Z will expect to be bound *only* by interests, held by third parties like X, which are *on* the Register. If Z cannot rely on section 29, this reliance on the Register will prove misplaced. He will find his registered title encumbered by *all* prior interests—whether or not overriding, and whether or not on the Register.

On the other hand, Z's position might, in principle, be considered also to align with B's in the ABC scenario. In both scenarios, the potential vulnerability of (respectively) B and Z stems from the voidness of the immediate and necessarily off-Register 'transaction' (the A–B transaction and the Y–Z transaction) which led to the acquisition of their respective registered titles. The validity of the A–B or Y–Z transactions is something to which the Register did not, and could not be expected to, speak. Accordingly, since Z's vulnerability stems from an off-Register problem in the Y–Z transaction, and not solely (if at all) from Z's misplaced reliance on the Register, it is not obvious that a well-functioning registration system *must* promise him priority over prior third party rights—although, of course, any registration system may choose to make promises beyond what is strictly necessary for its core operation.

Turning from principle to practice, the cases have offered conflicting views on this difficult question. A few cases have certainly *assumed* that section 29 or its broadly equivalent provision under the LRA 1925—section 20—cannot be triggered by a forged or other disposition from Y to Z that has no effect under the general law. In *Malory Enterprises Ltd v Cheshire Homes (UK) Ltd*,[97] a case decided under the LRA 1925, Arden LJ suggested that 'since the [forged transfer] … could not in law be of any effect in itself, … it cannot constitute a "disposition" of the … land [for the purposes of the provision]'. Newey J felt compelled to adopt the same interpretation of the LRA 2002 in *Fitzwilliam v Richall Holdings Services Ltd*.[98] Unfortunately, these decisions are not strongly persuasive. It was not technically necessary to decide the point in either case, and no extended reasons were given.

[97] *Malory Enterprises Ltd v Cheshire Homes (UK) Ltd* [2002] EWCA Civ 151, [2002] Ch 216 [65].

[98] *Fitzwilliam v Richall Holdings Services Ltd* [2013] EWHC 86 (Ch), [2013] 1 P & CR 19 [83]–[86]. Newey J considered that it was not open to him, in light of *Malory*, to give 'disposition' any wider interpretation under the LRA 2002, so that it could include a 'void' disposition.

A different view was more recently taken in *Swift 1st Ltd v Chief Land Registrar*,[99] where the Court of Appeal held that *Malory* was decided *per incuriam*. It had misunderstood the effect of section 69 of the LRA 1925 (the predecessor of section 58(1) of the LRA 2002), and it had also misread section 20 of the LRA 1925. In short, *Malory* had wrongly suggested that section 20 could not apply to a registered forged disposition. According to Patten LJ in *Swift*:[100]

> An important, perhaps even critical, part of Arden LJ's reasoning ... was that section 20 of the [LRA 1925] had no application to a forged disposition. But section 114[101] makes it clear that, although a registered disposition which would be fraudulent and void if unregistered remains fraudulent and void even if registered, this takes effect subject to the provisions of the [LRA 1925] with respect to registered dispositions for valuable consideration one of which is, of course, section 20. It is not therefore possible to construe section 20 as having no application to a fraudulent transfer for valuable consideration that is registered.

Patten LJ says nothing of the LRA 2002. Nevertheless, on the assumption that section 29 was not intended to effect any substantive change, one is left to assume that he would interpret section 29 similarly. It is regrettable that the Law Commission found it unnecessary to tackle this important point in its 2016 Consultation Paper.[102]

The better view may be that, in the interests of protecting innocent disponees like Z, an extended interpretation of section 29 should be preferred. This would assume that where a disposition is not a 'real' disposition under the general law—ie, it is void or otherwise of no legal effect—it may nevertheless qualify as a 'disposition' for the purposes of section 29 *if it is a disposition which, on completion by registration, would be treated as legally effective by the LRA 2002*. In other words, the meaning of 'disposition' here should be read in the light of the operation of section 58. If section 58 would deem the legal estate to be vested in the disponee, Z, on his registration as the proprietor of the estate (even if it would not otherwise be), then section 29 might also be triggered. This would have the benefit of more closely aligning the title and priority promises. In such cases, *registration* would have a presumptive effect in affording *title*, and a similar presumptive effect in affording *priority* over pre-existing interests in accordance with section 29.

In chapter sixteen we explain that the LRA 2002 goes beyond the irreducible core required for a well-functioning land registration regime, in extending the title promise in an ABC scenario not only to C (whose potential vulnerability to loss of title to A should have been, but was not, exposed on the Register), but also to B, whose vulnerability is not attributable to a Registry-error but arises from the invalidity of the *off-Register* A–B transaction. Given that the LRA 2002 extends its title promise beyond the necessary minimum, it seems proper for its priority promise to be similarly extended so as to benefit Z, whose potential vulnerability, like B's, arises not from a Register-error, but from the *off-Register* invalidity of the transaction (from Y to Z) which led to Z's acquisition of the registered title. On this

[99] *Swift 1st Ltd v Chief Land Registrar* [2015] EWCA Civ 330, [2015] Ch 602.

[100] ibid [44].

[101] LRA 1925, s 114: 'Fraudulent dispositions, how far to be void. Subject to the provisions in this Act contained with respect to indemnity and to registered dispositions for valuable consideration, any disposition of land or of a charge, which if unregistered would be fraudulent and void, shall, notwithstanding registration, be fraudulent and void in like manner.'

[102] Law Com CP No 227 (n 29).

view, if the LRA 2002 extends its title promise to a registered disponee via section 58, then consistency of treatment suggests that that party may also rely (if valuable consideration is proffered) on section 29's priority promise.[103]

Both promises are, of course, promises that may not be respected *in specie*, and may instead be given effect only via a money award in lieu. Thus, a registered disponee's acquisition of a title (via section 58) which is unencumbered (via section 29's clearing effect) is itself vulnerable to a schedule 4 application to alter the Register—most likely, in an XYZ case, by removing Z's interest from the Register. Z would lose both title and, with it, priority. Nevertheless, in this case, the presumptive applicability of section 58 (in affording title) and of section 29 (in affording priority) would mean that Z might qualify for a Registry indemnity, on the assumption that he was prejudicially affected by the rectification.

Note that, even on this extended view of section 29's application, it would not operate in favour of every disponee under a void disposition. First, it would only operate in favour of a disponee whose disposition was caught by section 58—ie, where the legal estate is deemed to be vested in the disponee, *by registration*, even if it would not otherwise be.[104] Secondly, Z must provide 'valuable consideration' to benefit from section 29's promise of priority. Thirdly, there must also be at least *some* semblance of a 'disposition' to Z, before section 29 can bite. It would not be triggered if there was no disposition of the relevant title to Z, and Z is registered as proprietor due to a spontaneous *Land Registry* error—eg if Z is registered with a title that was not the title purportedly conveyed, or that includes an area which is *outside* the title purportedly conveyed. This line seems comprehensible. What is the basis in such cases for protecting Z from prior encumbrances that burden the relevant title, when Z did not believe he was acquiring that title, when he would very likely have made no Register search in relation to it, and when he could not have legitimately placed reliance on what the Register did or did not disclose about prior encumbrances?

b. Fraudulent Disponees

A second important question concerns section 29's application to a disposition of Y's registered estate to Z, where Z is fraudulent. Will Z's fraud have any effect on his ability to benefit from section 29's priority promise? This clearly overlaps with the question whether a *real* disposition is required, but it is distinct. The relevant 'fraud' might involve, or result in:

(i) a *void* 'disposition' which is the product of Z's fraudulent conduct (eg, forgery by Z);
(ii) a *real* disposition to Z which is nevertheless *voidable* by Y disponor (eg, owing to a fraudulent misrepresentation by Z);
(iii) a *real* disposition to Z which is fully valid (and not even voidable) but was effected for some fraudulent *motive* (eg, to defeat the rights of a third party, X).

In cases (i) and (ii), the fraud *directly* impairs Z's acquisition of title from Y. If Y can re-gain title via an alteration claim, then any impact that section 29 might have had, in postponing prior interests to Z's previously-registered title, is reversed.[105] However, case (iii) raises

[103] For earlier recognition of the importance of aligning the title and priority promises, see Goymour, 'Resolving the Tension' (n 76).

[104] eg, it would not operate in favour of the grantee of a void equitable charge.

[105] If the relevant fraudulent transaction was *void*, then rectification can be sought under the LRA 2002, sch 4, para 2(1)(a)/para 5(1)(a), for the purpose of 'correcting a mistake'. *NRAM plc v Evans* [2017] EWCA Civ

different and difficult issues, which are the focus of this section. Here, the integrity of the Y–Z disposition—and section 29's prima facie effect—is not in doubt. The question that squarely arises is whether Z is prevented from relying on section 29 on grounds of bad faith or improper/fraudulent motives.

Consider the following facts.[106] Y, the registered freehold proprietor, holds his title subject to an option to purchase granted to X. X's option is not protected by a notice in the Register, nor is X in actual occupation of the relevant land. Knowing this, and for the purpose of defeating X's unprotected option, Y sells the land for a small sum to his wife, Z, who is registered as proprietor. On the face of it, Z can rely on section 29 to postpone—and in practice, defeat—X's right. Is there any basis for resisting that conclusion?

Section 29 does not *explicitly* incorporate any requirement for 'good faith' on the part of the disponee.[107] Nor, in the light of the Law Commission publications that preceded the LRA 2002, can any legitimately be *implied*.[108] The statutory omission was the product of a deliberate decision that the statutory priority rule embodied in section 29 should not be qualified. To this extent, the Law Commission indicated a clear preference for the approach taken in *Midland Bank Trust Co Ltd v Green*[109] (an unregistered land case), over Graham J's controversial decision in *Peffer v Rigg*[110] (a registered land case). In the former, the House of Lords had refused to imply any 'good faith' qualification into corresponding priority provisions of the Land Charges Act ('LCA') 1972, which on their face rendered an option, which was registrable as a Class C land charge[111] but was not in fact registered, 'void' 'as against a purchaser for money or money's worth of a legal estate in the land charged with it'.[112] On the facts of *Midland Bank v Green*, which concerned an unprotected option held by X, the conveyance of the burdened unregistered estate from Y to Z resulted in Z acquiring title free of X's option, *despite* Y and Z's common fraudulent motive of defeating X's option. In *Peffer*, by contrast, Graham J found a roundabout way of reading a 'good faith' requirement into section 20 of the LRA 1925—the provision of the LRA 1925 that achieved a clearing effect equivalent to section 29 of the LRA 2002.

Nevertheless, analysis cannot stop there. *Whatever* the effect of section 29 might be, it was never intended to be a complete regime. The Law Commission specifically envisaged that the *general law* would continue to have a role in mitigating section 29's operation, via the imposition on a disponee of what were ambiguously labelled 'personal remedies' or 'personal liabilities'.[113] Unfortunately, the Law Commission did not identify what it considered to be the legitimate parameters of those doctrines. The result is that the supposedly

1013 has recently confirmed that the registration of a merely *voidable* transaction does not involve a 'mistake' for this purpose, but that once a voidable transaction is rescinded, alteration can be sought for the purpose of 'bringing the register up to date' under para 2(1)(b)/para 5(b).

[106] These resemble those of *Midland Bank Trust Co Ltd v Green* [1981] AC 513 (HL).

[107] E Cooke and P O'Connor, 'Purchaser Liability to Third Parties in the English Land Registration System: a Comparative Perspective' (2004) 120 *LQR* 640, 650–659.

[108] This is clearest from Law Com No 254 (n 34) paras 3.44 ff; cf Law Com No 271 (n 36) paras 5.16 ff, where the discussion is very bare, and must be read in light of the discussion in the earlier paper.

[109] *Midland Bank v Green* (n 106).

[110] *Peffer v Rigg* [1977] 1 WLR 285.

[111] LCA 1972, s 2(4)(iv).

[112] LCA 1972, s 4(6).

[113] Law Com No 254 (n 34) para 3.48.

clear statutory rule is, in truth, a mirage. The priority afforded by section 29 does not *depend* on 'good faith', but it can be substantially negated via an un-/under-identified and unsystemised patchwork of general law principles. This represents a regrettable failure of legislative ambition in relation to a fundamental component of the registration regime—ie, the ambit of the regime's pivotal priority promise.

c. A Necessary Diversion: Alternative Ways of Dealing with Fraudulent Disponees

It follows from the last section that a full understanding of the position of fraudulent disponees requires an extended exploration of *general law principles*. Section 29 is not *itself* qualified by a 'good faith' requirement, expressly or impliedly, but there are three possible *general law* routes by which a decision might nevertheless be reached in favour of X, where Z disponee, who relies on section 29's effect, is fraudulent. They are:

(i) that X has a *direct right* against Z;
(ii) that section 29 can be *disapplied* vis-à-vis Z; or
(iii) that section 29 is not engaged, because Z did not provide the necessary *valuable consideration*.

Each of these routes has an uncertain ambit. They require close analysis.

Direct Rights Against the 'Fraudulent' Disponee

First, section 29 might be allowed to operate in favour of Z—thereby postponing X's pre-existing interest—but Z's conduct in relation to his acquisition might lead to his incurring a *new liability* to X: a 'direct right'.[114] This could involve Z's incurring a purely monetary liability to X. Or it could involve the imposition of a new obligation on Z to X, which affords X some form of right in relation to the estate or interest that Z has acquired via the disposition. This right might be purely personal, or be in the nature of a proprietary interest that encumbers Z's title. We explore the appropriate parameters of such claims further below.[115]

Disapplication of Section 29 vis-à-vis the 'Fraudulent' Disponee.

Secondly, it might be argued that Z should be *disabled* from relying on section 29 to achieve priority, where this reliance could be regarded as 'fraudulent'. This would not involve the recognition of any *new* direct liability or obligation for Z, but only the *disapplication* of section 29, and the concomitant persistence of X's pre-existing interest according to section 28's first-in-time rule. Some authors certainly assume that that conclusion could be reached by the invocation of what is sometimes assumed to be a general law 'doctrine' that statutes should not be used as an instrument of fraud.[116] There are, however, some hidden complications. The basis, ambit and effect of the 'doctrine' remains controversial.

[114] See also ch 16 of this book, section III(E).
[115] See section III(D)(ii) below.
[116] cf R Smith, *Property Law*, 8th edn (Harlow, Pearson, 2014) 253; M Dixon, *Modern Land Law* 10th edn (Abingdon, Routledge, 2016) 82. Cf also K Gray and SF Gray, *Elements of Land Law*, 5th edn (Oxford, OUP, 2008) paras 8.2.26 ff.

In the past, the most common invocation of the instrument of fraud 'doctrine' has been where a person claims to deny the existence of some right on the basis that statutory formality requirements, originating in the Statute of Frauds, are not satisfied.[117] In that context, the essential argument is that a statute enacted to *prevent* fraud, should not be allowed to be used as an *instrument* of fraud. However, this immediately generates three further issues.

First, on what assumption is such judicial intervention legitimate? If a statute's provisions are indeed to be disapplied, and effectively reworked, is this an *appropriate* incursion in view of the statute's underlying purpose, or would it thwart the statutory policies? The particular statute and its objectives are key. It seems dangerous to assume that there is a *general* doctrine that extends across all statutes, or, if there is, that it has uniform content.

Secondly, what does 'fraud' encompass in this context? In the Statute of Frauds cases, there is no objection *per se* to Z relying on the statute, to deny the existence of some right held by X; more is needed. This has typically comprised an attempt by Z to renege from an undertaking that he had given, that he would recognise and respect X's right, on the faith of which Z acquired property from Y, often at a knock-down price.[118] Nevertheless, it is not obvious that that *exhausts* the material forms of fraud. In the registration context, Lord Wilberforce found in *Midland Bank v Green*[119] that 'it is not "fraud" to rely on legal rights conferred by Act of Parliament'.[120] In *Lyus v Prowsa Developments Ltd*,[121] Dillon J acknowledged this, and its prima facie implications—ie, it would not be improper *per se* for Z, the transferee of a registered freehold title from Y, to claim to take free of an unprotected estate contract, held by X, by reliance on section 20 of the LRA 1925.[122] However, on the facts there was further conduct that amounted to 'fraud' of a similar nature to that reflected in the Statute of Frauds cases, which made 'all the difference'.[123] Z transferee was seeking to renege on an undertaking that it had given, on the basis of which it had acquired the land.[124] Once again, this leaves open what other forms of 'fraud' might suffice.

Thirdly, what exactly is the impact of any qualifying 'fraud', where present? More specifically, is the statute really *disapplied*, or does the fraud have some other impact? This controversy is evident in the Statute of Fraud cases that involve orally declared trusts of land. The relevant governing legislation prescribes that the declaration of trusts of land must be evidenced in signed writing.[125] Cases which give effect to *oral* declarations of trusts of land, in the face of this governing legislation, are susceptible to multiple interpretations. One view is that courts do indeed *wholly disapply* the statute in order to prevent fraud: they permit the admission of oral evidence to prove an express trust, which is then enforced.[126]

[117] eg, the requirements of what is now LPA 1925, s 53(1)(b), requiring a declaration of a trust of land to be evidenced by signed writing.

[118] eg, *Bannister v Bannister* [1948] 2 All ER 133 (CA); *Rochefoucauld v Boustead* [1897] 1 Ch 196 (CA). See too cases involving the enforcement of half-secret and fully-secret trusts, notwithstanding non-compliance with the Wills Act 1837 formalities. See generally B McFarlane, 'Constructive Trusts Arising on a Receipt of Property Sub Conditione' (2004) 120 *LQR* 667.

[119] *Midland Bank v Green* (n 106).

[120] ibid, 531; he proceeded to accept the 'validity of interpreting clear enactments as to registration and priority according to their tenor'.

[121] *Lyus v Prowsa Developments Ltd* [1982] 1 WLR 1044.

[122] ibid, 1054–1055.

[123] ibid, 1054.

[124] ibid, 1055.

[125] LPA 1925, s 53(1)(b).

[126] eg, *Rochefoucauld v Boustead* (n 118).

However, a second view, manifest in the same cases, is that the relevant fraud leads the law to recognise *new* rights, by operation of law—most likely, via a constructive trust.[127] This does not involve any disapplication of the statute, since the existence and operation of constructive trusts is unaffected by the statutory formality requirements.[128]

A similar ambiguity exists in the registration cases. In *Lyus v Prowsa*, Dillon J was clear that section 20 of the LRA 1925 would not enable the registered transferee, Z, to resist a claim to enforce X's unprotected estate contract.[129] However, in context, this can be understood in two ways:

(i) X's estate contract bound Z registered transferee *by virtue of its status as a pre-existing proprietary interest, which persisted against Z*. The prevention of fraud simply disabled the registered transferee from relying on the clearing effect of section 20 of the LRA 1925. The equivalent argument under what is now the LRA 2002 regime would mean that if section 29 is wholly inapplicable, then section 28's basic first-in-time rule will apply.

(ii) X's estate contract did *not* bind Z registered transferee by virtue of its status as a pre-existing proprietary interest. Section 20 of the LRA 1925 was not strictly *disapplied*: it was allowed to operate and clear Z's registered title of X's pre-existing encumbrance. However, the court recognised and enforced a new obligation *directly* against Z, in favour of X, because of the circumstances in which Z had obtained title.

The technical difference between these two analyses has an important bearing on their legitimacy, scope and effect. First, in terms of legitimacy, analysis (i) involves a more dramatic intervention: judicial *disapplication* of the governing statute's express terms. In contrast, analysis (ii) merely illustrates how section 29's effects are softened or qualified—but not *directly* contradicted—via various forms of direct (or *in personam*) liability. Indeed, on this view, the instrument of fraud 'doctrine' is not really an *independent* principle at all. Secondly, in terms of scope, analysis (ii) is naturally tied to the circumstances in which the courts recognise direct (or *in personam*) liabilities. In contrast, analysis (i) is not logically confined in this way—the fraud that engages the instrument of fraud 'doctrine' is susceptible to autonomous definition. Thirdly, in terms of practical effect, if section 29 is disapplied as analysis (i) suggests, the status of X's right—as a proprietary interest that encumbers the registered estate acquired by Z—is preserved via section 28's first-in-time rule. The right's status as a proprietary interest has obvious further significance for the persistence of X's right in the event of later dealings by Z with the registered estate. In contrast, adopting analysis (ii), matters are less clear-cut. Closer scrutiny of the nature of the particular direct (or *in personam*) liability is needed, to determine whether it yields an *in rem* interest which is capable of binding successors, rather than a merely *in personam* right.[130]

Some of the uncertainties just identified are evident in *Halifax plc v Curry Popeck (A Firm)*.[131] Joint registered proprietors of a bungalow, Tracy and John Whale, perpetrated frauds on mortgage lenders. The frauds occurred in several stages. First, Halifax was fraudulently

[127] eg, *Bannister v Bannister* (n 118).
[128] LPA 1925, s 53(2).
[129] *Lyus v Prowsa* (n 121) 1054–1055.
[130] See McFarlane, 'Constructive Trusts' (n 118).
[131] *Halifax plc v Curry Popeck (A Firm)* [2008] EWHC 1692 (Ch).

induced to loan monies to Tracy, ostensibly to *purchase* the bungalow, of which she and John were already joint registered proprietors. Although Halifax did not obtain the legal charge which it expected as security for this loan, it was assumed that Halifax acquired some form of proprietary estoppel-based equity vis-à-vis Tracy and John. Secondly, a second lender was fraudulently induced to loan monies to John, acting under an assumed name ('John Sinclair'), in order to fund his 'purchase' of the bungalow from himself and Tracy. The result was that John, as 'John Sinclair', became the sole registered proprietor, subject to a registered charge. Thirdly, Bank of Scotland was fraudulently induced to loan monies to 'John Sinclair'. Like Halifax, Bank of Scotland never obtained the legal charge which it expected as security, but it was able subsequently to obtain a charging order over 'John Sinclair's' registered title to the bungalow, to secure a judgment debt obtained against John. By the time of the proceedings before Norris J, the bungalow had been sold. The immediate question concerned the relative claims of Halifax and Bank of Scotland to the proceeds of sale.

Reduced to its essentials, the priority dispute presented itself as follows:

(i) Halifax had acquired an equity, via proprietary estoppel, as a result of the conduct of Tracy and John, which encumbered their joint registered title;
(ii) this registered title was subsequently conveyed to John, as 'John Sinclair', ostensibly via a sale, who became sole registered proprietor;
(iii) some time later, Bank of Scotland had acquired an equitable charge, via a charging order, over 'John Sinclair's' registered title.

Under section 28's basic first-in-time rule,[132] Halifax's estoppel equity would have priority to Bank of Scotland's later equitable charge. However, the question then arose as to whether section 29 had in fact *previously* been triggered by the transfer of the registered estate by John and Tracy to John alone, and therefore whether Halifax's prior unprotected estoppel equity had been postponed at that point. If it had, then John's registered estate would effectively be cleared of Halifax's prior equity, and would be subject only to Bank of Scotland's later equitable charge, which would necessarily prevail.

Norris J in fact concluded that section 29 was not engaged by the transfer from Tracy and John to John alone because there was no accompanying 'valuable consideration'.[133] However, assuming that section 29 *was* engaged, Norris J offered an interesting discussion as to whether a person like John might benefit from section 29's postponing effect in relation to a prior interest, held by a third party like Halifax, which he himself had been responsible (solely or jointly) for creating. Counsel for Halifax argued that section 29 would not affect equitable rights/obligations 'created' by the disponee (here John), or which arose vis-à-vis the disponee, either at the time of the disposition or before. As such, nothing in section 29 would enable John to claim title free from Halifax's pre-existing estoppel equity, which had previously arisen against Tracy and John whilst they were joint registered proprietors.[134] However, Norris J found more persuasive the different view, advanced by Bank of Scotland, that section 29 would have a more extensive effect. It would free John's title as registered disponee from Halifax's pre-existing estoppel equity even if John, the disponee,

[132] LRA 2002, s 28, discussed in section III(C) above.
[133] *Curry Popeck* (n 131) [42]–[46]; see further text to n 146 below.
[134] ibid [50].

was party to the creation of that interest. On this view, section 29's effect was the same as that of section 20 of the LRA 1925, despite its different wording. Thus:

> [Counsel] submits that, although the language of section 29 is different, its effect is entirely the same, namely that the section was not intended to keep alive equitable estates or interests which were unprotected at the date of the registration of a disposition. He readily acknowledged that in any system of registration such a rule was capable of manipulation and of conferring benefits on the unworthy. But ... that that should not mean that the plain words of the section should be accorded a contorted construction.[135]

However, this was subject to an important caveat:

> [T]he mere fact that the registration of a registrable disposition wiped the title clean of any prior unprotected equitable interests [via section 29] did not, of course, destroy the obligations themselves. All it did was to destroy the subsistence of those interests as *interests in land*, leaving them capable of enforcement as *personal rights* and leaving available the full range of remedies against the creators of the equitable obligations.[136]

Norris J accepted this argument, in the following terms:

> [That] analysis is the correct one. It is consistent with the policy to which the citation from the Law Commission Report refers. It is consonant with the plain meaning of the words of [section] 29 and it is consistent with the obvious meaning of section 20 of the Land Registration Act 1925. On the assumption of a transfer for valuable consideration, equitable interests binding the dispon[o]r do not bind the disponee *as interests in land*, even if the disponee was a party to the creation of those interests. This will mean that if the disponee then creates a subsequent equitable obligation binding the estate, there will be no question of competing equities. The [earlier] obligation which the disponee created will continue to bind him as a personal obligation.[137]

He gave an illustration involving an estate contract.

> Take the simple example of a contract. If [Y], as personal representative, contracts to sell Blackacre to X and he then for valuable consideration transfers Blackacre into his own name and then contracts to sell Blackacre to [Z], X will not be able to assert an equitable title to Blackacre against [Z]; but the contract that [Y] had made will continue to bind him; he will be liable for damages for such breach. If he had not created a contract in favour of [Z], it would have been enforceable against him by way of specific performance because he would not, as I think, be able to assert section 29 against X, being personally estopped from doing so on the grounds that he was using section 29 as an engine of fraud and the principle in *Rochefoucauld v Boustead* ... would have prevented him from asserting the section. But absent such a consideration as that, namely an estoppel which arises, the estate in land created by the contract between [Y] and X came to an end when the registered disposition to [Y] took effect.[138]

This is not straightforward. In essence, Norris J's assumptions were:

(i) section 29 *would* apply to the disposition by Y, acting as personal representative, to himself, acting in his personal capacity, so as to postpone X's unprotected earlier interest, and by that means, effectively extinguish it;

[135] ibid [48].

[136] ibid [49] (emphasis added).

[137] ibid [51] (emphasis added). Norris J claimed further support from the analysis in Law Com No 271 (n 36), examined in text to n 169 below, of unpaid vendor's liens: see ibid [52].

[138] ibid.

(ii) section 29 would have this postponing effect even though Y, the newly-registered disponee, was responsible for the creation of X's interest, *before* the disposition; and
(iii) thereafter, X's prior right would be enforceable against Y disponee *as a matter of personal obligation only*, and would no longer constitute a proprietary interest, encumbering Y disponee's *title*, which could potentially endure vis-à-vis a later disponee.

Applied to *Curry Popeck*, the result would have been that, if section 29 was triggered, Bank of Scotland's later equitable charge would prevail. This would not be because Bank of Scotland itself could take advantage of section 29's special priority rule, but because of section 29's perceived effect on Halifax's prior equity when Tracy and John effected the registrable disposition to John alone—section 29 would postpone Halifax's equity to John's registered estate, and effectively clear his estate of that pre-existing encumbrance. Thereafter, any claim that Halifax might have vis-à-vis John would have taken the form of a merely personal obligation. As such, there would be no question of competing *in rem interests* at all, when John subsequently granted the charge to Bank of Scotland: at that point, Bank of Scotland's charge would be the *only* proprietary interest encumbering his registered estate.

We are not convinced that Norris J's analysis is correct, for four reasons.

First, as we explain elsewhere,[139] it is not obvious *why* section 29 should enable a disponee to take free of pre-existing interests which he had created, or which arose directly against him by operation of law. This was certainly not the position adopted in the 1998 Law Commission Consultative Document.[140] If there was a change of heart by the time of the 2001 Law Commission Report,[141] the reason for it is not apparent.

Secondly, Norris J seems to recognise that a third party's prior right might persist vis-à-vis the registered disponee personally, but he seems—we think wrongly—to imagine that such direct rights can only exist as personal obligations. He can be forgiven for this, to the extent that the Law Commission used the language of '*personal* remedies' to mean 'direct rights', and in a manner that might be construed as meaning 'personal obligations *only*' rather than—in our view more correctly—'new obligations that may (in an appropriate case) comprise new proprietary interests that encumber the disponee's title'. On this latter view, section 29 might afford the registered disponee a title clear of the third party's prior interest. However, in addition, where that interest arose in response to the registered disponee's own conduct, section 29 will not allow that disponee to avoid the obligation that affects his own conscience. The law may give this obligation continuing effect, by recognising a *new* right *in rem* in favour of the earlier interest-holder, which encumbers the disponee's registered title.

Thirdly, Norris J's invocation of the instrument of fraud principle is surprising and misplaced. In his example, he relies on this idea to conclude that the contract to sell Blackacre which the registered disponee, Y, had previously made with X, would continue to bind Y and be enforceable by way of specific performance. Y disponee could not resist the claim, Norris J said, because he would be 'personally estopped' from relying on section 29, 'on the grounds that he was using section 29 as an engine of fraud'.[142] The difficulty with this is

[139] See ch 16 of this book, section III(E); also text to n 33 et seq of this chapter above, and section III(D)(ii) below.
[140] Law Com No 254 (n 34) paras 7.36–7.37.
[141] cf Law Com No 271 (n 36) para 5.10. See further section III(D)(ii) below.
[142] *Curry Popeck* (n 131) [51].

that it is unclear why section 29 would be relevant to the question in issue. Norris J assumed that Y disponee would continue to be bound by the contract he had made with X, and that this might yield a liability to pay damages. The puzzle is why he thought that the remedy of specific performance required any more elaborate explanation. Specific performance would be available to enforce *in specie* the positive contractual obligation towards X, undertaken by Y, to convey the relevant estate. Its availability would not depend on the relevant obligation additionally constituting an *encumbrance*, operating *in rem*, over the estate. Indeed, this highlights the oddity of Norris J's analysis of the proprietary position. *If* Y disponee remained subject to a contractual obligation to convey the estate to X, and *if* that obligation was susceptible to an order for specific performance, then equity would ordinarily anticipate the performance of the obligation, and recognise some form of equitable interest or title in favour of the beneficiary of the obligation, X. It might be suggested that this view could not be maintained in the face of section 29, but that supposition seems incorrect. X's equitable specific performance-based interest would not stem from the persistence of a pre-existing interest *per se*, but from the fact that Y disponee's *contractual* (*in personam*) duty to convey to X survives the disposition, and remains susceptible to *in specie* enforcement. For reasons that may already be apparent, section 29 does not prevent—and does not need to be disapplied to enable—the enforcement of such direct rights against a registered disponee.[143]

Fourthly, Norris J's invocation of the instrument of fraud principle is also puzzling from a different perspective. He imagines that the principle only operates via some form of personal estoppel. However, that cannot be accepted as universally, or even generally, correct. The 'disabling' of a party from relying on legislation may well have wider implications, depending on the effect of the particular provision which that party is disabled from invoking. In the cases on which Norris J placed reliance, the outcome has been the recognition of an interest in land, either by way of an express trust in X's favour (rendered enforceable despite lack of written evidence, as required by the governing legislation),[144] or by way of a constructive trust in X's favour (enforceable without written evidence).[145] In the present context, if the true effect of the instrument of fraud principle is that the disponee is disabled from relying on section 29, then it is not evident why the principle cannot have a larger effect—ie, *preventing* X's right from postponement vis-à-vis the fraudulent disponee's title, and leaving it enforceable as an *in rem encumbrance* over that title.

'No' Consideration

Thirdly, *Curry Popeck* contemplated that there may be XYZ priority disputes where the Y–Z transaction is fraudulent, and where its fraudulent character is such that there is *no consideration* proferred by Z. Here, section 29 cannot be relied on, not because of the fraud *per se*, but because of the non-fulfilment of one of section 29's explicit triggering conditions: the presence of 'valuable consideration'. This condition manifests a deliberate legislative policy choice that section 29's bounty—in the form of priority over X's prior interest—should only be available to those who, by paying, *deserve* to be privileged.

[143] See text to n 114 above and section III(D)(ii) below.
[144] eg, *Rochefoucauld v Boustead* (n 118).
[145] eg, *Bannister v Bannister* (n 118).

The absence of 'valuable consideration' was the real ground for the decision in *Curry Popeck*, where it was held that section 29 was not engaged. In his judgment, Norris J noted counsel's argument that there were 'only three possibilities' in determining whether 'valuable consideration' had been provided:

> either on the facts [1] it is a transfer for a nil consideration [which is axiomatically not 'valuable']; or [2] on the facts it is a transfer for a nominal consideration [which is not 'valuable'];[146] or [3] on the facts it is a transfer for valuable consideration.[147]

Norris J considered, however, that there was also a fourth possibility—'that the transfer is part of a fraudulent enterprise in which the concept of consideration is entirely meaningless'—which, like options 1 and 2, would fail to qualify as 'valuable' and would mean that section 29 is not engaged.[148] This fourth possibility was illustrated by the facts of *Curry Popeck*.[149] Although the stated consideration was £200,000, it was 'clear that … this was never paid' and was 'not a figure which [bore] any relationship to anything that is known to have happened in the real world'.[150] Norris J agreed with counsel that 'there was no genuine sale' or 'any underlying deal' between Tracy and John, as joint registered proprietors, and John, as the relevant disponee.[151] 'All that happened was that they carried out a re-shuffling of the legal title to the property in furtherance of their fraudulent enterprises'.[152] The idea that one cannot take advantage of the section 29 priority promise in the absence of a 'genuine sale' or a 'true deal' is consistent with the apparent policy premise of section 29—that only those who pay for the privilege deserve the promise of section 29.[153] It does, however, raise some interpretative difficulties, several of which were identified in the Law Commission's 2016 Consultation Paper.[154]

The fourth interpretation offered by Norris J—ie 'meaningless consideration'—presents particular difficulties. The judge regarded it as distinct from the first interpretation offered by counsel—ie, where there is 'nil consideration'. However, it is not clear how these ideas of 'nil' and 'meaningless' consideration actually differ and, to the extent that they do differ, to what situations the concept of 'meaningless consideration' might extend. Arguably 'valuable consideration' (which is defined by the statute to exclude 'nominal consideration in money')[155] either is present or is not: it is a binary matter. The concept of 'nil consideration' seems sufficient to capture all situations where there is 'no valuable consideration'. This being so, it is not obvious what role is left for a further concept of 'meaningless consideration': the consideration is either 'nil' or 'nominal' (neither of which count for section 29), or it is 'valuable' (which does count).

[146] LRA 2002, s 132(1): '*valuable consideration*' does not include marriage consideration or a nominal consideration in money.
[147] *Curry Popeck* (n 131) [42].
[148] ibid [43].
[149] ibid [46].
[150] ibid [44].
[151] ibid [46].
[152] ibid.
[153] This policy preference is not self-evidently correct. Some registration regimes do give even donees protection against pre-existing rights that are not entered on the Register, as the Law Commission has noted: see Law Com CP No 227 (n 29) paras 7.52–7.58.
[154] Law Com CP No 227 (n 29) ch 7.
[155] LRA 2002, s 132(1).

Norris J's so-called 'fourth' concept might perhaps be preserved as a distinct category if the label of 'nil consideration' were confined to the narrow category of situations where the Y–Z conveyance was *outwardly gratuitous*—as where Y intended a gift, and where this was obviously so on the face of the conveyance. Narrowed in this way, 'nil consideration' would not capture cases where the conveyance was expressed to be for valuable consideration, but where either: (a) the agreement to provide consideration was not genuinely intended, and no consideration was in fact provided; or (b) the agreement to provide valuable consideration *was* genuinely intended, but the obligation was not subsequently performed. *Curry Popeck* appears to classify scenario (a) as involving 'meaningless consideration'—it resembles the facts of *Curry Popeck* itself. However, *Curry Popeck* leaves it unclear whether Z disponee in scenario (b) would also be deprived of section 29's promise, as someone whose consideration was 'meaningless'. On the one hand, that disponee, Z, has not actually paid anything, and for that reason may not have earned the benefit of section 29's priority promise. On the other hand, Z has made a genuine contractual bargain with Y. He has thereby furnished sufficient *contractual* consideration, most likely in the form of his promise to pay, and he remains liable for that contract sum. As a matter of policy, the undertaking of this legally enforceable debt might be enough to qualify Z for section 29's promise.

On balance, the second view seems preferable. Z's contractual liability to pay a non-nominal sum to Y seems sufficient to justify his benefiting from section 29's priority promise. Furthermore, the second view seems less likely to cause uncertainty for the parties concerned. If we were to prefer the first view, the conveyance from Y to Z would always have the *potential* to trigger section 29. Nevertheless, it might not do so immediately on Z's registration if Z had not yet paid; and it might only do so *at some later point*, if and when Z finally pays. This could prove problematic. Z's payment, and the date of his payment, will necessarily be invisible from the face of the Register. This will make it difficult for others—including X, and any future disponees from Z—to know whether, and if so when, Z's title has benefited from section 29's clearing rule. The second view avoids causing this kind of protracted uncertainty.

d. Conclusions on the Triggering of the Section 29 Priority Promise

It is clear that many unanswered questions surround the threshold issue of when, and to whom, the section 29 priority promise is—and should be—made. The significance of this problem cannot be underestimated. In XYZ priority disputes, the potential persistence of undiscoverable off-Register third party encumbrances can threaten the enjoyment/security of a registered disponee's title, in just as harmful a way as can the loss of title by a disponee in an ABC title dispute. Despite this, the availability of the LRA 2002's priority promise has received comparatively little attention compared to its twin, section 58's title promise. To make matters worse, the uncertainty regarding the triggers for section 29 is compounded by further uncertainties that surround the effect of section 29's priority promise, where it is triggered. The following four sections, (ii)–(v), expose some of these concerns.

ii. A Disponee's Vulnerability to 'Direct Rights', Despite Section 29 Postponement

Even when section 29 is triggered, all is not as it immediately appears. Within its own terms, section 29 is absolute: its postponing effect applies in favour of Z registered disponee 'for valuable consideration', and there is no explicit requirement that the disponee be in *good faith*.

Nevertheless, there is a hidden chink in the armour, *by deliberate design*. Whilst section 29 on its face states an amoral rule, the Law Commission's 1998 Consultative Document[156] specifically envisaged that the provision's operation would be softened by the disponee's continuing vulnerability to what were described as 'personal liabilities' or 'personal remedies', arising outside the LRA 2002, under the general law.

This is a very important concession, with potentially dramatic ramifications for the reality of section 29's priority promise. It means that a disponee's position cannot be determined by reference to section 29 alone—it results from the combined effect of section 29 and general law doctrines. It is regrettable that the Law Commission did not provide any clear(er) steer, in the legislation or at least in its background reports, regarding the extent to which the general law might legitimately be drawn upon. A tap is, by implication, left open for these general law doctrines to intrude and impair the security of disponees who would otherwise be privileged by section 29's priority promise. Yet neither the Law Commission nor statute provides any explicit guidance as to when, and on what basis, that tap must be shut off. The courts therefore bear a heavy responsibility for exercising self-restraint in recognising and developing these so-called '*in personam*' liabilities, in order to avoid a position where section 29's priority promise is so widely undermined that it no longer ensures security for those who have a legitimate claim to rely on the Register—thereby frustrating a key objective of the registration system.

We cannot address these issues comprehensively here. Several observations are nevertheless warranted; these follow in the next section. We then proceed to examine these issues in context by reference to three problematic case examples.

a. Three Key Observations About '*In Personam*' Liability/Direct Rights

First, what *type* of rights might be created via the courts' imposition of '*in personam*' liability/direct rights? The terms in which the 1998 Law Commission discussed such liabilities[157] have sowed seeds of confusion. The Commission's language of 'personal liability' or 'personal remedies', and several of the key examples that it gave, might seem to suggest that the Commission only had in mind 'personal liability' in a very narrow sense—ie, a liability which is 'personal'/'*in personam*' in the dual sense: (i) that it is imposed in response to Z disponee's personal conduct, and (ii) that it would only take the form of a personal obligation, and could not also give rise to a *new* proprietary interest that encumbers Z disponee's title. However, that would be a misunderstanding of what the Law Commission meant. It would also be questionable both as a matter of policy, and as a representation of the general law's operation. In truth, the key line is between:

(a) claims held by X that reflect a *prior* encumbrance, which persists and binds Z disponee's title—claims whose existence and exigibility fall to be determined, first and foremost, by the registration regime's priority rules and promises (ie, sections 28 and 29); and
(b) claims held by X that involve the recognition of a *new* right, in direct response to the circumstances in which Z disponee acquired his title.

[156] Law Com No 254 (n 34) paras 3.48–3.49.
[157] ibid.

In case (b), the relevant *new* right might comprise an entitlement to a personal monetary remedy only—eg, an entitlement to compensation for loss wrongfully caused. Alternatively, it might comprise an entitlement to some form of *in specie* enjoyment of the land, in which case the further possibility arises that this right might be merely a personal right—eg, a mere contractual licence—or might confer an *in rem* interest in land that encumbers Z disponee's title—eg, via a trust, or as an estoppel equity.[158] To avoid perpetuating any confusion arising from the '*in personam*' nomenclature, we prefer to label these new rights—whether personal or proprietary—'direct rights'.

There is nothing inherent in the policies of the LRA 2002 regime to suggest that, where Z registered disponee who can rely on section 29 is subject to a direct right, the right can only legitimately take the form of a truly *in personam* right (to money, or relating to the land), as opposed to an *in rem* encumbrance. Section 29 only dictates that X's prior right, if postponed by section 29, must cease to affect Z registered estate *as a property right*. It does not mean that the circumstances of the disposition will never justify the recognition of a *new* proprietary right in favour of X or another, which encumbers the disponee's title. For example, if, under the general law, a thief holds stolen property/proceeds on constructive trust,[159] there is no obvious reason why B, who is able via forgery to 'steal' A's registered estate in land, should not be rendered an immediate constructive trustee of that registered estate for A—just as he would be if the estate had been unregistered.[160] The possibility that a direct right might arise by operation of law against the new registered proprietor, despite section 58's title promise, was mooted in chapter sixteen; and it is at least readily conceivable that a trust might be imposed on 'thief'-B's title despite section 58's vesting effect. A similar analysis might also be valid in some XYZ priority disputes. Even if X's prior right is postponed to Z's later registered estate under section 29, a constructive trust might be imposed on Z in X's favour. This could be the case if Z's conduct, which resulted in his fraudulently gaining an unencumbered title at X's expense via section 29's operation, can be relevantly equated with theft by Z of X's rights, and on that assumption, be treated as sufficient to justify the imposition of a *new* constructive trust over Z's title. This constructive trust could be a vehicle by which a new version of X's old right might be recognised over Z's title.[161]

Secondly, the incidence of direct rights assumes particularly acute significance for disponees like Z. Their imposition does not merely prejudice Z's position in relation to the land; it may also do so without hope of compensation from the Registry. The imposition of a direct right under the general law is not a Registry-indemnity justifying event: the Registry does not take responsibility for liabilities which arise off-Register, under the general law. Similarly, no indemnity would follow from any alteration to the Register which gave effect to the direct right: this would be a matter of 'bringing the Register up to date' and, as such,

[158] See further McFarlane, 'Constructive Trusts' (n 118).

[159] As suggested in *Westdeutsche* (n 63) 716 (Lord Browne-Wilkinson).

[160] It may not be a *necessary* remedy, to the extent that the victim of the theft (A) might achieve a similar outcome via an application for rectification of the Register. But there would be no clear sense in which the recognition of the trust would be inherently inconsistent with the LRA 2002 framework, and the operation of s 29. The dishonest immediate disponee (B) is not illegitimately prejudiced, but neither are any later disponees (C), since these can rely in the ordinary way on s 29.

[161] See generally, McFarlane, 'Constructive Trusts' (n 118).

a mere 'alteration' rather than any indemnity-supporting 'rectification'. Z's loss would arise from the recognition of a direct right affecting him under the general law, and not from the subsequent Register alteration. Nevertheless, the potentially detrimental effect of the recognition of such direct rights cannot be underestimated—whether the direct right results in a purely personal remedy against Z, or a new *in rem* encumbrance over Z's title. The latter clearly compromises Z's position, and serves in substance, if not in form, to stultify section 29's postponing effect. However, even the imposition of a purely personal liability on Z will be damaging to Z's position, and arguably compromises the reliability of the Register for Z—Z disponee's title and priority are secure, but Z may come under a personal liability to compensate parties who suffer loss as a result.

Thirdly, it remains uncertain when, as a matter of policy, direct rights can properly be recognised without unduly prejudicing the position of those who can legitimately rely on the Register. It might be inferred from the Law Commission's discussion that knowledge or notice (of any sort) of a prior and unprotected right should not be sufficient to justify the recognition of a new direct right.[162] *Something more* is needed. Unfortunately, no attempt has yet been made to develop a coherent, joined-up account of what that 'something more' might be—ie, to define the tipping-point at which a disponee cannot legitimately claim immunity from a prior interest, or from liability for the loss that would result from its subordination. All we have currently is an unsystematised patchwork of discrete, independently-developed liabilities. For example, it is uncontroversial that Z disponee might be subject to liability, despite section 29, in respect of promises that he previously made to X which are binding as contracts; or to prevent his unconscionably reneging from an undertaking that he has given to Y to respect some prior claim of X, especially where Z has taken the property at a 'knock-down' price;[163] or where alone, or conspiring with another, Z has acted with the intention of wrongfully prejudicing X's prior right;[164] or in some settings, where Z is knowingly implicated in another's improper dealings, which prejudice a prior right.[165] The threshold for incurring such liabilities is set relatively high, and so far, the courts have exercised self-restraint both in expanding them and in developing new bases of liability. However, if—together—these doctrines achieve an appropriate balance, then it is by chance rather than by conscious system design.

[162] cf Law Com No 254 (n 34) paras 3.39–3.50; Law Com No 271 (n 36) paras 5.16–5.21.

[163] eg, *Lyus v Prowsa* (n 121); *Ashburn Anstalt v Arnold* [1989] Ch 1 (CA); *Lloyd v Dugdale* [2001] EWCA Civ 1754, [2002] 2 P & CR 13; *HSBC Bank plc v Dyche* [2009] EWHC 2994 (Ch), [2010] 2 P & CR 4; *Chaudhary v Yavuz* [2011] EWCA Civ 1314, [2013] Ch 249; *Groveholt Ltd v Hughes* [2012] EWHC 3351 (Ch), [2013] 1 P & CR 20; Law Com No 254 (n 34) para 3.48(2). For general exploration of this species of trust, see McFarlane, 'Constructive Trusts' (n 118).

[164] eg, *Midland Bank Trust Co Ltd v Green (No 3)* [1982] Ch 529 (CA) (an unregistered land case involving the LCA 1972); *Lictor Anstalt v Mir Steel UK Ltd* [2014] EWHC 3316 (Ch) [283]–[295] (a registered land case involving the LRA 2002).

[165] eg, a liability for dishonest participation in a breach of trust, or for knowing receipt of misapplied trust property, as assumed in *Eagle Trust plc v SBC Securities Ltd* [1993] 1 WLR 484, 503–504; *Hollis v Rolfe* [2008] EWHC 1747 (Ch) [172]–[174]; *Haque v Raja* [2016] EWHC 1950 (Ch) [46]–[52]; Law Com No 254 (n 34) paras 3.48(2) and 3.49; Law Com No 271 (n 36) para 4.11. The role for these liabilities within the registration regime is, however, questioned in M Conaglen and A Goymour, 'Knowing Receipt and Registered Land', ch 5 in C Mitchell (ed), *Resulting and Constructive Trusts* (Oxford, Hart, 2009). Cf also *Arthur v AG of the Turks and Caicos Islands* [2012] UKPC 30.

b. Some Particularly Problematic Cases

The permissible range of direct rights requires close attention in the wake of Norris J's recent discussion in *Curry Popeck*.[166] As we have seen, the case posed the general question whether section 29 could afford a registered disponee a clean title, clear of an unprotected earlier interest to whose creation the registered disponee had himself been privy. Norris J was persuaded by counsel, and by his reading of the 1998 and 2001 Law Commission publications,[167] to conclude that section 29 had a surprisingly far-reaching effect. If triggered, it meant that the prior right could be postponed, and in practice, rendered no longer an interest encumbering the registered disponee's *title*. The disponee would still be subject to a personal obligation towards the prior interest-holder, but that would be all. That is, whilst there would be a direct right exigible against the disponee, Norris J seemed to assume that section 29 dictated that that right could *only* be a *personal* right against the disponee, and not an interest *in rem*.[168]

This is a surprising conclusion, which makes little sense in terms of policy or principle. If the disponee's conduct indeed justifies the recognition or preservation of a direct right against him, despite section 29's clearing effect, then it is hard to understand why that right can never take the form of a right *in rem* affecting the disponee's title. This is clearest in cases where the direct right would involve a claim against the disponee that the disponee should afford some use or other advantage in relation to his land—eg, an estoppel-based equity, or a claim based upon a contract by the disponee to convey an interest to another. In such cases, it ought to be possible for the law to respond to the disponee's conduct by recognising, where appropriate, a *new in rem* interest effective against his newly-acquired title. It is regrettable that Norris J thought otherwise in *Curry Popeck*.

Three hypothetical scenarios will usefully illustrate these points.

(i) Example 1

Whilst RP1 and RP2 were joint registered proprietors, an estoppel equity—which by section 116 of the LRA 2002 has the status of a (proprietary) interest in land—arose against their registered title as a result of their representation to X that X held a right of way over the land, which X subsequently relied on to his detriment. Some time later, the registered title is conveyed for valuable consideration into RP2's sole name.

Here, X's estoppel equity would be generated to prevent RP2's unconscionable departure from the representation that he made regarding X's rights. It reflects a continuing obligation *binding RP2's conscience* that should not, in principle, be cleared via section 29. Furthermore, if this obligation indeed continues to affect RP2 after he becomes the sole registered proprietor, it may have an *in rem* impact on RP2's registered title, despite section 29, via two distinct means. First, whilst section 29 might postpone the prior estoppel equity that previously encumbered the title of RP1 and RP2 as joint registered proprietors, the fact that the estoppel-based obligation will continue to affect RP2's conscience could justify the recognition of a *new* inchoate estoppel equity, with proprietary status, which encumbers RP2's title as sole registered proprietor from the outset. Secondly, in the ordinary way,

[166] *Curry Popeck* (n 131); see further section III(D)(i)(c) above.

[167] Law Com No 254 (n 34); Law Com No 271 (n 36).

[168] See the analysis at text to nn 131–145 above.

a court might subsequently satisfy this continuing obligation/inchoate estoppel equity by affording X some form of proprietary right over RP2's title.

(ii) Example 2

As joint registered proprietors, RP1 and RP2 jointly contract to convey their land to X. Some time later, the registered title is conveyed into RP2's sole name. X's estate contract is postponed by section 29, since it is protected neither by Registry entry nor as an overriding interest.

At first sight, it might appear that section 29's postponing effect means that RP2 obtains a clear title and that X effectively ceases to have any interest in the land. However, it is difficult to see how this can be so. The contract with X will have generated a continuing personal *obligation* which should continue to bind RP2 even after he becomes the sole registered proprietor—it is not affected by section 29. RP2's continuing contractual obligation to X obviously means, on orthodox contract law reasoning, that X can seek damages for its breach. In addition, whilst RP2 retains the registered title, X might well obtain a court order for specific performance of RP2's obligation to convey. This is highly significant. Where, as here, there is an existing contract to convey an interest to another which is susceptible to specific performance, equity will traditionally 'anticipate' the performance of this obligation, and afford the intended disponee, X, some form of equitable title or interest prior to the conveyance being executed. This should also be the case here. Section 29 cannot prevent the recognition of such an interest in favour of X, since this interest is generated by equity's response to the contractual obligation that *continues* to bind RP2.

(iii) Example 3

Y purchases X's registered title, but the purchase price is left unpaid. Under the general law, this would ordinarily support the recognition of an unpaid vendor's lien in favour of X, as vendor. It was assumed by the 2001 Law Commission that what is now section 29 would prevent X vendor from enforcing such a lien against Y, the newly-registered purchaser, unless the lien was protected by a notice against the registered title.[169] However, this conclusion is problematic for two reasons.

First, as we discuss below,[170] it is a mistake to think that section 29's priority promise operates in this kind of two-party scenario, where the concern is whether X's right binds an *immediate* disponee, Y. The better view is that section 29's promise only works in three-party scenarios, of the XYZ configuration.[171] *Ex hypothesi*, it is irrelevant where an unpaid vendor's lien is being enforced against the *immediate* purchaser.

Secondly, even if—contrary to our view[172]—section 29 could be applied in such two-party scenarios, the conclusion that X's lien is postponed to Y's registered estate would involve an unduly narrow conception of the nature of an unpaid vendor's lien, and of the grounds for its imposition. Properly understood, the lien appears to be a response to the underlying vendor-purchaser contract: it responds to the circumstance that X conveyed title to Y only on condition that Y paid the purchase price. That *contractual* condition continues

[169] Law Com No 271 (n 36) para 5.10.

[170] See section III(E) below.

[171] By analogy, the 'three-party' configuration includes cases where X's interest binds Y1/Y2, and then Y1/Y2 dispose to Y2, as occurred in, eg, *Curry Popeck* (n 131).

[172] See section III(E) below.

to bind Y as long as it remains unsatisfied, and will do so even after Y's registration as the new registered proprietor. Indeed, Y's registration means that the lien, which responds to his continuing contractual liability, can now bind his newly-acquired registered title. As we explain more fully in Section E, this would be a new lien, imposed afresh on Y's newly-registered title, as a result of Y's continuing failure to pay.

This conclusion, which directly contradicts the Law Commission's assumptions, can also be supported in principle. The opposite conclusion, which would allow Y to take free of an unprotected lien upon Y's registration, frustrates the purpose that underlies the general law's recognition of unpaid vendors' liens—ie, to protect vendors against non-payment, via a security interest that encumbers the estate conveyed. The Law Commission's interpretation could put in jeopardy the status of unpaid vendors' liens in the context of sales of registered land.[173] If that was intended, we might have expected a deeper discussion of the merits/demerits of such interests.

iii. The Vulnerability of Section 29 Postponement to Alteration via Schedule 4

A second important incursion upon section 29 has recently emerged as a result of *MacLeod v Gold Harp Properties Ltd.*[174] This is the result of judicial interpretation, rather than—as in the case of direct rights—deliberate design. *Gold Harp* effectively holds that section 29's ordering effect is *not final/conclusive.* It will be recalled that section 29 provides that prior interests affecting a registered estate, which are not protected by Register entry and do not amount to overriding interests, are postponed to a subsequent registered disposition for valuable consideration. Nevertheless, according to *Gold Harp*, this is subject to the operation of schedule 4, which may enable the Register to be altered in a manner that *changes*—and indeed negates—section 29's ordering effect, albeit only with prospective consequences.

The decision in *Gold Harp* amply illustrates the dramatic implications of this possibility. Reduced to its bare essentials, X's registered lease, which encumbered Y's registered title, was removed from the Register as a result of a mistake. Y thereafter granted a further registered lease to Z. If this was a disposition that triggered section 29, then Z's registered lease should have had priority to any interest that X might retain following his de-registration—which was not protected by any appropriate Registry entry or overriding. However, the Court of Appeal reached a contrary conclusion via schedule 4. First, the removal of X's registered lease from the Register was a 'mistake' by the Land Registry within the meaning of schedule 4. Secondly, schedule 4 conferred a jurisdiction to alter the Register *to correct the consequences of that mistake*, which could permit the *re*-registration of X's de-registered lease. In addition, and despite section 29's literal 'postponing' effect, the Register could also be adjusted in a manner that would afford X's lease priority over Z's lease—albeit only prospectively, from the date of the rectification order.[175]

[173] The Law Commission assumed that a timely notice would be needed, to preserve the lien's priority: see Law Com No 271 (n 36) para 5.10.

[174] *MacLeod v Gold Harp Properties Ltd* [2014] EWCA Civ 1084, [2015] 1 WLR 1249.

[175] It is arguable that these 'prospective' changes should be backdated to the date of the *application* for the alteration: see LRA 2002, s 74, which dates registrations generally from the date of the application for the relevant registration. See Goymour, 'Resolving the Tension' (n 76) 261, n 36.

It is difficult to over-state the significance of this decision. Inevitably, it forces us to reconsider the character of the priority promise reflected in section 29.

Section 29 is, in its express terms, unqualified. As such, it might seem to embody a guarantee which the regime respects *in specie*, and not merely via a money award: ie, a guarantee such that section 29 orders interests, by postponing certain prior interests, *conclusively*. However, for reasons that will already be apparent, all is not quite as it seems in practice. Thus, section 29's ordering effect in any event depends on the continuing registration of the triggering Y–Z disposition. If Z's registered title can itself be challenged via a schedule 4 application for alteration or rectification—eg, where the Y–Z 'disposition' is itself a forgery and Z's registration is thus a mistake—then section 29's effect is necessarily nullified. The cancellation of Z's registered title via Register alteration will mean that there is no longer a registered disposition, within the meaning of section 29, to which X's prior interest could be postponed.

The real significance of *Gold Harp* is that it suggests that even when the validity of the relevant Y–Z registered disposition *cannot* be challenged, the *priority* that section 29 confers on Z's interest, apparently without qualification, *can* be. If that is right, then the nature of section 29's priority promise is significantly altered. The LRA 2002 no longer guarantees priority *in specie* to registered disponees like Z. Indeed, a registered disponee's position is doubly precarious. He may be left merely with a monetary indemnity in lieu under schedule 8,[176] and even then, not necessarily so, because the jurisdiction to award an indemnity is itself qualified.[177] As such, the registration regime's priority promise necessarily becomes a diluted '*you will have priority, subject to its being appropriate to rectify the Register; in which event, you will be indemnified, but only in so far as the loss was not the result of your fraud or lack of proper care*'.

How should we view this development? Charles Harpum, the LRA 2002's architect, has been scathing in his criticism of *Gold Harp*.[178] He insists that this was never the intention—section 29's ordering effect was meant to be final, at least as long as the relevant Y–Z disposition remained on the Register. Furthermore, if schedule 4 is allowed to undermine section 29, then the Register's reliability is necessarily, and unjustifiably, compromised. A registered disponee for valuable consideration is no longer safe in assuming that on registration, he acquires not merely *title*, but also a title *subject only to the interests specified in section 29(2)*.

Notwithstanding these forceful criticisms, the *Gold Harp* holding has at least two arguments in its favour.

The first argument is that the *Gold Harp* interpretation is the more natural reading of schedule 4, paragraph 8. The stipulation that the court's/Registrar's powers to secure rectification of the Register extend to '*changing for the future the priority of any interest affecting the registered estate*' seems devoid of meaning, *unless* it allows for section 29's ordering effect to be adjusted—ie, if a *past* ordering can be altered, albeit only with prospective consequences. Harpum insists that this was not intended. But in answer to this, the *Gold Harp* Court of Appeal could rightly respond, in effect, 'if you intended what you say you intended, why bother including schedule 4, paragraph 8 at all?'. Indeed, one might wonder why paragraph 8

176 LRA 2002, sch 8, para 1(1)(a).
177 LRA 2002, sch 8, para 5.
178 See ch 8 of this book.

did not in fact say the opposite—ie, 'the powers under schedule 4 to rectify the Register *do* not *extend to changing the priority of any interest affecting the registered estate*'.

The wording of paragraph 8 may possibly be rendered comprehensible, consistently with Harpum's view of section 29, if it speaks to a different situation where rectification is sought in relation to title to a registered estate, of which some other interest is derivative. Consider, for example, a case where F is registered as freehold proprietor following a forged transfer of E's title, and F subsequently grants a registered derivative interest to G—eg a registered lease, charge or easement. In rectification proceedings brought by E, a court would be very likely to restore the registered freehold title to E. In such a case, the effect of schedule 4, paragraph 8 might be to confirm that a court could order E's re-registration, *free* of G's registered interest—thereby changing (by nullifying) 'the priority of [an] interest affecting the registered estate'. However, under the terms of paragraph 8, the status of G's registered interest could only be affected 'for the future'—prospectively, from the date of the rectification taking place.

There is a second argument in favour of the *Gold Harp* approach, which is an argument for coherence within the wider LRA 2002 framework. It is now widely acknowledged that section 58's title promise is not an absolute *in specie guarantee* of title, which promises mud rather than merely money in lieu. Even if not by the conscious design of its drafters, *the courts* have come to construe the LRA 2002 in a manner that means that a registered proprietor benefits neither from 'immediate indefeasibility', nor indeed 'deferred indefeasibility'. Neither B in AB title cases (involving only two parties), nor C in ABC title cases (involving three parties),[179] can safely rely upon section 58's apparent vesting effect.[180] Registration as the proprietor of a registered estate, although 'conclusive' as to the vesting of the estate in the proprietor via section 58's express terms, does not irreversibly achieve this effect, since it is (by implication) subject to schedule 4's alteration regime. Furthermore, as a result inter alia of an expansive interpretation of the court's/Registrar's-jurisdiction to alter the Register to correct a 'mistake'[181]—a concept deliberately left undefined by the Law Commission—a person like C, who acquires a registered interest via a disposition from B, the registered proprietor, has no cast-iron immunity from problems that infect the root of B's registered title. This is highly significant. A major driver for the implementation of the registration system was to remove the necessity for disponees to investigate the *root* of a disponor's title. As currently interpreted, the LRA 2002 only achieves this in a compromised way in ABC title cases. C's title *may* be vulnerable to rectification because of a problem that infects B's root of title. The only assurance which C receives, if his title is not protected *in specie*, is the lesser assurance of a monetary indemnity, and even then, only if C has not fraudulently or carelessly contributed to the mistake.

There is scope for legitimate debate about whether the courts' direction of travel in AB and ABC title cases is faithful to the intentions of the drafters of the LRA 2002 (which are inscrutable in important respects), or is otherwise 'correct' as a matter of policy. However, the present point is different. *As long as* the courts understand section 58's title promise as they currently do, and resolve ABC title cases as they currently do, a concern for *coherence*

179 For an explanation of this categorisation, see ch 16 of this book, section III(D).

180 See, in particular, the discussion in ch 16 of this book, section III(D).

181 ibid.

suggests that the *Gold Harp* reading must be correct. Indeed, this was one of the apparent motivations for the Court of Appeal's decision.[182] If the *title promise* which C enjoys when dealing with B registered proprietor is not a cast-iron promise, and may be realised only via a money indemnity if the Register is rectified in favour of A, what is the reason for treating the *priority* promise any differently? Why should the priority that section 29 affords be any more impregnable than the title which section 58 confers? In ABC title cases, C relies on the Register, and on B's registration as the conveying proprietor. This reliance is necessarily compromised insofar as schedule 4 allows rectification to reflect problems that relate to the root of B's title. In XYZ priority disputes, Z similarly relies on the Register and on the operation of section 29, as an assurance against the persistence of prior third party interests affecting Y's title. On Harpum's reading, Z is secure—resulting in an inexplicable differentiation in the strengths of the title and priority promises, and the reliability of the Register for C and Z respectively. Only the *Gold Harp* reading aligns these cases, leaving C and Z similarly secure/insecure.

Looking to the future, there is no evidence that the current state of play will change. The 2016 Law Commission seems to accept the courts' expansive view of what constitutes a 'mistake' for the purpose of schedule 4, and its implications for ABC title cases.[183] The Commission also seems to accept *Gold Harp*, and its implications for XYZ priority cases.[184] Indeed, a major strand of the Law Commission's reasoning in its 2016 Consultation Paper is that there is no good reason for treating these cases dramatically differently.[185] It necessarily follows that the priority promise, like the title promise, is inherently compromised. There is no absolute *in specie* guarantee of priority, but only a more qualified assurance. Priority under section 29, like the vesting of title via section 58, is susceptible to reversal via schedule 4—in which case, the assurance for Z, like that for C, is transmuted into a monetary indemnity at best.

Accepting this, one final point assumes crucial importance. In XYZ priority cases, just as in ABC title cases, the extent to which the title and priority promises are compromised depends substantially on the courts' readiness to find a 'mistake' which can justify correction under schedule 4. Real care is needed, in the context of XYZ priority cases, when identifying these circumstances.

'Mistake', as the courts have come to understand it, appears to assume some form of Land Registry act or omission, ordinarily in response to an application made to it.[186] The core circumstances likely to support rectification in XYZ priority cases are where, on an application to it, the Registrar fails correctly to enter X's interest against Y's registered title; or where the Registrar wrongly *removes* such an entry, as was the case in *Gold Harp*. In either case, the Registrar's omission or removal of a notice that *should* have been on the Register seems to be a 'mistake' that might be corrected via a schedule 4 order for rectification. Furthermore, since the absence of this entry may mean that the priority of X's interest is compromised by a later registered disposition by Y to Z that triggers section 29, the exercise

[182] *Gold Harp* (n 174) [98]. See also Goymour, 'Resolving the Tension' (n 76) 257; and Law Com CP No 227 (n 29) para 13.160.

[183] Law Com CP No 227 (n 29) paras 13.64–13.74, 13.77–13.82.

[184] ibid paras 13.189–13.195; see also paras 13.152–13.163.

[185] ibid paras 13.160–13.162.

[186] See text to n 45 above.

of correcting the mistake (and its consequences) may extend to re-ordering the priority position that has resulted.[187]

Crucially, the same reasoning cannot legitimately be extended to cases where X has himself *unilaterally failed* to seek the entry of a notice to preserve his interest's priority. It is difficult to see how this might constitute a 'mistake' by the Registrar sufficient to bring schedule 4 into play. If it did, then every disappointed interest-holder in X's position, who failed to seek such a notice, and whose unprotected interest is subsequently postponed to Z's interest via section 29, might attempt to challenge that outcome via schedule 4. This would nullify the key incentive for X to enter his interest on the Register (if it is not overriding), and thereby ensure the reliability of the Register: the risk of loss of priority. In short, the registration regime can and should protect X from problems not of his own making, and in particular, problems resulting from the registration *regime's* failings—ie, Land Registry acts or omissions. However, it could not comprehensibly protect X from problems caused by his own failure to take steps for his own protection, which under the registration framework remain *his* proper responsibility. The integrity of the regime requires the courts to avoid any temptation to protect X from his own failings, by adopting an appropriately narrow interpretation of alteration-justifying 'mistakes'.

iv. 'Overriding Interests' and Their Interpretation

A third source of instability in section 29's priority promise relates to the courts' interpretation of overriding interests.

It must immediately be recognised that promises are inherently circumscribed by their terms. The section 29 priority promise is of this nature. It promises priority to Z over X, but this is immediately qualified—priority is not conferred on Z if X's prior interest is either protected on the Register or overriding. The fact that the promise is structured in this way—as a 'big' promise which is inherently qualified—leads to the possibility that the general law might intrude into the interpretation not only of the 'big' promise, but also into the interpretation of its qualifications, with significant consequences for the parties' respective priority positions.

This can be seen most clearly in relation to the category of overriding interests. These constitute a deliberate qualification to the section 29 priority promise, which necessarily limits the reliability of the Register for registered disponees like Z. *Ex hypothesi*, these are proprietary interests, belonging to X, whose persistence against a later registered disponee, Z, does not depend upon any entry in the Register, and whose existence and extent are revealed, if at all, via off-Register inspections and inquiries. Furthermore, if such interests persist and compromise the title of Z, a later registered disponee, the disponee will not be compensated via a Registry-indemnity, as currently conceived. None of this goes to show that the registration regime's priority promise is in any sense 'broken'—only that, by design, it is inherently limited. No assurance is ever given to a party in Z's position of priority vis-à-vis this species of undisclosed interest.

The Law Commission were acutely aware of these problems when designing what might constitute an overriding interest in what became schedule 3 of the LRA 2002. The Commission adopted a range of familiar strategies in an effort to maximise the Register's

[187] This is the exercise which *Gold Harp* (n 174) suggests is made possible by LRA 2002, sch 4, para 8.

reliability, limit the extent of off-Register inquiries, and reduce the risk that registered disponees might be bound by interests whose existence they were neither aware of, nor reasonably capable of discovering.[188] These included: reducing the list of overriding interests contained in the former LRA 1925;[189] re-defining the most important and/or qualifying their status by the addition of further conditions;[190] and imposing duties on applicants for registration to disclose what might be overriding interests, with a view to permanently bringing them 'onto' the Register.[191]

The balance which the Law Commission sought to strike is particularly evident in the context of its major re-working of what became schedule 3, paragraph 2 (formerly, LRA 1925, section 70(1)(g)) and paragraph 3 (formerly, section 70(1)(a)). These provisions are well-known. For present purposes, the key point is that whilst the LRA 2002 attempts, via these devices, to strike a balance between prior interest-holders (X) who may not reasonably be expected to protect their right by Register entry, and later registered disponees (Z), it is a balance which is not susceptible to conclusive *statutory* regulation. Much will turn on the mindset with which the judiciary approach the application and interpretation of the overriding interest provisions; and this will ultimately depend upon their view of the balance that the LRA 2002 framework does or should strike between parties in the positions of X and Z. In particular, the priority that overriding status affords X interest–holder can be heavily compromised, for the benefit of Z registered disponee, by the courts' readiness to draw on and expansively interpret *general law* principles, which might mean that X's otherwise overriding prior interest will be postponed to Z's registered interest. For example, X's potential overriding status as a trust beneficiary in discoverable actual occupation may be compromised by the doctrines of overreaching, waiver, estoppel, or otherwise. It will also be heavily influenced by the courts' interpretation of the key statutory conditions in schedule 3, which may either reduce or extend Z registered disponee's exposure to X's unregistered prior right.[192]

v. Supplementary General Law Grounds for Postponement

A final source of uncertainty relates to the continuing significance of general law principles that, if applicable, may provide a reason, originating wholly outside of the LRA 2002, for subordinating X's earlier right to Z's later right.

[188] For comprehensive exploration, see generally Law Com No 254 (n 34) Parts IV–V; Law Com No 271 (n 36) Part VIII.

[189] cf LRA 1925, s 70 and LRA 2002, sch 3.

[190] See in particular the elimination of the former overriding interest that specifically protected squatters' rights (LRA 1925, s 70(1)(f)); the refinement of the lease overriding interest (cf LRA 1925, s 70(1)(k) and LRA 2002, sch 3, para 1); the modifications made to the overriding status of the rights of actual occupiers (cf LRA 1925, s 70(1)(g) and LRA 2002, sch 3, para 2); and the modifications made to the overriding status of certain easements/ analogous rights (cf LRA 1925, s 70(1)(a) and LRA 2002, sch 3, para 3).

[191] LRA 2002, s 71.

[192] See, eg, the stringency of the definition of 'actual occupation' in LRA 2002, sch 3, para 2, and the rigour with which the courts interpret and apply the 'exceptions' to the presumptive overriding status afforded to the 'interest' of a person in actual occupation (eg, sub-para (a) (whether an interest is one which its holder could 'reasonably' have been expected to disclose on inquiry); sub-para (b) (whether a person's occupation would have been 'obvious on a reasonably careful inspection of the land'); sub-para (c) (the criterion of 'actual knowledge' of the interest).

Although not presented as such in the statute, section 29 priority promise is, in effect, a promise of last resort. Z only needs to rely on *section 29* to obtain priority against X if he has not otherwise gained priority via some other means. Section 29 only comes into play if section 28's basic first-in-time rule would favour X's prior right. However, as we saw in Section C above, section 28's first-in-time rule itself seems to incorporate a number of general law principles that might cause the subversion of X's interest to Z's. These include: overreaching (if two trustees (Y1/Y2) hold on trust for X); waiver (express or implied); estoppel (where X is estopped from asserting priority); and rules that determine the timing of the creation of the two interests, etc. In such cases, the best view is that there is no work for section 29 to do. Section 28, and its necessary incorporation of the relevant general law postponement rules, is sufficient to give Z's interest priority.

The courts seem to have missed this important point: several cases have unnecessarily and inappropriately relied on such general law postponement rules to aid their interpretation of *section 29*. We see this, for example, in *Southern Pacific Mortgages Ltd v Scott,*[193] where the Supreme Court addressed the hypothetical question as to which interest—X's or Z's—might have arisen first in time under the general law in the context of a discussion of section 29 and schedule 3. Similarly, in *Credit and Mercantile plc v Kaymuu Ltd*[194] the Court of Appeal found that X had *waived* priority in the context of its discussion of section 29's priority rule. Other decisions have also used the concept of overreaching to explain why a beneficial interest arising under a trust cannot be an overriding interest, despite the beneficiary's actual occupation—a category of interest which is relevant only if the section 29 priority rule is in play.[195] Properly understood, however, the right location for these general law doctrines is section 28. If X's interest fails to arise before Z's, if its priority is waived, or if it is overreached, then Z has priority *under section 28* and there is no further postponing work to be done via section 29.

Our quibble with the courts' analyses may appear academic. Arguably the same results might be reached whether the general law is drawn into the interpretation of section 28 or section 29—eg, if X waives his interest, he might be seen as waiving it for the purpose of either provision. However, we consider that there are good reasons why the courts should confine their reliance on the general law's postponement rules to the appropriate provision, section 28, and should resist the temptation to incorporate them into section 29. Assuming that these external postponement rules (overreaching, waiver, estoppel etc) *should* remain relevant in relation to registered land, they should apply to *any* priority dispute, whether or not Z disponee falls into the privileged subset of disponees who benefit from section 29's priority promise. As such, section 28, which establishes the starting-point for *all* priority disputes, is the proper vehicle. Furthermore, section 28's basic rule, as drafted, can readily accommodate the general law's postponement rules without undue contortion.[196] The same is not necessarily true for section 29, bringing the risk that they are incorporated more sporadically at best. Thus, whilst the courts have certainly accepted that section 29 will yield

[193] *Southern Pacific Mortgages Ltd v Scott* [2014] UKSC 52, [2015] AC 385. See too *Abbey National v Cann* (n 85).

[194] *Credit and Mercantile plc v Kaymuu Ltd* [2015] EWCA Civ 655, [2015] 2 P & CR 15. See also *Woolwich Building Society v Dickman* (1996) 28 HLR 661 (CA) (noted at text to n 200 below) whose problematic result might in part be explained by the court's dealing with the effect of a waiver in relation to the forerunner of section 29, and not the forerunner of section 28.

[195] eg, *City of London Building Society v Flegg* (n 86) (concerned with equivalent provisions of the LRA 1925).

[196] See section III(C)(i)(c) above.

to the general law's doctrine of *overreaching* where X has a trust interest[197] or other species of overreachable right,[198] the extent to which courts might integrate other such postponement rules into their application of section 29 in other contexts is less clear.

What if, for example, X1, the holder of a restrictive covenant over Y's registered estate, protects his priority via a notice on the Register but X1 expressly waives his priority when Y conveys his estate to Z, who is duly registered as proprietor? Or what if X2 holds a two-year legal lease of Y's registered estate, and impliedly waives priority when Y landlord conveys his estate to Z? In the first case, section 29(2)(a)(i) appears to preserve X1's priority owing to the notice in the Register; in the second, section 29(2)(a)(ii) also appears to preserve X2's lease as a lease which is overriding within schedule 3, paragraph 1. However, if the general law doctrine of waiver *ought* to be incorporated into the LRA 2002 as a matter of policy, then Z, the new registered proprietor, should take priority. And yet, the courts may be reluctant to achieve this result via the vehicle of section 29, which outwardly confers priority on *X1/X2* in these situations, for good reasons—X1 deserves priority owing to the Register notice; X2's short lease deserves priority as an overriding interest, as the Law Commission explained, because it is not appropriate to require or even permit such short leases to be noted on the Register.[199] In such cases, the courts might be disinclined to rely on the general law's postponement rules to reach a result—priority for Z—which might *appear* to flatly contradict the result required by section 29—priority for X1/X2. In contrast, the waiver doctrine can be more naturally incorporated via section 28 in all cases, consistently with the legislation's express terms, and without so obviously appearing to flout Parliament's intentions.

The point might be illustrated by *Woolwich Building Society v Dickman*,[200] a case decided under the old LRA 1925. X, protected statutory tenants in occupation of a flat, had expressly waived their priority in writing when the landlord, Y, mortgaged his registered title to Z building society. Upon Y landlord's subsequent default, Z brought possession proceedings relying on its rights as registered mortgagee. X tenants successfully resisted this claim. The Court of Appeal held that, despite X tenants' express waiver of priority, their lease *continued* to bind Z's registered mortgage as an overriding interest within section 70(1)(g)—the forerunner to schedule 3, paragraph 2 of the LRA 2002.[201] According to Waite LJ, this was because section 70(1)(g) afforded X tenants, as persons in 'actual occupation' of the flat, 'mandatory rights' which could not be displaced/postponed even by an express waiver of priority, unless this was 'expressed on the register'—which was not the case.[202]

The *Dickman* conclusion is problematic. It ignores the inherent prerequisite that, to be 'overriding' within section 70(1)(g) of the LRA 1925 (and now schedule 3, paragraph 2 of

[197] eg, *City of London Building Society v Flegg* (n 86).

[198] *Sabherwahl* (n 86) (an estoppel equity); *Lambert* (n 86) (an equity to rescind a transfer of title).

[199] Law Com No 271 (n 36) para 8.9.

[200] *Woolwich Building Society v Dickman* (1996) 28 HLR 661 (CA).

[201] Via a complex process of reasoning, this paved the way for the further conclusion, that as the lease bound Z mortgagee, X could rely on s 98(1) of the Rent Act 1977, which prohibited a court from making any order for possession of a dwelling-house let on a protected tenancy, unless certain conditions were satisfied—which, on the facts, was not the case.

[202] *Dickman* (n 200) 668 (Waite LJ), 670–671 (Morritt LJ); Butler-Sloss LJ agreed with both. But note that Morritt LJ's judgment seems to suggest at 671 that the result *might* be different for tenancies which are not protected as secure statutory tenancies—on the assumption, it seems, that in these other settings, it would be sufficient to invoke an *inter partes* estoppel, based on the waiver, to prevent reliance on what would otherwise be an overriding interest under the terms of s 70(1) of the LRA 1925.

the LRA 2002), the relevant right must above all be a proprietary right which is capable of binding the relevant estate. A proprietary right whose priority is waived by its holder vis-à-vis a disponee ceases to be such a proprietary right, so far as the disponee is concerned, and so should be incapable of overriding the estate or interest acquired via the disposition. This point has been routinely accepted in proximate cases, decided under the LRA 1925 and the LRA 2002, involving beneficial interests arising under a trust of land of which Y is sole trustee. The courts have readily accepted that X beneficiary, who is in actual occupation and whose beneficial interest is prima facie overriding, can lose priority to Z registered disponee if X has expressly, or even impliedly, waived his priority.[203]

The difficult decision in *Dickman* may be the product of the Court of Appeal's focus on the detail of the overriding interest provision—X's right looked to be overriding because X was in actual occupation, and the waiver was not obviously relevant to that enquiry—at the expense of a close analysis of whether the relevant right was inherently *capable* of binding the disponees. It was not, owing to X's waiver. A case like *Dickman* would probably look very different within the new LRA 2002 framework, if X tenant's consent were treated as relevant to the operation of section 28, rather than section 29 and schedule 3.

It must finally be acknowledged that, whether the general law's postponement rules are incorporated via section 28 or via section 29, their application to XYZ priority disputes can significantly increase the vulnerability of X's pre-existing interest to later dispositions—and in a manner that is unlikely to be adequately compensated-for. This strengthens the position of a party like Z, who deals with Y registered proprietor, insofar as it affords Z the additional advantage that he will not be affected by a prior interest, even *beyond* the circumstances in which sections 28 and 29 expressly confer priority on Z. However, this incursion of the general law might also present a parallel risk in these XYZ priority cases to that noted by Thomas Mapp in the context of ABC title cases.[204] Put simply, where Z acquires an interest over Y's registered estate, any general law doctrinal incursion that reinforces the priority of Z's later-acquired right, vis-à-vis an interest previously held by X, affords additional *security* vis-à-vis such earlier interest-holders only at the risk of creating additional *insecurity* for Z's own interest, in the face of later dispositions of the registered estate. The same set of general law postponement rules that were invoked to subordinate *X's* interest (to Z's) could subsequently be invoked to subordinate *Z's* interest (to a future disposition of the estate by Y). This vulnerability does not directly undercut section 29's priority promise, which is only a promise of priority over *earlier* interests, and offers no guarantee of priority against future disponees.[205] Nevertheless the ongoing quality and security of the title afforded by sections 29 and 58 to a registered disponee is clearly threatened.

vi. Conclusions on the Applicability and Effect of Section 29 in XYZ Priority Disputes

The previous five sections have exposed many significant interpretative controversies surrounding the operation of section 29's priority promise. These controversies span a

[203] eg, *Mendelsohn* (n 87) (a case under the LRA 1925); *Kaymuu* (n 194) (a case under the LRA 2002).

[204] See T Mapp, *Torrens' Elusive Title: Basic Legal Principles of an Efficient Torrens's System* (Edmonton, University of Alberta, 1978).

[205] See section III(A) above.

wide spectrum of issues—including when section 29 applies, its immediate effect, its potential for stultification via direct rights, its vulnerability to schedule 4 alteration claims, and its troubled relationship with section 28. Three key conclusions are warranted.

First, uncertainty persists across all five controversies that affect section 29. This poses a serious risk that, as uncertainty is piled onto uncertainty, section 29's so-called 'promise' has a chameleon-like character—it is liable to change in strength and ambit depending how particular judges choose, in the case before them, to resolve the controversies we have identified. As we have seen, at times the priority promise may be absent or inapplicable; at other times, present but empty; and at yet other times, present and functioning as a cast-iron priority guarantee. There is a clear mismatch between the seemingly crystalline words of section 29's priority promise and the many interpretative controversies that lie beneath its apparently clear terms.

Secondly, this variability in the practical shape and realisation of section 29's priority promise is particularly problematic for two reasons: (1) without clear guiding principles as to how to resolve the interpretative controversies, there is a real risk of judges exercising an unbridled discretion, with the result that like cases are not always treated alike; (2) even if coherent principles can be developed to overcome problem (1), there will remain a gulf between the *appearance* of section 29's priority promise—as a strong and largely unqualified assurance—and the heavily qualified manner in which the promise is realised in practice. This mismatch risks undermining the public's confidence in the Register.

Thirdly, despite these concerns, it must be recognised that it is not *inherently* undesirable for the priority promise to be qualified in certain situations. However, looking to the future, it is essential: (1) that the vulnerabilities in the priority promise are fully appreciated, (2) that an open debate takes place regarding which should be tolerated as a matter of policy, and (3) that more attention is devoted to ensuring that the desired qualifications are formulated in transparent and clear terms. When doing so, and in particular, when addressing the normative question ((2)), it is vital that the priority promise is not considered in isolation. One must also have regard to the LRA 2002's other promises, and the extent to which these are, or should be, similarly qualified.

In this last respect, the Court of Appeal took a positive step in *Gold Harp* in recognising the importance of aligning the strength/vulnerability of section 58's title promise in ABC title cases, with the strength/vulnerability of section 29's priority promise in XYZ priority cases. This development, which arose in the context of each promise's vulnerability to schedule 4 alteration claims, is important, welcome and apt. Both C and Z will legitimately rely on the Register to ascertain whether any third party rights (held by A or X respectively) may encumber their title or otherwise render it insecure. It would be odd for one promise to be obviously more fragile than the other.

E. A Source of Confusion: The Operation of Sections 28 and 29 in 'Two-Party' Cases

A complete account of the LRA 2002's priority promise requires attention to be given to a surprising but persistent source of confusion in recent cases. This concerns the operation of section 29 in relation to so-called 'two-party' (rather than classic 'three-party') cases. The difference between these cases might be depicted as follows.

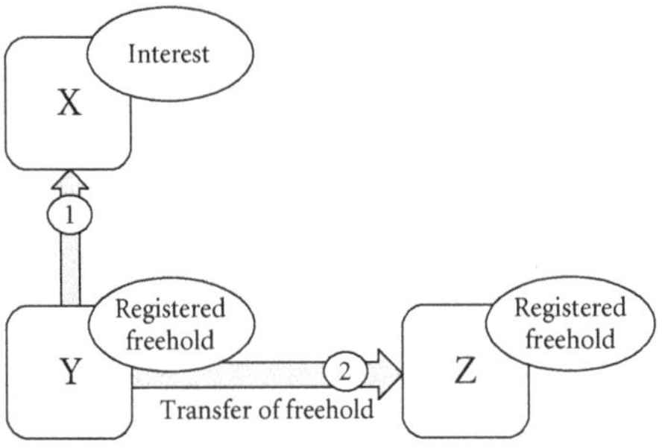

Three-party case

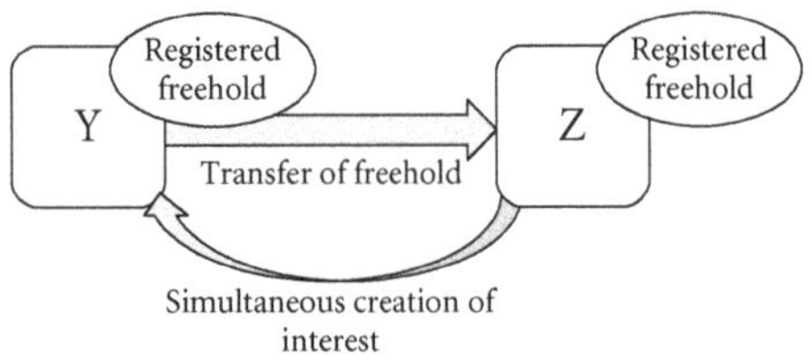

Two-party case

In a classic three-party XYZ priority case, Y's registered freehold estate is subject to X's interest, and Y subsequently effects a disposition of his registered estate to Z. This presents a priority problem in its ordinary sense: it concerns the persistence and priority of X's pre-existing right vis-à-vis the interest acquired by Z. The defining features of this classic scenario are: (a) that X's interest *affects* Y's estate; and (b) that it does so *prior* to the Y–Z disposition. In contrast, in what we call a two-party YZ case, the concern is with the enforceability of a right that Y has acquired *directly*, and for the first time, upon the disposition to Z. Important traps lie in wait unless it is clearly appreciated that these two-party cases raise *different* questions, and that the LRA 2002's priority promise, embodied in section 29, is not designed for them. In truth, these two-party cases do not involve a priority dispute at all.

As we have seen, section 29 provides a priority promise to a privileged class of disponees, like Z, who acquire an interest via a disposition by the registered proprietor, Y. The core problem to which section 29 is addressed is that Y's registered estate may be encumbered by a pre-existing interest which might persist and bind Z, as a subsequent disponee. A credible registration system, if it is to deliver the benefits of a reliable Register, must necessarily regulate the circumstances in which this is possible. The LRA 2002's strategy, which enables a privileged class of registered disponees for valuable consideration to *rely* on the Register, is a 'clearing' rule. If there is a pre-existing interest (held, eg, by X) which encumbers Y's estate *immediately before* the disposition to Z, it is postponed to the interest which Z disponee acquires under the disposition *unless* its priority is protected by Register entry, or by virtue of its status as an overriding interest.

For present purposes, the key point is that nothing in the policies that explain this special priority rule requires Z registered disponee to take free from rights that arise *directly* against him, *ab initio*, either: (i) as a result of his own dispositive acts, or (ii) otherwise, by operation of law. The reason why such rights bind the disponee is not because of the *priority rules* that govern the persistence and priority of a prior interest that encumbered the registered title of the disponor—whether found in sections 28 and 29, or elsewhere. Rather, such rights come into being and bind Z disponee *ab initio*, because of an effective exercise by Z disponee of his own dispositional powers; or because of a decision of the law to subject the disponee to an obligation or encumber his title *for some other reason*. There is no good reason why the LRA 2002's priority promise should have any bearing on the creation and enforceability of such *new direct* rights which arise, at the time of the Y–Z disposition, in favour of Y.

The inapplicability of section 29 to two-party cases is also consistent with section 29's express terms. Registration of the disposition of a registered estate by Y to Z 'has the effect of postponing to the interest under the disposition [to Z] any interest *affecting [Y's] estate immediately before the disposition* [to Z]', whose priority is not protected in one of the listed ways at the time of the Y–Z disposition.[206] Section 29's postponing effect is, in terms, confined to *pre-existing rights* that encumber Y's estate *before* the 'disposition' to Z. As such, nothing in section 29 would enable Z to avoid a trust that would arise against him *anew*, on his acquisition of an interest under the disposition, by operation of law—as a constructive or resulting trust. Nor would anything in section 29 enable Z to avoid the effect of any interest which he created on or after the time of disposition, as a result of the dispositional powers vested in him in the 'registration gap'—eg, a charge granted by Z over the estate conveyed to him, at the time of completion, pursuant to his 'owner's powers' under sections 23 and 24(b). Since these powers do not arise and become exercisable by Z any earlier than the 'disposition' date, the relevant interest would not 'affect' the relevant estate *immediately before* the disposition—but only on, or after. It follows that section 29 is *irrelevant* to a two-party case. It speaks neither to the creation of direct rights in Y's favour against Z, nor to their potential 'postponement' to Z's interest.

Despite this, some cases have applied section 29 in two-party cases—in our view inappropriately. One example is the *Swift 1st* case.[207] On its face, this involved an AB title dispute, where a stranger had forged the grant of a charge over A's registered title in favour of B. The litigation immediately raised the question whether the Land Registry was required to pay B an indemnity, if the charge was removed from the Register. This was thought to raise some important problems. On the Court of Appeal's analysis, A's statutory right to seek rectification of the Register was a proprietary right which was binding on B via section 29 and schedule 3, *because A was in actual occupation*. As such, the AB title dispute was, in effect, treated as a YZ two-party priority dispute. Ordinarily, this would have ruled out any indemnity for B, because B's registered charge was inherently, from the outset, subject to A's prior right: if there is no prejudice to B from alteration of the Register, the alteration is not rectification, and without rectification, there is no indemnity available under the LRA 2002. However, the Court of Appeal found a way of avoiding this outcome on the facts via schedule 8, paragraph 1(2). This deems there to be a loss, and therefore prejudice for the purposes of schedule 4, where a disponee whose title is altered had acquired that title 'in good faith under a forged disposition'. This deeming provision paved the way for the conclusion that the alteration was a loss-causing rectification for which an indemnity was available.

The result in *Swift 1st* seems just, but the reasoning is questionable. In particular, it is surprising that the Court of Appeal thought that the status of A's interest as an overriding interest was really in issue. Properly understood, A's right to seek rectification arose *on*, and *only on*, B's registration, and it was a right that arose *directly* vis-à-vis B's registered charge.

[206] LRA 2002, s 29 (emphasis added).
[207] *Swift 1st* (n 99).

As such, it was not a right that had affected A's registered estate at the time of the 'disposition' to B, and it was not a right that could be postponed to B's interest via section 29. Indeed, observably, the case did not raise a priority point at all: it did not concern the persistence of A's prior property right, as against later dispositions to a third party. Rather, the only question in issue concerned the proper resolution of A's claim to rectification that arose directly against B. Neither section 28 nor section 29 were in point, and it was irrelevant to ask whether A had an overriding interest. This would only have been necessary if the case raised a priority issue, and if it was necessary to preserve the priority of A's interest, which would otherwise be caught by section 29, from being postponed.[208]

This might seem to be a technical point. However, the mischaracterisation of the *Swift 1st* case as a priority dispute brings real practical dangers.

First, it creates unnecessary fragility for a claimant in *A*'s position. If A is not in actual occupation, then the logic of section 29 suggests that A's right, if not entered on the Register, is necessarily postponed to B's interest. The same analysis suggests that the resulting postponement of A's interest is an event that should attract no indemnity. This cannot be right, once the substance of A's complaint is seen for what it is: ie, a direct complaint about the mistaken registration of B's forged charge over A's title.

Secondly, the same process of reasoning can create unwarranted consequences for *B*. If A's claim to rectification is seen as a pre-existing property right, which can affect B as an overriding interest, then in the absence of any loss-deeming provision equivalent to schedule 8, paragraph 1(2)(b), the removal of B's charge will not involve rectification of the Register. This will prevent B from relying on the additional defences involved where rectification (rather than mere alteration) is in issue,[209] and from seeking an indemnity for any resulting losses. Again, the position would be otherwise if the substance of A's complaint is seen for what it is: ie, as a direct challenge to the mistaken registration of the forged charge over A's title.

Thirdly, taken to its logical conclusion, the reasoning in *Swift 1st* could bring within the ambit of section 29—and therefore schedule 3—any interest created by the law or by the parties, before or at registration. This would include a constructive trust arising in favour of A, as a response to *B's* unconscionable conduct.[210] The logic of *Swift 1st* would suggest that if A is not in actual occupation, then B—as a registered disponee for valuable consideration—might take free of that trust. This result is clearly perverse and defeats the very purpose of the imposition of this kind of trust—ie, it is imposed due to B's own unconscionable conduct.

Stepping back, it is vital that the courts do not fall into the *Swift 1st* trap, and that in future, they recognise that section 29 is *not* designed for two-party cases. The *Swift 1st*

[208] A genuine 'three-party' priority issue, engaging s 29 (or its equivalent, s 30, in the case of a transfer of a registered charge) might have arisen had B chargee subsequently effected a registered disposition to C. Then, it would be legitimate to ask whether A's right to seek rectification—understood in *Swift 1st* (n 99) to be proprietary—which had previously encumbered B's registered interest, would persist, or be postponed, vis-à-vis C's (ie, a third party's) interest.

[209] LRA 2002, sch 4, paras 3(2) and 6(2).

[210] See the cases, noted at n 163 above, where a trust is imposed to prevent B from unconscionably reneging from an undertaking he gave to respect another's—here A's—rights, on the basis of which B acquired title. Or see too the possible imposition of a constructive trust where B is equivalent to a 'thief' of A's title, noted at text to n 159 et seq above.

decision involves a misinterpretation of the clear words of the LRA 2002, which demand that to be governed by section 29 and schedule 3, the relevant interest must have 'affect[ed] the estate immediately before the disposition'. Manifestly, this could not be so on the facts of *Swift 1st*: A's right to rectify, even if proprietary, never affected *A's* registered estate, and only arose against *B's* charge on its registration. This misconception must be exposed and corrected. It assumes that the LRA 2002 speaks to issues which it was never designed to settle, and which it can only be forced to settle at the risk of unnecessary and unjustified consequences.

A second example of the same misapplication of section 29 is found in a surprising analysis in the 2001 Law Commission Report of the status of an unpaid vendor's liens.[211] Consider the following case. RP1 contracts to sell his estate to RP2. At this point, an unpaid vendor's lien arises in favour of RP1. A transfer to RP2 is then executed and registered, but part or all of the purchase price has not been paid. Can RP2 claim to take free of the lien, via section 29, unless the lien's priority is protected by the entry of a notice (or, unusually, the lien is otherwise overriding), at the time of registration of the disposition to RP2?

In the 1998 Law Commission Consultative Document,[212] the Commission considered that such a result would be undesirable as a matter of policy. Their provisional recommendation, subject to consultation, was therefore that RP2 should *not* take free of the lien—a conclusion that could have been readily reached via their broader provisional recommendation that a disponee would take his interest subject to interests to which he was a party.[213] However, the 2001 Law Commission Report seems to reveal a change of heart.[214] In this later report, the Commission seemed to assume that one authority, *Orakpo v Manson Investments Ltd*,[215] suggested that RP2 could take free of the unpaid vendor's lien via section 29's predecessor provision—section 20 of the LRA 1925. They considered, though, that the problem was a small problem in practice, which could be readily addressed if conveyancers were diligent in securing a timely notice entry in respect of a vendor's lien.

It is a pity that the Law Commission dealt with this matter in such a peremptory manner, for the following reasons.

First, on examination, *Orakpo* is a difficult decision, which is poor authority for the claimed proposition. C had borrowed monies from D licensed moneylender, inter alia, to enable him to complete contracts to buy two properties. The loan transactions, and the legal charges executed as security, were later found to be unenforceable for non-compliance with the Moneylenders Act 1927. The question then arose whether, in lieu of its bargained-for but unenforceable security, D was entitled to be subrogated to the unpaid vendors' liens which had been discharged via its advance. C resisted this, arguing that section 20(1) of the LRA 1925 meant that C took a clear title on his registration as proprietor of the purchased estate.[216] D responded that section 20(1) 'should be read in a modified manner, so as not to free a registered proprietor from liabilities or encumbrances to the creation of which he has himself been privy'.[217] Buckley LJ noted that Walton J appeared to have accepted

[211] Law Com No 271 (n 36) para 5.10.
[212] Law Com No 254 (n 34) paras 7.36–7.37.
[213] ibid, para 7.37.
[214] Law Com No 271 (n 36) para 5.10.
[215] *Orakpo v Manson Investments Ltd* [1977] 1 WLR 347 (CA).
[216] ibid, 359–360.
[217] ibid, 360.

that argument at first instance, but found it 'difficult [him]self to make that construction accord with the language of the subsection'.[218] Stopping there, it might appear that Buckley LJ considered that section 20(1) did indeed have the clearing effect assumed by the Law Commission. However, that was not in fact the ultimate effect of Buckley LJ's decision. He found that this clearing of D's lien could be 'put right if necessary by rectification': D could have the Register rectified, to secure the entry of notices of its subrogation rights.[219] This suggests that *even though* section 20(1) might appear to have had a title-clearing effect, that was not the whole story. If the relevant right and associated obligation arose directly against the new registered proprietor—in *Orakpo*, D's lien—it was not an obligation which he could be permitted to avoid, and a Register-amendment could be sought to give it effect.

Secondly, there are important distinctions between the language of section 20 of the LRA 1925 and that of its successor provision—section 29 of the LRA 2002. Section 20's clearing effect is expressed in very wide terms: *'free from all other estates and interests whatsoever'*.[220] In contrast, section 29 seems deliberately narrower and more nuanced. It has the effect of *postponing* only those rights that 'affected the [registered] estate' 'immediately before the disposition', subject to their priority being appropriately protected.

Thirdly, the application of section 29 to an unpaid vendor's lien remains unclear—it depends on some under-examined questions as to the nature of such liens. According to the Law Commission, the lien arises in favour of the vendor, RP1, when the contract of sale is made.[221] As such, it might seem to be an interest which pre-dates the disposition to the purchaser, RP2, which *could* be caught by section 29's clearing effect—as the Law Commission seemed to assume. However, whether that is indeed correct depends on identifying *when* the lien arises, and therefore *which* and *whose* estate/interest is in fact encumbered by it.

Section 29 can only catch the lien if the proper view is that the lien encumbers RP1's estate before or at the date of the *disposition* to RP2. This requires a rather elaborate analysis. In particular, it requires the assumption that, upon the contract of sale being made, RP1 holds his legal estate on some form of qualified trust for RP2, but that this legal estate is also simultaneously encumbered by a lien which secures debts owed by RP2 to RP1. This is not impossible, but does seem artificial.

The better and rather different view is that the lien never encumbers RP1's legal estate at all, but only the derivative interest that RP2 acquires at each stage of the conveyancing process. That is, it encumbers, successively: RP2's estate contract (upon the contract being made), RP2's full equitable title (upon disposition), and RP2's legal title (upon registration). In view of RP2's outstanding obligations to pay RP1, it does not seem that there is any moment in time—any *scintilla temporis*—during which RP2 has an unencumbered interest. As such, there is no obstacle to imagining that a new lien can fasten in turn, by operation of law, on each new interest that vests in RP2 in the course of the conveyancing process.

[218] ibid.

[219] ibid, 360–361.

[220] LRA 1925, s 20(1): 'In the case of a freehold estate registered with an absolute title, a disposition of the registered land or of a legal estate therein ... for valuable consideration shall, when registered, confer on the transferee or grantee [the relevant legal estate] ... subject—(a) to the incumbrances and other entries, if any, appearing on the register; and (b) unless the contrary is expressed on the register, to the overriding interests, if any, affecting the estate transferred or created, but free from all other estates and interests whatsoever ...'.

[221] Law Com No 271 (n 36) para 5.10, relying on *Barclays Bank plc v Estates & Commercial Ltd* [1997] 1 WLR 415 (CA) 419, 420 (Millet LJ).

The corollary of this view is that the lien never affects *RP1's estate* 'immediately before the disposition'. Between the date of the contract and completion/disposition, the lien affects the equitable interest that *RP2* acquires via the estate contract, and not RP1's legal estate. Between completion/disposition and registration, the lien affects the full equitable title that RP2 acquires via the transfer documents. On registration, a lien fastens anew on RP2's registered estate. In short, the lien is not a prior encumbrance that affects RP2's registered title in accordance with priority rules. It is an interest that arises *directly* against RP2, in response to the demands of his own conscience.

Drawing these threads together, there is a very good case to be made that the particular problem which the 2001 Law Commission identified in relation to unpaid vendor's liens rests on a misunderstanding. Whether or not that is right, it certainly seems regrettable that the 2001 Report failed to put the general question beyond doubt in a manner similar to that mooted by the 1998 Consultative Document: ie, by clarifying that notwithstanding section 29, a disponee will take his estate or interest subject to rights which are imposed on him directly by operation of law or to whose creation he was a party.[222]

IV. Future Challenges

To be credible, the LRA 2002 must offer some form of priority promise to disponees, as a necessary prop and companion for its title promise.[223] Parties dealing with a registered proprietor would be unable to safely rely on the Register without some substantial assurance, not only against undisclosed vices that might otherwise undermine their acquisition of title, but also against undisclosed prior encumbrances. This assurance must be robust if the Register is to command public confidence. It follows that the special priority rule which is established by section 29 for the benefit of later disponees of *already-registered* estates is pivotal to the realisation of the registration regime's objectives.

The picture looks different at first registration. A credible registration regime does not need to offer any *promise* of priority to the first registered proprietor, who *ex hypothesi* did not rely on the Register when acquiring his interest. The registration framework could opt simply to transpose—preserve or continue—the existing priorities of all pre-existing interests at first registration.[224] Nonetheless, this is not the way in which the LRA 2002, via the ordering rules found in sections 11 and 12, appears to work in practice. Some pre-existing interests may be cleared from the first registered title for the benefit of the first registered proprietor—sometimes by deliberate design, and sometimes because of Registry error. This can probably be tolerated as long as the Act can be interpreted—or if not, re-cast—so that this prejudice to the prior encumbrancer can be made good via a Register-indemnity.[225] If the migration of unregistered estates into the registration regime, which was instituted in order to give the *public* confidence in land transactions, causes loss to such *individuals*, it is a loss which should not go compensated.

[222] cf Law Com No 254 (n 34) para 7.37.
[223] See Goymour, 'Resolving the Tension' (n 76).
[224] See section II(A) above.
[225] See section II(C) above.

Looking ahead, first registration problems are of ever-diminishing significance. It is the priority promise offered to subsequent disponees of already-registered estates that is key to the enduring integrity of the registration regime. Unfortunately, as this chapter has shown, all is not necessarily well. Several challenging issues require attention.

First, which disponees of a registered estate properly benefit from the section 29 priority promise? In principle, the promise should only work in favour of those who 'deserve' it. But what exactly does this entail? On close inspection, the crystalline words of section 29 conceal some significant interpretative controversies concerning, inter alia: whether section 29 will avail a registered 'disponee', if the relevant 'disposition' was void under the general law;[226] the nature of the 'valuable consideration' that must be provided, to engage the section 29 rule;[227] and whether, and via what mechanisms, a disponee's 'fraud' will be a barrier to the invocation of section 29—despite the provision's silence on the point.[228] There is also a deeper set of questions concerning whether the balance struck by the authors of the LRA 2002 is in all respects the right one. Should section 29's operation be limited to *registered dispositions*?[229] Should it be always be necessary to provide value to trigger section 29?[230] Should section 29 be explicitly qualified by reference to disponee 'fault'—at least in the nature of 'fraud'? None of these questions is straightforward.

Secondly, where section 29 is engaged, what is, and should be, the strength of the resulting promise? It is commonplace that section 29's priority promise is inherently qualified by the provision's express terms, which preserve the priority of earlier rights entered in the Register or having 'overriding' status. But there are other less obvious ways in which the promise's impact may be affected, which any critical account of the law must attend to.

The first of these challenges relates to the correct mode of realisation of the promise. It has long been clear that the LRA 2002's title promise may not be realised *in specie*, as section 58's title-vesting effect can be reversed via schedule 4—in which case, the Act's promise of *title* is a promise that is only made good, at best, in money.[231] Following *Gold Harp*,[232] the same now appears to be true of the priority promise—section 29's ordering effect *might* also be reversed via schedule 4.[233] This may not be what the authors of the LRA 2002 intended[234]—it clearly weakens the strength of the priority promise, since section 29 will not offer a cast-iron *in specie* assurance of priority in all cases. But it does at least have the merit of symmetry. Disponees are not intolerably prejudiced if the schedule 4 jurisdiction is exercised with appropriate caution, and is reliably backed by a substantial Land Registry indemnity for a disponee who loses out as a result.

The second challenge arises from the continuing role of general law doctrines in determining the position of disponees—including the privileged sub-category of disponees who can rely on section 29's priority promise. On examination, it is clear that sections 28 and 29

226 See section III(D)(i)(a) above.
227 See section III(D)(i)(c) above.
228 See section III(D)(i)(b) and (c) above.
229 See text to n 73 et seq, above, noting the recent proposals in Law Com CP No 227 (n 29).
230 cf the recent discussion in Law Com CP No 227 (n 29) ch 7.
231 See ch 16 of this book, section III(D).
232 *Gold Harp* (n 174), discussed in section III(D)(iii) above.
233 See section III(D)(iii).
234 See ch 8 of this book.

do not provide anything like a complete statement of the principles that are required to understand the full priority 'picture'. Thus, a wide array of general law postponement principles appear implicitly to be incorporated and remain salient.[235] In addition, disponees, including those who benefit from section 29's operation, remain vulnerable to the imposition of so-called 'direct rights' via the general law.[236] This inevitably presents difficulties. In either case, the general law remains relevant, yet its role is not expressly regulated by the Act. More could be done to clarify the proper parameters in future. As things stand, it falls to the judiciary to forge an appropriate path, unguided. It is a heavy responsibility.

Wide-ranging deployment of general law postponement principles will not threaten the legislative ambition insofar as these principles tend to be applied, and generously interpreted, to *improve* the priority that a registered disponee enjoys *beyond* that afforded by section 29.[237] However, public confidence in the registration regime might be undermined for a different reason if these postponement principles are strained too far to that end—enhanced security for registered disponees can only be implemented at the cost of potentially uncompensated prejudice to those whose prior rights are thereby postponed/ compromised.

Direct rights pose a similar dilemma but for different reasons. There is no good reason why a registered proprietor should obtain a *comprehensive* immunity from direct rights, generated by his *own* conduct. Indeed, public confidence in the registration regime would be fatally undermined if that were so—eg, if even the fraudulent/dishonest were favoured in this way. At the same time, courts need to be alive to the risk that direct rights could sometimes be imposed in circumstances that might, via a side-wind, illegitimately stultify the security that the Act, via section 29, was intended to afford to registered disponees from prior interests—most obviously, if constructive or even actual knowledge of an unprotected prior right, *without more*, was sufficient to trigger the recognition of a new direct right against a registered disponee. It remains very unclear how, and where, this important line is to be drawn.

The third and related source of challenge comes at a more conceptual level. Put simply, section 29 and its priority promise must be kept within their proper sphere—ie, true 'priority' cases, where the question arises whether a prior incumbrance, which affected a registered estate, will persist to bind a later registered disponee, or will be postponed. There is no justification whatsoever in principle or policy for deploying section 29 in a 'two-party' setting to determine the status of a right that has arisen *directly* against the registered proprietor.[238] Ill-considered suggestions to the contrary in some recent decisions[239] must be exposed as errors.

[235] See section III(C)(i)(c) and section III(D)(v) above. This is also a theme of ch 13 of this work.
[236] See section III(D)(ii).
[237] This is, almost without exception, the reason for the courts' invocation of general law postponement principles in cases such as those noted in nn 85–87 above.
[238] See Section III(E).
[239] See in particular, *Swift 1st* (n 99).

18

A Tale of Three Promises: (3) The Empowerment Promise

STEPHEN WATTERSON AND AMY GOYMOUR

I. Introduction

In this chapter, we turn our attention to the third promise offered by the Land Registration Act ('LRA') 2002—what we call the 'empowerment promise'. The fundamental problem addressed by this promise is that a person, whilst nominally invested with title to an estate or interest, might have limits on their normal dispositional capacities (broadly-understood)—such that under the general law, a purported disposition by that person, which occurs beyond those limited capacities, might be vulnerable to challenge. This creates some obvious traps for disponees which the LRA 2002 was specfically intended to address. Broadly speaking, the validity of a disposition of a registered title was not to be called into question, if it occurred in contravention of a limit on the proprietor's dispositional capacities, unless that limit was reflected in the entry of a restriction in the Register. That might seem straightforward. However, close scrutiny reveals a number of hidden traps which, if not properly understood and publicised, may ensnare parties who deal on the basis that the Register is correct. The purpose of this chapter is to draw attention to the empowerment promise and expose these associated traps.

II. Basis of the Empowerment Promise

The empowerment promise is the product of several provisions of the LRA 2002. For dispositions involving a 'registered estate' or 'registered charge', they are found in sections 23–26; these are the focus of this chapter. For dispositions by a registered chargee involving the *property subject to the charge*—eg, the freehold estate subject to a charge—the equivalent provisions are found in sections 51–52.[1]

In summary, section 23 confers 'owner's powers' in relation to a registered estate; section 24 identifies who can exercise these owner's powers; section 25 prescribes their mode of exercise;

[1] See text to n 26 et seq below, for discussion of the relationship between these provisions in relation to registered chargees' powers.

and, finally, section 26 provides for the 'protection of disponees' who take from someone who exercises owner's powers. In combination, and at their widest, these provisions make a seemingly strong promise: registered proprietors (and certain others) are empowered to dispose of the registered estate, even if they are not empowered to do so under the general law, in such a way that the disponee's title will be free from challenge. However, like the title and priority promises examined in chapters sixteen and seventeen, the Act's empowerment promise is fragile in several key respects. These vulnerabilities are the focus of the following sections.

III. Key Vulnerabilities

A. The Purpose and Effect of Section 23

Our exploration of the empowerment promise must start with section 23, which defines the central concept of 'owner's powers'. What is its purpose and effect, when viewed within the overall scheme of sections 23–26?

If registration is not merely a necessary step in the acquisition of title, akin to an extra formality requirement, but is actually constitutive of a new form of title, then it might be argued that it is necessary for the legislation to define that title's content and implications: the title is, after all, a creature of the legislation.[2] Nevertheless, whilst true, this is insufficient to account for the shape of section 23 as drafted.

It is very clear that the LRA 2002 does not purport exhaustively, via its express terms, to give legal content to the rights and interests that it seeks to govern. In general, the Act is parasitic upon the general law's understanding of the basic nature and consequences of the various estates and interests that fall within its ambit—eg freehold estates, leases, restrictive covenants, etc. The Act's central concern is to provide a framework for parties who *deal* with land, and to facilitate *dynamic* transactional dealings. Consistently with this, it is necessary for the Act, via section 23, to speak to only one (admittedly important) aspect of the status of 'owner'—the *dispositional powers* associated with having title to a registered estate or charge. And it does so with a view to the facilitation of dispositions of such interests. The Act's strategy to this end, embodied in sections 23–26, has three key components:

(i) to identify an abstract bundle of dispositional powers associated with a registered estate or charge ('owner's powers');[3]
(ii) to render those 'owner's powers' exercisable not only by the nominal registered estate-owner or charge-holder, but also by those who are entitled to be registered as such;[4] and
(iii) to afford a substantial immunity for disponees from the risk that a particular proprietor's entitlement to exercise those 'owner's powers' might be subject to limits which could render a disposition vulnerable to challenge.[5]

[2] eg, E Cooke, *The New Law of Land Registration* (Hart Publishing, Oxford, 2003) 55–56.
[3] LRA 2002, s 23.
[4] LRA 2002, s 24(a), (b).
[5] LRA 2002, s 26.

Against this background, the fundamental question remains—what is the nature of the powers identified by section 23?

Section 23(1) provides in terms that an '[o]wner's powers in relation to a registered estate consist of—(a) power to make a disposition of any kind permitted by the general law in relation to an interest of that description, other than a mortgage by demise or sub-demise'. Section 23(2) correspondingly provides that an '[o]wner's powers in relation to a registered charge consist of—(a) power to make a disposition of any kind permitted by the general law in relation to an interest of that description, other than a legal sub-mortgage'.

The first point requiring re-emphasis is that section 23 is concerned narrowly with an owner's *dispositional* powers. It does not speak to the wider bundle of rights and powers ordinarily associated with title to the relevant estates or charges—eg, rights to use and enjoy the land. Consistently with this, sections 23–26 are expressly headed 'Powers of disposition'. The underlying purpose of these provisions points in the same direction—the aim is to facilitate transactions for the benefit of disponees, by enabling them to proceed on the reassuring basis that the registered proprietor has extensive (if not unlimited) dispositional powers. Some recent decisions have nevertheless overlooked this, and have given section 23 an inappropriately broader reach—eg, so as to encompass a landlord's power to give a notice to quit to a tenant,[6] or a chargee's powers to sell or lease the property subject to the charge.[7] That is an error. 'Owner's powers' only comprise powers of *disposition 'in relation to' the registered estate or charge*. The unwarranted extended reading given in these recent decisions threatens to create unintended and unwanted consequences, when combined with section 24(b)—as we explain below.[8]

Accepting that section 23 deals only with dispositional powers, the second key point concerns the Act's explicit reference back to the general law. Section 23 refers to a 'power to make a disposition of any kind *permitted by the general law* in relation to an interest of that description'. This seems to be both empowering (it confers powers, when taken together with section 24) and limiting (those powers are restricted in some sense to the powers recognised by the general law). The difficult question is—*how* limiting? More particularly, what general law limits, if any, are being incorporated by the Act's explicit reference to the 'general law'?

Although not completely free from doubt, the interpretation that seems most consistent with the Act's words, and most likely to realise the legislative ambition, is that the reference back to the 'general law' is intended to be only minimally restrictive. Section 23 isolates an abstract, disembodied bundle of dispositional powers. The reference is to the powers *generally* associated with an interest of the relevant quality—eg, if the interest is a registered freehold estate, the dispositional powers are those generally associated with a freehold estate. Crucially, the reference is not to those powers enjoyed by any particular *type of person* invested with title to such an interest, whose dispositional powers might be further limited. As such, 'owner's powers' are not limited by any *personal* transactional incapacity under which a particular proprietor might labour, under the general law. For example, someone who is mentally incapacitated acquires, upon registration as freehold proprietor, the full

[6] cf *Stodday Land Ltd v Pye* [2016] EWHC 2454 (Ch), [2016] 4 WLR 168. See further text to n 28 et seq below.

[7] cf *Skelwith (Leisure) Ltd v Armstrong* [2015] EWHC 2830 (Ch), [2016] Ch 345. See further text to n 26 et seq below.

[8] See section III(B) below.

array of dispositional owner's powers associated with a freehold estate; and his dispositional powers are prima facie unaffected by his mental incapacity.

What then is the purpose of section 23's reference to the 'general law'? Whilst it might seem, on one view, to incorporate an unidentified collection of general law constraints on a proprietor's dispositional capacities, the better view may be that the only limit necessarily implied by this phrase is in effect the limit imposed by the *numerus clausus* principle—that is, 'owner's powers' are powers to transfer or grant the same types of interests as are permitted by the general law, *and only those interests*. On this view, for example, a freeholder cannot grant an easement or a lease over his land unless the right conferred fits the general law's definition of an easement or a lease. It might be argued that this does no more than state the obvious. However, in a world of 'title by registration'—where registration is constitutive—the registration regime *creates* rights, and nothing can be taken for granted concerning their shape. Section 23's reference back to the 'general law' thus plays an important role in ensuring that the *numerus clausus* principle is incorporated into the land registration regime. This interpretation of section 23 seems broadly in line with the reading of section 23 recently offered by the Law Commission.[9]

B. The Purpose and Effect of Section 24

Whilst section 23 defines 'owner's powers', it is section 24 which identifies the person(s) in whom those powers are vested.

It is clearly vital to the LRA 2002 regime, and to the ability of potential disponees to rely on the Register, that a right to exercise 'owner's powers' is conferred on whoever is the registered proprietor for the time being. This is achieved by section 24(a). However, section 24 also has an extended empowering effect, which cannot be explained in the same terms: the same right to exercise owner's powers is conferred by section 24(b) on a person who is merely 'entitled to be' registered as proprietor, and who therefore, for the time being, is not yet the registered proprietor. This seems to encompass two major categories of person. First, a disponee under a 'registrable disposition'[10] which has not yet been completed by 'registration', and who, pending such registration, therefore has only an equitable estate or interest. This person inhabits—albeit usually only temporarily—the so-called 'registration gap' that exists between the times of disposition and registration.[11] Secondly, section 24(b) also seems to capture a person who obtains the legal estate *without* registration, by a disposition

[9] See Law Commission, *Updating the Land Registration Act 2002—A Consultation Paper* (Law Com CP No 227, 2016) para 5.62, and in particular the following passage: 'The limit imposed in section [23(1)(a)] and (b) by reference to "a disposition of any kind permitted by the general law in relation to an interest of that description" refers to the types of disposition a freehold owner can make ... This interpretation is buttressed by the exceptions that immediately follow: in section 23(1)(a) "other than a mortgage by demise or sub-demise" and in section 23(2)(a) "other than a legal sub-mortgage". These are types of disposition, not circumstances in which types of dispositions can be made. The reference to the "general law" was not intended to restrict owner's powers to the principle of *nemo dat* or restrictions imposed by common law, equity or statute'.

[10] LRA 2002, s 27.

[11] The Law Commission consider, we think correctly, that the relevant powers are not acquired in this case before *completion* of the relevant disposition: see Law Com CP No 227 (n 9) para 5.26. They consider that this is consistent with the assumption in *Southern Pacific Mortgages Ltd v Scott* [2014] UKSC 52, [2015] AC 385 [79] that purchasers cannot create proprietary rights until completion of their purchase transaction.

that occurs by operation of law, and does not amount to a 'registrable disposition'—eg, a transfer on the death or bankruptcy of a registered proprietor.[12] Authorities have divided as regards the proper interpretation of section 24(b).

The first and better view is that in combination, sections 23 and 24(b) achieve a statutory departure from what might otherwise be the general law's starting-point, reflected in the maxim *nemo dat quod non habet*—a person 'cannot grant a greater interest than he or she possesses'.[13] This maxim finds specific expression in the general principle that an owner with a merely equitable title 'cannot grant anything larger than an equitable interest'.[14] However, on this first view, section 24(b) mandates a different outcome. Any person who is 'entitled to be registered as proprietor' can exercise the same full range of dispositional owner's powers in relation to the registered (*legal*) estate or charge, as can the registered proprietor. As such, a disponee might, from the date of disposition to him, *himself* effect a registrable disposition to another of the interest which he is in the process of acquiring that could operate *at law*—even though, pending his own registration as proprietor of the registered estate or charge, he may only have an equitable estate or interest. The upshot is that the disponee (B) from the registered proprietor (A) is empowered, for the benefit of a subsequent disponee (C), to transfer or grant something greater than he has, and the general law's *nemo dat* principle is statutorily overridden.

Morgan J implicitly adopted this first reading in *Bank of Scotland plc v King*.[15] There, B purchaser of a registered title from A had purported to charge the title to C during the 'registration gap'. Completion by registration of the A–B transfer had never in fact occurred. Nevertheless, B purchaser was assumed to be empowered by section 24(b) to grant a charge over the registered title to C which, upon its registration, would take effect as a registered charge.

Doubt has, unfortunately, been cast on Morgan J's decision by a line of subsequent cases, which insist that sections 23 and 24(b) must be read more restrictively, and in a manner that respects—rather than departs from—the *nemo dat* maxim.[16] According to these cases, whilst a person (B) who is entitled to be registered as proprietor is 'entitled to exercise owner's powers',[17] those powers are more limited than those of a registered proprietor, because they are implicitly limited by the general law *nemo dat* maxim. This approach makes the quality of B's interest crucial. If, pending registration, B disponee has only an equitable title, then his powers of disposition to C are limited to those which would be available to a person with such an equitable title under the general law. *Ruoff and Roper* explain the effect of these post-*King* decisions in the following terms:[18]

> [A] person's right to exercise owner's powers, by virtue of being entitled to be registered as proprietor, does not mean that he has unlimited powers of disposition. The fact that he has acquired such a right under a registrable disposition which has not yet been completed by registration, and which therefore takes effect in equity only until registered, of itself means that his powers of disposition

[12] LRA 2002, s 27(5)(a)-(c).
[13] eg, *Mortgage Business plc v O'Shaughnessy* [2012] EWCA Civ 17, [2012] 1 WLR 1521 [59].
[14] ibid [61].
[15] *Bank of Scotland v King* [2007] EWHC 2747 (Ch), [2008] 1 EGLR 65.
[16] See *O'Shaughnessy* (n 13); *Skelwith* (n 7); *Stodday* (n 6).
[17] LRA 2002, s 23.
[18] *Ruoff & Roper—Registered Conveyancing* (London, Sweet & Maxwell, loooseleaf) para 13.003.04 (August 2017 release).

> under the general law are limited. In particular, by the maxim *nemo dat quod non habet*, under which a person 'cannot grant a greater estate than he possesses'. In the case of an equitable owner of a registered estate or charge, this manifests itself in the general principle that such an equitable owner cannot grant a legal interest.

The consequence of this second interpretation is that B purchaser of A's registered estate, who had not yet been registered as proprietor, would be unable in the 'registration gap' effectively to transfer the registered estate via a sub-sale; or grant a registrable (legal) lease or an immediately effective non-registrable (legal) lease;[19] or grant a charge which could take effect as a registered (legal) charge.[20] This might well bring unfortunate knock-on consequences. In particular, it might increase the vulnerability of later disponees, like C, who—if unable to acquire a registered interest—might themselves be denied the benefit of the Act's title, priority and empowerment promises. The better view is that these post-*King* decisions involve a wrong-turning.[21] Section 24(b) *was* intended to depart from the *nemo dat* principle—arming a person, like B, who was merely entitled to be registered as proprietor, with the full array of 'owner's powers'. This might not be required to ensure the reliability of the Register for disponees, like B, who enjoy these powers, but it does appear to have other, good practical ambitions. As the Law Commission has explained, it facilitates some commonplace conveyancing transactions: in particular, acquisition mortgages and sub-sales.[22]

Some of the contorted reasoning in the recent decisions could arguably have been avoided if the courts had more clearly appreciated that the statutory concept of 'owner's powers' is limited. As explained earlier in this chapter,[23] it does not encompass *every* power associated with ownership of a legal estate or charge, but only a relevant owner's *dispositional* powers, *in relation to the registered estate or charge*. This assumes particular significance for the immediate discussion, because it is only these so-called 'owner's powers' which are made exercisable, via section 24(b)'s extended effect, by a person, like B, who is entitled to be registered as proprietor. In other words, if B registrable disponee relies on section 24(b), he does not *himself* have a legal estate unless and until registered, and he is not empowered to do anything *as if* he had the legal estate, *except* for the purpose of effecting dispositions.

This point was misperceived in two recent decisions, with malign consequences. In *Skelwith (Leisure) Ltd v Armstrong*,[24] and again in *Stodday Land Ltd v Pye*,[25] section 23 was given wider prima facie effect. Then, to avoid any perceived over-reach, section 24(b) was cut back. In neither case, however, was this necessary. The correct answer should have been that 'owner's powers' were not in issue.

In *Skelwith*,[26] Newey J confronted the question whether B, the unregistered assignee of a registered charge, could exercise a power of sale over the charged registered title in favour of a purchaser, C. He concluded that the assignee might do so—notwithstanding that the

[19] cf *O'Shaughnessy* (n 13).
[20] cf *King* (n 15).
[21] See, for a similar view, Law Com CP No 227 (n 9) paras 5.18 ff.
[22] ibid, para 5.22.
[23] See section III(A) above.
[24] *Skelwith (Leisure) Ltd v Armstrong* [2015] EWHC 2830 (Ch), [2016] Ch 345.
[25] *Stodday Land Ltd v Pye* [2016] EWHC 2454 (Ch), [2016] 4 WLR 168.
[26] *Skelwith* (n 24).

assignee had, for the time being, only an equitable title to the charge. However, this conclusion, whilst correct, was reached via an unnecessarily circuitous route:

(i) 'Owner's powers' in respect of a registered charge, as defined by section 23(2), *included a chargee's general law powers to deal with the charged property*, and in particular, the power to sell the charged property conferred by section 101 of the Law of Property Act ('LPA') 1925.
(ii) Section 24 identified the persons by whom those powers were exercisable.
(iii) Prima facie, section 24(b) meant that those powers were also exercisable by B, an unregistered assignee of the relevant registered charge.
(iv) However, the concept of 'owner's powers' in section 23 was impliedly qualified by the general law *nemo dat* maxim, which meant that B unregistered assignee's powers were not automatically equated to those which B assignee would acquire on registration. They would encompass a power of sale only if such a power was exercisable by an equitable assignee, positioned as B was, under the general law. Newey J ultimately found that this was the case.

None of this contortion was in fact necessary.

Newey J's initial and primary mistake in *Skelwith* came at stage (i), when he assumed that a chargee's powers to sell or otherwise dispose of the *property subject to the charge*—such as those conferred by the LPA 1925, section 101—are 'owner's powers' within the meaning of section 23. This is incorrect. Sections 23–26 deal only with an owner's powers to deal with the *registered estate or charge*—ie, powers to transfer or charge the existing registered charge. These provisions say nothing about the registered chargee's powers to dispose of the *property subject to the registered charge*—eg, to deal with the freehold estate over which a charge subsists, as where a chargee seeks to realise its security by exercising its power to sell the charged property. Instead, the power to deal with the property subject to the charge is conferred by sections 51–52, acting in tandem. Section 51 ensures that any registered charge takes effect as a 'charge by deed by way of legal mortgage'—the only form of legal mortgage now permitted by the LRA 2002.[27] By necessary implication, the registered chargee has all the powers associated with a charge by deed by way of legal mortgage under the general law. However, this still brings risks, since the 'general law' permits a chargee's powers of disposition to be limited in ways that could render a disposition of the charged property vulnerable to challenge, and thereby prejudice the disponee's position—eg, because a chargee's default power of leasing has been excluded. Section 52 seeks to neutralise the risks that such a limitation might present for any disponee from the chargee, via a targeted immunity operating for the disponee's benefit which mirrors that provided by section 26. Crucially, sections 51–52 serve to empower the *registered chargee*, and no-one else—there is no provision corresponding to section 24(b), which extends the powers to a person who is *entitled to be registered* as proprietor of the charge, eg following an assignment of the charge. It follows that the answer to the question of what powers are exercisable by the unregistered assignee of a registered charge *in relation to the property subject to the charge* is simply not resolved by the LRA 2002—by neither sections 23–26 nor sections 51–52. It is purely a matter for the general law.

[27] LRA 2002, s 23(1)(a) (excluding the grant of mortgages by demise or sub-demise from 'owner's powers').

A similar error infects *Stodday*,[28] where B, the transferee of a registered freehold reversion subject to a lease, claimed to have served an effective notice to quit on an agricultural tenant during the 'registration gap'—ie, before he was registered as the new proprietor of the freehold reversion. The tenant contended that it was not open to the new landlord, B, as an *unregistered* disponee, to give such a notice. B countered that section 24(b) enabled such a notice to be given: the ability to give a notice to quit was a 'power' encompassed by section 23, which was extended to B, though not-yet-registered, by section 24(b).[29] The simple and correct answer should have been that section 23, and therefore section 24(b), were simply not relevant. The power to give a notice to quit was not an 'owner's power', because it had nothing to do with a 'disposition' of property. As such, and as in *Skelwith*, the question would simply be for the general law, unregulated by the LRA 2002: could an equitable owner of a freehold reversion subject to a lease serve an effective notice to quit? Unfortunately, Norris J's reasoning was more contorted. Apparently assuming that section 23 'owner's powers' in relation to a registered estate *might* encompass the power to give a notice to quit, he then went on to conclude—following *Skelwith*—that it would not be included in the powers rendered exercisable by an equitable owner of the freehold reversion by virtue of section 24(b), unless the same power was available to such an equitable owner under the general law.[30]

C. The Purpose and Effect of Section 26

The preceding discussion has arguably been only preliminary, since on one reading, it is section 26 which is (substantially) the 'operative' provision when it comes to the LRA 2002's empowerment promise—as betrayed by the fact that it is section 26 which bears the explicit heading, '[p]rotection of disponees'. It warrants quotation in full:

> 26 Protection of disponees
>
> (1) Subject to subsection (2), a person's right to exercise owner's powers in relation to a registered estate or charge is to be taken to be free from any limitation affecting the validity of a disposition.
> (2) Subsection (1) does not apply to a limitation–
>   (a) reflected by an entry in the register, or
>   (b) imposed by, or under, this Act.
> (3) This section has effect only for the purpose of preventing the title of a disponee being questioned (and so does not affect the lawfulness of a disposition).

Several important questions arise out of section 26. The most important relate to its express terms (the focus of Subsection i below) and its interaction with the Act's other two promises—the title and priority promises (the focus of Subsection ii). Some other thorny issues relating to the ambit of section 26 are tackled in Subsection iii. The answers given to all of these questions have a fundamental bearing on the nature, strength and ambit of the Act's empowerment promise.

[28] *Stodday* (n 25).
[29] ibid [33].
[30] ibid [37]–[39].

i. The Nature and Strength of the Empowerment Promise

The empowerment promise embodied in section 26 finds technical expression via a form of a protective 'immunising' or 'cleansing' rule, which addresses the possibility that a person's 'right to exercise owner's powers' might be subject to a 'limitation affecting the validity of a disposition'. The right is 'taken to be free' from any such limitation,[31] though only for the limited purpose of 'preventing the title of the disponee being questioned'.[32] What exactly is the nature and strength of this cleansing rule?

a. An Extended Category of Benefited Parties—*All* Disponees ...?

The first noteworthy question concerns the categories of party who benefit from section 26's cleansing effect.

Assume that B registered proprietor has owner's powers. On its face, section 26 applies, without qualification, to (all) 'disponees' from B—ie, C. This is consistent with section 23's expansive definition of 'owner's [dispositional] powers', which encompasses powers to transfer or grant *any* interest, legal or equitable, and registrable or not.[33] It seems to follow from this that section 26 can have the same cleansing effect in favour of the grantee of a merely equitable, unregistered interest (eg an equitable charge), and indeed, in favour of a disponee of *any* permitted type of disposition, even if no consideration is provided by C disponee. This is explicable in policy terms—it enhances the ability of *any* disponee to rely on the Register as an indicator of the dispositional capacities of the registered proprietor. Nevertheless, this comes at the expense of the holder of a pre-existing interest, X (eg, where X is the beneficiary of a trust, of which B is trustee) which the limit on the registered proprietor's dispositional powers was designed to secure. Section 26 effectively overrides these interests, which receive protection, if at all, via other means—eg, via monetary claims for compensation for losses caused by the 'unlawful' but effective disposition to C. Note too that the effect of section 26 seems to be that even those who obtain *unregistered* interests via a disposition by the registered proprietor receive the benefit of a limited form of 'Midas touch'. For, even if the LRA 2002 does not generally provide any assurance of the validity of such interests (even when protected by entry of a notice),[34] disponees of such interests, if created *by* a registered proprietor, are insulated via section 26 from one potential 'vice' in their creation—ie, lack of *vires* of the registered proprietor/disponor.

Section 26's expansive ambit is particularly noteworthy for two reasons. First, the benefited parties are more generously defined than the beneficiaries of section 58's title promise: the latter is essentially limited to those who become registered proprietors of *registrable* (legal) interests—in particular, freehold/leasehold estates or registered charges.[35] Secondly, section 26's cleansing effect also extends beyond the category of parties who are favoured by the priority promise which is reflected in section 29's special priority rule.

[31] LRA 2002, s 26(1).

[32] LRA 2002, s 26(3).

[33] LRA 2002, s 23(1); see section III(A) above.

[34] LRA 2002, s 32(3).

[35] LRA 2002, s 58(1), which applies in terms only on the entry of a person in the Register '*as the proprietor of a legal estate*'—'legal estate' is defined expansively by reference to the LPA 1925, s 1, to include any estate in land, interest or charge that is capable, under the terms of s 1, of subsisting at law (see LRA 2002, s 132(1)).

As we have discussed in chapter seventeen, the LRA 2002's starting-point is that a later disposition takes effect subject to a prior interest.[36] A later disposition only benefits from the special priority rule that postpones an unprotected prior interest to the disposition—for practical purposes 'cleansing' the later interest—if the later disposition is a 'registered disposition' 'for valuable consideration'.[37] In contrast, section 26's cleansing effect works, on the face of it, in favour of any disponee, registered or not, and whether or not for value.

b. An Unchallengeable or Guaranteed Title ...?

Section 26's extended ambit becomes all the more significant if the 'promise' which it embodies is a *strong* promise—ie, if the disponee's title is indeed rendered unchallengeable. This problem can be illuminated by two comparisons, reflecting our analysis in chapters sixteen and seventeen of the title and priority promises.

First, as we have explained in chapter sixteen, the title promise, as applied by the courts, has not proved to be impregnable in practice. In what have been termed ABC title cases[38]—where B obtains the registered title pursuant to a 'disposition' from A, and B later effects a registered disposition to C—any registered title that C might appear to receive via B as registered proprietor is not wholly immune from defects in the root of B's registered title, eg, as where the A–B 'disposition' was forged. A will sometimes be able to seek rectification as against C's title under schedule 4. If successful, the title promise is only given meaning for C, if at all, via an indemnity award under schedule 8.

Secondly, as we have also explained in chapter seventeen, the priority promise now seems to be similarly vulnerable in what have been termed XYZ priority cases[39]—ie, where Y holds a registered title subject to X's prior right, and Y subsequently effects a disposition to Z. The priority rules applicable at *first* registration may afford Z, as first registered proprietor, priority over X's prior interest. Nevertheless, the apparent postponing effect of sections 11–12 may well be vulnerable to challenge by X, via a schedule 4 application.[40] A similar position now appears to prevail where Z acquires his interest via a disposition of Y's *already-registered* title.[41] In these cases, if viewed in isolation, section 29's special priority rule might seem to confer priority on Z's interest, over X's prior right, unless X's right was relevantly protected by a Register entry or was an overriding interest. The 2001 Law Commission may have taken the view that this ordering effect of section 29 is final and irreversible.[42] However, the courts, and in particular the Court of Appeal in *MacLeod v Gold Harp Properties Ltd*,[43] have read the LRA 2002 differently.[44] On this view, which appears to

[36] LRA 2002, s 28; see ch 17 of this book, section III(C).

[37] LRA 2002, s 29(1) (extended by s 29(4)); see ch 17 of this book, section III(D).

[38] For this language, see A Goymour, 'Resolving the Tension Between the Land Registration Act 2002's "Priority" and "Alteration" Provisions' [2015] *Conv* 253.

[39] See ibid.

[40] See ch 17 of this book, especially sections II(B)(ii) and II(B)(iii).

[41] See ch 17 of this book, section III(D)(iii).

[42] This does not *clearly* emerge from the 2001 Report: Law Commission, *Land Registration for the Twenty-First Century–A Conveyancing Revolution* (Law Com No 271, 2001). However, it does seem to be the view of Charles Harpum, the Law Commissioner who led the Commission's land registration project, as expressed in ch 8 of this book.

[43] *MacLeod v Gold Harp Properties Ltd* [2014] EWCA Civ 1084, [2015] 1 WLR 1249.

[44] See ch 17 of this book, section III(D)(iii).

be accepted by the Law Commission in its 2016 Consultation Paper,[45] section 29's operation is also subject to reversal via schedule 4. Assuming the presence of a qualifying 'mistake' by the Land Registry—eg, in de-registering X's interest, where there was no valid basis for doing so—section 29's effect in postponing X's interest to Z's interest can be reversed via the rectification jurisdiction, such that X's interest can be re-entered on the Register, binding Z's title prospectively. In that event, section 29's priority promise is given meaning for Z, for the future, only via an indemnity award under schedule 8.

How strong, relative to these other promises, is the empowerment promise? Section 26 provides that a 'person's right to exercise owner's powers' is 'to be taken to be free from any limitation affecting the validity of a disposition', which is not reflected by an entry in the Register or imposed by or under the LRA 2002.[46] The (limited) purpose, manifest in section 26(3), is to 'prevent [...] the title of [the] disponee being questioned'. This is susceptible to several possible readings.

The strongest reading is that the disponee's title is *absolutely* immune from any challenge mounted on the basis that the disposition infringed some material limit on the disponor's right to exercise owner's powers. On this view, section 26 ousts any argument that, under the general law, the disposition might be void or voidable—section 26 *nullifies* the effect that infringement of the relevant limit would otherwise have on the disponee's title. As such, the Registrar, in registering such a disposition, would appear to be acting *as the LRA 2002 framework requires*—ie, giving effect to the disposition as a disposition that is not infected by the relevant 'limit'. If correct, this would seem to rule out any argument that the disponee's registration should be reversed by a process of alteration or rectification. This reversal would not bring the Register 'up to date'—the very point of section 26, on this reading, is that the disponee has a good title. Neither has the Registrar made a rectification-justifying 'mistake'—he has performed the duties required of him.

This bold reading might be supported in policy terms. On the one hand, it enhances the Register's reliability. *Any* disponee, registered or not, could rely on the Register as an accurate picture of the dispositional powers of the registered proprietor—whether a natural person, a company, or a statutory body. Such disponees would enjoy *in specie* immunity—and not a mere monetary guarantee—from any risk that there might be a limit on the registered proprietor's dispositional powers which is not publicised by any Register entry. On the other hand, the same rule could also create incentives for registered owners with limited dispositional powers—or more likely, their officers or agents—to ensure that those limits are observed, or at least are made visible via Register entry.[47] It is likely that the 2001 Law Commission did indeed intend section 26 to supply this sort of *in specie* immunity.[48]

Notwithstanding what has just been said, intervening case law provides some fuel for a weaker reading of section 26 and its empowerment promise. This is, in particular, a product of the courts' expansive interpretation and application of the schedule 4 alteration jurisdiction, which might allow an argument to be made that where a disposition infringes

[45] Law Com CP No 227 (n 9) paras 13.152–13.163.

[46] LRA 2002, s 26(1), (2).

[47] A proprietor which acts outside its dispositional power may risk being subject to personal liability for breach of its duties to relevant stakeholders.

[48] See, in particular, Law Com No 271 (n 42) para 4.10.

a material general law limit on the registered proprietor's dispositional powers, registration of the disposition involves a rectification-justifying 'mistake'. If schedule 4 is indeed given this extended effect, then some categories of (registered) disponee may find their interest is nullified, despite the terms of section 26, which suggest that their title should not be called into question. In such cases, the Act's empowerment promise would be given effect in favour of the disponee, if at all, only via a Registry-indemnity.

If this is the likely direction of travel of the case law, it is imperative to develop a rigorous account of the circumstances in which a rectification-justifying mistake can and should properly be identified. With that aim in mind, the remainder of this section considers the appropriate analysis of three hypothetical cases. Each involves a registered proprietor, RP, whose dispositional powers would ordinarily be limited *under the general law*. The question in each case is whether the cleansing effect of section 26's empowerment promise can be reversed via the application of schedule 4—thereby denying the disponee an *in specie* immunity and compelling him, at best, to seek a Registry-indemnity in lieu.

Case 1: RP Effects a Registered Disposition Contrary to a Limit Not Reflected in a Restriction

In Case 1, RP effects a registered disposition contrary to a limit which is not reflected in a restriction in the Register. This cannot be a sufficient basis to call into question the validity of the disposition from RP to a disponee, B. In the absence of a restriction, section 26 cleanses the RP–B disposition, *for the benefit of B disponee*, of what would otherwise be a vice rendering the disposition void or voidable. It would also seem, crucially, that the RP–B disposition is not susceptible to reversal via schedule 4's alteration provisions—neither on the ground of 'correcting a mistake', nor as a means of bringing the Register 'up to date'. Whilst *RP* might have made a 'mistake' in effecting a disposition that infringes the limits on his powers, and may have acted in breach of duty, the prevailing interpretation of rectification-justifying mistakes holds that there must be a mistake *by the Land Registry*.[49] There is no relevant Registry mistake here. Even if the RP–B disposition would have been void under the general law, the voidness is cured by section 26 for the benefit of B, and hence the Registry would not not be mistaken in registering B—the Registry, like B, can treat the RP–B disposition as being relevantly flawless. Neither, seemingly, can it be argued that the Register is out of kilter with the true legal position, and so requires bringing 'up to date' via schedule 4. Even if RP's acting *ultra vires* rendered the RP–B disposition void or voidable under the general law, any resulting invalidity is cured for B's benefit by section 26, which provides that B's title is good. It follows that the Registry acted properly in registering the RP–B disposition, which is now irreversible.

Further thought suggests that the appropriateness of the analysis just offered might depend on closer investigation into the particular reason for the absence of the restriction in the Register. There are several variations on Case 1, which might warrant different outcomes:

(a) where RP failed to seek a relevant restriction;
(b) where the Land Registry failed to enter a restriction, when it ought to have done so; or
(c) where the Land Registry failed to enter a restriction, when requested to.

[49] See ch 17 of this book, text to n 45 et seq and n 186 et seq.

Beginning with Case 1(a), what if the reason for the absence of the restriction is that RP could have—or even should have—sought a restriction to reflect the limit on his dispositional powers, yet failed to do so? RP's omission here does not seem to be a sufficient basis to call into question any later disposition to B, in breach of the limit which the restriction would record. It does not involve any mistake *by the Land Registry*, as would be required for rectification under schedule 4.

Case 1(b) poses more difficulties. There will be certain circumstances in which, on an application made to it and on material before it, the Land Registry *should* have entered a restriction, yet failed to do so. For example, it might be normal procedure, on the registration of a company as a registered proprietor, to inquire into whether there are limits on the company's corporate capacities, which should be reflected in the Register. If the Registrar unreasonably fails to identify such limits, or having identified them, fails to enter a restriction to reflect them, then there are good reasons for thinking that there is a rectifying-justifying 'mistake'. Rather more difficulty arises, however, in explaining the form that any consequential Register-correction might take.

On the one hand, B disponee, who received an interest pursuant to a registered disposition by RP that breached limits that were not entered in the Register, might legitimately say that *his registration* was not a mistake. Section 26 renders the RP–B disposition immune from challenge for infringement of a limit on RP's dispositional powers that was not recorded via a restriction. On this view, the Registrar's mistake in failing to enter a restriction is not rectification-justifying.

On the other hand, it might be argued (i) that the Registrar *did* make a mistake in not entering a restriction, prior to the disposition to B, and (ii) that the rectification jurisdiction may allow the remoter *consequences* of that earlier mistake—ie, B's subsequent registration—to be reversed.

The case law on the availability of rectification in ABC title cases[50] contains traces of both strands of reasoning, but ultimately seems to lean towards the availability of rectification in favour of the earlier interest-holder. In such cases, courts have contemplated that the combined effect of sections 58 and section 23 might mean that C's registration is not itself mistaken, and yet C might nevertheless be vulnerable to de-registration on the basis this is required to correct the consequences of an *earlier* mistake—ie, the registration of B.[51]

Whether the approach adopted in ABC title cases is legitimate in the context of the empowerment promise depends on the strength of the assurance which the legislature intended that promise to offer. The stronger view, discussed above, suggests that section 26 will insulate a disponee from any attempt to argue that the registration of his disposition was a mistake, or that his title should be compromised to correct the *consequences* of the Registry's earlier mistake, in omitting a restriction. This would leave any relevant stakeholders prejudiced by the disposition (whom the power limitations were supposed to protect) to seek a Registry-indemnity for the consequences of the 'mistake'—the omission of the restriction—which is left uncorrected. The weaker view would suggest that RP might

[50] See ch 16 of this book, section III(D)(ii).

[51] eg, *Ajibade v Bank of Scotland plc* [2008] EWLandRA 2006_0163; *Knights Construction (March) Ltd v Roberto Mac Ltd* [2011] EWLandRA 2009_1459, [2011] 2 EGLR 123; *Barclays Bank plc v Guy (No 2)* [2010] EWCA Civ 1396, [2011] 1 WLR 681; *Patel v Freddy's Ltd* [2017] EWHC 73 (Ch). See also our discussion in ch 16 of this book, section III(D)(ii).

invoke a similar line of reasoning to that employed in the ABC title cases, noted in the preceding paragraphs. RP (or other interested stakeholders) might then succeed in a rectification claim vis-à-vis B disponee. If so, any empowerment promise made by section 26 to B disponee is only realised, if it all, via a Registry-indemnity.

There is no obviously right answer as to which of the two views should be preferred. It must ultimately depend on whether it is thought that there is a private (or even public) interest in ensuring that limits on a registered proprietor's dispositional powers are *specifically* enforced—by enabling any disposition that infringes them to be unwound/nullified—which overwhelms the disponee's claim to specific protection. Is it appropriate, for example, for the law to sanction the irreversible alienation of land belonging to a public authority or a charity, which may have flouted its own constitutional limits?[52]

Turning finally to Case 1(c), there is little more that needs to be said. Case 1(c) is substantially equivalent to Case 1(b). In both cases, an omission by the Registry, in circumstances where the Registry *should* have acted, has meant that a limit that would otherwise have been reflected in the Register, is not. This has subsequently enabled a disposition to occur and be registered, which would not otherwise be possible. The two variations warrant similar treatment.

Case 2: The Land Registry Overlooks a Restriction

Case 1 concerned problems arising from a failure to enter a restriction in the Register. A different type of problem arises in Case 2, where RP's registered title *is* subject to a restriction, which the Registry subsequently overlooks. As a result of this oversight, a disposition by RP to B is registered, in breach of the restriction. Here, it seems clear that B's registration was a 'mistake', and that it should be susceptible to correction via schedule 4. Arguably, no indemnity should be available to B, since the empowerment promise is not even engaged. B is given no immunity, via the express terms of section 26, from the effect of limits that are reflected in a restriction recorded in the Register.[53]

Case 3: RP Makes a Disposition to B, Beyond His General Law Dispositional Powers, Which is Not Registered

Two further puzzles are raised by our earlier observation that section 26's empowerment promise extends, on its face, to *any* disponee from RP, registered or unregistered.[54] The puzzles are illustrated by Case 3—where RP effects a disposition to B, in breach of his general law dispositional powers, which is *not registered.*

The first condundrum concerns the significance of restrictions in the Register. In relation to registrable dispositions by RP, restrictions are an obvious, concrete way of giving legal force to the limit on RP's dispositional powers. A restriction is technically a mode of

[52] The 2001 Law Commission seems to have had in mind these kinds of limits, in recommending what became s 26 of the LRA 2002: Law Com No 271 (n 42) para 4.3; see too the discussion in C Harpum and J Bignall, *Registered Land: Law and Practice under the Land Registration Act 2002* (Bristol, Jordans, 2004) para 7.1. Of course, even if the alienation is irreversible, the parties responsible for the *ultra vires* disposition *might* still incur a personal liability—a possibility preserved by the limited terms of s 26(3). See Law Com No 271 (n 42) para 4.11.

[53] LRA 2002, s 26(2).

[54] See section III(C)(i)(a) above.

Register-entry that regulates *Registry*-behaviour—ie, the circumstances in which a disposition should, or more likely should not, be registered. However, what happens where a disposition is effective *without registration*—as where the disposition is not a 'registrable' disposition (eg, the creation of a short lease[55] or the creation of an inherently equitable interest), or is registrable but is nonetheless effective in equity prior to its registration (eg, the express creation of an easement)? Where such an unregistered disposition from RP to B is effective without registration, is there any way of limiting RP's dispositional powers, within the terms of section 26, bearing in mind that the very same provision deems those powers to be unimpeded? The best answer is that, within the context of section 26, the entry of a restriction has a modified significance. It is significant not only as a mechanism for ensuring that the RP–B disposition will not be *registered* in breach of the terms of the restriction. The restriction also has the further, indirect effect, through section 26(2), of qualifying section 26(1)'s empowering rule. Section 26(1) provides, in terms, that a relevant limit will not affect the validity of a disposition. However, and crucially, section 26(2) then excludes from this curative provision a limit which is made visible by the restriction—whether or not the RP–B disposition could be, and is, ultimately registered.

A second condundrum, related to the first, concerns the legal status of an unregistered disposition which is effected in favour of B, in breach of general law limits on RP's dispositional powers. Manifestly, there is no role for schedule 4 (and thus schedule 8) here, since there is no *Registry entry* in favour of B that is susceptible to reversal by any process of Register amendment. Can the RP–B disposition nevertheless be treated as invalid? Our conclusions in the preceding paragraph suggest that the answer may depend on whether a relevant restriction had been entered in the Register prior to the RP–B disposition: section 26's cleansing effect in favour of *any* disponee is inherently qualified by the restriction, whether or not the RP–B disposition could be, and is, ultimately registered. It follows that the unregistered disposition to B should still be treated as void/voidable under the general law, despite section 26: because of the restriction, the empowerment promise has never been made to this category of disponee. It also follows, conversely, that if a relevant restriction had not been entered in the Register, section 26 would mean that RP's dispositional powers were unlimited, and the RP–B disposition would stand.

c. Conclusions as to the Nature and Strength of the Empowerment Promise

Two conclusions could be drawn from the preceding discussion. First, section 26's empowerment promise serves to cure the RP–B disposition from invalidity, but only to the extent that the limits on RP's dispositional powers are not reflected by a restriction in the Register. Secondly, B benefits from this promise whether or not the RP–B disposition is registered. Crucially, in this latter regard, the empowerment promise extends more broadly than do the title and priority promises, whose benefits are confined only to *registered* proprietors/disponees.[56]

[55] ie, the grant of lease for a term of seven years or less, which (subject to a narrow list of exceptions) is not a 'registrable disposition' (LRA 2002, s 27(1), (2)(b)(i)).

[56] There is one notable exception: the priority promise afforded via s 29 is extended to grantees of leases with terms of seven years or less, which are not registrable dispositions (LRA 2002, s 29(4)).

ii. The Relationship Between the Empowerment Promise and the Act's Other Promises

Important additional light may be cast on the LRA 2002's empowerment promise via an investigation of its relationship to the Act's other two promises. The Law Commission's 2001 Report suggests that the Commission appreciated that what we have termed the title, priority and empowerment promises were targeted at three different mischiefs.[57] Each has a distinct technical statutory basis within the resulting LRA 2002. However, it is also a feature of the Act that the substantive triggering conditions for each of the promises, and their nature and strength, differ. One resulting question is whether these differences are justified. A second set of questions is considered in this section. Is it clear which promise, if any, is engaged on any given facts? And what is each promise's proper scope, relative to the other promises? If the answers to these questions are not clear, cases may be resolved inappropriately.

Within the LRA 2002, it is the empowerment promise that, at first sight, appears the most emphatic of the three promises. In terms, section 26 expresses an intention to provide a strong measure of immunity from title-challenges to disponees as a general class—an immunity which is unusually strong and wide, and certainly stronger and wider than the title and priority promises, as drafted and interpreted in practice by the courts.[58] This difference makes it crucial that section 26 is not over-extended. An over-expansive interpretation of the 'limitations' that are cleared by section 26 might result in section 26 overlapping with and contradicting the Act's other clearing provisions—and the promises which they embody.

To understand the proper ambit of section 26, relative to those other provisions, we must return to the three underlying mischiefs to which the promises, and their associated statutory provisions, are properly addressed.

The first problem concerns whether a person who is named in the Register as proprietor (RP1) has a title which is free from defects. A risk of defects arises in any system in which title is most frequently acquired derivatively, via transfer from a prior owner: unless and until any defect is 'cured', there is a risk that the party (RP1) who might appear to be the owner may in fact have either a flawed title, or no title at all. According to the *title promise*, analysed in chapter sixteen, registration of RP1 as proprietor is constitutive of title. Whilst RP1 is not thereby necessarily immunised from problems with the *transaction* by which he acquired his title from the immediately preceding owner, parties who later deal with RP1 as registered proprietor (ie RP2, etc) certainly obtain protection from problems with the root of RP1's registered title—eg problems that might, under the general law, render the transfer of title to RP1 void or voidable.[59]

The second problem, analysed in chapter seventeen, concerns whether the title of a registered proprietor, RP1, is encumbered by any prior interests belonging to another party, X,

[57] Law Com No 271 (n 42) paras 4.2 and 9.29 ff.

[58] See section III(C)(i) above, considering the nature and strength of the empowerment promise; cf our discussion of the title and priority promises, in chs 16 and 17 of this book, respectively.

[59] As explained elsewhere, the nature of this protection is not pre-ordained. It could involve an immunity from loss of title, or only a monetary guarantee/indemnity: see, eg, ch 16 of this book, section I, and ch 17 of this book, sections II(B)(ii) and III(D)(iii).

and whether such encumbrances will persist against a later disponee of the registered title (ie, RP2) or of a derivative interest. If the Register is to offer a reliable picture of the state of title to land for third parties dealing with RP1, then these parties must have some immunity from prior interests that affected the registered title but were not disclosed in the Register. This is the effect of the *priority* promise. A limited class of third party disponees taking from RP1 is privileged by an assurance of priority over all prior interests affecting RP1's registered title, other than those encumbrances which are protected by entry in the Register or qualify as overriding interests.

The third problem, and the focus of this chapter, concerns whether RP1's own powers to deal with the registered title are limited in ways that would render a purported disposition to a disponee vulnerable to challenge—void or voidable, at law or in equity. This seems to be the target of the *empowerment* promise. A third party dealing with the registered proprietor, RP1, can assume that he is invested with the full range of owner's dispositional powers, and that these are exercisable by him without limitation. A limitation cannot be invoked vis-à-vis the disponee, to invalidate the disposition to him, unless it was made visible to the disponee via an entry in the Register.

Although the empowerment promise's limited function seems clear, there is nevertheless a real risk that it might be over-extended unless care is taken when interpreting section 26 of the LRA 2002. The main danger of such over-extension is that the empowerment promise might then interfere with, and even eclipse, the operation of the other two promises—with potentially detrimental and unintended consequences. The most troublesome boundary, in practice, lies between the empowerment and the priority promises.

Recall that section 26 provides that RP1's right to exercise owner's powers is 'taken to be free from any limitation affecting the validity of a disposition'. What exactly is a relevant 'limitation' which is cleared by this provision? More specifically, could it be argued that *any* prior encumbrance affecting a registered proprietor's title (eg an easement held by X) is a relevant 'limitation' on a registered proprietor's dispositional powers, because the existence of the encumbrance means that any disposition by RP1 to another will take effect subject to the priority rules found in sections 28–30? Such an expansive reading of section 26's clearing rule must be resisted—it would undermine the operation of the priority promise afforded by sections 29 and 30. For example, it would mean that where RP1's registered title is subject to an unregistered prescriptive easement in favour of X, RP1 could confer an unencumbered title on any disponee via the empowerment promise, free from X's easement. This would eclipse the operation of the priority rules in sections 28–29 which would ordinarily afford priority to such a prior legal easement, even against a registered disponee who paid valuable consideration, owing to the easement's status as a protected overriding interest.[60]

Is it possible to avoid this unpalatable conclusion? Section 26's ambit might be restrained via three possible interpretations of the provision.

[60] LRA 2002, sch 3, para 3. This overriding status is subject to certain express qualifications: such an easement will not override unless: (i) it was within the actual knowledge of the disponee at the time of the disposition; (ii) it would have been obvious on a reasonably careful inspection of the servient land at the time of the disposition; or (iii) it has been exercised during a period of one year that ends with the day of disposition.

a. A Strained Reading of Section 26(2)(b)

First, it might be possible to prevent the empowerment promise from invading the territory of the priority promise via a strained reading of section 26(2)(b). This states that section 26(1) will not deem a registered proprietor's right to exercise owner's powers to be free from a limitation which is 'imposed by, or under, this Act'. If the priority rules in sections 28–30, which may protect prior encumbrancers like X, are themselves regarded as a 'limitation' imposed by the Act on a registered proprietor's powers, then the empowerment promise must itself yield to the priority rules. However, this is not a natural interpretation of section 26(2)(b), and it may not persuade the courts.

b. Prior Encumbrances are not 'Limits' Cleared by Section 26

Secondly, and more securely, the empowerment promise could be reined back to the same extent via the assumption that a prior encumbrance is not *in itself* a relevant 'limitation' on the 'right to exercise owner's powers'—prior encumbrances, as a general category, do not inherently affect the *validity*, as opposed to the *priority*, of a disposition. On that assumption, if RP1 is the registered freehold proprietor subject to X's lease, the question whether a transferee of the registered freehold title is bound by the lease turns on the application of the priority rules in sections 28–29. This is a priority issue, and not a *vires* (or empowerment) issue. The registered proprietor *can* lawfully transfer the freehold, and X's lease does not impair the validity of that transfer. The transfer simply takes effect subject to X's lease, if at all, in accordance with the LRA 2002's priority rules. The transferee of the freehold cannot rely on section 26 to achieve any larger cleansing effect.

This narrower reading of section 26 seems consistent with dicta in the Court of Appeal's recent decision in *Mortgage Express v Lambert*.[61] There, the two joint registered proprietors (Y1/Y2) had purchased a registered lease (subject to lease-back) from X, in circumstances that enabled X to ask that the transaction be set aside as an 'unconscionable bargain'. The question arose whether Z's registered charge, which had been granted by the joint registered proprietors (Y1/Y2), might be subject to X's equity to rescind, on the basis that—as X had remained in occupation—X's equity might have the status of an overriding interest under schedule 3, paragraph 2. The Court of Appeal ultimately held that it did not. Schedule 3, paragraph 2—which is, of course, part of the LRA 2002's priority rules—did not *enhance* the priority of an earlier right, like X's. It merely *preserved* its priority, to the extent of preventing its subordination via the operation of section 29. It would not elevate the prior right if the right would *otherwise* be postponed—ie, if the right was inherently subordinate to the disposition by Y1/Y2 to Z, on general law principles. That was the case on the facts: X's right was overreached by the grant of the mortgage pursuant to the provisions of section 2(1)(ii) of the LPA 1925.

For present purposes, the real interest in *Lambert* lies in the discussion of section 26 earlier in Lewison LJ's judgment. Having first explained that the joint registered proprietors (Y1/Y2) had been entitled, *from the time of completion*, to exercise 'owner's powers', which

[61] *Mortgage Express v Lambert* [2015] EWCA Civ 555, [2017] Ch 93.

included the 'power to charge the estate at law with the payment of money',[62] Lewison LJ went on to quote from section 26, before continuing:[63]

> There was no limitation in the register at the time of the mortgage; nor was there a limitation on the validity of the disposition imposed by the Act itself. If there were an overriding interest that interest would not affect the *validity* of the disposition consisting of the grant of the mortgage. The mortgage would take effect subject to it.

Though rather elliptical, this passage seems to reveal an implicit assumption that it is a mistake to treat any prior encumbrance, to which a disposition might otherwise be subject, as a limitation on the right to exercise owner's powers which can be cleared by section 26. The thrust of Lewison LJ's words is that where Y registered proprietor's title is subject a prior interest in favour of X, this interest will often not technically prevent or invalidate a further disposition by Y in favour of Z. For example, a transfer of freehold title or the grant of a lease by Y to Z would not technically be *invalidated* by a pre-existing easement in favour of X. The Y–Z disposition would be valid, but simply take effect subject to X's prior right, via the Act's priority rules. In such a case, the prior encumbrance, which does not affect the validity of the Y–Z disposition, would not be a 'limitation' within the clearing effect of section 26. That must be right. A more expansive view could bring any classic XYZ priority dispute within the ambit of section 26, and would run the risk of subverting the targeted priority rules found in sections 28–30.

c. Prior Encumbrances Are Not 'Limits' Cleared by Section 26, Except Where They Take the Form of a Right to Challenge the Disponor's Acquisition of Title

There are, however, passages in *Lambert* that might betray some receptivity to a third and intermediate position, which holds that section 26 will clear a disponee's title of some, but not all, prior encumbrances. A few lines further on in his judgment, Lewison LJ found 'strong support' in the Law Commission's 2001 Report for the view expressed by Z chargee's counsel, that section 26's purpose was to prevent the disponee's title from being called into question, and that:[64]

> in effect this means that if a right is asserted as an overriding interest, and that right is a right to impugn the title acquired by the disponee, then section 26 defeats that right.

This seems to imply that whilst not *every* prior encumbrance belonging to X is cleared by section 26, there may be some forms of prior right—consisting of a right to call into question the title of Y registered proprietor-disponor—which would be. This would potentially encompass a wide range of possible rights/claims held by X:

(i) a right/equity to rescind a transfer of title by X to Y on conventional grounds (eg, for misrepresentation, duress, undue influence, or on the basis that it is part of an 'unconscionable bargain');

[62] ibid [26], noting ss 23(1)(b), 24(b) LRA 2002; '[o]nce completion of the TR1 had taken place [Y1/Y2] were entitled to be registered as proprietors. Consequently, they were entitled to exercise owner's powers, which includes power to charge the estate at law with the payment of money: sections 23(1)(b) and 24(b) of the Land Registration Act 2002'.

[63] ibid [27] (emphasis in original).

[64] ibid [27], apparently endorsed ibid [28].

(ii) an equity to rectify a conveyance of title by X to Y, on the ground of mistake;
(iii) a statutory claim of X to rectify the Register as against Y.

Each of these involves a claim via which X might impugn Y's title, and potentially also that of Z, Y's disponee. On the law as currently understood, each of these claims affords X some form of proprietary 'interest' that affects Y's registered estate, and might in turn bind Z, if X's right is afforded protection by the priority rules found in sections 28 and 29—ie, X's right may persist against Z, a later registered purchaser, if X's interest is protected via a notice in the Register, or is overriding. However, counsel in *Lambert*—with Lewison LJ's apparent support—appears to have argued that the result which would be reached via the Act's priority provisions must be read subject to the operation of section 26, which would effectively clear X's interest from the title conveyed by Y to Z disponee, if X's interest entitled him to call into question the validity of his earlier disposition to Y.

With respect, this third interpretation does not seem to be a legitimate reading of the LRA 2002. It deploys cleansing provisions that were designed for one mischief, to address a different mischief. Where X has a right to call Y's title into question, the underlying problem, which the LRA 2002 must address, is whether a later disposition by Y to Z is affected by the defect in the 'root' of Y's statutory registered title—whether the defect arises because Y acquired title pursuant to a forged transaction, or a voidable transaction, or otherwise. This was not the mischief which the Law Commission intended section 26's empowerment promise to address. The Commission's central concern was with situations in which there was no basis for challenging the *vesting* of title in Y, but where Y nevertheless had *limited dispositional powers*, reflecting Y particular character/status—eg, as a statutory body with limited statutory powers, as a company with corporate capacities limited by its articles of association, or as a trustee with limited equitable powers. The focus was a problem related to the *vires* of the registered proprietor, and not his *title* per se.

d. Which is the Preferable Interpretation?

Stepping back, it seems that the second and narrower interpretation of section 26—which would not permit section 26 to cleanse the Y–Z transfer from *any* prior encumbrance—seems to better accord with the provision's purpose. This preference is also reinforced by five further considerations.

First, the third view does not represent a very natural interpretation of section 26. A right/equity to rescind is certainly a circumstance that can render Y disponor's title vulnerable to challenge, and if allowed wider ambit, could infect the title acquired by a later disponee, Z. As such, it is certainly a circumstance that might be said to '*affect the validity*' of the subsequent Y–Z disposition. But is it also right to regard it as a 'limitation' on Y disponor's 'right to exercise owner's powers'? A case where X has a right/claim to impair Y's title as registered proprietor via an equity to rescind is rather different from a case where title is properly vested in Y as registered proprietor subject to an express trust for X. In this latter case, Y trustee's powers/authority to deal with the registered estate may well be limited, and Y trustee will be acting wrongfully/unlawfully in dealing with the registered estate outside his authority or otherwise in breach of his duties as a fiduciary. In contrast, a person whose title is merely *voidable* is differently placed. He has full powers to deal with the property under the general law; he is not a fiduciary; and pending a legally effective act of or order for rescission, he has no other duties that can limit his dealings.[65] No onward dealing by him with that property can be regarded as 'unlawful' or 'wrongful'. If that is right, then it is difficult to see how it can be said that there is any relevant limitation on Y's 'right' to exercise owner's powers. And if X's right/equity to rescind is not such a limitation, it is not a vice whose effect can be cleared via section 26 without more—even if the right/equity allows X to challenge the validity of any X–Y transaction, pursuant to which Y obtained his registered title.

Secondly, if a right/equity to rescind a transfer of title is a relevant limitation which is cleared by section 26, then the role of section 116 within the LRA 2002 regime is greatly reduced. This provision confirms that such an equity is an 'interest capable of binding successors in title'. If the third interpretation were adopted, this statutory confirmation of the equity's status might be material only in enabling the priority of that interest to be preserved via the entry of a notice—on the assumption that a limitation consisting of an interest made visible via entry in the Register would be excepted by section 26(2) from section 26(1)'s effect. An equity to rescind, if not protected in that way, would effectively be overridden by section 26's clearing effect; and it could not be re-elevated in priority via reliance on its status as an overriding interest.

The Law Commission's 2001 Report does not suggest that section 26 was meant to operate in this expansive way. Indeed, a significant number of cases might be decided or certainly reasoned differently, if it were the intended effect. In particular, numerous cases that have assumed that a right to rescind might be an overriding interest would be wrongly decided. Furthermore, elaborate discussions of whether there may be a basis for 'rectification' in ABC title cases, if the A–B transaction is voidable—eg, is there any mistake that might support rectification of the title that C acquired via the transaction with B?[66]—might seem unnecessary. The short answer would be: that B was registered proprietor; that B had owner's powers; that the limit on B's right to exercise those owner's powers, consisting of A's equity to have the A–B transaction set aside, is cleared by section 26 for the benefit of disponees from B; that as a matter of express provision in the LRA 2002, C's title therefore cannot be called into question.

Thirdly, a similar point can be made about other kinds of claim that X might have, which might result in a challenge to Y's title. These would include an equity to rescind a transfer of title to Y on any conventional grounds,[67] as well as an equity to rectify a conveyance for mistake, which has previously been regarded as an interest that can exist as an overriding interest, including by Lewison LJ himself.[68] The same process of reasoning would also suggest an obvious answer to a (controversial) line of cases which have assumed that a *statutory* right to rectify Y's title might amount to an overriding interest, binding a later disponee who could otherwise rely on section 29's special priority rule.[69] The answer would be that *any* disponee would be secure, in any case, as a result of section 26. If that were indeed the case,

[65] See, eg, the limited view adopted of the position of a party subject to a right/equity to rescind in *Lonrho plc v Fayed (No 2)* [1992] 1 WLR 1, 11–12 (Millett J).

[66] See recently, *NRAM plc v Evans* [2017] EWCA Civ 1013.

[67] eg, misrepresentation, duress, undue influence, unconscionable bargains.

[68] See *Cherry Tree Investments Ltd v Landmain Ltd* [2012] EWCA Civ 736, [2013] Ch 305.

[69] *Malory Enterprises Ltd v Cheshire Homes (UK) Ltd* [2002] EWCA Civ 151, [2002] Ch 216 [68]–[70].

then the Law Commission has misperceived the required solution in its 2016 Consultation Paper, where it was thought necessary to clarify that the statutory right to rectify cannot be an overriding interest.[70]

Fourthly, an expansive interpretation of section 26 will render the most common species of equity—an equity to rescind—unusually insecure. Under general property law, a mere equity has traditionally been treated as a more fragile species of interest, to the extent that a bona fide purchaser of any competing interest, legal or equitable, could take free from it. In its 2001 Report, the Law Commission seemed to consider that there was no reason from a priority point of view why such an equity should be inherently more fragile than a full equitable interest.[71] And yet the suggested interpretation of section 26 would indirectly produce exactly this result: such equities would in practice be *even more* fragile. Except in the fairly unlikely event that they are the subject of a Register-entry, they would be of no avail against *any* later disponee—whether of a registrable/registered interest or of an unregistered interest, and whether or not for value.

Finally, the *Lambert* decision itself cannot be regarded as good authority for an expansive interpretation of section 26. The case was actually decided on the basis that X's equity to rescind could not have overriding status, and so would not have priority vis-à-vis the registered charge that Z obtained by grant from Y1/Y2 joint registered proprietors, because X's equity had been *overreached* by that conveyance. However, had the expansive interpretation of section 26 been correct, then the Court of Appeal's elaborate analysis of section 29, and of the conditions for overreaching, would have been wholly unnecessary. Section 26 alone would have given the registered chargee—and indeed any other disponee—a title that was immune from challenge.

To sum up, the persistence of a prior encumbrance affecting a registered title raises a priority problem, which is appropriately resolved via the LRA 2002's priority rules and the Act's priority promise. Courts should avoid any over-extended reading of section 26's ambit, which would capture some or all of the same situations.

e. A Further Problem: The Impact of the Doctrine of Overreaching

There is one further issue concerning the boundary between the Act's three promises that requires analysis. This concerns how the general law's concept of overreaching and associated statutory provisions (including sections 2 and 27 of the LPA 1925) interrelate with the three key promises made by the LRA 2002—and in particular the empowerment promise that section 26 underpins. Section 26 is obviously *relevant* to overreaching, to the extent that—according to the dominant view in recent times[72]—overreaching is the consequence of a dispositional power. The central question is whether section 26 actually ensures that a relevant disposition has overreaching effect, or merely *facilitates* the process by addressing one key obstacle to the operation of overreaching under the general law.

[70] Law Com CP No 227 (n 9) paras 13.60–13.63, 13.83–13.87 (dealing with what is labelled the 'Malory 2' argument).

[71] Law Com No 271 (n 42) paras 5.32–5.36.

[72] This 'modern' view can be traced to C Harpum, 'Overreaching, Trustees' Powers and the Reform of the 1925 Legislation' [1990] *CLJ* 277.

This issue can be tested by imagining a case where Y's title as registered proprietor is subject to a trust in favour of X. Y thereafter purports to *gift* his title to Z. What is Z's position?

If this situation is directly analysed via the LRA 2002's priority rules, then the answer seems to be as follows. Section 29 could not apply: Z, as a donee, would not have provided the 'valuable consideration' needed to trigger section 29's special priority rule. Section 28 would instead govern. As such, X's prior interest might prevail vis-à-vis Z unless postponed by *some other rule*. And that immediately raises the question—*what other rule might be material?* In particular, to what extent, and on what assumption, might section 26 be material, if at all?

The short answer to this question is that section 26 is indeed material, but that its role—what we have described as its cleansing or clearing effect—is subtler than might first appear. As explained above,[73] section 26 does not embody a priority rule—ie, it is not intended to enable a disponee, Z, to acquire an interest free from a prior encumbrance which affected the registered title of the disponor, Y, and might otherwise affect him. Nor does section 26 embody a more limited title-clearing provision addressed to problems which infect the root of the registered title of the disponor, Y—ie, it is not designed to immunise the disponee, Z, from a right/claim of X to call Y disponor's title into question. Rather, section 26 is a provision narrowly focused on circumstances that affect the *vires* of Y, the registered proprietor-disponor, rather than his *title*. Any *vires* limit, if not reflected in a Registry entry, is effectively overridden, for the benefit of disponees like Z.

It follows from this that if section 26 has implications for X's ability to assert his beneficial interest against Z, more careful analysis is needed. The existence of the trust has two concurrent, but different, implications. It means: (i) that X beneficiary has an *interest* in the registered estate; and (ii) that Y trustee's *equitable powers/authorities* to deal with the trust subject-matter are limited. X's beneficial *interest*—(i)—is not itself a 'limitation' on Y's 'right to exercise owner's powers', within the meaning of section 26, which that provision directly serves to clear. If there is a relevant 'limitation' on B trustee's 'right to exercise owner's powers', within the meaning of section 26, it comes from (ii)—from limitations on Y's *equitable powers/authorities* as trustee to deal with the trust subject-matter. It is these limits, and not X's beneficial interest as such, that section 26 immediately affects and serves to clear for the benefit of disponees, like Z.

If we view X's interest simply as a prior encumbrance affecting Y's registered title, then it is the priority rules in sections 28–29 that are immediately engaged. Since section 29 is not triggered by Y's gratuitous disposition to Z, X's interest prima facie prevails. Crucially, however, section 29 does not exhaust the circumstances in which an earlier interest might be subordinated to a later interest; other principles, derived from the general law and preserved by the LRA 2002, can have this effect.[74] One of these is the familiar device of overreaching.

Overreaching is by nature a priority principle, insofar as it involves the subordination of a prior interest to a later disposition involving the same title.[75] Section 26 is not inherently a priority rule, for reasons already explained, but it can have priority consequences, insofar

[73] See section III(C)(ii)(b) above.

[74] For extended discussion of this point, see ch 17 of this book, section III(C)(i)(c) above.

[75] See, eg, *City of London Building Society v Flegg* [1988] AC 54 (HL), where the grant of registered charge by joint registered proprietors was effective to overreach the beneficial interests of third parties; those interests were thereby postponed/subordinated to the registered charge, and could not re-gain priority as overriding interests, based on the beneficiaries' actual occupation.

as it may *facilitate* the overreaching of a prior interest, such as the beneficial interest of X. The mechanism by which it does so is rather subtle.

Section 26 does not expressly provide that 'the disposition shall, without more, be treated as valid', nor that 'the disposition shall, without more, be effective to overreach the prior right'. What section 26 states is that 'a person's right to exercise owner's powers in relation to a registered estate or charge is taken to be free from any limitation affecting the validity of a disposition'. In other words, in a case where overreaching might be in issue, section 26 merely address the problem that the registered proprietor's dispositional powers may be limited. It does not go further, and guarantee that overreaching occurs—because there may be other requirements for overreaching to operate, which are not addressed by section 26, and may remain unsatisfied. The question that must be asked is a simple one: if there was no such limitation on the registered proprietor's powers, could X's interest be overreached by the disposition according to the general law's principles of overreaching? There will inevitably be some situations where the fact that the 'limitation' on the powers of Y registered proprietor is effectively overridden by section 26 will not be sufficient to free Z from X's prior interest. This would be so, for example, if X's interest is not by its nature overreachable, or if there are other conditions for overreaching to operate which have not been observed—in particular, those found in section 2 of the LPA 1925, examined further below.[76]

These points can be illustrated by reference to the example, given earlier, where Y, who holds the registered estate as sole trustee for X, gifts the registered title to Z. In general, such a gratuitous disposition of a trust asset is likely to be *ultra vires* and a breach of trust. Section 26 seems to cure this *vires* problem, for the benefit of any disponee, like Z—the relevant 'limitation' on Y trustee's equitable power/authority is effectively overridden. That removes one major problem that might render Y's disposition to Z incapable of overreaching X's interest. Nevertheless, it does not necessarily remove all problems, and so cannot ensure that Z will get a clear title. This would depend, in the first instance, on whether X's interest is a type of interest that is susceptible to being overreached by this type of disposition. If it is not, then the curing of the *vires* problem for Z's benefit will not suffice to enable overreaching to occur—the disposition will potentially be subject to X's prior interest, on ordinary priority principles. If, in contrast, it *is* an overreachable type of interest—as is certainly true of beneficial interests arising under a trust—then the curing of the *vires* problem may enable overreaching to occur, but only if any other conditions for overreaching are satisfied. This inevitably raises some difficult questions, which are imperfectly resolved in the authorities and the literature, as to what those other conditions might be.[77] One particularly important question concerns whether section 2 of the LPA 1925 exhaustively defines the circumstances in which overreaching is possible. If it does, is there any general need for two trustees to effect the conveyance, as one reading of section 2 might suggest, or is this merely a product of the capital monies payment rule in section 27 of the LPA 1925? If the former is the right view, and two trustees are generally required, then it must follow that Y's disposition to Z could not overreach X's interest, despite section 26's effect in curing the *vires* problem: because only one trustee is involved there would be an outstanding obstacle

[76] See section III(C)(iii)(c) below.

[77] ibid.

to overreaching under the general law. If, however, the latter view is the right one, then Y's disposition *might* overreach X's interest: since the transaction is a gift, the capital monies payment rule is not engaged, two trustees are not required, and a gratuitous conveyance by one alone might be overreaching.[78]

Stepping back, the positions of X, Y and Z might be summarised as follows. Section 26 nullifies any equitable limitations on Y's powers to dispose of the subject-matter of the trust, imposed by the terms of the trust or by the general law. Once those limitations have been cleared by section 26 for the benefit of a disponee like Z, it becomes a question for the *general law* whether the Y–Z disposition has overreaching effect. Any confusion or controversy as to when overreaching is permissible under the general law is not something which section 26's empowerment promise can or should resolve. It is a matter for resolution exclusively by the general law.

iii. Other Limitations on the Ambit of the Empowerment Promise

The significance of the empowerment promise within the LRA 2002 framework is a product of not only its force, but also of its *ambit*. It is a targeted promise, whose ambit is limited by design. Some limits follow from the express terms of sections 23–26 and—being part and parcel of the land registration legislation—do not compromise the legislative ambitions. However, there are also some other implicit limits that must be clearly perceived. There is a delicate balance to be struck by the LRA 2002. If these implicit limitations are not recognised—and if section 26's operation is therefore over-extended—there is a risk that greater security for disponees is achieved only at the expense of others' interests, or that section 26 may undermine other provisions of the Act that are specifically targeted at the relevant mischief. In this section, which builds on some of our earlier discussion in this chapter, we expose five limits on the ambit of section 26's empowerment promise—some explicit, others implicit.

a. Limits Reflected By An 'Entry in the Register' or 'Imposed By, or Under, this Act'

First, section 26(2) expressly qualifies section 26(1), by excluding limitations that are: (i) reflected by an entry in the Register, or (ii) imposed by or under the LRA 2002. Neither exception is surprising. They make it clear that the Act is not intended to supply an *absolute* guarantee of dispositional capacities—but only, primarily, to address the risk of *concealed* vulnerabilities. Dispositional powers can still be effectively limited, if this is done in a manner that brings the limitation to a disponee's attention—first and foremost, by the entry of a restriction. The ambit of (ii) is more inscrutable, although its basic aim seems legitimate—ie, to prevent stultification of other provisions of the Act, and therefore to defer to the operation of those other provisions.

b. The Allocation of the 'Right to Exercise Owner's Powers'

Secondly, section 26(1) should also be read subject to the effect of section 24. In short, it will not protect a disponee from the risk that the purported disponor is not a person who,

[78] See *State Bank of India v Sood* [1997] Ch 276 (CA).

under section 24, has the 'right to exercise' owner's powers—ie someone who is either the registered proprietor,[79] or entitled to be registered as proprietor.[80]

It is very unlikely that section 26 was intended to absolve a disponee of the need to verify that the party with whom he is dealing *is* the registered proprietor, for the purpose of section 24(a). No-one has so far suggested that in the case of, eg, a forged disposition apparently effected by the registered proprietor, but in fact effected by a fraudster, the disponee can invoke section 26 to insulate himself from the fact that the fraudster is not a person entitled to exercise owner's powers.

Similarly, it is very unlikely that section 26 was intended to protect a disponee from the need to verify that the party with whom he is dealing, D, who is *not* presently the registered proprietor, is nonetheless *entitled to be* registered as proprietor within the meaning of section 24(b). Such an entitlement will arise as a consequence of 'off-Register' events, which are not susceptible to discovery by Register inspection. There are thus 'off-Register' investigations that will still legitimately be needed, eg, into whether the registered proprietor is bankrupt and D is indeed his trustee in bankruptcy, or into whether there has been a formal disposition to D which is valid under the general law, but which has not yet been completed by registration.

The conclusion that the disponee will not benefit from the LRA 2002's empowerment promise in such circumstances could be reached via two routes. First, and most obviously, the empowerment promise is simply not engaged if the relevant disponor was not invested with owner's powers by section 24. More technically, section 26(1) simply does not bite: the circumstance that a person is not a person who is invested with a right to exercise owner's powers is not a relevant 'limitation' on the right to exercise owner's powers which section 26(1) is designed to cure. Secondly, and alternatively, the same conclusion could be reached in any event via section 26(2)(b). Section 26(1) cannot override the limitation 'imposed by' the LRA 2002, which is reflected in the express terms of section 24: the right to exercise owner's powers is conferred—and conferred only—on the person who really 'is' the registered proprietor or, if not, who really 'is entitled to be' registered as proprietor.

c. The General Law's Overreaching Conditions

Thirdly, it remains a difficult question whether the general law's limitations on overreaching might be overcome by section 26(1). Any answer to this question is made complicated because of thorny underlying debates about the nature and basis of the concept of overreaching within land law. It is further complicated by the failure of the Law Commission, in its publications that preceded the LRA 2002, to engage explicitly with those debates, and more particularly, to explain how (if at all) the concept of overreaching fitted within what became the overall LRA 2002 scheme.

Modern discussion of overreaching in English law tends to begin with Charles Harpum's influential 1990 article.[81] Key insights included: (i) that 'overreaching' was a concept that had a wide general law basis, and was the corollary of a *power of disposition*; (ii) that section 2 of the LPA 1925 did not alter the basic general law position that an *ultra vires* disposition

[79] LRA 2002, s 24(a).
[80] LRA 2002, s 24(b).
[81] Harpum, 'Overreaching, Trustees' Powers and the Reform of the 1925 Legislation' [1990] *CLJ* 277.

by trustees would not overreach; (iii) that the conditions expressed or incorporated by section 2 of the LPA 1925—in particular, the requirement found in section 27(2)[82] to pay any capital monies to at least two trustees—were *additional* requirements that limited the overreaching effect even of what might be an *intra vires* disposition.

In the context of land held on what, since the Trusts of Land and Appointment of Trusts Act ('TLATA') 1996, is known as a 'trust of land', this understanding of overreaching suggested that disponees might face a significant risk—a disposition by trustees, if *ultra vires* their limited powers of disposition, would not overreach. Harpum argued that the 1925 draftsman's distinctive solution, in the context of *registered land*, involved arming registered proprietors with unlimited dispositional powers, in the absence of the entry of a restriction in the Register—a role he attributed to section 18 of the LRA 1925. Harpum's account was later challenged by Graham Ferris and Graham Battersby, who insisted that it overlooked the distinction, material in the context of trusts, between (i) legal capabilities and (ii) equitable authorities.[83] In their view, section 18 of the LRA 1925 dealt only with the *legal* capabilities of a registered proprietor. The *equitable* powers/authorities of trustees, as unregistered or registered proprietors of an estate in land, were dealt with elsewhere—by section 28 of the LRA 1925.[84] Ferris and Battersby argued that this analysis brought particularly serious implications following the enactment of the TLATA 1996. Whilst the TLATA 1996 undoubtedly *extended* trustees' default powers of disposition,[85] it also arguably *qualified* those powers in ways that—in a significant but uncertain range of circumstances—could render a disposition by trustees *ultra vires*, and *ex hypothesi*, incapable of overreaching the beneficiaries' interests.[86] Purchasers from trustees of *unregistered* land were afforded specific protections by the TLATA 1996; but purchasers from trustees of *registered* land were not.[87] Accordingly, if Ferris and Battersby were right, and if section 18 of the LRA 1925 did not have the effect that Harpum believed, purchasers of registered land were significantly more exposed to the risk that dispositions might not overreach beneficiaries' interests than was widely assumed. Such purchasers could not, as might otherwise be the case, rely merely on the fact that they had dealt with two registered proprietors/trustees of land; they also had to ensure the trustees had acted *intra vires* the terms of the trust.

This particular controversy is probably now only of historic interest. Although the Law Commission did not specifically advert to this underlying debate in its 2001 Report, it is generally assumed—including by Ferris and Battersby—that the LRA 2002 was intended to address the problem, and make good the perceived deficiency in the protections afforded to parties dealing with trustees of registered land. The LRA 2002's protection for disponees from invalidating circumstances is explicit: in contrast to the LRA 1925, it is not left to be inferred from a general grant of dispositional powers (now 'owner's powers') to a registered

[82] LPA 1925, s 27(2), incorporated via s 2(1)(ii).

[83] See especially G Ferris and G Battersby, 'The Impact of the Trusts of Land and Appointment of Trustees Act 1996 on Purchasers of Registered Land' [1998] *Conv* 168; G Ferris and G Battersby, 'The General Principles of Overreaching and the Reforms of 1925' (2002) 118 *LQR* 270; G Ferris and G Battersby, 'The General Principles of Overreaching and the Modern Legislative Reforms, 1996–2002' (2003) 119 *LQR* 94. Cf G Ferris, 'Making Sense of Section 26 of the Land Registration Act 2002' in E Cooke (ed), *Modern Studies in Property Law—Volume 2* (Hart Publishing, Oxford, 2003).

[84] See LPA 1925, s 28.

[85] TLATA 1996, s 6(1).

[86] ibid, ss 6(2)–(8), 8.

[87] ibid, s 16; cf s 16(7) ('This section does not apply to registered land').

proprietor. As we have seen, section 26 provides, in terms, that a person's right to exercise owner's powers is to be taken to be 'free from any limitation affecting the validity of the disposition'. The Law Commission's 2001 Report that preceded the LRA 2002 indicates that section 26 was intended, inter alia, to encompass limits on trustees' (equitable) powers/authorities—eg, a provision of a trust deed, which required certain consents for the exercise of trustees' powers, which were not in fact obtained.[88]

It follows that the position now seems to be reached that, in the absence any restriction in the Register, a disponee who deals with trustees of registered land can effectively proceed on the basis that their *equitable* dispositional authority is co-extensive with their *legal* dispositional capability (to borrow the Ferris/Battersby terminology): ie, that any disposition, pursuant to the 'owner's powers' invested in the trustees as registered proprietors, is within their equitable authority.

Nevertheless, there is one outstanding and rather important problem. What is the relationship between section 26 of the LRA 2002 and sections 2 and 27(2) of the LPA 1925, which restrict the ambit of overreaching in the context of land transactions? On one view, section 26 protects disponees *regardless* of whether the requirements of sections 2 and 27(2) are satisfied. On another view, compliance with sections 2 and 27(2) remains a fundamental requirement for a disposition by trustees of registered land to overreach, notwithstanding the general terms of section 26. If the former is the correct view, then *Williams & Glyn's Bank Ltd v Boland*[89] would now be decided differently, and many cases decided under the LRA 2002 must have been decided *per incuriam*. A disponee would take free of a beneficiary's interest under a pre-existing trust, even if the disposition was by a sole trustee of land and the capital monies (if any) were not paid as directed by section 27(2) of the LPA 1925.

In fact, almost no-one believes that that is the intended effect of section 26.[90] Indeed, it is clear that the Law Commission in 2001, and more recently in 2016, takes the view that sections 2 and 27(2) of the LPA 1925 remain conditions for overreaching. However, the outstanding problem is that the Law Commission has never explained *how* that conclusion be achieved within the terms of the LRA 2002 as enacted, and consistently with prevailing accounts of how overreaching works.[91] We think that an answer can be found, as follows.

Section 26(1)'s protective effect is expressly limited to circumstances that bear on a person's '*right* to exercise owner's powers', that might call into question the validity of a disposition. These words are apt to encompass a trustee, who—whilst invested with owner's powers—might have more limited equitable authority. Under the general law's rules on overreaching, of which section 2 of the LPA 1925 is a key component, a disposition which is *ultra vires* cannot overreach. This particular vulnerability is cured by section 26(1) of the LRA 2002, in the context of dealings by trustees of a *registered* estate—it effectively requires the relevant disposition to be *treated as* an authorised disposition, and thus capable of overreaching, for the purposes of determining its proprietary effects. However, it is far

88 Law Com No 271 (n 42) para 4.10.

89 *Williams & Glyn's Bank v Boland* [1981] AC 487 (HL).

90 cf the different arguments of Nicola Jackson, which yield the same conclusions regarding the intended effect of the LRA 1925 and the LRA 2002: N Jackson, 'Overreaching in Registered Land Law' (2006) 69 *MLR* 214; N Jackson, 'Overreaching and Unauthorised Dispositions of Registered Land' [2007] *Conv* 120.

91 cf the important, sustained exploration of the proper interpretation of the LRA 2002, s 26, addressed principally to resolving this conundrum, offered in Ferris, 'Making Sense of Section 26' (n 83).

less obvious that section 26(1) is also addressed to a further, distinct problem that might prevent overreaching, namely non-compliance with sections 2 and 27(2) of the LPA 1925.

The key to unlocking this problem is to see that section 26(1) does not speak to and cure problems that do not bear on a person's '*right*' to exercise owner's powers. If the question is asked, 'what is overreaching?', the answer is that overreaching is *not in itself* properly described *as a power of disposition*, nor *a fortiori*, *as an 'owner's power'*, to use the language of sections 23, 24 and 26. Rather, overreaching is in effect a priority or ordering principle which is potentially engaged by the exercise of a power of disposition. Consistently with this, it is a mistake to think that the conditions in section 2 of the LPA 1925 can fall within the clearing effect of section 26(1). They are not 'limitations' that affect a registered proprietor's '*right*' to exercise 'owner's [dispositional] powers' (which in the context of registered proprietors who are trustees, describes their equitable authorities). They are conditions that limit the overreaching consequences that could otherwise follow, *as a corollary of the due exercise of those dispositional powers.* In short, and reinforcing conclusions that we have drawn above,[92] whilst section 26(1) may remove the obstacle to overreaching presented by an *ultra vires* disposition (ie a disposition that breaches the terms of the trust), it does not remove the need to comply with section 2 of the LPA 1925, if overreaching is to occur.

d. The Authority of Persons Acting For a Registered Owner

Fourthly, even within its sphere of application, section 26's empowerment promise only speaks to the dispositional powers of the proprietor of a registered estate or charge, and not to the authority of those who may appear to be acting on the proprietor's behalf (eg, an agent) to alter the owner's legal position. The LRA 2002 regime has nothing to say about this.[93] Take, for example, a situation where T, purporting to act as A's agent, makes an unauthorised 'disposition' of A's registered title to B. If registered as proprietor, B can take advantage of the title promise offered by section 58. However, section 26's empowerment promise is not engaged. B is not assured by the LRA 2002 that T disponor, being neither the registered proprietor, nor someone entitled to be registered as proprietor, had dispositional owner's powers. Crucially, this means that B's registered title is vulnerable to reversal via schedule 4's alteration regime. A is entitled to argue that T lacked dispositional capacity, and that B's registration was unauthorised and should be reversed.

Note that the line between the registered proprietor's capacity and an agent's authority to act for the owner is potentially troublesome. For example, in the case of a company: (i) the company's capacity to dispose of its land might be subject to limitations under its constitution; or (ii) (more likely) the company's capacity might be relevantly unlimited, but the officers to whom its dispositional powers are delegated might themselves have limited authority. On a narrow view, which seems consistent with the examples given by the Law Commission,[94] section 26 at best addresses problem (i). If that is right, then

[92] See section III(C)(ii)(e) above.

[93] This statement remains good notwithstanding LRA 2002, s 24(b). Section 24(b) does not operate by investing the party entitled to be registered as proprietor with authority to act for the still-registered proprietor. It invests him with distinct dispositional powers, exercisable on his own behalf, and for his own benefit. Indeed, in a typical case, where the registered proprietor has conveyed his title to another, who has not yet become registered in his place, the still-registered proprietor technically retains dispositional powers but may hold them in the capacity as trustee for the transferee.

[94] Law Com No 271 (n 42) para 4.3.

section 26 has a limited application and curative effect. No promise is given that officers, when acting as agents for a company, have authority to bind the company to transactions involving the company's land that fall within the company's corporate capacity. As such, it falls on disponees, or their legal advisers, to satisfy themselves that the relevant agent is indeed authorised/deemed to be authorised under the general law to effect the disposition.

e. The Powers of Holders of Unregistered Interests

Fifthly and finally, the empowerment promise embodied in sections 23–26 and 51–52 extends only to the dispositional powers of proprietors of '*registered* estates' or '*registered* charges'. *Ex hypothesi*, it does not speak to the powers of proprietors of *unregistered* interests. It follows that the disponee of an unregistered interest remains vulnerable in accordance with the general law's rules. In this respect, the LRA 2002 is justifiably consistent across all three key promises. Such unregistered interests, which are not investigated and verified by the Registry, do not benefit from the title promise;[95] dispositions involving such interests do not trigger the priority promise;[96] and disponees are not afforded any empowerment promise as regards the dispositional powers of the unregistered disponor.

IV. Future Challenges

Although pivotal within the LRA 2002 registration regime, the empowerment promise has been the least discussed and litigated of the three promises. This is unfortunate.

Closer investigation of sections 23–26 reveals a wide range of interpretative difficulties concerning the ambit of the empowerment promise. We have seen, for example, that the courts have not always understood that section 23, and thus section 26, deals only with the *dispositional* powers ordinarily associated with the status of owner of a relevant estate or charge.[97] They have not always seen that section 24(b) was intended to achieve an exception to the general law's *nemo dat* starting-point, to enable a person who is not yet the registered proprietor to effect a disposition *as if they were*.[98] They have also not yet closely investigated the nature of the general law 'limitations' on dispositional powers which section 26 was, and was not, designed to cure for the benefit of disponees.[99] The risks of error can be significant and will cut more than one way. In some cases, section 26's curative operation will be unduly confined to the detriment of disponees. More often, the risk is the opposite—of unjustified over-extension, to the detriment of prior interest-holders.

These problems assume heightened significance owing to two other features of the section 23–26 framework. First, the empowerment promise benefits a wider category of disponees than the Act's title and priority promises. *Any* disponee, whether or not registered,

[95] See ch 16, section III(A).

[96] See ch 17, section II(A) (concerning first registration) and section III(D)(i) (concerning dispositions of registered titles). Note the exception concerning the creation of certain short unregistrable leases: section 29(4) extends, via a fiction of registration, the priority promise to such leases, provided that valuable consideration is paid.

[97] See section III(A) above.

[98] See section III(B) above.

[99] See section III(C)(ii), (iii) above.

and whether or not for valuable consideration, seems to benefit from section 26's curative effect.[100] Secondly, it remains unclear whether the empowerment promise is a stronger promise than the title and priority promises.[101] Will section 26's curative operation be final, as the 2001 Law Commission probably intended, or will future courts decide that the effect of section 26 can be reversed via a schedule 4 application—as is true of sections 58 and 29? If the latter, then the empowerment promise, like the title and priority promises, will turn out to be a promise that is sometimes realised via a Registry-indemnity at best.

Looking ahead, it will be important for future reform discussions of the LRA 2002 to consider whether these differences can be justified, and if not, how the Act's three promises should be more closely aligned. In the meantime, the courts must take particular care not to over-extend section 26's curative operation beyond its legitimate ambit and ambitions. Above all, this will require them to resist an over-expansive interpretation of the '*limitations*' on owners' dispositional powers that will be cleared for the benefit of disponees. Such caution is vital to preserve the internal integrity of the registration regime—preventing the empowerment promise from invading territory that is properly within the remit of the other promises.[102] But it is also important to ensure the Act's due interaction with the general law.

The most difficult area of intersection, and the intersection that seems most often salient in practice, is the relationship between section 26's operation and the general law's concept of overreaching. In particular, which general law limits on overreaching are overridden via section 26, and which (if any) remain unaffected?[103] In part, the problem here stems from a consistent failure of law reformers to address this key intersection explicitly and in depth.[104] However, the far bigger problem, which has indirectly emerged from this chapter's exploration of the empowerment promise, is not in truth a problem with the promise, or with section 26, or indeed with the wider LRA 2002 framework, at all. Rather, it is the continuing uncertainty that surrounds the *general law's* concept of overreaching in this context—its precise nature and ambit, and its legitimate sphere of operation in modern land law, and in particular, within our modern registration framework. This uncertainty cannot be tolerated. When it operates, overreaching is a potent mechanism through which prior rights can be subordinated to later dispositions, *beyond* the circumstances in which this is provided for by the LRA 2002's priority rules, and potentially without compensation.[105] Without a clear steer from modern law reformers, and forced to apply inscrutable provisions of the LPA 1925[106]—now almost a century old—there has been a consistent trend in recent decades of courts giving overreaching an *extended* reach.[107] Whether they have always been right to have done this as a matter of law, or as a matter of sound policy, is far from clear. Independently of the problems presented by sections 23–26 and the empowerment promise, it is high-time that overreaching in land law was looked at comprehensively afresh.

[100] See section III(C)(i)(a) above.
[101] See section III(C)(i)(b) above.
[102] See section III(C)(ii) above.
[103] See sections III(C)(ii)(e) and III(C)(iii)(c) above.
[104] ibid.
[105] See esp ch 17 of this book, sections III(C)(i)(c) and III(D)(v).
[106] LPA 1925, ss 2, 27.
[107] See, in particular, *Flegg* (n 75); *Sood* (n 78); *Birmingham Midshires Mortgage Services Ltd v Sabherwal* (2000) 80 P & CR 256; *Lambert* (n 61); *Baker v Craggs* [2016] EWHC 3250 (Ch), [2017] 2 WLR 1483.

E

The Mechanical Challenges of Land Registration in a Modern Society

19

Lessons from Scottish Land Registration Reform: Changes Under the Bonnet

EMMA WARING[1]

I. Introduction

Scotland holds the oldest public land register in the world, the General Register of Sasines ('the Sasine Register') dating back to 1617. The Sasine Register is a register of copies of deeds, which currently operates in parallel with the map-based Scottish Land Register established by the Land Registration (Scotland) Act 1979 (the '1979 Act'). The Land Register now operates under the Land Registration etc (Scotland) Act 2012 (the '2012 Act') and remains a map-based register of titles. The Keeper of the Land Register ('the Keeper') has overall responsibility for various registers, including both the Sasine Register and the Land Register, which are held and managed by the Registers of Scotland ('RoS').[2] RoS is a non-ministerial department of the Scottish administration and holds trading fund status.

On 8 December 2014, the 2012 Act introduced sweeping legal changes, which fundamentally shifted the basis of the registration system in Scotland. The land registration reforms contained in the 2012 Act followed many of the recommendations made by the Scottish Law Commission ('SLC'). The aim of the 2012 Act was to bring registration law explicitly into alignment with property law. Significant changes were introduced that affected: the mirroring of property rules and registration systems; approaches to defective applications; cadastral mapping; the realignment of rights; and the extent of state guarantee of title.

[1] I am grateful to Martin Dixon, Amy Goymour and Stephen Watterson for inviting me to the Cambridge Private Law Centre and Cambridge Centre for Property Law's conference on Land Registration in 2014. I also owe a great debt of gratitude to the Keeper and staff at the Registers of Scotland for their warm welcome, patience, and erudite explanations of Scottish land registration practices. Thanks also to Caroline Hunter and Richard Nolan for discussions relating to the chapter. All errors and omissions are my own.

[2] RoS actually holds 17 public registers including: the Land Register; the General Register of Sasines; Chancery and Judicial Registers (Register of Inhibitions, Register of Deeds and Probative Writs in the Books of Council and Session, Register of Judgments); the Crofting Register; Register of Sites of Special Scientific Interest; Register of Community Interests; Register of Protests; Register of Service of Heirs; Register of the Great Seal; Register of the Cachet Sea; Register of the Prince's Seal; Register of the Quarter Seal; Register of Crown Grants; Register of Sheriffs Commissions; and the Register of Hornings.

The SLC vividly described the proposed changes to the 1979 Act as being 'a matter merely of engineering' or a change 'under the bonnet'.[3] The SLC's stated aim for the 2012 Act was that it should 'improve the performance and reliability of the engine and keep to a minimum the new things that the driver will have to learn'.[4] The SLC recommended that the 1979 system be 'stripped down and rebuilt so as to enable it to deliver according to high performance specifications'.[5] Despite the SLC averring that the process involved merely 'changes under the bonnet' or tinkering with technical rules, the 2012 Act *was* a significant—albeit much-needed—overhaul of the internal workings of the Scottish land registration system. Whilst the work of RoS and its products under the 2012 Act might appear to much of the outside world to be very similar, there has in fact been a sea change in how the final product is created.

This chapter considers the 'changes under the bonnet' introduced by the 2012 Act from two perspectives. First, the chapter surveys the background to the 2012 Act and some of the key technical legal 'changes under the bonnet' that it brings about. The second section of the chapter shifts focus to consider the implementation of the 2012 Act from a viewpoint which will be less familiar to doctrinal scholars: that of RoS staff. This approach seeks to illuminate a different type of change 'under the bonnet' involved during the transition process to the new regime: changes in thinking and approach.

II. Scottish Registration Regimes

Land registration is a highly technical and opaque world to almost everyone other than those working directly in the field. However, it is of fundamental importance both for individual property owners and for society at large. Despite this, the work carried out by land registries and their staff is frequently misunderstood and often all but invisible to the outside world. In one sense, this apparent invisibility is a testament to the success of a land registration system. As the SLC aptly noted, '[m]uch law is like plumbing: useful but unexciting and seldom thought about except when it goes wrong'.[6] Nowhere is this more true than when considering land registration rules. The ideal registration system should work seamlessly and invisibly, just like plumbing. It is at its very best when it can be relied upon to such an extent that the engineering and efforts required to obtain reliable, comprehensive, timely and efficient results are unobtrusive.

As noted above, Scotland operates the Sasine Register and the Land Register. Eventually, the Sasine Register will be phased out altogether as the triggers for first registration start to bite further and remaining properties transfer across to the Land Register.[7] Alongside

[3] Scottish Law Commission, *Discussion Paper on Land Registration: Void and Voidable Titles* (Scot Law Com DP No 125, 2004) para 5.43.

[4] Scottish Law Commission, *Report on Land Registration—Volume 1* (Scot Law Com No 222, 2010) para 37.1.

[5] ibid, para 1.5.

[6] Scots Law Com No 222 (n 4) para 1.1.

[7] See, eg, the closure of the Sasine Register to standard securities on 1 April 2016. New securities must now be added to the Land Register, thus triggering first registration of the affected plot. It is no longer possible to record in the Sasine Register deeds including a disposition, a lease, an assignation of a lease or any other deed relating to a registered plot of land or to a lease registered in the Land Registers.

existing triggers such as changes in ownership, there are several other methods that should increase the number of registered titles. These include: (i) the possibility of voluntary registration;[8] (ii) Keeper-Induced Registration ('KIR'), where the Keeper has a power under the 2012 Act to move titles from the Sasine Register onto the Land Register, without an owner-initiated application; and (iii) extended triggers for first registration, including the closure of the Sasine Register to standard securities.[9]

There are obvious inefficiencies in operating two registers that are governed by completely different legislation and approaches, in addition to the practical challenges posed by first registrations, so there is great sense in encouraging Sasines titles to move to the Land Register. There is, nevertheless, still some way to go: by the end of December 2015 title coverage had reached 59.3%, representing around 27.8% of the land mass in Scotland.[10] However, the registration rate is poised to accelerate significantly following the Scottish Ministers' 'invitation' in May 2014 for the Keeper to complete the Land Register by 2024, and the stated aim of registering all public sector land in Scotland by 2019.[11] Whether or not these goals will be achieved is still a moot point. The difficulties faced by RoS in registering all land in Scotland should not be underestimated, given the number of titles that do not even appear on the Sasine Register, and the significant quantities of coastal and tidal land. Early indications are, however, promising.[12] The changes introduced by the 2012 Act, some of which will be discussed in this chapter, will play a large part in making the goal of total registration possible.

A. The General Register of Sasines

The Registration Act 1617 established the legal basis for the General Register of Sasines and ordained that any transfer of land after this time had to be recorded in it. The copies of deeds contained in the Sasine Register can be searched by name or by property address, but there is no instant answer to questions about ownership. Instead, title has to be deduced by interpreting the deeds—an often complex and laborious process which requires a detailed and expert understanding, and which offers no guarantee of title at the end of the process. It is also worth noting that there continue to be significant parcels of land in Scotland that have never appeared on the Sasine Register, because their ownership last changed hands before the General Register of Sasines was created, and there has not been a deed in the subsequent 400 years. These parcels of land include the Universities of St Andrews, Glasgow and Aberdeen. The University of Edinburgh, which was founded in 1583, predates the Sasine Register, but Old College had been owned by the City Council, so a deed exists

[8] This is advantageous since a 25% discount for voluntary application fees has been guaranteed until mid-2019.

[9] A standard security is the only fixed charge available over land in Scotland and is the Scots law equivalent of an English legal mortgage. Standard securities were introduced by the Conveyancing and Feudal Reform (Scotland) Act 1970 and apply to 'heritable property' (equivalent to freehold property in English law) and leasehold property with a term of more than 20 years. Individuals, companies and limited liability partnerships may grant a standard security.

[10] Registers of Scotland, *10-Year Property Market Report 2006-2016*, 3 (2016). See <www.ros.gov.uk/property-data/property-statistics/the-10-year-report> accessed May 2017.

[11] <news.gov.scot/news/target-set-to-register-all-of-scotlands-land> (25 May 2014).

[12] See J King, 'Completion of the Land Register: The Scottish Approach' in F McCarthy, J Chalmers and S Bogle (eds), *Essays in Conveyancing and Property Law in Honour of Professor Robert Rennie* (Cambridge, Open Book Publishers, 2015) ch 16.

for this transfer.[13] In acting as a record of deeds, the Sasine Register understandably could say nothing about either the underlying validity of the recorded deeds or the quality of the title as a whole. All of this changed under the 1979 Act, as described below.

B. The 1979 Act

The advantages of a land registration system were obvious and led to the enactment of the 1979 Act, which revolutionised Scottish land registration practices. The 1979 Act was particularly brief due to pressures of parliamentary time—it amounted to only 30 sections in total, with even fewer than that concerning land registration itself. Whilst legislative brevity can be good, it became apparent that the statute was too brief to be completely fit for purpose: the 1979 Act was criticised for containing so many holes that it was disparagingly described as resembling 'a Swiss cheese'.[14] The relative absence of statutory guidance meant that RoS *had* to take the lead in putting flesh on the bare bones of the 1979 Act. Thus it can truly be said that RoS 'to a remarkable extent' invented the Scottish system of land registration under the 1979 Act.[15]

Whereas the Sasine Register merely recorded deeds and said nothing about their underlying soundness, or about the validity of the title as a whole, the 1979 Act instituted a wholly different approach. The mere act of registration itself took on constitutive effect, no matter whether there were underlying defects in the transactional documents or in the title itself. The 1979 Act took a bright line rule approach to determining title by giving the Keeper the so-called 'Midas touch'.[16] As in the famous myth, the Keeper's 'touch', or decision to register, turned a title into perfect 'gold'. But it could also, as in the original myth, have an unfortunately indiscriminate effect—everything would become 'golden' or unassailable by virtue of registration even where the transaction was in effect 'dross' or based on an underlying deed that was voidable or even void. This led to problems because land registration law in Scotland would operate to give title in circumstances where normal property law rules would not have done so. In particular, the 'Midas touch' contradicted long-held notions of *nemo dat*, which prevent a non-owner in property law terms passing on ownership to anyone else. The SLC criticised this contradictory result as an example of unhelpful 'bijuralism',[17] which led to overly complex and confused rules.

The immediate indefeasibility of title created by the 1979 Act produced a simulacrum of certainty but created other problems. O'Connor rightly notes that immediate indefeasibility undermines general property law rules by 'neutralising their sanctions', given that an invalid transfer will be 'cured' by registration. O'Connor convincingly argues that purchasers in this type of system have 'little incentive' to query documents, since registration cures every fault. As such, the 'likely result is that more forgeries and invalid instruments will slip through to registration, causing more losses'.[18] It is not in a client or practitioner's interest

[13] Scot Law Com No 222 (n 4) para 33.13, n 25.
[14] ibid, para 3.5.
[15] ibid, para 3.6.
[16] Scottish Law Commission, DP No 125 (n 3) para 5.34.
[17] ibid, para 1.11.
[18] P O'Connor, 'Registration of Invalid Dispositions: Who Gets the Property?' in E Cooke (ed), *Modern Studies in Property Law—Volume 3* (Oxford, Hart Publishing 2005) ch 3, 60–61.

in this type of system to query the underlying documents. Instead, the focus is on getting the transaction 'past' the registration hurdles and getting it entered onto the Register, at which point it becomes 'golden' and the affected parties can heave a sigh of relief.

These problems were compounded under the 1979 Act by the protection against rectification offered to a proprietor in possession. Where the proprietor was registered, particularly in the absence of a qualification on indemnity,[19] their position was nearly unassailable. This was partly because the 1979 Act system greatly favoured the proprietor in possession: it made it almost impossible, save for very limited circumstances, to rectify the Register where this would prejudicially affect the proprietor in possession, unless they consented—which was unlikely in practice.[20]

C. Calls for Reform and the Genesis of the 2012 Act

These and other problems with the 1979 Act soon became evident. Prime among them was its underlying conceptual hollowness. The 1979 Act was legitimately criticised by Professor George Gretton, a former Law Commissioner at the SLC, as having all of the 'intellectual sharpness of a mashed potato'.[21] The 1979 Act created a new world of registered land in Scotland, but unfortunately did so in the abstract, divorcing the registration system from underlying rules of Scottish property law. As such, under its system of 'bijuralism', incoherence reigned. It is fair to say that RoS itself was well aware of the problems with the registration law and its practices. Over time calls for reform grew more pressing.

At the Keeper's request, the SLC was asked to review the 1979 Act and the SLC's Sixth Programme in 2000 included land registration, although work did not begin until 2003. Over the course of the SLC's work on land registration, two members of staff from RoS—Martin Corbett and John Glover—were seconded directly to the SLC. Additionally, staff from the Scottish Government Legal Directorate and the Office of the Scottish Parliamentary Counsel joined RoS on secondment to ensure that channels of communication between all institutions were as transparent and open as possible.

Three Discussion Papers[22] were produced during Professor Kenneth Reid's tenure as a Law Commissioner. A Report,[23] including a draft Land Registration (Scotland) Bill, was published in February 2010 under his successor, Professor George Gretton. The SLC's discussion papers and reports are notable throughout for the clarity and immediacy of their language when dealing with the highly technical area of land registration law. The colourful phrases, analogies and metaphors employed by the SLC proved to be of significant help in

[19] A 'qualification on indemnity' will arise where the Keeper will not guarantee a title or part of it due to a lack of evidence during the registration process about whether the title is wholly valid and marketable. The new owner will normally take out indemnity insurance and/or wait until the passage of time (eg, 10 years) cures the defect in title.

[20] 1979 Act, s 9(3).

[21] GL Gretton, 'Comment on *Kaur v Singh*' 1997 SCLR 1075, 1085.

[22] Scottish Law Commission, *Discussion Paper on Land Registration: Void and Voidable Titles* (DP No 125, 2004); Scottish Law Commission, *Discussion Paper on Land Registration: Registration, Rectification and Indemnity* (DP No 128, 2005); and Scottish Law Commission, *Discussion Paper on Land Registration: Miscellaneous Issues* (DP No 130, 2005).

[23] Scot Law Com No 222 (n 4).

translating registration law for a wider audience. Notable examples include their descriptions of the Keeper's role in registration as being akin to the 'Midas touch'; their labelling of the new approach to lodgment of correct applications as the 'one-shot principle'; and their presentation of the battle between good faith purchasers and dispossessed owners as a battle about who got the 'mud or money'.[24]

Canny law reformers are aware of the value that colourful phrases may have not only in explicating reform proposals, but also in harnessing political support for legislative change. Professor MacQueen, one of the SLC's current Law Commissioners, observed that it was a 'vital necessity' on joining the SLC to consider how projects and proposals would benefit Scottish society and the economy. Accordingly, the analogy between plumbing and land registration in the SLC's Report echoed governmental economic concerns and 'played into ... the SNP Government's self-image of managerial competence' with terms that had been fortuitously 'written to catch the prevailing wind in government'.[25]

The SLC's Report was thus implemented by the Land Registration etc (Scotland) Act 2012, and came into force on 8 December 2014. The 2012 Act has been described as 'a chip off the Gretton and Reid block' where '[i]ncoherence is replaced with coherence and brevity with appropriate depth'.[26] The stated aim of the 2012 Act was to 'improve the performance and reliability of the engine and to keep to a minimum the new things that the driver will have to learn'.[27] The SLC recommended that the 1979 Act system be 'stripped down and rebuilt so as to enable it to deliver according to high performance specifications'.[28]

III. Legal Changes Brought About by the 2012 Act: Stripping Down and Rebuilding the Engine

The 2012 Act places much of RoS's practice under the 1979 Act into statutory form. This chapter takes a deliberately impartial stance towards the innovations introduced by the 2012 Act, since substantive neutrality is a central tenet of the author's ongoing research into decision-making processes at RoS. However, for the purposes of placing the qualitative research data discussed later in this chapter into context, the main legal changes introduced by the 2012 Act are outlined below.

Under the 2012 Act, the component parts of the Register are explicitly specified as being: (a) the title sheet record; (b) the cadastral map; (c) the archive record; and (d) the application record.[29] Every plot of registered land has a searchable title sheet that defines the property extent on the Ordnance Survey map and includes details of price, current owners,

[24] This phrase originated in TW Mapp, *Torrens' Elusive Title: Basic Legal Principles of an Efficient Torrens' System* (Edmonton, University of Alberta, Faculty of Law, 1978) para 4.24.

[25] E Cooke and H MacQueen, 'Law Reform in a Political Environment: The Work of the Law Commissions' in D Feldman (ed), *Law in Politics, Politics in Law* (Oxford, Hart Publishing, 2013) 148.

[26] AJM Steven, 'A Golden Era? The Impact of the Scottish Law Commission on Property Law' in W Barr (ed), *Modern Studies in Property Law—Volume 8* (Oxford, Hart Publishing, 2015) ch 2, 29.

[27] Scot Law Com No 222 (n 4) para 37.1.

[28] ibid, para 1.5.

[29] 2012 Act, s 2.

mortgage details and any conditions affecting the property. Previously, the cadastral map, the archive record and the application record were not specified by legislation and had arisen as a matter of administrative practice within RoS. The 2012 Act thus explicitly recognised and endorsed the inclusion of these elements within the land registration scheme.

The archive record consists of copies of all documents submitted to the Keeper, those that the Keeper has to include under Land Register rules and other documents that the Keeper deems to be appropriate.[30] However, despite the archive record's acknowledged existence, parties relying on the title sheet record are not deemed to have constructive knowledge of the archive record's content.[31]

The application record is a snapshot at any one time of any pending applications for registration and extant advance notices existing in relation to the title sheet.[32] Every registered plot of land (including separate legal tenements,[33] such as mineral rights or a flat in a tenement building), as well as registered leases, now has their own title sheet that contains all of the registration information about that property. The title sheet itself contains a property section, proprietorship section, securities section and a burdens section, much as in the English registration system.

A. Cadastral Map

The 'cadastral map' is an important innovation that is explicitly provided for by the 2012 Act. This comprises a map showing the 'totality of registered geospatial data' for each cadastral unit—or registered plot of land. The RoS use a digital mapping service ('DMS') which enables plans staff to map and display the extent of cadastral units based on information drawn from the property address, grid reference or map name. The underlying 'base map' is specified in the 2012 Act as being the Ordnance Map produced by the Ordnance Survey, or another mapping system or combination of systems satisfying the requirements ordered or prescribed by the Scottish Ministers.[34] There are naturally areas of Scotland which have not been mapped by the Ordnance Survey but which might still be registered, such as seabed titles, and provision is made for these to be registered with a dataset of co-ordinates if necessary. There are also other properties that are notoriously difficult to map, such as individual flats and shopping centre units and the 2012 Act makes provision for tenements and flatted buildings in section 16. In summary, for each unit or property, the cadastral map shows that unit's unique identifying number, the boundaries of the unit and the title number of any

[30] 2012 Act, s 14(1).

[31] 2012 Act, s 14(4).

[32] An advance notice provides protection for a deed intended to be registered in the Land Register. In Scotland, a real right is only created when the deed detailing the right is registered in the Land Register. Between delivery of the deed and registration the purchaser is vulnerable to the granter becoming insolvent, or the registration of a competing deed over the same plot. An advance notice does not freeze the Land Register, but does give a 35-day period of protected priority for a deed between two parties, eg, disposition, standard security of deed of servitude. An advance notice cannot be used for a unilateral deed, eg, deeds of conditions.

[33] A tenement normally describes a building or part of a building containing two or more flats separated horizontally and designed to be in separate ownership. Mineral rights can also be owned separately from the land itself and as such can be described in Scots law as a 'separate tenement' as can other rights such as rights of salmon fishing.

[34] 2012 Act, s 11(6).

registered leases pertaining to the unit. The cadastral map may also depict other registered rights, such as extents of servitudes; and section 11(3) permits, but does not compel, three-dimensional mapping which allows for future technological developments.

B. Abolition of the Midas Touch

Under the 1979 Act, the predominant concern of conveyancers was not whether or not the title being sold and purchased was good, but rather whether or not the Keeper would accept it for registration. Once entered on the Register, everything, dross or not, became perfect or 'golden', and (virtually) impregnable as a consequence of the Keeper's Midas touch. The 2012 Act operates as a legislative version of the Pactolus River, effectively washing away the Keeper's Midas touch.[35] As discussed below in more detail, mere entry on the Land Register does not now provide automatic protection by perfecting defective titles. Instead, a system of deferred indefeasibility now reigns. Nonetheless, the 2012 Act continues to provide a state guarantee of title by Keeper's warranty, where the Keeper offers this. The default position, as set out in section 73(1) of the 2012 Act, is that full warranty is given when registration is complete, unless the Keeper decides to limit or exclude warranty,[36] for example where there is an existing caveat on the title sheet,[37] or the examination of title has been limited or restricted in some way.

C. 'One-Shot' Rule

Before an application for registration could be accepted under the 1979 Act, the application had to comply with criteria set out in section 4 of the 1979 Act. Where there were problems with the application form—for example, an incorrect fee supplied, an error in the deed, or missing supporting documents—the application could be taken onto the application record whilst requisitions were made. This limbo-like status was described as being in 'Standover'. An application could remain in Standover for up to 60 days until the changes were made or issues resolved, and for applications after September 2010, an extension of 15 days could also be requested. The decision of RoS to enter a faulty application in the Application Record was significant because in the event that the application was eventually accepted, the change to the Register (in accepting the application) would operate retrospectively and the registration date would be based on the original date of the original (faulty) application. In 2009, RoS reported that of the applications for first registration that went through the plans and legal stages of registration, 36% were put into Standover.[38]

Under the 2012 Act, in contrast, applicants are required to get their applications right first time; bad applications are simply to be rejected immediately under the 'one-shot rule'.

[35] In Ovid's *Metamorphoses*, Midas is instructed by Bacchus to journey to Sardis, the ancient capital of Lydia, and to wash in the Pactolus River to remove the golden touch. The Pactolus River (near the Aegean coast of Turkey) was famous in ancient times for the gold deposits to be found in the sand of the riverbed.

[36] 2012 Act, s 75(1)(b).

[37] 2012 Act, s 67. A caveat is placed on the title sheet as a warning that a court action has been raised in respect of that registered title.

[38] <www.ros.gov.uk/__data/assets/pdf_file/0007/5938/update28.pdf> accessed May 2017.

If the applicant satisfies the Keeper that the conditions of acceptance have been met at the date of application, then the Keeper must accept it under section 21(2) of the 2012 Act. The one-shot rule requires practitioners to provide all of the documents and information necessary for registration, from the outset, rather than relying on RoS staff to fill in the blanks and perfect imperfect applications. Where an application is rejected under the 2012 Act one-shot rule, the applicant will pay a flat fee of £30. The applicant can still reapply later with an amended application despite the initial rejection decision. However, the resubmitted amended application will be given a new (later) registration date since there is no provision for the revival of a previously rejected application.

The Keeper's conditions of application can be general—for example, that the fee has been paid, the application is in the prescribed form, that the application must not relate to a souvenir plot[39] and so on. It appears that most applications so far have been rejected for simple documentary reasons rather than a lack of conveyancing knowledge (such as misunderstanding the nature of the evidence required to support an application). The requirement that plans be provided has sometimes proved to be problematic, but the main reasons why applications are rejected under the 'one-shot' rule are for simple errors such as unsigned documents, unsigned cheques and so on.

The one-shot rule is a pragmatic attempt to ensure that trained conveyancers deal fully with the conveyancing process, rather than leaving it to RoS staff to spot errors and then mitigate or fix them. It also seeks to bring property and registration law into line with each other since logically, a transaction which is faulty to the extent that it cannot pass title in property law, should not act to pass title as a matter of registration law.

D. Responsibility of Solicitors

It will be apparent from the one-shot rule that practitioners are now required to take a more active role in land registration under the 2012 Act. The new Act entails greater responsibility on the part of practitioners to ensure that they themselves have understood and followed the registration requirements, rather than relying on RoS staff to pick up the pieces or fill in the figurative blanks.

The Keeper's former 'Midas touch' under the 1979 Act has been credited with being in danger of reducing the role of practitioners to 'that of a clerk, filling in forms, collecting documents, and awaiting with anxiety the verdict from Meadowbank House'.[40] In the 1979 Act world, the priority was to 'get the title past the Keeper'—once that had been accomplished, there was little for conveyancers or their clients to worry about.[41] In the new 2012 Act world the Keeper takes a positively 'hands off' role, which is summed up in the 'tell me, don't show me' mantra of the Keeper's guidance to conveyancers. Whilst this approach is

[39] 2012 Act, s 22(2) defines a 'souvenir plot' as a 'plot of land which is of inconsiderable size and no practical utility, and is neither a registered plot, nor a plot the ownership of which has, at any time, separately been constituted or transferred by a document recorded in the Register of Sasines'. Souvenir plots of a square foot of land in Scotland have been offered for sale for years, with the promise that ownership of the plot carries with it the right to call oneself Lady, Lord or Laird.

[40] KGC Reid, '"Tell Me Don't Show Me" and the Fall and Rise of the Conveyancer' in McCarthy, Chalmers and Bogle (eds) (n 12) ch 2, 15. Meadowbank House is the Edinburgh home of RoS.

[41] ibid, 16.

a significant change from the 1979 Act world, it is in fact consistent with the terms of that statute: since the 1979 Act said nothing at all about there being any obligation on the Keeper to carry out title examination, this was 'just done in order to preserve the integrity of the Land Register and the Keeper's liability under the indemnity'.[42]

Now, when an application for an unregistered plot is made, the applicant will be asked to identify deeds in which burdens are contained and to highlight any burdens that have been extinguished. The Keeper relies on the information provided and will not search for other deeds that might affect the plot, unless it is in a so-called 'Research Area' where preparatory work has been carried out by RoS, and in relation to which other deeds containing burdens have already been identified.[43] Where a Research Area is involved, the Keeper continues to disclose any discovered burdens in the title sheet, despite the applicant not including them. With the exception of Research Areas, the onus is now firmly on the applicant to satisfy the Keeper that the application meets with the general application conditions and the conditions of registration. The applicant certifies that the application satisfies the relevant conditions and the Keeper relies on this certification when registering the application. The Keeper will not carry out further investigation—eg, into whether the deed being registered is valid, because the granter has title and capacity to grant the deed.

The renewed centrality of the conveyancer is underlined by the statutory duty of care set out in section 111 of the 2012 Act. This states that a person granting a deed intended to be registered, and a person acting in connection with the grant as a solicitor or other legal advisor to the granter owes a statutory duty to the Keeper to take reasonable care to ensure that the Keeper does not inadvertently make the Register inaccurate. Where someone knowingly or recklessly makes materially false or misleading statements, or fails to disclose material information, when submitting an application to the Keeper, they will be committing a criminal offence under section 112 of the 2012 Act. The offence provisions apply to applicants for registration and to their solicitors and legal advisors, but are not aimed at capturing those making erroneous registration applications where the errors are genuine, and the relevant parties are neither knowing nor reckless. Thus, neither an applicant nor their solicitor or legal advisor will commit an offence if they give the Keeper information in good faith having taken all reasonable precautions to disclose material information.

E. Rectification of Inaccuracies

The SLC wryly observed that the amount of attention paid to mistakes and inaccuracies in its publications should 'not lead the reader to suppose that the Land Register is a mass of inaccuracy, that conveyancers do not understand their business, that fraud is rife, or that the staff at the Department of the Registers are less than competent. Far from it.'[44] This caveat is merited. Land registration reform necessarily raises the spectre of inaccuracy, but as the SLC rightly noted, 'the size of the problem should not be judged from the amount of attention it must necessarily receive' in reform proposals.[45]

[42] R Rennie, 'Land Registration—Who is in Charge?' (2016) 142 *Property Law Bulletin* 7, 8.
[43] Research Areas are discussed in greater detail below.
[44] Scot Law Com No 222 (n 4) para 17.4.
[45] ibid.

One of the difficulties under the 1979 Act was that it was 'not obvious how the Register can be inaccurate'[46] due to the Midas touch transmuting base materials into unassailable 'golden' registered proprietary rights. The 1979 Act used the term 'inaccuracy' to refer to two different scenarios: (i) where the Register states something that is untrue ('actual' inaccuracy); and (ii) where the Register states that something is true under the terms of the registration regime, but which is false in general law terms ('bijural' inaccuracy).

'Actual' inaccuracies included situations where land had been registered in the name of a company that did not exist. As the SLC comments, the Keeper's Midas touch '[could] confer ownership even on someone with no right at all to the property, but it [could not] confer ownership on *no one*, which is what registration in favour of a non-existent person [would be]'.[47] 'Bijural' inaccuracies [were] more complicated. The SLC gives the example of a disposition from A to C that was registered, but where it emerged that A's signature on the disposition had been forged. According to general property rules, such a deed would be void and ineffective at passing title. However, under the 1979 Act the fact of registration activated the Keeper's Midas touch and C would be the owner nonetheless. In general law terms, the Register entry would be inaccurate, but according to the registration rules, the Register would be accurate because it would record the effect of the Keeper's Midas touch. The problem of having two different legal systems at play and interacting in this way is stark. Under the 1979 Act, the Keeper's Midas touch would mean that the Register entry prevails, unless rectification occurs; and this could only occur under the 1979 Act where rectification would not prejudice a proprietor in possession, unless the inaccuracy was wholly or substantially caused by the proprietor's fraud or carelessness.[48] The Keeper's inability to correct the Register where there was a proprietor in possession who had not caused the inaccuracy themselves was an absolute rule with no judicial discretion, unlike the corresponding English provision.[49]

The approach taken to inaccuracies is significantly different under the 2012 Act. Usefully, section 65 of the 2012 Act attempts to define the meaning of 'inaccuracy'. This is a change from the 1979 Act, which used the term in section 9(1) but did not attempt to define its meaning. Section 65 states that a title sheet is inaccurate so far as it 'misstates what the position is in law or in fact, omits anything required, by or under an enactment, to be included in it, or includes anything the inclusion of which is not expressly or impliedly permitted by or under an enactment'.[50]

Similarly, the cadastral map may be inaccurate in ways which mirror the title sheet inaccuracies; in short, this might involve saying something that is wrong, or omitting something that should have been said. Thus, the cadastral map is inaccurate if it 'wrongly depicts or shows what the position is in law or in fact, omits anything required, by or under an enactment, to be depicted or shown on it, or depicts or shows anything the depiction or showing of which is not expressly or impliedly permitted by or under an enactment'.[51]

[46] ibid, para 17.5.
[47] ibid, para 17.10.
[48] 1979 Act, s 9(3)(a)(iii).
[49] O'Connor, 'Registration of Invalid Dispositions' (n 18) 61. See Land Registration Act 2002, sch 4, paras 3(3) and 6(3), which provide that alteration of the Register might not be effected if the circumstances are 'exceptional'.
[50] 2012 Act, s 65(1).
[51] 2012 Act, s 65(2).

A misstatement of the legal position might include omitting rights in land which have arisen impliedly, such as a prescriptive servitude (easement), or a factual misstatement might include failing to reflect the terms of a deed in the title sheet. The errors and inaccuracies contained in section 65 of the 2012 Act are ones that the Keeper potentially has the power to amend by rectification. Other errors (other than minor clerical mistakes) cannot be rectified.

Applicants seeking rectification under the 2012 Act have a number of hurdles to cross before they can bring a successful claim for rectification. First, as noted above, there must be an 'inaccuracy' under section 65 of the 2012 Act. Secondly, the inaccuracy, and its solution, must be 'manifest'. This is because, subject to some limited restrictions,[52] the Keeper only has a legal duty to rectify the Register where the Keeper becomes aware of a 'manifest inaccuracy'[53] in the title sheet or cadastral map, provided that the solution is also manifest.[54] The use of the term 'manifest' sets a high evidential burden.[55] The inclusion of the term 'manifest' indicates that the Keeper need only act where the inaccuracy of the position is beyond doubt or has otherwise been established clearly—for example, where a court has already decided the case underlying the rectification request. It is for the Keeper to determine whether or not an inaccuracy is 'manifest'.

Not only must an applicant demonstrate that a 'manifest' inaccuracy exists, but they must also show that the *solution* to the inaccuracy is also 'manifest' or clear. For example, where the individual shares in common property do not add up to a whole, it will be obvious that an inaccuracy exists. However, it may not be possible for the Keeper to determine which of the individual shares is faulty and which of them should be altered. In these circumstances, there is a manifest inaccuracy in the title, but the solution is not manifest because it is not clear which title should be altered or rectified. Unless the solution is clear, the Keeper must reject the claim as being impossible to rectify, and should enter a note on the title sheet or the cadastral map alerting third parties to the inaccuracy.[56] The Land Register remains inaccurate unless and until a solution becomes manifest (for example, the common owners agree on their relative shares or further evidence comes to light), or prescription acts to realign property rights. In practice, parties in this situation are likely to come to come to an agreed practical solution because the effect of a note of inaccuracy on their title will affect its marketability and potential value by putting off purchasers.

F. Realignment of Rights

The Keeper is not deemed to be 'aware' of an inaccuracy until such time as it is manifest within the meaning of section 80. The precise timing of when the Keeper becomes aware of an inaccuracy can have a significant effect on the realignment of property rights under the terms of the 2012 Act, and can dictate who gets the mud and who gets the money.

52 For example, where rectification would interrupt prescriptive possession under the 2012 Act, s 81.
53 2012 Act, s 80(1).
54 2012 Act, s 80(2).
55 See the SLC's discussion of this higher evidential standard in Scot Law Com No 222 (n 4) para 12.59.
56 2012 Act, s 80(3).

The classic scenario involves a person ('A') who is 'not the proprietor of a registered plot of land' but is registered as proprietor and is in possession of the land.[57] A may not be the proprietor of the land for a number of reasons, for example, the real owner of the land ('O') may has been the victim of a fraud by 'F' and O's signature on the relevant deed is in fact a forgery and the deed void. Here, when A is registered, A's name is entered in the proprietorship section of the title sheet and A will benefit from the Keeper's warranty, so long as this has not been expressly limited or excluded. However, as a matter of property law, A does not become the owner because a void deed does not have legal effect. The Land Register will be inaccurate from the outset and will remain inaccurate (in recording A as the proprietor rather than O) until O shows that she is owner and that the Register has a manifest inaccuracy that can be manifestly resolved by rectification of the Register and O's entry as proprietor on the title sheet.

A will then be left with a claim for indemnity against the Keeper, because A has been deprived of his rights. The Keeper is liable to pay compensation where an inaccuracy is rectified under section 84, but this liability is excluded in the circumstances listed in section 85. For example, among others, the Keeper has no liability to pay compensation where the inaccuracy is caused other than by a change made by the Keeper to a title sheet or the cadastral map; if the inaccuracy was based on an error in the cadastral map and the error was made in reasonable reliance on the base map (ie, the Ordnance Survey map was to blame); where the inaccuracy is caused by an act or omission by the claimant or where the claimant could have avoided loss by taking reasonable steps; or the connection between the claimant's loss and the inaccuracy is too remote.[58]

In practice, the situation may well be more complex since A (the non-owning but registered proprietor) will often have conveyed the disputed land to a good faith third-party, 'B', by the time that the inaccuracy becomes known. Part 9 of the 2012 Act applies in this situation. Here, exceptionally, despite legal or factual inaccuracies in the Land Register, rectification is not provided. Instead, the property rights themselves are (in limited circumstances) altered to mirror the inaccurate entries on the Land Register. As such, section 86 of the 2012 Act, which deals with the realignment of rights, has been fairly described as a 'Midas touch light'.[59]

Section 86 applies where a non-owning registered proprietor dispones[60] or conveys land to a third party who is in good faith. A's lack of title in property will not prevent B from gaining title both in property law and registration law to the disputed land, as long as various statutory requirements are met. Section 86 will allow B to acquire ownership *if* B can demonstrate that: (i) the land was in A's possession, openly, peaceably and without judicial interruption for a continuous period of at least 1 year, or the possession of A and B for periods which together constituted 1 year; and (ii) that at no time during that year did the Keeper become aware that the Register was inaccurate in recording A (or B) as the

[57] 2012 Act, s 86(1).

[58] 2012 Act, s 85.

[59] A Stewart and E Sinclair, *Conveyancing Practice in Scotland* (Haywards Heath, Bloomsbury Professional, 2016) 50.

[60] 'Dispone' is a Scots word used when transferring ownership of land. It was traditionally essential to use the word 'dispone' to give validity to any deed transferring ownership in land and variants of it (disponor, disponee) continue to be used in Scots land and registration law.

proprietor; and (iii) that B was in good faith; and (iv) that the disposition to B would have conferred ownership on B had A been proprietor when the land was disponed or conveyed; and that (v) at no time during the 1 year period was the title sheet subject to a caveat or a statement under section 30(5);[61] and (vi) the Keeper warrants or is to be taken to warrant A's title. Where all of these elements are met, realignment occurs by operation of law and B will gain title to the disputed land without any fear of rectification taking place. Where another party has been deprived of their land as a result of the application of principles in Part 9 of the 2012 Act, compensation can be paid. Any payment of compensation by the Keeper will be on condition that the claimant, here O, assigns to the Keeper any rights that O might have against someone else in respect of the loss. This statutory provision allows the Keeper to proceed against others who have contributed to O's loss, particularly conveyancers, since these claims are not extinguished by payment of compensation by the Keeper.[62]

The idea of deferred indefeasibility contained in section 86 is sensible. It allows third parties, in certain circumstances, to negotiate based on seemingly established facts clearly noted in the Register. If in fact it later transpires that the Register is inaccurate, then the ousted owner, if out of possession, has a year in which to complain and tell the Keeper that the Register is inaccurate. Where an owner has not done this and an innocent third party is registered as owner, then the Register stays good at this point rather than unravelling. The 2012 Act flips the Register back to following registration law rather than the original property law solution that arose at the time of the initial transaction.[63]

G. Advance Notices

Part 4 of the 2012 Act introduced a system of so-called 'advance notices' for conveyancing transactions. These were intended to provide greater protection for purchasers in the period between delivery and registration of a deed disponing or conveying an interest in land. During this 'gap risk' or registration gap, a purchaser is potentially exposed to the risks that: (a) another party might register a competing deed before the purchaser and take priority; and (b) that the seller might become insolvent and the property might be seized by creditors. Under the 1979 Act, these risks were mitigated by insurance, but the 2012 Act introduced a 'warning' system of advance notices under section 56 of the 2012 Act to alert third parties to the purchaser's interest and thereby provide some protection in this registration gap. An advance notice can be applied for by the person who will grant the protected deed,[64] or any person with their consent.[65] So, the owner of a house could apply for an advance notice to operate in in favour of the prospective purchaser. The purchaser would

[61] 2012 Act, s 30(5) relates to a qualifying statement on the title sheet noting that the name and designation of the proprietor was not known with reasonable certainty.

[62] 2012 Act, s 94(4).

[63] 2012 Act, ss 86–93 set out the circumstances in which the Register is inaccurate but will not be rectified and where realignment can occur, provided that the conditions laid down in the relevant sections are satisfied. It will be for the courts to determine that realignment conditions have been satisfied—eg, possession and good faith requirements.

[64] 2012 Act, s 57(2)(a).

[65] 2012 Act, s 57(2)(b).

be able to apply for an advance notice, with the consent of the owner, in favour of the lender who would be providing the mortgage monies for the purchase.

The entry of an advance notice in the application record of the Land Register referring to a registrable deed ensures that no disposition or competing advance notice can take priority during the 35-day advance notice period (the 'protected period').[66] After this period has elapsed, the Keeper removes the advance notice and adds it to the archive record.[67] It is possible to apply for a further advance notice for another 35-day period, but this will be a separate period of protection rather than an extension of the original priority period. Thus, it is possible that a competing disposition could exist which the second advance notice would not be able to protect against. In these circumstances, before entering a second advance notice, the purchaser should search the Land Register for any competing dispositions before continuing with the transaction. Advance notices can also be discharged earlier than this—for example, if a sale has fallen through.[68]

H. Legislative Changes Under the Bonnet—a Reprise

It will be evident from the foregoing discussion that the 2012 Act introduced major reforms to the system of land registration operating in Scotland. To the outside world the eventual product of the registration process—a registered title—may seem the same. In fact, the quality of this title is different because deferred indefeasibility has replaced the Keeper's immediately effective 'Midas touch'. Additionally, the way in which the title is produced has changed significantly since the conveyancer has once again been placed at the very heart of the process, rather than RoS staff. These are significant technical changes 'under the bonnet', whose legal effects on the underlying integrity of the Land Register have yet to be fully determined. This chapter does not examine this question further, however. In the following section, it turns instead to consider some of the mental changes required by some participants in the land registration process—and more specifically, the RoS staff.

IV. Changes in Thinking and Approach: Transitional Attitudes to the New 2012 Regime

As set out in the first section of this chapter, the 2012 Act introduced significant changes to the way in which land registration rules operate in Scotland. Clearly, all parties involved have had to adjust to new rules and ways of doing business under the 2012 Act, no matter whether they are conveyancers, RoS staff, academics, judges, students, banks, or citizens. However, this section of the chapter deliberately focuses on one specific group and the mental gymnastics required of its members as the 'changes under the bonnet' came into effect: staff charged with implementing the 2012 Act at RoS. The focus on RoS to the exclusion

[66] 2012 Act, s 58.
[67] 2012 Act, s 62.
[68] 2012 Act, s 63.

of other groups affected by the 2012 Act is not intended to minimise the significance of the legislation on other stakeholders.[69] It is, however, a valuable opportunity to explore an often-overlooked area of land law by examining attitudes within a land registry to land registration practices, at a particular legal transition point.

To this end, the latter section of this chapter draws on some preliminary results drawn from qualitative research carried out at RoS over a period of 12 months running up to and including the commencement day of the 2012 Act. It does not examine the work of RoS following the Act's commencement, since the research project is still ongoing and final results have not yet been collated and analysed. Nonetheless, the research undertaken during the pre-commencement period usefully illustrates not only the technical legal challenges of changing land registration approaches, but also the mental 'changes under the bonnet' required of staff who must implement new legislation.

A. Methodology

As noted above, the 1979 Act was a rather skeletal statute, which left RoS with a lot of room to manoeuvre in practice. Inevitably, RoS had to fill in the detail and create its own workable practices within the general framework of the 1979 Act. These practices were predominantly rational, valid and sensible, but they also had the effect of creating significant pockets of discretion. For instance, under the 1979 Act, the Keeper could accept an application for registration if 'accompanied by such documents and other evidence as he may require'.[70]

The optimum role of discretion in administrative decision-making, and the point at which administrative decision-making acquires a legal character, can be contentious. The research project took a deliberately neutral stance on the desirability or otherwise of RoS practices and the content of registration decisions and aimed instead at observing *how* decisions were made. Thus, the project considered both 'day-to-day' simple registration decisions, as well as those that are more complex, including first registrations as well as overlap and underlap scenarios.

Throughout the process, the Keeper and RoS staff were uniformly welcoming, patient and helpful, and the project could not have taken place without their willingness and engagement. Interestingly, the very lack of detailed Scots land law knowledge on the part of the interviewer appeared to stimulate rich responses in semi-structured interviews and interactions; RoS staff immediately appreciated that questions stemmed from genuine attempts to understand the registration principles, rather than as veiled criticism.

The project involved undertaking a qualitative study of the land registration decision-making processes in action before the implementation of the 2012 Act. The research utilised a mixed-method approach, combining documentary analysis, observation, and

[69] S Brymer, 'Looking Forward—With One Eye on the Past', (2016) 142 *Property Law Bulletin* 2, 2: 'Given that the reform of the 1979 Act came "hot on the heels" of the abolition of the feudal system; the codification of the law of real burdens; the reform of the law of the tenement; and not to forget the introduction of standard missives etc, one has to have sympathy with certain older members of the profession who wished that their retiral date could be advanced'.

[70] 1979 Act, ss 4(1), (2). See Reid, '"Tell Me Don't Show Me"' (n 40) 22, for comparison with the 2012 Act, where under s 21 the Keeper *must* accept an application where the 'application conditions are met'.

semi-structured face-to-face interviews with a variety of staff from different grades and roles within RoS. Observations and interviews were conducted using an intentionally stratified and purposeful sampling method which involved observing and interviewing a wide variety of staff including: plans staff; the 2012 project team; policy team members; the Wiki (RoS 2012 manual) team; risk and corporate business specialists; standard dealings staff; complex dealings; research area specialists; and training team members, among others.[71] Additionally, a fieldwork diary was kept which was both analytical and descriptive. This allowed for observations, interactions and discussions to be recorded and supported a coding scheme, which is still subject to re-analysis as the project continues into the post-2012 Act phase.[72]

The comments set out in the following section are drawn from some of the semi-structured interviews forming part of the initial research project, and are illustrative of common themes that arose throughout conversations with staff at this stage of the research project. The findings are representative in that they provide instances of views and attitudes held by specific participants in the case-studies at a particular point in the transition to the 2012 regime, but are not 'generalisable'.[73]

Participants in the project gave informed consent and were offered anonymity. Since the precise employment background, role and team membership of participants at given stages of the research could indirectly allow for their identification, this information is not provided below. All comments have been taken verbatim from recorded and transcribed semi-structured interviews, but with potentially identifying details removed.

B. Initial Qualitative Research Findings

With the caveat that the research project is still ongoing, a number of common themes arose in semi-structured face-to-face interviews undertaken as part of the initial phase, which indicate the mental changes required of participants. Many of the mental changes required by the introduction of new legislation will be familiar to practitioners, Land Registry staff, citizens, academics, students, banks and other stakeholders in England who experienced the far-reaching reforms to English land law effected by the Land Registration Act 2002.

i. The RoS Staff

It is worth noting initially that RoS is in the highly enviable position of still having a significant number of long-serving staff members. They have a depth of knowledge and experience that may not be fully appreciated by outsiders, and together, contribute to a valuable institutional memory. Despite early retirements and restructuring over a number of years, the staff at RoS comprises a number of highly-specialised and knowledgeable plans and legal experts who are capable of dealing with the Sasine Register and undertaking complex

[71] The number of participants will not be finalised until the project ends, but at this transition stage some 35 staff members had been interviewed and/or observed.

[72] The full dataset, once this has been accumulated, including interview transcripts will be analyzed using NVivo and subjected to thematic coding.

[73] L Webley, 'Qualitative Approaches to Empirical Legal Research' in P Cane and HM Kritzer (eds), *The Oxford Handbook of Empirical Legal Research* (Oxford, OUP, 2010) ch 38, 934–35.

first registration, and have experience of a wide variety of property rights including fishing rights and minerals.

Many of the interviewees who took part in the interviews, whatever their employment grade or specialism, had been part of the organisation for a significant period of time—often decades. As retirement age beckons in the future for many of the most experienced staff members, there is an acknowledged need to ensure that expertise and knowledge are not lost. The registration complexities tackled by some staff members are extremely challenging. Those dealing with both plans and legal aspects of first registrations of particularly complex deals, such as shopping centres, harbours, and foreshores, require immense patience, technical skill and applied knowledge. Several interviewees talked about RoS colleagues in glowing terms, with one stating that:

> X is like an oracle of knowledge [laughs], but no, but there's a lot you know when you've been here a long time you really do understand a lot of the [issues], you've got a lot of appreciation for how things were in the past and different resources that you may not have thought about and people there's a lot of people you think "oh I'll go and talk to so-and-so and they'll know" they're a specialist on a certain topic, those things take years like to figure out.

In an attempt to retain at least some of the institutional knowledge being built up under the 2012 Act, RoS has transformed its previous 1979 Act practice manual into a more collaborative and flexible 'Wiki' product to facilitate learning and knowledge exchange about the 2012 Act registration practice. This IT solution is an admirable and noteworthy attempt to engage staff and provide varying levels of information—all of which can be accessed by anyone within RoS, but also members of the conveyancing profession and the public.[74] Additionally, most of the interviewees had worked in a number of different departments in RoS—for example, starting in the Sasine Register 'minuting' or translating a six or eight page deed into a précised paragraph using highly formalised syntax and boilerplate phrases, before moving to other areas of the organisation. Individuals often had a variety of front-facing roles dealing with the public, as well as less outwardly visible roles.

ii. Outward-Looking Collaboration

Whilst this project was limited to a view from inside RoS and did not ask the profession what it thought of RoS and its work, some common themes arose in interviews. One was the very strong desire to communicate the work of RoS better to the outside world. The 2012 Act, and the reforms it introduced, necessitated a surprising amount of collaboration between RoS and different stakeholders in the registration process, as well as education. As the terms of what became the 2012 Act emerged, one interviewee noted that RoS:

> [s]tarted to go out and talk to solicitors, talk to councils, talk to housing associations, talk to utility companies, all sorts of things we did you know a whole segmentation of our stakeholders to see who they were and who they could be, because there's lots of people out there who don't actually know what we do or what we could do to help them.

RoS staff who had been engaged with groups that might have been expected to understand their work and role appeared to have uniformly enjoyed the chance to talk about their

[74] The 2012 Act Wiki can be accessed at www.rosdev.atlassian.net/wiki/display/2ARM/Home.

work and the upcoming changes. Staff responses to research questions in semi-structured interviews became noticeably longer and more detailed once they sensed that they were talking to an interested interlocutor. When referring to the number of roadshows and the scale of public engagement involved in the lead-in to the 2012 Act, interviewees were uniformly proud of their efforts to talk about RoS's work. One interviewee proudly stated that the roadshow team had been 'everywhere from Edinburgh, Glasgow, Shetland, Dumfries, Fort William ... all "airts and pairts" of Scotland, as they say, but over and above that, we've gone face-to-face with 380 firms in the last two months [before the commencement of the 2012 Act].'

iii. Acceptance and Relative Responsibilities

There can sometimes be a perceived tension between conveyancers and other parties in the land registration process. Different stakeholders have to collaborate whilst operating under different regimes and pressures. Despite the sense that practitioners may historically have been somewhat wary of RoS, and may have viewed staff as difficult-to-please gatekeepers under the 1979 Act, RoS interviewees were uniformly sympathetic to the practical realities of life for many conveyancers. In talking about why there had been relatively little feedback from consultation exercises, one participant commented that they felt some practitioners had little or no time to consider legislative changes until they were forced to do so. They felt that the practitioners with whom they dealt were:

> [G]ood people, they're hardworking, these conveyancers don't have any spare time, their margins are nightmarishly thin, competition is brutal, people leave at a whim and there's an awful lot of specialism. You know, if you think conveyancing's easy, you're doing it wrong.

Alongside this evident respect for practitioners was an understanding that for many practitioners, all but routine interactions with RoS would be unusual. Difficult or complex registration issues would be challenging for any practitioner, no matter what their practice was like, because they would be unlikely to be 'repeat players' in the way that RoS staff would be in complex situations. One interviewee who had experience of being in practice observed that 'you can do really complicated transactions [in practice] and then you might never do one again for ten years ... a lot of the experience lies here [at RoS by comparison] in people seeing things every day'. Another compared the internal support available to the bigger conveyancers with the more limited resources available to rural and smaller conveyancers, and said that 'I have huge sympathy for what they try to deal with ... coming across something once in a blue moon, "what on earth do I do with this"'.

Despite RoS staff being understanding and tolerant of practitioner pressures and mistakes, many felt that the balance of responsibility had swept too far the other way under the 1979 Act. Several interviewees commented that the 1979 Act had encouraged conveyancers to focus less on 'getting a good title for their client' and more on getting 'a title the Keeper will fall for'. One went so far as to say, explicitly, that:

> it's not a game of football, you know, they [conveyancers] shouldn't have to 'get it past' us ... they should be instructing us because they're, you know, conveyancing solicitors are the experts, so you know it's just putting it back that way really, which is the way it probably always should have been but it evolved differently.

Others commented on the historically paternalistic approach taken by RoS, whereby no matter how skilled the conveyancer, the Keeper and staff double-checked information in great detail—with the consequence that 'there was an enormous duplication of the work done by solicitors' to produce a 'Rolls Royce product under the 1979 Act' and that going forward 'we've still got a good product but we care very much more than parties, and that doesn't seem quite right'. There have been points in RoS's history where there have been significant backlogs of first registrations, but even when under pressure, the focus was on 'very old-fashioned land registration—"it will be right"—and we would correspond with solicitors backwards and forwards ten/fifteen/twenty times …'.

One interviewee felt that practitioners did not need to be worried about the 2012 Act,

> but they are a bit afraid of it … a little bit is the paternalistic nature of the Keeper over the last thirty years where the Keeper's been really good at checking people's homework and people, some people, in the profession perhaps have become a little bit reliant on that.

There was some surprise before the commencement of the 2012 Act that the profession's attention had focused predominantly on the duty of care under section 111, and the offence created by section 112.

Another interviewee observed wryly that they felt that much more fundamental changes such as 'getting rid of bijuralism and removing the Keeper's Midas touch were ignored. All of the interest was in section 111 and 112'. Others commented that they felt that practitioners, even those dealing with conveyancing, 'focused on the high-level things and their eye was drawn to the thing that frightened them most and they didn't actually unpick lots of other parts and also it [the Bill] was enormous to read so the bigger it was the harder it was, but certainly the … comments on consultation were minimal'. The general feeling was that conveyancers who were honest and doing their best did not need to be concerned about the duty of care or offence provisions in the new Act, because they merely stated what would happen already.

> [E]arly on in our interactions we did find that a wee bit frustrating that we were having to steer people away from that and say 'well look, you know if you're not breaking the law then why are you concerned *what* we call the law? You know, it doesn't matter whether it's specifically mentioned in here, or if it's just part of a bigger fraud law, you know that you're not doing anything wrong.' … I think it was just that whole feeling that the solicitors perhaps felt that we were just changing things, that shift of emphasis away from 'we'll always fix everything for you, wherever we can' to 'actually *you* need to get this right'.

Interestingly, several RoS staff explicitly mentioned academics and referred to phrases from cases, comments by the SLC, conversations with other academics and academic journal articles. It may be that these references were occasioned by knowledge of the interlocutor's role as an academic—but staff had clearly engaged deeply with the arguments made and demonstrated an enthusiasm to consider intricate complexities and hypotheticals of registration law and practice.

iv. Rebalancing Roles in the Registration Process

RoS has a history of proactively undertaking projects to enhance the quality of the Land Register. Perhaps one of the best examples of this approach can be seen in the 35,000 so-called 'Research Areas'. These are areas where a group of RoS staff—the New Area Preparation ('NAP') team—identified areas of land on the Base Map (normally roughly an acre in size) that had been, or were likely to be, split up into units of six or more properties, and shared some common burdens. RoS was proactive in identifying and creating Research Areas, such that in 2009–2010, 506 Research Areas were created containing some 6,680 properties.

Having identified such areas, the NAP prepared what were effectively template burdens entries[75]—including instructions on their use—with the objective of facilitating first registration, and of ensuring consistency of burden entries where that would be appropriate. Not all common burdens in a Research Area would necessarily attach to all individual titles in the area. Where a plot of land in a Research Area is registered, the general RoS policy is for a registration officer to follow the Research Area instructions concerning entries in the burdens section of the title sheet. Where, however, the application form states explicitly that specified deeds in the Research Area do not apply to the plot in question, or where the application form states that specific burdens in the Research Area do not subsist or do not affect the plot, then the registration officer does not need to follow the Research Area instructions. In all other situations, the registration officer will follow the Research Area NAP instructions on burdens. Queries or wrinkles in the documents relating to a Research Area can be referred by a registration officer to a referral officer.

The justification for creating these Research Areas was tied to efficiency savings. As one interviewee noted:

> It was about efficiency, most of it was driving efficiency and cases could be settled at an appropriate grade if they could be, and also it avoided duplication of work because every property in here essentially has the same burden … then maybe like a month after this property is sold, this one could come in, you might have to order new deeds, it just made sense really, you know, so you're not wasting everybody's time looking at the same deeds over and over again.'

It should be noted that there are likely to be differences in the burdens recorded by conveyancers of properties neighbouring Research Areas, and those recorded by RoS for Research Area units. These differences may be more meaningful in theory rather than practice, since burdens may no longer be extant, or the extent of the burdened element of the property may be relatively minor. It is, in any case, unnecessary to examine this variation further here. The key point is that Research Areas exemplify the proactive, analytical and detailed approach historically taken towards the Register by RoS staff.

The 2012 Act now renders unnecessary much of this type of detailed, proactive enquiry—RoS staff are to rely on the 'show me, don't tell me' approach, whereby the conveyancer, and not RoS, has the ultimate responsibility for carrying out enquiries. The substantive desirability or otherwise of this approach, and its effect on the underlying integrity of the Land Register, are important questions that will need to be addressed on a later occasion. What is beyond doubt is that the 2012 Act will force a change in RoS work.

Staff discussed some of the changes that they felt the transition to the 2012 Act required. Whilst being positive about the 2012 Act, several staff members appeared to be nostalgic and somewhat rueful that the more interesting aspects of RoS work would now be undertaken

[75] Real burdens in Scots property law impose either positive obligations or negative obligations on land. The obligation will run with the land in perpetuity. Typical examples include obligations for upkeep, or prohibitions on using property for business purposes analogous to covenants in English law.

by conveyancers. There were, for example, some concerns that under the 2012 Act the land registration process, apart from first registrations, might be:

> a slightly more boring job, it's a more functional administrative job whereas … [under] the [19]79 Act registration you took a whole pile of stuff and you made a product … you added your knowledge and expertise in property registration and you made, there was judgement calls all the way through to form a land certificate.

For some interviewees there was a concern that the changes under the 2012 Act might be hard because 'the brain will engage and … [RoS staff] will be questioning things and most of the time they're not meant to be using their brain in that way [under the 2012 Act], they're just meant to be registering'. Others noted that 'there's still that transition period where everybody's got to readjust how they do things, they've got to think of things in a slightly different way and that's always, you know, a period of pain to make'.

One of the interesting aspects of the interviews was interviewees commenting that they would almost need to think about change in terms of holding themselves back from solving problems that they would formerly have dealt with. For instance, one interviewee said that 'it's almost about training people in what they don't do any more'. Another interviewee felt that it would be a big shift to get conveyancers to step forward, and that RoS staff 'shouldn't be guarding that door, we should be saying "look if you are comfortable, you're the expert, you know the client, you know the circumstances" and therefore you shouldn't then see it as another obstacle to get it registered'.

Others rightly noted that RoS staff had been trained to be cautious in investigating title under the 1979 Act, with one person saying that they had probably 'been trained over the years to be a pedant'. One participant observed that it would be hard to step back from making requisitions because:

> I think we've, like, come from a place where we've got so much expertise and by our nature we investigate everything whether we need to or not, so I think it's just difficult the change is going to be a wee learning curve or they'll get used to it you know … I'm going to be in a different world but I think we'll get used to it, it's just to stop ourselves, you know, from, we have … just to stop ourselves from looking into things too much.

Despite the imminent changes, there was a great deal of enthusiasm and 'buy-in' for the 2012 Act among RoS staff, perhaps because RoS staff had been so fully included in the land registration reform process. One commented that 'I'm now starting to accept the reasoning behind the process changes … you almost do have to learn to accept a new regime by mentally accepting the underlying reasoning.' Another interviewee excitedly said:

> We're changing the world! Yes, absolutely. I mean what has happened is that for a lot of people they've depended on that [RoS 1979 Act processes] as a double-check of what they do and I think that is a bit of a learning curve for everyone involved. For our staff too, because they're used to saying "look this is not quite right, but let's see if we can fix it" when actually the legislation now is all about "we don't really have the power to do that, we shouldn't be doing that"'.

Under the new 'one-shot rule' RoS staff will not actively engage with the (sometimes) drawn-out requisition process, to amend or complete faulty applications, that became common under the 1979 Act. But there are ambitious projects afoot in Scotland that should provide plenty of scope for staff to continue to use their expertise. For example, the ambitious target for completion of the Land Register is likely to rely heavily on Keeper-Induced

Registrations to move titles from the Sasine Register onto the Land Register. The interviewees were not questioned about this aspect of the RoS's work, post-2012 Act. It is, however, evident that these first registrations will require complex and expert interpretative skills—indeed, some first registrations will be pre-Sasines, and should involve some of the most challenging and interesting land registration issues in Scotland. The staff at RoS are well-placed to undertake this mammoth task.

V. Conclusion

This chapter has outlined some of the main technical legal changes to land registration in Scotland introduced by the 2012 Act. These changes 'under the bonnet' have been considerable—particularly their emphasis upon abolishing the Keeper's Midas touch, and reinstating the centrality of the conveyancer in the registration process. It has also highlighted some initial findings of a qualitative research project carried out at RoS prior to the commencement of the 2012 Act, into the changes of thinking and approach required by the transition to the 'new' regime, from key participants in the registration process. A deliberately neutral stance was taken towards the substantive content and desirability of the 2012 changes. Nevertheless, several common themes emerged from RoS interviewees.

There was a noticeable outward-looking focus among staff—albeit that they acknowledged that the work of land registries was not well-understood or appreciated. Staff appeared to enjoy their work and the challenges posed by investigating titles under the 1979 Act. The changes introduced by the 2012 Act were acknowledged to be significant, and whilst there was considerable understanding of the pressures faced by conveyancers in practice, there was also a sense among RoS staff that the 2012 Act changes would rightly reinstate conveyancers to their once central role in the conveyancing process. In reversing the centrality of the Keeper under the 1979 Act, the 2012 Act effectively mirrors the Sasines world where the conveyancer took the lead in land transactions. The interviewees at RoS acknowledged that the 'changes under the bonnet' introduced by the 2012 Act would be a learning process for all parties, not just in learning new technical rules but also in absorbing and implementing new ways of thinking about land registration.

20

Automating State Guarantee of Title Systems: System Design and Possible Outcomes—Australasian Thoughts

ROD THOMAS, ROUHSHI LOW AND LYNDEN GRIGGS*

I. Introduction

The automation of Land Registry dealings is a topical subject.[1] The drivers for change seem to be irresistible. As we move towards twenty-first century 'online' systems, existing paper-based systems are regarded as outmoded and unsafe.[2] In light of modern expectations, they are slow to operate, cumbersome and expensive. Being paper-based, they are also open to abuse, in a way not envisaged before computer imaging and photocopying became commonplace.[3] In line with government directives to modernise, automation is a top contender for the 'action now' basket.

* We would like to thank the following for their comments and thoughts: Ed Johnson, Emeritus Fellow, Wolfson College, Cambridge; Ross Anderson, University of Cambridge; Nick Bohm, of the UK-based Foundation for Information Policy Research; Allan Beever, Mary-Rose Russell and Shananne Joyce of AUT University; Peter Gutmann of the University of Auckland, and Stephen Styants, Solicitor, Auckland. The substance of this chapter has been published by the authors in 'Designing an Automated Torrens System—Baseline Criteria, Risks and Possible Outcomes' [2015] *NZ L Rev* 452 which follows on from an article by the authors, 'Australasian Torrens Automation, Its Integrity, and the Three Proof Requirements' [2013] *NZ L Rev* 227. Responsibility for content remains with the authors.

1 The literature includes: R Thomas, 'Fraud, Risk and the Automated Register' in D Grinlinton (ed), *Torrens in the Twenty-first Century* (Wellington, LexisNexis, 2003) 349, 359–61; J Greenwood and T Jones, 'Automation of the Register: Issues Impacting on the Integrity of Title' in Grinlinton (ed) (ibid) 323; R Muir, 'Electronic Registration: The Legislative Scheme and Implications for the Torrens System in New Zealand' in Grinlinton (ed) (ibid) 311; R Thomas, R Low and L Griggs, 'Australasian Torrens Automation, Its Integrity, and the Three Proof Requirements' [2013] *NZ L Rev* 227; R Thomas, L Griggs and R Low, 'Electronic Conveyancing in Australia—Is Anyone Concerned about Security?' (2014) 23 *Australian Property LJ* 1; G Brennan, '*The Impact of eConveyancing on Title Registration: A Risk Assessment*' (Switzerland, Springer, 2015); P Rosier, 'Electronic Conveyancing: A New Age' (2013) 51(11) *L Society J* 61; M McCutcheon, 'Farewell to Paper: Electronic Conveyancing to go National' (2013) 87(10) *L Institute J* 40.

2 Thomas, Low and Griggs, 'Three Proof Requirements' (n 1).

3 ibid 235.

However, automation has brought with it casualties[4] and false starts.[5] This suggests that any initial rush of enthusiasm needs to be accompanied by a clear understanding of both the issues and associated risks. This is especially so if the system being automated is Torrens-based. This is because a key component of Torrens (at least in Australia, New Zealand, Singapore and certain other jurisdictions) is that registration of title is guaranteed by the state and compensation is payable if that guarantee is not met and if the new title-holder is not found guilty of fraud.[6]

Ultimately, there are two major concerns with automation. The first relates to public confidence in the land titles system. The second is who carries the risk under any automation proposal. If any increased risk of abuse or misuse is passed from the state to conveyancers, as the operators of the system, this will lead to an increase in transactional costs,[7] if increased conveyancing fees are charged to compensate for increased exposure to liability claims.

II. Where We Have Come From

The deeds system reflected policy decisions that prior legal rights should be favoured over transactional security, based on standard *nemo dat* principles[8] that your title is only as good as that of your predecessor.[9]

This policy decision, coupled with the possibility of the assertion of undocumented third party title claims, led to uncertainty of tenure. Such uncertainties resulted in high transactional costs with the possibility of conveyancers being held accountable for client losses arising out of 'off Register' claims.

Automation is not a large concern under a deeds-oriented system. It is relatively easy to design a system that is no more than a 'mere recordation of deeds'.[10] Such a system is relatively easy to implement and inexpensive to run, since registration would provide no definitive assurance of result. There can be no objection to reversing a transaction subsequently found to be defective based on standard *nemo dat* principles. Thus, the system design requirements may be no different from (say) an online product order system, or an automated system for calculating leave entitlements.[11]

[4] It is reported that the England and Wales Land Registry wrote off nearly £11 million in funds, expended in developing automation proposals. See, eg, C Baksi, 'Land Registry Drops e-Transfer Move' *Law Society Gazette* (7 July 2011). See also the comments detailed in Land Registry, *Report on Responses to e-Conveyancing Secondary Legislation Part 3* (2011); and Land Registry, *Annual Report and Accounts 2010/11* (HC 1158, 2011) 55.

[5] A former scheme in Victoria, Australia, failed after expenditure of an estimated AUD$40–AUD$50 million. The failure was attributed to institutional lenders not being willing to endorse and back the introduction of the scheme. See Thomas, Low and Griggs, 'Three Proof Requirements' (n 1) 249.

[6] P Butt, *Land Law*, 6th edn (Pyrmont (NSW), Thomson Reuters, 2010) paras 20-67–20-77.

[7] See generally the economics argument presented in B Arruñada, 'Leaky Title Syndrome?' [2010] *NZLJ* 115.

[8] *Nemo dat quod non habet*, literally meaning 'no one gives what he does not have'.

[9] See the general discussion in Butt (n 6) para 19-10.

[10] B Arruñada, *Institutional Foundations of Impersonal Exchange: Theory and Policy of Contractual Registries* (Chicago, University of Chicago Press, 2012) 62.

[11] Except the registration may be a public way of best demonstrating one's claim to title to the world. See the Deeds Registration Act 1908 (NZ), s 35.

III. The Argument for Transactional Security

A. Security of Tenure

It can be argued that a government should provide for the security of the housing stock occupied by its citizens, by means of a sound and reliable registration system. This is certainly seen by the World Bank as a central plank for development of underperforming economies.[12]

The Torrens system was introduced from the late 1850s[13] to provide for certainty of tenure, as a reaction to the uncertainties attendant on the operation of the deeds system.[14] Its operation amounts to an adoption of a set of business rules, focused on security of transactions, rather than the protection of pre-existing interests. Thus, in the interests of transactional certainty, there are clear winners and losers. Once the dynamic security associated with the purchase process is guaranteed to the newly minted indefeasible interest, that interest becomes liable to be defeated by a later purchaser acting without fraud. Benefits of transactional security come at the burden of passive ownership.[15] If a registered interest is lost because of the operation of these rules, the state will pay compensation, which (hopefully)[16] is fair recompense.

However, some have suggested that the benefits of certainty of outcome produced by the operation of Torrens principles under a paper-based system were overstated, and that a fair system should allow for hard cases.[17]

To what extent, then, is this premium on certainty of outcome defensible? Is a less secure system in terms of predictable outcomes nevertheless successful, in terms of system design, provided that incidents of abuse are not common? This thinking is somewhat similar to the Kaldor-Hicks criterion,[18] where a change in policy or policy regime can be viewed as beneficial if the overall gains made are more significant than the total of the losses. Such thinking lay behind the recent New Zealand Law Commission proposal to allow registration to be overturned in the absence of a fraud finding, where an instance of 'manifest injustice' can be shown.[19]

[12] This comment is often directed by the World Bank to developing countries. Current initiatives including countries like Brazil, Kenya, and Morocco can be found at The World Bank, 'Projects & Operations' (available via www.web.worldbank.org). The principles also remain true for developed countries that are looking to re-establish the principles of recording land transactions. A more recent example is Greece, where lack of a credible land registration system is seen as a major impediment to economic recovery. See P Taylor and L Papadimas, 'Insight—Typically Greek, Delayed Land Register is Never-Ending Epic', Thomson Reuters, 18 October 2015 (available online via www.uk.reuters.com).

[13] Real Property Act 1858 (South Australia); see generally Butt (n 6) para 20-04.

[14] Butt (n 6) paras 20–01–20–04.

[15] See P O'Connor, 'Deferred and Immediate Indefeasibility: Bijural Ambiguity in Registered Land Title Systems' (2009) 13 *Edin LR* 194.

[16] In *Burmeister v Registrar-General of Land* [2014] NZHC 631, (2014) 15 NZCPR 91, the Registrar-General successfully argued compensation awarded under s 172(b) of the Land Transfer Act 1952 (NZ) was pegged at the value of the land at the date of deprivation. This led to a significant under-recovery by victims of cynical fraud.

[17] A Mason, 'Indefeasibility—Logic or Legend?' in Grinlinton (ed) (n 1) para 17–19; and Greenwood and Jones (n 1) 345–47.

[18] For a discussion of the application of Kaldor-Hicks to Torrens transactions, see L Arrieta-Sevilla, 'A Comparative Approach to the Torrens Title' (2012) 20 *Australian Property LJ* 31.

[19] New Zealand Law Commission, *A New Land Transfer Act* (NZLC R116, 2010) paras 2.11–2.16.

Such arguments would be challenged by proponents of pure Torrens simplicity, who argue that public confidence is, ultimately, linked to certainty of outcome leading to reduced transactional costs.[20] Such proponents point out that this is a much-acknowledged reason for the success of the Torrens system over the prior deeds registration system.[21]

Further, a system has integrity because it is soundly engineered. The extent to which that system has (or has not) been made the subject of recorded abuses is really a matter of secondary importance. A system that is open to abuse will eventually invite abuse. This secondary issue is one of timing, and such a timing issue cannot sensibly be relevant in terms of system design.[22] Indeed, even if statistically low incidents of abuse are recorded (and, therefore, can be justified in terms of savings in operating costs) the issue may have consequences in terms of loss of public confidence that 'homes' are protected and safe from fraud and registration abuses.[23] As Arruñada notes, such a lack of confidence is clearly an economics issue:

> Everybody agrees that security of property is essential for development. All owners want their rights to be universally respected. If they do not feel secure, if their rights are weak, they will be unwilling to invest, and this will hinder economic growth.[24]

Faced with transactional uncertainty, an award of monetary compensation for loss in a few high profile cases may be considered to be an inadequate response. Thus, the issue of system design becomes critical.

B. The Associated Issue of Cost and Risk

The paper-based Torrens system was designed to enable dealings to be placed for registration by the parties themselves, without the need for specialist assistance.[25] This simplicity was promoted as a means of reducing transactional costs for consumers as the ultimate beneficiaries of the system. This was not considered likely to lead to an increased risk of abuse, due to the state accepting the responsibility for policing it.

This point is amply illustrated by the absence of any known prosecutions of parties who presented casual or incorrect dealings for registration under the Australasian paper-based Torrens systems over the last 160 or so years.[26] This is telling, given that users over that

[20] See generally R Thomas, 'Reduced Torrens Protection: The New Zealand Law Commission Proposal for a New Land Transfer Act' [2011] *NZ L Rev* 715.

[21] New Zealand Law Commission R116 (n 19) iv.

[22] We are indebted to Ross Anderson, Professor of Security Engineering, Computer Laboratory, Cambridge University for making this clear to us. The New Zealand 'Landonline' system, discussed in section VI(B) of the main text below, has previously been suggested to be unsafe in terms of system design. See generally Thomas, Low and Griggs, 'Three Proof Requirements' (n 1). There may be other reasons than system design to explain abuse or lack of abuse of a system.

[23] This may be why a Kaldor-Hicks criterion analysis may not be useful. For a Kaldor-Hicks criterion analysis to be useful, surely we have to measure the *risk* of abuse as a component part of the 'losses', in order to then assess how losses may then be measured against the 'gains'? Indeed, even a few instances of vulnerable people losing their homes, or of property of unique national or regional significance being transferred out of public ownership, could affect public confidence in the integrity of the 'system'.

[24] Arruñada, *Institutional Foundations* (n 10) 21.

[25] Land Transfer Regulations 1966 (NZ), reg 15 (revoked).

[26] The Torrens system was first introduced in South Australia in the late 1850s.

period have been required to certify to the Registrar that the presented dealing was correct and could be relied upon.[27] Indeed, the zealous protection of the Registry staff easily led to perceptions of 'over-policing' of the Register.[28]

A key indicator of the success of the operation of this paper-based Torrens system is found in the 2010 New Zealand Law Commission Report proposing the introduction of a new Land Transfer Act. It described Land Transfer system as 'one of the great legal reforms of the nineteenth century. It gave people security in their dealings with land'.[29]

IV. The Need for Change

No argument can seriously be raised against the proposition that the paper-based Torrens systems are now outdated.[30] It is accepted that the manual system had credibility, but only in terms of the operating environment of the late nineteenth and early twenty-first centuries.

From the late 1960s onwards, stresses in the operation of paper-based systems became patently obvious. The advent of computers and document copying facilities made issues of security tenuous under a paper-based system.[31] In Australasian jurisdictions, there were known examples of prolonged delays in processing paper-based registration, of up to 12 months. This is discussed elsewhere.[32] Given the extent of change in the operational environment, any automated system may need to be more than a generational update. It will be required to operate in a different environment, which is not paper-based.

V. Tools for Analysis

In earlier writing,[33] we have suggested that the credibility of any registration process must be assessed under three headings. These are: 'proof of identity', 'proof of ownership', and 'proof of authority to deal'.

'Proof of identity' (perhaps better expressed as 'proof of name')[34] is the need for people wishing to deal with an interest in the land to identify themselves. A passport or a driver's

[27] Patently such claims could be made. Most Australasian systems require certification from the party deriving the benefit of the registered transaction that the dealing was 'correct for the purposes of [the Land Transfer Act]': see for New Zealand, s 164 of the Land Transfer Act 1952 (NZ) which in subs (3) additionally provides for prosecutions where such certificates are given 'falsely or negligently'.

[28] Thomas, Low and Griggs, 'Three Proof Requirements' (n 1) 238–39.

[29] New Zealand Law Commission R116 (n 19) iv.

[30] See generally Thomas, Low and Griggs, 'Three Proof Requirements' (n 1) 238–39.

[31] ibid, 235.

[32] R Thomas, 'Land Transfer Fraud and Unregistered Interests' [1994] *NZ Recent L Rev* 218, n 60. Having said this, the New South Wales Registry still has encoded outstanding duplicate titles which need to be presented with dealings as authority to register. This overcomes many concerns raised in this article dealing with issues such as 'proof of ownership' and some aspects of 'proof of authority to deal', which will be discussed further.

[33] See generally, Thomas, Low and Griggs, 'Three Proof Requirements' (n 1).

[34] We are thankful to Nick Bohm, counsel and trustee of the Foundation for Information Policy Research, for pointing out that proof of 'identity' is somewhat misleading, as it is always context-driven, and therefore can be a confusing expression. A driver's licence is not proof of identity, per se, but proof a driver's licence has been issued

licence issued in the name of John Smith, properly understood, is evidence only that the person before you has a passport or driver's licence in that name, with a photographic licence embedded within that document. At best, it is not by itself proof (indeed any proof at all) that the person before you is a particular 'John Smith' for other purposes.

'Proof of ownership' is the next requirement. This is proof that the John Smith before you is the same 'John Smith' who owns the interest he or she wishes to deal with. This proof provides unique challenges in the automated environment where any system is intended to operate solely 'online'.

The third proof, 'proof of authority to deal' (or 'proof of entitlement') is multi-faceted. Three examples of this proof are that transactions placed for registration are:

(i) made by parties who have legal capacity; and
(ii) not in contravention of legal requirements; and
(iii) made with authority obtained from an appropriate title custodian.

This proof requirement traverses areas of expertise which were (and may still be) the province of experienced Registry staff.[35] It raises issues of how such experience under a paper-based system can adequately be translated under an automated registration experience where (say) a virtual Registry is operated by conveyancers acting as de facto Registrars, without any third party involvement.[36]

VI. Australasian Automation Proposals

The Australian and New Zealand automation procedures have previously been assessed under these three proof requirements.[37] Conclusions were drawn that Australian and New Zealand proposals are not credible in terms of proof of ownership and of proof of authority to deal.[38] Indeed, on reflection, the assessment of proof of name—the first proof requirement—may be less secure than was previously thought to be the case.

A. Current Approaches to Proof of Name

All the Australasian systems place a primary focus on proof of name as the key issue for accessing automated registration, at the expense of the other two proof requirements.[39] As governments already have various means of establishing identity, be they passports, drivers'

to a person whose name is given on the issued licence. Proof of name (which may be tendered by producing a driver's licence) is a more accurate descriptor of what we intend.

[35] In Thomas, Low and Griggs, 'Three Proof Requirements' (n 1) 237–38, we make the argument that experienced Registry staff undertook a role under a paper-based Torrens system that was greater than mere processers of paper-based materials placed for registration.

[36] This is the New Zealand 'Landonline' experience ('Landonline' is discussed in section VI(B) below).

[37] See generally, Thomas, Low and Griggs, 'Three Proof Requirements' (n 1).

[38] ibid 254.

[39] See generally, Thomas, Griggs and Low, 'Electronic Conveyancing in Australia' (n 1).

licences, or other such equivalents, this appears to be an easy 'win' in terms of automation proposals. However, on further consideration, such confidence may be misplaced.

We argue that drivers' licences or passports cannot be treated by conveyancers as credible proofs of name. Given modern technological advances,[40] manufactured approximates of both may be made with relative ease.[41] Indeed, the authenticity of such forms of identification as passports rely on embedded codes to be scanned by appropriate machines. However, given conveyancers are not issued with scanners,[42] the presentation of (say) a passport as a means of proof is as inherently unsafe as the presentation of an outstanding duplicate title under the old, now discredited, paper-based system.[43]

Given this, it is unrealistic—if not unsatisfactory—to place on conveyancers the burden of certifying proof of name by production of such identification, without also issuing them with the means to read embedded electronic codes as the real means of proving authenticity.[44]

Whilst even embedded electronic codes may not ultimately be safe from hacking,[45] the technology required to undertake such an exercise successfully requires some degree of sophistication. The result is surely safer than the mere production of documents—or a facsimile of the same—for visual inspection.

B. Current Approaches to Proof of Ownership

Under the New Zealand 'Landonline' system, the Registrar-General requires the conveyancer to give an undertaking as to proof of ownership, which the Registrar then relies upon.[46]

[40] For examples, see Thomas, Low and Griggs, 'Three Proof Requirements' (n 1) 235, 242 and 251. This was due to the advent of computer imaging and photocopiers, enabling credible approximates of an original to be manufactured. The Council of Australian Governments (COAG) agreed in 2012 that work should be undertaken to develop a national measurement framework for identity crime to better inform efforts to implement the National Identity Security Strategy (NISS): www.ag.gov.au/rightsandprotections/identitysecurity/pages/nationalidentitysecuritystrategy.aspx (accessed 16 January 2017).

[41] In July 2012 the promoters of 'Confidential Access' (a now defunct website) were convicted at the Old Bailey of identity theft on an 'industrial scale' and of 'providing fraudsters with all the tools needed to create false identities'. They charged £50 for a utility bill and £800 for a set of professional sealed and certified trading accounts with a reference. See P McCloy, 'Title Fraud' *Law Society Gazette* (16 August 2012).

[42] Arguably, such readers may be readily available and reasonably inexpensive. The Australian Government has recognised the problems surrounding identity theft and document verification and its Document Verification Service is available for private sector access on a fee-for-service basis. This access can ensure the verification of passports, visas, medicare cards, citizenship and drivers' licences. See also Australian Government Attorney-General's Department, 'Document Verification Service' (www.dvs.gov.au).

[43] Thomas, Low and Griggs, 'Three Proof Requirements' (n 1) 235.

[44] Identification of name can be carried out by a certification provided by Australian Post. Property Exchange Australia (PEXA, discussed further at n 58 below) announced on its website in 2014 that '[f]rom September [2014], Property Lawyers and Conveyancers can send their clients to an Australia Post branch to have their identity verified if a face-to-face meeting isn't an option—a huge step forward for the growth of the industry': PEXA, 'PEXA announces Verification of Identity options' (www.pexa.com.au/news/article/pexa-ltd-announces-verification-of-identity-options/103). The announcement also suggests that this (somehow) 'also provides more secure evidence of ownership and right to deal and, critically, that the person transacting with the property is the person named in the Register of Land as the registered proprietor'.

[45] See generally, S Murdoch, S Drimer, R Anderson and M Bond, 'Chip and PIN is Broken' (paper delivered to IEEE Symposium on Security and Privacy, Oakland, 2010) (see www.cl.cam.ac.uk/research/security/banking/nopin/oakland10chipbroken.pdf).

[46] See generally Thomas, Low and Griggs, 'Three Proof Requirements' (n 1) 240–49.

The Registrar has published 'standards for verification',[47] intended to deal with common transactions. For 'routine transactions', proof of ownership may be satisfied by production to the practitioner of a copy of a local body rates notice, bank statement or utilities account addressed to the client at the property as acceptable proof of the client's link to the property.[48]

It must be said that production of such secondary documents is not proof of anything, let alone the best proof. In this regard, in New Zealand—as indeed must be the case in many overseas jurisdictions—local body rates notices, power accounts and bank statements are electronically produced.[49] Even if the produced document was original, arguably it could have been intercepted in the mail.[50] Alternatively, the produced document could easily have been manufactured with little skill by an imaginative use of photocopiers and computers to create an approximation of an original.

The question may be asked: in an automated environment where it is reasonably accepted that the outstanding duplicate title no longer serves as reliable proof of ownership, is the production of a printed local body rates notice or a printed bank statement any better form of proof?

In Australian systems, there is equally an onus on the conveyancer to provide proof of ownership. However, to date, little guidance has been published as to how this should be achieved has been published, though titles offices are beginning to recognise and address this issue.[51]

C. Current Approaches to Proof of Authority to Deal

Under the New Zealand Landonline system, the conveyancer stands in the position of the Registrar when determining what dealings may be accepted for registration.[52] Again, open-ended undertakings are given that the presented conveyance does not breach known statutory prohibitions against alienation.

By gazette notice, the Registrar-General has published some 23 different statutory provisions to be complied with by practitioners before certifying that the dealing can be accepted for automated registration.[53] This is discussed elsewhere.[54] This is an 'offline' list, in the

[47] ibid, 243.

[48] New Zealand Law Society, 'Property Transactions and E-Dealing: Practice Guidelines', 59–62 (available via www.lawsociety.org.nz to members). See also Land Information New Zealand, *Standard for Verification of Identity for Registration under the Land Transfer Act 1952* (LINZS20002, 2013).

[49] In New Zealand, local body rates are normally payable by the owner or lessee of the property: Local Government (Rating) Act 2002 (NZ), ss 11–12.

[50] For instance, one of the authors is aware of a fraud perpetrated where the fraudster caused mail addressed to the property to be redirected to him, apparently in an attempt to prove ownership of land by production of original mail.

[51] New South Wales is the leading jurisdiction in Australia on this issue. It has issued verification of identity guidelines which other states have already substantially adopted, or are likely to replicate in the future. See, eg, NSW Government (Land & Property Information), 'How Do I Verify the Identity of a Person Claiming a Right to Deal with Land?' <www.lpi.nsw.gov.au>. The guidelines are constantly updated.

[52] Greenwood and Jones (n 1).

[53] Thomas, Low and Griggs, 'Three Proof Requirements' (n 1) 245. See also Land Infomration New Zealand, 'Statutory Requirements, Forms of Electronic Instruments, and Requirements for the Retention of Evidence' (2008) 114 *Supplement to New Zealand Gazette* 3925.

[54] Thomas, Low and Griggs, 'Three Proof Requirements' (n 1) 244–46.

sense that the list is not itemised within the online system, nor is it brought to the attention of the practitioner when this 'global' undertaking is given. Instead, the undertakings are covered by the rather bland online certification that 'statutory requirements specified by the Registrar for that class of instrument' have been satisfied.[55] The Registrar accepts such undertakings as a substitution for the involvement of staff experienced in processing registration. The conveyancer undertakes this additional responsibility without the benefit of any training in both recognising and overcoming difficulties that commonly arise during a registration process.

In terms of the Australian experience, an initial report obtained by the New South Wales Registry leading to automation[56] at least recognised some of these issues by introducing the concept of 'CoRD' ('control of the right to deal'). This concept was intended to operate as an acknowledgment that a third party (for example, a mortgagee) will control the right to register.[57] However, in the rollout of Property Exchange Australia ('PEXA'),[58] it is unclear how this concept is to be applied and whether it is intended to extend to control of dealings affecting other third parties, or where registration conflicts with any legislative regime.

Examples where the CoRD principle may be usefully applied would be land transferred in breach of trustee obligations, assets vested by operation of law in an official assignee, or land which by virtue of its legal status requires consent of a third party before it is transferred.[59] Remember that under a Torrens based system, in the absence of title fraud by the party deriving the benefit, registration is good title by virtue of principles of certainty of registration.[60]

It appears that under most Australian automation proposals, Registry staff will be retained. This is markedly different from the New Zealand Landonline solution, which is to create a virtual Registry controlled by the conveyancers. However, it is not clear what the continued role of Registry staff under Australian systems will be, even if they are retained.[61] Hopefully, the level of care exercised by Registry staff will match in some way the

[55] The language refers back to the wording of the Land Transfer Act 1952 (NZ), s 164A(3)(c).

[56] NSW Government (Land & Property Information), 'Certificate of Title Solution for Concurrent Electronic & Paper-based Conveyancing' (2012) (available via www.lpi.nsw.gov.au).

[57] See ibid, para 4.1 ff. As noted in NSW Government (Land & Property Information), 'NEC News: More Q & A' (available via www.lpi.nsw.gov.au) (3 November 2012): 'A party has CoRD when that party has authority to consent to the registration of a subsequent interest in land. CoRD has been traditionally evidenced by legitimate possession of the paper Certificate of Title'. This is noted in NSW Government (Land & Property Information), 'Using Certificates of Title for eLodgment' (available via www.lpi.nsw.gov.au), a 'party has Control of the Right to Deal (CoRD) when that party has authority to consent to the registration of a subsequent interest in land, eg, a second mortgage, lease or plan. Evidence of CoRD is either legitimate possession of the paper certificate of title (CT); or an eCT on the land title where the mortgagee has elected not to hold a CT'.

[58] Part Two of the Electronic Conveyancing (Adoption of National Law) Act 2012 (NSW) establishes the Electronic Lodgement Network (ELN), with this to be known by the acronym of PEXA (Property Exchange Australia). This system stemmed from the work of Property Exchange Australia Ltd, an unlisted public company owned by some of Australia's largest financial institutions, together with the Governments of Victoria, New South Wales, Queensland, and Western Australia. Property Exchange Australia Ltd will run the national property exchange and will be open to non-shareholders though separate from direct Government oversight.

[59] This may be conservation land, land set aside for Public Housing, or, in the New Zealand context, Māori protected land.

[60] This realisation is important as it appears (at least in terms of the operation of Landonline) that there are presently fewer recorded incidents of fraud than was the case under the operation of the manual system.

[61] The operating and participation rules for PEXA have focused on conveyancers as the subscribers to the system. The Land Titles Offices of each state have been involved in the process through ARNECC (Australian Registrars' National Electronic Conveyancing Council) (see www.arnecc.gov.au).

guardianship role accepted by the Registry in operating a manual system which required more 'hands on' manual processing.

D. What Does This Tell Us About Existing System Designs?

In many respects, this overemphasis on proof of name, at the expense of proof of ownership and proof of authority to deal, is irresponsible. As already noted, good system engineering is about automating the hard part first, and not the easy part. Unless a credible means of overcoming obstacles concerning all the three proofs is achievable, questions should be raised about whether an automation process should proceed at all.

VII. What is the Difference in Risk?

A. Manual Processing

In the past, those charged with operating a manual system may often have acted as an effective check against fraud and irresponsible behaviour, certainly in terms of systematic fraud.[62]

Being a Recorder or Registrar[63] under a paper-based system was often a chosen, lifelong vocation. Not unnaturally, those serving as Registrars had different perspectives on how the system operated and developed different skill sets.[64] Any registration may involve multiple low-level checks assessing the credibility of a dealing. Intuitively, if something did not look 'right', further investigation and collaborative teamwork might be applied to 'brainstorm' a possible solution. Although personal quirks of various Registrars when querying the actions of conveyancers may well have caused frustrations, such foibles and unpredictable uncertainties often acted as a barrier to systematic fraud or abuse.

B. Computers[65]

In terms of system operation, the user of an automated system is in the hands of the architect or designer of the programme. The programmer sets the nature of the discourse. A computer-based system operates at its interface through simple binary choices. It consists of a number of programmed processes and choices laid out within the algorithm behind the programme. The programming of the system may not be apparent to users in terms of any hidden 'interactive' codes or possible viruses. Under the pre-set processes, a number of given possibilities are offered at every stage of the programmed sequence. One of the proffered solutions must be accepted or rejected in order to move on to the next stage, or

[62] A more detailed explanation of the workings of the manual Australasian Torrens systems is provided in Thomas, Low and Giggs, 'Three Proof Requirements' (n 1) 231–39.

[63] 'Registrar or Recorder' is the term used in Australian jurisdictions; 'Assistant Land Registrar' in New Zealand.

[64] See also, the general discussion in Thomas, Low and Griggs, 'Three Proof Requirements' (n 1) 236–39.

[65] The authors are indebted to suggestions and comments made by Ed Johnson, Emeritus Fellow of Wolfson College, Cambridge, on this section of the article.

the user must return to a previous stage in the programme. For this reason, a query cannot arise unless conceived at the design stage by the architect of the system as an issue requiring a programmed response.[66]

Unlike a human brain, a computer is unlikely to be able to compare and judge multiple forms and lines of evidence or undertake simultaneous reasoning. Unless the programmer at the design stage perceives a particular set of circumstances as being a threat which requires a programmed response, the computer will not comprehend that threat. Although computers make an excellent adjunct to human endeavours, this should not blind us to what they cannot do. It is dangerous to assume that they are the equivalent of—or provide a satisfactory substitute for—the exercise of human discretion and judgement.

C. Different Risks

The risk paradigm under a manual system and an automated system do not operate in parallel. If a fraudster understands the detail of computer programming, he or she may be able to overcome its inbuilt controls with catastrophic consequences in terms of the operation of the system. One abuser striking at a point of vulnerability may create, over a short period, mayhem. This may be compared with risk under a manual system, which may encounter 'one off' instances of different forms of fraud or abuse, from time to time.

VIII. Recognition of the Influence of the Reasons to Automate

Obviously, a combination of factors will drive any automation project. However, the prime reason to automate will inevitably affect or drive the design parameters. Three possible key reasons for automation are identified. These serve as a framework for discussion of possible choices made in any automation proposal.

A. Politics

Automation can be politically driven. A government may see automation as a public manifestation of its desire to be seen as progressive and business friendly. The danger of such a directive in terms of system design is that delivery in a timely manner can become an issue of political credibility, causing difficult design issues to be minimised or bypassed.

Although we do not claim that this is necessarily an illustration of the impact of political deadlines, the Australian Government has announced that by 2017 virtually all government services will be 'online' as a key part of its economic development strategy.[67] Perhaps in a

[66] Whilst it may be conceivable that computer programmes of more sophistication exist, an issue may well be whether they are sufficiently stable in terms of operating functionability, or achievable in terms of available funding.

[67] J Bajkowski, 'Coalition Promises "Virtually All" Government Services to be Online by 2017' *Government News* (2 September 2013) (available via www.governmentnews.com.au). This is an Australian Government initiative to enable online dissemination of Government news and initiatives to members of the Australian Public.

similar vein, the Land Registration Act 2002 (UK) ('LRA 2002') was legislated under a government directive to automate.[68]

B. Efficiencies and Savings

Another driver of automation could be a desire to achieve savings. Here, land registration may be treated primarily as a processing system, which can be more efficiently undertaken if computerised. On this basis, physical Registries may be closed and Registry staff made redundant. Following this line of reasoning, system choices may be influenced by savings made in volume processing, which can then be passed on to the consumer. Released statistics often herald the success in terms of the speed with which 'low lying fruit', such as registration of simple transfers, mortgages or discharges of mortgages, are achieved.[69]

The difficulty of this approach is, again, a design issue. As previously discussed, the credibility of any system should be determined by the way it handles difficult conceptual issues, rather than bulk. Although issues such as fraud and abuse may infrequently occur, when they do, the result may be catastrophic in terms of continued public confidence. If a weak link is found under a computerised system, a single operator can create havoc.

The New Zealand Landonline Registry may be seen as such an example. In essence, it is no more than a simple data processing system. The integrity of the Register is achieved (in so far as it has integrity) by requiring conveyancers, licensed to operate the system, to certify to the Registrar that they, as users, will not abuse the system. In this way, those users underwrite the credibility of the registration result, thereby removing the need for the system to be more sophisticated or comprehesive in terms of its design. This reduces the need for system designers to provide solutions to conceptually difficult registration issues, and lessens difficulties that may later emerge arround discovered design defects.

C. Outmoded Systems

Finally, the principal reason to automate may be recognition that manual, paper-based registration practices, designed for nineteenth century conditions, are now both unsafe to operate and outmoded. This realisation is important, as it accepts automation is inevitable. The issue is then how to make the best choices to achieve the desired result, as opposed to proceeding with automation proposals without due recognition of possible risks.

Two key deficiencies in manual, paper-based practices, are now evident. First, the physical task of processing vast amounts of paper in a time-efficient manner has proved difficult.

[68] See generally C Harpum, S Bridge and M Dixon, *Megarry and Wade: The Law of Real Property*, 8th edn (London, Sweet and Maxwell, 2012) para 7-157. The LRA 2002 created a framework for the introduction of a system of paperless conveyancing. As the authors note, automation was 'postponed'. This was due, in part, to concerns about whether the integrity of the Register could be maintained under an automated system. However, in 2016, HM Land Registry initiated a project for the purposes of updating the Land Registration Act 2002: Law Commission, *Updating the Land Registration Act 2002—A Consultation Paper* (Law Com CP No 227, 2016). Ch 20 discusses electronic conveyancing, including the possibility of re-examining the legislative framework in the Land Registration Act 2002 to see how it could be adapted to facilitate and support the future development of electronic conveyancing (see para 20.10). The consultation period ran from 31 March 2016 to 30 June 2016; the final report is to be published in 2017.

[69] Muir (n 1) 311 states: 'The ability to electronically lodge and instantly register title transactions will revolutionise conveyancing practice'. See also New Zealand Law Society, 'Land*online* Hits the Road to Increase Uptake of e-Dealing' (2004) 627 *LawTalk* 12.

Secondly, controls designed to deter fraud under nineteenth century paper conditions, prior to the introduction of computers, photocopiers and document imaging, are now patently clumsy, unsuitable and indeed unsafe.[70]

IX. Who Carries the Risk of Abuse Under Automated Systems?

The question as to who carries the risk of abuse under automated systems is, ultimately, key. If the state no longer accepts the responsibility of policing an automated system against abuse, and conveyancers become the ultimate indemnifiers against abuse, the purpose of registration will be to determine which of these parties—the state or the conveyancer—bears the loss.[71] If we then conclude, as a result of such an analysis, that under automation the outcome of registration may be unsafe, we must then consider in terms of Australasian law whether such such an outcome can still be considered 'Torrens' in nature.

Existing writing to date on New Zealand and Australian automation has focused on the transfer of risk from the Registry back to the party presenting the dealing for registration.[72] Conveyancers given access to the Register effectively underwrite the integrity of the system against abuse or misuse by providing a form of warranty that the transactions satisfy the three proof requirements.

This transfer of risk occurs in a twofold manner. First, the conveyancer or other authorised user invariably has to certify that the dealing presented for registration complies with all legal requirements.[73] Although this feature may have been common to manual paper-based systems, that undertaking did not result in findings of culpability and the Registrar seeking indemnification for negligent certification.[74] Instead, access rights to automated registers have been withdrawn from negligent conveyancers in New Zealand, irrespective of any loss having been suffered.[75]

[70] Thomas, Low and Griggs, 'Three Proof Requirements' (n 1) 235.

[71] Indeed, it is arguable that the operation of the old deeds system provided a greater assurance of result than the operation of a Torrens regime which, as a result of automation, produces less secure registration results. Under the old deeds system, the title of the prior owner was invariably to be preferred over that of the new purchaser, unless a better title could be proved. Such an analysis would bring into operation constructive trust principles applying in equity, found to operate on the 'concience' of the new purchaser. In the conveyancing context, such principles were invariably applied by a court of equity under fairly well established principles. Thus, determining who bore the ultimate risk was a more predictable exercise. However, under an automated 'State guarantee' system which enables titles to be overturned on general gounds of unfairness being shown, the registration result is less certain. This adds an increased element of risk for conveyancers who may bear the risk of underwriting to the state any risk of abuse of the system again misuse or abuse.

[72] Thomas, 'Fraud, Risk and the Automated Register' (n 1) 362–63; and Thomas, Low and Griggs, 'Three Proof Requirements' (n 1) 246–49.

[73] Thomas, Low and Griggs, 'Three Proof Requirements' (n 1) 241.

[74] ibid, 236.

[75] The New Zealand Law Society publication, *LawTalk*, recorded in 2013 that a Law Society Lawyers Standards Committee investigated 'on its own motion' a practitioner who failed to provide correct certifications to Land Information New Zealand (LINZ) in accordance with its published e-dealing requirements: New Zealand Law Society, 'Fined for ongoing non-compliance with e-dealing requirements' (2013) 825 *LawTalk* 33. The Committee imposed a censure and fined the practitioner $7,500 (and awarded costs) stating that the practitioner had 'created a risk to the efficacy of the land transfer system'. The New Zealand Registrar General of Land had already

Secondly, there is a largely unnoted form of further indemnification. It is something of an industry standard for users of online systems to undertake to the service provider that the online system will not be abused as a condition of being granted online access.[76] In this manner, the small-print of online access agreements often imposes personal liability on conveyancers in the event that any abuse of the electronic system occurs. This is an added layer of indemnification not duplicated under a manual, paper-based system.[77]

By way of illustration, under Landonline, the 'Landonline terms and conditions'[78] clearly shift the risk of abuse onto the user,[79] in terms of access to the system by use of 'Security Measures'.[80] The consequences of breach are also clearly set out. By clause 27 of those terms, Land Information New Zealand (LINZ)[81] excuses itself from liability under the access agreements for any issues due to the fault of the user.[82]

'suspended' the practitioner's user rights to sue Landonline. There was no suggestion that the practitioner's actions led to any damage or loss as a result of this casual certification. L Griggs, R Low and R Thomas in 'The Changing Face of Conveyancing Responsibility' (2015) 5 *Prop L Rev* 109, 111, refer to the circumstances of a fraud carried out on the New Zealand Landonline system by a Mr Sharma. He was disciplined and struck off.

[76] In New South Wales, the relevant provision is found in the Electronic Conveyancing (Adoption of National Law) Act 2013 (NSW):

> 26 Subscribers required to comply with participation rules:
>
> (1) A subscriber who is authorised under a participation agreement to use an ELN [Electronic Lodgement Network] must comply with the participation rules relating to that ELN.
> (2) If a subscriber contravenes those participation rules, the Registrar may:
> (a) if the Registrar operates the ELN, restrict, suspend or terminate the subscriber's use of the ELN, or
> (b) if an ELNO [Electronic Lodgmenet Network Operator] operates the ELN, direct the ELNO to restrict, suspend or terminate the subscriber's use of the ELN.
> (3) Subsection (2) does not limit or affect any right, power, authority or remedy that the Registrar or an ELNO has under the operating requirements, the participation rules, a participation agreement or any other law of this jurisdiction in relation to contravention of the participation rules.

[77] This issue has been largely bypassed or overlooked in discussions on automation. Instead, the automation dialogue invariably focuses on cost and time savings to conveyancers in terms of achieving immediacy of result as a result of online registration—which in turn is heralded as enabling savings to be passed on to their clients as consumers.

[78] Land Information New Zealand ('LINZ'), 'Landonline Terms and Conditions' (available via www.landonline.govt.nz).

[79] LINZ (n 78) cl 17 provides as follows: 'Any use of Landonline by any person with access to the Security Measures used or made available to you or any of your people (whether authorised by you or not) constitutes sufficient authority for LINZ to: [17.1] act on any enquiries, provide such information, update its registers or to otherwise transact such dealings, with or under the instruction of that person ….'

[80] LINZ (n 78). '"Security Measures" means logon names, passwords, private keys used in relation to Digital Certificates or other measures provided to you or your people by LINZ or the LINZ Registration Authority from time to time to enable access or continued access to Landonline'.

[81] The Government body directed to control land registration dealings.

[82] LINZ (n 78) cl 27 provides: 'Your obligations to LINZ: (1) You shall be liable to LINZ for reasonably foreseeable costs (including settlement and legal fees), damages, losses or expenses that LINZ may incur, suffer or become liable for as a result of:

> 1. 29.1. your breach of this agreement;
> 2. 29.2. your or any of your peoples intentional misuse of Landonline;
> 3. 29.3. your or any of your peoples negligent acts errors or omissions; or
> 4. 29.4. any claim, suit, action or proceeding brought by a third party against LINZ as a result of the matters set out in paragraphs 29.1–29.3. except to the extent that LINZ is at fault through any act or omission … except to the extent of LINZ's obligations under statute to provide compensation in the circumstances prescribed by such *statute* or statutes.'

The potency of such undertakings is yet to be realised in Australasian Torrens systems. It will remain academic until (or unless) the state seeks indemnification and compensation from users because of breaches by users of the LINZ User Agreement Terms, or the Australian equivalent.

This previously uncommented-on issue is critical in terms of transfer of risk. In summary, where the state does not seek indemnification from the system users,[83] then the end result may be no different to what it is now. The conveyancer will be able to stand behind his client, who has the benefit of indefeasability. However, given the state now has a contractual right to seek indemnification from system users for breaches of the user agreement, it is surely more likely that the state will seek to pass on any increased liability to users who may be thought to have breached the contractual user terms.

Consequentially, by a process which has not been made the subject of discussion and yet which clearly has significant policy implications in terms of who carries the ultimate burden of risk, the responsibility for the registration result may move from the state to the system users.

To date, evidence of such a possibility is signalled by the New South Wales[84] and Queensland[85] Governments, which have imposed increased responsibility on mortgagees where they fail to act with due care in verifying the party before them.[86]

This realisation is given more potency when the issue of privatisation of registries is considered. A private registry operator will no doubt be driven by profit imperatives. Given this, a privatised or commercialised operator may be unwilling to absorb any increased financial exposure in the operation of the registration process, if that financial risk can be hedged, or passed onto other stakeholders in the conveyancing process, such as conveyancers.

X. How Automated Systems are Introduced into Operation

Research to date indicates that unless an automated system has widespread support, it will not succeed unless introduced by compulsion.[87] In this vein, Landonline was introduced into New Zealand as a compulsory registration system for most purposes.[88] No other known country has been bold enough to force automation in this way. Consequentially, conveyancers in New Zealand have been forced to accept the proffered User Agreement Terms in order to be able to continue to offer conveyancing services.

Automation proposals in England and Wales, as well as those in Australia, are understood to be optional in terms of use, and will operate in conjunction with the existing manual system. In order to engender support, many automated systems are initially introduced on a trial basis, alongside the continued operation of the manual system.

[83] The Registrar may instead suspend or remove access privileges.

[84] Real Property Act 1900 (NSW), s 56C.

[85] See Land Title Act 1994 (Qld), s 11A(2).

[86] The New Zealand Law Commission proposed that a similar regime also be introduced under the (then) proposed new Land Transfer Act. See New Zealand Law Commission R116 (n 19) paras 2.19 and 2.24.

[87] See, eg, I Bour, 'Electronic Identities in Europe: Overview of E-ID Solutions Connecting Citizens to Public Authorities' (Underwriters Laboratories, The ID Management Competence Centre, 2013) 4–7.

[88] See generally R Thomas, 'Fraud, Risk and the Automated Register' (n 1) 349, 359–61.

However, operation of any dual system must be regarded as inherently problematic as this practice may produce inconsistent outcomes between the two systems, and unsafe results.[89] This may arise because an automated system operates in parallel with a manual system. In this regard, it should be remembered that Torrens systems operate strictly in terms of priority being afforded to dealings presented for registration from the date of receipt.[90] No dealing can be processed until a prior lodged document has either been registered or rejected. However, with manual registration occurring alongside automated registration, we have two incompatible systems operating on the same Register. A remotely set up automated dealing will trump any manual dealings that have been posted in the mail for processing.[91] Such outcomes must sit uneasily with the hopes of providing a single robust system that ensures fair, safe and predictable outcomes. It would also follow that where a private individual wishes to undertake manual registration, both parties must do so. Alternatively, a conveyancer acting for one of the parties must be prepared to give undertakings to act for both parties in processing the dealing as an automated transaction.

Practically, if automation cannot be forced on conveyancers—as it has been in New Zealand—a more subtle means of ensuring compliance is available. This may occur where major lending banks are persuaded to endorse an automated system which has benefits in terms of speed of transactions and reduced operating and transactional costs. Where such lenders require automated registration as a standard pre-condition for them to be part of the transaction, lesser players will follow suit. Thus, in a relatively short period of time, the key financial institutions in the mortgage market may drive a cultural change that results in automation becoming the norm. Indeed, an earlier automation proposal in Victoria failed to obtain traction after major banks refused to endorse that proposal.[92]

XI. Four Possible Proposals

Given the preceding discussion, what are some of the options presently available to automate a Torrens system? Four are suggested, dictated by the extent to which the state will accept responsibility for the consequences of the act of registration. The proposals are:

(1) diluting the benefits of registration;
(2) delaying the benefit of registration;
(3) transferring responsibility for registration; or
(4) accepting the risk of abuse.

[89] ibid, 359–61.

[90] In terms of New Zealand, see the Land Transfer Act 1952 (NZ), ss 37 and 41.

[91] Under an automated system, the registration can occur at the same time the funds are released. Thus registration is almost instantaneous, and closely follows the financial transaction between the parties. In New Zealand, following automation, nearly all physical land registries have been closed. Thus if a manual dealing is being undertaken, it invariably has to be posted to the Registry. If the settlement funds are handed over in consideration for the right to manually present dealings for registration, pending receipt by the Registry of your documents through the mail, there is no way of knowing whether a competing automated dealing may at any time trump your registration.

[92] Thomas, Low and Griggs, 'Three Proof Requirements' (n 1) 249, n 106.

None of these bear a direct correlation to responsibility and risk undertaken under operation of a 'pure' paper-based Torrens system.[93]

A. Diluting the Benefits of Registration—Extension of Overriding Interests

Although the nature of indefeasibility has been much heralded, in practice all Torrens regimes allow many 'off Register' exceptions to the indefeasibility regime.[94] In most regimes, acknowledged exceptions range from the application of local government ordinances, town planning regimes, taxes, Public Works acquisitions, territorial authority rating sales, adverse possessory interests and others of a similar nature.

The LRA 2002 (UK) expressly exempts certain 'overriding interests' (as they are colloquially known) from the state guarantee.[95] These include interests of third parties in actual occupation, short-term leases,[96] certain legal easements and profits-à-prendre, customary and public rights, local land charges, certain mines and minerals, and manorial rights.[97]

If implementation of a fully secure state guarantee of title system is untenable in the short term, then state guarantee of the registration result may still be provided, but made expressly subject to a number of stated exceptions. Examples may consist of exceptions related to control of right to deal, or CoRD principles.[98] These may be dealings which need certain statutory consent requirements to be complied with before they are deemed to be effective at law, or even (say) transactions in breach of trustee powers. However, such exceptions must also have a bearing on the issue of system integrity. Patently, too many exceptions to the state guarantee coming into operation affect not only the quality of title, but also impact on transactional costs. The parties to any transaction will have to absorb or insure against the increased cost of undertaking preliminary investigations of potential 'off register' interests, before committing to the transaction.

B. Delaying the Benefit of Registration—Introduction of Delayed or Discretionary Indefeasibility

The introduction of delayed indefeasibility protection potentially provides a safer, equally low-cost option, compared to diluting the benefits of registration.

Under such a proposal, a registered dealing may not become fully 'indefeasible' until a settled period of time passes after registration has occurred.[99] This gives a period of grace

[93] See also Thomas, Griggs and Low, 'Electronic conveyancing in Australia' (n 1) 14–16. None of the four proposals in this article include private PIN numbers being issued to the holders of registered land interests. At the time of writing, such an option is not considered realistic and appears unlikely to be endorsed or favoured by the public—or indeed safe from abuse. See generally, Bour (n 87).

[94] E Cooke, *The New Law of Land Registration* (Oxford, Hart Publishing, 2003) 76–77.

[95] See generally ibid 78 and 164; also LRA 2002, ss 28, 29 and sch 3.

[96] These are for 7 years or less.

[97] LRA 2002, schs 1 and 3.

[98] See section VI(C) above.

[99] A similar idea to this was suggested by the Scottish Law Commission. See Scottish Law Commission, *Land Registration: Void and Voidable Titles* (DP Paper No 125, 2004) 84.

for the registration to be challenged by an affected party.[100] After all, any new registrant will probably have either attempted to take possession, sought to receive the benefits of the receipts of the land such as rentals or, if a mortgagee, will have an expectation of receiving mortgage interest payments. Under any one of these situations, there is an increased likelihood or opportunity of discovering fraud or improper dealing within a short period following the act of registration. To assist this process, flags may be hidden within the system, which identify behaviour the programmer associates with system abuse, falling short of purchaser fraud. These flags may either also serve the function of warning Registry staff that vunerable titles are (or have been) dealt with, or constitute online notifications to holders of registered interests that an interest on the issued title has been altered.[101]

The New Zealand Law Commission recommended the introduction of delayed indefeasibility,[102] and this recommendation merits some consideration. It proposed an interim period following the registration event, where a court may overturn a title where a claim of 'manifest injustice' has been made out. Thirteen grounds were provided to guide the court. However, given the required grounds focus on an 'injustice' to the dispossessed interest-holder, the new registrant may not be aware of the relevance—or indeed existence—of these grounds until the issue is put before the court. Most of the grounds favoured the return of the land to the dispossessed landowner.[103]

Nevertheless, the Law Commission proposal was open to criticism in one key respect, which arguably has the effect of negating a key aspect of indefeasibility. If registration is challenged, the new registrant must fund the cost of defending his or her registered status. This means that the hapless registrant may have no assurance of whether the registration will be respected or not, pending the matter being resolved by a court determination. This unfortunate registrant (who is not guilty of fraud) will consequently have to absorb the cost of defending his or her title—and on grounds which he or she may not have been aware of at the time of registration. Given this, even if the new registrant is successful, he or she will be financially worse off, as the New Zealand Torrens State Guarantee only applies where the registered interest is lost.

Arguably, such a proposal would be more palatable if the state (and not the new owner) funded the owner's litigation costs under such proceedings. After all, the proposed 'manifest injustice' test is separate from that of Torrens fraud, so surely the principle of indefeasibility should cover the risk of unsuccessful challenges where no fraud is pleaded.[104]

[100] Somewhat analogously, Part III Division 4 of the Land Titles Act 1980 (Tas), provides a system of qualified Torrens title. Where land is being brought under the Torrens Act for the first time, and the Recorder of Titles is not convinced that the applicant is entitled to the estate that is claimed, a qualified title can be issued. The 'caution' issued in relation to the title will lapse after twenty years. See also Real Property Act 1900 (NSW), s 28B. A similar initiative was legislated in New Zealand by the Land Transfer (Compulsory Registration of Titles) Act 1924, which provided for the Government to issue Torrens titles, limited as to 'parcels' or as to 'title'. This is now Part 12 of the Land Transfer Act 1952.

[101] These flags will be too late to enable registration to be overturned, if the system in question is an immediate indefeasibility system as is presently operable in both New Zealand and Australian jurisdictions.

[102] This is argued to be the effect of the New Zealand Law Commission Report (n 19) paras 2.11–2.16, even though the report referred to the proposal as 'immediate indefeasibility with limited judicial discretion'. See further R Thomas, 'Automated Registration and Deferred Indefeasibility' *Property Pot Pourri 1*, Auckland District Law Society Incorporated, 8 May 2014, Ellerslie Convention Centre, Auckland. See now Land Transfer Act 2017 (NZ), ss 54–57.

[103] See generally R Thomas, 'Reduced Torrens Protection' (n 20).

[104] Again, the hapless registrant may not be aware of the asserted grounds being argued to overturn the registration. The proceedings are plaintiff-orientated and do not favour retention of the registered status.

C. Transferring Responsibility for Registration—Reliance on Third Party Undertakings

This is the equivalent of introducing something akin to a simple data processing system, which places the risk on the conveyancers, where those parties give undertakings to the Registrar—as a condition of being granted access to the system—that the system will not be abused. Such a system has a patent attraction in terms of design simplicity and ease of implementation. Indeed, it can be argued that the conveyancers' increased obligations are essentially an effective guard against abuse.[105]

With such considerations in mind, the New Zealand implementation of Landonline has some appeal. It relies for its integrity almost exclusively on undertakings given by conveyancers.[106] If a key driver to implement automation is to provide an online system by a set target date, or under severe budgetary constraints, such a system may offer the best alternative. However, over time, the transfer of risk of registration abuse or misuse to conveyancers will in all likelihood lead to higher transactional costs.[107]

Under such a proposal, the state still plays a role in auditing compliance with the system. However, of necessity this 'policing' function now occurs after the registration event has taken place. At this stage, the abuse may not be reversible, given the nature of indefeasibility.[108]

Unless such a system can be forced onto conveyancers,[109] it is hard to see that such an option is viable. After all, the risk of abuse and misuse is placed squarely back on the users with an attendant increase in financial risk for those parties.

D. Accepting the Risk of Abuse

Under this proposal, the Registry will not require 'open-ended' indemnifications from conveyancers. Instead, conveyancers will have discharged their responsibilities to the state if

[105] This will be true, pending abuse occurring. Sceptics may consider that an increased opportunity to abuse the system will inevitability (over time) lead to greater abuse. New Zealand is a relatively small country with a population of just over 4.5 million. A fraud of significant proportions could have significant repercussions in terms of continued public confidence. However, it has to be accepted that as at 2011, the New Zealand Registrar-General confirmed recorded incidents of fraud had lessened under the automated system from those previously recorded under the old, paper-based system. See, eg, R Thomas 'Reduced Torrens Protection' (n 20) 735, n 94.

[106] Thomas, Low and Griggs, 'Three Proof Requirements' (n 1) 244–46.

[107] Title insurance could be used as a mechanism to mitigate against this increased risk. An innovative response found in New Zealand has been to combine these two elements. At least one known legal practice promotes title insurance as a standard conveyancing cost. If a client elects not to carry insurance, the conveyancing fee is increased by the firm as an acknowledgment of the increased risk it absorbs in being engaged to carry out the title registration, including risks arising from the operation of the automated system.

[108] Under New Zealand's Landonline, the Registrar-General audits compliance with conveyancers' record-keeping to check for compliance with the key issues of proof of name, ownership, and authority to deal. However, this event occurs only after the registration event has occurred and thus the results may be irreversible. See also *LawTalk* (n 75).

[109] As noted, this is the result of the introduction of such a system in New Zealand. An alternative would be for the main institutional banks operating in the jurisdiction to endorse such a system, causing other, lesser players to follow their lead. This trend will only occur if the banks consider that they are, in turn, protected from risk of abuse and misuse of the system. Such protection will presumably arise from undertakings the banks receive from conveyancers retained to represent their interests.

published prescriptive checklists are followed. Assuming that they are followed, the risk of abuse will therefore remain with the state.[110]

This is more akin to the operation of a manual system, where the state effectively policed the system and absorbed the risk of abuse.[111] Illustrations of how such principles could translate in an automated environment follow, by use of the Landonline proof requirements.

In terms of proof of name, this would be satisfied where the conveyancers' requirement to verify identity is satisfied by completion by the conveyancers of one of a number of prescribed checks, rather than assenting to an open-ended undertaking to the Registrar. Thus, the need to verify identity is met where a credible passport or other form of identification card such as a driver's licence is produced to the conveyancer.[112] Likewise, in terms of proof of ownership, it might be sufficient to produce a printed local body rates notice, or other printed document addressed to the owner at the property.[113] The issue of authority to deal could likewise be met by the conveyancer answering 'yes' to an online list of direct questions on compliance with CoRD issues of competency and issues of statutory compliance.

Under such a proposal, registration comes with more risk for the state, so it would appear prudent for Registry staff to be retained. The Registrar may then determine which party's title registration is protected, and which party is entitled to indemnification from the state. In terms of continued public confidence in the integrity of the system, where a contest arises between an individual and a mortgagee, the mortgagee can reasonably be expected to be compensated with a monetary payment.

XII. Concluding Remarks

Good, functional design of a land administration system is critical. One should be wary of emulating Quentin Blake's Mrs Armitage's bicycle:[114] when she enthusiastically added too many gadgets, her bike became unstable with obvious results. However, one can avoid Mrs Armitage's fate. Steps can be made to move incrementally towards automation, with manual processing remaining embedded at critical stages. Then, over time, as online systems develop in sophistication and become more commercially secure, other parts may be automated.

The preceding discussion enables us to offer for consideration seven guidelines for architects of any automation proposal.

(1) A system that transfers risk from the state to users is not a continuation of a conventional state guarantee of title system. If risk transfers back to the users, we may revert to the problems of increased conveyancing costs and uncertainty of title tenure which the state guarantee system was introduced to overcome.

[110] Alternatively, additional proof criteria could be required of banks, given the prevalence of identity fraud issues.

[111] Thomas, Low and Griggs, 'Three Proof Requirements' (n 1) 236–40.

[112] Thus, if the passport is subsequently found to be a forged approximate, the risk of this abuse is a matter for the registry and not the conveyancer.

[113] This is presently the standard of proof for more straightforward dealings.

[114] Quentin Blake, *Mrs Armitage on Wheels* (London, Random House, 1999).

(2) A straightforward comparison of the risks inherent in a manual system and an automated system is fraught with difficulty as the two systems are designed to satisfy different operating conditions.
(3) Existing automated systems invariably rely on proof of name as proof that the dealing is by the correct party and that that party is authorised to undertake the required transaction. This is seen to be a fundamental design fault in the operation of those systems.
(4) The credibility of any automation proposal needs to be determined in the light of how it deals with the hard issues, such as fraud, and not its ability to transact volume at low cost.
(5) Continued public confidence in the security of land tenure should be a key criterion in determining the success of any automated system, as opposed to the limited extent of any recorded abuses.
(6) There is a difference between a homeowner losing their house, and a mortgagee their investment. The mortgagee's loss is more compensable than the homeowner's, in terms of any financial payment.
(7) If the drivers to automate are irresistible and a sound system cannot be introduced, some form of staged introduction should be considered. In this regard, reference is made to the four proposals set out in this chapter.

In line with these guidelines, this chapter has suggested that any one of the four measures may be introduced as interim steps, pending more secure operating systems becoming viable. Again, these are:

(1) diluting the nature of the indefeasibility protection offered by introducing further 'overriding interests' or more extensive exceptions being legislated to the offered indefeasibility protection;
(2) delaying the benefit of indefeasibility protection for a stipulated period of time after the registration event, by the reintroduction of the concepts of 'delayed' or 'discretionary' indefeasibility;
(3) the state accepting that, given an automated system is more open to abuse, users of the system will in future underwrite any abuse in consideration for being given the privilege of access to the system; or
(4) introducing a system where immediate indefeasibility is offered (as is the case under many Torrens regimes) but the state makes a policy decision to absorb the risk of any increases abuse or misuse. Under such a proposal, users of the system would not provide to the state open-ended undertakings that the automated system would not be abused. Instead, they would only be liable if they failed to follow prescriptive operating procedures required by the state in terms of operating procedures. The state would also have a role in deciding where the monetary compensation should be paid, which, in many cases will be better directed to the mortgagee and not the innocent defrauded landowner who has lost his or her home.

It should be noted that these four measures do not operate independently, one from the other. For example, the greater the number of overriding interests, the more delayed or discretionary indefeasibility will need to be considered in terms of system design. Furthermore, a realisation of increased risk involved in the conveyancing exercise calls for frank dialogue of how any increased liability for abuse or misuse is to be allocated between the stakeholders—being mortgagees, conveyancers, consumers, the state and (perhaps) any privatised system operator.

Ultimately, what this leads to, is that increased risks come with automation. Title insurance is thus likely to become a more significant issue as automation proposals are introduced. Indeed, Ontario, as one of the first Torrens systems to automate (albeit as a deferred indefeasibility regime) has an established practice of landowners obtaining title insurance as a standard cost of any conveyance.[115]

One is left to ask again whether—if risk is transferred from the state to the user, and the outcomes are not safe—the introduced system can truly be considered unchanged, in terms of its original construct, as a state guarantee of title regime? We would suggest not.

[115] In Australia, the focus of the title insurers has been working with the mortgagees and in insuring against their risk. The experience in Ontario is that most transactions are accompanied by title insurance on the recommendation of the parties' lawyers. Email from C Yonis (General Counsel, First Title Insurance, Sydney) to Rouhshi Low (QUT University) concerning the prevalence of title insurance in Ontario (8 September 2014). In New Zealand, title insurance is available but is not commonly taken out.

INDEX

Lightning Source UK Ltd.
Milton Keynes UK
UKHW030054010323
417837UK00005B/397

9 781509 906031